Street by Street

NEWCAS⬛⬛⬛⬛NE
SUNDERLAND
DURHAM, GATESHEAD,
SOUTH SHIELDS, TYNEMOUTH

Blyth, Chester-le-Street, Cramlington, North Shields, Peterlee, Ponteland, Seaham, Stanley, Washington, Whitley Bay

2nd edition March 2002
lst edition May 2001

© Automobile Association Developments
Limited 2002

Ordnance Survey® This product includes map data licensed from Ordnance Survey® with the permission of the Controller of Her Majesty's Stationery Office. © Crown copyright 2002. All rights reserved. Licence No: 399221.

All rights reserved. No part of this publication may be reproduced, stored in a retrieval system, or transmitted in any form or by any means– electronic, mechanical, photocopying, recording or otherwise – unless the permission of the publisher has been given beforehand.

Published by AA Publishing (a trading name of Automobile Association Developments Limited, whose registered office is Millstream, Maidenhead Road, Windsor, Berkshire SL4 5GD. Registered number 1878835).

The Post Office is a registered trademark of Post Office Ltd. in the UK and other countries.

Mapping produced by the Cartographic Department of The Automobile Association. A01227

A CIP Catalogue record for this book is available from the British Library.

Printed by G. Canale & C. s.p.a., Torino, Italy

The contents of this atlas are believed to be correct at the time of the latest revision. However, the publishers cannot be held responsible for loss occasioned to any person acting or refraining from action as a result of any material in this atlas, nor for any errors, omissions or changes in such material. The publishers would welcome information to correct any errors or omissions and to keep this atlas up to date. Please write to Publishing, The Automobile Association, Fanum House (FH17), Basing View, Basingstoke, Hampshire, RG21 4EA.

Ref: MD051z

Key to map symbols — ii

Key to map pages — 1

Enlarged scale pages — 2-5

Street by Street — 6-209

Index – towns & villages — 210-211

Index – streets — 212-269

Index – featured places — 269-278

Junction 9	Motorway & junction
Services	Motorway service area
	Primary road single/dual carriageway
Services	Primary road service area
	A road single/dual carriageway
	B road single/dual carriageway
	Other road single/dual carriageway
	Minor/Private road, access may be restricted
← ←	One-way street
	Pedestrian area
=======	Track or footpath
	Road under construction
	Road tunnel
AA	AA Service Centre
P	Parking
P+	Park & Ride
	Bus/Coach station
	Railway & main railway station
	Railway & minor railway station
	Underground station
	Light Railway & station
++++++	Preserved private railway
LC	Level crossing
	Tramway

--------	Ferry route
....	Airport runway
-·-·-·-	Boundaries - borough/district
	Mounds
93	Page continuation 1:17,500
7	Page continuation to enlarged scale 1:10,000
	River/canal, lake, pier
	Aqueduct, lock, weir
465 ▲ Winter Hill	Peak (with height in metres)
	Beach
	Coniferous woodland
	Broadleaved woodland
	Mixed woodland
	Park
	Cemetery
	Built-up area
	Featured building
	City wall
A&E	24-hour Accident & Emergency hospital
PO	Post Office
	Public library
i	Tourist Information Centre
	Petrol station Major suppliers only
†	Church/chapel

	Toilet
	Toilet with disabled facilities
PH	Public house AA recommended
	Restaurant AA inspected
	Theatre or performing arts centre
	Cinema
	Golf course
▲	Camping AA inspected
	Caravan Site AA inspected
	Camping & Caravan Site AA inspected
	Theme park
	Abbey, cathedral or priory
	Castle
	Historic house or building
Wakehurst Place NT	National Trust property
M	Museum or art gallery
	Roman antiquity
	Ancient site, battlefield or monument
	Industrial interest
	Garden
	Arboretum
	Farm or animal centre
	Zoological or wildlife collection
	Bird collection
	Nature reserve
V	Visitor or heritage centre
	Country park
	Cave
	Windmill
	Distillery, brewery or vineyard

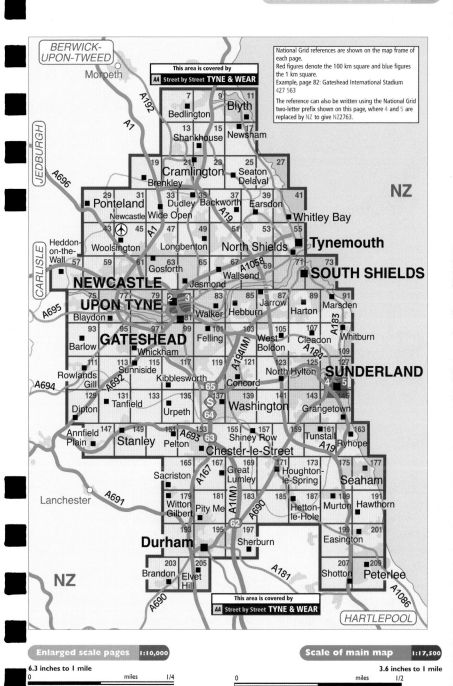

BERWICK-UPON-TWEED

Morpeth

This area is covered by
AA **Street by Street** TYNE & WEAR

National Grid references are shown on the map frame of each page.
Red figures denote the 100 km square and blue figures the 1 km square.
Example, page 82: Gateshead International Stadium
427 563

The reference can also be written using the National Grid two-letter prefix shown on this page, where 4 and 5 are replaced by NZ to give NZ2763.

JEDBURGH

CARLISLE

7   9   11

Bedlington   Blyth

13   15   17

Shankhouse   Newsham

19   21   23   25   27

Cramlington   Seaton Delaval

Brenkley

29   31   33   35   37   39   41

Ponteland   Dudley   Backworth   Earsdon

Newcastle   Wide Open

NZ

43   45   47   49   51   53   55   Whitley Bay

Heddon-on-the-Wall   Woolsington   Longbenton   North Shields   Tynemouth

57   59   61   63   65   67   69   71   73

Gosforth   Wallsend   SOUTH SHIELDS

NEWCASTLE   Jesmond

UPON TYNE   75   77   79   2   3   83   85   87   89   91

Blaydon   Walker   Hebburn   Jarrow   Harton   Marsden

81

93   95   97   99   101   103   105   107   Whitburn

Barlow   Whickham   Felling   West Boldon   Cleadon

GATESHEAD   109

111   113   115   117   119   121   123   125   127

Rowlands Gill   Sunniside   Kibblesworth   Concord   North Hylton   SUNDERLAND

129   131   133   135   137   139   141   143   4   5

Dipton   Tanfield   Urpeth   Washington   Grangetown

64

147   149   151   153   155   157   159   161   163

Annfield Plain   Stanley   Pelton   Shiney Row   Tunstall   Ryhope

63

Chester-le-Street

165   167   169   171   173   175   177

Sacriston   Great Lumley   Houghton-le-Spring   Seaham

179   181   183   185   187   189   191

Witton Gilbert   Pity Me   Hetton-le-Hole   Murton   Hawthorn

Lanchester   62

193   195   197   199   201

Durham   Sherburn   Easington

203   205   207   209

NZ   Brandon   Elvet Hill   Shotton   Peterlee

This area is covered by
AA **Street by Street** TYNE & WEAR

HARTLEPOOL

Enlarged scale pages 1:10,000

6.3 inches to 1 mile
0   miles   1/4
0   1/4   kilometres   1/2

Scale of main map 1:17,500

3.6 inches to 1 mile
0   miles   1/2
0   1/2   kilometres   1

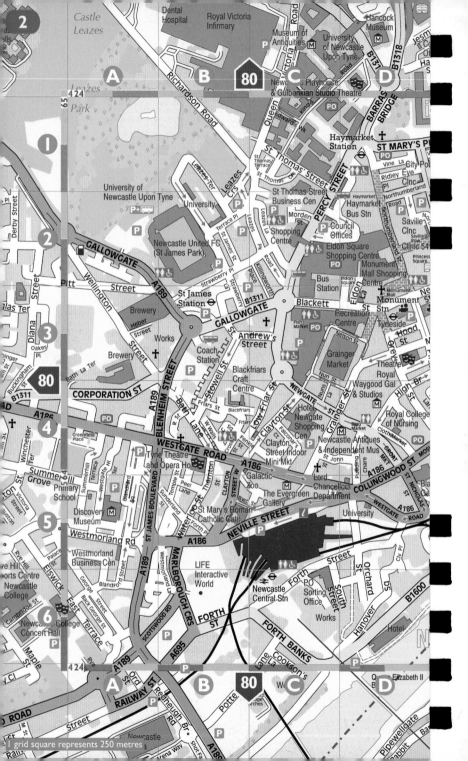

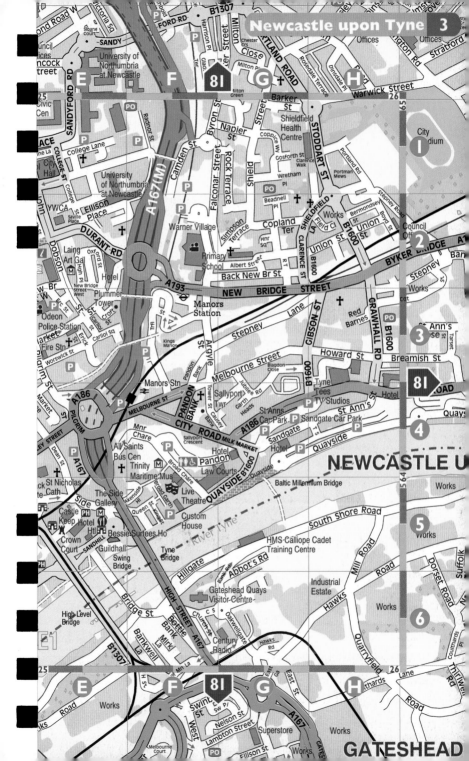

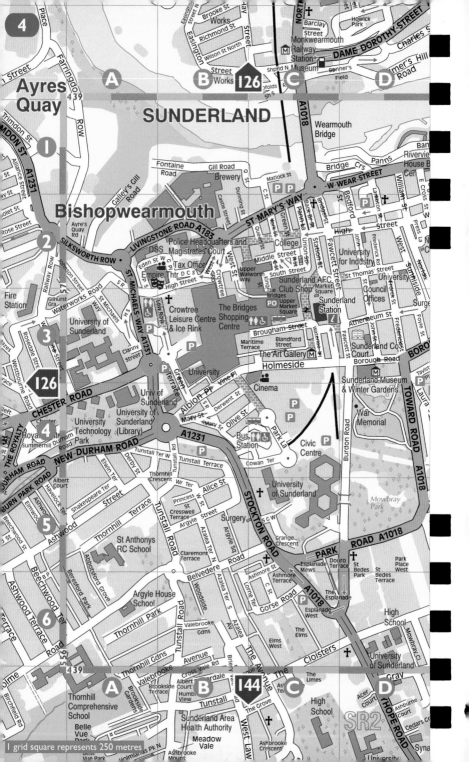

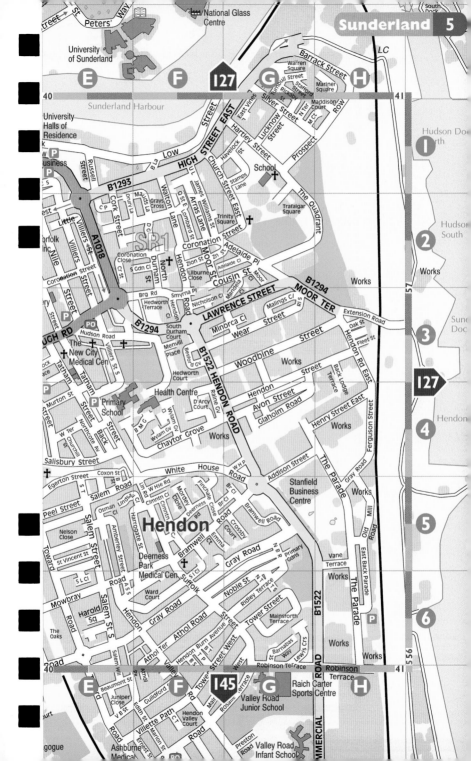

6

A 424 B C

I

Burnt House

83

2

Netherton Lane

Blue House Farm

York Gv
Ripley Cl
Ayton Ct
Knaresborough Cl
Skipton
Warwick Gv
Dover Close
Hylton Cl
Conway Cl

3

North Farm
82 B1331
The Grange
Oakdale
Hallwood
South Farm

NETHERTON LANE
North Ridge
Meadowdale
Netherton Lane
Red House Farm

B1

Cemetery

Nedderton

4

Westlea

581

5

6

HARTFORD ROAD

Netherton Moor Farm

A 424 B C
A192 **I2** DS
Plessey Woods

I grid square represents 500 metres

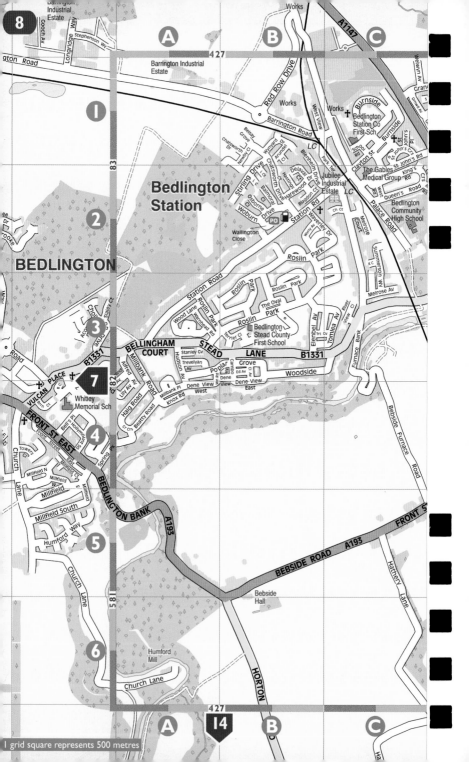

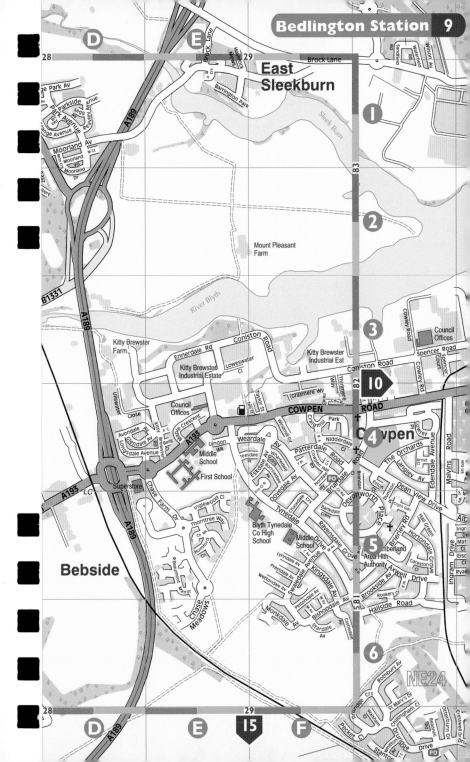

12

Netherton Moor Farm

(A) **6** (B) (C)
424

I

East Moor

Plessey Woods Country Park

Hartford Dr

Hartford Hall

SHIELDS ROAD

A192

80

Hartford Bridge

2

HARTFORD BANK

A1068

3

79

Shotton Lane

4

North Ne Industr Estate

Windmill Industrial Estate

Works

Nel

Nelson Industrial Estate

Baker Road

Nelson Road

5

5 78

Road

Shotton Lane

FISHER LANE

A1068

6

Bolam Business Park

Bassington Industrial Estate

Bassington Lane

Bassington Drive

Bassingt

(A) **20** (B) (C)
424

Bassin Industr Estate

1 grid square represents 500 metres

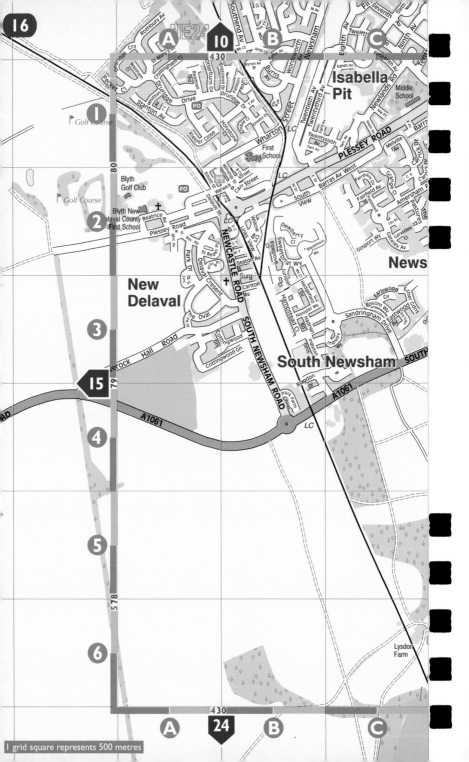

D E F

22 23

Works

1

77

Plessey North Moor Farm

Moor Plantation

Fusilier Plantation

2

South Drive

Shotton Grange

3

76

20

Waterloo Plantation

4

Plessey South Moor Farm

A1068

Hoys Wood

A1(T)

5

Seven Mile House Farm

575

A1(T)

Hotel

6

FISHER LANE

A1068

22 23 32

D E F

B1518 FR

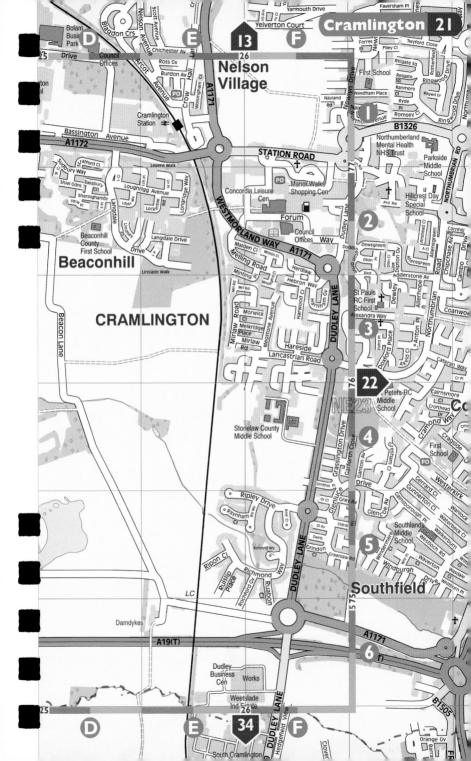

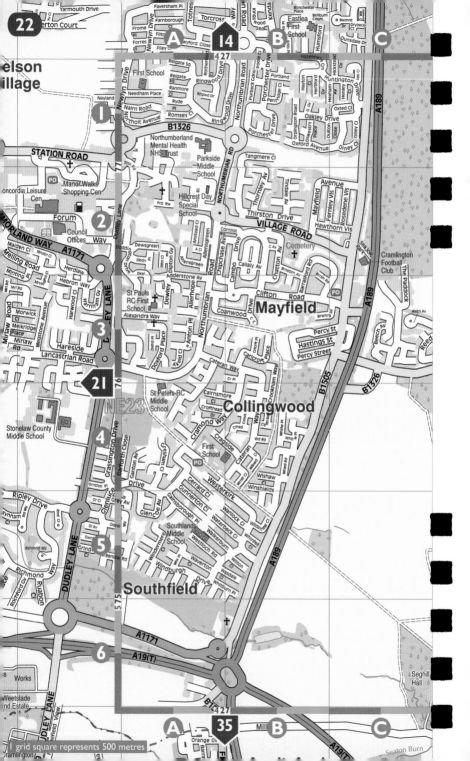

1 grid square represents 500 metres

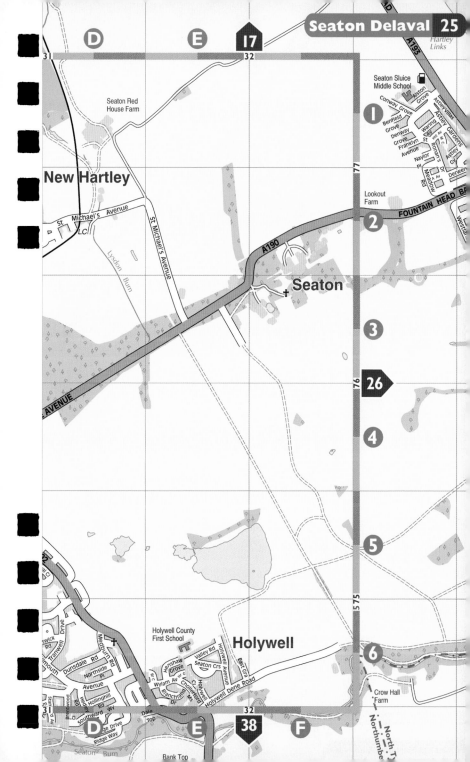

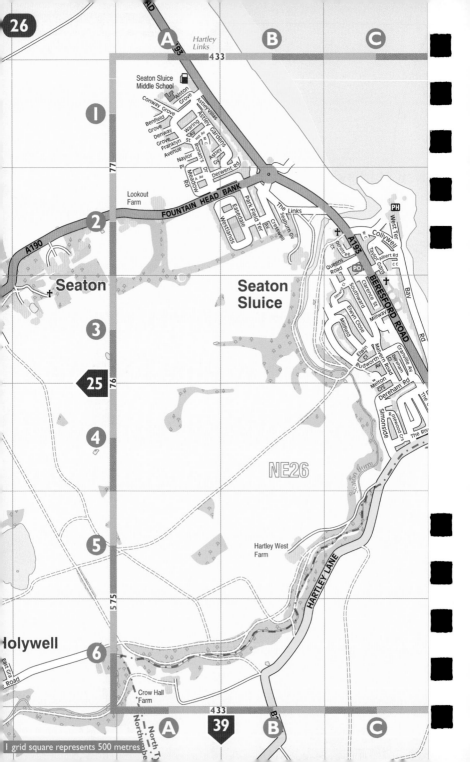

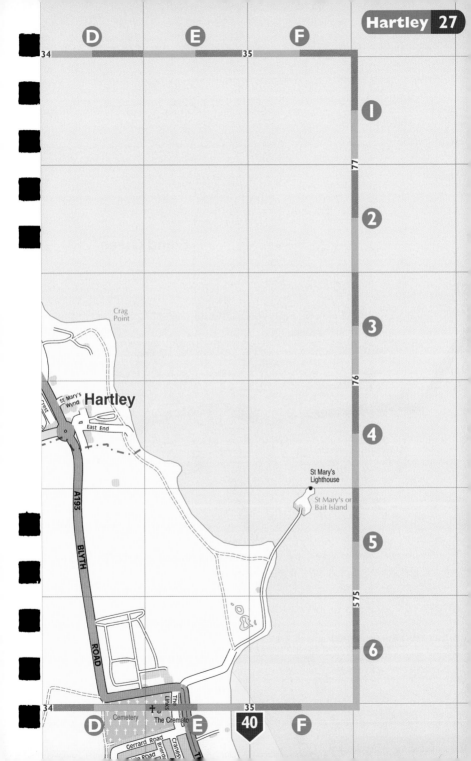

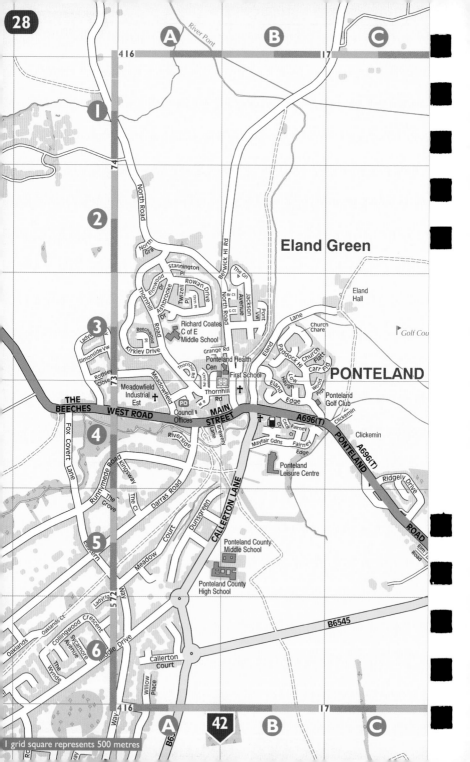

River Pont

A   B   C

416   17

1

74

North Road

2

North Gra

North Road

Stannington Pl

Elwood Dr

Thornhill Road

Ashbrooke Dr

Twizell Pl

Rowan Drive

Berwick Hill Rd

The Gn

Jackson Avenue

North Road

Pont Vw

Eland Green

Eland Hall

Golf Cou

Lane

Church Chare

3

Ladyw

Simonside Vw

Beechwood Pl

Kirkley Drive

Richard Coates C of E Middle School

Grange Rd

Ponteland Health Cen

First School

Eland

Paddock Hl

Church

Flatt

Carr Fld

Wood

Frds

PONTELAND

Rothley Close

Meadowfield

Thornhill Rd

Thornhill Rd

Eland

High

Eland Edge

Low

Ponteland Golf Club

THE BEECHES

WEST ROAD

Meadowfield Industrial Est

PO

Council Offices

MAIN STREET

Brewery Lane

Riverside

A696(T)

Fairney Cl

Fairney Edge

Clickemin

Clickemin

4

Fox Covert Lane

Rummymede Road

Kingsway

The Cl

Darras Road

The Grove

Mayfair Gdns

Ponteland Leisure Centre

PONTELAND

A696(T)

Ridgely Drive

Ridgely Drive

ROAD

5

Eastern

Meadow

Court

Dungsreen

CALLERTON LANE

Ponteland County Middle School

Elm I

Road

572

Way

Ladyrig

Ponteland County High School

B6545

6

Oaklands Cl

Collingwood Crescent

Sycamore Avenue

Middle Drive

The Wynde

Willow Place

Callerton Court

Oaklands

Rd

416   17

Way

B6

A   42   B   C

I grid square represents 500 metres

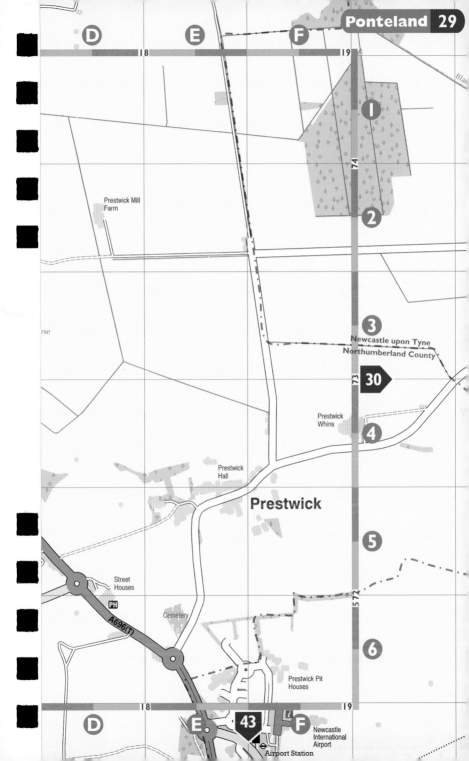

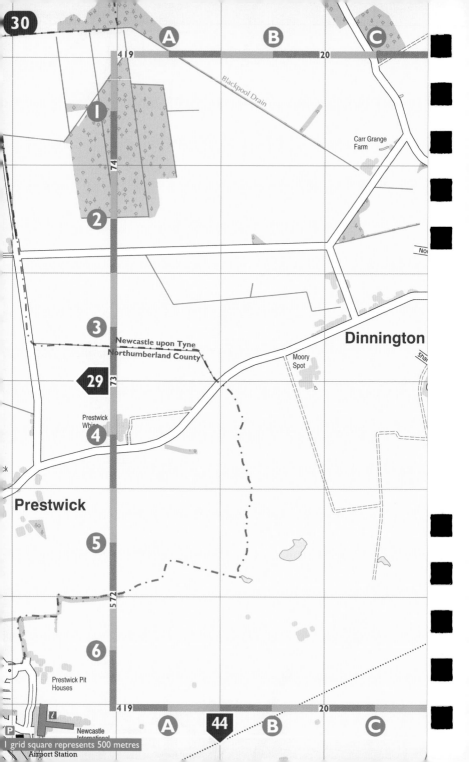

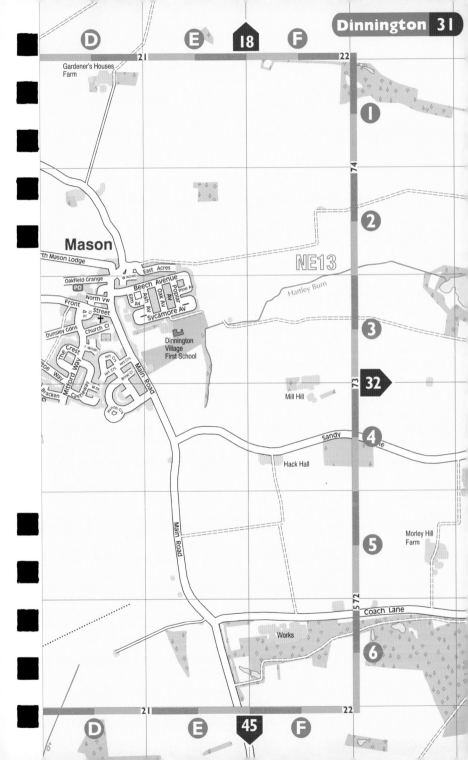

D E **18** F

22

I

74

2

Gardener's Houses
Farm

21

Mason

th Mason Lodge

NE13

Hartley Burn

Oakfield Grange

PO

East Acres

W Acres

Beech Avenue

North Vw

Poplar Av

Pine Av

Oak Av

Ash Av

Elm Av

3

Front Street

Sycamore Av

Dunsley Gdns

Church Cl

73

32

The Crest

Mitford Way

Castleway

Hrt Crs

Hrt Crs

Hrt Crs

M Dr

Birtel Cl

Dinnington
Village
First School

Mill Hill

oe Way

Main Road

Sandy

4

Bracken
Cl

Hack Hall

Morley Hill
Farm

5

Main Road

72

Coach Lane

Works

6

21

22

D E **45** F

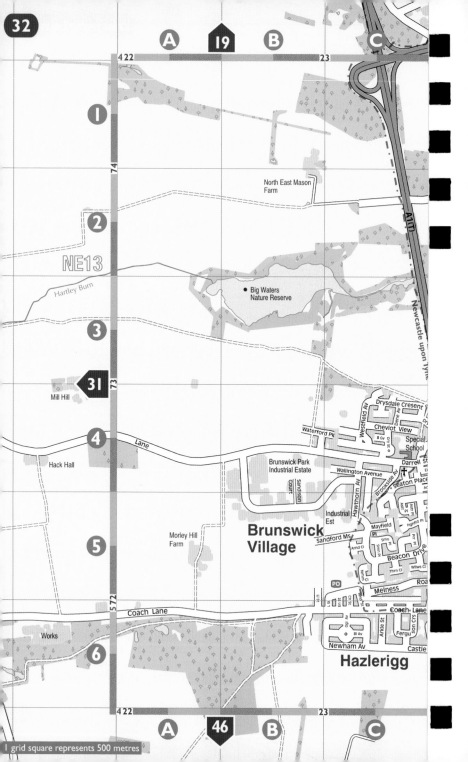

A 19 B C

4 22 23

1

74

2

NE13

Hartley Burn

North East Mason Farm

● Big Waters
Nature Reserve

3

31 73

Mill Hill

A1(T)

Newcastle upon Tyne

4 Lane

Hack Hall

Waterford Pk

Drysdale Cresent

Westfield Av

Dene Av

Cheviot View

B Gv

Special
School

Darrell St

Wallington Avenue

Brunswick Park
Industrial Estate

Sandison
Court

Hawthorn Av

Brookside Av

Seaton Place

Industrial
Est

Mayfield
Pl

5

5 72

Morley Hill
Farm

Brunswick
Village

Sandford Ms

Arnd Cl

Beacon Drive

Thrn Cl Wllws Cl

PO

Melness

Road

Coach Lane

Works

6

Newham Av

Arkle St

Fergu son Crs

Coach Lane

Castle

Hazlerigg

4 22 23

A 46 B C

1 grid square represents 500 metres

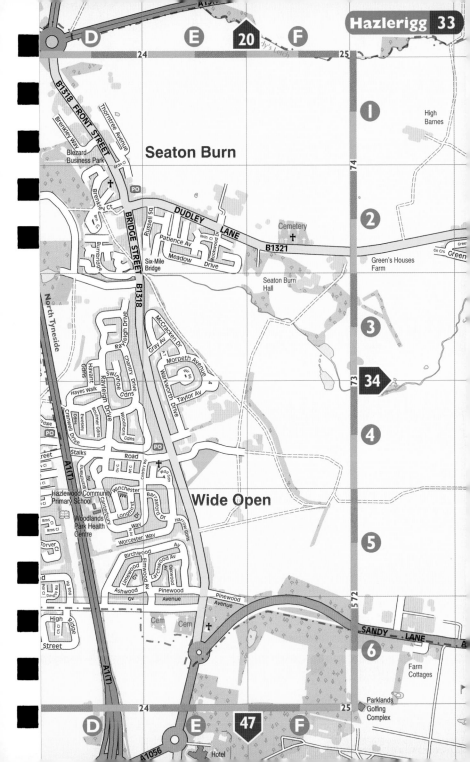

D E 20 F

24 25

ly's Letch

I

High Barnes

B1318 FRONT STREET

Thorntree Avenue

Brenkley Way

Blezard Business Park

Seaton Burn

Gran Cl

PO

Brenkle Ct

BRIDGE STREET

Russell Sq

DUDLEY LANE

Patience Av

Meadow Drive

Nrln Cl

Brookwood Dr

Cemetery

2

B1321

Green's Houses Farm

Grn Crs Green

Burns de

Six-Mile Bridge

B1318

North Tyneside

Seaton Burn Hall

3

McCracken Dr

Gray Av

Morpeth Avenue

Ravensdon Drive

Chantry Drive

Swinhoe Gdns

Ravleigh Drive

Warkworth Drive

Taylor Av

73

34

Havant Gdns

Hayes Walk

Boumer Gdns

Ewesley Gdns

Cranwell Drive

Woodhorn Gdns

PO

4

Street

A1(T)

PO

Stalks

Road

Cranbry Way

Dale

Rms Cl Rms Cl

Hazlewood Community Primary School

Woodlands Park Health Centre

Canterbury

Longhirst

Winchester Dr

Way

Barrasford Dr

Wide Open

Harlow Gdns

5

Torver Cl

Worcester Way

Birchwood Av

Limewood Av

Elmwood Av

Larchwood Av

Oakwood

Ashwood Gv

Pinewood Avenue

Pinewood Avenue

72

High Ridge Street

A1(T)

Cem Cem

SANDY LANE

6

Farm Cottages

24 25

D E 47 F

A1056

Hotel

Parklands Golfing Complex

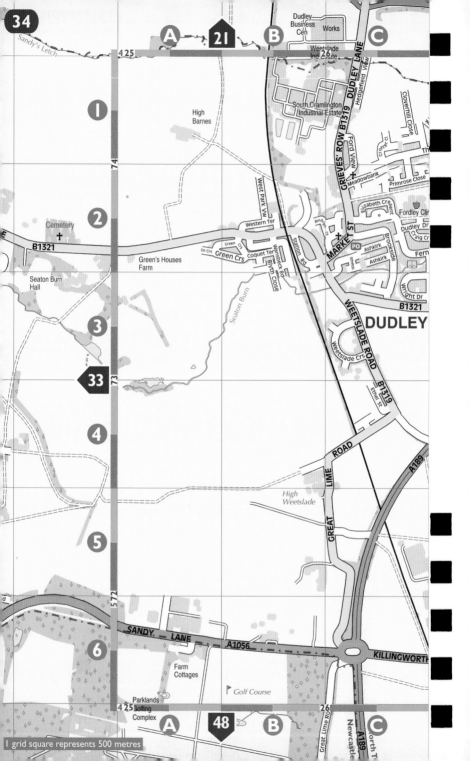

34

Sandy's Letch

A **21** **B** **C**

425

Dudley
Business
Cen   Works

Weetslade
Ind Estate **26**

Hedgefield View

DUDLEY LANE

I

74

High
Barnes

Clovernill Close

South Cramlington
Industrial Estate

GRIEVES' ROW B1319

Ford View

Coffer Cl

Meadowbank

Primrose Close

2

Cemetery

Elizabeth Cresent

Fordley Clin

Dudley Dr

West Park VW

Western Ter

B1321

Brookside

Ashkirk

MARKET ST

PO

Green's Houses
Farm

Green
Cs

Green Crs

Cn Crs

Coquet Ter

Wansbeck Rd

Blyth Close

Seaton Rd

Ashkirk

Wright Dr

Seaton Burn
Hall

B1321

DUDLEY

Seaton Burn

3

WEETSLADE ROAD

Weetslade Crs

33

73

B1319

Ethel St

4

A189

High
Weetslade

ROAD

5

572

LIME

GREAT

A189

6

SANDY   LANE

A1056

KILLINGWORTH

Farm
Cottages

Golf Course

Parklands
Golfing
Complex

425

A **48** **B** **26** **C**

Great Lime Road

A189

Newcastle

North T

I grid square represents 500 metres

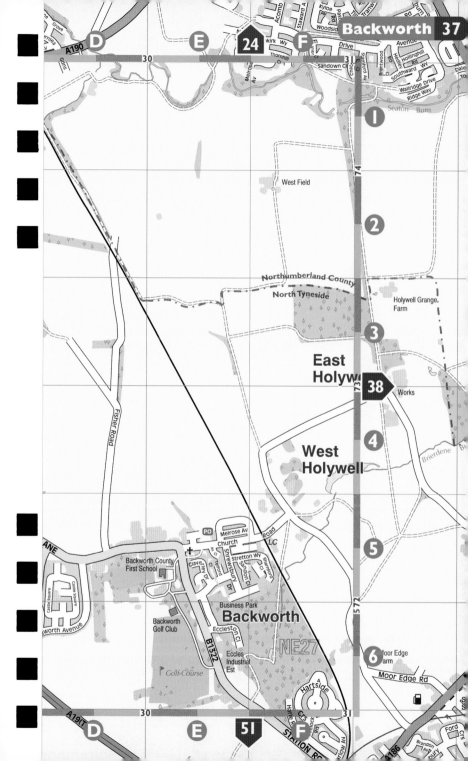

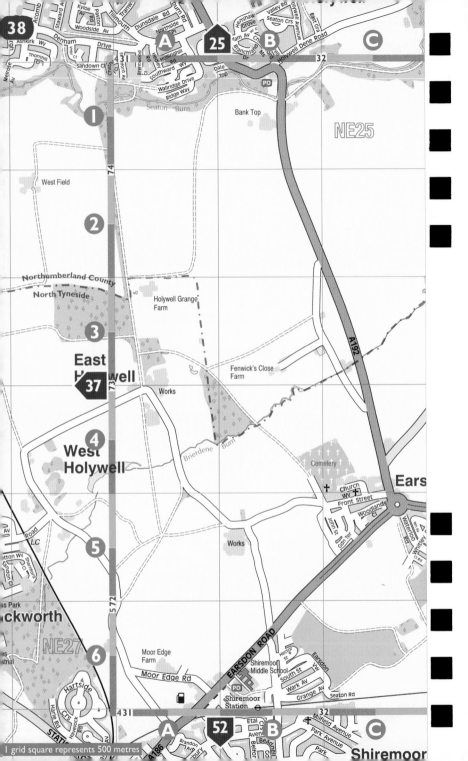

Crow Hall Farm

North Tyneside
Northumberland County

B1325

26

I

Brier Dene Farm

Brierdene Burn

Cemetery

Gerrard Road

Garsdale Road

Westley

Hastir

Brier Dene

PO

Golf Course

Whitley Bay Golf Club

Glebe School

Whitley Lodge First School

2

St Lucia Close

Woodburn Drive

Woodburn Drive

Carolyn Wy

Carolyn

Willoughby Drive

Longridge Drive

Monkridge

Surge

3

PO

HARTLEY LANE

Beaumont

Huntly Rd

Haddington

Gainsborough

Dilston

Dacre

Crevington Gy

40

Earnshaw Way

Hilsden Rd

Cranthorpe

MONKSEATON

Whitley Bay High School

Well Rd

Well Rd

Hertford Cl

Caxton

Hascombe Cl

First School

Surgery

Hepscott Dr

4

The Ivanhoe

Denebank

Denehom

Westgate

Red House

The Ridings

Ridge

Berwick Hill Gy

Mill Dyke

Ashbury

Thornbury

Chedon

Melburn Dr

Monkseaton

Langdale

Hartley Avenue

don

A192

Monkseaton Rd

Holly Av

Hesleyside Rd

EARSDON ROAD

MONKSEATON DR

Nw Cl

Chatwll Gv

Blaxdale

Valley Gardens

Upplands

Hazelbank

Valehead

Hermiston

Windsor Road

Ashborde

5

Seaton

Burnbank

Warwick Rd

Kielder Hoxoxy

Ludlow Dr

Hatfield

Wentworth Gdns

Superstore

Carnoustie Wy

Rosemount Wy

Turnberry

Newsteads

Sandown

Fairways

Mwfield

Muirfield

Andrew

Pykerley

Elmwood Rd

Woodleigh

Back La

Percy

Front

PO

Kielder Road

First School

PO

Wilton Gdns

Arundel Drive

Sandringham Drive

Marina

Church

Melville

West Monkseaton Station

Sunningdale

Brantwood Av

Belmont

Beechwood

Oakland

Meadow Rd

Monkseaton Clinic

Middle School

6

Thorntree

Marina

Drive

Harewood Crs

Fairfield Gn

Eastward Gn

Holm

Fairfield Drive

EARSDON ROAD

Mitchell Av

Westfield Av

Eastfield Rd

Ironwood Av

Dale Rd

Caldwell Crs

Crawford Av

Paignton

Wembley Avenue

Avenue

Closefield Grove

First School

Medical Cen

PO

Vernon Drive

Churchill

Grange Park

Monks Av

Cauldwell Avenue

Drumoyne

Langley A34

A192

Townsville Av

Selwyn Av

Gardens

Bromley Avenue

Springfield

Seatonville Crs

Melbourne Crs

Seatonville

SEATON

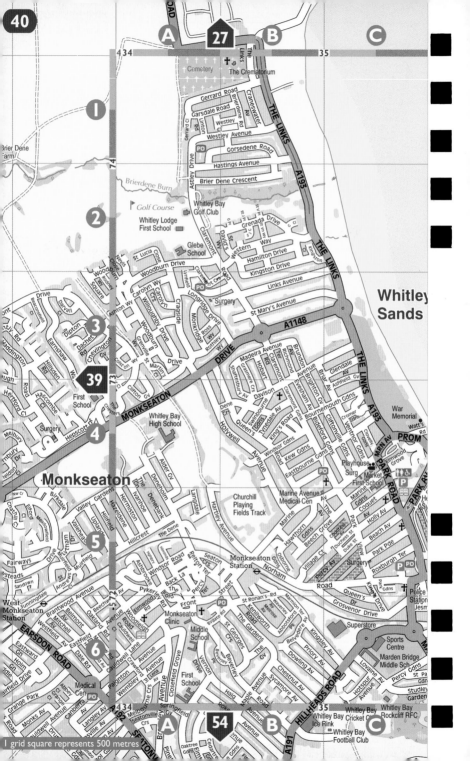

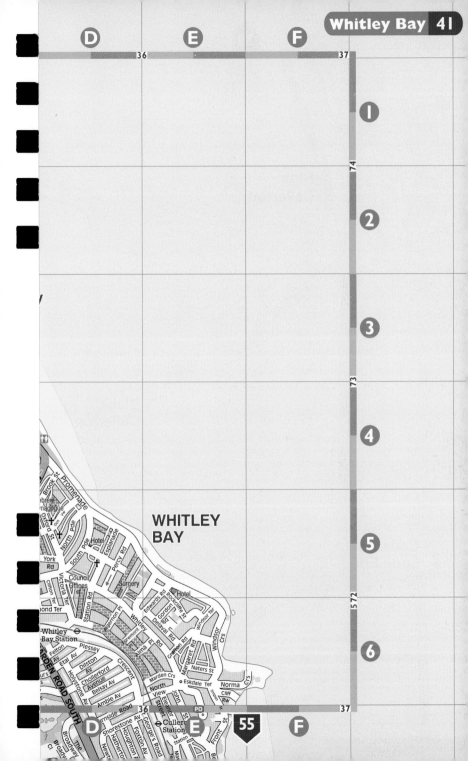

D   E   F

36   37

1

74

2

3

73

4

WHITLEY
BAY

5

5 72

6

37

D   E   55   F

Promenade
ebrew
nagogue
Brook St
Oxford St
York
Rd
North Pde
South Pde
Esplanade
Hotel
Council
Offices
Surgery
Percy Rd
Victoria Ter
Crifton Ter
ond Ter
Station Rd
Whitley
Bay Station
Plessey
Felton
Av
Etal Av
Dilston
Av
Chollerford
Avenue
Belsay Av
Amble Av
rnside Road
Shorestone Av
Hartherton
Houghton
Newt
The
Broadway
Cl
RDEN ROAD SOUTH
Jesmond Pl
Whitley Rd
Claremont
Crescent
Alma Pl
Margaret Rd
North
View
Marden Crs
Edwards Rd
Gordon Sq
Radcliffe Rd
Oxlaval Rd
Windsor Ter
Windsor Crs
Grafton Rd
Naters St
Eskdale Ter
Norma Cts
Cliff
RW
John
Eleanor
Street
St George's Road
Cullerc
Station
Front St
PO
Station
Hotel
Mai
Be

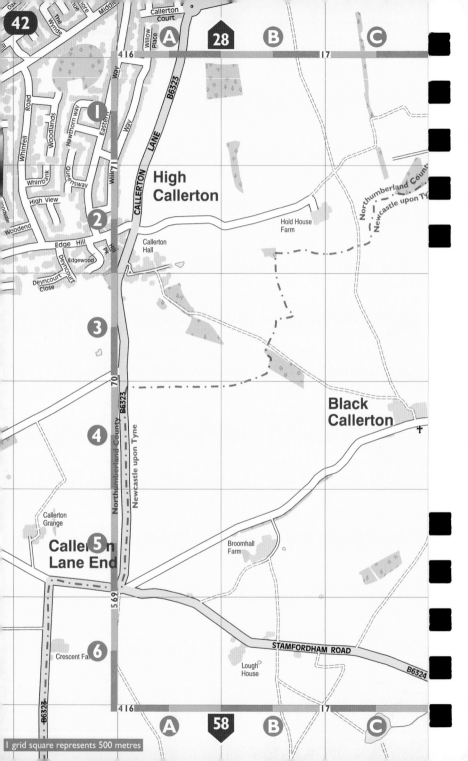

42

The Wynde
Oak
Middle

Callerton
Court

Willow Place

416 17

Way
Hawthorn way
Eastern Way
Way
Willn'71
CALLERTON LANE
B6323

1

Whinfell Road
Woodlands
Queensway
Whin'bank
High View

High
Callerton

2

Woodend
Edge Hill
Edgewood
Deyncourt Close
Deyncourt close

Callerton Hall

Hold House Farm

Northumberland County
Newcastle upon Ty

3

70
B6323

Black
Callerton

†

Northumberland County
Newcastle upon Tyne

4

Callerton Grange

5
Callerton
Lane End

Broomhall Farm

569

6
Crescent Fa

Lough House

STAMFORDHAM ROAD
B6324

B6323

416 17

1 grid square represents 500 metres

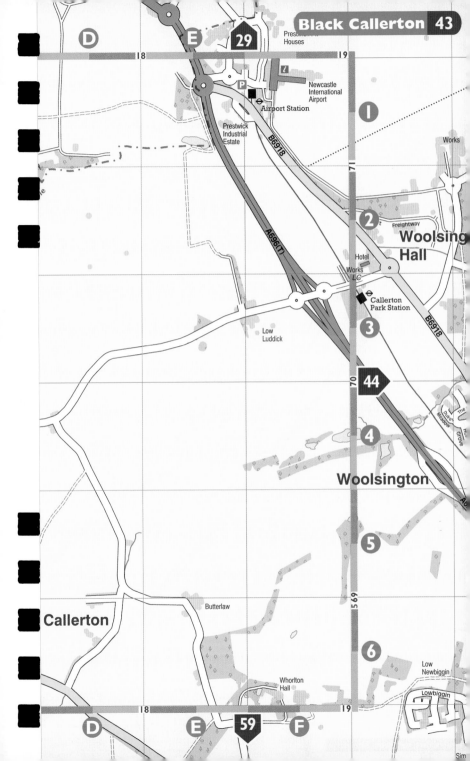

D
E
29
I

Prestwick Houses

Newcastle International Airport

P
Airport Station

Prestwick Industrial Estate

B6918

A696(T)

Works

2
Freightway

Woolsing Hall

Hotel
Works
LC

Callerton Park Station

3

B6918

Low Luddick

70

44

The Hut
Dukes Meadow
Grove

4

Woolsington

A6

5

5 69

Callerton

Butterlaw

Low Newbiggin

6

Lowbiggin

Whorlton Hall

D
E
59
F

Sim

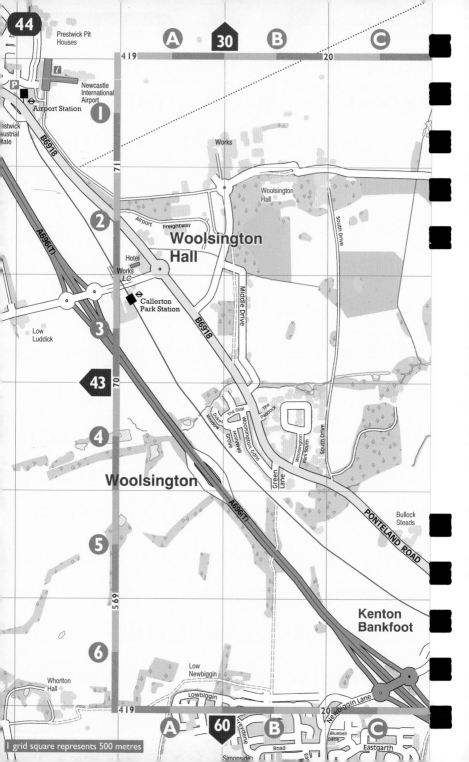

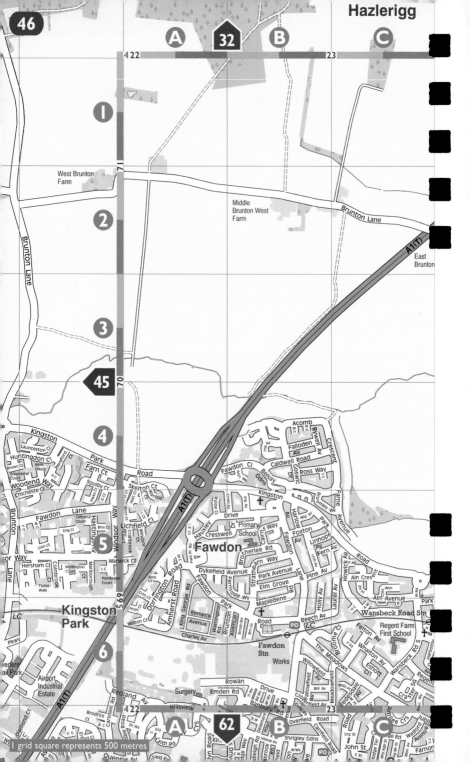

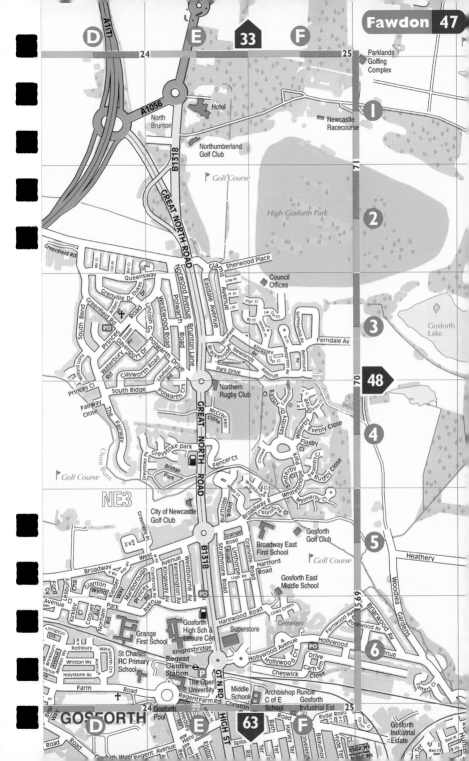

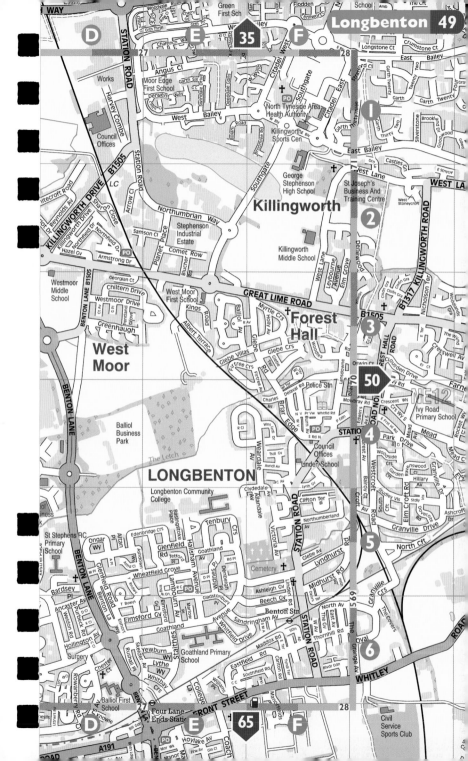

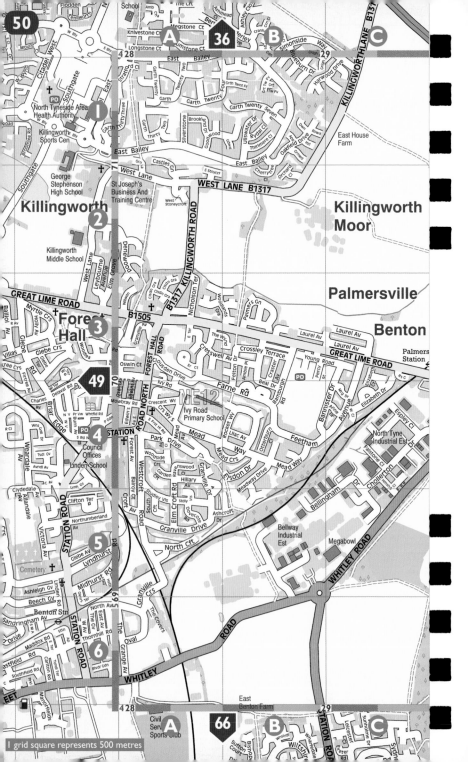

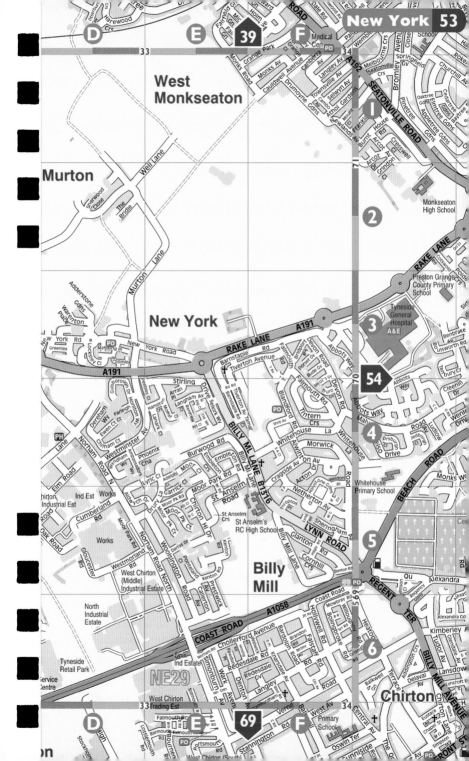

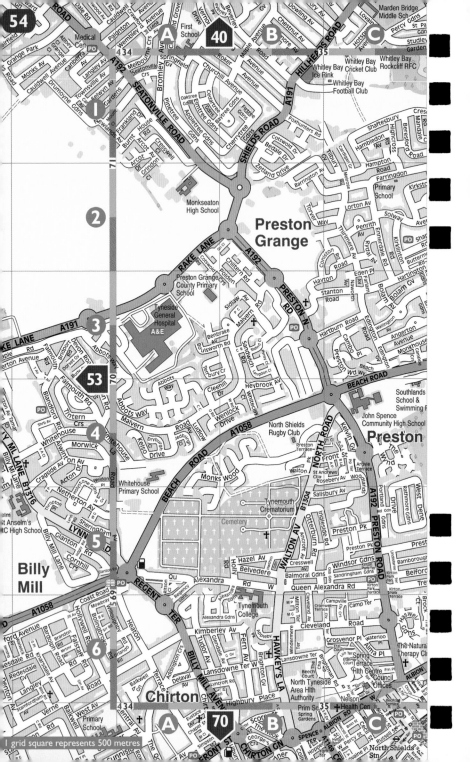

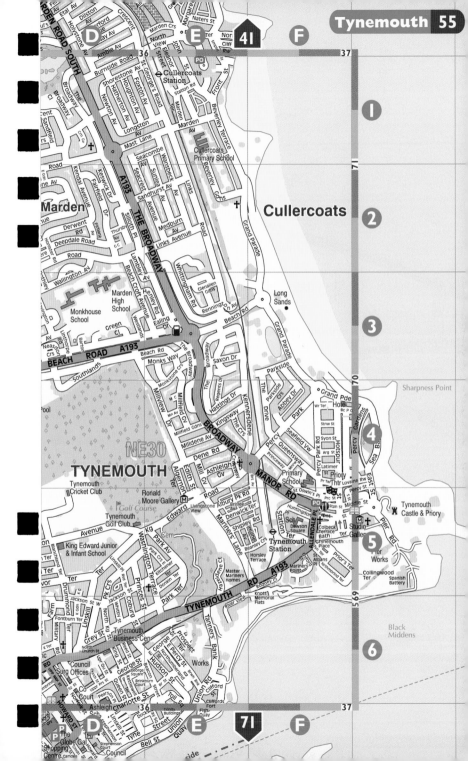

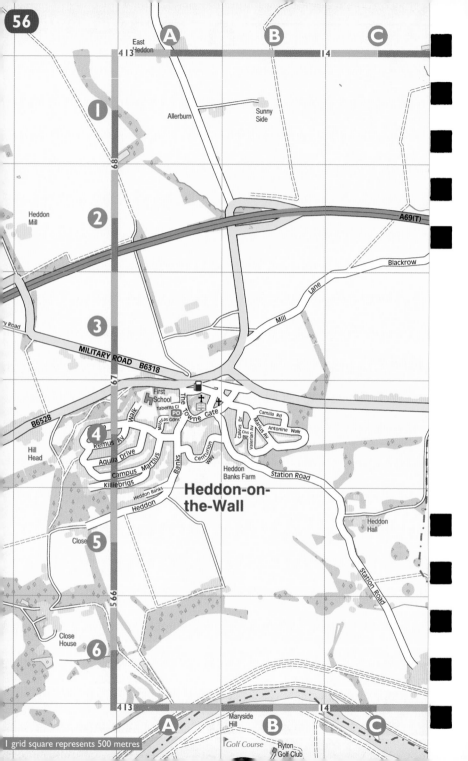

56

East Heddon

A
B
C

4 1 3

1 4

1

68

Allerburn

Sunny Side

2

Heddon Mill

A69(T)

Blackrow

Mill Lane

3

Y Road

MILITARY ROAD B6318

67

First School

The Towne Gate

Taberna Cl

PO

Sas Gdns

Camilia Rd

Calvus Dr

Valentus Av

Martius Av

Antonine Walk

B6528

4

Remus Av

Aquila Drive

Campus Martius

Killiebrigs

Banks

Centurion Way

Heddon Banks

Heddon Banks Farm

Station Road

Hill Head

Heddon Banks

Heddon

Heddon-on-the-Wall

Heddon Hall

5

Close

566

Station Road

6

Close House

4 1 3

1 4

A
B
C

Maryside Hill

Golf Course

Ryton Golf Club

1 grid square represents 500 metres

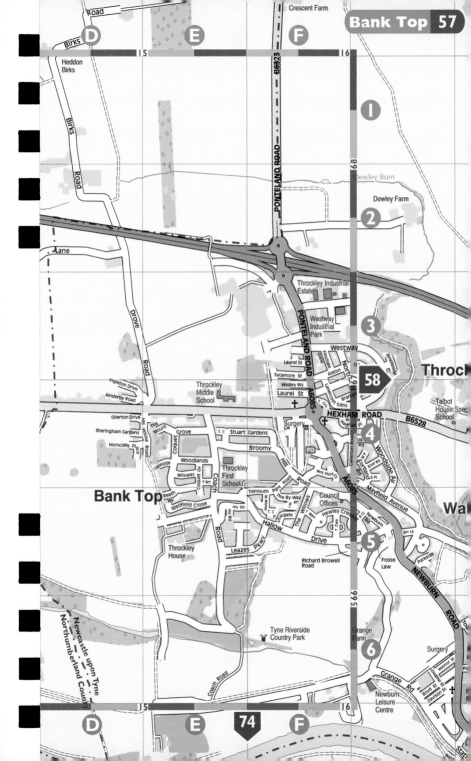

Crescent Farm

Lough House

B6324

A **42** **B** **C**

416 17

PONTELAND ROAD

B6323

1

68

Dewley Burn

Dewley Farm

Fell House Farm

2

Throckley Industrial Estate

North Walbottle

North Walbottle

West Indu Park

3

PONTELAND ROAD

Westway

A6085

Finchdale Gdns

Laurel St

Sycamore St

Ambleside

A6085

Wesley Wy

Brampton Gdns

Laurel St

Cost Gdns

Throckley

57

HEXHAM ROAD

Hadrian Pl

Clarton Road

Vallum Rd

B6528

Talbot House Special School

Surgery

4

Woodside Av

Ponteland

Elm Rd

E Pl

Primary School

George Street

Whitehall Rd

HAWTHORN

N Walbottle Rd

North Walbottle Road

cuart Gardens

Broomy

Mnt Pleast C

ckley

Tillmouth

Hill Road

The By-Way

Park Road

The Willows

A6085

Mayfield Avenue

Newburn

Walbottle

Grove Rd

The Green

PO

The Paddock

Percy Way

Queens Road

Queen's Ct

ckley

ol

Hewley Cresent

Council Offices

C

D

Dri

Hallow

5

Err La

New Burn

Walbottle

Bells Rd

Walbottle Road

eazes

Pkwy

Richard Browell Road

Fosse Law

Parkside

NEWBURN ROAD

566

6

Tyne Riverside Country Park

Grange Farm

Surgery

Newburn Hall Motor Mus

Townfield Gdns

Altwick St

Park Rd

First School

Works

Newburn

Grange Rd

Boyd St

Wemtoz St

Dawson St

Council Offices

Works

Newburn Leisure Centre

416 17

A **75** **B** **C**

PO

Church Rd

Millfield Lane

Burnha

HIGH ST

Station

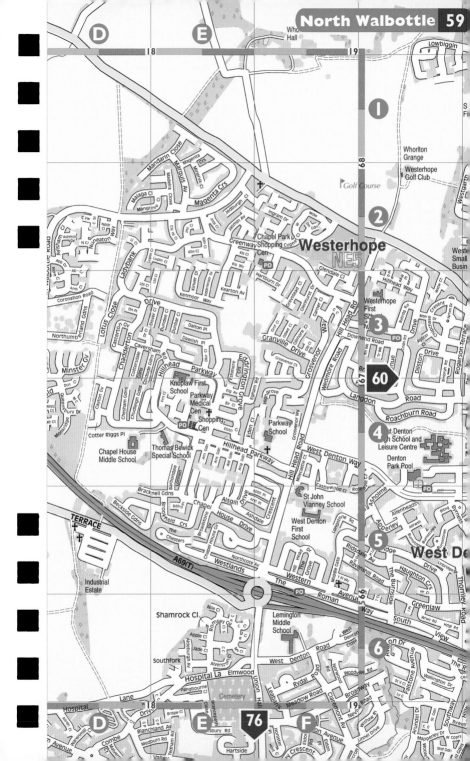

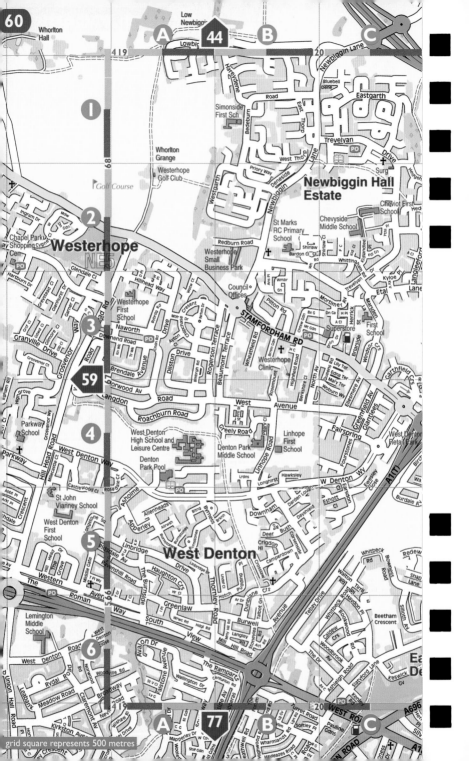

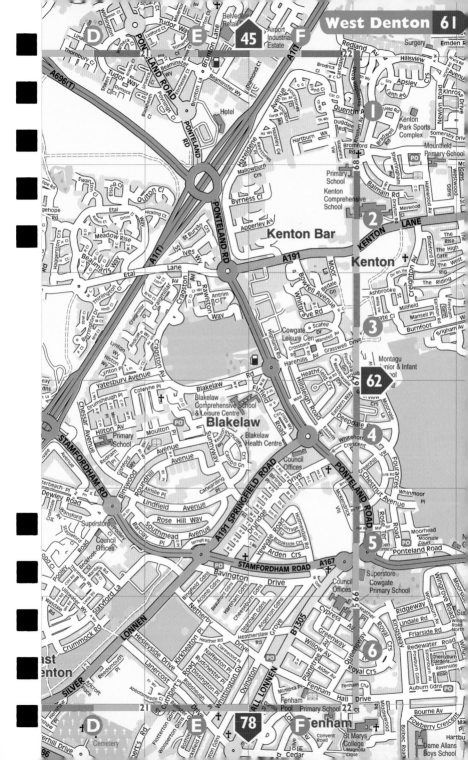

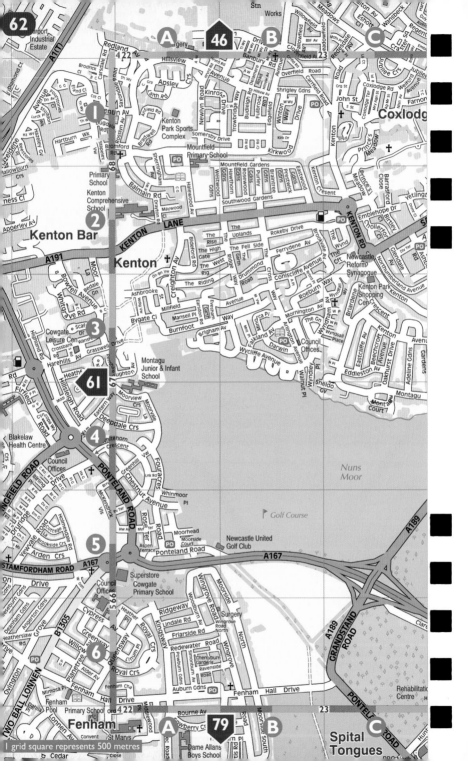

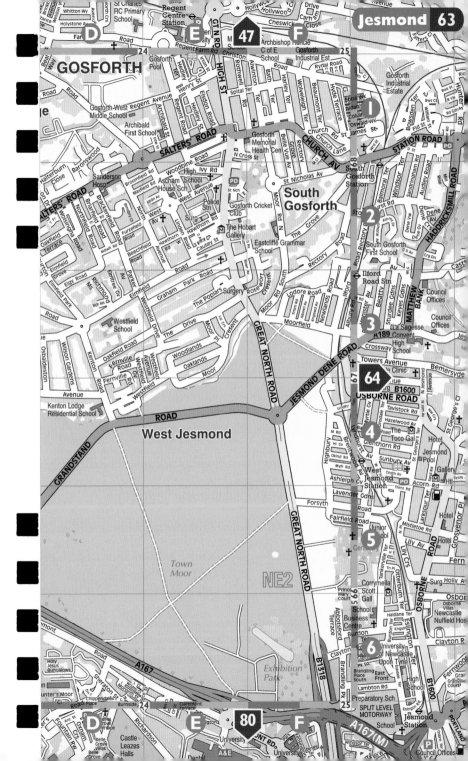

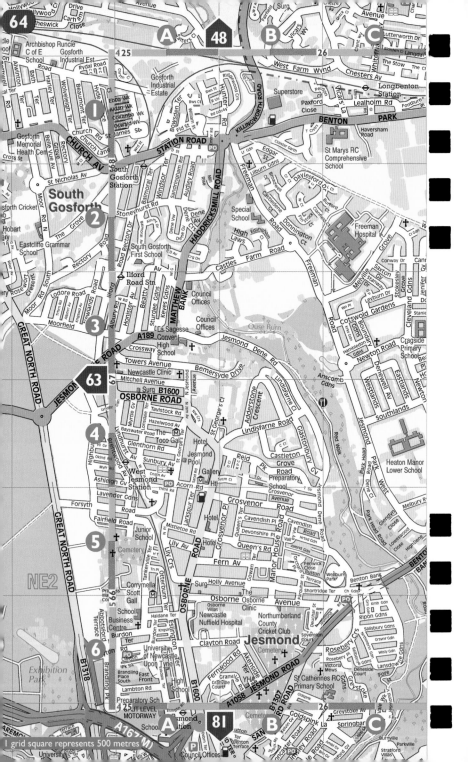

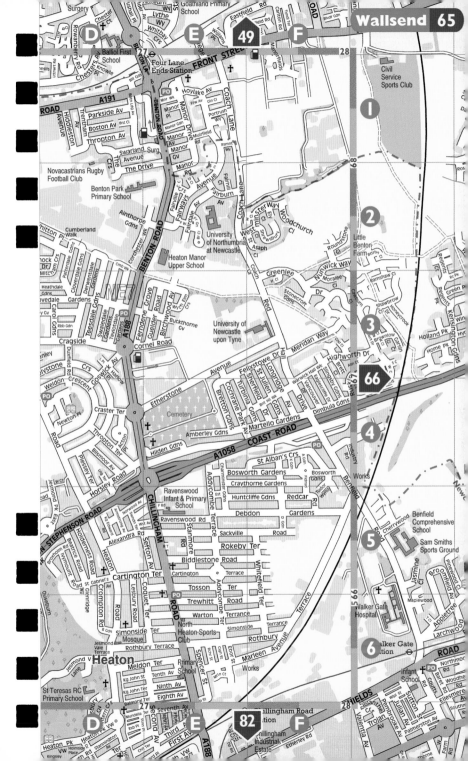

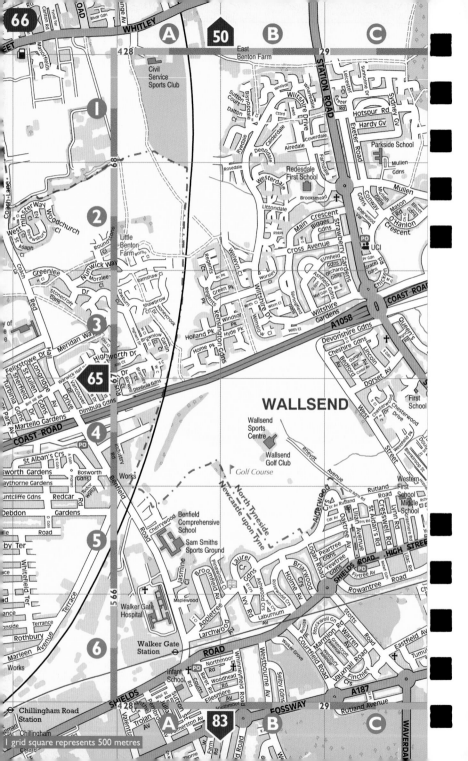

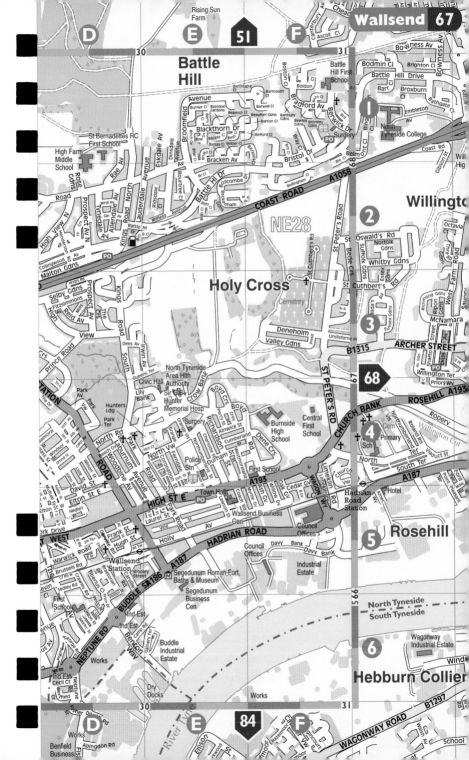

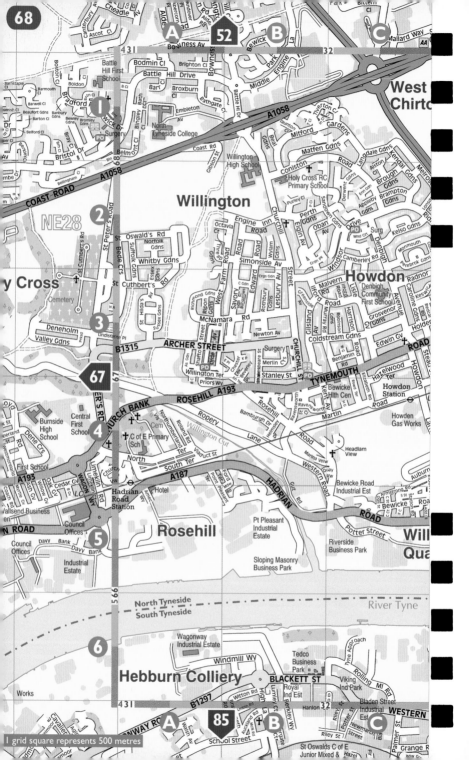

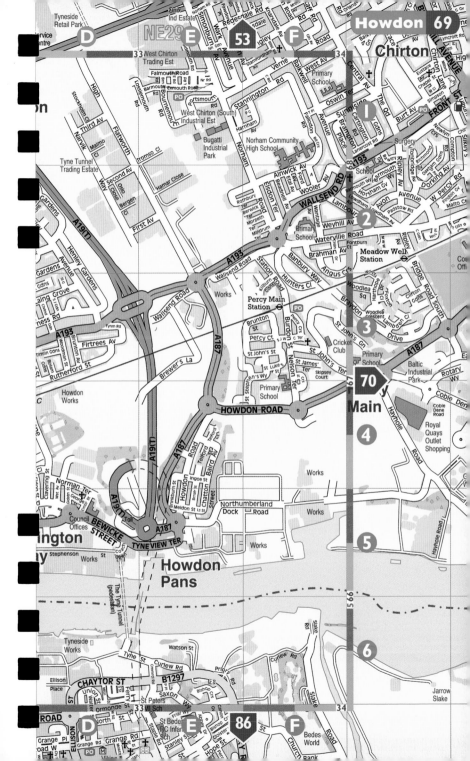

A   B   C

437   38

South Pier

Hotel

Harbour Vw
Beacon St

DRIVE B1344

Lawe Road

Fort
PO
Trajan St   Trajan Av
Vespasian
Cleveland St   Julian Av
Julian St   Fairles St
Tura

The Lawe

SEA ROAD

Coston Dr
Pollard St
Salmon St
St Aidan's Rd
Henry Nelson St

Pier
Pole   Hotel

Westovian
Theatre Society

Herd
Sand

OCEAN RD   A185
Dale
Chatsworth
Court
Blenheim
Walk
Flagg Court
Petworth Close   Longstone Gardens
Seafield Ter

SEA RD

Council
Offices
Mus &
Art Gall

Health
Centre

JMI
School
Wallington
Crove
Harefield
Square
Woodbine
Mariners
Cottages

Beach   Bents
Marina   Drive
Salisbury Pl
Marine Ap
Sea Way

Promenade

Amphitheatre
The Bents

Sandhaven Caravan
& Camping Park

South
Foreshore

SEA ROAD
A183

71

Town Hall
Civic
Offices
Surg

Broughton

Candlish

Erskine

Erskine Wy

SOUTH SHIELDS

Park   Road

Promenade

Sports &
Recreation Hall
Cemetery

NE33

Dartford Road
Kingsway

Wharton St
Hyde St
Sponr

Leighton   Street
Osborne   Road

St

Vincent

Coleridge   Av

Mowbray   Wentworth

Birkdale

HORSLEY HLRD

Eairvals Rd

COAST ROAD
A183

Bamburgh

Kelvin Gv

B1301

Westoe Rd
Imeary St

Robert St
Madeira
Chichester Rd E
Osborne Av
Readhead Av
Michael St

Westoe Dr
Manor Court
Silverton
Gardens

Northfiel
Road

Sheldon Rd

Southfield Road

Garth Crs
Hemsley Rd

Infant
School

Cheviot
County
Mixed S

Gateshead & South Tyneside
Hlth Authority
Surgery

Westoe Village

Westoe

South Tyneside
College

Northfield
Gardens
Fountain Gv

HIGHFIELD ROAD

Allendale Dr

Cheviot

St Cuthberts

Chichester
Stn

B1301   DEAN RD
Surg

Northcote St

CHICHESTER ROAD

STANHOPE ROAD

Morthfield
Oxford St
Alverthorpe
Crandall St
Dulverton
Wantage

Farrington St
Canterbury St
Marlborough St
Banbury
Greta
Hescott Ter
Lisburn

High
School

SUNDERLAND ROAD

Grosvenor

Grosvenor
Road

Tynedale   Readhead
Rd   Road

Horsley
Hill

Highfield Drive

High Meadow

Midhurst Av

Cemetery

Vale

WESTHOPE

Norham Av N

CHEVIOT
B1301

A   89   B   C

South Tyneside
Area Hlth Authority

Trow
Point

The
Leas

Frenchman's
Bay

A183 COAST ROAD

Junior
School

90

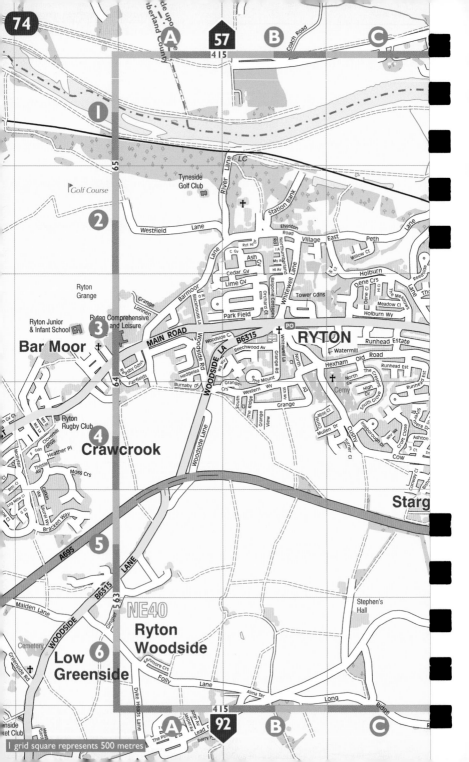

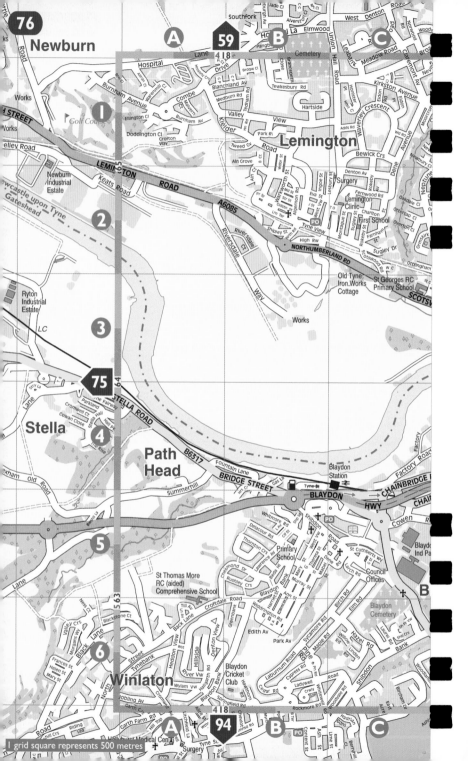

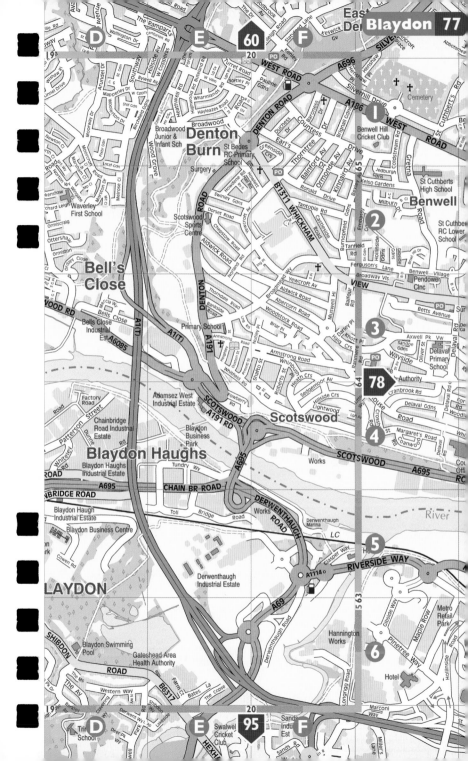

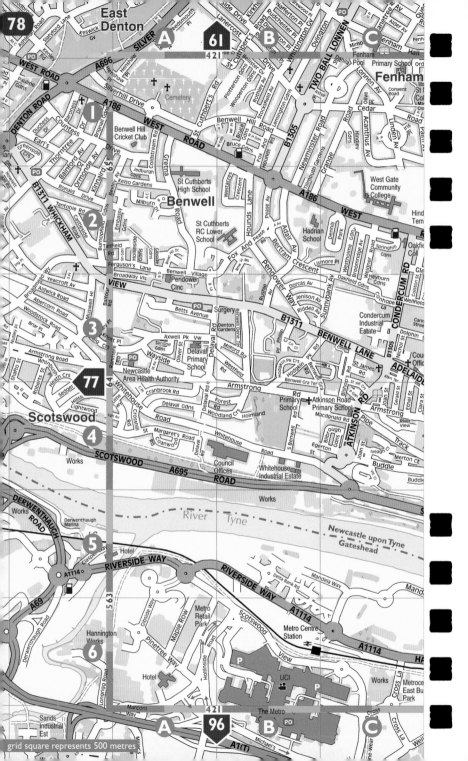

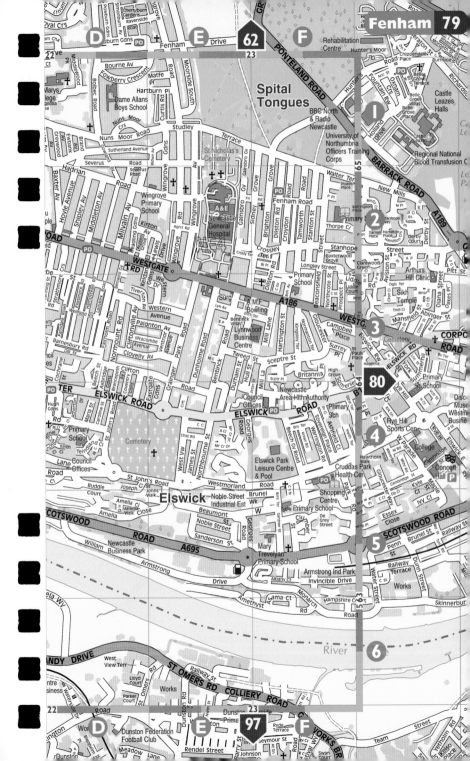

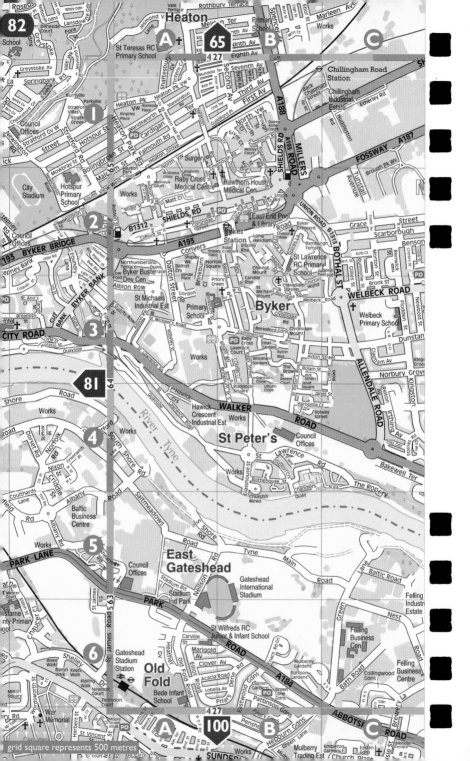

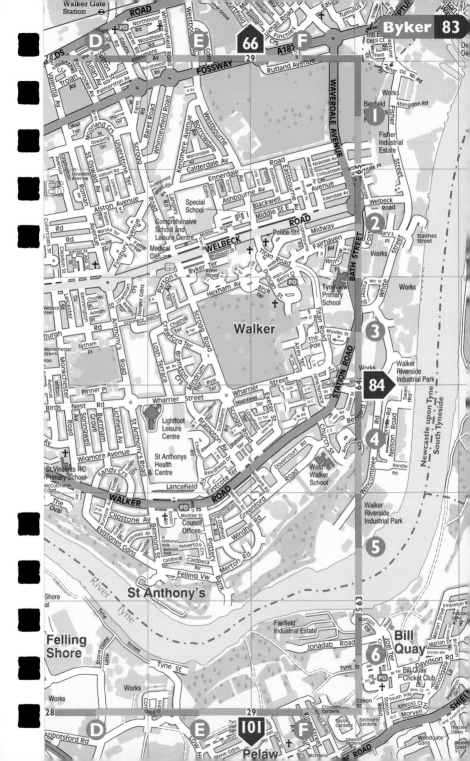

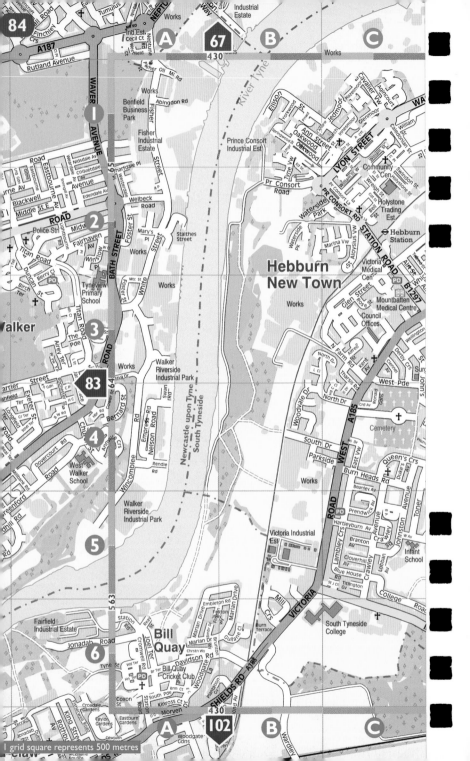

1 grid square represents 500 metres

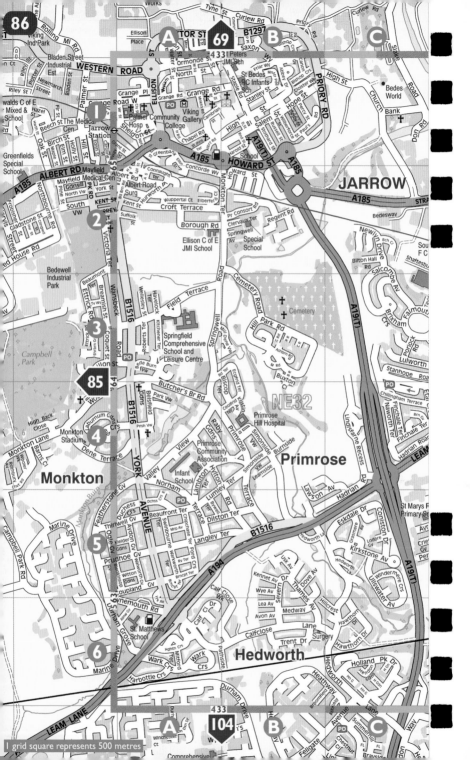

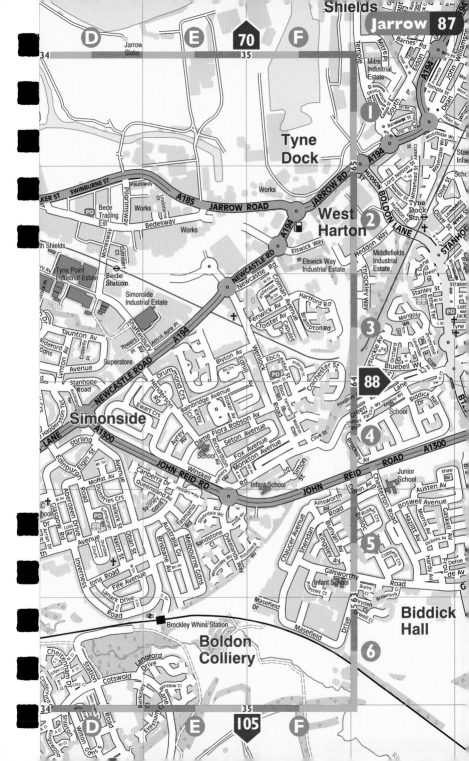

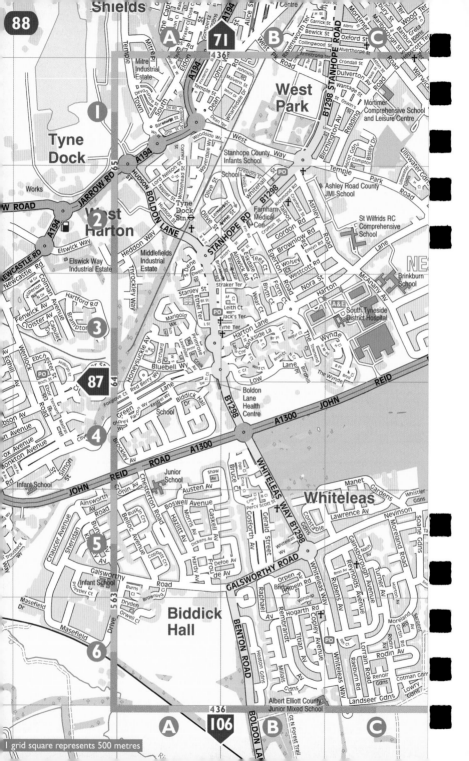

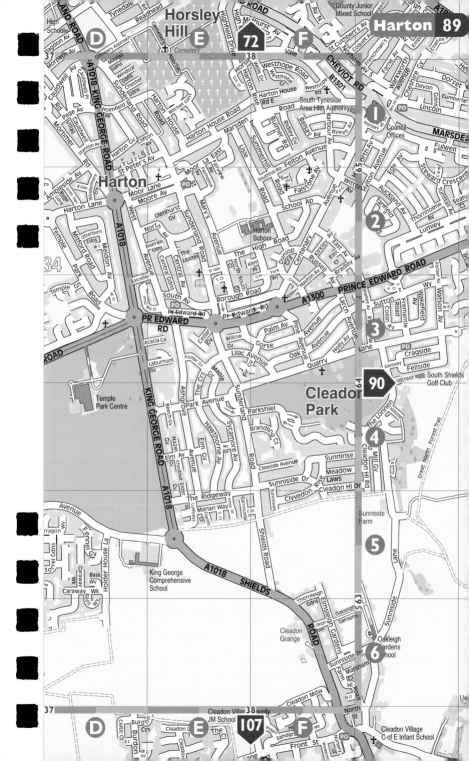

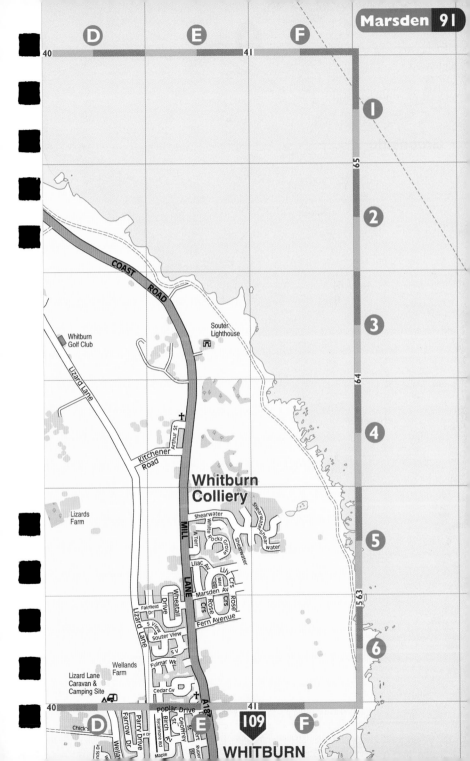

D E F

40 41

1

65

2

COAST ROAD

3

Souter
Lighthouse

Whitburn
Golf Club

64

4

Lizard Lane

Kitchener
Road

**Whitburn
Colliery**

St murs st

5

Lizards
Farm

Shearwater

White Terr
Cocks Gr Vw
Shearwater
Shearwater
water

Lilac Av

Lily Crs
May Gn

MILL LANE

Marsden Av

Rose
Crs

Rose Crs

5 63

Fairfield
Dri

Wheatall
Drive

Fern Avenue

Lizard Lane

S View

Souter View

6

S V

Wellands
Farm

Fulmar Wk

Lizard Lane
Caravan &
Camping Site

Cedar Gv

A183

40 41

Poplar Drive

Chick's

D E F

Farrow Dr
Parry Drive

Geoffrey
St

Birch
St

Sycamore Rd

Rupert

Wella

109

WHITBURN

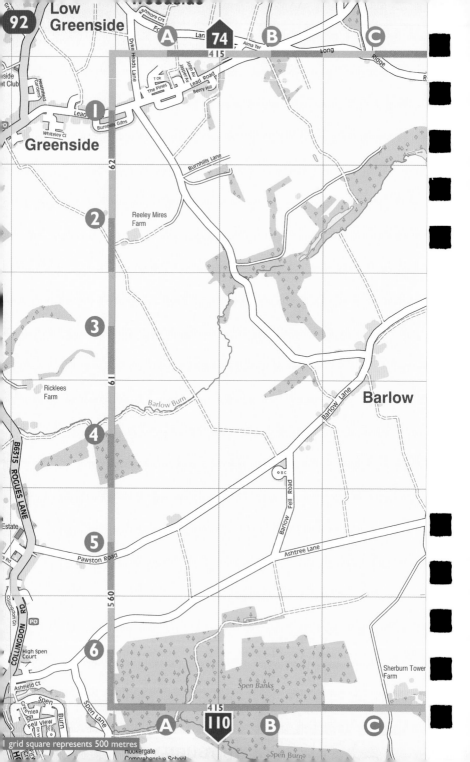

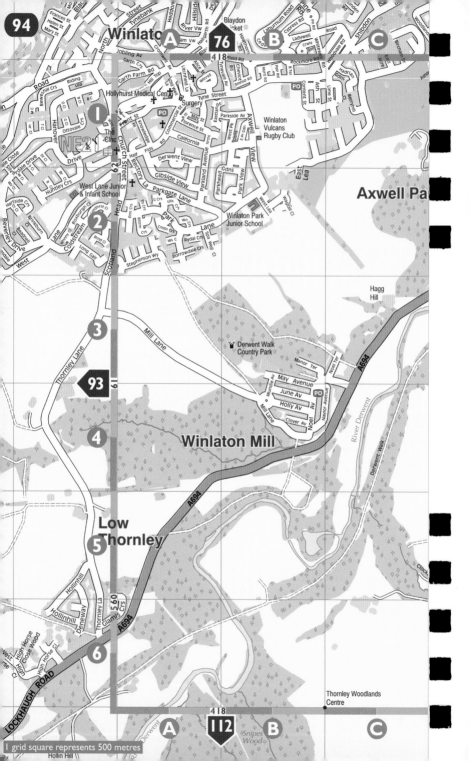

Winlaton **A** 76 **B** **C**

Blaydon
Racket

Hollyhurst Medical Cent
Surgery

Tyne Street

Winlaton
Vulcans
Rugby Club

NE21

The Elms

California

Derwent View

Gibside View

West Lane Junior
& Infant School

Winlaton Park
Junior School

Axwell Pa

Hagg
Hill

Mill Lane

Derwent Walk
Country Park

93

Manor Ter

Noel Ter

A694

May   Avenue

June Av

Holly Av

Clover Av

Winlaton Mill

River Derwent

Derwent Walk

**Low
Thornley**

A694

A694

Thornley Woodlands
Centre

A 112 **B** **C**

Snipes
Wood

I grid square represents 500 metres

Hollin Hill

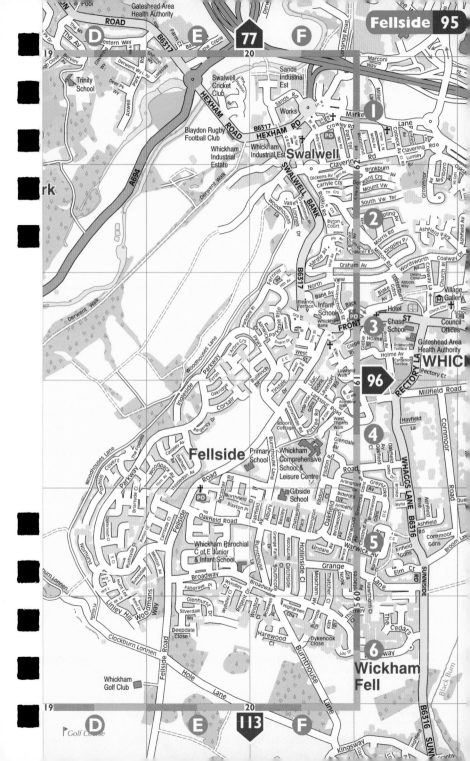

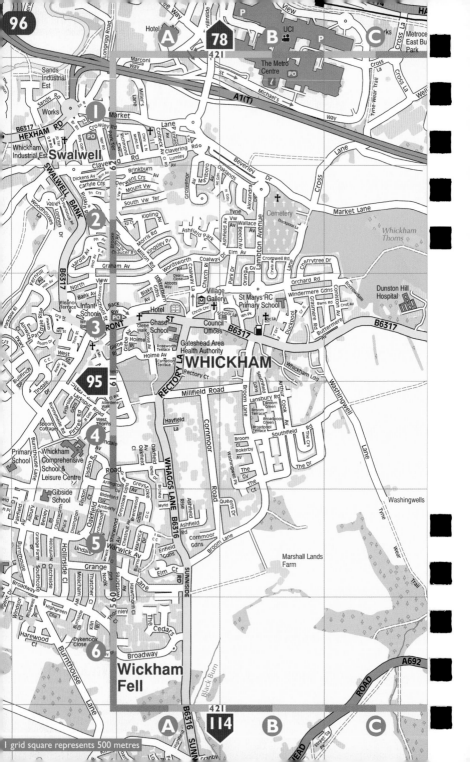

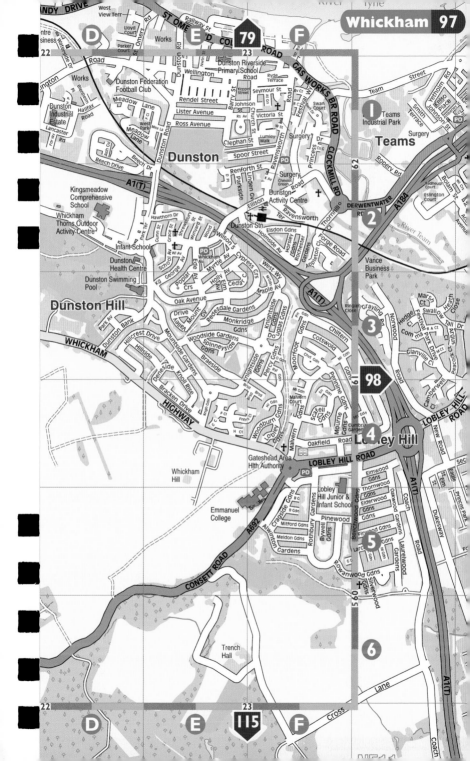

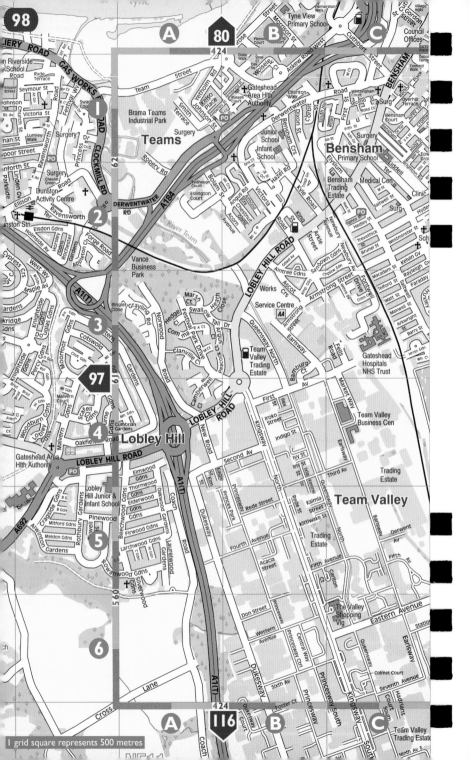

I grid square represents 500 metres

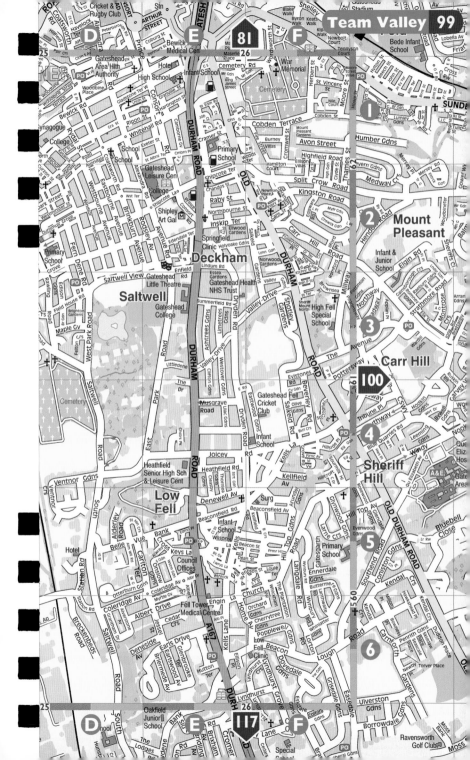

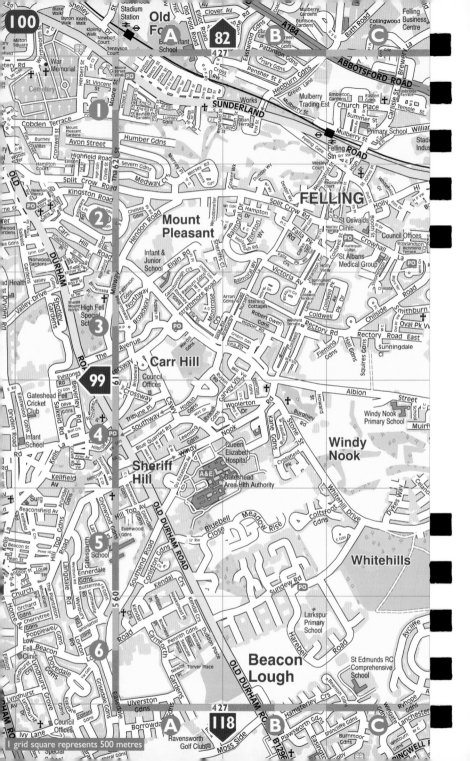

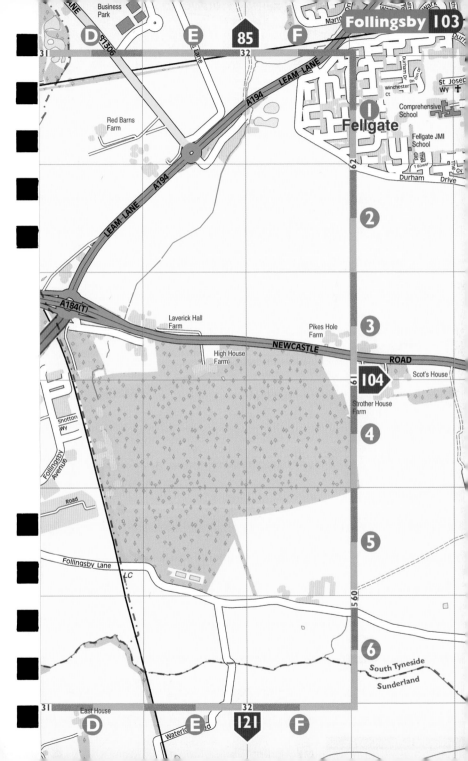

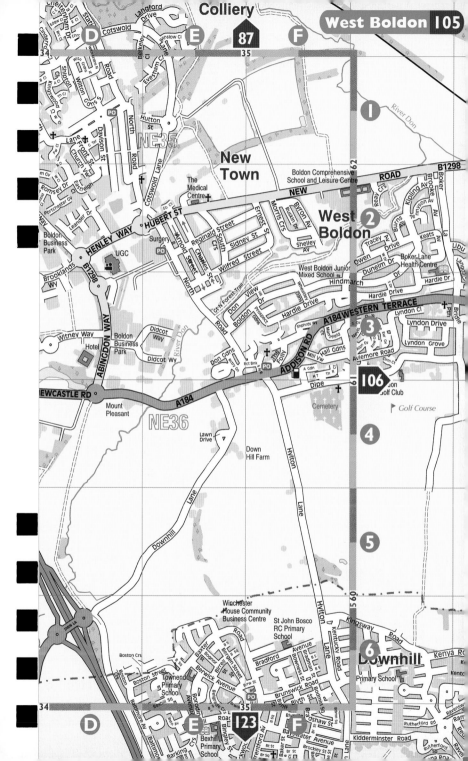

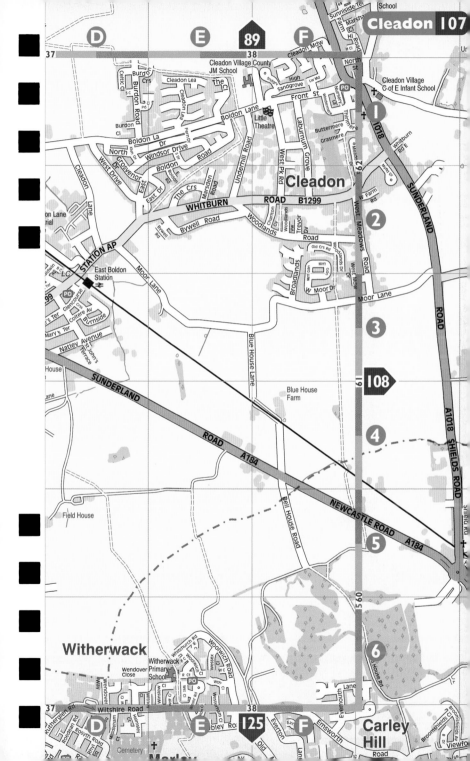

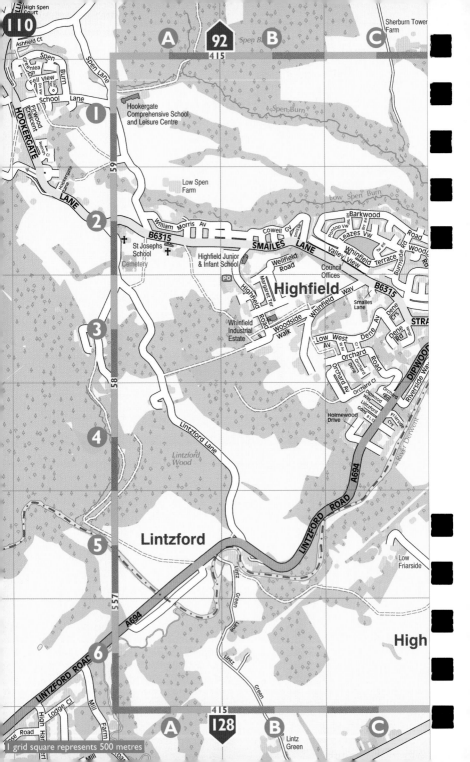

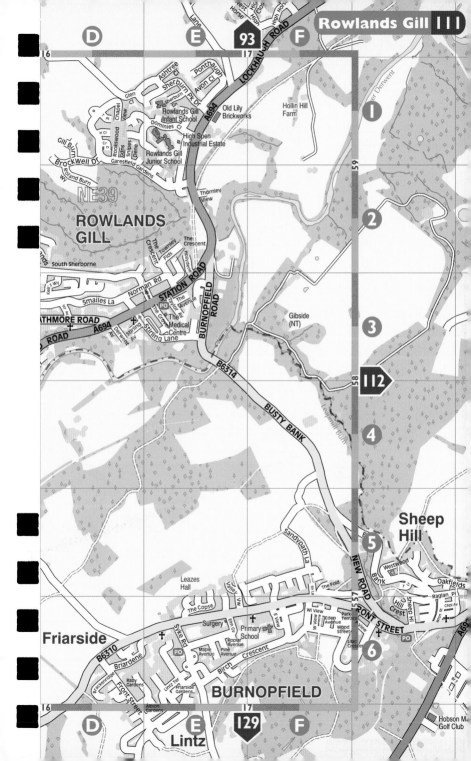

112

LOCKHAUGH ROAD

94
418

Thornley Woodla
Centre

Snipes Dene
Wood

River Derwent

Hollin Hill
Farm

ily
works

59

Gibside
Hillhead

Cut
Thorn

Hillhead
Lane

West Lane

Gibside
(NT)

58

III

BUSTY BANK

LOBLEYHILL

Byermoor RC Aided
Junior & Infant School

Fellside Road

Byermoor Industrial
Estate

Byerm

Gateshead

Durham County

Sheep
Hill

Sandyvath La

Busty
Bank

Westwood

Oakfields

The Close

NEW ROAD

Raglan Pl

Crookbank
Farm

Primary
School

W View
Eden Avenue
Wood Street

The Fold

Park Terrace

FRONT STREET

Hill
Crest

Sheep Hill

Chpl Av

A692

E View

Crescent

Lilac
Crescent

PO

RNOPFIELD

Crookgate
Bank

418
130

Barcusclose Lane

Field Fare
Court

1 grid square represents 500 metres

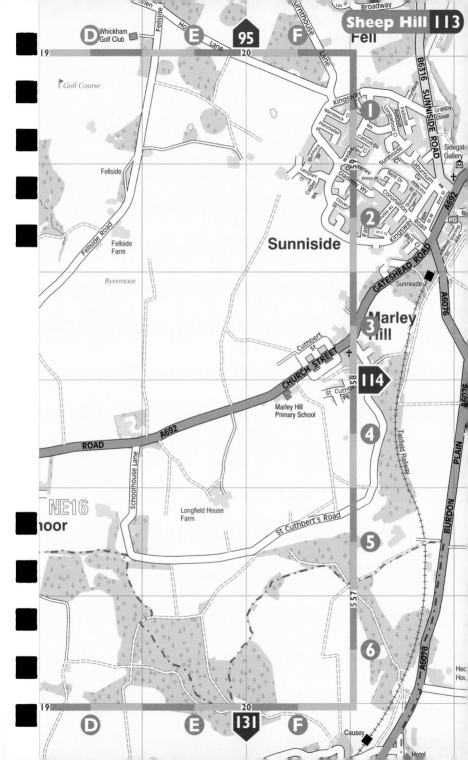

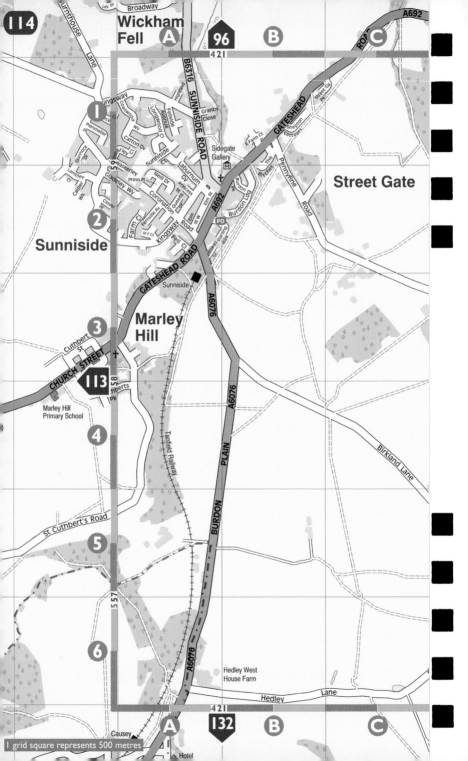

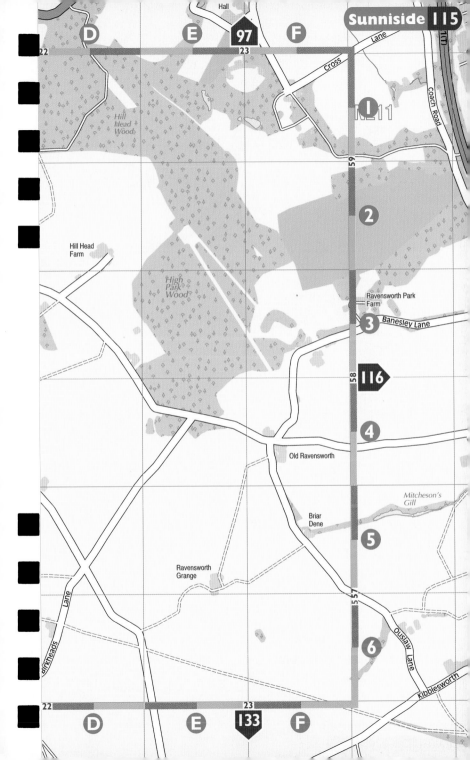

Hall

D   E   **97**   F

22   23

Hill Head Wood

I **211**

59

2

Hill Head Farm

High Park Wood

Ravensworth Park Farm

3 Banesley Lane

58 **116**

4

Old Ravensworth

Mitcheson's Gill

Briar Dene

5

Ravensworth Grange

55 57

6

Ouslaw Lane

Birkheads Lane

Cross Lane

Coach Road

Kibblesworth

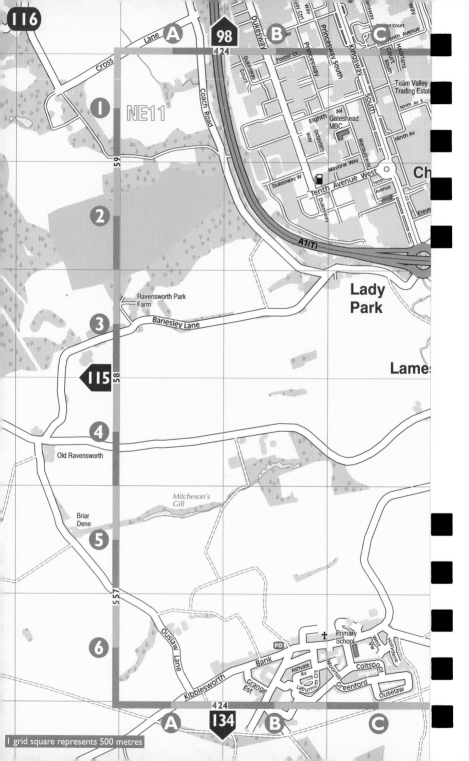

116

98
424

A   B   C

Lane

Cross

1   NE11

59

2

Dukesway
Foster ct.
Princesway south
Princesway
Kingsway
Street Court
Tenth Avenue
Highians
Court
South

Dukeway

Dukesway
Court

Eighth
AV
Octavian
Way

AV
Gateshead
MBC

Ninth Av E

Ninth Av

Mayoral Way

Dukesway W

Tenth Avenue West
Dukesway
Tenth
Avenue

Ch

Team Valley
Trading Estate

Eleven

Coach Road

A7(T)

Lady
Park

Ravensworth Park
Farm

3   Banesley Lane

Lames

115   58

4

Old Ravensworth

Mitcheson's
Gill

Briar
Dene

5

557

6

Ouslaw Lane

Kibblesworth

424
134

Bank

PO

Ashvale
AV

Grange
Est

Laburnum Crs

†
Primary
School

Moorhill

Holycene

West
AV

Coltspo

Creenford

Ouselaw

A   B   C

I grid square represents 500 metres

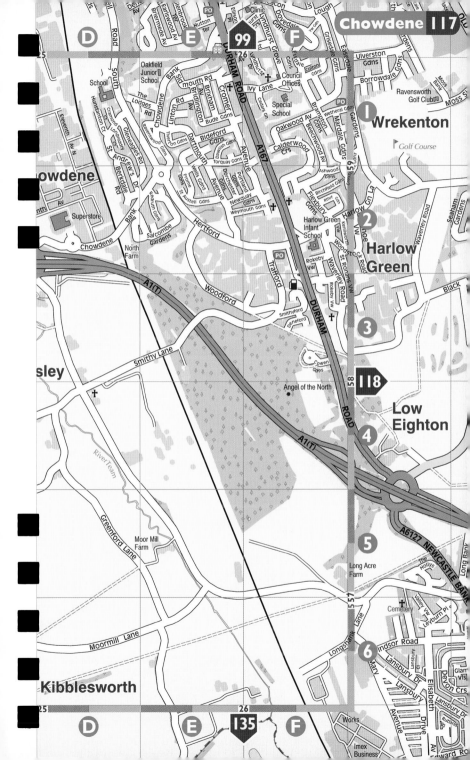

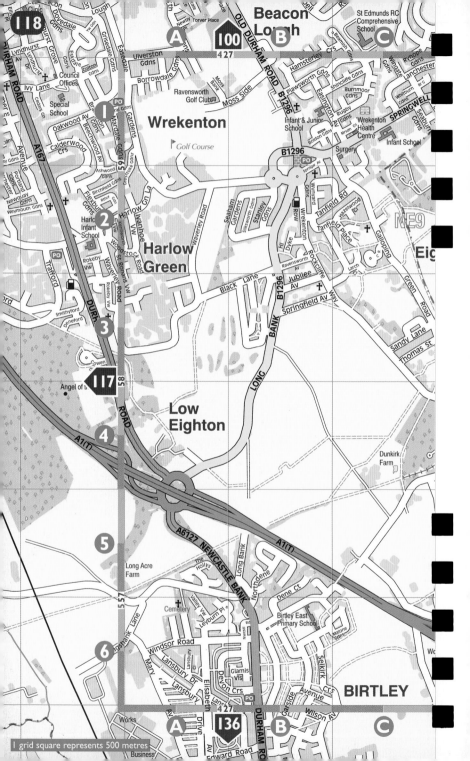

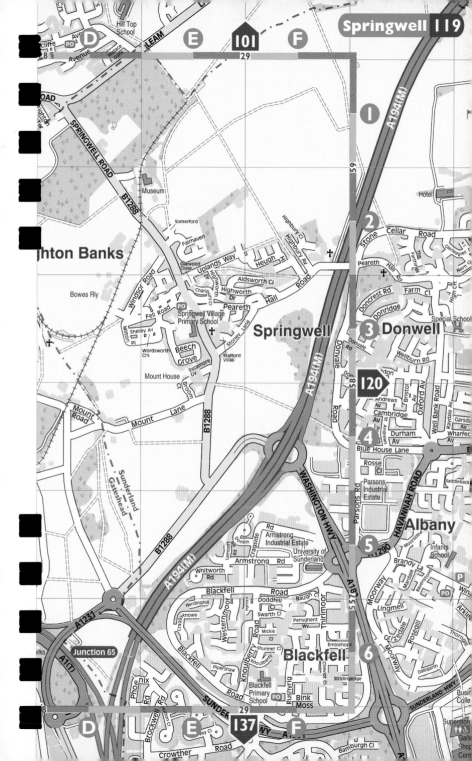

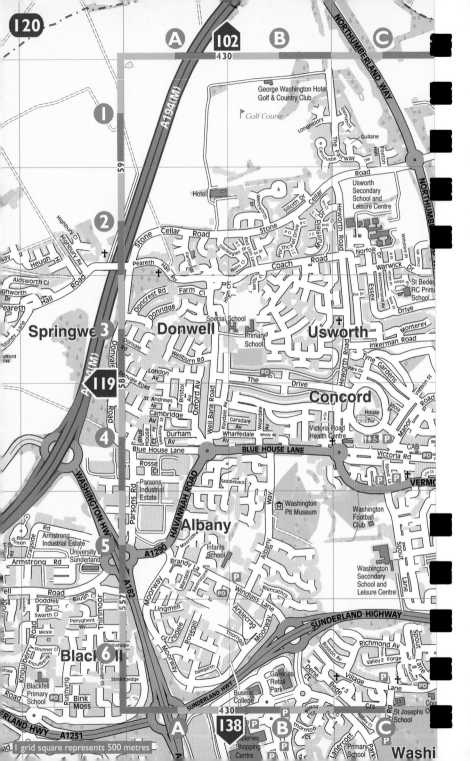

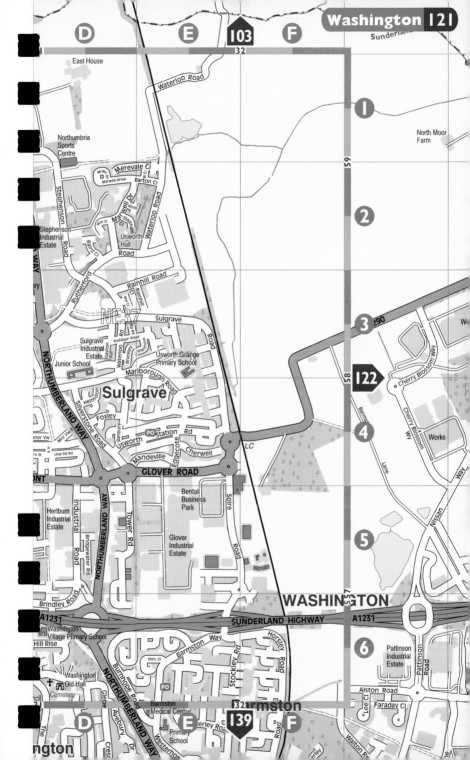

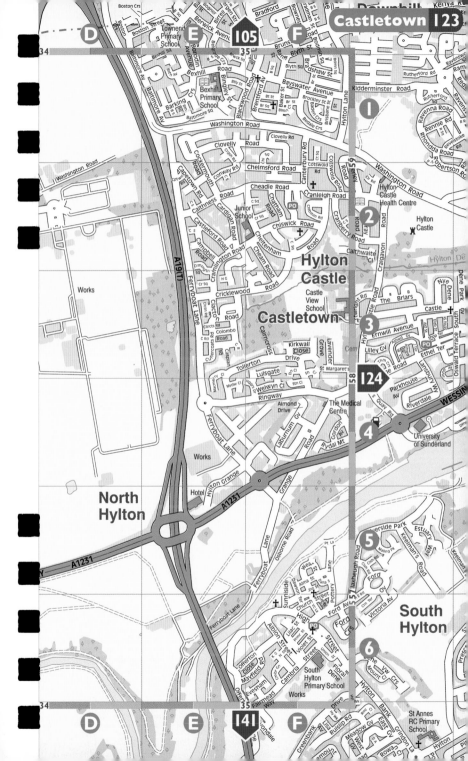

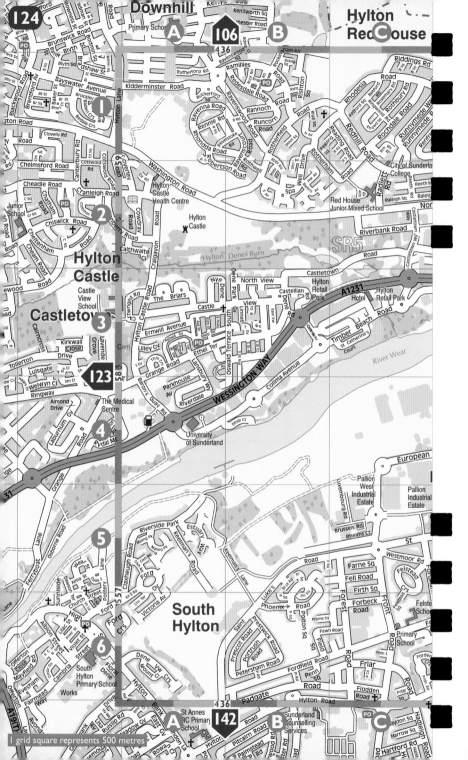

I grid square represents 500 metres

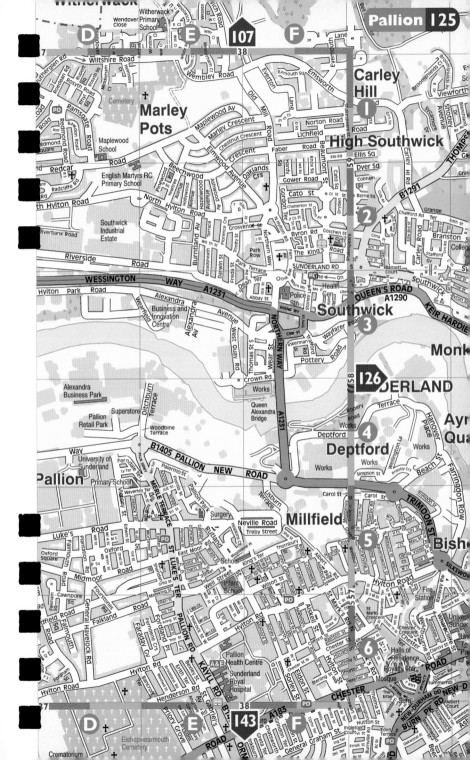

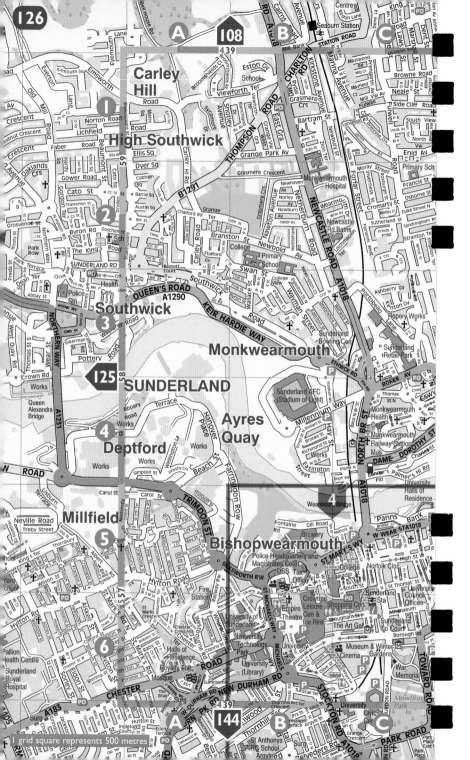

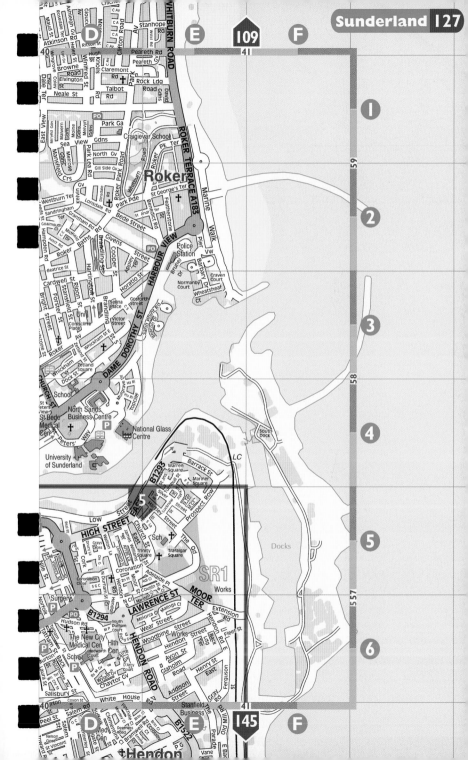

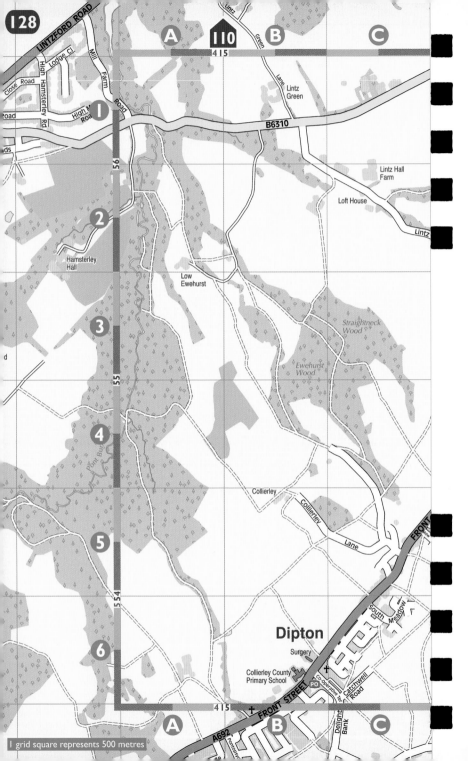

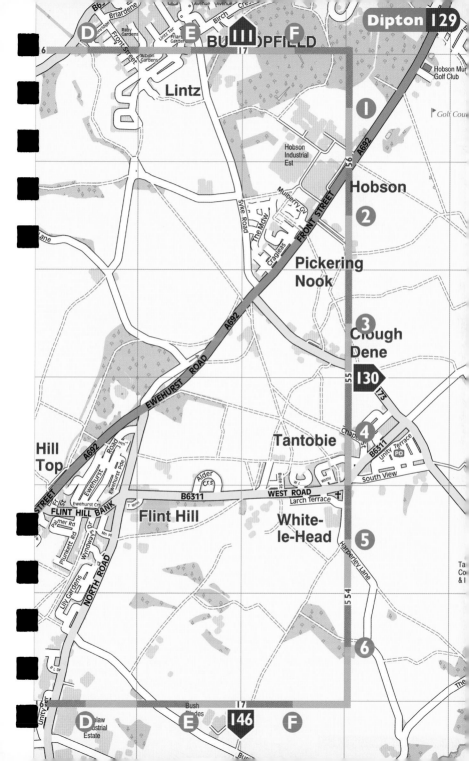

D   Briardene

Raby Gardens

Lintz Ter
Friars Garden

E   BU[■]PFIELD
17

F

Innridge

Front Street

Albion Gardens

Lintz

Hobson Mur Golf Club

Golf Cour

1

A692

56

FRONT STREET

Hobson Industrial Est

Mulberry Gv

Syke Road

The Maw

Craglea

Hobson

2

Pickering Nook

A692

EWEHURST ROAD

Clough Dene

3

55

130

173

Chapel St

4

B6311

Unity Terrace

PO

Hill Top

A692

Ewehurst Road

Ewehurst Pde

Ewehurst Crs

FLINT HILL BANK

Palmer Rd

Wyndway Dr

Mill Pl

T Mews

Tantobie

Barns St

W L

Wshi

South View

Alder Crs

B6311

WEST ROAD

Larch Terrace

STREET

Ft St

Plunkett Rd

Lily Gardens

NORTH ROAD

Flint Hill

White-le-Head

5

55 54

Harperley Lane

Ta Co & I

B L Dr

6

The

Unity Street

D   Delaw Industrial Estate

E   Bush Blades

17

146

F

Bush

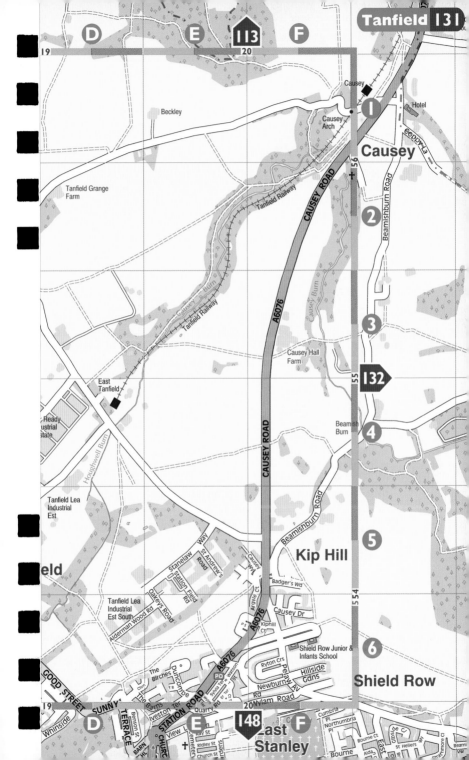

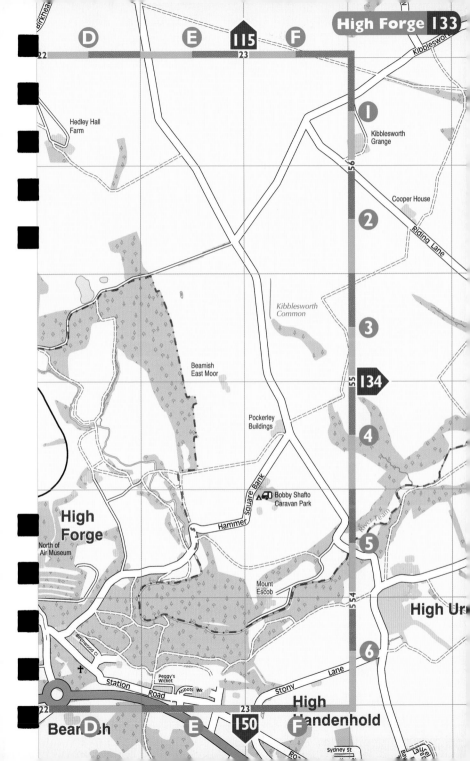

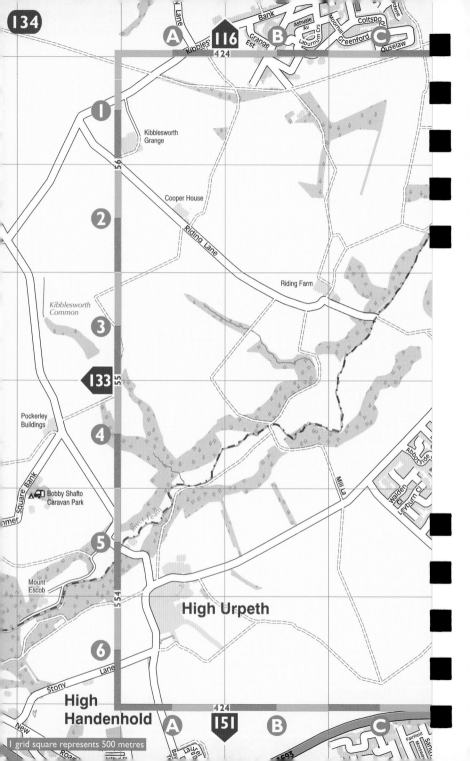

134

A Kibbles Lane 116 424 B Bank Ashvale Av Laburnum Crs Grange Est Moorhill Greenford Coltspo C Ouselaw

1

56

Kibblesworth Grange

Cooper House

2

Riding Lane

Riding Farm

Kibblesworth Common

3

133 55

Pockerley Buildings

4

Abbotsyde

Walden Cl Leybun Cl Mill La

Square Bank

Bobby Shafto Caravan Park

nmer River Team

5

Mount Escob

54

High Urpeth

6

Stony Lane

High Handenhold

New Road A 424 151 B B693 C Fairfield Mosswood Sanu Bay Laurel St Arthur St

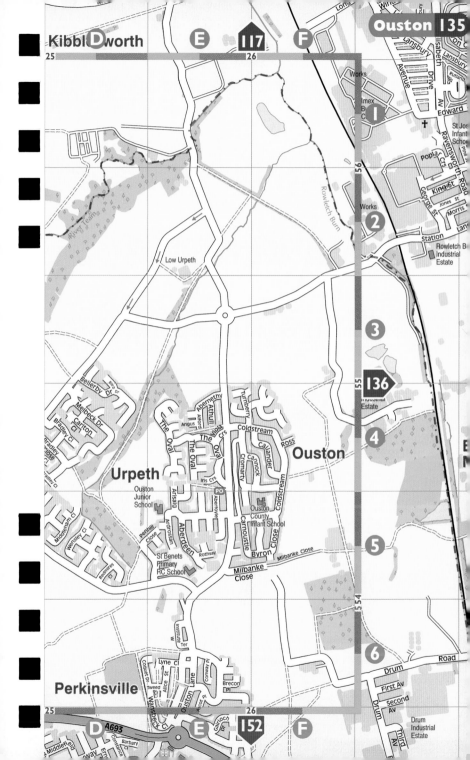

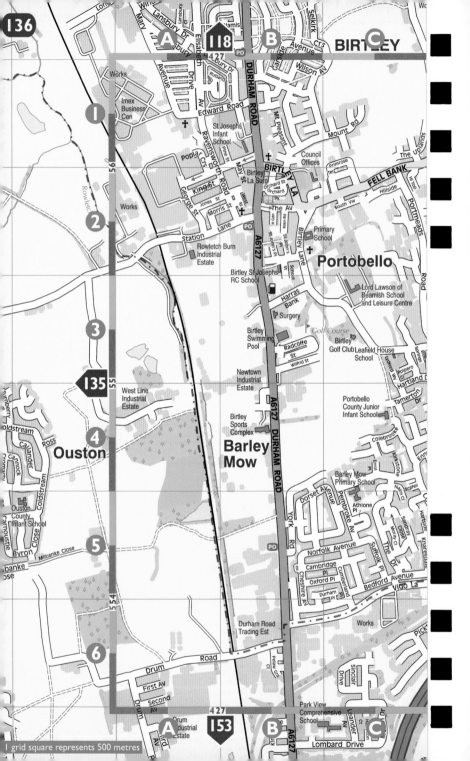

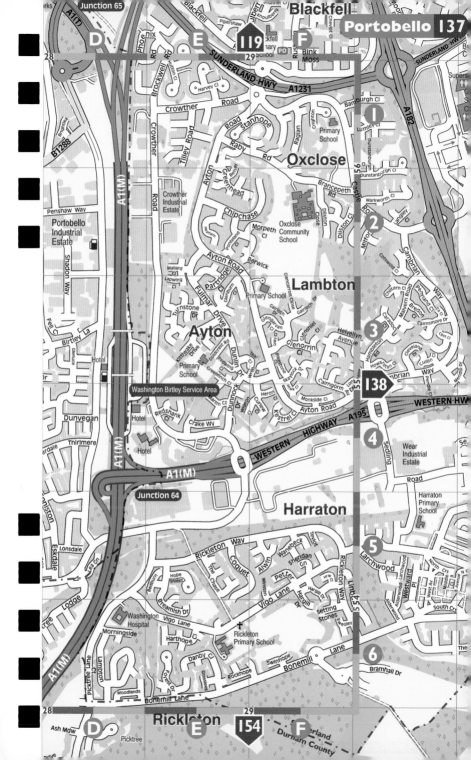

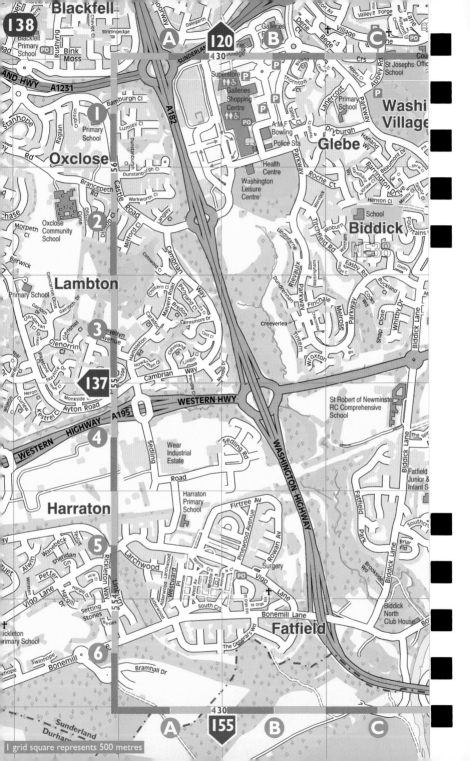

1 grid square represents 500 metres

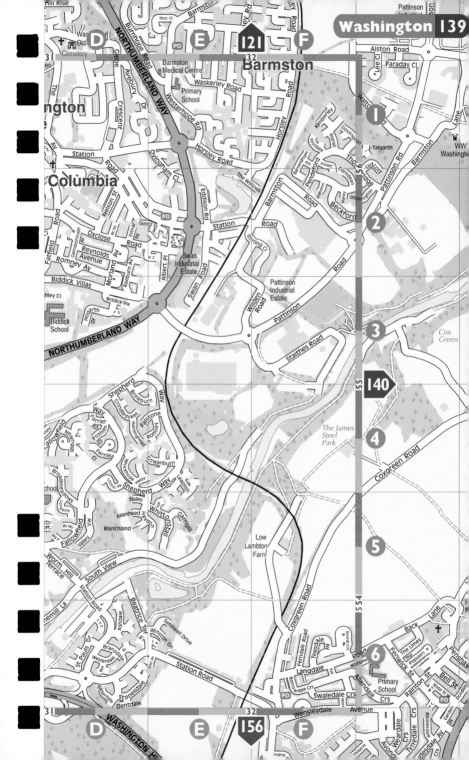

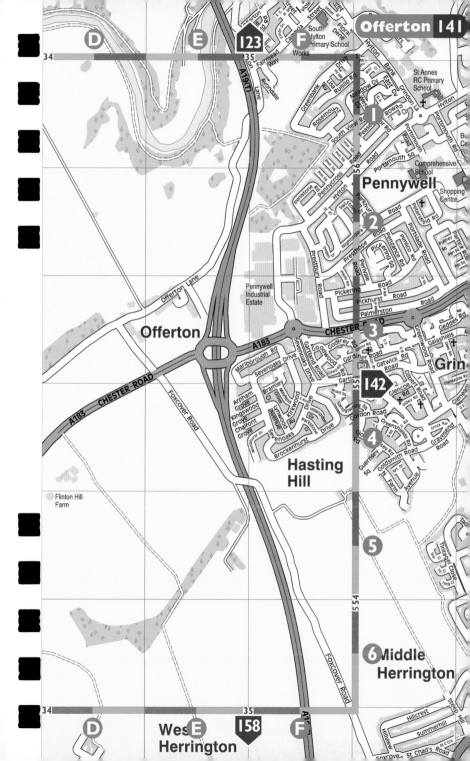

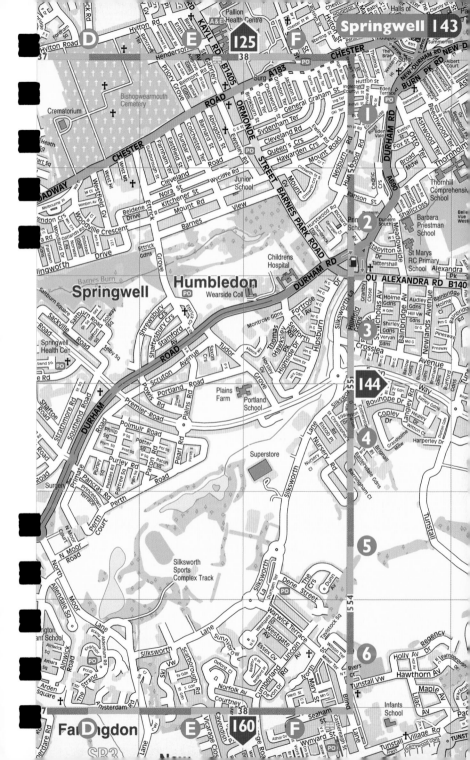

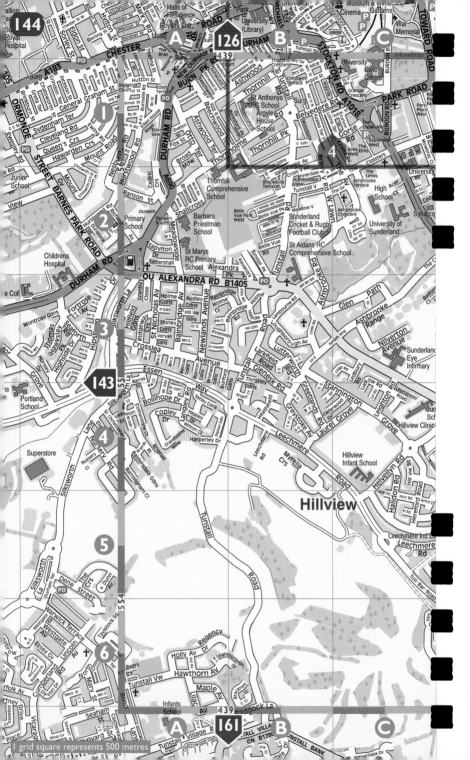

I grid square represents 500 metres

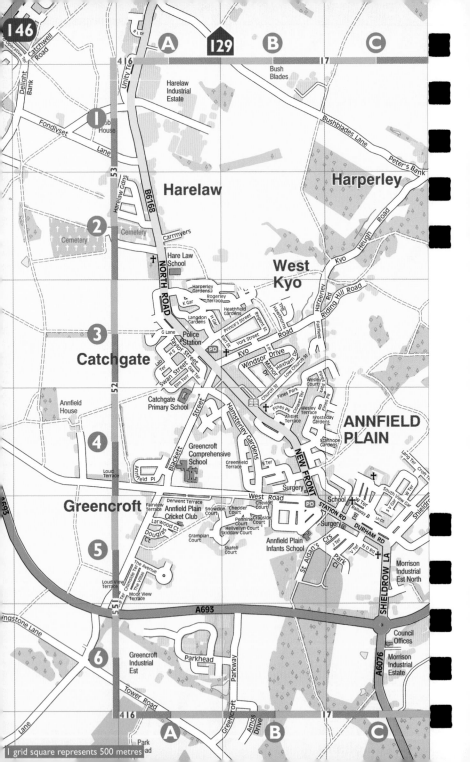

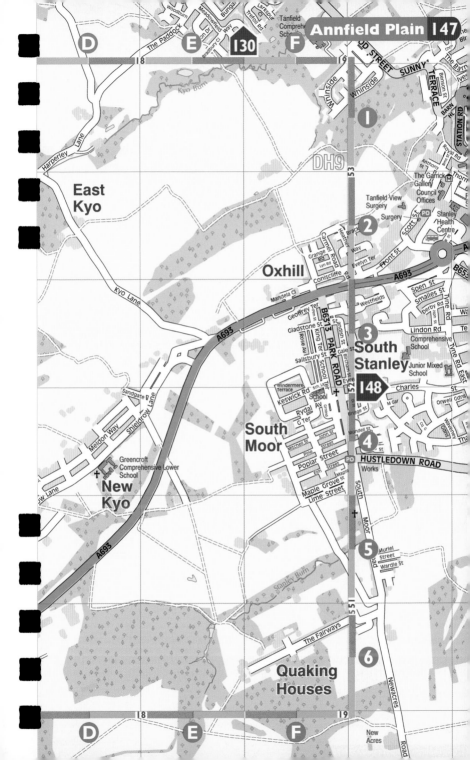

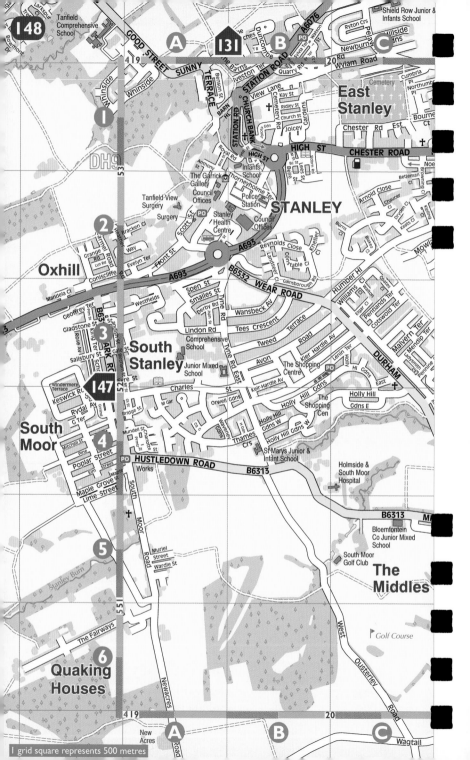

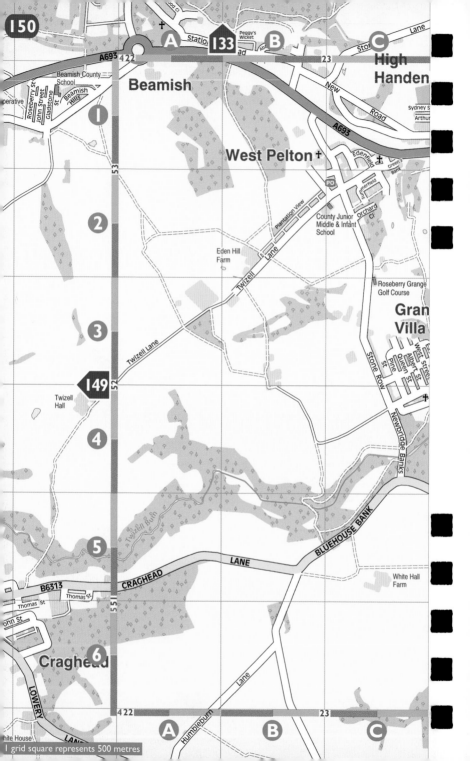

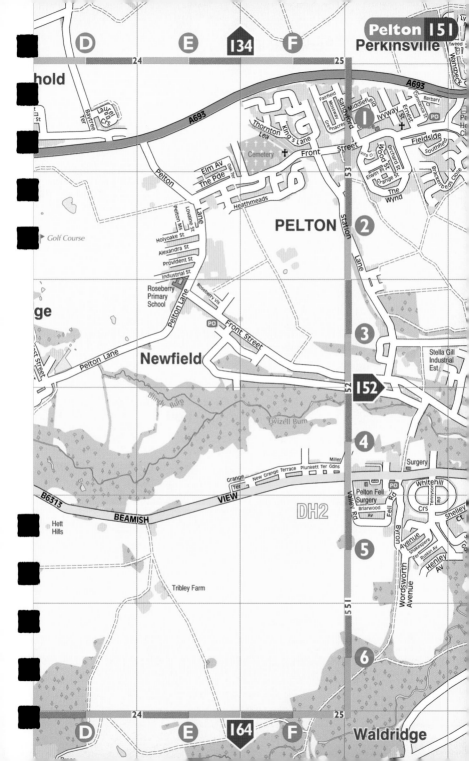

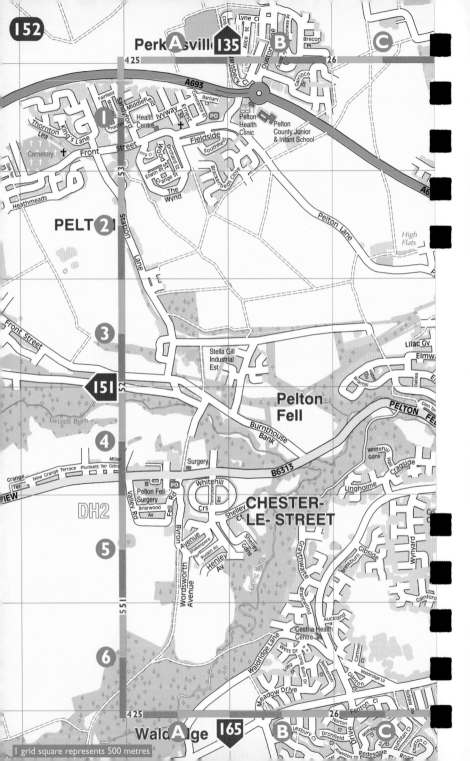

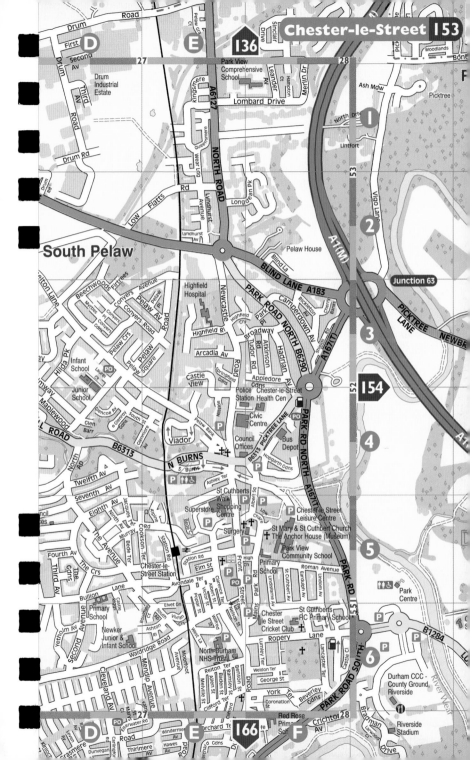

136

166

154

Junction 63

South Pelaw

Picktree

Woodlands

Park View Comprehensive School

Lombard Drive

Drum Industrial Estate

Pelaw House

Lintfort

Ash Mdw

Highfield Hospital

BLIND LANE A183

Camperdown Av

Highfield Rd

Arcadia Av

Broadway

Appledore

Police Station

Chester-le-Street Health Cen

Civic Centre

Council Offices

Bus Depot

Viador

N BURNS

Castle View

Infant School

Junior School

Glen Barr

Twelfth Av

Seventh Av

Eighth Av

Fourth Av

Third Av

The Crs

Superstore

St Cuthberts Walk Shopping Centre

Surgery

Chester-le-Street Station

Chester le Street Leisure Centre

St Mary & St Cuthbert Church
The Anchor House (Museum)

Park View Community School

Primary School

Roman Avenue

Park Centre

Bullion Primary School

Newker Junior & Infant School

North Durham NHS Trust

Chester le Street Cricket Club

St Cuthberts RC Primary School

Ropery

Lumley Ter

Weldon Ter

George St

York Ter

Red Rose Prima School

Coronation St

Crichton

B1284

Durham CCC County Ground, Riverside

Riverside Stadium

PARK ROAD SOUTH 151

PARK ROAD NORTH

A167(T)

A1(M)

A1671(T)

PICKTREE LANE

NEWBR

North Drive

Vigo Lane

Sinclair Drive

Leander Av

Hampton

Merlin Dr

Drum Road

First

Second Av

Third Av

Drum Rd

Low Flatts Rd

North Road

A6127

Wear Lodge

Lyndhurst Avenue

Lyndhurst Av

Longdean Pk

Beechwoods

Firtrees

Convers Avenue

Pelaw Av

Convers Road

Pelaw Crs

Pelaw Square

Hilda Pk

Maplewood

B6313

Cleveland Av

Mendip Avenue

Waldridge Road

Second Avenue

The Avenue

Station Rd

Front Street

High Rd

Mains Rd

Newcastle Rd

Park Road North B6290

Hadrian Av

Shields Rd

Ricketon

Cherry Banks

PICKTREE LANE

B6313

Hopgarth Gdns

Albert Sq

Low Chare

Elm St

Avondale Ter

Clarence Ter

Victor St

Ashton

Vivian

West La

Reiton Ter

Ramsey St

Allen St

Melville St

Clifford Ter

Benson Rd

Bradman Drive

River Wear

Lanwood Rd

Orchard Gdns

Windermere Av

Hawes Rd

Thirlmere

27

28

27

28

D

E

D

E

F

I

2

3

4

5

6

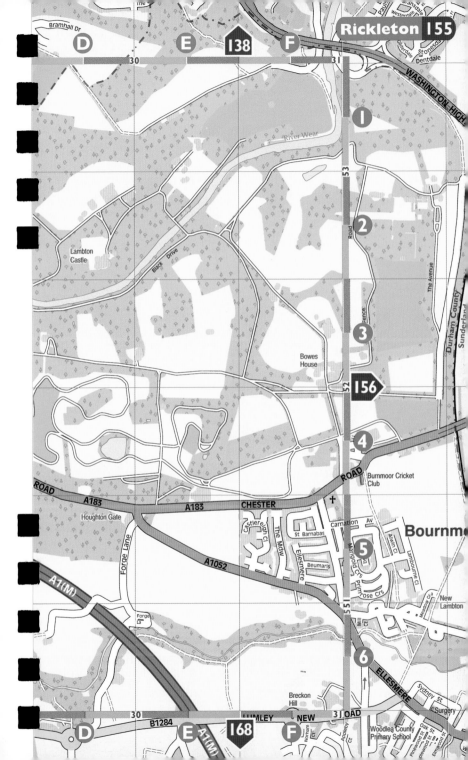

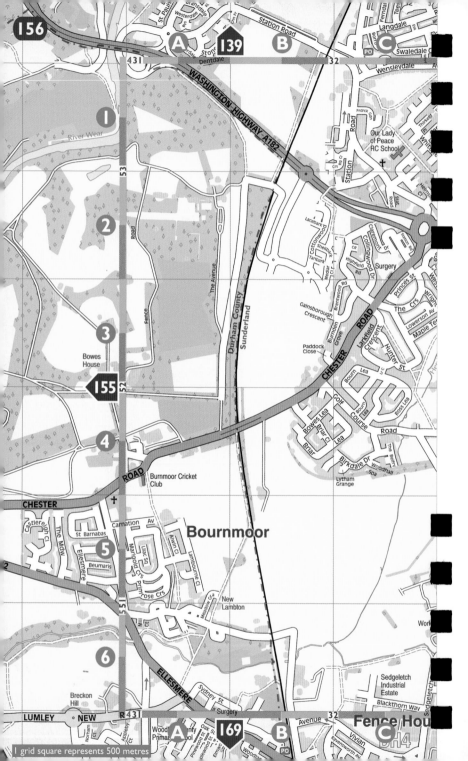

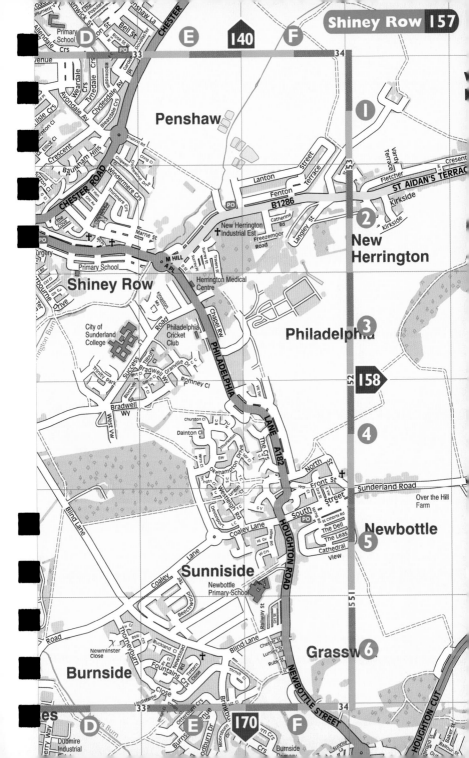

160

Farringdon Junior School

Farringdon School and Leisure Centre

Farringdon

SR3

New Silksworth

143

Silksworth Rd
Church View Medical Cen
Silksworth Health Cen

Silksworth Road

Silksworth Road

East Herrington

CITY WAY

Brenlynn Cl
Maclynn Cl
Goldlynn
Morval Cl

DOXFORD PK WY

DOXFORD PARK WAY

Benedict Biscop C of E Sch

Moorside

159

Knollside Cl
Brookbank Cl
Bishops Wy
Canonsfield Cl
Hall Farm Road
Priesthield
Treecone Cl
Honeysuckle Cl
Badger Cl
Foxlair

Dox

A19(T)

Burdon Lane

Thristley House Farm

Hangmans Lane

Salter's

Old Burdon

Warden Law North Farm

437

173

437

A **B** **C**

A **B** **C**

1 grid square represents 500 metres

Orkney Dr
Langhurst Ct
Hewitt
Eaton
Lyndthorpe
Lyngrove
Lynthorpe
Leechmere Way
Works

A 145 Leechmere **B** Queen
Lansdowne **C**

440
Golf
Course
Ryhope
Golf Course

Rye View
Road
Callington Dr
Ocean Vw
Penmale Dr

**Ryhope
Colliery**

Bankside
Shaftesbury Av
Western Hill
B1286
Ryhope
Health
Centre
Rosslyn Avenue
Black Rd
Ridley Av

1

Brick Rw
Chester Av
Back Ryhope
RYHOPE STREET
Western Hill
Roselea Av
Atheistan
Rigg
Byron
Ter
Cliff Road
B1287

PO
Infant School
Trotter Ter
Dine
Dene St
Smith Street
Primary Sch
Colin Ter
**THE
VILLAGE**
Scotland
George
PO
St

Wraith
Terrace
Fee
Terrace
Thomas Street
Station Road
Byron
SEA VIEW

Blyton Avenue
Stewart
Av
Bevan
Hylton
Terrace
Williams
Terrace
Burdoch
Crescent
School
Thomas St
Richardson
Ter
F Ter
Brewer
Terrace
Arnol Cdns

2

Wilkinson
Av
Smith Gv
Ryhope
Cemetery
Ryhope
Dinsdale St
South
Martindale
Jm Cl
Martville W
Arthur Av
Country
Regent Road

Esdale
Lane
Esdale
Burdon
Esdale
Martville E

161 52

STOCKTON ROAD
Wexworth Rd
STOCKTON RD

Ryhope
General
Hospital

3

Cherry
Knowle
Hospital
A1018

4

Sunderland
Durham County

551

5

A1018
STOCKTON
ROAD
Seaham
Grange

6

Chipchase
Enterprise
Way
Chevychase
Court
Dene

Seaham
Grange
Industrial
Estate
Partnership
Court
Hall
STOCKTON
South Gra Pk
LC

440
A 175 **B** B1285 **C**
Lord Byrons Walk
41
Neasham

I grid square represents 500 metres

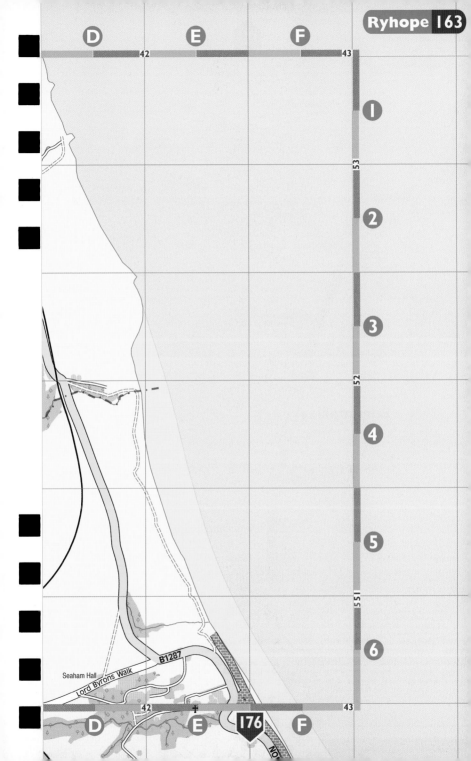

D E F

42 43

1

53

2

3

52

4

5

551

6

42 43

D E F 176

Seaham Hall

B1287

Lord Byrons Walk

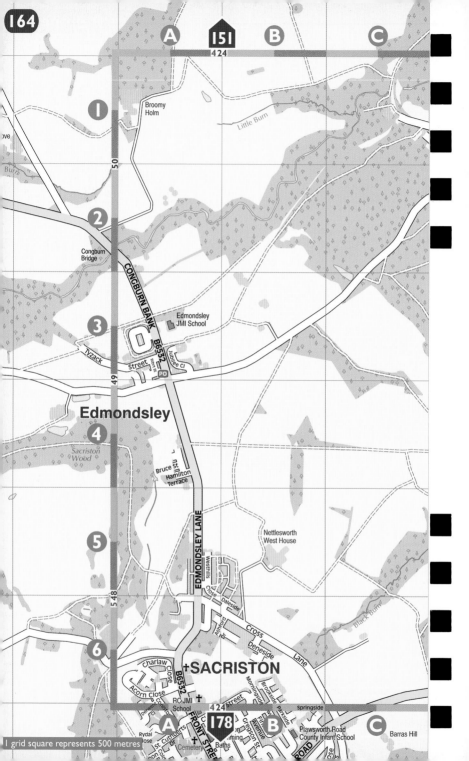

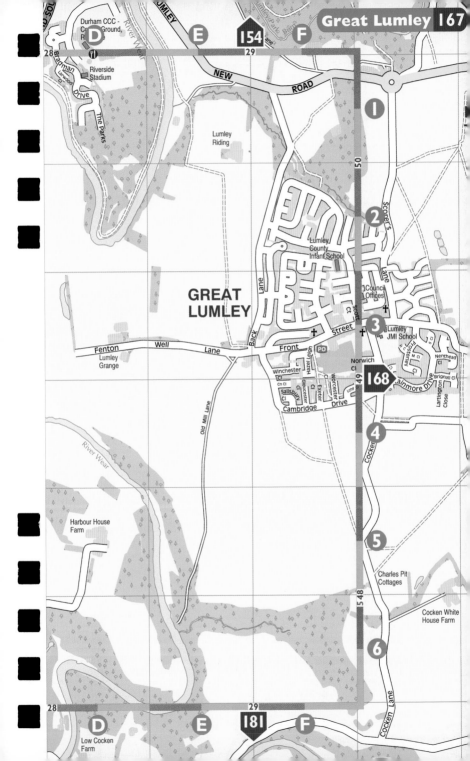

154

GREAT LUMLEY

Durham CCC - County Ground, R

Riverside Stadium

New Road

Lumley Riding

Lumley County Infant School

Council Offices

Scorer's Lane

Lumley JMI School

168

Fenton Lumley Grange

Well Lane

Back Lane

Front Street

PO

Scott St

Winchester Cl

Cn Cl

Salisbury Cl

Cambridge

Gloucester Cl

Exeter

Worcester Drive

Norwich Cl

Nenthead Cl

Brignall Cl

Lartington Close

Ainmore Drive

Old Mill Lane

River Wear

Harbour House Farm

Charles Pit Cottages

Cocken White House Farm

Cocken Lane

181

Low Cocken Farm

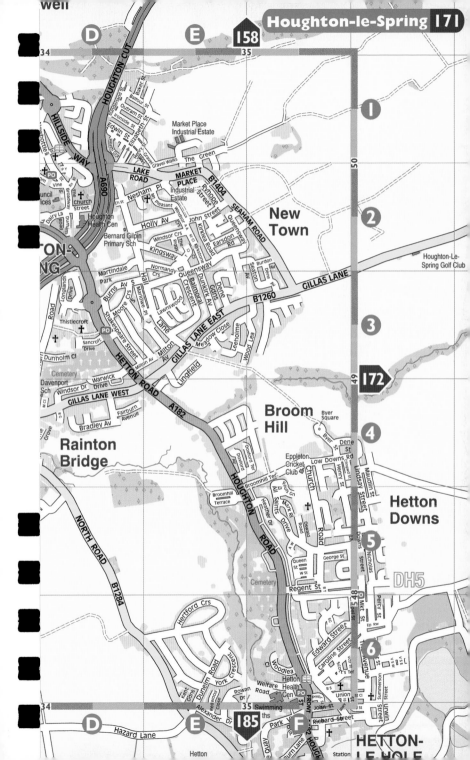

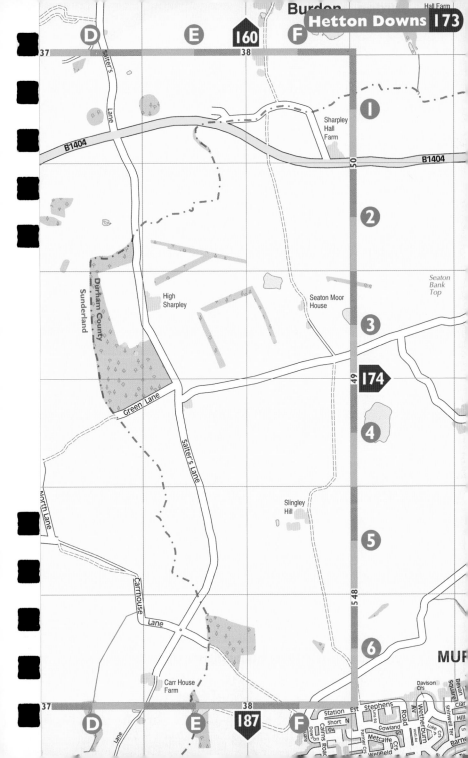

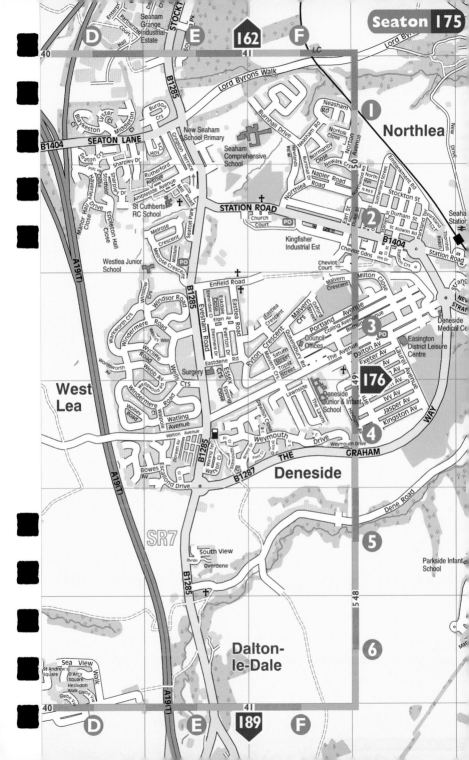

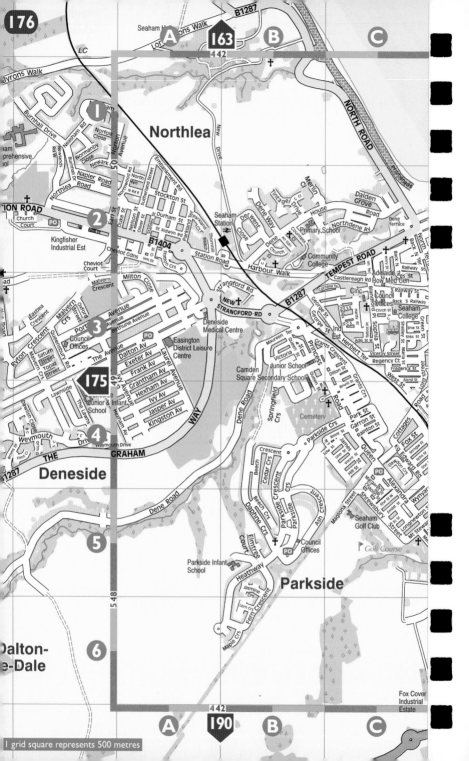

D E F

1

50

2

Police Station

SEAHAM
PO

3

Foundry
Road
Primary
School

49

Albert St
Alfred St
Stewart St
Candlish
Ter
Fenwick
Row

Gas Works Road
Bottle Works Rd

4

Embankment

Hill Crs

Street
Street
Road

Dawdon

LC   Edith Street

Nose's
Point

548

5

Dawdon
Industrial
Estate

6

43   A182
D   E   **191**   F

44

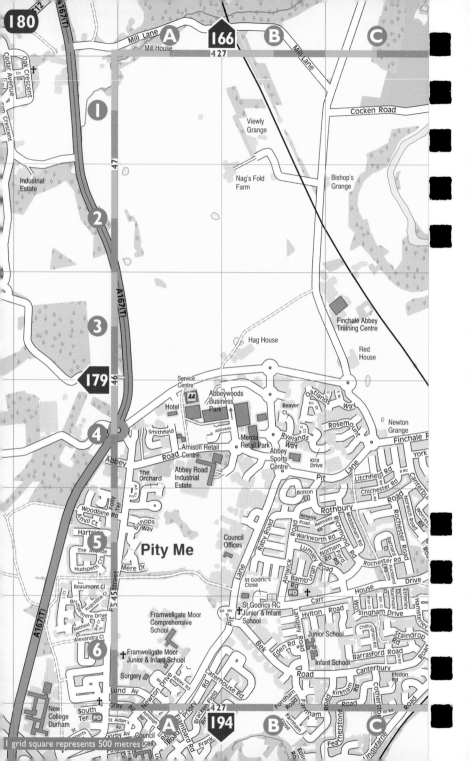

184

West Rainton

Middle Rainton

Rainton

Holly Haven

The Dene

Benridge Bank

The Meadows

Church Street

Cem

Fieldside

Robin Lane

Robin House

Field House Farm

183

Pitfield House

High Moorsley

Pittington Road

Moorsley Road

Station Rd

Front Street   High Street

Hillside

Pittington

Lady's Piece

Coalford Lane

Elemore St

St Lawrence

St Lawrence

Newby Lane

170

1 grid square represents 500 metres

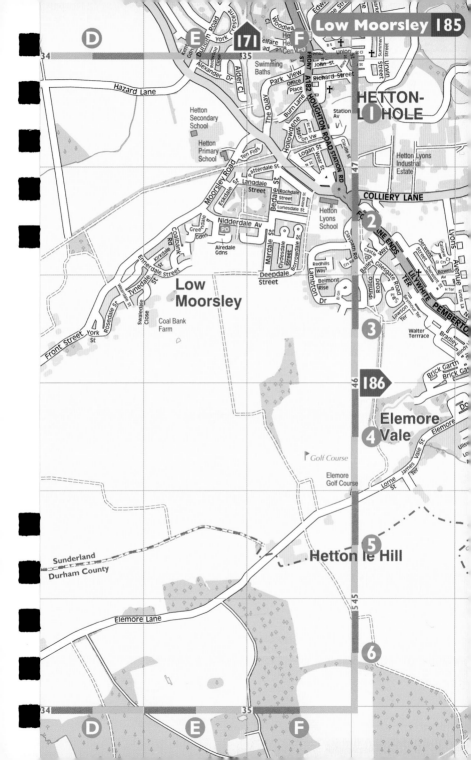

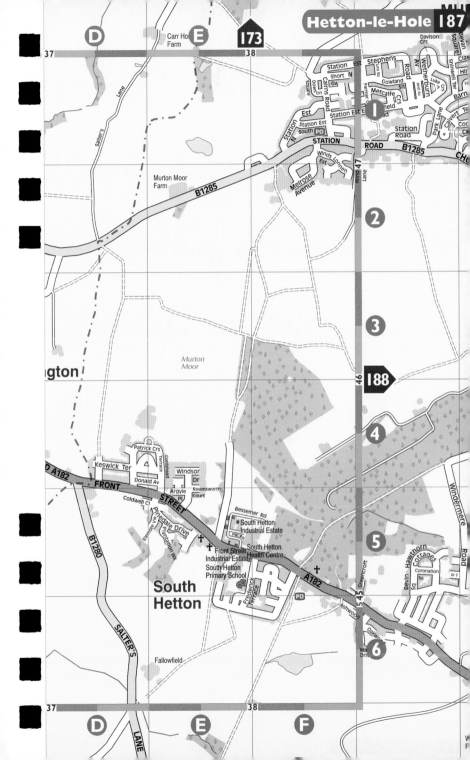

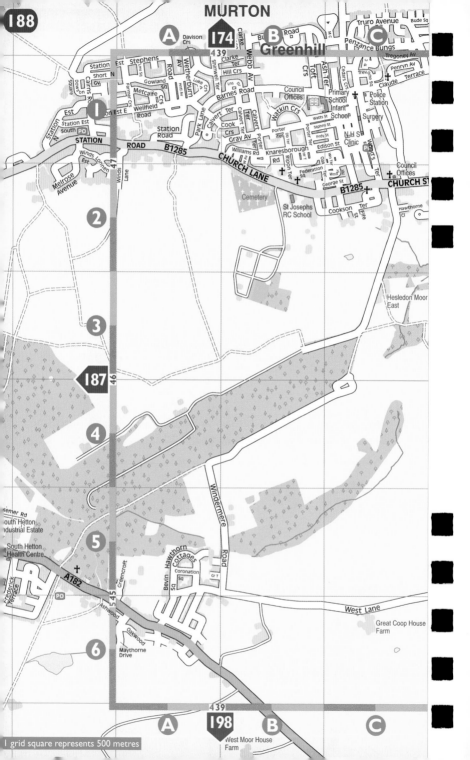

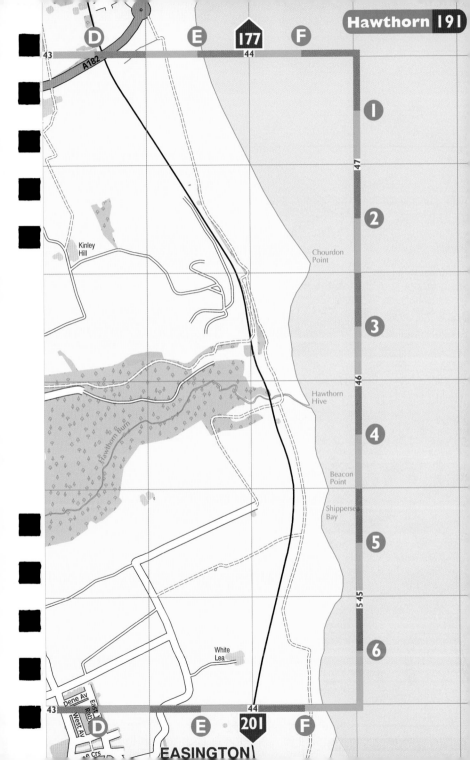

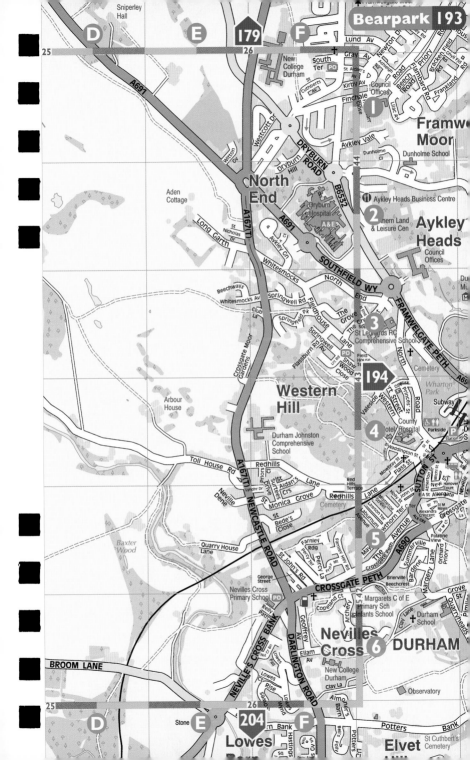

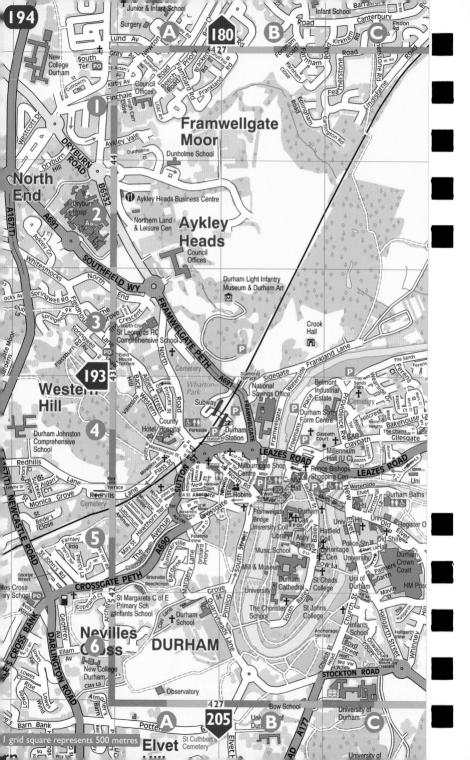

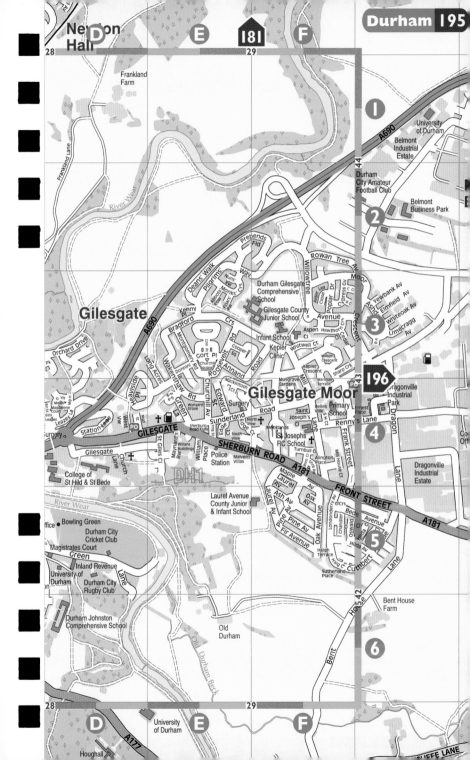

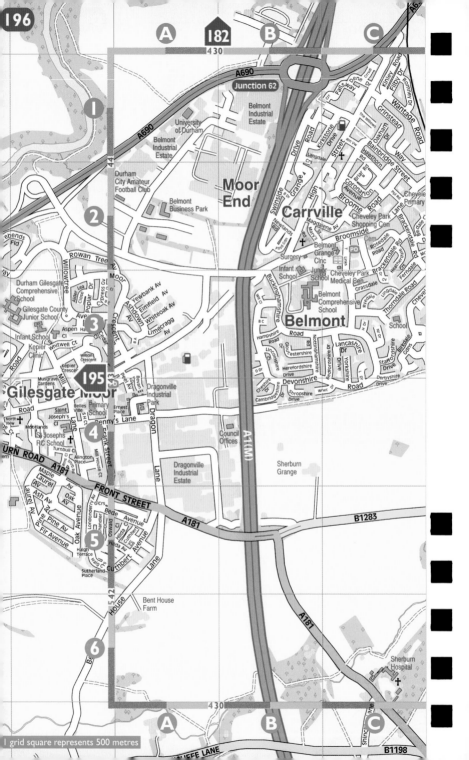

31 **32**

D Ramside Hall
    Hotel
Ramside Hall
Golf Club
Golf Course

E

183

F

Lady's Piece Lane

Coalford Lane
Elemore St
St Lawrence
PO

Pittington Lane

Fatfield
House

I

Priors Grange

Hallgarth Lane

44

2

Hallgarth

Broomside
House

3

Coalford Beck

Whitegates
Road
Dowsey
Cummings
Avenue

Lady Anne
Rd
Usher Av

Forster
Av

43

4

Gray Avenue

Beech
Road
Kidd Avenue
Lddl Av

Forster Av

Cookshold Lane

Sports
Centre

Stanley
Close
Liddle
AV

Hallgarth Street

King St

George St

Milford Dr
Whalton
Cl

Meldon
AV

Sherburn

5

Railway
Close
smith
Man's Drive
St
Talisman
Close

Cem
Church
Wynd
St Cuthberts

PO

Hope St

FRONT
STREET

Mill Lane

The Crescent

Chapel
Ct

B1283

L

42

Sherburnhouse Beck

6

31 **32**

D E F

Mill
Lane

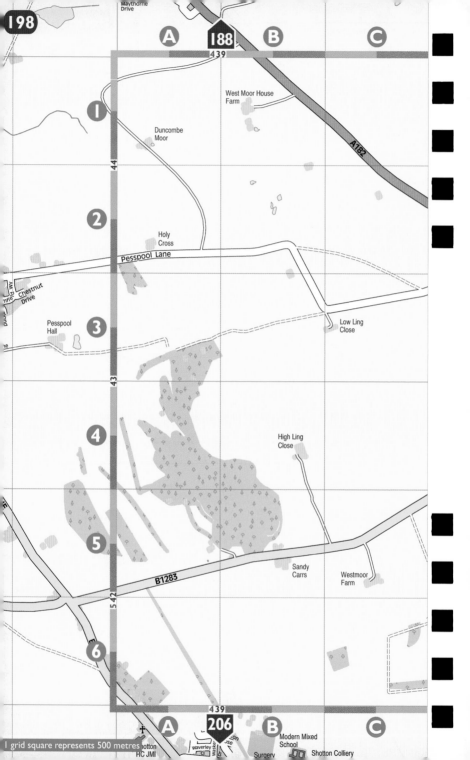

A **188** B C
439

1

44

West Moor House
Farm

Duncombe
Moor

A182

2

Holy
Cross

Pesspool Lane

Mn Dr Chestnut
Drive

3

Pesspool
Hall

Low Ling
Close

43

4

High Ling
Close

5

B1283

542

Sandy
Carrs

Westmoor
Farm

6

439

A **206** B C

Waverley
Cl Walker
Dr

Modern Mixed
School

Surgery Shotton Colliery

Shotton
RC JMI

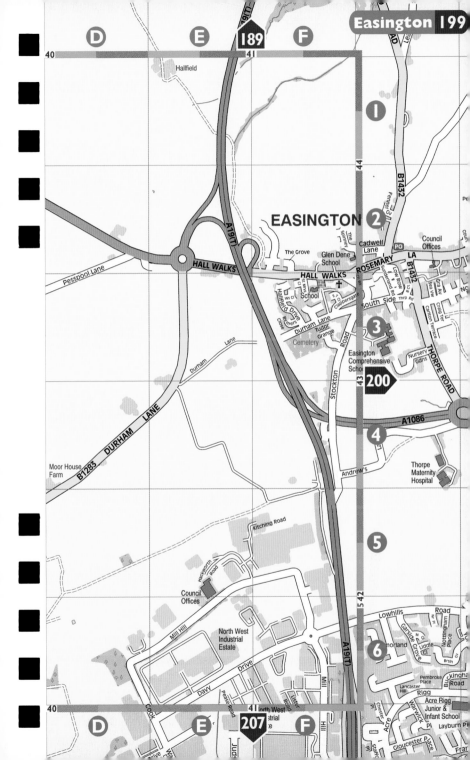

191
44

EASINGTON COLLIERY

Dene Av
East View
Raby Av
West Av
The Crs
Lane
Thomas St
Thorpe St
Jom Street
North Road
Cem
Memorial Avenue
School Street
B1283
Welfare Close
Memorial Avenue

Tower St
Alan St
Abbot St
Ashton St
Ascot St
Andrews St
Ashley St
Allison St
BYRON ST
PO
Browning St
Peele Street
Barwick
Bradley
Bolam
Boyd St
Blake St
Beaty St
Butler St
Baldwin St
Bostron St
STATION ROAD

Office Street
Charles St
Castle St
court St
Camp St
Cornwall St
Carole St
Corbett St

Paradise

Horden Burn

Spencer Terrace
Carville Terrace
Angus Terrace
Elliott Terrace
Maritime Crs
Maritime St
Culloden Ter

SUNDERLAND ROAD

Horden Point

1
44
2
3
43
4
5
542
6

A1086
Thorpe Road
Horden & Easington RC Primary School
Kilburn
Webb Sq
Beaumont Cres
Corvets Crescent
Wilkinson Rd
Smillie Road
Faraday Road
Bruce
Kirkup Road
McAllister Cl
Nisbitt St
Naisbitt Av
Yoden Crs
A 1086

Belford St
Alnwick St
Morpeth St
Rothbury St
Newcastle St
Sunderland Av
Northumberland St
Durham Av
PO
Sea View Industrial Estate
Timber Rd
Drive
Blackhills
Thompson Rd

Council Offices
Brier W Avenue
Rise
Lane
A43
Eden Hall Infant School
Horden
D
Wallflower Avenue
Snowdrop Avenue
Primrose Avenue
E
SUNDERLAND
209
44
F
PO
Surgery
Park Rd
Sea View Crs
Eden Street
Caton

D
E
191
44

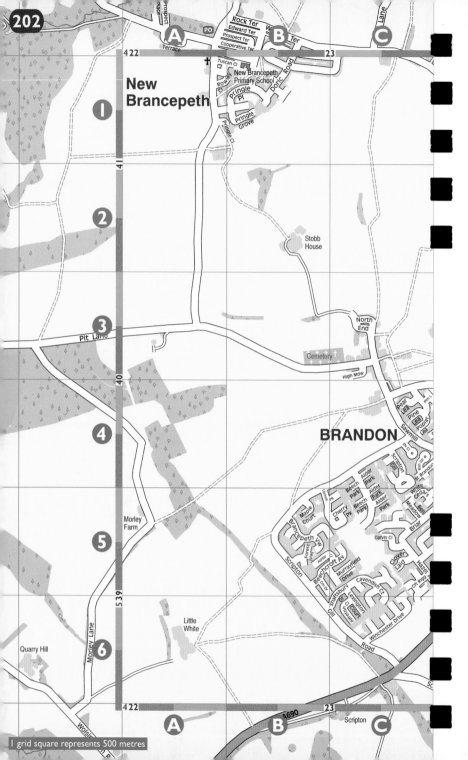

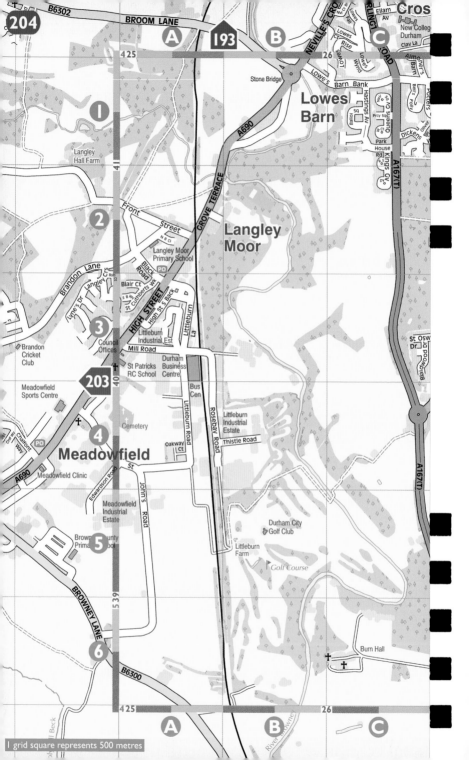

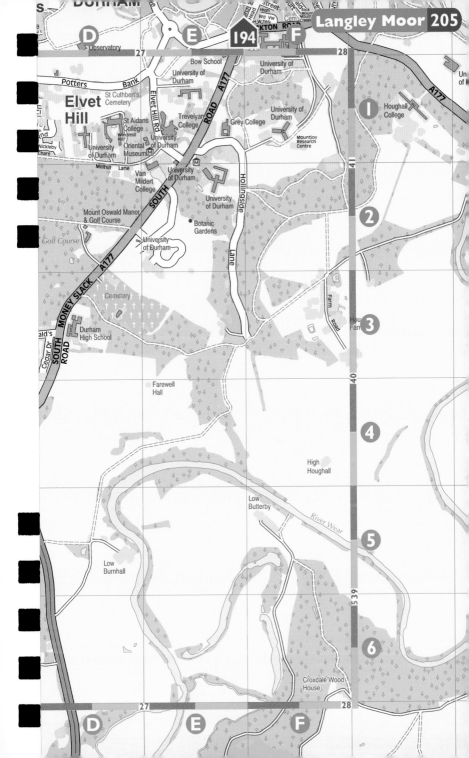

DURHAM

Observatory

Potters Bank

Elvet Hill

St Cuthbert's Cemetery

St Aidans College

Windmill Hill

University of Durham

Oriental Museum

Millhill Lane

Wickleby Chare

Bow School

University of Durham

Elvet Hill Rd

Trevelyan College

Grey College

University of Durham

University of Durham

Mountjoy Research Centre

Houghall College

Van Mildert College

University of Durham

University of Durham

Botanic Gardens

Mount Oswald Manor & Golf Course

Hollingside Lane

Golf Course

Cemetery

Durham High School

MONEY SLACK

SOUTH ROAD

Cedar Dr

ald's

Farewell Hall

Farm Road

Farm

High Houghall

Low Butterby

River Wear

Low Burnhall

Croxdale Wood House

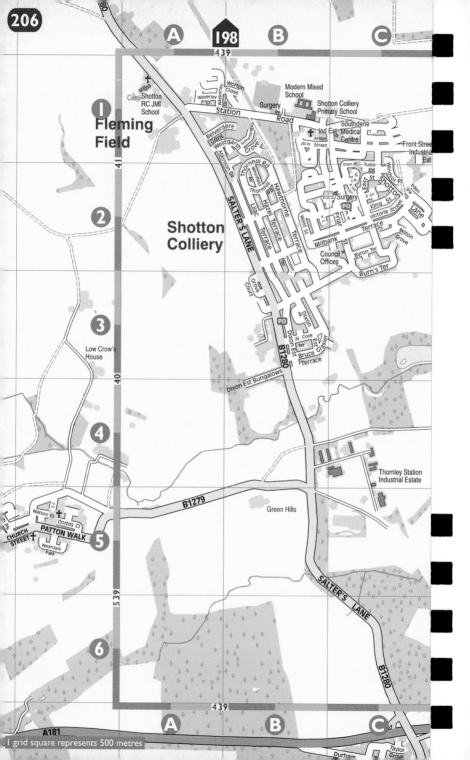

A **198** B C
439

I

Cem

Shotton
RC JMI
School

**Fleming
Field**

41

Belverdere
Gdns
Westgarth
Atkinson Ct

Waverley
Cl

Worton
Close

Waverley

Station

Road

Grove

Sutherland St

Modern Mixed
School

Surgery

Shotton Colliery
Primary School

Southdene

Front Street
Industrial
Est

Ind Est
Arden
Street

JbI Pl

Medical
Centre

Dnlm Pl Tudor

Windsor Pl

Windsor

2

**Shotton
Colliery**

SALTER'S LANE

Thornhill Rd

Wynnmdg Rd

Thornhill

Hawthorne

Lilac
Terrace

Hazel Terrace

West St

Webster

Terrace

East
St

Surgery

PO

Friars

King St

Victoria Street

Terrace

Milbank

Council
Offices

Byron Ter

Burn's Ter

East
Pl

Eden
Pl

SHOTTON

LANE

Milton
Grove

Grove
Court

Dixon

PO

Dixon Est

AJ Cook
Ter

Bruce
Terrace

Glazier

B1280

3

40

Low Crow's
House

Dixon Est Bungalows

4

Thornley Station
Industrial Estate

Watson Cl

B1279

Green Hills

Dodds Cl

5

CHURCH
STREET

PATTON WALK

Weardale
Park

539

SALTER'S LANE

6

B1280

439

A B C

A181

Taylor
Grove

Durham

1 grid square represents 500 metres

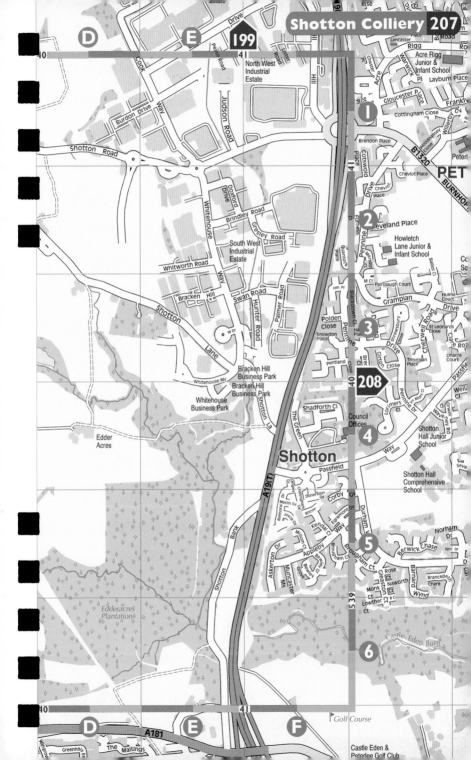

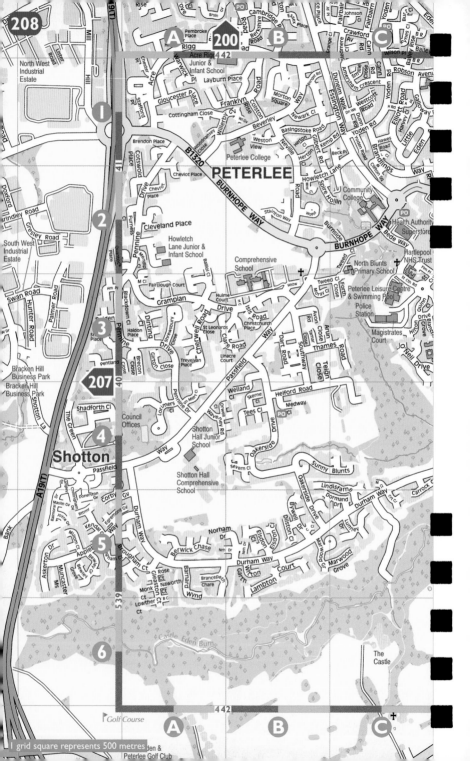

201

Horden

Eden Hall
Infant School

Council
Offices

Cotsford
Junior School

Cotsford
Yoden Primary
School

Cotsford
County Infant School

Cotsford
Estates

Dixon
Rise

Dene House
County Mixed
Modern School

Eastfield

Garth
Cornfield

Community Care

Brakespeare
Place

Adrian
Place

Hatfield
Place

Hawthorns Hospital

Bellister Pk

Dene
Leazes

Castle Eden Dene
Nature Reserve

Hardwick
Hall Farm

Hesleden
County Junior

Sycamore
Drive

SUNDERLAND ROAD
SHOTTON RD
COTSFORD LA
COAST ROAD
YODEN WAY
SURTEES ROAD
HESLEDEN ROAD
B1320
B1281
A1086

D E F I 2 3 4 5 6

Albany	120 A5
Annfield Plain	146 C4
Annitsford	35 E1
Axwell Park	94 C2
Aykley Heads	194 A2
Ayres Quay	126 A4
Ayton	137 E3
Backworth	37 E6
Bank Top	57 D5
Barley Mow	136 B4
Barlow	92 C4
Barmston	139 E1
Battle Hill	67 E1
Beaconhill	21 D2
Beacon Lough	100 B6
Beamish	150 A1
Bearpark	192 B3
Bebside	9 D5
Bedlington	7 F2
Bedlington Station	8 A2
Bell's Close	77 D2
Belmont	196 B3
Bensham	98 C1
Benton Square	50 C3
Benwell	78 A2
Biddick	138 C2
Biddick Hall	88 A6
Bill Quay	84 A6
Billy Mill	53 F5
Birtley	118 C6
Bishopwearmouth	126 A5
Black Callerton	42 C4
Blackfell	119 F6
Blakelaw	61 E4
Blaydon	76 C5
Blaydon Burn	93 D1
Blaydon Haughs	77 D4
Blyth	10 B6
Boldon Colliery	87 E6
Bournmoor	156 A5
Brandon	202 B4
Brenkley	18 B5
Broom Hill	171 F4
Broompark	192 C6
Brunswick Village	32 B5
Burdon	161 D5
Burnopfield	111 E6
Burnside	157 D6
Burradon	35 D5
Byermoor	112 C5
Byker	82 B3
Callerton	43 D6
Camperdown	35 E5
Carley Hill	126 A1
Carr Hill	100 A3
Carrville	196 B2
Castletown	123 F3
Causey	132 A1
Chester-le-Street	152 B5
Chester Moor	165 F3
Chilton Moor	170 A3
Chirton	54 A6
Chowdene	116 C2
Cleadon	107 F2
Cleadon Park	89 F4
Clough Dene	130 A3
Cold Hesledon	190 A2
Colliery Row	170 B2
Collingwood	22 A4
Columbia	139 D2
Concord	120 B4
Cowpen	10 A4
Coxlodge	62 C1
Craghead	149 F6
Cramlington	21 D3
Crookgate Bank	112 B6
Crookhill	75 D3
Cullercoats	55 F2
Dalton-le-Dale	175 E6
Dawdon	177 D5
Deckham	99 E2
Deneside	175 F4
Denton Burn	77 D1
Deptford	125 F4
Dinnington	30 C3
Dipton	128 B6
Donwell	120 A3
Downhill	106 A6
Doxford Park	160 C4
Dudley	34 C3
Dunston	97 E1
Dunston Hill	97 D3
Durham	194 A6
Earsdon	38 C4

Easington	199 F2
Easington Colliery	201 E1
Easington Lane	186 C3
East Boldon	106 B2
East Cramlington	23 D3
East Denton	60 C6
East Gateshead	82 A5
East Hartford	14 A3
East Herrington	159 F2
East Holywell	37 F3
East Kyo	147 D2
East Rainton	170 C6
East Sleekburn	9 F1
East Stanley	148 C1
Eighton Banks	118 C2
Eland Green	28 B2
Elemore Vale	186 A4
Elswick	79 E5
Elvet Hill	205 D1
Farringdon	160 A1
Fatfield	138 B6
Fawdon	46 A5
Fellgate	103 F1
Felling	100 B2
Felling Shore	83 D6
Fellside	95 E4
Fence Houses	169 F1
Fenham	78 C1
Flint Hill	129 E5
Follingsby	102 C5
Fordley	35 D3
Forest Hall	49 F3
Framwellgate Moor	194 A1
Fulwell	108 B6
Gateshead	81 E5
Gilesgate	195 D3
Gilesgate Moor	195 E4
Glebe	138 B1
Gosforth	63 D1
Grangetown	145 D5
Grange Villa	150 C3
Grasswell	157 F6
Great Eppleton	172 C5
Great Lumley	167 E3
Greenhill	174 B6
Grindon	142 A3
Hallgarth	197 F2
Harelaw	146 A2
Harlow Green	118 A2
Harperley	146 C2
Harraton	137 F5
Hartley	27 D4
Harton	89 D2
Hasting Hill	141 F4
Hawthorn	190 A5
Hazlerigg	32 C6
Heaton	65 D6
Hebburn	85 D3
Hebburn Colliery	68 A6
Hebburn New Town	84 B2
Heddon-on-the-Wall	56 A5
Hedworth	86 B6
Hendon	5 F5
Hetton Downs	172 A5
Hetton-le-Hill	185 F5
Hetton-le-Hole	186 A1
Heworth	101 E2
High Callerton	42 A2
High Dubmire	170 A2
Highfield	110 B3
High Forge	133 D5
High Friarside	110 C6
High Handenhold	150 C1
High Moorsley	184 C4
High Shields	70 C6
High Southwick	125 F1
High Urpeth	134 A6
Hill Top	129 D4
Hillview	144 B5
Hobson	130 A2
Holy Cross	67 E3
Holywell	25 E6
Horden	209 D1
Horsley Hill	72 B6
Houghton-le-Spring	170 C2
Howdon	68 C3
Howdon Pans	69 E5
Humbledon	143 E3
Hylton Castle	123 F2
Hylton Red House	106 C6
Isabella Pit	16 C1
Jarrow	86 C2
Jesmond	64 B6
Kenton	61 F2

Kenton Bankfoot	44 C6
Kenton Bar	61 F2
Kibblesworth	117 D6
Killingworth	49 F2
Killingworth Moor	50 C2
Killingworth Village	36 A6
Kimblesworth	179 D1
Kingston Park	45 F6
Kip Hill	131 F5
Lady Park	116 C3
Lambton	137 F3
Lamesley	116 C3
Langley Moor	204 B2
The Lawe	71 F2
Leam Lane	101 F4
Leamside	183 D2
Lemington	76 B1
Lintz	129 E1
Lintzford	110 A5
Little Thorpe	200 B4
Lobley Hill	98 A4
Longbenton	49 E4
Low Eighton	118 A4
Lowes Barn	204 B1
Low Fell	99 E5
Low Moorsley	185 E3
Low Thornley	93 F5
Lumley Thicks	168 B1
Lyons	186 B2
Marden	54 C2
Marley Hill	114 A3
Marley Pots	125 E1
Marsden	90 B3
Mason	31 D2
Mayfield	22 B3
Meadowfield	203 F4
Middle Herrington	142 A6
Middle Rainton	184 B1
The Middles	148 C5
Mill Dam	70 C5
Millfield	125 F5
Monkseaton	39 F4
Monkton	85 F4
Monkwearmouth	126 A3
Moor End	196 B2
Mount Pleasant	100 A2
Murton	53 D2
Murton	174 A6
Nedderton	6 A4
Nelson Village	21 E1
Nettlesworth	165 D6
Nevilles Cross	193 F6
Newbiggin Hall Estate	60 B2
Newbottle	158 A5
New Brancepeth	202 A1
Newburn	58 C6
Newcastle upon Tyne	3 H4
New Delaval	16 A3
Newfield	151 E3
New Hartley	25 D2
New Herrington	158 A2
New Kyo	147 D4
Newsham	16 C2
New Silksworth	160 B1
Newton Hall	181 D6
New Town	105 E1
New Town	171 F2
New York	53 E3
North Blyth	11 D2
North End	193 E2
North Hylton	123 D5
Northlea	176 A1
North Shields	71 D1
North Walbottle	58 C3
Offerton	141 D3
Old Burdon	160 C6
Old Fold	82 A6
Ouston	135 F4
Oxclose	137 F1
Oxhill	147 F2
Pallion	124 C4
Palmersville	50 C3
Parkside	176 B5
Path Head	76 A4
Pelaw	101 E1
Pelton	151 F2
Pelton Fell	152 B4
Pennywell	142 A2
Penshaw	157 E1
Percy Main	70 A4
Perkinsville	135 D6
Peterlee	208 A2
Philadelphia	157 F3
Pickering Nook	129 F2

Pittington 184 A6	South Bents 109 D4	Wardley 102 A2
Pity Me 180 A5	Southfield 22 A5	Washington 121 F6
Plawsworth 165 F6	South Gosforth 63 F2	Washington Village 138 C1
Ponteland 28 C3	South Hetton 187 E5	West Allotment 52 A3
Portobello 136 B2	South Hylton 124 A6	West Boldon 105 F2
Preston 54 C4	South Moor 147 F4	West Chirton 68 C1
Preston Grange 54 B2	South Newsham 16 B3	West Denton 60 A5
Prestwick 29 F5	South Pelaw 153 D2	Westerhope 59 F2
Primrose 86 B4	South Shields 72 A4	Western Hill 193 F4
Quaking Houses 147 F6	South Stanley 148 A3	West Harton 87 F2
Rainton Bridge 171 D4	Southwick 125 F3	West Herrington 158 B1
Rainton Gate 183 D3	Spital Tongues 79 F1	West Holywell 37 F4
Rickleton 154 B1	Springwell 119 F3	West Jesmond 63 D4
Roker 127 E2	Springwell 143 D3	West Kyo 146 B2
Rosehill 68 A5	Stanley 148 B2	Westlea 6 C4
Rowlands Gill 111 D2	Stargate 74 C5	West Lea 175 D4
Ryhope 162 B2	Stella 75 F4	West Monkseaton 53 E1
Ryhope Colliery 162 A1	Stony Gate 158 C4	West Moor 49 D3
Ryton 74 B3	Street Gate 114 C2	Westoe 72 A5
Ryton Woodside 74 A6	Sulgrave 121 D4	West Park 88 B1
Sacriston 164 A6	Sunderland 4 A1	West Pelton 150 B1
St Anthony's 83 D5	Sunderland 125 F4	West Rainton 183 F1
St Peter's 82 B4	Sunniside 113 F2	Whickham 96 A3
Saltwell 99 C1	Sunniside 157 E5	Whitburn 109 E1
Scotswood 77 F4	Swalwell 95 F1	Whitburn Colliery 91 E4
Seaham 177 D3	Tanfield 130 C2	Whitehills 100 C5
Seaton 25 F3	Tanfield Lea 130 C5	Whiteleas 88 B5
Seaton 174 C2	Tan Hills 165 E6	White-le-Head 129 F5
Seaton Burn 33 E1	Tantobie 129 F4	Whitley Bay 41 E5
Seaton Delaval 24 B4	Teams 98 A1	Whitley Sands 40 C3
Seaton Sluice 26 B3	Team Valley 98 C5	Wickham Fell 96 A6
Seghill 36 B1	Thorney Close 142 B5	Wide Open 33 E5
Shankhouse 14 B5	Throckley 58 A3	Willington 68 A2
Sheep Hill 112 A5	Tunstall 161 D2	Willington Quay 68 C5
Sherburn 197 F5	Tyne Dock 87 F1	Windy Nook 100 C4
Sheriff Hill 100 A4	Tynemouth 55 D4	Winlaton 75 F6
Shield Row 132 A6	Urpeth 135 D4	Winlaton Mill 94 A4
Shiney Row 157 D3	Usworth 120 B3	Witherwack 107 D6
Shiremoor 52 C1	Walbottle 58 A5	Witton Gilbert 178 B3
Shotton 207 F4	Waldridge 165 D1	Woolsington 43 F4
Shotton Colliery 206 A2	Walker 83 E3	Woolsington Hall 44 A3
Simonside 87 D4	Wallsend 66 B4	Wrekenton 118 A1
South Beach 17 F2		

USING THE STREET INDEX

Street names are listed alphabetically. Each street name is followed by its postal town or area locality, the Postcode District, the page number, and the reference to the square in which the name is found.

Standard index entries are shown as follows:

Abbay St *SWCK/CAS* SR5 ....**125** F3

Street names and selected addresses not shown on the map due to scale restrictions are shown in the index with an asterisk or with the name of an adjoining road in brackets:

Abbot Ct *GATE* * NE8 ....**81** E5

Abbey Ms
BDN/LAN/SAC (off Priory Ct) DH7....**178** B2

GENERAL ABBREVIATIONS

ACC	ACCESS	COLL	COLLEGE	EST	ESTATE
ALY	ALLEY	COM	COMMON	EX	EXCHANGE
AP	APPROACH	COMM	COMMISSION	EXPY	EXPRESSWAY
AR	ARCADE	CON	CONVENT	EXT	EXTENSION
ASS	ASSOCIATION	COT	COTTAGE	F/O	FLYOVER
AV	AVENUE	COTS	COTTAGES	FC	FOOTBALL CLUB
BCH	BEACH	CP	CAPE	FK	FORK
BLDS	BUILDINGS	CPS	COPSE	FLD	FIELD
BND	BEND	CR	CREEK	FLDS	FIELDS
BNK	BANK	CREM	CREMATORIUM	FLS	FALLS
BR	BRIDGE	CRS	CRESCENT	FLS	FLATS
BRK	BROOK	CSWY	CAUSEWAY	FM	FARM
BTM	BOTTOM	CT	COURT	FT	FORT
BUS	BUSINESS	CTRL	CENTRAL	FWY	FREEWAY
BVD	BOULEVARD	CTS	COURTS	FY	FERRY
BY	BYPASS	CTYD	COURTYARD	GA	GATE
CATH	CATHEDRAL	CUTT	CUTTINGS	GAL	GALLERY
CEM	CEMETERY	CV	COVE	GDN	GARDEN
CEN	CENTRE	CYN	CANYON	GDNS	GARDENS
CFT	CROFT	DEPT	DEPARTMENT	GLD	GLADE
CH	CHURCH	DL	DALE	GLN	GLEN
CHA	CHASE	DM	DAM	GN	GREEN
CHYD	CHURCHYARD	DR	DRIVE	GND	GROUND
CIR	CIRCLE	DRO	DROVE	GRA	GRANGE
CIRC	CIRCUS	DRY	DRIVEWAY	GRG	GARAGE
CL	CLOSE	DWGS	DWELLINGS	GT	GREAT
CLFS	CLIFFS	E	EAST	GTWY	GATEWAY
CMP	CAMP	EMB	EMBANKMENT	GV	GROVE
CNR	CORNER	EMBY	EMBASSY	HGR	HIGHER
CO	COUNTY	ESP	ESPLANADE	HL	HILL

HLS	HILLS
HO	HOUSE
HOL	HOLLOW
HOSP	HOSPITAL
HRB	HARBOUR
HTH	HEATH
HTS	HEIGHTS
HVN	HAVEN
HWY	HIGHWAY
IMP	IMPERIAL
IN	INLET
IND EST	INDUSTRIAL ESTATE
INF	INFIRMARY
INFO	INFORMATION
INT	INTERCHANGE
IS	ISLAND
JCT	JUNCTION
JTY	JETTY
KG	KING
KNL	KNOLL
L	LAKE
LA	LANE
LDG	LODGE
LGT	LIGHT
LK	LOCK
LKS	LAKES
LNDG	LANDING
LTL	LITTLE
LWR	LOWER
MAG	MAGISTRATE
MAN	MANSIONS
MD	MEAD
MDW	MEADOWS
MEM	MEMORIAL
MKT	MARKET
MKTS	MARKETS
ML	MALL
ML	MILL
MNR	MANOR
MS	MEWS
MSN	MISSION
MT	MOUNT
MTN	MOUNTAIN
MTS	MOUNTAINS
MUS	MUSEUM

MWY	MOTORWAY
N	NORTH
NE	NORTH EAST
NW	NORTH WEST
O/P	OVERPASS
OFF	OFFICE
ORCH	ORCHARD
OV	OVAL
PAL	PALACE
PAS	PASSAGE
PAV	PAVILION
PDE	PARADE
PH	PUBLIC HOUSE
PK	PARK
PKWY	PARKWAY
PL	PLACE
PLN	PLAIN
PLNS	PLAINS
PLZ	PLAZA
POL	POLICE STATION
PR	PRINCE
PREC	PRECINCT
PREP	PREPARATORY
PRIM	PRIMARY
PROM	PROMENADE
PRS	PRINCESS
PRT	PORT
PT	POINT
PTH	PATH
PZ	PIAZZA
QD	QUADRANT
QU	QUEEN
QY	QUAY
R	RIVER
RBT	ROUNDABOUT
RD	ROAD
RDG	RIDGE
REP	REPUBLIC
RES	RESERVOIR
RFC	RUGBY FOOTBALL CLUB
RI	RISE
RP	RAMP
RW	ROW
S	SOUTH
SCH	SCHOOL

SE	SOUTH EAST
SER	SERVICE AREA
SH	SHORE
SHOP	SHOPPING
SKWY	SKYWAY
SMT	SUMMIT
SOC	SOCIETY
SP	SPUR
SPR	SPRING
SQ	SQUARE
ST	STREET
STN	STATION
STR	STREAM
STRD	STRAND
SW	SOUTH WEST
TDG	TRADING
TER	TERRACE
THWY	THROUGHWAY
TNL	TUNNEL
TOLL	TOLLWAY
TPK	TURNPIKE
TR	TRACK
TRL	TRAIL
TWR	TOWER
U/P	UNDERPASS
UNI	UNIVERSITY
UPR	UPPER
V	VALE
VA	VALLEY
VIAD	VIADUCT
VIL	VILLA
VIS	VISTA
VLG	VILLAGE
VLS	VILLAS
VW	VIEW
W	WEST
WD	WOOD
WHF	WHARF
WK	WALK
WKS	WALKS
WLS	WELLS
WY	WAY
YD	YARD
YHA	YOUTH HOSTEL

POSTCODE TOWNS AND AREA ABBREVIATIONS

ASHBK/HED/RY	Ashbrooke/Hedon/Ryhope
BDLGTN	Bedlington
BDN/LAN/SAC	Brandon/ Lanchester/Sacriston
BLAY	Blaydon
BLYTH	Blyth
BOL	Boldon
BOLCOL	Boldon Colliery
BW/LEM/TK/HW	Benwell/Lemington/ Throckley/Heddon-on-the-Wall
BYK/HTN/WLK	Byker/Heaton/Walker
CLDN/WHIT/ROK	Cleadon/Whitburn/Roker
CLS/BIR/GTL	Chester-le-Street/Birtley/ Great Lumley
CLSW/PEL	Chester-le-Street west/Pelton
CNUT	Central Newcastle upon Tyne
CRAM	Cramlington
DHAM	Durham
DIN/WO	Dinnington/Wide Open
DUN/TMV	Dunston/Team Valley

ELS/FEN	Elswick/Fenham
FELL	Felling
GATE	Gateshead
GOS/KPK	Gosforth/Kingston Park
HAR/WTLS	Harton/Whiteleas
HEBB	Hebburn
HLH	Hetton-le-Hole
HLS	Houghton-le-Spring
JES	Jesmond
JRW	Jarrow
LGB/HTN	Longbenton/Heaton
LGB/KIL	Longbenton/Killingworth
LWF/SPW/WRK	LowFell/ Springwell/Wrekenton
MLFD/PNYW	Millfield/Pennywell
MONK	Monkseaton
NSHW	North Shields west
PLEE/EAS	Peterlee/Easington
PONT/DH	Ponteland/Darras Hall
RDHAMSE	Rural Durham south & east

RHTLP	Rural Hartlepool
ROWG	Rowlands Gill
RYTON	Ryton
SEA/MUR	Seaham/Murton
SMOOR	Shiremoor
SSH	South Shields
STKFD/GP	Stakefold/Guide Post
STLY/ANP	Stanley/Annfield Plain
SUND	Sunderland
SUNDSW	Sunderland southwest
SWCK/CAS	Southwick/Castletown
TYNE/NSHE	Tynemouth/North Shields east
WASHN	Washington north
WASHS	Washington south
WBAY	Whitley Bay
WD/WHPE/BLK	West Denton/ Westerhope/Blakelaw
WICK/BNPF	Wickham/Burnopfield
WLSD/HOW	Wallsend/Howdon

A

Abbay St SWCK/CAS SR5	125	F3
Abbey Cl MONK NE25	39	F6
WASHS NE38	138	C1
Abbey Ct GATE NE8	99	E1
Abbey Dr JRW NE32	86	B1
TYNE/NSHE NE30	55	F4
WD/WHPE/BLK NE5	59	D2
Abbey Ms		
BDN/LAN/SAC (off Priory Ct) DH7	178	B2
Abbey Rd DHAM DH1	179	F4
WASHS NE38	138	C1
Abbeywoods DHAM DH1	180	A4
Abbot Ct GATE * NE8	81	E5
Abbotsfield Cl SUNDSW SR3	160	B3
Abbotsford Gv ASHBK/HED/RY SR2	4	A5
Abbotsford Pk MONK NE25	40	B6
Abbotsford Rd FELL NE10	100	C1

Abbotsford Ter JES NE2	63	F6
Abbotside Cl CLSW/PEL DH2	134	C4
Abbotside Pl WD/WHPE/BLK NE5	59	E5
Abbotsmeade Cl		
WD/WHPE/BLK NE5	61	D6
Abbot's Rd GATE NE8	3	G6
Abbots' Rw DHAM DH1	195	E3
Abbot St PLEE/EAS SR8	201	D4
Abbots Wk STLY/ANP DH9	133	E6
Abbots Wy NSHW NE29	54	A4
WICK/BNPF NE16	96	A3
Abbs St SWCK/CAS SR5	126	C3
Abercorn Pl WLSD/HOW NE28	52	A6
Abercorn Rd		
BW/LEM/TK/HW NE15	77	F3
SUNDSW SR3	142	C5
Abercrombie Pl		
WD/WHPE/BLK NE5	61	D4
Aberdare Rd SUNDSW SR3	159	F1
Aberdeen CLSW/PEL DH2	135	E5
Aberdeen Ct DIN/WO NE13	45	F4

Aberdeen Dr JRW NE32	87	D4
Aberford Cl WD/WHPE/BLK NE5	59	D3
Aberfoyle CLSW/PEL DH2	135	E5
Aberfoyle Ct STLY/ANP DH9	149	D2
Abernethy CLSW/PEL DH2	135	E4
Abingdon Ct GOS/KPK * NE3	45	F5
Abingdon Rd BYK/HTN/WLK NE6	84	A1
Abingdon Sq CRAM NE23	14	B5
Abingdon St MLFD/PNYW SR4	143	E1
Abingdon Wy BOL NE36	105	D3
BOLCOL NE35	104	C1
Abinger St ELS/FEN NE4	80	A3
Aboyne Sq SUNDSW SR3	142	C5
Acacia Av HLS DH4	169	F1
Acacia Gv HAR/WTLS NE34	89	D3
HEBB NE31	85	D4
Acacia Rd FELL NE10	82	A6
Acacia St DUN/TMV NE11	98	B5
Acanthus Av ELS/FEN NE4	78	C1
Acer Ct ASHBK/HED/RY SR2	144	C2
Acklam Av ASHBK/HED/RY SR2	145	E5

Acomb Av *MONK* NE25 ....24 C6
  WLSD/HOW NE28 ....51 F5
Acomb Ct *ASHBK/HED/RY* SR2 .....145 C5
  BDLGTN NE22.................................7 F3
Acomb Crs *GOS/KPK* NE3 ....46 B4
Acomb Gdns *WD/WHPE/BLK* NE5 ...61 G6
Acorn Av *BDLGTN* NE22......................7 F4
  GATE NE8 ....98 B2
Acorn Cl *BDN/LAN/SAC* DH7 ....164 A6
Acorn Pl *BDN/LAN/SAC* DH7 ....203 D6
Acorn Rd *JES* NE2 ....64 A4
Acre Rigg Rd *PLEE/EAS* SR8 ....208 A1
Acton Dene *STLY/ANP* DH9 ....149 E2
Acton Pl *LGB/HTN* NE7 ....65 D4
Acton Rd *NSHW* NE29 ....53 F4
Adair Av *BW/LEM/TK/HW* NE15 ....78 B2
Ada St *BYK/HTN/WLK* NE6 ....83 D2
  SSH NE33 ....71 F5
Adderstone Av *CRAM* NE23 ....22 A3
Adderstone Crs *JES* NE2 ....64 B4
Adderstone Gdns *NSHW* NE29 ....53 D3
Addington Crs *NSHW* NE29 ....54 A6
Addington Dr *BYK/HTN* NE24 ....17 D1
  WLSD/HOW NE28 ....51 F5
Addison Cl *BYK/HTN/WLK* * NE6 ....82 A2
Addison Gdns *FELL* NE10 ....102 A2
Addison Rd *BOL* NE36 ....105 F3
  BW/LEM/TK/HW NE15 ....76 C1
Addison St *ASHBK/HED/RY* SR2 ....5 C5
  NSHW NE29 ....70 C2
Addycombe Ter
  BYK/HTN/WLK NE6 ....65 E5
Adelaide Cl *SUND* SR1 ....5 F2
Adelaide Ct *GATE* * NE8 ....81 D5
Adelaide Pl *SUND* SR1 ....5 G2
Adelaide Rw *SEA/MUR* * SR7 ....176 C3
Adeline Gdns *GOS/KPK* NE3 ....62 C4
Adelphi Cl *NSHW* NE29 ....53 E4
Adelphi Pl *BYK/HTN/WLK* NE6 ....83 D5
Adelphi Pl *PLEE/EAS* SR8 ....208 C1
Admiral Wy *SUNDSW* SR3 ....159 E6
Adolphus St *CLDN/WHIT/ROK* SR6 ...109 E1
Adrian Pl *PLEE/EAS* SR8 ....209 D1
Adventure La *HLS* DH4 ....183 E1
Affleck St *GATE* NE8 ....81 D6
Afton Ct *HAR/WTLS* NE34 ....88 B3
Afton Wy *GOS/KPK* NE3 ....62 A1
Agar Rd *SUNDSW* SR3 ....142 C6
Agincourt *HEBB* NE31 ....84 C1
  LGB/KIL NE12 ....35 F6
Agnes Maria St *GOS/KPK* NE3 ....62 C1
Agnes St *STLY/ANP* DH9 ....148 B1
Agricola Ct *SSH* NE33........................71 E2
Agricola Gdns *WLSD/HOW* NE28 ....51 F6
Agricola Rd *ELS/FEN* NE4 ....79 C3
Aidan Av *WBAY* NE26 ....26 A2
Aidan Cl *DIN/WO* NE13 ....32 C4
  LGB/KIL NE12 ....51 E3
  STLY/ANP DH9 ....149 D1
Aidan Wk *GOS/KPK* NE3 ....63 F1
Aiden Wy *HLH* DH5 ....171 F5
Ailesbury St *MLFD/PNYW* SR4 ....125 F5
Ainderby Rd
  BW/LEM/TK/HW NE15 ....57 D4
Ainsdale Gdns *WD/WHPE/BLK* NE5 ...59 E4
Ainsley St *DHAM* DH1 ....194 A4
Ainslie Pl *WD/WHPE/BLK* NE5 ....61 D5
Ainsworth Av *HAR/WTLS* NE34 ....87 F5
Ainthorpe Cl *SUNDSW* SR3 ....161 D1
Ainthorpe Gdns *LGB/HTN* NE7 ....65 D2
Aintree Gdns *GATE* NE8 ....98 B2
Aintree Rd *SUNDSW* SR3 ....142 C6
Airedale *WLSD/HOW* NE28 ....66 B1
Airedale Gdns *HLH* DH5 ....185 E2
Aireys Cl *HLS* DH4 ....170 B2
Airey Ter *BYK/HTN/WLK* NE6 ....83 F3
  GATE NE8 ....98 C1
Airport Freightway *DIN/WO* NE13 ......44 A2
Airville Mt *SUNDSW* SR3 ....160 C4
Aisgill Cl *CRAM* NE23 ....22 A3
Aisgill Dr *WD/WHPE/BLK* NE5 ....59 E5
Aiskell St *MLFD/PNYW* SR4 ....125 F6
AJ Cook Ter *RDHAMSE* DH6 ....206 B3
Akeld Cl *CRAM* NE23 ....22 A3
Akenside Hl *CNUT* NE1 ....3 E5
Akenside Ter *JES* NE2 ....64 B6
Alamein Av *HLH* DH5 ....171 G4
Alan St *PLEE/EAS* SR8 ....201 E1
Alansway Gdns *SSH* NE33 ....71 F6
Albany Av *LGB/KIL* * NE12 ....49 F4
Albany Ct *ELS/FEN* NE4 ....79 C5
Albany Rd *GATE* NE8 ....81 F5
Albany St East *SSH* NE33 ....71 F4
Albany St West *SSH* NE33 ....71 F6
Albany Wy *WASHN* NE37 ....120 B5
Albatross Wy *BLYTH* NE24 ....17 D3
Albemarle Av *JES* NE2 ....63 F3
Albemarle St *SSH* NE33 ....71 E3
Albert Av *WLSD/HOW* NE28 ....67 D4
Albert Ct *ASHBK/HED/RY* SR2 ....144 A1
Albert Dr *LWF/SPW/WRK* NE9 ....99 D6
Albert Pl *LWF/SPW/WRK* NE9 ....99 E6

  WASHS NE38 ....139 E3
Albert Rd *BDLGTN* NE22 ....8 C2
  JRW NE32 ....86 A1
  MLFD/PNYW SR4 ....125 F5
  WBAY NE26 ....26 C2
Albert St *CLS/BIR/GTL* DH3 ....153 E5
  CLSW/PEL DH2 ....150 C3
  DHAM DH1 ....194 A3
  HEBB NE31 ....84 C1
  JES NE2 ....3 G2
  SEA/MUR SR7 ....176 C4
Albert Ter *LGB/KIL* NE12 ....49 E3
Albion Ct *SSH* NE33 ....71 E2
Albion Gdns *WICK/BNPF* NE16 ....129 E1
Albion Pl *SUND* SR1 ....4 B4
Albion Rd *TYNE/NSHE* NE30 ....70 C1
Albion Rd West *NSHW* NE29 ....70 C1
Albion Rw *BYK/HTN/WLK* NE6 ....82 A2
Albion St *FELL* NE10 ....100 C4
  MLFD/PNYW SR4 ....123 F6
Albion Ter *NSHW* NE29 ....54 C6
Albion Wy *BLYTH* NE24 ....10 B5
  CRAM NE23 ....14 C5
Albury Park Rd *TYNE/NSHE* NE30 .....55 E5
Albury Pl *WICK/BNPF* NE16 ....95 F5
Albury Rd *JES* NE2 ....63 F3
Albyn Gdns *SUNDSW* SR3 ....143 F5
Alconbury Cl *BLYTH* NE24 ....17 D1
Alcote Gv *RDHAMSE* DH6 ....206 C3
Alcroft Cl *WD/WHPE/BLK* NE5 ....59 D2
Aldborough St *BLYTH* NE24 ....11 D5
Aldbrough Cl *ASHBK/HED/RY* SR2 ...162 B2
Aldbrough St *HAR/WTLS* NE34 ....87 F3
Aldeburgh Av
  WD/WHPE/BLK NE5 ....59 E4
Aldenham Rd *SUNDSW* SR3 ....143 D6
Alder Av *ELS/FEN* NE4 ....61 F6
Alder Cl *HLS* DH4 ....185 E1
Alder Crs *STLY/ANP* DH9 ....129 E4
Alder Ct *BDN/LAN/SAC* * DH7 ....192 B5
Alder Gv *MONK* NE25.........................40 A4
Alder Lea Cl *DHAM* DH1 ....195 F3
Alderley Cl *ASHBK/HED/RY* SR2 ....145 E4
  BOLCOL NE35 ....105 D1
Alderley Dr *LGB/KIL* NE12 ....36 B6
Alderley Rd *LWF/SPW/WRK* NE9 ....99 D5
Alderley Wy *CRAM* NE23 ....14 C5
Alderman Wood Rd
  STLY/ANP DH9 ....131 D6
Alderney Gdns
  WD/WHPE/BLK NE5 ....59 E4
Alder Pk *BDN/LAN/SAC* DH7 ....202 C4
Alder Rd *NSHW* NE29 ....52 C5
  WLSD/HOW NE28 ....52 A6
Aldershot Rd *SUNDSW* SR3 ....159 F1
Aldershot Sq *SUNDSW* SR3 ....159 F1
Alder St *SWCK/CAS* SR5 ....124 A3
Alder Wy *LGB/KIL* NE12 ....35 E6
Alderwood *WASHS* NE38 ....138 A5
Alderwood Crs *BYK/HTN/WLK* NE6 ...68 B5
Alderwyk *FELL* NE10 ....102 A4
Aldhome Ct *DHAM* DH1 ....179 F6
Aldsworth Cl *LWF/SPW/WRK* NE9 ....119 E3
Aldwick Rd *BW/LEM/TK/HW* NE15 .....77 F2
Aldwych Dr *NSHW* NE29 ....53 D5
Aldwych Rd *SUNDSW* SR3 ....159 F1
Aldwych Sq *SUNDSW* SR3 ....159 F1
Aldwych St *SSH* NE33 ....72 A4
Alexander Dr *HLH* DH5 ....185 E1
Alexander Ter
  CLDN/WHIT/ROK SR6 ....126 C1
Alexandra Av *SWCK/CAS* SR5 ....125 E3
Alexandra Cl *DHAM* DH1 ....179 F3
Alexandra Crs *DHAM* DH1 ....194 A5
Alexandra Dr *WICK/BNPF* NE16 ....96 C3
Alexandra Gdns *NSHW* NE29 ....54 A6
Alexandra Pk
  ASHBK/HED/RY SR2 ....144 B2
  SUNDSW SR3 ....144 A2
Alexandra Rd *BYK/HTN/WLK* NE6 .....65 D5
  GATE NE8 ....99 D2
Alexandra St *CLSW/PEL* DH2 ....151 E2
  WLSD/HOW NE28 ....67 D4
Alexandra Wy *CRAM* NE23 ....22 A3
Alexandria Crs *DHAM* DH1 ....194 A5
Alexandrina St *SEA/MUR* SR7 ....176 A3
Alford *CLSW/PEL* DH2 ....135 E4
Alfred Av *BDLGTN* NE22 ....8 A3
Alfred St *BYK/HTN/WLK* NE6 ....83 D2
  HEBB NE31 ....84 C1
  PLEE/EAS SR8 ....201 D1
  SEA/MUR SR7...............................177 D4
Alfreton Cl *BDN/LAN/SAC* DH7 ....202 C6
Algernon *LGB/KIL* NE12 ....35 F5
Algernon Cl *BYK/HTN/WLK* * NE6 ......82 B7
Algernon Pl *WBAY* NE26 ....41 D6
Algernon Rd
  BW/LEM/TK/HW NE15 ....76 B2
  BYK/HTN/WLK NE6 ....82 B1
Algernon Ter *TYNE/NSHE* NE30 ....55 E4
Algiers Rd *SUNDSW* SR3 ....159 E1
Alice St *ASHBK/HED/RY* SR2 ....4 B7
  BLAY NE21 ....94 A1
  CLSW/PEL DH2 ....135 E6
  SSH NE33 ....71 E6

Aline St *SEA/MUR* SR7 ....177 D3
  SUNDSW SR3 ....161 D1
Alington Pl *DHAM* DH1 ....195 F4
Alison Dr *BOL* NE36 ....106 C3
Allandale Av *LGB/KIL* NE12 ....49 F5
All Church *BW/LEM/TK/HW* NE15 ....78 A2
Allandale Av *WLSD/HOW* NE28 ....67 D2
Allendale Crs *HLS* DH4 ....139 F6
  SMOOR NE27 ....52 C1
Allendale Dr *HAR/WTLS* NE34 ....72 C4
Allendale Pl *TYNE/NSHE* NE30 ....55 F5
Allendale Rd *BDN/LAN/SAC* DH7 ......203 E4
  BLYTH NE24 ....11 E6
  BYK/HTN/WLK NE6 ....82 C3
  SUNDSW SR3 ....159 F1
Allendale Sq *SUNDSW* SR3 ....143 D5
Allendale St *HLH* DH5 ....185 F2
Allendale Ter *BYK/HTN/WLK* NE6 ......83 C3
Allenheads *WASHS* NE38 ....139 D3
Allenheads *MONK* NE25 ....40 A4
  WD/WHPE/BLK NE5 ....60 A5
Allensgreen *CRAM* NE23 ....22 A2
Allen St *CLS/BIR/GTL* DH3 ....153 E6
Allerdean Cl *BW/LEM/TK/HW* NE15 ...76 A1
Allerdene Wk *WICK/BNPF* NE16 ....96 A3
Allergate *DHAM* DH1 ....194 A5
Allergate Ter *DHAM* * DH1 ....194 A5
Allerhope *CRAM* NE23 ....22 A3
Allerton Gdns *BYK/HTN/WLK* NE6 .....65 F4
Allerwash *WD/WHPE/BLK* NE5 ....60 A5
Allhusen Ter *GATE* NE8 ....100 A3
Alliance Pl *MLFD/PNYW* SR4 ....126 A5
Alliance St *MLFD/PNYW* * SR4 ....126 A5
Allingham Ct *LGB/HTN* NE7 ....65 F3
Allison Ct
  WICK/BNPF
  (off Metrocentre) 96 A1
Allanville *LGB/KIL* NE12 ....35 F5
Alloa Rd *SUNDSW* SR3 ....142 C6
Allonby Wy *WD/WHPE/BLK* NE5 ....61 D6
All Saints Dr *HLH* DH5 ....171 F4
Allwork Ter *WICK/BNPF* * NE16 ....96 A3
Alma Pl *HLS* DH4 ....157 E2
  NSHW NE29 ....54 C6
  WBAY NE26 ....41 D6
Alma St *MLFD/PNYW* SR4 ....123 F5
Almond Crs *GATE* NE8 ....98 A2
Almond Dr *SWCK/CAS* SR5 ....123 F4
Almond Pl *ELS/FEN* NE4 ....78 C1
Almoner's Barn *DHAM* DH1 ....193 F6
Aln Av *GOS/KPK* NE3 ....46 C5
Aln Ct *BW/LEM/TK/HW* NE15 ....76 B2
Aln Crs *GOS/KPK* NE3 ....46 C5
Aln Gv *BW/LEM/TK/HW* NE15 ....76 B1
Alnham Ct *NSHW* NE29 ....69 F2
Alnmouth Av *NSHW* NE29 ....69 F2
Alnmouth Dr *GOS/KPK* NE3 ....64 A2
Aln St *HEBB* NE31 ....84 C2
Aln Wk *GOS/KPK* NE3 ....46 B5
Alnwick Av *NSHW* NE29 ....69 F2
Alnwick Cl *CLSW/PEL* DH2 ....165 F1
  WICK/BNPF NE16 ....95 F3
Alnwick Gv *JRW* NE32 ....86 A6
Alnwick Rd *DHAM* DH1 ....180 B5
  HAR/WTLS NE34 ....88 B2
  SUNDSW SR3 ....143 D6
Alnwick Sq *SUNDSW* SR3 ....143 D6
Alnwick St *BW/LEM/TK/HW* NE15 ......58 B2
  PLEE/EAS SR8 ....201 E5
  PLEE/EAS SR8 ....201 D1
  WLSD/HOW NE28 ....67 E4
Alnwick Ter *DIN/WO* NE13 ....33 F3
Alpine Ct *CLSW/PEL* DH2 ....153 E5
Alpine Gv *BOL* NE36 ....106 A3
Alpine Wy *SUNDSW* SR3 ....143 F5
Alresford *LGB/KIL* NE12 ....35 F6
Alston Av *BYK/HTN/WLK* NE6 ....83 D2
  CRAM NE23 ....22 C3
Alston Cl *NSHW* NE29 ....53 E5
  WLSD/HOW NE28 ....68 C2
Alston Crs *CLDN/WHIT/ROK* SR6 ......108 B3
Alston Gdns *BW/LEM/TK/HW* NE15 ...77 F3
Alston Gv *WBAY* NE26 ....26 A1
Alston Rd *MONK* NE25 ....24 C2
  WASHS NE38 ....122 A5
Alston St *GATE* NE8 ....98 B1
Alston Wk *PLEE/EAS* SR8 ....209 D1
Alston Wy *BDN/LAN/SAC* DH7 ....203 E4
Altan Pl *LGB/KIL* NE12 ....49 D5
Alum Well Rd *LWF/SPW/WRK* NE9 .....99 D5
Alverston Cl
  BW/LEM/TK/HW NE15 ....59 E6
Alverstone Av *LWF/SPW/WRK* NE9 ....99 D5
Alverthorpe St *SSH* NE33 ....71 F6
Alvin Gra *JRW* * NE32 ....85 E1
Alwin *WASHS* NE38 ....137 F5
Alwin Cl *HLS* DH4 ....156 A5
Alwinton Av *NSHW* NE29 ....53 F4
Alwinton Cl *BLYTH* NE24 ....11 D6
  WD/WHPE/BLK NE5 ....60 C2
Alwinton Dr *CLSW/PEL* DH2 ....165 F1
Alwinton Gdns *DUN/TMV* NE11 ....97 F5
Alwinton Rd *SMOOR* NE27 ....52 C1
Alwinton Ter *GOS/KPK* NE3 ....63 F1

Amara Sq SUNDSW SR3 ....**143** D6
Ambassadors Wy NSHW NE29 ....**53** D4
Amber Ct BLYTH NE24 ....**10** B6
Ambergate Cl WD/WHPE/BLK NE5 ....**60** C3
Amberley Cha LGB/KIL NE12 ....**36** A6
Amberley Cl WLSD/HOW * NE28 ....**68** C2
Amberley Gdns LGB/HTN NE7 ....**65** E4
Amberley St ASHBK/HED/RY SR2 ....**5** E5
   GATE NE8 ....**98** A1
Amberley St South
   ASHBK/HED/RY NE4 ....**5** E5
Amberley Wy BLYTH NE24 ....**17** D1
Amberly Gv WICK/BNPF NE16 ....**95** F5
Amble Av HAR/WTLS NE34 ....**73** D6
   MONK NE25 ....**55** D1
Amble Cl BLYTH NE24 ....**16** B1
Amble Gv JES NE2 ....**81** F1
Amble Pl LGB/KIL NE12 ....**50** B3
Ambleside BW/LEM/TK/HW NE15 ......**58** A3
Ambleside Av HAR/WTLS NE34 ....**89** D2
   SEA/MUR SR7 ....**175** D2
Ambleside Cl MONK NE25 ....**24** C5
   PLEE/EAS SR8 ....**209** D1
Ambleside Ter
   CLDN/WHIT/ROK SR6 ....**108** B6
Amble Wy GOS/KPK NE3 ....**47** D6
Ambridge Wy GOS/KPK NE3 ....**62** B1
Ambrose Pl BYK/HTN/WLK NE6 ....**84** A2
Ambrose Rd SUNDSW SR3 ....**142** C6
Amec Wy WLSD/HOW NE28 ....**68** A5
Amelia Cl ELS/FEN NE4 ....**79** D5
Amelia Gdns SUNDSW SR3 ....**159** D1
Amelia Wk ELS/FEN NE4 ....**79** D5
Amen Cnr
   CNUT
   (off St. Nicholas Chambers) NE1 ....**2** D5
Amersham Crs PLEE/EAS SR8 ....**208** C1
Amersham Pl WD/WHPE/BLK NE5 ......**61** D4
Amersham Rd BLYTH NE24 ....**16** C2
Amesbury Cl WD/WHPE/BLK NE5 ......**59** D3
Amethyst Rd ELS/FEN NE4 ....**79** E6
Amethyst St MLFD/PNYW SR4 ....**125** E5
Amherst Rd GOS/KPK NE3 ....**46** A6
Amos Ayre Pl HAR/WTLS NE34 ....**87** E3
Amsterdam Rd SUNDSW SR3 ....**143** D6
Amy St SWCK/CAS SR5 ....**126** A2
Ancaster Av LGB/KIL NE12 ....**49** D6
Ancaster Rd WICK/BNPF NE16 ....**95** F5
Anchorage Ter DHAM DH1 ....**194** B6
Ancona St MLFD/PNYW SR4 ....**125** E4
Ancroft Av NSHW NE29 ....**54** B5
Ancroft Pl WD/WHPE/BLK NE5 ....**61** D6
Ancroft Rd MONK NE25 ....**24** A5
Ancroft Wy GOS/KPK NE3 ....**46** B4
Ancrum St JES NE2 ....**80** A1
Anderson St SSH NE33 ....**71** F3
Andover Pl WLSD/HOW NE28 ....**52** A6
Andrew Rd SUNDSW SR3 ....**159** D1
Andrew's La PLEE/EAS SR8 ....**199** F4
Andrew St PLEE/EAS SR8 ....**201** D1
Anfield Pl STLY/ANP DH9 ....**146** A4
Anfield Rd CRAM NE23 ....**14** A4
Annie St CLDN/WHIT/ROK SR6 ....**108** C6
Annitsford Dr CRAM NE23 ....**35** D2
Ann's Rw BLYTH NE21 ....**11** D3
Ann St BLAY NE21 ....**76** B5
   GATE NE8 ....**81** E6
   HEBB NE31 ....**84** B1
Annville Crs BYK/HTN/WLK NE6 ....**83** F4
Anscomb Gdns LGB/HTN NE7 ....**64** B3
Anson Cl SSH NE33 ....**71** D6
Anson Pl WD/WHPE/BLK NE5 ....**60** D3
Anstead Cl CRAM NE23 ....**22** A2
Anthony Rd SUNDSW * SR3 ....**159** F1
Anthony St PLEE/EAS SR8 ....**201** E1
   STLY/ANP DH9 ....**148** A1
Antlift Ter STLY/ANP DH9 ....**146** B4
Antonine Wk
   BW/LEM/TK/HW NE15 ....**56** B4
Anton Pl CRAM NE23 ....**22** A3
Antrim Cl WD/WHPE/BLK NE5 ....**61** E3
Antrim Gdns SEA/MUR SR7 ....**176** B3
Antwerp Rd SUNDSW SR3 ....**159** E1
Anvil Ct DHAM DH1 ....**179** F5
Apperley WD/WHPE/BLK NE5 ....**60** A5

Apperley Av GOS/KPK NE3 ....**61** E2
Appian Pl BW/LEM/TK/HW NE15 ....**58** A4
   LWF/SPW/WRK NE9 ....**100** A3
Appleby Ct HLS DH4 ....**168** C1
   NSHW NE29 ....**70** B1
Appleby Gdns WLSD/HOW NE28 ......**68** C2
Appleby Pk NSHW NE29 ....**54** B6
Appleby Rd SUNDSW SR3 ....**159** F1
Appleby Sq SUNDSW SR3 ....**159** F1
Appleby St NSHW NE29 ....**70** C2
Appleby Wy PLEE/EAS SR8 ....**207** F5
Apple Cl BW/LEM/TK/HW NE15 ....**59** E6
Appledore Gdns
   CLS/BIR/GTL DH3 ....**153** F3
Appledore Rd BLYTH NE24 ....**17** D1
Appleforth Av
   ASHBK/HED/RY SR2 ....**145** F5
Appleton Cl DUN/TMV NE11 ....**97** F2
Appletree Gdns
   BYK/HTN/WLK NE6 ....**66** A6
   MONK NE25 ....**54** A1
Applewood LGB/KIL NE12 ....**50** B1
Appley Ter CLDN/WHIT/ROK SR6 ......**127** D3
Apsley Crs GOS/KPK NE3 ....**62** A1
Arbroath Rd SUNDSW SR3 ....**142** C6
Arcade
   TYNE/NSHE (off Front St) NE30 ....**55** F5
The Arcade
   CLS/BIR/GTL (off Front St) DH3 ....**153** E5
   WICK/BNPF
   (off Metrocentre) NE16 ....**78** B6
Arcadia Av CLS/BIR/GTL DH3 ....**153** E3
Arcadia Ter BLYTH NE24 ....**11** D6
Archbold Ter JES NE2 ....**81** D1
Archer Rd SUNDSW SR3 ....**142** C6
Archer Sq SUNDSW SR3 ....**142** C6
Archer St WLSD/HOW NE28 ....**68** A3
Archery Ri DHAM DH1 ....**193** F6
Archibald St GOS/KPK NE3 ....**63** E1
Arcot Av CRAM NE23 ....**21** D1
   MONK NE25 ....**54** A1
Arcot Dr MONK NE25 ....**54** A2
   WD/WHPE/BLK NE5 ....**60** B6
Arden Av GOS/KPK NE3 ....**47** D3
Arden Cl WLSD/HOW NE28 ....**51** F5
Arden Crs WD/WHPE/BLK NE5 ....**61** F5
Arden Sq SUNDSW SR3 ....**143** D6
Arden St RDHAMSE DH6 ....**206** B1
Ardrossan CLSW/PEL DH2 ....**135** E5
Ardrossan Rd SUNDSW SR3 ....**159** F1
Arena Wy ELS/FEN NE4 ....**80** B5
Argent St PLEE/EAS SR8 ....**201** D1
Argus Cl DUN/TMV NE11 ....**98** A3
Argyle Rd SUNDSW SR3 ....**159** D1
Argyle Pl ASHBK/HED/RY SR2 ....**4** B5
   RDHAMSE DH6 ....**187** E5
Argyle Sq ASHBK/HED/RY SR2 ....**4** B5
Argyle St ASHBK/HED/RY SR2 ....**4** B5
   CNUT NE1 ....**3** F3
   HEBB NE31 ....**85** D1
   TYNE/NSHE NE30 ....**55** F4
Argyle Ter NSHW NE29 ....**54** C4
Arisaig CLSW/PEL DH2 ....**135** E4
Arklecrag WASHN NE37 ....**116** B5
Arkleside Pl WD/WHPE/BLK NE5 ......**59** E5
Arkle St DIN/WO NE13 ....**32** C6
   GATE NE8 ....**98** B2
Arkwright St GATE NE8 ....**98** C3
Arlington Av GOS/KPK NE3 ....**62** B3
Arlington Ct
   GOS/KPK (off Kenton Av) NE3 ......**62** C3
Arlington Gv CRAM NE23 ....**14** A4
   WICK/BNPF NE16 ....**95** F4
Arlington Rd HEBB NE31 ....**85** E4
Arlington St MLFD/PNYW SR4 ....**125** E6
Armstrong Av BYK/HTN/WLK NE6 ......**65** D5
   HAR/WTLS NE34 ....**89** D1
Armstrong Dr LGB/KIL NE12 ....**49** D2
Armstrong Rd
   BW/LEM/TK/HW NE15 ....**77** E3
   ELS/FEN NE4 ....**78** C4
   PLEE/EAS SR8 ....**200** C6
   WASHN NE37 ....**119** E5
   WLSD/HOW NE28 ....**68** C5
Armstrong St DUN/TMV NE11 ....**98** B3
   GATE NE8 ....**98** B3
Armstrong Ter SSH NE33 ....**71** E6
Arncliffe Av MLFD/PNYW SR4 ....**143** D2
Arncliffe Gdns WD/WHPE/BLK NE5 ....**59** E4
Arndale Houses
   CLS/BIR/GTL
   (off Durham Rd) DH3 ....**136** B2
Arnham Gv MLFD/PNYW SR4 ....**141** E4
Arnold Gv STLY/ANP DH9 ....**148** C3
Arnold Rd SUNDSW SR3 ....**142** C6
Arnold St BOLCOL NE35 ....**105** C2
Arran Ct SUNDSW * SR3 ....**160** C2
Arran Dr JRW NE32 ....**87** D5
Arran Gdns FELL NE10 ....**100** B3
Arran Pl NSHW NE29 ....**53** E4
Arras La SUND SR1 ....**5** F2
Arrow Cl LGB/KIL NE12 ....**49** D2
Arther Ter CLDN/WHIT/ROK SR6 ....**91** E5
Arthur Av ASHBK/HED/RY SR2 ....**162** C2
Arthur Cook Av WICK/BNPF NE16 ......**96** B3

Arthur St BLYTH NE24 ....**11** D4
   CLDN/WHIT/ROK SR6 ....**91** E4
   GATE NE8 ....**81** E6
   JRW NE32 ....**86** A2
   STLY/ANP DH9 ....**150** C1
Arun Cl PLEE/EAS SR8 ....**208** B3
Arundel Cl BDLGTN NE22 ....**8** B1
   DIN/WO NE13 ....**32** C5
Arundel Dr BW/LEM/TK/HW NE15 ......**77** D1
   MONK NE25 ....**39** D6
Arundel Gdns LWF/SPW/WRK NE9 ....**99** F5
   SUNDSW SR3 ....**159** E1
Arundell Ct GOS/KPK * NE3 ....**45** C5
Arundel Rd SUNDSW SR3 ....**142** C6
Arundel Wy BDN/LAN/SAC DH7 ....**203** E4
Asama Ct ELS/FEN NE4 ....**79** F6
Ascot Cl WLSD/HOW NE28 ....**51** F6
Ascot Ct GOS/KPK NE3 ....**45** C5
   SUNDSW SR3 ....**159** F1
Ascot Crs GATE NE8 ....**98** B3
Ascot Gdns HAR/WTLS NE34 ....**88** C2
Ascot Pl CLSW/PEL DH2 ....**152** B1
Ascot St PLEE/EAS SR8 ....**201** E2
Ash Av DHAM DH1 ....**195** F5
   DIN/WO NE13 ....**31** D3
Ashberry Gv
   CLDN/WHIT/ROK SR6 ....**126** C3
Ashbourne Av BYK/HTN/WLK NE6 ......**83** E2
Ashbourne Cl SMOOR NE27 ....**37** D5
Ashbourne Rd JRW NE32 ....**86** B3
Ashbrook Cl BDN/LAN/SAC DH7 ......**202** B5
Ashbrooke MONK NE25 ....**40** A5
Ashbrooke Crs
   ASHBK/HED/RY SR2 ....**144** C2
Ashbrooke Cross
   ASHBK/HED/RY * SR2 ....**144** B3
Ashbrooke Dr PONT/DH NE20 ....**28** A3
Ashbrooke Gdns WLSD/HOW NE28 ....**68** A3
Ashbrooke Mt
   ASHBK/HED/RY * SR2 ....**144** B2
Ashbrooke Range
   ASHBK/HED/RY SR2 ....**144** B3
Ashbrooke Rd
   ASHBK/HED/RY SR2 ....**144** C2
Ashbrooke St WD/WHPE/BLK NE5 ....**62** A3
Ashbrooke Ter
   ASHBK/HED/RY SR2 ....**144** C2
Ashburne Ct ASHBK/HED/RY SR2 ....**144** C2
Ashburn Rd WLSD/HOW NE28 ....**52** A6
Ashburton Rd GOS/KPK NE3 ....**62** C2
Ashbury MONK NE25 ....**39** E4
Ashby St ASHBK/HED/RY SR2 ....**145** E3
Ashcroft Dr LGB/KIL NE12 ....**50** A5
Ashdale HLS DH4 ....**139** D6
Ashdale Crs WD/WHPE/BLK NE5 ......**59** E5
Ashdown Av DHAM DH1 ....**196** A3
Ashdown Cl LGB/KIL NE12 ....**49** D5
Ashdown Rd SUNDSW SR3 ....**142** C6
Ashdown Wy LGB/KIL NE12 ....**49** D5
Asher St GATE NE8 ....**100** A1
Ashfield JRW NE32 ....**104** C1
Ashfield Av WICK/BNPF NE16 ....**96** B2
Ashfield Cl ELS/FEN NE4 ....**79** F4
Ashfield Gdns WLSD/HOW NE28 ......**66** B3
Ashfield Gv NSHW NE29 ....**54** C6
   WBAY NE26 ....**32** C3
Ashfield Pk WICK/BNPF NE16 ....**96** A3
Ashfield Ri WICK/BNPF NE16 ....**96** A5
Ashfield Rd GOS/KPK NE3 ....**62** C5
   WICK/BNPF NE16 ....**96** A5
Ashfield Ter FELL * NE10 ....**101** E1
Ashford Cl BLYTH NE24 ....**17** D1
Ashford Dr BDN/LAN/SAC DH7 ....**164** A6
Ashford Gv WD/WHPE/BLK NE5 ....**59** D2
Ashford Rd SUNDSW SR3 ....**159** F1
Ash Gv CLDN/WHIT/ROK SR6 ....**109** F1
   DUN/TMV NE11 ....**97** D1
   RYTON NE40 ....**74** B2
   WLSD/HOW NE28 ....**67** F4
Ashgrove Av HAR/WTLS NE34 ....**89** E4
Ashgrove Ter GATE * NE8 ....**99** D1
Ashkirk CRAM NE23 ....**34** C2
Ashkirk Cl CLSW/PEL DH2 ....**165** F1
Ashkirk Wy MONK NE25 ....**24** C6
Ashleigh Av DHAM DH1 ....**194** A1
Ashleigh Cl BLAY NE21 ....**94** C1
Ashleigh Crs WD/WHPE/BLK NE5 ......**60** C6
Ashleigh Gv CLDN/WHIT/ROK SR6 ..**109** D6
   JES NE2 ....**72** E4
   LGB/KIL NE12 ....**49** F5
   TYNE/NSHE NE30 ....**55** E4
Ashleigh Rd WD/WHPE/BLK NE5 ......**60** C6
Ashley Cl LGB/KIL NE12 ....**36** B6
   WASHS NE38 ....**138** C3
Ashley Rd HAR/WTLS NE34 ....**88** B2
Ashley Ter CLS/BIR/GTL DH3 ....**153** E4
Ashmead Cl LGB/KIL NE12 ....**36** A6
Ash Mdw CLS/BIR/GTL DH3 ....**154** A1
Ashmore St ASHBK/HED/RY SR2 ....**4** C6
Ashmore Ter ASHBK/HED/RY SR2 ......**4** C6
Asholme WD/WHPE/BLK NE5 ....**60** A5
Ashridge Cl HAR/WTLS NE34 ....**90** A3
Ashridge Ct FELL NE10 ....**102** A3
Ash St BLAY NE21 ....**94** B1
Ash Ter SEA/MUR SR7 ....**188** B1

Ashton Ct *RYTON* NE40 ......74 C4
Ashton Ri *CLSW/PEL* DH2 ......153 E6
　PLEE/EAS SR8 ......209 D1
Ashton St *PLEE/EAS* SR8 ......201 E4
Ashton Wy *SUNDSW* SR3 ......159 E2
　WBAY NE26 ......39 F3
Ashtree Cl *ELS/FEN* NE4 ......79 E4
　ROWG NE39 ......111 E1
Ash Tree Dr *BDLGTN* NE22 ......7 E2
Ashtree La *BLAY* NE21 ......92 B5
Ashvale Av *DUN/TMV* NE11 ......116 B6
Ashwell Rd *SUNDSW* SR3 ......159 F1
Ashwood *RDHAMSE* DH6 ......157 F6
Ashwood Av *SWCK/CAS* SR5 ......125 E2
Ashwood Cl *CRAM* NE23 ......14 A4
　LGB/KIL NE12 ......50 A4
Ashwood Crs *BYK/HTN/WLK* NE6 ......66 B5
Ashwood Cft *HEBB* NE31 ......84 C1
Ashwood Gdns
　LWF/SPW/WRK NE9 ......117 F2
Ashwood Gv *DIN/WO* NE13 ......33 D5
　SWCK/CAS SR5 ......124 A3
Ashwood St *ASHBK/HED/RY* SR2 ......144 A1
Ashwood Ter *ASHBK/HED/RY* SR2 ......144 A1
Askern Av *ASHBK/HED/RY* SR2 ......145 E5
Askerton Dr *PLEE/EAS* SR8 ......207 F5
Askew Rd *GATE* NE8 ......80 C6
Askew Rd West *GATE* NE8 ......98 B1
Askrigg Av *ASHBK/HED/RY* SR2 ......145 E5
　WLSD/HOW NE28 ......51 F5
Aspen Cl *DHAM* DH1 ......195 F3
Aspen Ct *SUNDSW* * SR3 ......160 A2
Aspen Ter *WD/WHPE/BLK* NE5 ......62 A5
Aspley Cl *SUNDSW* SR3 ......160 C2
Association Rd
　CLDN/WHIT/ROK SR6 ......127 D2
Aster Pl *ELS/FEN* NE4 ......78 B1
Astley Dr *WBAY* NE26 ......40 A2
Astley Gdns *MONK* NE25 ......24 B5
　WBAY NE26 ......26 A1
Astley Gv *WBAY* NE26 ......26 A1
Astley Rd *MONK* NE25 ......24 B4
Astley Vls *WBAY* NE26 ......26 A1
Aston Sq *SUNDSW* SR3 ......159 F1
Aston St *SSH* NE33 ......88 C1
Athelhampton *WASHS* NE38 ......139 F1
Athelstan Rigg
　ASHBK/HED/RY SR2 ......162 C1
Athenaeum St *SUND* SR1 ......4 D3
Atherton Dr *ELS/FEN* NE4 ......79 D4
　HLS DH4 ......169 F3
Atherton St *DHAM* DH1 ......194 A5
Athlone Pl *CLS/BIR/GTL* DH3 ......136 C5
Athol Gdns *ASHBK/HED/RY* SR2 ......162 C2
　MONK NE25 ......53 F1
Athol Gn *DUN/TMV* NE11 ......97 F1
Athol Gv *SUNDSW* SR3 ......160 C1
Atholl Gdns *LWF/SPW/WRK* NE9 ......100 A3
Athol Pk *ASHBK/HED/RY* SR2 ......145 D2
Athol Rd *ASHBK/HED/RY* SR2 ......5 F6
Athol Ter *ASHBK/HED/RY* SR2 ......5 F6
Athull *CLSW/PEL* DH2 ......135 E4
Atkinson Gdns *NSHW* NE29 ......70 C3
Atkinson Gv *RDHAMSE* DH6 ......206 A1
Atkinson Rd *CLDN/WHIT/ROK* SR6 ......108 C4
　CLS/BIR/GTL DH3 ......153 F3
　ELS/FEN NE4 ......78 C4
Atkinson St *WLSD/HOW* NE28 ......67 D5
Atkinson Ter *ELS/FEN* NE4 ......78 C3
　WLSD/HOW NE28 ......67 D5
Atkin St *LGB/KIL* NE12 ......35 D5
Atlantis Rd *SUNDSW* SR3 ......142 B6
Atley Wy *CRAM* NE23 ......13 D4
Attlee Cl *CRAM* NE23 ......35 D5
Attlee Gv *ASHBK/HED/RY* SR2 ......145 D6
Attwood Gv *SWCK/CAS* SR5 ......126 A3
Aubone Av *DUN/LEM/TK/HW* NE15 ......78 B2
Auburn Cl *WLSD/HOW* NE28 ......68 C4
Auburn Gdns *ELS/FEN* NE4 ......62 A6
Auckland *CLSW/PEL* DH2 ......152 B5
Auckland Av *HAR/WTLS* NE34 ......90 A2
Auckland Rd *DHAM* DH1 ......180 C5
　HEBB NE31 ......85 E1
Auckland Ter *JRW* NE32 ......87 D4
Auden Gv *ELS/FEN* NE4 ......79 D2
Audley Gdns *SUNDSW* SR3 ......144 A5
Audley Rd *GOS/KPK* NE3 ......64 A2
Audouins Rw *GATE* * NE8 ......98 C2
Augusta Ct *WLSD/HOW* NE28 ......52 A6
Augusta Sq *SUNDSW* SR3 ......159 F1
Augustine Cl *DHAM* DH1 ......179 F6
August Pl *SSH* NE33 ......71 F5
Augustus Dr *BDLGTN* NE22 ......7 D2
Austen Av *HAR/WTLS* NE34 ......88 A5
Austen Pl *STLY/ANP* DH9 ......148 C4
Austin Sq *SWCK/CAS* SR5 ......126 A2
Australia Gv *HAR/WTLS* NE34 ......87 E5
Austral Pl *DIN/WO* NE13 ......32 C5
Autumn Cl *WASHS* NE38 ......120 C6
Avalon Dr *BW/LEM/TK/HW* NE15 ......60 A6
Avalon Rd *SUNDSW* SR3 ......142 C6
Avebury Dr *WASHS* NE38 ......139 D1
Avebury Pl *CRAM* NE23 ......14 B5
Avenue Rd *GATE* NE8 ......99 E2
　MONK NE25 ......24 B5

Avenue Ter *ASHBK/HED/RY* SR2 ......144 B2
The Avenue *ASHBK/HED/RY* SR2 ......4 B6
　BLAY NE21 ......77 D6
　CLS/BIR/GTL DH3 ......136 B2
　CLS/BIR/GTL DH3 ......156 A3
　CLSW/PEL DH2 ......153 D5
　DHAM DH1 ......179 F5
　DHAM DH1 ......194 A5
　HLH DH5 ......172 A6
　LWF/SPW/WRK NE9 ......99 F3
　MONK NE25 ......24 C4
　ROWG NE39 ......111 E3
　SEA/MUR SR7 ......75 F3
　STLY/ANP DH9 ......146 A5
　WASHS NE38 ......139 D1
　WBAY NE26 ......40 B5
　WLSD/HOW NE28 ......67 D5
Avenue Vivian *HLS* DH4 ......169 E1
Aviemore Rd *BOL* NE36 ......106 A3
Avison St *ELS/FEN* NE4 ......80 A3
Avison Pl *ELS/FEN* NE4 ......80 A3
Avon Cl *ELS/FEN* * NE4 ......80 A2
Avocet Cl *BLYTH* NE24 ......17 D3
Avolon Ct *ELS/FEN* * NE4 ......80 A2
Avolon Pl *ELS/FEN* NE4 ......80 A2
Avolon Wk *ELS/FEN* * NE4 ......80 A2
Avon Av *JRW* NE32 ......86 B6
　NSHW NE29 ......70 A2
Avon Cl *ROWG* NE39 ......111 E1
　WLSD/HOW NE28 ......51 F6
Avon Ct *HLS* DH4 ......169 F2
Avon Crs *HLS* DH4 ......169 F2
Avoncroft Cl *SEA/MUR* SR7 ......174 C2
Avondale *MLFD/PNYW* SR4 ......141 F1
　HLS DH4 ......157 D1
　LGB/KIL NE12 ......49 F4
Avondale Cl *BLYTH* NE24 ......9 E4
Avondale Gdns *BOL* NE36 ......105 F3
Avondale Ri *BYK/HTN/WLK* * NE6 ......82 B3
Avondale Rd *BYK/HTN/WLK* NE6 ......82 B3
Avondale Ter *CLSW/PEL* DH2 ......153 C5
　GATE NE8 ......99 D2
Avonlea Wy *WD/WHPE/BLK* NE5 ......61 E3
Avonmouth Rd *SUNDSW* SR3 ......159 E1
Avonmouth Sq *SUNDSW* SR3 ......159 F1
Avon Rd *HEBB* NE31 ......85 D4
　PLEE/EAS SR8 ......208 B3
　STLY/ANP DH9 ......148 B3
Avon St *GATE* NE8 ......99 F1
　SUND SR1 ......5 G4
Awnless Ct *HAR/WTLS* NE34 ......88 B5
Axbridge Gdns *ELS/FEN* NE4 ......79 D4
Axminster Cl *CRAM* NE23 ......14 B5
Axwell Dr *BLYTH* NE24 ......10 A5
Axwell Park Cl *WICK/BNPF* * NE16 ......95 F3
Axwell Park Rd *BLAY* NE21 ......95 D1
Axwell Park Vw
　BW/LEM/TK/HW NE15 ......78 A3
Axwell Ter *WICK/BNPF* * NE16 ......95 F1
Axwell Vw *BLAY* NE21 ......94 B1
　WICK/BNPF NE16 ......95 F3
Aycliffe Av *LWF/SPW/WRK* NE9 ......100 C6
Aycliffe Crs *LWF/SPW/WRK* NE9 ......100 C6
Aydon Gv *JRW* NE32 ......86 A5
Aykley Ct *DHAM* DH1 ......193 F2
Aykley Gn *DHAM* DH1 ......193 F2
Aykley Rd *DHAM* DH1 ......180 A5
Aykley V *DHAM* DH1 ......193 F1
Aylesbury Dr *SUNDSW* SR3 ......160 A3
Aylesbury Pl *LGB/KIL* NE12 ......49 D5
Aylesford Sq *BLYTH* NE24 ......17 D1
Aylsham Cl *WD/WHPE/BLK* NE5 ......59 D2
Aylsham Ct *SUNDSW* SR3 ......160 C4
Aylyth Pl *GOS/KPK* NE3 ......62 B3
Ayr Dr *JRW* NE32 ......86 C5
Ayre's Quay Rd *SUND* SR1 ......4 A2
Ayre's Ter *NSHW* NE29 ......54 C6
Ayrey Av *HAR/WTLS* NE34 ......87 E4
Aysgarth Av *ASHBK/HED/RY* SR2 ......145 E4
　WLSD/HOW NE28 ......51 F5
Ayton Av *ASHBK/HED/RY* SR2 ......145 E5
Ayton Cl *BDLGTN* NE22 ......6 C2
Ayton Ri *BYK/HTN/WLK* NE6 ......82 B3
Ayton Rd *WASHS* NE38 ......137 F2
Ayton St *BYK/HTN/WLK* NE6 ......82 B3
Azalea Av *ASHBK/HED/RY* SR2 ......4 B6
Azalea Ter North
　ASHBK/HED/RY SR2 ......4 B5
Azalea Ter South
　ASHBK/HED/RY SR2 ......4 B6

Back
　JES (off Osborne Ter) NE2 ......81 D1
Back Bridge St *SUND* SR1 ......4 C2
Back Chapman St
　BYK/HTN/WLK NE6 ......82 B1
Back Croft Rd *BLYTH* NE24 ......11 D5

Back Eccleston Rd *SSH* * NE33 ......72 A4
Back George St *ELS/FEN* NE4 ......2 A6
Back Goldspink La *JES* NE2 ......81 E1
Back Heaton Park Rd
　BYK/HTN/WLK NE6 ......82 A2
Back La *BLAY* NE21 ......76 A6
　CLS/BIR/GTL DH3 ......167 F3
　HLS DH4 ......140 A6
　MONK NE25 ......40 A5
Back Lodge Ter *SUND* SR1 ......5 H3
Back Maling St
　BYK/HTN/WLK NE6 ......81 F3
Back Mitford St *ELS/FEN* NE4 ......80 B5
Back Mount Joy *DHAM* DH1 ......194 C6
Back New Bridge St *CNUT* NE1 ......3 G2
Back North Bridge St
　SWCK/CAS SR5 ......126 C4
Back North Railway St
　SEA/MUR SR7 ......176 C2
Back North Ter *SEA/MUR* SR7 ......176 C2
Back Percy Gdns *TYNE/NSHE* NE30...55 F4
Back Rw *WICK/BNPF* NE16 ......95 F3
Back Ryhope St
　ASHBK/HED/RY SR2 ......162 A1
Back Silver St *DHAM* DH1 ......194 B4
Back South Railway St
　SEA/MUR SR7 ......176 C3
Back Stephen St
　BYK/HTN/WLK NE6 ......81 F2
Back St *BLAY* NE21 ......93 F1
Back Walker Rd
　BYK/HTN/WLK NE6 ......83 F4
Back Western Hl *DHAM* DH1 ......194 A3
Back Woodbine St *GATE* NE8 ......98 C5
Backworth La *CRAM* NE23 ......36 B2
Baden Crs *SWCK/CAS* SR5 ......123 F1
Baden Powell St
　LWF/SPW/WRK NE9 ......99 F3
Baden St *CLS/BIR/GTL* DH3 ......153 E6
Badger Cl *SUNDSW* SR3 ......160 C3
Badger's Wd *STLY/ANP* DH9 ......131 F5
Badminton Cl *BOLCOL* NE35 ......105 D1
Baffin Ct *SUNDSW* SR3 ......160 B2
Baildon Cl *WLSD/HOW* NE28 ......67 E2
Bailey Ri *PLEE/EAS* SR8 ......200 C6
Bailey Sq *SWCK/CAS* SR5 ......105 F6
Bailey Wy *HLH* DH5 ......186 A2
Bainbridge Av *HAR/WTLS* NE34 ......87 F3
　SUNDSW SR3 ......144 A3
Bainbridge Holme Cl
　SUNDSW SR3 ......144 A3
Bainbridge Holme Rd
　SUNDSW SR3 ......144 B3
Bainbridge St *DHAM* DH1 ......196 C1
Bainford Av
　BW/LEM/TK/HW NE15 ......77 F2
Baird Av *WLSD/HOW* NE28 ......69 E4
Baird Cl *WASHN* NE37 ......121 D2
Baird Ct *GATE* * NE8 ......100 A1
Baird St *SWCK/CAS* SR5 ......123 F1
Bakehouse La *DHAM* DH1 ......194 C4
Baker Gdns *DUN/TMV* * NE11 ......97 E1
　FELL NE10 ......102 A2
Baker Rd *CRAM* NE23 ......12 C5
Baker St *HLH* DH5 ......171 D1
　SWCK/CAS SR5 ......123 F1
Bakewell Ter *BYK/HTN/WLK* NE6 ......82 C4
Baldersdale Gdns *SUNDSW* SR3 ......144 A6
Baldwin Av *BOL* NE36 ......106 C3
　ELS/FEN NE4 ......79 E1
Baldwin St *PLEE/EAS* SR8 ......201 E2
Balfour Rd *BW/LEM/TK/HW* NE15 ......77 F2
Balfour St *BLYTH* NE24 ......10 C3
　GATE NE8 ......98 C1
　HLH DH5 ......171 D1
Balgonie Cottages *RYTON* NE40 ......74 B3
Baliol Sq *DHAM* DH1 ......204 C1
Balkwell Av *NSHW* NE29 ......69 F1
Balkwell Gn *NSHW* NE29 ......54 A6
Ballast Hl *BLYTH* NE24 ......11 E4
Ballast Hill Rd *NSHW* NE29 ......70 C3
Ballater Cl *STLY/ANP* DH9 ......149 D2
Balliol Av *LGB/KIL* NE12 ......49 E3
Balliol Cl *PLEE/EAS* SR8 ......208 A2
Balliol Gdns *BDLGTN* NE7 ......65 D1
Balmain Rd *GOS/KPK* NE3 ......62 A2
Balmoral Av *GOS/KPK* NE3 ......64 A2
　JRW NE32 ......87 D5
Balmoral Cl *BDLGTN* NE22 ......8 B2
Balmoral Ct *SWCK/CAS* SR5 ......125 F1
Balmoral Crs *HLH* DH5 ......171 E2
Balmoral Dr *FELL* NE10 ......100 B2
　PLEE/EAS SR8 ......207 F5
Balmoral Gdns *NSHW* NE29 ......54 B5
Balmoral St *WLSD/HOW* NE28 ......67 D4
Balmoral Ter *ASHBK/HED/RY* SR2 ......145 E4
　BYK/HTN/WLK NE6 ......82 A1
　GOS/KPK NE3 ......64 A2
　SUNDSW SR3 ......159 E1
Balmoral Wy *FELL* NE10 ......100 B3
Balroy Ct *LGB/KIL* NE12 ......50 A4
Baltic Millennium Br *CNUT* NE1 ......3 G5
Baltic Rd *FELL* NE10 ......82 C5
Baltimore Av *SWCK/CAS* SR5 ......105 D6
Baltimore Sq *SWCK/CAS* SR5 ......123 E1

Bamborough Ct *CRAM* NE23 ....**34** B2
Bamborough Ter
  TYNE/NSHE NE30 ....**54** C5
Bambro' St *ASHBK/HED/RY* SR2 ....**5** F6
Bamburgh Av *SSH* NE33 ....**72** B5
  WASHS NE38 ....**137** F1
Bamburgh Cl *BLYTH* NE24 ....**10** B5
  WLSD/HOW NE28 ....**68** B3
Bamburgh Ct *DUN/TMV* NE11 ....**98** B3
Bamburgh Dr *FELL* NE10 ....**84** A6
  WLSD/HOW NE28 ....**68** B3
Bamburgh Gdns *SUNDSW* SR3 ....**144** A3
Bamburgh Rd *DHAM* DH1 ....**180** D5
  LGB/KIL NE12 ....**50** B4
  WD/WHPE/BLK NE5 ....**60** A4
Bamburgh Ter *BYK/HTN/WLK* NE6 ....**82** B2
Bampton Av
  CLDN/WHIT/ROK SR6 ....**108** B5
Banbury *WASHN* NE37 ....**121** D4
Banbury Gdns *WLSD/HOW* NE28 ......**67** F1
Banbury Rd *GOS/KPK* NE3 ....**46** B6
Banbury Ter *SSH* NE33 ....**71** F6
Banbury Wy *BLYTH* NE24 ....**16** C1
  NSHW NE29 ....**69** F2
Bancroft Ter *MLFD/PNYW* SR4 ....**125** E6
Banesley La *DUN/TMV* NE11 ....**116** A3
Banff St *SWCK/CAS* SR5 ....**105** F6
Bank Av *WICK/BNPF* NE16 ....**95** F3
Bank Ct *TYNE/NSHE* * NE30 ....**71** D1
Bankdale Gdns *BLYTH* NE24 ....**9** F5
Bankhead Rd
  BW/LEM/TK/HW NE15 ....**58** B5
Bankhead Ter *HLS* DH4 ....**169** F1
Bank Rd *GATE* NE8 ....**3** G6
Bankside Cl *ASHBK/HED/RY* SR2 .....**162** A1
Bankside La *HAR/WTLS* NE34 ....**88** B3
Bankside Rd
  BW/LEM/TK/HW NE15 ....**77** E3
Bank Top Hamlet
  WICK/BNPF * NE16 ....**95** F3
Bankwell La *GATE* NE8 ....**3** F6
Bannister Dr *LGB/KIL* NE12 ....**50** B4
Bannockburn *LGB/KIL* NE12 ....**35** E6
Barbara St *ASHBK/HED/RY* SR2 ......**145** E3
Barbary Cl *CLSW/PEL* DH2 ....**152** A1
Barbary Dr *CLDN/WHIT/ROK* SR6 ....**127** E2
Barbondale Lonnen
  WD/WHPE/BLK NE5 ....**59** E5
Barbour Av *HAR/WTLS* NE34 ....**89** F1
Barclay Pl *WD/WHPE/BLK* NE5 ....**61** D5
Barclay St *SWCK/CAS* SR5 ....**126** C4
Barcusclose La *WICK/BNPF* NE16 ...**112** B6
Bardolph Rd *NSHW* NE29 ....**53** F6
Bardon Cl *WD/WHPE/BLK* NE5 ....**60** B2
Bardon Crs *MONK* NE25 ....**25** E6
Bardsey Pl *LGB/KIL* NE12 ....**49** D6
Barehirst St *SSH* NE33 ....**88** A1
Barents Cl *WD/WHPE/BLK* * NE5 ......**60** B4
Baret Rd *BYK/HTN/WLK* NE6 ....**66** A6
Barford Dr *CLSW/PEL* DH2 ....**165** F1
Baring St *SSH* NE33 ....**71** E2
Barker St *JES* NE2 ....**3** G1
Barking Crs *SWCK/CAS* SR5 ....**123** E1
Barking Sq *SWCK/CAS* SR5 ....**123** E1
Barkwood Rd *ROWG* NE39 ....**110** C2
Barleycorn Pl
  SUND (off Laura St) SR1 ....**4** D4
Barlow Crs *BLAY* NE21 ....**92** B4
Barlow Fell Rd *BLAY* NE21 ....**92** B5
Barlowfield Cl *BLAY* NE21 ....**93** F2
Barlow La *BLAY* NE21 ....**92** C4
Barmoor La *RYTON* NE40 ....**74** A3
Barmouth Cl *WLSD/HOW* NE28 ....**67** F1
Barmouth Rd *NSHW* NE29 ....**69** F2
Barmouth Wy *NSHW* NE29 ....**69** F2
Barmston La *WASHN* NE37 ....**122** B3
  WASHS NE38 ....**140** A1
Barmston Rd *WASHS* NE38 ....**139** F2
Barmston Wy *WASHS* NE38 ....**121** E6
Barnard Cl *BDLGTN* NE22 ....**6** C3
  DHAM DH1 ....**180** C5
Barnard Crs *HEBB* NE31 ....**85** D1
Barnard St *BLYTH* NE24 ....**11** D5
  MLFD/PNYW SR4 ....**143** E2
Barnard Wynd *PLEE/EAS* SR8 ....**208** A5
Barnesbury Rd *ELS/FEN* NE4 ....**79** D3
Barnes Park Rd *MLFD/PNYW* SR4 ...**143** F2
Barnes St *SEA/MUR* SR7 ....**188** A3
  SSH NE33 ....**71** D6
Barnes St *HLH* DH5 ....**171** F6
Barnes Vw *MLFD/PNYW* SR4 ....**143** E2
Barnett Ct *SWCK/CAS* SR5 ....**126** A2
Barn Hl *STLY/ANP* DH9 ....**148** A1
Barningham *WASHS* NE38 ....**139** F2
Barningham Cl *SUNDSW* SR3 ....**144** A4
Barns Cl *JRW* NE32 ....**85** F4
Barnstaple Cl *WLSD/HOW* NE28........**67** E1
Barnstaple Rd *NSHW* NE29 ....**53** E5
The Barns *STLY/ANP* DH9 ....**113** D6
Barnton Rd *FELL* NE10 ....**101** D4
Barnwood Cl *WLSD/HOW* NE28 ....**67** E1
Baroness Dr
  BW/LEM/TK/HW NE15 ....**77** F1

Baron's Quay Rd *SWCK/CAS* SR5 .....**124** A4
Baronswood *GOS/KPK* NE3 ....**63** D2
Barrack Rd *ELS/FEN* NE4 ....**80** A1
Barrack St *SUND* SR1 ....**127** E4
Barras Av *BLYTH* NE24 ....**16** C1
  CRAM NE23 ....**35** D1
Barras Av West *BLYTH* NE24 ....**16** B2
Barras Br *CNUT* NE1 ....**2** D1
Barras Dr *SUNDSW* SR3 ....**144** A4
Barrasford Cl *GOS/KPK* NE3 ....**62** C2
Barrasford Dr *DIN/WO* NE13 ....**33** E5
Barrasford Rd *CRAM* NE23 ....**22** B2
  DHAM DH1 ....**180** C6
Barrasford St *WLSD/HOW* NE28 ....**69** E5
Barrass Av *CRAM* NE23 ....**36** A1
Barr Cl *WLSD/HOW* NE28 ....**68** A1
Barrie Sq *SWCK/CAS* SR5 ....**126** A2
Barrington Av *TYNE/NSHE* NE30 ....**54** B2
Barrington Ct *BDLGTN* NE22 ....**7** F4
Barrington Dr *WASHS* NE38 ....**138** C1
Barrington Pk *BDLGTN* NE22 ....**9** E1
Barrington Pl *ELS/FEN* NE4 ....**79** F2
  GATE NE8 ....**80** C6
Barrington Rd *BDLGTN* NE22 ....**8** B1
  STKFD/GP NE22 ....**7** E1
Barrington St *SSH* NE33 ....**71** E3
Barrington Ter *HLH* DH5 ....**171** F5
Barron St South *SWCK/CAS* SR5 .....**124** B3
Barrowburn Pl *CRAM* NE23 ....**36** C1
Barrow St *SWCK/CAS* SR5 ....**105** E6
Barry St *DUN/TMV* NE11 ....**97** E1
  GATE NE8 ....**98** C3
Barsloan Gv *PLEE/EAS* SR8 ....**200** A6
Barton Cl *TYNE/NSHE* NE30 ....**55** D3
  WASHN NE37 ....**121** D3
  WLSD/HOW NE28 ....**67** F1
Barton Ct *CLDN/WHIT/ROK* * SR6 ....**108** B5
Bartram Gdns *GATE* NE8 ....**99** D3
Bartram St *SWCK/CAS* SR5 ....**126** B1
Barwell Cl *WLSD/HOW* NE28 ....**67** F1
Barwell Ct *LGB/HTN* NE7 ....**66** A3
Barwick St *PLEE/EAS* SR8 ....**201** E2
Basildon Gdns *WLSD/HOW* NE28 ......**67** E1
Basil Wy *HAR/WTLS* NE34 ....**89** D1
Basingstoke Pl *LGB/KIL* NE12 ....**49** E5
Basingstoke Rd *PLEE/EAS* SR8 ....**208** B1
Baslow Gdns *SUNDSW* SR3 ....**144** A3
Bassett Cl *ELS/FEN* NE4 ....**80** A2
Bassington Cl *CRAM* NE23 ....**12** C6
Bassington Dr *CRAM* NE23 ....**12** C6
Bassington La *CRAM* NE23 ....**12** C6
Bates La *BLAY* NE21 ....**77** E2
Bath Cl *WLSD/HOW* NE28 ....**68** A1
Bathgate Cl *WLSD/HOW* NE28 ....**68** A1
Bathgate Sq *SWCK/CAS* SR5 ....**123** E1
Bath La *BLYTH* NE24 ....**11** E5
  CNUT NE1 ....**2** B4
Bath Rd *FELL* NE10 ....**82** C6
  HEBB NE31 ....**85** D5
Bath Ter *BYK/HTN/WLK* NE6 ....**83** F5
Bath Ter *BLYTH* NE24 ....**11** E5
  GOS/KPK NE3 ....**63** F1
  TYNE/NSHE NE30 ....**55** F5
Batley St *SWCK/CAS* SR5 ....**123** E1
Battle Hill Dr *WLSD/HOW* NE28 ....**68** B1
Baugh Cl *WASHN* NE37 ....**119** F6
Baulkham Hills *HLS* DH4 ....**157** D2
Bavington *FELL* NE10 ....**101** F5
Bavington Dr *WD/WHPE/BLK* NE5 ....**61** E5
Bavington Gdns *TYNE/NSHE* NE30 ...**54** C3
Bavington Rd *MONK* NE25 ....**24** C5
Bawtry Gv *NSHW* NE29 ....**70** A1
Baxter Av *ELS/FEN* NE4 ....**79** D2
Baxter Rd *SWCK/CAS* SR5 ....**105** E6
Baxter Sq *SWCK/CAS* SR5 ....**105** E6
Baxterwood Gv *ELS/FEN* NE4 ....**79** F2
Baybridge Rd *WD/WHPE/BLK* NE5 ....**60** A3
Baysdale *HLS* DH4 ....**139** D6
Bayswater Av *SWCK/CAS* SR5 ....**123** F1
Bayswater Rd *GATE* NE8 ....**100** A2
  JES NE2 ....**64** A4
Bayswater Sq *SWCK/CAS* SR5 ....**123** F1
Baytree Gdns *MONK* NE25 ....**54** A1
Baytree Ter *STLY/ANP* DH9 ....**151** D1
Baywood Gv *WLSD/HOW* NE28 ....**67** E1
Beach Av *WBAY* NE26 ....**40** C5
Beach Croft Av *TYNE/NSHE* NE30 .....**55** D2
Beachcross Rd
  MLFD/PNYW * SR4 ....**144** A1
Beach Gv *PLEE/EAS* SR8 ....**209** F2
Beach Rd *NSHW* NE29 ....**54** A5
  SSH NE33 ....**71** F4
  TYNE/NSHE NE30 ....**54** C4
Beach St *MLFD/PNYW* SR4 ....**126** A4
Beachville St *MLFD/PNYW* SR4 ....**144** A1
Beachway *BLYTH* NE24 ....**17** E2
Beach Wy *TYNE/NSHE* NE30 ....**54** C3
Beacon Dr *CLDN/WHIT/ROK* SR6 .....**127** E3
  DIN/WO NE13 ....**32** C5
Beacon Old *HAR/WTLS* NE34 ....**90** B2
Beacon La *CRAM* NE23 ....**20** C2
Beacon Lough Rd
  LWF/SPW/WRK NE9 ....**99** F6

Beaconsfield Av
  LWF/SPW/WRK NE9 ....**99** F5
Beaconsfield Cl *MONK* NE25 ....**39** F3
Beaconsfield Crs
  LWF/SPW/WRK NE9 ....**99** F5
Beaconsfield Rd
  LWF/SPW/WRK NE9 ....**99** E5
Beaconsfield St *BLYTH* NE24 ....**11** E5
  ELS/FEN NE4 ....**79** F3
  STLY/ANP DH9 ....**148** B1
Beaconside *HAR/WTLS* NE34 ....**90** B2
Beacon St *LWF/SPW/WRK* NE9 ....**99** E5
  SSH NE33 ....**71** E2
  TYNE/NSHE NE30 ....**55** D6
Beadling Gdns *ELS/FEN* NE4 ....**79** D2
Beadnell Av *NSHW* NE29 ....**69** F2
Beadnell Cl *BLAY* NE21 ....**93** F2
Beadnell Gdns *SMOOR* NE27 ....**52** B1
Beadnell Pl *JES* NE2 ....**3** G2
Beadnell Rd *BLYTH* NE24 ....**16** A1
Beadnell Wy *GOS/KPK* NE3 ....**62** C1
Beal Cl *BLYTH* NE24 ....**10** B5
Beal Dr *LGB/KIL* NE12 ....**50** B4
Beal Gdns *WLSD/HOW* NE28 ....**68** B1
Beal Rd *SMOOR* NE27 ....**52** B1
Beal Ter *BYK/HTN/WLK* NE6 ....**83** E4
Beal Wy *GOS/KPK* NE3 ....**63** D1
Beaminster Wy *GOS/KPK* NE3 ....**61** E1
Beamish Av *GOS/KPK* NE3 ....**61** E1
Beamishburn Rd *STLY/ANP* DH9 ......**131** F5
Beamish Cl *WLSD/HOW* NE28 ....**67** E1
Beamish Gdns
  LWF/SPW/WRK NE9 ....**100** C6
Beamish Hills *STLY/ANP* DH9 ....**149** F1
Beamish St *STLY/ANP* DH9 ....**148** A1
Beamish Vw *CLSW/PEL* DH2 ....**151** D5
  STLY/ANP DH9 ....**149** D1
Beaney La *CLSW/PEL* DH2 ....**165** E4
Beanley Av *HEBB* NE31 ....**84** C4
Beanley Crs *TYNE/NSHE* NE30 ....**55** E5
Beanley Pl *LGB/HTN* NE7 ....**64** C3
Bearpark Colliery Rd
  BDN/LAN/SAC DH7 ....**192** A2
Beatrice Av *BLYTH* NE24 ....**16** A3
Beatrice Gdns *BOL* NE36 ....**106** C3
  HAR/WTLS NE34 ....**89** D2
Beatrice St *CLDN/WHIT/ROK* SR6 ....**127** D3
Beatrice Ter *HLS* DH4 ....**139** D5
Beattie St *HAR/WTLS* NE34 ....**88** A3
Beatty Av *JES* NE2 ....**64** A3
Beatty Rd *BDLGTN* NE22 ....**8** A4
Beatty St *PLEE/EAS* SR8 ....**201** E2
Beaufort Cl *HLS* DH4 ....**157** D3
  WD/WHPE/BLK NE5 ....**61** D5
Beaufort Gdns *WLSD/HOW* NE28 ....**67** F1
Beaufront Cl *FELL* NE10 ....**102** A4
Beaufront Gdns *GATE* NE8 ....**100** A1
  WD/WHPE/BLK NE5 ....**61** D5
Beaufront Ter *JRW* NE32 ....**86** A5
  SSH NE33 ....**71** E6
Beauly *WASHS* NE38 ....**138** C3
Beaumaris Gdns *SUNDSW* SR3 ....**159** E1
Beaumaris Wy
  WD/WHPE/BLK NE5 ....**61** D2
Beaumont Cl *DHAM* DH1 ....**179** F5
Beaumont Crs *PLEE/EAS* SR8 ....**201** D5
Beaumont Dr *MONK* NE25 ....**39** E3
  WASHS NE38 ....**138** C2
Beaumont Mnr *BLYTH* NE24 ....**9** E5
Beaumont Pl *PLEE/EAS* SR8 ....**209** D3
Beaumont St *ASHBK/HED/RY* SR2 ...**145** E3
  BLYTH NE24 ....**10** C4
  ELS/FEN NE4 ....**79** E5
  NSHW NE29 ....**70** C1
  SWCK/CAS SR5 ....**125** F1
Beaumont Ter *GOS/KPK* NE3 ....**63** F1
  JRW NE32 ....**85** F3
  WD/WHPE/BLK NE5 ....**60** B4
Beaver Cl *DHAM* DH1 ....**180** B4
Bebdon Ct *BLYTH* NE24 ....**10** B6
Bebside Furnace Rd *BLYTH* NE24 ....**8** C4
Bebside Rd *BLYTH* NE24 ....**8** B5
Beckenham Av *BOL* NE36 ....**106** C3
Beckenham Cl *BOL* NE36 ....**107** D2
Beckenham Gdns
  WLSD/HOW NE28 ....**67** E2
Beckett St *GATE* NE8 ....**81** F4
Beckfoot Cl *WD/WHPE/BLK* NE5 ....**61** D5
Beckford *WASHS* NE38 ....**139** F2
Beckford Cl *WLSD/HOW* NE28 ....**67** E1
Beck Pl *PLEE/EAS* SR8 ....**208** C1
Beckside Gdns
  WD/WHPE/BLK NE5 ....**59** D5
Beckwith Rd *SUNDSW* SR3 ....**142** B6
Beda Hl *BLAY* NE21 ....**76** B5
Bedale Cl *DHAM* DH1 ....**196** C2
  WLSD/HOW NE28 ....**67** E1
Bedale Crs *SWCK/CAS* SR5 ....**123** F1
Bedale Dr *MONK* NE25 ....**54** B1
Bedale Gn *WD/WHPE/BLK* NE5 ....**61** F3
Bedale St *HLH* DH5 ....**185** F2
Bedburn *WASHS* NE38 ....**137** E5
Bede Av *DHAM* DH1 ....**195** F5
Bede Burn Rd *JRW* NE32 ....**86** A2
Bedeburn Rd *WD/WHPE/BLK* NE5 .....**60** B1

Bede Burn Vw JRW NE32 ....**86** A3
Bede Cl LGB/KIL NE12 ....**51** D4
Bede Ct CLS/BIR/GTL DH3 ....**153** E5
   GATE NE8 ....**81** F6
Bede Crs WASHS NE38 ....**120** B6
   WLSD/HOW NE28 ....**67** F2
Bede St CLDN/WHIT/ROK SR6 ...**127** D2
   PLEE/EAS SR8 ....**201** E2
Bedesway JRW NE32 ....**86** C2
Bede Ter BOL NE36 ....**106** C3
   CLSW/PEL DH2 ....**153** D5
   JRW NE32 ....**86** A3
Bede Wk HEBB NE31 ....**85** E3
Bede Wy DHAM DH1 ....**180** A6
   PLEE/EAS SR8 ....**208** C2
Bedford Av CLS/BIR/GTL DH3 ....**136** C5
   SSH NE33 ....**71** E5
   WLSD/HOW NE28 ....**66** C3
Bedford Ct NSHW NE29 ....**71** D1
Bedford Pl SUNDSW SR3 ....**143** F6
   WD/WHPE/BLK NE5 ....**59** E5
Bedford St NSHW NE29 ....**71** D1
   SUND SR1 ....**4** D1
Bedford Ter NSHW NE29 ....**54** C6
Bedford Wy NSHW NE29 ....**70** C1
Bedlington Bank BDLGTN NE22 ......**7** F4
Beech Av CLDN/WHIT/ROK SR6 ..**109** F1
   CRAM NE23 ....**22** C3
   DIN/WO NE13 ....**31** D3
   GOS/KPK NE3 ....**46** B6
   HLS DH4 ....**170** C1
   WICK/BNPF NE16 ....**96** E3
Beechburn Wk ELS/FEN NE4 ....**79** F3
Beech Cl DHAM DH1 ....**181** D4
   GOS/KPK NE3 ....**47** E3
Beech Ct NSHW NE29 ....**54** B6
Beech Crs SEA/MUR SR7 ....**176** E4
Beechcrest DHAM DH1 ....**194** A5
Beechcroft Av BDN/LAN/SAC DH7 ..**202** B5
   GOS/KPK NE3 ....**62** C3
Beechcroft Cl DHAM DH1 ....**195** F3
Beech Dr DUN/TMV NE11 ....**97** D1
The Beeches
   ELS/FEN (off Clumber St) NE4 ...**79** F5
   LGB/KIL (off Eastfield Rd) NE12 ....**49** F6
Beechfield Gdns WLSD/HOW NE28 ...**66** C3
Beechfield Rd GOS/KPK NE3 ....**63** D2
Beech Gv BDN/LAN/SAC DH7 .....**192** B6
   HAR/WTLS NE34 ....**89** C4
   LGB/KIL NE12 ....**49** F6
   LWF/SPW/WRK NE9 ....**119** E3
   WBAY NE26 ....**40** B5
   WLSD/HOW NE28 ....**67** D4
Beech Grove Rd ELS/FEN NE4 .....**79** F4
Beech Pk BDN/LAN/SAC DH7 ....**202** C5
Beech Rd DHAM DH1 ....**194** A1
   RDHAMSE DH6 ....**197** F3
Beech Sq WASHS NE38 ....**139** D2
Beech St ELS/FEN NE4 ....**79** D4
   GATE NE8 ....**100** A1
   JRW NE32 ....**85** F1
Beech Ter BLAY NE21 ....**94** B1
   STLY/ANP DH9 ....**149** D5
Beech Wy LGB/KIL NE12 ....**35** E6
Beechways DHAM DH1 ....**193** E3
Beechwood Av
   LWF/SPW/WRK NE9 ....**117** F1
   MONK NE25 ....**39** F6
   RYTON NE40 ....**74** B3
Beechwood Cl JRW NE32 ....**86** C2
Beechwood Crs SWCK/CAS SR5 .**125** E2
Beechwood Gdns DUN/TMV NE11 ...**98** A5
Beechwood Pl PONT/DH NE20 ......**28** A3
Beechwoods CLSW/PEL DH2 ....**153** D3
Beechwood St
   ASHBK/HED/RY SR2 ....**144** A1
Beechwood Ter
   ASHBK/HED/RY SR2 ....**144** A1
   HLS DH4 ....**157** E6
Beeston Av SWCK/CAS SR5 ....**123** E1
Beetham Crs WD/WHPE/BLK NE5 ..**60** C6
Beethoven St SSH NE33 ....**71** F4
Begonia Cl HEBB NE31 ....**85** D5
Bek Rd DHAM DH1 ....**180** B6
Beldene Dr MLFD/PNYW SR4 .....**143** D2
Belford Av SMOOR NE27 ....**52** B1
Belford Cl ASHBK/HED/RY SR2 ...**144** C3
   WLSD/HOW NE28 ....**67** F1
Belford Ct
   BLYTH (off Devonworth Pl) NE24 ..**10** A5
Belford Gdns DUN/TMV NE11 ......**97** F5
Belford Rd ASHBK/HED/RY SR2 ..**145** D3
Belford St PLEE/EAS SR8 ....**201** E6
Belford Ter BYK/HTN/WLK NE6 ...**83** D3
   TYNE/NSHE NE30 ....**54** C5
The Belfry HLS DH4 ....**156** C4
Belgrade Cl SWCK/CAS SR5 ......**105** E6
Belgrade Sq SWCK/CAS SR5 .....**123** E1
Belgrave Crs BLYTH NE24 ....**11** E5
Belgrave Pde ELS/FEN NE4 ....**80** A4
Belgrave Ter FELL NE10 ....**100** C3
   SSH NE33 ....**71** F3
Bellburn Ct CRAM NE23 ....**14** B6

Belle Grove Pl JES NE2 ....**80** A1
Belle Grove Ter JES NE2 ....**80** A1
Belle Grove Vls JES NE2 ....**80** A1
Belle Gv West JES NE2 ....**80** A1
Bellerby Dr CLSW/PEL DH2 ....**135** D3
Belles Ville DHAM DH1 ....**195** F4
Belle St STLY/ANP DH9 ....**148** B1
Belle Vue Av GOS/KPK NE3 ....**63** F1
Belle Vue Bank
   LWF/SPW/WRK NE9 ....**99** D5
Belle Vue Ct
   DHAM (off Claypath) DH1 ....**194** C4
Bellevue Crs CRAM NE23 ....**14** A4
Belle Vue Crs SSH NE33 ....**88** C3
Belle Vue Gv LWF/SPW/WRK * NE9 ..**99** E5
Belle Vue Pk ASHBK/HED/RY SR2 ..**144** B2
Belle Vue Pk West
   ASHBK/HED/RY SR2 ....**144** B2
Belle Vue Rd ASHBK/HED/RY SR2 ..**144** B2
Belle Vue Ter NSHW NE29 ....**70** C2
Bellfield Av GOS/KPK NE3 ....**46** B6
Bellgreen Av GOS/KPK NE3 ....**47** F3
Bell Gv LGB/KIL NE12 ....**35** E6
Bell House Rd SWCK/CAS SR5 ...**107** F5
Bellingham Cl WLSD/HOW NE28 ...**67** F2
Bellingham Ct BDLGTN NE22 ....**8** A3
   GOS/KPK* NE3 ....**61** F1
Bellingham Dr LGB/KIL NE12 ....**50** B5
Bellister Gv WD/WHPE/BLK NE5 ...**61** E6
Bellister Pk PLEE/EAS SR8 ....**209** D4
Bellister Rd NSHW NE29 ....**53** F6
Bell Meadow BDN/LAN/SAC DH7 ..**202** C5
Belloc Av HAR/WTLS NE34 ....**88** A5
Bells Cl BLYTH NE24 ....**9** E4
   BW/LEM/TK/HW NE15 ....**77** D3
Bell's Folly DHAM DH1 ....**204** C1
Belshill Cl WLSD/HOW NE28 ....**52** A6
Bell's Pl BDLGTN NE22 ....**7** F4
Bell St HEBB NE31 ....**84** C2
   HLS DH4 ....**140** A6
   MLFD/PNYW SR4 ....**125** E6
   TYNE/NSHE NE30 ....**71** D1
   WASHS NE38 ....**139** E2
Belmont FELL NE10 ....**101** F5
Belmont Av MONK NE25 ....**39** F6
Belmont Cl WLSD/HOW NE28 ....**67** F1
Belmont Ri HLH DH5 ....**185** F3
Belmont Rd MLFD/PNYW SR4 .....**143** E1
Belmont St BYK/HTN/WLK NE6 ....**83** E5
Belmont Wk BYK/HTN/WLK NE6 ...**83** E5
Belmount Av GOS/KPK NE3 ....**47** F3
Belper Cl WLSD/HOW NE28 ....**67** E1
Belsay WASHS NE38 ....**137** E2
Belsay Av DIN/WO NE13 ....**32** C6
   HAR/WTLS NE34 ....**89** F1
   MONK NE25 ....**41** D6
Belsay Cl WLSD/HOW NE28 ....**67** E1
Belsay St BLYTH NE24 ....**10** B5
Belsay Gdns DUN/TMV NE11 ....**97** F5
   GOS/KPK NE3 ....**46** B4
   MLFD/PNYW SR4 ....**143** E1
Belsay Pl ELS/FEN NE4 ....**79** D2
Belsfield Gdns JRW NE32 ....**86** A4
Belsize Pl BYK/HTN/WLK NE6 ....**66** B6
Beltingham WD/WHPE/BLK NE5 ...**60** A6
Belvedere Av MONK NE25 ....**40** B6
Belvedere Ct BYK/HTN/WLK * NE6 ..**82** B2
Belvedere Gdns LGB/KIL NE12 ......**49** F6
Belvedere Pkwy GOS/KPK * NE3 ...**45** E5
Belvedere Rd ASHBK/HED/RY SR2 ..**144** B2
Belverdere Gdns RDHAMSE DH6 ..**206** A1
Bemersyde Dr JES NE2 ....**64** A3
Benbrake Av NSHW NE29 ....**54** A3
Bendigo Av HAR/WTLS NE34 ....**87** E5
Benedict St CLDN/WHIT/ROK SR6 ..**127** E2
Benfield Gv WBAY NE26 ....**26** A1
Benfield Rd BYK/HTN/WLK NE6 ....**65** F4
Benjamin Rd WLSD/HOW NE28 ....**68** C3
Benridge Bank HLS DH4 ....**183** E2
Bensham Av GATE NE8 ....**98** C1
Bensham Ct GATE NE8 ....**81** D6
   HAR/WTLS NE34 ....**88** B3
Bensham Crs GATE NE8 ....**98** B1
Bensham Pl GATE NE8 ....**81** D6
Bensham Rd GATE NE8 ....**81** D6
Benson Pl BYK/HTN/WLK * NE6 .....**82** B2
Benson Rd BYK/HTN/WLK NE6 .....**82** C2
Benson St CLS/BIR/GTL DH3 ....**153** E6
   STLY/ANP DH9 ....**148** A1
Benson Ter FELL * NE10 ....**100** C2
Bent House La DHAM DH1 ....**195** F6
Bentinck Crs ELS/FEN * NE4 ....**79** E4
Bentinck Rd ELS/FEN NE4 ....**79** E4
Bentinck Vls ELS/FEN NE4 ....**79** E3
Benton Bank JES NE2 ....**64** C5
   LGB/HTN NE7 ....**65** C5
Benton Cl LGB/HTN NE7 ....**65** D1
Benton Hall Wk LGB/HTN NE7 ....**65** F4
Benton La LGB/KIL NE12 ....**49** D5
Benton Lodge Av LGB/HTN NE7 ....**65** D1
Benton Park Rd LGB/HTN NE7 ....**64** B1
Benton Rd HAR/WTLS NE34 ....**88** B6
   LGB/HTN NE7 ....**65** E1

SMOOR NE27 ....**51** F2
Benton Ter JES NE2 ....**81** E1
Benton Wy WLSD/HOW * NE28 ....**67** D5
Bents Cottages SSH NE33 ....**72** A4
Bents Park Rd SSH NE33 ....**72** A3
Benwell Cl
   BW/LEM/TK/HW
   (off Benwell Gra) NE15 ....**78** C3
Benwell Dene Ter
   BW/LEM/TK/HW NE15 ....**78** B3
Benwell Grange Av
   BW/LEM/TK/HW NE15 ....**78** C3
Benwell Grange Rd
   BW/LEM/TK/HW NE15 ....**78** B3
Benwell Grange Ter
   BW/LEM/TK/HW NE15 ....**78** B3
Benwell Gv ELS/FEN NE4 ....**79** D3
Benwell Hall Dr
   BW/LEM/TK/HW NE15 ....**78** A2
Benwell Hill Gdns
   WD/WHPE/BLK NE5 ....**78** B1
Benwell Hill Rd
   WD/WHPE/BLK NE5 ....**78** A1
Benwell La
   BW/LEM/TK/HW NE15 ....**78** A3
Benwell Village
   BW/LEM/TK/HW NE15 ....**78** A2
Benwell Village Ms
   BW/LEM/TK/HW NE15 ....**78** B2
Beresford Av HEBB NE31 ....**85** D5
Beresford Gdns
   BYK/HTN/WLK NE6 ....**82** B3
Beresford Pk ASHBK/HED/RY SR2 ....**4** A5
Beresford Rd TYNE/NSHE NE30 ...**54** C1
   WBAY NE26 ....**26** C3
Bergen Cl NSHW NE29 ....**69** D2
Bergen Sq SWCK/CAS SR5 ....**105** E6
Bergen St SWCK/CAS SR5 ....**105** E6
Berkdale Rd LWF/SPW/WRK NE9 .**117** D2
Berkeley Cl BOLCOL NE35 ....**105** D1
   LGB/KIL NE12 ....**36** A6
   SUNDSW SR3 ....**159** E1
Berkeley Sq GOS/KPK NE3 ....**47** D5
Berkely St SSH NE33 ....**71** F4
Berkhamstead Ct FELL * NE10 .....**102** B3
Berkley Av BLAY NE21 ....**77** D6
Berkley Cl WLSD/HOW NE28 ....**67** F1
Berkley Rd NSHW NE29 ....**53** F6
Berkley St BW/LEM/TK/HW NE15 ..**58** B6
Berkley Wy HEBB NE31 ....**85** E4
Berkshire Cl DHAM DH1 ....**196** B3
   WD/WHPE/BLK NE5 ....**60** B4
Berkshire Rd PLEE/EAS SR8 ....**200** B6
Bermondsey St JES NE2 ....**3** H2
Bernard St BYK/HTN/WLK NE6 .....**83** F4
   HLS DH4 ....**170** C2
Berrington Dr WD/WHPE/BLK NE5 ..**61** D3
Berrishill Gv MONK NE25 ....**39** E4
Berry Cl BYK/HTN/WLK NE6 ....**83** E7
   WLSD/HOW NE28 ....**68** E1
Berryfield Cl SUNDSW SR3 ....**160** C3
Berry Hl RYTON NE40 ....**92** A1
Berryhill Cl BLAY NE21 ....**94** C1
Bertram Crs
   BW/LEM/TK/HW NE15 ....**78** B2
Bertram St SSH NE33 ....**71** E6
Berwick WASHS NE38 ....**137** E2
Berwick Av SWCK/CAS SR5 ....**105** E6
Berwick Cha PLEE/EAS SR8 ....**208** A5
Berwick Cl BW/LEM/TK/HW NE15 ..**75** F1
Berwick Ct PONT/DH NE20 ....**28** B3
Berwick Dr WLSD/HOW NE28 ....**67** F1
Berwick Hill Rd PONT/DH NE20 .....**28** A3
Berwick Sq SWCK/CAS SR5 ....**105** E6
Berwick Ter NSHW NE29 ....**69** F2
Besford Gv SUND SR1 ....**5** E5
Bethune Av SEA/MUR SR7 ....**175** F3
Betjeman Cl STLY/ANP DH9 ....**148** C2
Betts Av BW/LEM/TK/HW NE15 ....**78** A3
Beumaris HLS DH4 ....**155** F5
Bevan Av ASHBK/HED/RY SR2 ....**162** A1
Bevan Gdns FELL NE10 ....**101** F2
Bevan Gv DHAM DH1 ....**196** A3
Bevan Sq SEA/MUR SR7 ....**174** B6
Beverley Cl GOS/KPK NE3 ....**47** D2
Beverley Crs LWF/SPW/WRK NE9 ..**99** F1
Beverley Dr BLAY NE21 ....**93** E2
   WICK/BNPF NE16 ....**96** B1
Beverley Gdns CLS/BIR/GTL DH3 .**153** F6
   TYNE/NSHE NE30 ....**55** E1
Beverley Pk MONK NE25 ....**40** A6
Beverley Pl WLSD/HOW NE28 ....**68** B4
Beverley Rd ASHBK/HED/RY SR2 .**145** E4
   LWF/SPW/WRK NE9 ....**99** F2
   MONK NE25 ....**40** B6
Beverley Ter BYK/HTN/WLK NE6 ...**83** F7
   TYNE/NSHE NE30 ....**55** E1
Beverley Wy PLEE/EAS SR8 ....**208** B7
Bevin Sq RDHAMSE DH6 ....**188** A5
Beweshill Crs BLAY NE21 ....**93** C3
Bewick Cl CLSW/PEL DH2 ....**165** F2
Bewick Crs BW/LEM/TK/HW NE15 ..**76** F2
Bewicke Rd WLSD/HOW NE28 ....**68** C3
Bewicke St WLSD/HOW NE28 ....**69** D5
Bewick Pk WLSD/HOW NE28 ....**52** B6

Bewick Rd *GATE* NE8 ....99 D1
Bewick St *CNUT* NE1 ....2 B5
  SSH NE33 ....71 E6
Bewley Gdns *WLSD/HOW* NE28 ...67 F1
Bewley Gv *PLEE/EAS* SR8 ....207 F5
Bexhill Rd *SWCK/CAS* SR5 ....123 E1
Bexhill St *JRW* NE32 ....17 D1
  SWCK/CAS SR5 ....123 E1
Bexley Av *BW/LEM/TK/HW* NE15 ....77 F2
Bexley PI *WICK/BNPF* NE16 ....95 F5
Bexley St *MLFD/PNYW* SR4 ....125 E6
Bickington Ct *HLS* * DH4 ....157 E5
Biddick Hall Dr *HAR/WTLS* NE34 ....88 A4
Biddick La *WASHS* NE38 ....138 C3
Biddick Vw *WASHS* NE38 ....139 D3
Biddick Vls *WASHS* NE38 ....139 D3
Biddlestone La *NSHW* NE29 ....69 F1
Biddlestone Rd
  BYK/HTN/WLK NE6 ....65 E5
Bideford Gdns *HAR/WTLS* NE34 ...72 C5
  JRW NE32 ....86 C3
  LWF/SPW NE9 ....117 E1
  WBAY NE26 ....40 B4
Bideford Gv *WICK/BNPF* NE16 ....95 F5
Bideford Rd *GOS/KPK* NE3 ....62 A2
Bideford Rd *ASHBK/HED/RY* SR2 .145 E4
Bigbury Cl *HLS* DH4 ....157 E6
Bigges Gdns *WLSD/HOW* NE28 .....66 B2
Bigg Market *CNUT* NE1 ....2 D4
Bilbrough Gdns *ELS/FEN* NE4 ......78 C4
Billy Mill Av *NSHW* NE29 ....54 A6
Billy Mill La *NSHW* NE29 ....53 F5
Bilsdale *CLDN/WHIT/ROK* SR6 ....109 E3
Bilsdale PI *LGB/KIL* NE12 ....48 B6
Bilsmoor Av *LGB/HTN* NE7 ....65 D4
Bilton Hall Rd *JRW* NE32 ....86 C2
Binchester St *HAR/WTLS* NE34 .....87 F1
Bingfield Gdns
  WD/WHPE/BLK NE5 ....61 E6
Bingley Cl *WLSD/HOW* NE28 ....68 A1
Bingley St *SWCK/CAS* SR5 ....123 E1
Bink Moss *WASHN* NE37 ....119 F6
Binswood Av *WD/WHPE/BLK* NE5 ..61 D5
Bircham Dr *BLAY* NE21 ....76 C6
Bircham St *STLY/ANP* DH9 ....147 F3
Birch Av *CLDN/WHIT/ROK* SR6 ....109 E3
  FELL NE10 ....101 F3
Birch Ct *SUNDSW* SR3 ....160 A2
Birch Crs *WICK/BNPF* NE16 ....111 E6
The Birches *STLY/ANP* DH9 ....131 E6
  WICK/BNPF NE16 ....114 B1
Birchfield *WICK/BNPF* NE16 ....96 A4
Birchfield Gdns
  BW/LEM/TK/HW NE15 ....77 D3
  LWF/SPW NE9 ....117 F2
Birchfield Rd *ASHBK/HED/RY* SR2 .144 A2
Birchgate Cl *BLAY* NE21 ....93 F1
Birch Gv *WLSD/HOW* NE28 ....67 E1
Birchgrove Av *DHAM* DH1 ....196 A3
Birchington Av *SSH* NE33 ....88 B1
Birch Rd *BLAY* NE21 ....76 C6
Birch St *JRW* NE32 ....85 F1
Birch Ter *BYK/HTN/WLK* NE6 ....83 F3
Birchvale Av *WD/WHPE/BLK* NE5 ..60 C4
Birchwood Cl *CRAM* NE23 ....36 A1
  STLY/ANP DH9 ....133 E6
Birdhill PI *HAR/WTLS* NE34 ....88 A4
Birds Nest Rd *BYK/HTN/WLK* NE6 ..83 D4
Bird St *TYNE/NSHE* NE30 ....55 E6
  SSH NE33 ....39 F5
Birkdale *MONK* NE25 ....39 F5
Birkdale Av *CLDN/WHIT/ROK* SR6 .109 D3
Birkdale Cl *LGB/HTN* NE7 ....65 E2
  WLSD/HOW NE28 ....67 D2
Birkdale Dr *HLS* DH4 ....156 C4
Birkdale Gdns *DUN/TMV* NE11 ....115 D6
Birkland La *WICK/BNPF* NE16 ......114 C4
Birkland Cl *WICK/BNPF* NE16 ....57 D1
Birling PI *WD/WHPE/BLK* NE5 ....61 F4
Birnam Gv *JRW* NE32 ....87 D2
Birnie Cl *ELS/FEN* NE4 ....79 D4
Birrell Sq *SWCK/CAS* SR5 ....105 E6
Birrell St *SWCK/CAS* SR5 ....105 E6
Birtley Av *TYNE/NSHE* NE30 ....55 F4
Birtley Cl *GOS/KPK* NE3 ....62 C2
Birtley La *CLS/BIR/GTL* DH3 ....136 B3
Birtwistle Av *HEBB* NE31 ....84 C5
Biscop Ter *JRW* NE32 ....86 A3
Bishop Crs *JRW* NE32 ....69 E6
Bishopdale *HLS* DH4 ....139 D6
  WLSD/HOW NE28 ....66 B1
Bishopdale Av *BLYTH* NE24 ....9 F4
Bishop Morton Gv *SUND* SR1 ....5 F4
Bishop Ramsay Ct
  HAR/WTLS NE34 ....89 F2
Bishop Rock Dr *LGB/KIL* NE12 .....48 C6
Bishop Rock Rd *LGB/KIL* NE12 ....48 C6
Bishop's Av *ELS/FEN* NE4 ....79 F3
Bishops Cl *WLSD/HOW* NE28 ....68 A4
Bishops Dr *RYTON* NE40 ....74 C5
Bishops Meadow *BDLGTN* NE22 ....7 D3

Bishop's Rd *ELS/FEN* NE4 ....78 C4
Bishops Wy *DHAM* DH1 ....180 A5
  SUNDSW SR3 ....160 B3
Bishopton St *ASHBK/HED/RY* SR2 ...5 E5
Bisley Dr *HAR/WTLS* NE34 ....88 C1
Bittern Cl *WLSD/HOW* NE28 ....52 C6
Black Boy Rd *HLS* DH4 ....169 D3
Blackburn Gn *FELL* NE10 ....100 D3
Blackdown Cl *LGB/KIL* NE12 ....48 C6
  PLEE/EAS SR8 ....208 A3
Black Dr *CLS/BIR/GTL* DH3 ....155 E2
Blackettbridge
  CNUT (off Eldon Sq) NE1 ....2 C3
Blackett St *CNUT* NE1 ....2 C3
  HEBB NE31 ....68 B6
  STLY/ANP DH9 ....146 A4
Blackfell Rd *WASHN* NE37 ....119 E5
Blackfriars *CNUT* NE1 ....2 C3
Blackfriars Ct *CNUT* * NE1 ....2 C3
Blackfriars Wy *LGB/KIL* NE12 ......48 C5
Blackheath Cl *WASHN* NE37 ....120 B2
Blackheath Ct *WD/WHPE/BLK* NE5 ...61 D1
Blackhill Av *WLSD/HOW* NE28 ......52 A5
Blackhill Crs *LWF/SPW/WRK* NE9 ..100 C6
Blackhills Rd *PLEE/EAS* SR8 ....201 F6
Blackhouse La *RYTON* NE40 ....74 A3
Black La *BLAY* NE21 ....75 F6
  LWF/SPW/WRK NE9 ....118 A3
Black Rd *ASHBK/HED/RY* SR2 .....162 B1
  BDN/LAN/SAC DH7 ....204 A2
  HEBB NE31 ....85 E1
Blackrow La
  BW/LEM/TK/HW NE15 ....56 C2
Blackstone Cl *BLAY* NE21 ....75 F6
Blackthorn Dr *WLSD/HOW* NE28 ...67 E1
Blackthorn Pl *ELS/FEN* NE4 ....80 A5
Blackthorn Wy *BLYTH* NE24 ....16 B2
  HLS DH4 ....156 C6
Blackwood Rd *SWCK/CAS* SR5 ...123 E1
Bladen St *JRW* NE32 ....85 F1
Blagdon Av *HAR/WTLS* NE34 ....72 A6
Blagdon Cl *CNUT* NE1 ....3 G3
Blagdon Cl *BDLGTN* NE22 ....8 B2
Blagdon Crs *CRAM* NE23 ....13 D6
Blagdon Dr *BLYTH* NE24 ....16 B4
Blaidwood Dr *DHAM* DH1 ....204 C3
Blair Cl *RDHAMSE* DH6 ....197 E5
Blair Ct *BDN/LAN/SAC* DH7 ....204 A3
Blake Av *WICK/BNPF* NE16 ....96 A3
Blakelaw Rd *WD/WHPE/BLK* NE5 ...61 D4
Blakemoor Pl *WD/WHPE/BLK* NE5 ..61 A5
Blakes Cl *PLEE/EAS* SR8 ....201 E2
Blake Wk *GATE* NE8 ....81 F6
Blanche Gv *PLEE/EAS* SR8 ....208 C3
Blanchland *WASHS* NE38 ....139 D5
Blanchland Av
  BW/LEM/TK/HW NE15 ....76 A1
  DHAM DH1 ....181 D6
  DIN/WO NE13 ....33 D4
Blanchland Cl *WLSD/HOW* NE28 ...67 F2
Blanchland Dr *MONK* NE25 ....25 E6
  SWCK/CAS SR5 ....126 B1
Blanchland Ter *TYNE/NSHE* NE30 ..55 D5
Blandford Rd *NSHW* NE29 ....53 F5
Blandford Sq *CNUT* NE1 ....2 A6
Blandford St *CNUT* NE1 ....2 A6
  SUND SR1 ....4 C3
Blaxton Pl *WICK/BNPF* NE16 ....95 F5
Blaydon Bank *BLAY* NE21 ....76 A6
Blaydon Hwy *BLAY* NE21 ....76 B5
Blaykeston Cl *SEA/MUR* SR7 ......175 D1
Bleachfield *FELL* NE10 ....101 E4
Bleasdale Crs *HLS* DH4 ....157 D1
Blencathra *WASHN* NE37 ....120 B5
Blenheim Cl *LGB/KIL* NE12 ....35 F6
Blenheim Dr *BDLGTN* NE22 ....8 B1
Blenheim Pl *DUN/TMV* NE11 ....97 D1
Blenheim St *CNUT* NE1 ....2 A6
Blenheim Wk *SSH* NE33 ....71 F3
Blenkinsop Ct *PLEE/EAS* SR8 .....208 A6
Blenkinsopp Ct *PLEE/EAS* SR8 ...208 A6
Blenkinsop St *WLSD/HOW* NE28 ...66 B2
Blind La *CLS/BIR/GTL* DH3 ....155 F2
  HLS DH4 ....157 D5
  SUNDSW SR3 ....143 F6
Blindy La *HLH* DH5 ....186 B3
Bloomfield Dr *HLH* DH5 ....184 C1
Bloomsbury Ct *GOS/KPK* NE3 .....63 D2
Blossom Gv *HLS* DH4 ....157 D4
Blount St *BYK/HTN/WLK* NE6 ....82 C2
Blucher Rd *LGB/KIL* NE12 ....49 E1
  NSHW NE29 ....70 B3
Blue Anchor Cl *CNUT* * NE1 ....3 F3
Bluebell Cl *LWF/SPW/WRK* NE9 ..100 A5
Bluebell Dene *WD/WHPE/BLK* NE5 ..60 C1
Bluebell Wy *HAR/WTLS* NE34 ....88 A3
Blueburn Dr *LGB/KIL* NE12 ....36 B5
Blue Coat Ct *DHAM* DH1 ....194 C4
Bluehouse Bank *STLY/ANP* DH9 ..150 B3
Blue House Buildings
  DHAM (off High St) DH1 ....196 B2
Blue House La *WASHN* NE37 ......120 A4
Blue House La
  CLDN/WHIT/ROK SR6 ....107 E3

  WASHN NE31 ....120 A4
Blue Quarries Rd
  LWF/SPW/WRK NE9 ....100 A4
Blyth Cl *CRAM* NE23 ....34 B2
Blyth Ct *BW/LEM/TK/HW* NE15 .....76 B1
  HAR/WTLS NE34 ....88 B3
Blyth Rd *WBAY* NE26 ....27 D5
Blyth Sq *SWCK/CAS* SR5 ....123 F1
Blyth St *MONK* NE25 ....24 B4
  SWCK/CAS SR5 ....123 F1
Blyton Av *ASHBK/HED/RY* SR2 ....162 A1
  HAR/WTLS NE34 ....87 E3
Bodlewell La *SUND* SR1 ....5 F1
Bodley Cl *GOS/KPK* NE3 ....61 F1
Bodmin Cl *WLSD/HOW* NE28 ....68 A1
Bodmin Rd *NSHW* NE29 ....53 E4
Bodmin Sq *SWCK/CAS* SR5 ....123 F1
Bodmin Wy *GOS/KPK* NE3 ....46 B6
Bognor St *SWCK/CAS* SR5 ....105 E6
Bohemia Ter *BLYTH* NE24 ....11 D6
Boker La *BOL* NE36 ....106 A2
Bolam Av *BLYTH* NE24 ....10 C3
  TYNE/NSHE NE30 ....54 C3
Bolam Gdns *WLSD/HOW* NE28 .....69 D3
Bolam Gv *TYNE/NSHE* NE30 ....54 C3
Bolam Rd *LGB/KIL* NE12 ....49 E1
Bolam St *BYK/HTN/WLK* NE6 ....82 B3
  GATE NE8 ....98 A2
  PLEE/EAS SR8 ....201 E2
Bolam Wy *BYK/HTN/WLK* NE6 ......82 B3
  MONK NE25 ....24 B5
Bolbec Rd *ELS/FEN* NE4 ....79 D1
Bolburn *FELL* NE10 ....101 F3
Boldon Cl *WLSD/HOW* NE28 ....67 F1
Boldon Dr *BOL* NE36 ....105 E3
Boldon Gdns *LWF/SPW/WRK* NE9 ..118 A1
Boldon La *CLDN/WHIT/ROK* SR6 ..107 D1
  HAR/WTLS NE34 ....88 B4
Boldon North Br *BOL* NE36 ....106 B2
Bolingbroke Rd *NSHW* NE29 ....53 F6
Bolingbroke St *BYK/HTN/WLK* NE6 ..83 F1
  SSH NE33 ....71 F4
Bollihope Dr *SUNDSW* SR3 ....144 A4
Bolton Cl *DHAM* DH1 ....180 B5
Bonchester Cl *BDLGTN* NE22 ....7 F2
Bonchester Pl *CRAM* NE23 ....14 B6
Bond Cl *SWCK/CAS* SR5 ....126 B3
Bond Ct *ELS/FEN* * NE4 ....78 C3
Bondene Av *FELL* NE10 ....101 D2
Bondene Av West *FELL* NE10 ....100 C2
Bondene Wy *CRAM* NE23 ....14 A4
Bondfield Gdns *FELL* NE10 ....101 F2
Bondicar Pl *WD/WHPE/BLK* NE5 ...61 F5
Bondicar Ter *BLYTH* NE24 ....10 C5
Bond St *ELS/FEN* * NE4 ....78 C3
Bonemill La *CLS/BIR/GTL* DH3 ....137 D6
  WASHS NE38 ....138 B6
Bonington Wy
  WD/WHPE/BLK NE5 ....61 D4
Bonner's Rd *SWCK/CAS* SR5 ....126 C4
Bonnivard Gdns *CRAM* NE23 ....36 C1
Booth St *FELL* NE10 ....101 D2
  MLFD/PNYW SR4 ....125 F5
Bootle St *SWCK/CAS* SR5 ....123 F1
Bordeaux Cl *SUNDSW* SR3 ....160 A2
Border Rd *WLSD/HOW* NE28 ....67 D5
Boreham Cl *WLSD/HOW* NE28 ......67 F1
Borodin Av *SWCK/CAS* SR5 ....105 E6
Borough Rd *HAR/WTLS* NE34 ....89 E3
  JRW NE32 ....86 A2
  NSHW NE29 ....70 C1
  SUND SR1 ....4 D3
Borrowdale *WICK/BNPF* NE16 ....96 C3
Borrowdale Av *BLYTH* NE24 ....9 F4
  BYK/HTN/WLK NE6 ....83 E1
  CLDN/WHIT/ROK SR6 ....108 B5
Borrowdale Cl *BOL* NE36 ....106 B2
  DHAM DH1 ....197 D2
Borrowdale Crs *BLAY* NE21 ....94 A2
  HLS DH4 ....139 F6
Borrowdale Dr *DHAM* DH1 ....196 B2
Borrowdale Gdns
  LWF/SPW/WRK NE9 ....118 A1
Borrowdale St *HLH* DH5 ....185 F2
Boscombe Dr *WLSD/HOW* NE28 ...67 E2
Boston Av *LGB/HTN* NE7 ....65 D1
  WASHS NE38 ....120 B6
Boston Cl *WLSD/HOW* NE28 ....67 F1
Boston Crs *BOL* NE36 ....105 D6
  SWCK/CAS SR5 ....105 D6
Boston St *PLEE/EAS* SR8 ....201 E2
  SWCK/CAS SR5 ....105 D6
Boswell Av *HAR/WTLS* NE34 ....88 A5
Bosworth *LGB/KIL* NE12 ....35 E6
Bosworth Gdns
  BYK/HTN/WLK NE6 ....65 E4
Bothal St *BYK/HTN/WLK* NE6 ....82 C2
Bottle Bank *GATE* NE8 ....3 H7
Bottlehouse St *BYK/HTN/WLK* NE6 ..82 B4
Bottle Works Rd *SEA/MUR* SR7 ...177 D3
Boundey Cl *SUNDSW* SR3 ....161 E1
The Boulevard
  WICK/BNPF
  (off Metrocentre) NE16 ....78 B6

Boulmer Av *CRAM* NE23 ....**14** A4
Boulmer Cl *GOS/KPK* NE3 ....**46** B4
Boulmer Ct *CLSW/PEL* DH2 ....**153** E6
Boulmer Gdns *DIN/WO* NE13 ....**33** D4
Boulsworth Rd *NSHW* NE29 ....**54** A3
Boundary Gdns *LGB/HTN* NE7 ....**64** C5
Boundary St *SWCK/CAS* SR5 ....**126** B2
Bourne Av *ELS/FEN* NE4 ....**79** D1
Bourne Ct *STLY/ANP* DH9 ....**148** C1
Bournemouth Dr *SEA/MUR* SR7 ....**175** E4
Bournemouth Gdns *WBAY* NE26 ....**40** B4
  WD/WHPE/BLK NE5 ....**60** B3
Bournemouth Rd *NSHW* NE29 ....**69** E1
Bourn Lea *HLS* DH4 ....**156** C3
Bourtree Cl *WLSD/HOW* NE28 ....**67** C2
Bowburn Av *SWCK/CAS* SR5 ....**124** B2
Bowburn Cl *FELL* NE10 ....**102** B3
Bower St *CLDN/WHIT/ROK* SR6 ....**108** C6
The Bower *JRW* NE32 ....**104** A2
Bowes Av *SEA/MUR* SR7 ....**175** D4
Bowes Cl *WICK/BNPF* NE16 ....**114** A2
Bowes Lea *HLS* DH4 ....**156** B4
Bowes Lyon Cl *ROWC* NE39 ....**110** C4
Bowes St *BLYTH* NE24 ....**10** C5
  GOS/KPK NE3 ....**64** A1
Bowfell Av *WD/WHPE/BLK* NE5 ....**61** F3
Bowfell Cl *WD/WHPE/BLK* NE5 ....**61** F3
Bowfield Av *GOS/KPK* NE3 ....**47** E3
Bow La *DHAM* DH4 ....**194** B5
Bowlynn Cl *SUNDSW* SR3 ....**160** A2
Bowman Dr *CRAM* NE23 ....**35** D2
Bowman Pl *SSH* NE33 ....**71** E5
Bowman St *CLDN/WHIT/ROK* SR6 ....**109** E1
Bowmont Dr *CRAM* NE23 ....**14** C6
  STLY/ANP DH9 ....**130** B6
Bowness Av *WLSD/HOW* NE28 ....**52** A6
Bowness Cl *BOL* NE36 ....**92** A5
  PLEE/EAS SR8 ....**209** D1
Bowness Pl *LWF/SPW/WRK* NE9 ....**100** A6
Bowness Rd *WD/WHPE/BLK* NE5 ....**60** C5
  WICK/BNPF NE16 ....**96** B3
Bowness St *SWCK/CAS* SR5 ....**105** F6
Bowsden Ct *GOS/KPK* NE3 ....**64** A1
Bowsden Ter *GOS/KPK* NE3 ....**64** A1
Boyd Crs *WLSD/HOW* NE28 ....**67** E4
Boyd Rd *WLSD/HOW* NE28 ....**67** E4
Boyd St *BW/LEM/TK/HW* NE15 ....**58** A6
  DHAM DH1 ....**194** C6
  JES NE2 ....**3** H2
  PLEE/EAS SR8 ....**201** E2
Boyne Ct *BDN/LAN/SAC* DH7 ....**203** F3
  BLYTH NE24 ....**11** D4
Brabourne St *HAR/WTLS* NE34....**88** B2
Bracken Av *WLSD/HOW* NE28 ....**67** E1
Bracken Cl *DIN/WO* NE13 ....**30** C4
  STLY/ANP DH9 ....**147** F2
Brackendale Rd *DHAM* DH1 ....**196** C2
Brackendene Dr
  LWF/SPW/WRK NE9 ....**99** D5
Bracken Dr *DUN/TMV* NE11 ....**97** E4
Bracken Field Rd *DHAM* DH1 ....**194** A1
Brackenfield Rd *GOS/KPK* NE3 ....**63** D2
Bracken Hl *PLEE/EAS* SR8 ....**207** E3
Brackenside *WICK/BNPF* NE16....**111** D6
Bracken St *GOS/KPK* NE3 ....**47** E3
Brackenwood Gv
  ASHBK/HED/RY SR2 ....**144** B4
Brackley *WASHN* NE37 ....**121** D3
Bracknell Cl *SUNDSW* SR3 ....**144** B6
Bracknell Gdns
  WD/WHPE/BLK NE5 ....**59** D5
Brack Ter *FELL* NE10 ....**84** A4
Bradbury Cl *FELL* NE10 ....**102** B3
  STLY/ANP DH9 ....**130** B6
Bradbury Ct *MONK* NE25 ....**24** C2
Bradford Av *SWCK/CAS* SR5 ....**105** F6
  WLSD/HOW NE28 ....**67** F1
Bradford Crs *DHAM* DH1 ....**195** E3
Bradley Av *HAR/WTLS* NE34 ....**89** F3
  HLH DH5 ....**171** D4
Bradley Cl *CLSW/PEL* DH2 ....**134** C4
Bradley Lodge Dr *STLY/ANP* DH9....**129** D6
Bradley St *PLEE/EAS* SR8 ....**201** E2
Bradley Ter *HLH* DH5 ....**186** A3
Bradman Dr *CLS/BIR/GTL* DH3 ....**154** A6
Bradman Sq *SWCK/CAS* SR5 ....**105** F6
Bradman St *SWCK/CAS* SR5 ....**105** F6
Bradshaw St *SWCK/CAS* SR5 ....**123** F1
Bradwell Rd *GOS/KPK* NE3 ....**62** A1
Bradwell Wy *HLS* DH4 ....**157** D3
Brady Sq *WASHS* NE38 ....**139** E2
Brady St *MLFD/PNYW* SR4 ....**125** E5
Braebridge Pl *GOS/KPK* NE3....**62** B2
Braemar Ct *FELL* NE10....**84** A4
Braemar Dr *HAR/WTLS* NE34 ....**72** C6
Braemar Gdns *SUNDSW* SR3 ....**144** A3
  SUNDSW SR3 ....**159** F2
Braeside *ASHBK/HED/RY* SR2....**144** A2
  DUN/TMV NE11 ....**97** F4
The Brae *MLFD/PNYW* SR4 ....**126** A6
Brahman Av *NSHW* NE29 ....**69** F2
Braintree Gdns *GOS/KPK* NE3 ....**62** B2
Braithwaite Rd *PLEE/EAS* SR8 ....**209** E2

Brakespeare Pl *PLEE/EAS* SR8 ....**209** D3
Bramble Dykes
  NE15 ....**78** A3
Bramhall Dr *WASHS* NE38 ....**138** A6
Bramley Cl *MLFD/PNYW* SR4 ....**141** F4
Bramley Ct *LGB/HTN* NE7 ....**66** A3
Brampton Av *BYK/HTN/WLK* NE6 ....**83** E4
Brampton Ct *PLEE/EAS* SR8 ....**200** A3
Brampton Gdns
  BW/LEM/TK/HW NE15 ....**57** F4
  LWF/SPW/WRK NE9 ....**117** F1
  WLSD/HOW NE28 ....**68** C2
Brampton Pl *NSHW* NE29 ....**69** F1
Brampton Rd *HAR/WTLS* NE34 ....**87** F3
Bramwell Rd *ASHBK/HED/RY* SR2 ....**5** F1
  HLS DH4 ....**169** F1
Brancepeth Av *ELS/FEN* NE4 ....**79** D4
Brancepeth Chare *PLEE/EAS* SR8 ....**208** A5
Brancepeth Cl
  BW/LEM/TK/HW NE15 ....**59** E6
  DHAM DH1 ....**181** D6
Brancepeth Rd *HEBB* NE31 ....**68** B6
  WASHS NE38 ....**137** F2
Brancepeth Ter *JRW* NE32 ....**86** A5
Brancepeth Vw
  BDN/LAN/SAC DH7 ....**202** B5
Branch St *BLAY* * NE21 ....**94** A1
Brancpeth Cl *BDN/LAN/SAC* DH7 ....**192** B5
Brand Av *ELS/FEN* NE4 ....**79** D1
Brandling Ct *FELL* * NE10 ....**100** C1
  HAR/WTLS NE34 ....**89** F3
Brandling La *FELL* NE10 ....**100** C1
Brandling Pk *JES* NE2 ....**63** F5
Brandling Pl *FELL* NE10 ....**100** C1
  *JES** NE2 ....**64** A6
Brandling Pl South *JES* NE2 ....**64** A6
Brandling St
  CLDN/WHIT/ROK SR6 ....**127** D2
Brandling St South
  CLDN/WHIT/ROK * SR6 ....**127** D3
Brandlings Wy *PLEE/EAS* SR8....**208** C1
Brandon Av *SMOOR* NE27 ....**52** A1
Brandon Cl *BLAY* NE21 ....**93** F2
  BLYTH NE24 ....**10** A4
  DHAM DH1 ....**170** C2
Brandon Gdns
  LWF/SPW/WRK NE9 ....**118** C1
Brandon Gv *JES* NE2 ....**81** E1
Brandon La *BDN/LAN/SAC* DH7 ....**203** F3
Brandon Rd *GOS/KPK* NE3 ....**46** B6
  NSHW NE29 ....**53** F6
Brandy La *WASHN* NE37 ....**120** A5
Brannen St *NSHW* NE29 ....**70** B1
Bransdale *HLS* DH4 ....**139** D6
Bransdale Av
  CLDN/WHIT/ROK SR6 ....**109** D3
Branston St *SWCK/CAS* SR5 ....**105** F6
Branton Av *HEBB* NE31 ....**84** C5
Brantwood *CLSW/PEL* DH2 ....**152** B5
Brantwood Av *MONK* NE25 ....**39** F6
Branxton Crs *BYK/HTN/WLK* NE6 ....**83** E3
Brass Thill *DHAM* DH1 ....**194** A5
Bray Cl *WLSD/HOW* NE28 ....**67** E1
Braydon Dr *NSHW* NE29 ....**69** F3
Brayside *JRW* NE32 ....**104** C1
Breamish Dr *WASHS* NE38....**137** E6
Breamish St *CNUT* NE1 ....**3** H3
  JRW NE32 ....**85** F3
Brearley Wy *FELL* NE10 ....**100** B2
Breckenbeds Rd
  LWF/SPW/WRK NE9 ....**99** D6
Brecken Wy *BDN/LAN/SAC* DH7....**203** E4
Brecon Cl *PLEE/EAS* SR8 ....**208** A5
  WD/WHPE/BLK NE5 ....**61** D2
Brecon Pl *CLSW/PEL* DH2 ....**135** E6
Brecon Rd *DHAM* DH1 ....**181** D5
Bredon Cl *WASHS* NE38 ....**138** A3
Brendale Av *WD/WHPE/BLK* NE5....**59** F3
Brendon Pl *PLEE/EAS* SR8....**208** A1
Brenkley Av *SMOOR* NE27 ....**52** A2
Brenkley Cl *DIN/WO* NE13 ....**31** D3
Brenkley Ct *DIN/WO* NE13 ....**33** D3
Brenkley Wy *DIN/WO* NE13 ....**33** D1
Brenlynn Cl *SUNDSW* SR3 ....**160** A2
Brennan Cl *BW/LEM/TK/HW* NE15 ....**78** A2
Brentford Sq *SWCK/CAS* SR5 ....**123** F1
Brentford Av *SWCK/CAS* SR5 ....**123** F1
Brentwood Av *JES* NE2 ....**63** F4
Brentwood Ct *MONK* NE25 ....**38** A1
Brentwood Gdns *SUNDSW* SR3 ....**144** A3
  WICK/BNPF NE16 ....**96** B5
Brentwood Av *WLSD/HOW* NE28 ....**67** F5
Brentwood Pl *SSH* * NE33 ....**71** F4
Brentwood Rd *HLS* DH4 ....**156** C3
Brett Cl *LGB/HTN* NE7 ....**65** F3
Bretton Gdns *LGB/HTN* NE7 ....**65** E4
Brewer's La *NSHW* NE29 ....**69** E3
Brewer Ter *ASHBK/HED/RY* SR2 ....**162** C2
Brewery Bank *WICK/BNPF* NE16 ....**96** F1
Brewery La *FELL* NE10 ....**100** C1
  PONT/DH NE20 ....**28** A4
  *SSH** NE33 ....**71** D4
  *WICK/BNPF** NE16 ....**95** F1

Brewhouse Bank
  TYNE/NSHE NE30 ....**55** E6
Briar Av *BDN/LAN/SAC* DH7 ....**202** C5
  HLS DH4 ....**170** C2
  WBAY NE26 ....**40** B3
Briar Cl *CLSW/PEL* DH2 ....**179** E1
  HLS DH4 ....**156** B4
  WLSD/HOW NE28 ....**67** E1
Briardale *BDLGTN* NE22 ....**7** D3
Briardale Rd *BLYTH* NE24 ....**9** F5
Briardene *DHAM* DH1 ....**194** A5
  WICK/BNPF NE16 ....**111** D6
Briardene Cl *SUNDSW* SR3 ....**159** E2
Briardene Crs *GOS/KPK* NE3 ....**62** C3
Briardene Dr *FELL* NE10 ....**102** C3
Briar Edge *LGB/KIL* NE12 ....**49** F4
Briar Fld *WASHS* NE38 ....**138** C5
Briarfield Rd *GOS/KPK* NE3 ....**63** D2
Briarhill *CLSW/PEL* DH2 ....**152** C5
Briar La *BW/LEM/TK/HW* NE15 ....**58** A5
Briar Lea *BDN/LAN/SAC* DH7 ....**178** A3
  HLS DH4 ....**156** B4
Briar Pl *BW/LEM/TK/HW* NE15 ....**77** F3
Briar Rd *DHAM* DH1 ....**196** C2
  ROWC NE39 ....**110** C2
Briarside *WD/WHPE/BLK* NE5 ....**60** C3
The Briars *SWCK/CAS* SR5 ....**124** A3
Briarsyde Cl *WICK/BNPF* NE16 ....**95** D5
Briarwood *CRAM* NE23 ....**35** D2
Briarwood Av *CLSW/PEL* DH2 ....**152** A5
  GOS/KPK NE3 ....**48** A6
Briarwood Crs *BYK/HTN/WLK* NE6 ....**66** B5
Briarwood Rd *BLYTH* NE24 ....**11** E6
The Briary *BW/LEM/TK/HW* NE15 ....**57** E4
Brick Garth *HLH* DH5 ....**186** A3
Brick Rw *ASHBK/HED/RY* SR2 ....**162** A1
Bridge *HAR/WTLS* NE34 ....**88** B5
Bridge Cottages *CRAM* NE23 ....**35** D2
Bridge Crs *SUND* SR1 ....**4** C1
Bridgemere Dr *DHAM* DH1 ....**179** F6
Bridge Pk *GOS/KPK* NE3 ....**47** E4
Bridge Rd South *NSHW* NE29 ....**70** A2
The Bridges *SUND* SR1 ....**4** C3
Bridge St *BLAY* NE21 ....**76** A4
  BLYTH NE24 ....**11** E5
  DHAM DH1 ....**194** A4
  DIN/WO NE13 ....**33** D2
  GATE NE8 ....**3** E6
  STLY/ANP DH9 ....**147** F4
  SUND SR1 ....**4** C2
Bridgewater Cl
  BW/LEM/TK/HW NE15 ....**76** B1
  WLSD/HOW NE28 ....**67** E2
Bridgewater Rd *WASHN* NE37 ....**121** D5
Bridle Pth *BOL* NE36 ....**106** B3
  SUNDSW SR3 ....**142** B6
The Bridle *SMOOR* NE27 ....**53** D2
Bridlington Av *WLSD/HOW* NE28 ....**67** F1
Bridlington Av
  LWF/SPW/WRK NE9 ....**117** E1
Bridport Rd *NSHW* NE29 ....**53** F3
Brier Av *PLEE/EAS* SR8 ....**201** E6
Brier Dene Crs *WBAY* NE26 ....**40** A1
Brierdene Rd *WBAY* NE26 ....**40** B1
Brierley Rd *BLYTH* NE24 ....**10** A5
Briermede Av *LWF/SPW/WRK* NE9 ....**99** E6
Brierville *DHAM* DH1 ....**194** A5
Brieryside *WD/WHPE/BLK* NE5 ....**61** F4
Briery Vale Rd *ASHBK/HED/RY* SR2 ....**4** A6
Brigham Av *GOS/KPK* NE3 ....**62** A3
Brigham Pl *SSH* NE33 ....**71** E5
Brightlea *CLS/BIR/GTL* DH3 ....**137** D3
Brightman Rd *NSHW* NE29 ....**54** B6
Brighton Cl *WLSD/HOW* NE28 ....**68** A1
Brighton Gdns *GATE* NE8 ....**99** D3
Brighton Gv *ELS/FEN* NE4 ....**79** F2
  NSHW NE29 ....**54** B6
  WBAY NE26 ....**40** B3
Brighton Rd *GATE* NE8 ....**98** C2
Bright St *CLDN/WHIT/ROK* SR6....**127** D3
  SSH NE33 ....**71** F3
Brignall Cl *CLS/BIR/GTL* DH3 ....**168** A4
Brignall Gdns
  BW/LEM/TK/HW NE15 ....**77** F1
Brignall Ri *SUNDSW* SR3 ....**144** A4
Brindley Rd *PLEE/EAS* SR8 ....**207** E2
  WASHN NE37 ....**121** D6
Brinkburn *CLSW/PEL* DH2 ....**152** C5
  WASHS NE38 ....**139** D4
Brinkburn Av *BLYTH* NE24 ....**11** E6
  CRAM NE23 ....**22** B2
  GATE NE8 ....**99** D2
  GOS/KPK NE3 ....**47** D6
  WICK/BNPF NE16 ....**95** F2
Brinkburn Cl *BLAY* NE21 ....**93** F2
  BYK/HTN/WLK NE6 ....**82** A3
Brinkburn Ct *BYK/HTN/WLK* * NE6 ....**82** A3
  TYNE/NSHE NE30 ....**55** D6
Brinkburn Crs *HLS* DH4 ....**157** E6
Brinkburn La *BYK/HTN/WLK* * NE6 ....**82** A3
Brinkburn Pl *BYK/HTN/WLK* * NE6....**82** A2
Brinkburn Sq *BYK/HTN/WLK* * NE6 ....**82** A3
Brinkburn St *BYK/HTN/WLK* NE6 ....**82** A2
  HAR/WTLS NE34 ....**88** A2

MLFD/PNYW SR4 ....**143** F1
WLSD/HOW NE28 ....**69** E5
Brinkburn St South
BYK/HTN/WLK NE6 ....**82** B3
Brisbane Av *LWF/SPW/WRK* NE34 .....**87** E5
Brisbane Ct *GATE* * NE8 ....**81** D5
Brisbane St *SWCK/CAS* SR5 ....**123** F1
Brislee Av *TYNE/NSHE* NE30 ....**55** E5
Bristlecone *SUNDSW* SR3 ....**160** A3
Bristol Av *WASHN* NE37 ....**120** A4
Bristol Dr *WLSD/HOW* NE28 ....**67** F1
Bristol St *MONK* NE25 ....**24** B3
Bristol Ter *ELS/FEN* NE4 ....**79** F4
Britannia Ct *ELS/FEN* * NE4 ....**79** F4
Britannia Pl *ELS/FEN* NE4 ....**79** F3
Britannia Rd *SUNDSW* SR3 ....**160** C1
Brixham Av *LWF/SPW/WRK* NE9 ....**117** E1
Brixham Cl *SEA/MUR* SR7 ....**175** F4
Brixham Crs *JRW* NE32 ....**86** C3
Brixham Gdns *SUNDSW* SR3 ....**144** A4
Broad Chare *CNUT* NE1 ....**3** F4
Broadfield Pl *HAR/WTLS* NE34 ....**88** C3
Broad Garth *CNUT* NE1 ....**3** F5
Broad Landing *SSH* NE33 ....**71** D3
Broadlands *CLDN/WHIT/ROK* SR6 ....**107** F3
Broadlea *FELL* NE10 ....**102** A2
Broadmayne Av
MLFD/PNYW SR4 ....**142** C2
Broadmayne Gdns
MLFD/PNYW SR4 ....**142** C2
Broad Mdw *ASHBK/HED/RY* SR2 ......**144** A1
Broadmeadows *SUNDSW* SR3 ....**159** D2
WASHN NE38 ....**139** D4
Broadmead Wy
BW/LEM/TK/HW NE15 ....**77** E3
Broadoak *FELL* NE10 ....**102** A1
Broadpark *FELL* NE10 ....**102** A2
Broadpool Gn *WICK/BNPF* NE16 ....**96** B4
Broadpool Ter *WICK/BNPF* NE16 ....**96** B4
Broadsheath Ter *SWCK/CAS* SR5 ....**125** E5
Broadside *FELL* NE10 ....**102** A2
Broadstairs Ct *MLFD/PNYW* SR4 ....**142** C2
Broadstone Gv
WD/WHPE/BLK NE5 ....**59** E5
Broadwater *FELL* NE10 ....**102** A1
Broadway *BLYTH* NE24 ....**11** D6
BW/LEM/TK/HW NE15 ....**59** F6
CLS/BIR/GTL DH3 ....**153** F1
LWF/SPW/WRK NE9 ....**100** A3
TYNE/NSHE NE30 ....**55** E4
WICK/BNPF NE16 ....**95** E5
Broadway Cl *MONK* NE25 ....**55** D1
Broadway Crs *BLYTH* NE24 ....**11** D6
Broadway East *GOS/KPK* NE3 ....**47** D5
The Broadway *HLS* DH4 ....**171** D2
MLFD/PNYW SR4 ....**142** B2
TYNE/NSHE NE30 ....**55** D1
Broadway Vis
BW/LEM/TK/HW NE15 ....**78** A3
Broadway West *GOS/KPK* NE3..............**47** D5
Broadwell Ct *GOS/KPK* NE3 ....**64** B2
Broadwood Rd
BW/LEM/TK/HW NE15 ....**77** E1
Brockenhurst Dr
MLFD/PNYW SR4 ....**141** F4
Brock Farm Ct *TYNE/NSHE* NE30 ....**54** C6
Brockhampton Cl *BOLCOL* NE35 ....**87** D6
Brock La *BDLGTN* NE22 ....**9** E1
Brockley Av *HAR/WTLS* NE34 ....**88** B4
Brockley St *SWCK/CAS* SR5 ....**123** F1
Brock Sq *BYK/HTN/WLK* * NE6 ....**82** A3
Brock St *BYK/HTN/WLK* * NE6 ....**82** A3
Brockwell Cl *BLAY* NE21 ....**93** F1
Brockwell Ct *BLYTH* NE24 ....**16** B2
Brockwell Dr *ROWG* NE39 ....**111** D1
Brockwell Rd *WASHN* NE38 ....**137** E1
Brodie Cl *GOS/KPK* NE3 ....**61** F1
Brodrick Cl *GOS/KPK* NE3 ....**61** F1
Brodrick St *SSH* NE33 ....**71** F3
Brokenheugh *WD/WHPE/BLK* NE5 ....**60** B5
Bromford Rd *GOS/KPK* NE3 ....**61** F1
Bromley Av *MONK* NE25 ....**54** A1
Bromley Ct *GOS/KPK* NE3 ....**45** F5
Bromley Gdns *BLYTH* NE24 ....**17** D1
WLSD/HOW NE28 ....**67** F1
Brompton Pl *DUN/TMV* * NE11 ....**97** F2
Bromsgrove Cl *WLSD/HOW* NE28 ....**68** A1
Bronte Pl *STLY/ANP* DH9 ....**149** D4
Bronte St *GATE* NE8 ....**100** A1
Brookbank Cl *SUNDSW* SR3 ....**160** B3
Brook Ct *BDLGTN* NE22 ....**7** F4
Brookdale *DHAM* DH1 ....**197** D3
Brooke Av *BOLCOL* NE35 ....**106** A2
WICK/BNPF NE16 ....**95** F2
Brooke St *SWCK/CAS* SR5 ....**126** B4
Brookfield Crs
WD/WHPE/BLK NE5 ....**59** E5
Brookfield Ter *FELL* * NE10 ....**101** F1
Brookland Dr *LGB/KIL* NE12 ....**50** A1
Brookland Rd *MLFD/PNYW* SR4 ....**125** E6
Brooklands Wy *BOLCOL* NE35 ....**104** C2
Brookside *BDN/LAN/SAC* DH7 ....**164** B6
BDN/LAN/SAC DH7 ....**178** A4
CRAM NE23 ....**34** C2
Brookside Av *BLYTH* NE24 ....**10** A5

DIN/WO NE13 ....**32** C5
Brookside Crs *WD/WHPE/BLK* NE5 .....**61** F5
Brookside Gdns
ASHBK/HED/RY SR2 ....**144** B2
Brookside Ter
ASHBK/HED/RY SR2 ....**144** B2
Brookside Vis
SEA/MUR
(off Dene House Rd) SR7 ....**176** C2
Brookside Wd *WASHS* NE38 ....**138** C5
Brooksmead *WLSD/HOW* NE28 ....**66** B2
Brook St *BYK/HTN/WLK* NE6 ....**82** C3
WBAY NE26 ....**41** D5
Brookvale Av *GOS/KPK* NE3 ....**62** B3
Broom St *STLY/ANP* DH9 ....**149** D1
WICK/BNPF NE16 ....**96** B4
Broome Cl *GOS/KPK* NE3 ....**46** C6
Broome Rd *DHAM* DH1 ....**196** C2
Broomfield *JRW* NE32 ....**104** B1
Broomfield Av *BYK/HTN/WLK* NE6 ....**66** A5
WLSD/HOW NE28 ....**67** E1
Broomfield Rd *GOS/KPK* NE3 ....**63** D2
Broom Gn *WICK/BNPF* NE16 ....**96** B4
Broom Hall Dr
BDN/LAN/SAC DH7 ....**192** A5
Broomhill Gdns
WD/WHPE/BLK NE5 ....**61** F5
Broomhill Ter *HLH* DH5 ....**171** E5
Broom La *BDN/LAN/SAC* DH7 ....**192** A5
WICK/BNPF NE16 ....**96** A5
Broomlea *NSHW* NE29 ....**53** D3
Broomlee Rd *LGB/KIL* NE12 ....**49** F1
Broomley Ms *GOS/KPK* NE3 ....**46** B5
Broomridge Av
BW/LEM/TK/HW NE15 ....**78** C3
Broomshields Av *SWCK/CAS* SR5 .....**126** A1
Broomshields Cl *SWCK/CAS* SR5 ......**126** A1
Broomside La *DHAM* DH1 ....**196** C2
Broom Ter *WICK/BNPF* NE16 ....**96** B4
WICK/BNPF NE16 ....**112** A6
Broomy Hill Rd
BW/LEM/TK/HW NE15 ....**57** F4
Brotherlee Rd *GOS/KPK* NE3 ....**46** B5
Brougham Ct *PLEE/EAS* SR8 ....**207** F5
Brougham St *SUND* SR1 ....**4** C3
Brough Ct *BYK/HTN/WLK* * NE6 ....**82** B1
Brough Gdns *WLSD/HOW* NE28 ....**68** C2
Brough St *BYK/HTN/WLK* NE6 ....**82** B1
Broughton Rd *SSH* NE33 ....**71** F4
Brough Wy *BYK/HTN/WLK* * NE6 ....**82** B1
Browbank *BDN/LAN/SAC* DH7 ....**178** C3
Browne Rd *CLDN/WHIT/ROK* SR6 .....**126** C1
Browney La *BDN/LAN/SAC* DH7 ....**203** E1
Browning Cl *HAR/WTLS* NE34 ....**88** A6
STLY/ANP DH9 ....**148** C1
Browning St *PLEE/EAS* SR8 ....**201** E2
Brownlow Cl *LGB/HTN* NE7 ....**66** A3
Brownlow Rd *HAR/WTLS* NE34 ....**88** B2
Brownrigg Dr *CRAM* NE23 ....**22** B3
Brownsea Pl *LWF/SPW/WRK* NE9 ....**99** F3
Browntop Pl *HAR/WTLS* NE34 ....**88** B3
The Brow *BYK/HTN/WLK* NE6.................**82** B3
Broxburn Cl *WLSD/HOW* NE28 ....**68** A1
Broxburn Ct *WD/WHPE/BLK* NE5 ....**61** D3
Broxholm Rd *BYK/HTN/WLK* NE6 ....**65** F5
Bruce Cl *HAR/WTLS* NE34 ....**88** B4
WD/WHPE/BLK NE5 ....**60** B1
Bruce Gdns *WD/WHPE/BLK* NE5 ....**78** B1
Bruce Glasier Ter *RDHAMSE* DH6 .....**206** B3
Bruce Kirkup Rd *PLEE/EAS* SR8 ....**201** D6
Bruce Pl *PLEE/EAS* SR8 ....**200** B6
Bruce St *BDN/LAN/SAC* DH7 ....**164** A4
Brundon Av *WBAY* NE26 ....**40** B3
Brunel Dr *CLDN/WHIT/ROK* SR6 ....**127** E3
Brunel St *ELS/FEN* NE4 ....**80** A5
GATE NE8 ....**98** C2
Brunswick Gv *DIN/WO* NE13 ....**32** C4
Brunswick Rd *SMOOR* NE27 ....**52** B2
SWCK/CAS SR5 ....**105** F6
Brunswick St *SSH* NE33 ....**71** E5
Brunton Av *GOS/KPK* NE3 ....**46** B6
WLSD/HOW NE28 ....**67** D5
Brunton Cl *SMOOR* NE27 ....**52** B2
Brunton Gv *GOS/KPK* NE3 ....**46** B6
Brunton La *DIN/WO* NE13 ....**46** C2
GOS/KPK NE3 ....**45** D5
Brunton Rd *DIN/WO* NE13 ....**45** C5
Brunton St *NSHW* NE29 ....**69** F3
Brunton Ter *MLFD/PNYW* SR4 ....**125** F6
Brunton Wy *CRAM* NE23 ....**14** A4
FELL NE10 ....**84** A6
Brussels Rd *MLFD/PNYW* SR4...........**124** C5
WLSD/HOW NE28 ....**67** D5
Bryden Ct *HAR/WTLS* NE34 ....**88** C3
Bryers St *CLDN/WHIT/ROK* SR6 ....**109** E1
Bryon St *PLEE/EAS* SR8 ....**201** D2
Buchanan Gn *DUN/TMV* * NE11 ....**97** F1
Buckingham *SUNDSW* SR3 ....**143** D6
Buckingham Cl
CLDN/WHIT/ROK SR6 ....**109** E2

Buckingham Rd *PLEE/EAS* SR8 ....**200** A6
Buckinghamshire Rd *DHAM* DH1 ......**196** B3
Buckingham St *ELS/FEN* NE4...............**80** A3
Buckland Cl *HLS* DH4 ....**157** E6
WASHS NE38 ....**138** C3
Buckthorne Gv *LGB/HTN* NE7 ....**65** E3
Buddle Cl *ELS/FEN* NE4 ....**78** C4
PLEE/EAS SR8 ....**200** C6
Buddle Ct *ELS/FEN* NE4 ....**79** D4
Buddle Rd *ELS/FEN* NE4 ....**78** C4
Buddle St *WLSD/HOW* NE28 ....**67** D6
Buddle Ter *ASHBK/HED/RY* SR2 ....**5** F6
Bude Gdns *LWF/SPW/WRK* NE9 ....**117** E1
Bude Gv *NSHW* NE29 ....**53** F3
Bude Sq *SEA/MUR* SR7 ....**174** C6
Budle Cl *BLYTH* NE24 ....**10** B5
Budleigh Rd *GOS/KPK* NE3 ....**62** B1
Budworth Av *WBAY* NE26 ....**26** C3
Buford Ct
DHAM (off Western Hl) DH1 ....**194** A5
Bullfinch Dr *WICK/BNPF* NE16 ....**95** F4
Bullion La *CLSW/PEL* DH2 ....**153** D5
Bulman's La *NSHW* NE29 ....**54** C4
Bulmer Rd *HAR/WTLS* NE34 ....**89** F1
Bungalows
FELL (off Sunderland Rd) NE10 ....**101** D2
The Bungalows
CLS/BIR/GTL
(off Lansbury Dr) DH3 ....**118** A6
PLEE/EAS
(off Sunderland Rd) SR8 ....**201** E6
RDHAMSE
(off Dixon Est) DH6 ....**206** B3
STLY/ANP DH9 ....**130** B6
WLSD/HOW NE28 ....**68** A3
Bunyan Av *HAR/WTLS* NE34 ....**87** F5
Burdale Av *WD/WHPE/BLK* NE5............**60** C5
Burdock Crs *ASHBK/HED/RY* SR2 ......**162** A2
Burdon Av *CRAM* NE23 ....**21** E1
HLH DH5 ....**171** F2
Burdon Cl *CLDN/WHIT/ROK* SR6 ....**107** D1
Burdon Crs *CLDN/WHIT/ROK* SR6 .....**107** D1
SEA/MUR SR7 ....**175** E1
Burdon Dr *PLEE/EAS* SR8 ....**207** F1
Burdon Gv *SUNDSW* SR3 ....**161** D1
Burdon Hall Pk
SUNDSW (off Burdon) SR3................**161** D5
Burdon La *ASHBK/HED/RY* SR2 ....**162** A2
SUNDSW SR3 ....**160** C4
Burdon Main Rw *NSHW* NE29 ....**70** C2
Burdon Pk *WICK/BNPF* NE16 ....**114** B2
Burdon Pl *PLEE/EAS* SR8 ....**209** D2
Burdon Pln *WICK/BNPF* NE16 ....**114** A5
Burdon Rd *ASHBK/HED/RY* SR2 ....**4** D4
CLDN/WHIT/ROK SR6 ....**107** D1
SUNDSW SR3 ....**161** D2
Burdon St *NSHW* NE29 ....**69** F3
Burdon Ter *JES* NE2 ....**63** F6
Burford Ct *LGB/HTN* NE7 ....**64** C2
Burford Gdns *SUNDSW* SR3 ....**144** A4
Burghley Rd *FELL* NE10 ....**100** B4
Burke St *SWCK/CAS* SR5 ....**123** F1
Burlawn Cl *ASHBK/HED/RY* SR2 ....**145** E6
Burleigh St *SSH* NE33 ....**71** F4
Burlington Cl *ASHBK/HED/RY* SR2......**5** F5
Burlington Ct *WLSD/HOW* NE28 ....**52** A5
Burlington Gdns
BYK/HTN/WLK NE6 ....**65** D6
Burlison Gdns *FELL* NE10 ....**82** B6
Burnaby Dr *RYTON* NE40 ....**74** A4
Burnaby St *MLFD/PNYW* SR4 ....**143** F1
Burn Av *LGB/KIL* NE12 ....**49** F4
Burnbank Av *MONK* NE25 ....**39** D5
Burnbridge *DIN/WO* NE13 ....**33** D2
Burn Crook *HLH* DH5 ....**170** C4
Burnden Gv *HLS* DH4 ....**156** B3
Burnel Cl *WLSD/HOW* NE28 ....**67** E1
Burney Vis *GATE* NE8 ....**99** F1
Burnfoot Wy *GOS/KPK* NE3 ....**62** A3
Burn Gdns *PLEE/EAS* SR8 ....**200** B2
Burnhall Dr *SEA/MUR* SR7 ....**175** F1
Burnham Av
BW/LEM/TK/HW NE15 ....**75** F1
Burnham Cl *BLYTH* NE24 ....**17** D1
Burnham Gv *BOL* NE36 ....**106** C3
BYK/HTN/WLK NE6 ....**83** D4
Burnham St *HAR/WTLS* NE34 ....**88** B2
Burn Heads Rd *HEBB* NE31 ....**84** C4
Burnhills La *RYTON* NE40 ....**92** A2
Burnhope Dr *SWCK/CAS* SR5 ....**126** A1
Burnhope Rd *WASHS* NE38 ....**121** D6
Burnhope Wy *PLEE/EAS* SR8 ....**208** A2
Burnip Rd *SEA/MUR* SR7 ....**174** B6
Burn La *HLH* DH5 ....**185** F1
Burnlea Gdns *CRAM* NE23 ....**23** F6
Burnley St *BLAY* NE21 ....**76** B6
Burnmoor Gdns
LWF/SPW/WRK NE9 ....**118** C1
Burnopfield Gdns
BW/LEM/TK/HW NE15 ....**77** F2
Burnopfield Rd *ROWG* NE39 ....**111** E3
Burn Park Rd *ASHBK/HED/RY* SR2.....**144** A1
HLS DH4 ....**170** B2
Burn Prom *HLS* DH4............................**170** C2

Burn Rd BLAY NE21 ....93 E1
Burns Av BLYTH NE24 ....16 B1
  BOLCOL NE35 ....106 A2
Burns Av South HLH DH5 ....171 D3
Burns Cl HAR/WTLS NE34 ....88 A5
  HLS DH4 ....183 F2
  STLY/ANP DH9 ....148 C2
  WICK/BNPF NE16....................96 A5
Burns Crs WICK/BNPF NE16 ......95 F2
Burnside BDLGTN NE22 ....8 C1
  BDN/LAN/SAC DH7 ....178 A4
  BOL NE36 ....107 D3
  JES NE2 ....80 A1
  JRW NE32 ....86 B4
  MONK (off Hesleyside Rd) NE25 ...39 D5
  PLEE/EAS SR8 ....208 B2
Burnside Av CRAM NE23 ....35 D2
  HLS DH4 ....170 B1
  PLEE/EAS SR8 ....209 F2
Burnside Cl BLYTH NE24 ....10 A4
  WICK/BNPF NE16....................95 F6
Burnside Rd GOS/KPK NE3 ....47 E5
  ROWG NE39 ....110 C3
  TYNE/NSHE NE30 ....55 D1
The Burnside WD/WHPE/BLK NE5...60 A5
Burnside Vw CRAM NE23 ....36 A1
Burns St JRW NE32 ....86 A1
Burn's Ter RDHAMSE DH6 ....206 C3
Burnstones WD/WHPE/BLK NE5...60 A5
Burn Ter HEBB NE31 ....84 B6
Burnthouse Bank CLSW/PEL DH2 ...152 B4
Burnthouse Cl BLAY NE21 ....93 F2
Burnthouse La WICK/BNPF NE16 ...95 F6
Burnt House Rd MONK NE25 ......54 A1
Burntland Av SWCK/CAS SR5 ...125 E2
Burn Vw
  BOLCOL (off Foxhomes) NE35...104 C2
  CRAM NE23 ....35 D2
Burnville BYK/HTN/WLK NE6 .....81 F1
Burnville Rd MLFD/PNYW SR4 ...144 A1
Burnville Rd South
  MLFD/PNYW SR4...................144 A1
Burradon Rd CRAM NE23 ....35 D4
Burrow St SSH NE33 ....71 E3
Burscough Crs
  CLDN/WHIT/ROK SR6 ....126 C2
Burstow Av BYK/HTN/WLK NE6 ...83 D5
Burt Av NSHW NE29 ....70 A1
Burt Cl PLEE/EAS SR8................200 C6
Burt Crs CRAM NE23 ....35 D2
Burt Rd BDLGTN NE22 ....9 D1
Burt St BLYTH NE24 ....11 D4
Burwell Av WD/WHPE/BLK NE5 ...60 B6
Burwood Rd BYK/HTN/WLK NE6...83 E5
  NSHW NE29 ....53 E4
Busblades La STLY/ANP DH9 .....16 B1
Buston Ter JES NE2 ....64 B5
Busty Bank WICK/BNPF NE16 ...111 F4
Butcher's Bridge Rd JRW NE32 ...86 A4
Buteland Rd
  BW/LEM/TK/HW NE15 ....77 D1
Bute St STLY/ANP DH9 ....129 F4
Butler St PLEE/EAS SR8 ....201 E3
Butsfield Gdns SUNDSW SR3 ...144 A4
Butterburn Cl LGB/HTN NE7 ......66 C2
Buttermere CLDN/WHIT/ROK SR6 ...107 F1
  FELL NE10 ....101 F2
  PLEE/EAS SR8 ....207 F5
Buttermere Av HLH DH5 ....186 B4
  WICK/BNPF NE16....................96 B3
Buttermere Cl BLAY NE21 ....94 A2
Buttermere Crs BLAY NE21 ....94 A2
Buttermere Gdns HAR/WTLS NE34 ...89 D2
  LWF/SPW/WRK NE9 ....99 F5
Buttermere Rd TYNE/NSHE NE30 ...54 C2
Buttermere St
  ASHBK/HED/RY SR2 ....145 D4
Buttermere Wy BLYTH NE24 ......10 A3
Buxton Cl JRW NE32 ....86 B3
Buxton Gdns SUNDSW SR3 ......144 A3
  WD/WHPE/BLK NE5 ....60 B3
Buxton Rd JRW NE32 ....86 B3
Byers Cl SUNDSW SR3 ....144 A6
Byer Sq HLH DH5 ....171 F4
Byer St HLH DH5 ....171 F4
The Byeways LGB/KIL NE12 ....49 D6
Bygate Cl WD/WHPE/BLK NE5 ...62 A3
Bygate Rd MONK NE25 ....40 A6
Byker Bk BYK/HTN/WLK NE6 .....81 F3
Byker Br CNUT NE1 ....3 H2
Byker Buildings
  BYK/HTN/WLK NE6 ....81 F2
Byker Crs BYK/HTN/WLK NE6 ....82 B2
Byker St BYK/HTN/WLK NE6 .....83 E2
Byker Ter BYK/HTN/WLK NE6 ....83 E2
Byland Cl HLS DH4 ....157 E6
Byland Ct BDN/LAN/SAC DH7 ...192 A3
  WASHS NE38 ....138 B1
Byland Rd LGB/KIL NE12 ....48 B6
Byony Toft ASHBK/HED/RY SR2...162 C1
Byrness WD/WHPE/BLK NE5 .....60 A5
Byrness Cl GOS/KPK NE3 ....61 E2

Byron Av BLYTH NE24 ....16 B1
  BOLCOL NE35 ....105 F2
  CLSW/PEL DH2.....................152 A5
  HEBB NE31 ....85 E2
Byron Cl CLSW/PEL DH2 ....135 F5
Byron Ct WICK/BNPF NE16 ....95 F2
Byron Rd SWCK/CAS SR5 ....125 F2
Byron St JES NE2 ....3 F1
  SWCK/CAS SR5 ....126 A3
Byron Ter RDHAMSE DH6 ....206 C2
Byron Wk GATE NE8 ....81 F6
The By-Way BW/LEM/TK/HW NE15...57 F5
Bywell Av BW/LEM/TK/HW NE15...77 D1
  GOS/KPK NE3 ....46 B4
  HAR/WTLS NE34 ....89 F1
  SWCK/CAS SR5 ....126 B1
Bywell Dr PLEE/EAS SR8 ....208 B5
Bywell Gdns DUN/TMV NE11 .....97 F5
  LWF/SPW/WRK NE9 ....100 A4
Bywell Rd CLDN/WHIT/ROK SR6...107 E2
Bywell St BYK/HTN/WLK NE6 .....82 C3
Bywell Ter JRW NE32 ....86 A5

C

Cadleston Ct CRAM NE23 ....14 C6
Cadwell La PLEE/EAS SR8 ....200 A6
Caernarvon Cl WD/WHPE/BLK NE5...61 D2
Caernarvon Dr SUNDSW SR3 ...159 E2
Caer Urfa Cl SSH NE33 ....71 E2
Caesars Wk SSH NE33 ....71 E2
Cairncross SWCK/CAS SR5 ......123 F5
Cairnglass Gn CRAM NE23 ....14 C6
Cairngorm Av WASHS NE38 .....137 F3
Cairnmore Cl CRAM NE23 ....22 A4
Cairnsmore Dr WASHS NE38 ....138 A3
Cairns Rd SEA/MUR SR7 ....187 F1
  SWCK/CAS SR5 ....108 B6
Cairns Sq SWCK/CAS SR5 ....108 B6
Cairns Wy GOS/KPK NE3 ....46 B5
Cairo St ASHBK/HED/RY SR2 ....145 D2
Caithness Rd SWCK/CAS SR5 ...123 E2
Caithness Sq SWCK/CAS SR5 ...123 E2
Calais Rd SWCK/CAS SR5 ....123 E3
Caldbeck Av BYK/HTN/WLK NE6...83 E5
Caldbeck Cl BYK/HTN/WLK NE6...83 E5
Calderbourne Av
  CLDN/WHIT/ROK SR6 ....109 D6
Calderdale WLSD/HOW NE28 .....66 B3
Calderdale Av BYK/HTN/WLK NE6...83 E2
Calder Wk WICK/BNPF NE16....113 F2
Calderwood Crs
  LWF/SPW/WRK NE9 ....117 F1
Caldew Ct HLH DH5 ....186 A2
Caldew Crs WD/WHPE/BLK NE5...60 C6
Caldwell Rd GOS/KPK NE3 ....46 B4
Caledonian St HEBB NE31 ....84 C1
Caledonia St BYK/HTN/WLK NE6...83 F4
Calfclose La JRW NE32 ....86 A6
Calf Close Wk JRW NE32 ....86 A5
California BLAY NE21 ....94 A1
Callaley Av WICK/BNPF NE16 ....95 E4
Callaly Av CRAM NE23 ....22 B2
Callaly Wy BYK/HTN/WLK NE6 ...82 C4
Callander CLSW/PEL DH2 ....135 F4
Callerdale Rd BLYTH NE24 ....9 F4
Callerton Cl LGB/KIL NE12 ....35 F5
Callerton Av NSHW NE29 ....53 E5
Callerton Ct PONT/DH NE20 .....28 A6
  WD/WHPE/BLK
  (off Marsden La) NE5 ....60 C3
Callerton La PONT/DH NE20 .....28 A5
  WD/WHPE/BLK NE5 ....42 A4
Callerton Rd
  BW/LEM/TK/HW NE15 ....58 A4
Callerton Vw WD/WHPE/BLK NE5...59 D3
Calley Cl PLEE/EAS SR8 ....208 B5
Callington Dr ASHBK/HED/RY SR2...162 B1
Calthwaite Cl SWCK/CAS SR5 ...123 F2
Calvert Ter SEA/MUR SR7 ....188 A1
Calvus Dr BW/LEM/TK/HW NE15...56 B4
Camberley Cl SUNDSW SR3 .....144 B6
Camberley Dr BDN/LAN/SAC DH7...202 B5
Camberley Rd WLSD/HOW NE28...68 C2
Camberwell Cl DUN/TMV NE11 ...98 A4
Camberwell Wy SUNDSW SR3 ...159 F5
Cambo Av BDLGTN NE22
  MONK NE25 ....53 F1
Cambo Cl BLYTH NE24 ....10 B5
  GOS/KPK NE3 ....63 F1
  WLSD/HOW NE28 ....51 F6
Cambo Dr CRAM NE23 ....22 B3
Cambo Gn WD/WHPE/BLK NE5 ...61 E4
Cambo Pl TYNE/NSHE NE30 ......54 C3
Camborne Gv GATE NE8 ....99 E1
Camborne Pl GATE NE8 ....99 E1
Cambourne Av
  CLDN/WHIT/ROK SR6 ....109 D6
Cambria Gn MLFD/PNYW SR4 ...123 F6
Cambrian St JRW NE32 ....86 A1
Cambrian Wy WASHS NE38 ......138 A2

Cambria St MLFD/PNYW SR4 ....123 F6
Cambridge Av HEBB NE31 ....85 E3
  LGB/KIL NE12 ....49 F4
  WASHN NE37 ....120 A4
  WLSD/HOW NE28 ....66 C3
Cambridge Dr CLS/BIR/GTL DH3...167 F4
Cambridge Pl CLS/BIR/GTL DH3...136 B5
Cambridge Rd PLEE/EAS SR8 ...200 B3
  SUNDSW SR3 ....160 C1
Cambridgeshire Dr DHAM DH1 ...196 B3
Cambridge St ELS/FEN NE4 ....80 A4
Cambridge Ter * NE8 ....99 D1
Camden Av NSHW NE29 ....71 D1
Camden St JES NE2 ....3 F1
  SWCK/CAS SR5 ....125 F3
  TYNE/NSHE NE30 ....71 D1
Camelford Ct
  BW/LEM/TK/HW NE15 ....59 E6
Camelot Cl SEA/MUR SR7 ....176 B2
Cameron Cl HAR/WTLS NE34 .....88 B5
Cameron Wk
  WICK/BNPF
  (off Metrocentre) NE16 ....78 B6
Camerton Pl WLSD/HOW NE28 ...52 A5
Camilla Rd BW/LEM/TK/HW NE15...56 B4
Camilla St GATE NE8 ....99 E1
Campbell Park Rd HEBB NE31 ...85 D2
Campbell Pl ELS/FEN NE4 ....79 F3
Campbell Rd SWCK/CAS SR5 ...123 E2
Campbell St HEBB NE31 ....84 C1
Camperdown WD/WHPE/BLK NE5...60 B5
Camperdown Av
  CLS/BIR/GTL DH3 ....153 F3
Campion Dr STLY/ANP DH9 .....130 C6
Campion Gdns FELL NE10 ....100 C5
Camp Rd WLSD/HOW NE28 ....67 D6
Campsie Cl WASHS NE38 ....138 A3
Campsie Crs TYNE/NSHE NE30 ...54 C3
Camp St PLEE/EAS SR8 ....201 E2
Camp Ter NSHW NE29 ....54 C6
Campville NSHW NE29 ....54 C6
Camsey Cl LGB/KIL NE12 ....48 B6
Canberra Av MONK NE25 ....53 F1
Canberra Dr HAR/WTLS NE34 ...87 D3
Canberra Rd MLFD/PNYW SR4...142 C2
Candelford Cl LGB/HTN NE7 ......65 F3
Candlish St SSH NE33 ....71 F4
Candlish Ter SEA/MUR SR7 ......177 D4
Canning St ELS/FEN NE4 ....78 C3
  HEBB NE31 ....85 D3
Cannock CLSW/PEL DH2 ....135 E4
  LGB/KIL NE12 ....35 F6
Cannon Dr LGB/HTN NE7 ....64 C2
Cannon St GATE NE8 ....3 F6
Cann Rd PLEE/EAS SR8 ....200 C6
Canon Cockin St
  ASHBK/HED/RY SR2 ....145 D2
Canon Gv JRW NE32 ....86 B1
Canonsfield Cl SUNDSW SR3 ...160 B3
Canterbury Av WLSD/HOW NE28...51 F6
Canterbury Cl CLS/BIR/GTL DH3...167 F4
  LGB/KIL NE12 ....48 C6
Canterbury Rd DHAM DH1 ....180 C4
  SWCK/CAS SR5 ....123 F2
Canterbury St BYK/HTN/WLK NE6...82 C2
  SSH NE33 ....71 F6
Canterbury Wy DIN/WO NE13 ...33 E4
Capetown Rd SWCK/CAS SR5 ...123 E2
Caplestone Cl WASHS NE38 .....138 A3
The Captains Rw SSH NE33 ......71 D6
Captains Whf SSH NE33 ....71 D3
Capulet Gv HAR/WTLS NE34 .....87 F5
Capulet Ter ASHBK/HED/RY SR2...145 D2
Caradoc Cl WASHS NE38 ....138 A3
Caragh Rd CLSW/PEL DH2 ....166 B1
Caraway Wk HAR/WTLS NE34 ...89 D5
Carden Av HAR/WTLS NE34 ......90 A3
Cardiff Sq SWCK/CAS SR5 ....123 E3
Cardiff St PLEE/EAS SR8 ....201 E2
Cardigan Gv TYNE/NSHE NE30...54 C1
Cardigan Rd SWCK/CAS SR5 ...123 E2
Cardigan Ter BYK/HTN/WLK NE6...82 C1
Cardinal Cl LGB/KIL NE12 ....48 C6
  WD/WHPE/BLK NE5 ....59 D3
Cardinals Cl SUNDSW SR3 ......160 B3
Cardonnel St NSHW NE29 ....70 C2
Cardwell St CLDN/WHIT/ROK SR6...127 D3
Careen Crs SUNDSW SR3 ....159 D1
Carham Av CRAM NE23 ....22 B2
Carham Cl GOS/KPK NE3 ....47 F6
Carisbrooke BDLGTN NE22 ....7 E2
Caris St GATE NE8 ....99 F2
Cariby Wy CRAM NE23 ....13 E4
Carlcroft Pl CRAM NE23 ....22 B3
Carley Hill Rd SWCK/CAS SR5 ...126 A1
Carley Rd SWCK/CAS SR5 ....126 A2
Carlingford Rd CLSW/PEL DH2 ...166 A1
Carlington Ct
  BLAY (off Factory Rd) NE21 ....77 D1
Carliol Sq CNUT NE1 ....3 F3
Carliol St CNUT NE1 ....3 E3
Carlisle Cl FELL * NE10 ....100 C1
Carlisle Crs HLS DH4 ....156 C1
Carlisle Rd DHAM DH1 ....181 D5
Carlisle St FELL NE10 ....100 C1

Carlisle Wy *LGB/KIL* NE12 ....**51** E3
Carlton Av *BLYTH* NE24 ....**16** B3
Carlton Cl *CLSW/PEL* DH2 ....**135** D4
　GOS/KPK* NE3 ....**62** C3
Carlton Ct *DUN/TMV* NE11 ....**98** B5
Carlton Crs *SUNDSW* SR3 ....**159** E1
Carlton Gdns
　BW/LEM/TK/HW NE15 ....**77** D1
Carlton House
　BDLGTN (off Glebe Rd) NE22 ....**7** E4
Carlton Rd *LGB/KIL* NE12 ....**49** F6
Carlton St *BLYTH* NE24 ....**11** E5
Carlton Ter *LWF/SPW/WRK* NE9..........**99** D5
　NSHW NE29.....................................**70** B1
　PLEE/EAS SR8 ....**200** A3
Carlyle Ct *WLSD/HOW* NE28 ....**68** C5
Carlyle Crs *WICK/BNPF* NE16 ....**95** F2
Carlyle St *WLSD/HOW* NE28 ....**68** C5
Carlyon St *ASHBK/HED/RY* SR2 ....**4** C6
Carmel Gv *CRAM* NE23 ....**13** F5
Carmel Rd *STLY/ANP* DH9 ....**147** F2
Carnaby Rd *BYK/HTN/WLK* NE6 ....**83** E4
Carnation Av *HLS* DH4 ....**155** F5
Carnation Ter *WICK/BNPF* NE16.........**96** A3
Carnegie Cl *HAR/WTLS* NE34 ....**88** D1
Carnegie St *ASHBK/HED/RY* SR2 ......**145** E4
Carnforth Cl *WLSD/HOW* NE28............**51** F5
Carnforth Gdns
　LWF/SPW/WRK NE9 ....**100** A6
　ROWG NE39 ....**111** D1
Carnforth Gn *GOS/KPK* NE3 ....**62** A2
Carnoustie *CLSW/PEL* DH2 ....**135** E5
　HAR/WTLS NE34 ....**89** E5
　WASHN NE37 ....**120** B1
Carnoustie Cl *LGB/HTN* NE7 ....**65** E2
Carnoustie Ct *MONK* NE25 ....**39** E5
Carnoustie Dr *HAR/WTLS* NE34 ....**89** E5
Carol Gdns *LGB/HTN* NE7 ....**65** D3
Caroline Gdns *WLSD/HOW* NE28 ....**68** C3
Caroline St *ELS/FEN* NE4....................**79** D4
　HLH DH5 ....**171** F6
　JRW NE32 ....**85** F1
　SEA/MUR SR7.................................**176** C3
Carol St *MLFD/PNYW* SR4 ....**125** F5
Carolyn Cl *LGB/KIL* NE12 ....**49** E6
Carolyn Crs *WBAY* NE26 ....**40** A3
Carolyn Wy *WBAY* NE26 ....**40** A3
Carpenter St *SSH* NE33 ....**71** D4
Carr Av *BDN/LAN/SAC* DH7 ....**203** D4
Carrfield Rd *GOS/KPK* NE3 ....**46** B6
Carr Hill Rd *LWF/SPW/WRK* NE9 ....**99** F3
Carr House Dr *DHAM* DH1 ....**180** B6
Carrhouse La *HLH* DH5 ....**173** D5
Carrick Dr *BLYTH* NE24 ....**16** C1
Carrigill Pl *LGB/KIL* NE12 ....**48** C6
Carrington Cl *CRAM* NE23 ....**36** B1
Carrmere Rd *ASHBK/HED/RY* SR2 ....**145** D5
Carrmyers *STLY/ANP* DH9 ....**146** A2
Carrock Cl *PLEE/EAS* SR8 ....**208** C5
Carrowmore Rd *CLSW/PEL* DH2 ....**166** A1
Carrsdale *DHAM* DH1 ....**196** C1
The Carrs
　DHAM (off Old Pit La) DH1 ....**180** B5
Carr St *BLYTH* NE24 ....**16** B3
　HEBB NE31 ....**84** C1
Carrsway *DHAM* DH1 ....**196** C1
Carrsyde Cl *WICK/BNPF* NE16.............**95** E5
Carsdale Rd *GOS/KPK* NE3 ....**61** C3
Cartington Ct *PLEE/EAS* SR8 ....**208** C5
Cartington Ct *GOS/KPK* NE3................**46** A5
Cartington Rd *DHAM* DH1 ....**194** B1
　NSHW NE29 ....**70** B1
Cartington Ter *BYK/HTN/WLK* NE6 ......**65** D5
Cartmel Ct *CLSW/PEL* DH2 ....**152** C6
Cartmel Gv *GATE* NE8 ....**98** C3
Cartmel Pk *FELL* NE10 ....**101** F1
Cartwright Rd *SWCK/CAS* SR5 ....**124** A3
Carville Ri *BYK/HTN/WLK* NE6 ....**82** B3
Carville Rd *WLSD/HOW* NE28 ....**67** D5
Carville St *FELL* NE10 ....**82** A6
Carvill Gdns *WLSD/HOW* NE28 ....**67** D6
Carvis Cl *BDN/LAN/SAC* DH7 ....**202** C5
Carwarding Pl *WD/WHPE/BLK* NE5......**61** E5
Caseton Cl *MONK* NE25 ....**39** E4
Caspian Av * NE32.................................**86** B3
Caspian Rd *SWCK/CAS* SR5 ....**123** E3
Caspian Sq *SWCK/CAS* SR5 ....**123** E3
Castellian Rd *SWCK/CAS* SR5 ....**124** B3
Casterton Gv *WD/WHPE/BLK* NE5.......**59** D3
Castle Chare *DHAM* DH1 ....**194** B4
Castle Cl *CLS/BIR/GTL* DH3 ....**153** F6
　HLH DH5 ....**186** A2
　WICK/BNPF NE16............................**95** F3
Castledale Av *BLYTH* NE24 ....**9** F6
Castledene Ct *GOS/KPK* NE3 ....**64** B2
Castle Dene Gv *HLS* DH4 ....**170** C2
Castleford Rd *SWCK/CAS* SR5 ....**123** E2
Castlegate Gdns *GATE* NE8.................**97** F1
Castle Leazes *JES* NE2 ....**80** A1
Castlenook Pl
　BW/LEM/TK/HW NE15 ....**77** E1
Castlereagh St *SUNDSW* SR3 ....**160** C1

Castlereigh Cl *HLS* DH4 ....**155** F5
Castle Riggs *CLSW/PEL* DH2 ....**153** D5
Castle Rd *WASHS* NE38 ....**137** F2
Castles Farm Rd *LGB/HTN* NE7 ....**64** A2
Castles Gn *LGB/KIL* NE12 ....**50** A1
Castleside Rd
　BW/LEM/TK/HW NE15 ....**77** F2
Castle Sq *SMOOR* NE27 ....**37** D6
Castle St *DIN/WO* NE13 ....**32** C6
　PLEE/EAS SR8 ....**201** E2
　SUND SR1 ....**4** B2
Castle St South *SWCK/CAS* SR5 ....**124** B3
Castleton Cl *CRAM* NE23 ....**13** F5
　JES NE2..**64** B4
Castleton Gv *JES* NE2 ....**64** B4
Castleton Rd *JRW* NE32 ....**86** B3
Castletown Rd *SWCK/CAS* SR5 ....**124** B3
Castletown Wy *SWCK/CAS* SR5 ....**124** B3
Castle Vw *BDN/LAN/SAC* DH7 ....**192** B5
　CLS/BIR/GTL DH3...........................**153** E3
　SWCK/CAS SR5.............................**124** A3
Castleway *DIN/WO* NE13 ....**31** D4
Castlewood Cl
　WD/WHPE/BLK NE5 ....**59** F4
Catchside Cl *WICK/BNPF* NE16 ....**95** F5
Catchwell Rd *STLY/ANP* DH9 ....**128** C6
Cateran Wy *CRAM* NE23 ....**22** B4
Caterhouse Rd *DHAM* DH1 ....**180** A6
Catharine St West
　MLFD/PNYW SR4 ....**125** F6
Cathedral Ct *GATE ** NE8 ....**81** F5
Cathedral Vw *BDN/LAN/SAC* DH7 .....**178** C2
　HLS DH4 ....**157** F5
Catherine Cookson Ct *SSH* NE33.......**72** A5
Catherine Rd *HLS* DH4 ....**157** F2
Catherine St *SSH* NE33 ....**71** F3
Catherine Ter *STLY/ANP* DH9 ....**131** E6
Catholic Rw *BDLGTN* NE22 ....**7** D4
Cato Sq *SWCK/CAS* SR5 ....**125** F2
Cato St *SWCK/CAS* SR5......................**125** F2
Catton Gv *WICK/BNPF* NE16 ....**114** A1
Catton Pl *WLSD/HOW* NE28 ....**52** A6
Cauldwell Av *HAR/WTLS* NE34 ....**89** E1
　MONK NE25 ....**53** F1
Cauldwell Cl *MONK* NE25 ....**40** A6
Cauldwell La *MONK* NE25 ....**39** F6
Cauldwell Pl *HAR/WTLS* NE34 ....**89** D1
Cauldwell Vls *HAR/WTLS* NE34...........**89** D1
Causeway *CLDN/WHIT/ROK* SR6 ......**126** C4
　LWF/SPW/WRK NE9 ....**100** A4
The Causeway
　BW/LEM/TK/HW NE15 ....**57** F5
　LWF/SPW/WRK NE9 ....**99** F2
Causey Bank *CNUT* NE1 ....**3** F4
Causey Dr *STLY/ANP* DH9 ....**131** F6
Causey Rd *STLY/ANP* DH9 ....**131** F4
Causey St *GOS/KPK* NE3 ....**63** C2
Causey Wy *STLY/ANP* DH9 ....**131** E5
Cavalier Vw *HEBB* NE31 ....**84** C1
Cavalier Wy *SUNDSW* SR3 ....**160** B1
Cavell Sq *PLEE/EAS* SR8 ....**200** C1
Cavendish Ct *BDN/LAN/SAC* DH7 .....**202** C5
Cavendish Pl *JES* NE2 ....**64** B5
　SUNDSW SR3 ....**160** B1
Cavendish Rd *JES* NE2 ....**64** B5
Caversham Rd
　WD/WHPE/BLK NE5 ....**59** D3
Cawburn Cl *LGB/HTN* NE7 ....**66** A3
Cawdell Ct *TYNE/NSHE ** NE30............**71** D1
Cawnpore Sq *MLFD/PNYW* SR4 ....**125** D2
Cawthorne Ter *NSHW ** NE29...............**54** C4
Caynham Cl *NSHW* NE29 ....**54** A4
Cayton Gv *WD/WHPE/BLK* NE5 ....**59** D3
Cecil Ct *PONT/DH* NE20 ....**28** B4
　WLSD/HOW NE28 ....**67** D6
Cecil St *NSHW* NE29 ....**70** C1
Cedar Av *CLSW/PEL* DH2 ....**165** E6
Cedar Cl *BDLGTN* NE22 ....**7** E2
　DHAM DH1....................................**195** F3
Cedar Crs *DUN/TMV* NE11 ....**97** E3
　LWF/SPW/WRK NE9 ....**99** E6
　SEA/MUR SR7................................**176** B4
Cedar Dr *DHAM* DH1 ....**205** D3
Cedar Gv *CLDN/WHIT/ROK* SR6 ....**91** E6
　HAR/WTLS NE34 ....**89** D5
　HEBB NE31 ....**85** D5
　RYTON NE40 ....**74** B3
　WLSD/HOW NE28 ....**67** F5
Cedar Rd *BLAY* NE21 ....**76** B6
　ELS/FEN NE4 ....**78** C1
Cedars *ASHBK/HED/RY* SR2 ....**144** C2
Cedars Crs *SEA/MUR* SR7 ....**188** C3
Cedars Gn *LWF/SPW/WRK* NE9 ....**117** F1
Cedars Pk *ASHBK/HED/RY* SR2 ....**145** D3
The Cedars *ASHBK/HED/RY* SR2 ....**144** C2
　WICK/BNPF NE16 ....**96** A6
Cedartree Gdns *MONK* NE25 ....**54** A1
Cedarway *FELL* NE10 ....**101** D5
Cedar Wy *LGB/KIL ** NE12 ....**50** A4
Cedarwood Av
　BYK/HTN/WLK NE6 ....**66** C5
Cedarwood Gv
　ASHBK/HED/RY SR2 ....**144** B4
Cedric Crs *ASHBK/HED/RY* SR2........**144** A2

Celadon Cl *BW/LEM/TK/HW* NE15 ......**59** E6
Celandine Cl *GOS/KPK* NE3 ....**47** F5
Celandine Wy *FELL* NE10 ....**100** C4
Celtic Cl *CLDN/WHIT/ROK* SR6 ....**107** D1
Cemetery Ap *HAR/WTLS* NE34 ....**72** A6
Cemetery Rd *GATE* NE8 ....**99** E1
　JRW NE32.......................................**86** B3
　STLY/ANP DH9 ....**148** B1
Centenary Av *HAR/WTLS* NE34 ....**89** F2
Centenary Ct *ELS/FEN* NE4.................**79** E4
Central Av *BDN/LAN/SAC* DH7 ....**203** E5
　CLDN/WHIT/ROK SR6 ....**109** D2
　HAR/WTLS NE34 ....**89** E2
　NSHW NE29 ....**70** A1
Central Gdns *HAR/WTLS* NE34 ....**89** E2
Central Station
　CNUT (off Neville St) NE1 ....**2** C5
Centurian Wy *BDLGTN* NE22 ....**7** D2
Centurion Rd
　BW/LEM/TK/HW NE15 ....**60** A6
Centurion Wy
　BW/LEM/TK/HW NE15 ....**56** A4
　LWF/SPW/WRK NE9 ....**100** A4
Ceolfrid Ter *JRW* NE32.........................**86** B4
Chacombe *WASHS* NE38 ....**138** B3
Chadderton Dr
　WD/WHPE/BLK NE5 ....**59** D3
Chadwick St *WLSD/HOW* NE28 ....**67** D5
Chadwick Wk *GATE* NE8 ....**80** B6
Chaffinch Wy *LGB/KIL* NE12 ....**35** E6
Chainbridge Rd *BLAY* NE21 ....**76** C5
Chain Bridge Rd *BLAY* NE21 ....**77** E5
The Chains *DHAM* DH1 ....**194** C4
Chalfont Gv *MLFD/PNYW* SR4 ....**141** E4
Chalfont Rd *BYK/HTN/WLK* NE6 ....**83** E4
Chalfont Wy *BDN/LAN/SAC* DH7 ....**203** E4
Chalford Rd *SWCK/CAS* SR5 ....**126** A2
Chamberlain St *BLYTH* NE24 ....**11** E6
Chandler Cl *DHAM* DH1 ....**195** F5
Chandlers Ford *HLS* DH4 ....**139** E6
Chandlers Quay
　BYK/HTN/WLK NE6 ....**82** B4
Chandless St *GATE ** NE8.....................**81** E5
Chandos *SUNDSW* SR3 ....**160** C4
Chandos St *GATE* NE8 ....**99** E2
Chandra Pl *WD/WHPE/BLK* NE5...........**61** D4
Chantry Cl *SUNDSW* SR3 ....**160** A3
Chantry Dr *DIN/WO* NE13 ....**33** D4
Chapel Av *WICK/BNPF* NE16 ....**112** A6
Chapel Cl *GOS/KPK* NE3 ....**47** F3
Chapel Ct *RDHAMSE* DH6 ....**197** F5
Chapel Hill Rd *PLEE/EAS* SR8 ....**209** D1
Chapel House Dr
　WD/WHPE/BLK NE5 ....**59** E5
Chapel House Ov
　BW/LEM/TK/HW NE15 ....**59** E5
Chapel Ms *DHAM* DH1 ....**195** D4
Chapel Rd *JRW* NE32 ....**86** A1
Chapel Rw *HLS* DH4 ....**157** E3
Chapel St *HLH* DH5 ....**171** F6
　NSHW NE29 ....**70** A1
　STLY/ANP DH9 ....**129** F4
Chapel Vw *HLS* DH4 ....**183** E3
　ROWG NE39 ....**111** D1
Chapman St *CLDN/WHIT/ROK* SR6....**109** D6
Chapter Rw *SSH* NE33 ....**71** E3
The Chare *CNUT ** NE1...........................**2** C2
Charlaw Cl *BDN/LAN/SAC* DH7 ....**164** A6
Charlbury Cl *LWF/SPW/WRK* NE9 .....**119** E3
Charlcote Crs *BOL* NE36 ....**106** C3
Charles Av *GOS/KPK* NE3 ....**46** A6
　LGB/KIL NE12.................................**48** A5
Charles Baker Wk *HAR/WTLS* NE34....**90** A2
Charles Ct *BYK/HTN/WLK ** NE6 ....**82** B1
Charles Dr *CRAM* NE23 ....**35** D2
Charles St *BOLCOL* NE35 ....**105** E2
　CLDN/WHIT/ROK SR6 ....**126** C4
　DIN/WO NE13..................................**32** C5
　GATE NE8 ....**81** E6
　PLEE/EAS SR8 ....**201** E2
　STLY/ANP DH9 ....**148** A4
　SUND SR1 ....**4** D1
Charleswood *GOS/KPK* NE3 ....**47** F4
Charlotte Cl *ELS/FEN* NE4...................**80** A5
Charlotte Ms *CNUT ** NE1 ....**2** B4
Charlotte Sq *CNUT* NE1 ....**2** B4
Charlotte St *SSH* NE33.........................**71** E3
　STLY/ANP DH9 ....**148** A4
　TYNE/NSHE NE30 ....**71** D1
　WLSD/HOW NE28 ....**67** E4
Charlotte Ter *SSH ** NE33 ....**71** F4
Charlton Gv *CLDN/WHIT/ROK* SR6 ....**107** F2
Charlton Rd *SWCK/CAS* SR5 ....**126** B1
Charlton St *BW/LEM/TK/HW* NE15 ......**76** C2
Charlton Wk *GATE* NE8 ....**98** B1
Charman St *SUND* SR1 ....**4** C2
Charminster Gdns
　BYK/HTN/WLK NE6 ....**65** E4
Charnwood Av *LGB/KIL* NE12 ....**48** C6
Charnwood Ct
　SSH (off Leighton St) NE33 ....**72** A4
Charter Dr *SUNDSW* SR3 ....**159** E1
Chasedale Crs *BLYTH* NE24 ....**9** F5
Chase Farm Dr *BLYTH* NE24 ....**9** E4

Chase Mdw *BLYTH* NE24 ....9 E6
Chase Ms *BLYTH* NE24 ....9 E5
The Chase *LGB/KIL* NE12 ....48 C2
  NSHW NE29 ....54 B6
  WASHS NE38 ....137 E5
Chatham Cl *MONK* NE25 ....37 F1
Chatham Rd *SWCK/CAS* SR5 ....123 F2
Chathill Cl *MONK* NE25 ....39 E5
Chathill Ter *BYK/HTN/WLK* NE6 ....83 E3
Chatsworth Ct *SSH* NE33 ....71 F3
Chatsworth Crs *MLFD/PNYW* SR4 ......143 F2
Chatsworth Dr *BDLGTN* NE22 ....8 B1
Chatsworth Gdns
  BYK/HTN/WLK NE6 ....82 C4
  WD/WHPE/BLK NE5 ....60 B3
Chatsworth Pl *WICK/BNPF* NE16 ....95 F5
Chatsworth Rd *BLAY* NE21 ....86 B3
Chatsworth St *MLFD/PNYW* SR4 ....143 F1
Chatsworth St South
  MLFD/PNYW SR4 ....143 F1
Chatton Av *SWCK/CAS* SR5 ....125 F1
Chatton Av *CRAM* NE23 ....22 B3
  HAR/WTLS NE34 ....73 D6
Chatton Cl *CLSW/PEL* DH2 ....165 F1
Chatton Wd *WLSD/HOW* NE28 ....69 E5
Chatton Wynd *GOS/KPK* NE3 ....46 C5
Chaucer Av *HAR/WTLS* NE34 ....87 F5
Chaucer Cl *GATE* NE8 ....81 F6
  STLY/ANP DH9 ....148 C2
Chaucer Rd *WICK/BNPF* NE16 ....95 F2
Chaytor Gv *SUND* SR1 ....5 F4
Chaytor St *JRW* NE32 ....69 D6
Cheadle Av *CRAM* NE23 ....13 F5
  WLSD/HOW NE28 ....51 F6
Cheadle Rd *SWCK/CAS* SR5 ....123 F2
Cheam Cl *WICK/BNPF* NE16 ....96 A5
Cheam Rd *SWCK/CAS* SR5 ....123 F2
Chedder Ct *STLY/ANP* DH9 ....146 B5
Cheeseburn Gdns
  WD/WHPE/BLK NE5 ....61 G3
Cheldon Cl *MONK* NE25 ....39 E4
Chelford Cl *WLSD/HOW* NE28 ....52 A5
Chelmsford Gv *JES* NE2 ....81 F1
Chelmsford Rd *SWCK/CAS* SR5 ....123 F2
Chelmsford Sq *SWCK/CAS* SR5 ....123 F2
Chelsea Gdns *GATE* NE8 ....100 A2
Chelsea Gv *ELS/FEN* NE4 ....79 F3
Cheltenham Dr *BOLCOL* NE35 ....87 D6
Cheltenham Rd *SWCK/CAS* SR5 ....123 F2
Cheltenham Sq *SWCK/CAS* SR5 ....123 F2
Cheltenham Ter
  BYK/HTN/WLK NE6 ....82 A1
Chelton Cl *DIN/WO* NE13 ....33 D6
Chepstow Gdns *GATE* NE8 ....98 B3
Chepstow Rd
  BW/LEM/TK/HW NE15 ....77 E2
Chepstow St *MLFD/PNYW* SR4 ....126 A6
Cherry Banks *CLS/BIR/GTL* DH3 ....153 F3
Cherry Blossom Wy *WASHN* NE37 ......122 A4
Cherryburn Gdns *ELS/FEN* NE4 ....62 A6
Cherry Gv *LGB/KIL* NE12 ....35 E6
Cherry Pk *BDN/LAN/SAC* DH7 ....202 C5
Cherrytree Cl *LGB/KIL* NE12 ....50 B2
Cherrytree Ct *BDLGTN* NE22 ....8 C2
Cherry Tree Dr *BDLGTN* NE22 ....7 E3
Cherrytree Dr *WICK/BNPF* NE16 ....96 B2
Cherrytree Gdns
  LWF/SPW/WRK NE9 ....99 F6
  MONK NE25 ....54 B1
Cherry Trees *BLYTH* NE24 ....10 C6
Cherry Tree Sq
  ASHBK/HED/RY SR2 ....145 D1
Cherry Wy *HLS* DH4 ....170 A1
Cherrywood *BYK/HTN/WLK* NE6 ....66 A5
Cherrywood Gdns *SUNDSW* SR3 ....161 D1
Cherwell *WASHN* NE37 ....121 E4
Cherwell Rd *PLEE/EAS* SR8 ....208 A3
Chesham Gdns
  WD/WHPE/BLK NE5 ....59 D4
Cheshire Av *CLS/BIR/GTL* DH3 ....136 B5
Cheshire Dr *DHAM* DH1 ....196 B4
Cheshire Gdns *WLSD/HOW* NE28 ....66 C3
Cheshire Gv *HAR/WTLS* NE34 ....90 A1
The Chesils *LGB/KIL* NE12 ....64 C1
Chesmond Dr *BLAY* NE21 ....76 A5
Chessar Av *WD/WHPE/BLK* NE5 ....61 D4
Chester Av *WLSD/HOW* NE28 ....68 B3
Chester Ct *LGB/KIL* NE12 ....49 D6
Chester Crs *JES* NE2 ....81 E1
  SUND SR1 ....126 A1
Chesterfield Rd *ELS/FEN* NE4 ....79 E4
Chester Gdns *HAR/WTLS* NE34 ....89 D1
Chester Gv *BLYTH* NE24 ....10 B6
  CRAM NE23 ....36 A1
Chester Ov *ASHBK/HED/RY* SR2 ....126 A6
Chester Pl *GATE* NE8 ....80 C1
  PLEE/EAS SR8 ....200 A6
Chester Rd *CLS/BIR/GTL* DH3 ....154 C3
  HLS DH4 ....155 F5
  MLFD/PNYW SR4 ....141 D4
  STLY/ANP DH9 ....143 D1
Chester Road Est *STLY/ANP* DH9 ....148 C1
Chesters Av *LGB/KIL* NE12 ....48 C6
Chesters Pk *LWF/SPW/WRK* NE9 ....99 E4

The Chesters *MONK* NE25 ....39 F4
  WD/WHPE/BLK NE5 ....59 E5
Chester St *HLS* DH4 ....157 F6
  JES NE2 ....81 E1
  MLFD/PNYW SR4 ....125 F6
Chester St East *MLFD/PNYW* SR4 ......126 A6
Chester St West *MLFD/PNYW* SR4 ......125 F6
Chester Ter *SUND* SR1 ....126 A6
Chester Ter North
  MLFD/PNYW SR4 ....126 A6
Chesterton Rd *HAR/WTLS* NE34 ....88 A4
Chesterwood Dr *WLSD/HOW* NE28 ....66 C4
Chesterwood Ter *FELL* * NE10 ....102 A1
Chestnut Av *BLYTH* NE24 ....10 C3
  MONK NE25 ....40 B6
  WD/WHPE/BLK NE5 ....62 A4
  WICK/BNPF NE16 ....96 A5
Chestnut Cl *JRW* NE32 ....104 C1
  LGB/KIL NE12 ....35 D6
Chestnut Crs *SWCK/CAS* SR5 ....125 E1
Chestnut Gdns *GATE* NE8 ....98 B3
Chestnut Gv *HAR/WTLS* NE34 ....89 D4
Chestnut Gv *WLSD/HOW* NE28 ....67 E5
Cheswick Dr *GOS/KPK* NE3 ....47 F6
Cheveley Wk *DHAM* DH1 ....196 C3
Chevin Cl *BYK/HTN/WLK* NE6 ....66 C5
Chevington *FELL* NE10 ....101 F4
Chevington Gdns
  WD/WHPE/BLK NE5 ....61 F5
Chevington Gv *MONK* NE25 ....39 F3
Cheviot Cl *WASHN* NE37 ....119 F6
Cheviot Ct *SEA/MUR* SR7 ....175 F2
  STLY/ANP DH9 ....146 B5
Cheviot Gdns *DUN/TMV* NE11 ....97 F3
  SEA/MUR SR7 ....175 F2
Cheviot Gra *CRAM* NE23 ....35 E4
Cheviot Gn *DUN/TMV* NE11 ....97 F2
Cheviot La *ASHBK/HED/RY* SR2 ....162 A1
Cheviot Mt *BYK/HTN/WLK* NE6 ....82 B2
Cheviot Pl *PLEE/EAS* SR8 ....208 A2
Cheviot Rd *BLAY* NE21 ....94 B1
  HAR/WTLS NE34 ....72 C6
  JRW NE32 ....85 E4
Cheviot St *MLFD/PNYW* SR4 ....125 E5
Cheviot Vw *CLSW/PEL* DH2 ....165 F2
  DIN/WO NE13 ....32 C4
  SMOOR (off West St) NE27 ....51 F3
The Chevron
  BYK/HTN/WLK * NE6 ....82 A3
Chevy Cha
  CNUT (off Eldon Sq) NE1 ....2 C2
Chevychase Ct *SEA/MUR* SR7 ....162 B6
The Cheyne *SUNDSW* SR3 ....160 C3
Chichester Av *CRAM* NE23 ....13 E6
Chichester Cl *GATE* * NE8 ....81 D6
  GOS/KPK NE3 ....45 E5
Chichester Gv *BDLGTN* NE22 ....7 E2
Chichester Pl *SSH* NE33 ....71 E6
Chichester Rd
  CLDN/WHIT/ROK SR6 ....109 D6
  DHAM DH1 ....180 C5
  SSH NE33 ....71 F5
Chichester Rd East *SSH* NE33 ....71 F5
Chicken Rd *WLSD/HOW* NE28 ....66 C3
Chick's La *CLDN/WHIT/ROK* SR6 ....109 D1
Chigwell Cl *HLS* DH4 ....157 D1
Chilcote *FELL* NE10 ....100 C3
Chilcrosse *FELL* NE10 ....101 E3
Chilham Ct *NSHW* NE29 ....53 D4
Chillingham Cl *BLYTH* NE24 ....16 A1
Chillingham Ct
  BYK/HTN/WLK * NE6 ....82 B1
  NSHW NE29 ....69 F2
Chillingham Dr *CLSW/PEL* DH2 ....165 F2
  NSHW NE29 ....69 F2
Chillingham Gv *PLEE/EAS* SR8 ....207 F4
Chillingham Rd *BYK/HTN/WLK* NE6 ......65 E5
  DHAM DH1 ....180 C6
Chillingham Ter *JRW* NE32 ....86 C4
Chilside Rd *FELL* NE10 ....100 C3
Chiltern Cl *WASHN* NE38 ....138 A3
Chiltern Dr *LGB/KIL* NE12 ....49 D3
Chiltern Gdns *DUN/TMV* NE11 ....97 F3
Chiltern Rd *NSHW* NE29 ....54 B2
Chilton Gdns *HLS* DH4 ....169 F2
Chilton Garth *PLEE/EAS* SR8 ....209 E3
Chilton St *SWCK/CAS* SR5 ....126 B3
Chimside Ter *STLY/ANP* DH9 ....146 A5
China St *ASHBK/HED/RY* SR2 ....145 D2
Chipchase Av *CRAM* NE23 ....22 A3
Chipchase Cl *BDLGTN* NE22 ....6 C3
Chipchase Ct *HLS* DH4 ....168 C1
  MONK NE25 ....24 B2
  SEA/MUR SR7 ....162 B6
Chipchase Crs *WD/WHPE/BLK* NE5 ....60 A3
Chipchase Ter *JRW* NE32 ....86 A3
Chippendale Pl *JES* NE2 ....63 D6
Chirton Av *HAR/WTLS* NE34 ....90 B2
  NSHW NE29 ....70 B1
Chirton Dene Quays *NSHW* NE29 ....70 B4
Chirton Dene Wy *NSHW* NE29 ....70 B3
Chirton Gn *NSHW* NE29 ....70 B1
Chirton Gv *HAR/WTLS* NE34 ....90 B2
Chirton Hill Dr *NSHW* NE29 ....53 E5

Chirton La *NSHW* NE29 ....54 A6
Chirton West Vw *NSHW* NE29 ....70 B1
Chirton Wynd *BYK/HTN/WLK* NE6 ....82 B3
Chislehurst Rd *HLS* DH4 ....157 D1
Chiswick Gdns *GATE* NE8 ....99 F2
Chiswick Rd *MONK* NE25 ....24 C6
  SWCK/CAS SR5 ....123 F2
Chollerford Av *MONK* NE25 ....41 D6
  NSHW NE29 ....53 E6
Chollerford Cl *GOS/KPK* NE3 ....62 C2
Chollerford Ms *MONK* NE25 ....25 E6
Chollerton Dr *BDLGTN* NE22 ....7 F3
  LGB/KIL NE12 ....50 C5
Choppington Rd *STKFD/GP* NE62 ....7 E1
Chorley Pl *BYK/HTN/WLK* NE6 ....83 D3
Chowdene Bank *DUN/TMV* NE11 ....117 D2
Christal Ter *CLDN/WHIT/ROK* SR6 ....109 D2
Christchurch Pl *PLEE/EAS* SR8 ....208 B3
Christle Ter *BYK/HTN/WLK* NE6 ....83 E3
Christon Cl *GOS/KPK* NE3 ....64 A1
Christon Rd *GOS/KPK* NE3 ....63 E1
Christon Wy *FELL* NE10 ....84 A6
Christopher Rd *BYK/HTN/WLK* NE6 ....83 D1
Chudleigh Gdns
  WD/WHPE/BLK NE5 ....59 D4
Church Av *GOS/KPK* NE3 ....63 F1
Church Bank
  BW/LEM/TK/HW NE15 ....75 C1
  JRW NE32 ....86 C1
  STLY/ANP DH9 ....148 B1
  SWCK/CAS SR5 ....125 F3
  WLSD/HOW NE28 ....67 F4
Church Chare *PONT/DH* NE20 ....28 B3
  WICK/BNPF NE16 ....96 A3
Church Cl *BDLGTN* NE22 ....7 E4
  DIN/WO NE13 ....31 D3
  MONK NE25 ....39 E6
  PLEE/EAS SR8 ....209 D5
  SEA/MUR SR7 ....176 B2
Church Ct *BDLGTN* NE22 ....7 E4
  FELL * NE10 ....100 C1
  SEA/MUR SR7 ....175 F2
Churchdown Cl *BOLCOL* NE35 ....87 D6
Church Dr *LWF/SPW/WRK* NE9 ....99 F4
Churcher Gdns *WLSD/HOW* NE28 ....66 C2
Church Flatt *PONT/DH* NE20 ....28 B3
Church Gn *SEA/MUR* SR7 ....176 B2
Churchill Av *DHAM* DH1 ....195 E4
  MONK NE25 ....54 A1
  SWCK/CAS SR5 ....125 F2
Churchill Gdns *JES* NE2 ....64 C5
Churchill Ms *BYK/HTN/WLK* NE6 ....82 B5
Churchill Sq *DHAM* DH1 ....195 E3
  HLS DH4 ....170 A2
Churchill St *SUND* SR1 ....5 E4
  WLSD/HOW NE28 ....68 B2
Church La *BDLGTN* NE22 ....7 F4
  CLDN/WHIT/ROK SR6 ....109 E2
  DHAM DH1 ....194 C6
  GOS/KPK NE3 ....63 F1
  LWF/SPW/WRK NE9 ....100 A4
  SEA/MUR SR7 ....188 A1
Church Pl *FELL* NE10 ....100 C1
Church Ri *RYTON* NE40 ....75 D3
  WICK/BNPF NE16 ....96 A3
Church Rd *BW/LEM/TK/HW* NE15 ....75 C1
  HLH DH5 ....171 F4
  LWF/SPW/WRK NE9 ....99 E6
  SMOOR NE27 ....37 E5
Church St *BDN/LAN/SAC* DH7 ....178 A1
  BLAY NE21 ....93 F1
  BYK/HTN/WLK NE6 ....83 F4
  DHAM DH1 ....194 C6
  DUN/TMV NE11 ....97 F1
  GATE NE8 ....3 F6
  HEBB NE31 ....84 C1
  HLH DH5 ....171 D2
  HLS DH4 ....171 D2
  HLS DH4 ....183 F2
  MLFD/PNYW SR4 ....123 F6
  SEA/MUR SR7 ....188 A1
  STLY/ANP DH9 ....146 B4
  STLY/ANP DH9 ....148 B1
  SWCK/CAS SR5 ....126 A2
  TYNE/NSHE NE30 ....55 D6
  HLS DH4 ....113 F4
Church St East *SUND* SR1 ....5 F1
Church Street Head *DHAM* DH1 ....194 B6
Church St North
  CLDN/WHIT/ROK SR6 ....126 C3
  DHAM DH1 ....194 C6
Church Street Vis *DHAM* * DH1 ....105 D1
Church Vw *BOLCOL* NE35 ....105 D1
  CLSW/PEL DH2 ....179 F1
  SUNDSW SR3 ....160 C1
  WLSD/HOW NE28 ....67 F4
Church Wk *PLEE/EAS* SR8 ....199 F3
Church Wy *MONK* NE25 ....38 C4
  NSHW NE29 ....54 C6
  SSH NE33 ....71 F3
Church Wynd *RDHAMSE* DH6 ....197 E5
Churston Cl *HLS* DH4 ....157 E4
Cinderford Cl *BOLCOL* NE35 ....86 C6
Cirencester St *MLFD/PNYW* SR4 ....126 A5
Citadel East *LGB/KIL* NE12 ....49 F1

Citadel West LGB/KIL NE12......................49 F1
City Rd CNUT NE1...................................3 F4
City Wy SUNDSW SR3.........................159 D3
Civic Ct HEBB NE31................................85 E3
Clacton Rd SWCK/CAS SR5..................123 E3
Clanfield Ct LGB/HTN NE7.....................64 B2
Clanny St SUND SR1..................................4 A3
Clanton Cl FELL NE10...........................102 B3
Clapham Av BYK/HTN/WLK NE6..............82 C3
Clappersgate PLEE/EAS SR8................199 E3
Clara St ELS/FEN NE4..............................78 C4
   SEA/MUR SR7...............................176 A2
Claremont Av
   BW/LEM/TK/HW NE15.......................59 F6
   CLDN/WHIT/ROK SR6.....................127 D1
Claremont Crs WBAY NE26......................40 C2
Claremont Dr HLH DH4.........................156 C2
Claremont Gdns BOL NE36...................106 C3
   WBAY NE26.......................................40 B4
Claremont North Av GATE * NE8............81 D6
Claremont Pl GATE * NE8.......................99 D1
   JES* NE2...80 B1
Claremont Rd
   CLDN/WHIT/ROK SR6.....................127 D1
   JES NE2...62 C6
   WBAY NE26.......................................40 A2
Claremont South Av GATE * NE8...........81 D6
Claremont St GATE * NE8........................99 D1
   JES...80 B1
Claremont Ter ASHBK/HED/RY SR2.......10 A5
   BLYTH NE24.......................................10 C5
   FELL* NE10..84 A6
   JES NE2...80 B1
Claremount Ct BOL NE36......................106 A3
Clarence St JES NE2.................................3 C2
   SWCK/CAS SR5...............................125 F2
   WBAY NE26.......................................26 C3
Clarence Ter CLS/BIR/GTL DH3............153 E5
Clarence Wk JES NE2................................3 G1
Clarendon Sq SWCK/CAS SR5..............126 A1
Clare Rd PLEE/EAS SR8.........................208 A3
Clarewood Av HAR/WTLS NE34...............72 C6
Clarewood Gn ELS/FEN NE4....................80 A2
Clarewood Pl WD/WHPE/BLK NE5..........61 E6
Clarke Ter FELL NE10.............................100 B2
   SEA/MUR SR7...................................174 B6
Clarks Hill Wk
   BW/LEM/TK/HW NE15.......................75 E1
Clasper St ELS/FEN NE4..........................80 A5
Clasper Wy WICK/BNPF NE16..................77 E5
Claude St HLH DH5.................................185 F1
Claude Ter SEA/MUR SR7......................188 C1
Claudius Ct SSH NE33..............................71 E2
Claverdon St WD/WHPE/BLK NE5...........59 D2
Clavering Pl CNUT NE1..............................2 D5
Clavering Rd WICK/BNPF NE16...............96 A1
Clavering Sq DUN/TMV * NE11................97 E2
Clavering St WLSD/HOW * NE28..............69 D5
Clavering Wy BLAY NE21..........................93 D1
Claverley Dr SMOOR NE27.......................58 C5
Claxheugh Rd MLFD/PNYW SR4............124 A5
Claxton St PLEE/EAS SR8......................209 F1
Clay La DHAM DH1.................................193 F6
Claymere Rd ASHBK/HED/RY SR2.........145 D3
Claypath Ct DHAM DH1..........................194 B4
Claypath La SSH NE33.............................71 E4
Claypath Rd HLH DH5............................185 F2
Claypath St BYK/HTN/WLK NE6...............81 F2
Claypool Ct HAR/WTLS NE34...................88 B3
Clayton Park Sq JES NE2........................64 A6
Clayton Rd JES NE2.................................63 F6
   JRW NE32..86 A1
Clayton St BDLGTN NE22...........................8 C2
   CNUT NE1...2 C4
Clayton St West CNUT NE1........................2 B5
Clayton Ter FELL * NE10........................100 B4
Claywortn Rd GOS/KPK NE3....................47 D5
Cleadon Hill Dr HAR/WTLS NE34............89 F5
Cleadon Hill Rd HAR/WTLS NE34............90 A4
Cleadon La BOL NE36.............................107 D2
   CLDN/WHIT/ROK SR6.....................108 B1
Cleadon Lea CLDN/WHIT/ROK SR6......107 E1
Cleadon Mdw
   CLDN/WHIT/ROK SR6.....................107 F1
Cleadon St BYK/HTN/WLK NE6................83 D2
Cleadon Towers
   HAR/WTLS (off the Lonnen) NE34......90 A3
Cleasby Gdns LWF/SPW/WRK NE9..........99 E4
Cleaside Av HAR/WTLS NE34....................89 F4
Cleehill Dr NSHW NE29............................54 A4
Cleeve Ct WASHS NE38..........................138 B1
Cleghorn St BYK/HTN/WLK NE6..............65 E6
Clement Av BDLGTN NE22..........................8 B3
Clementina ASHBK/HED/RY SR2...............5 F5
Clement St LWF/SPW/WRK NE9...............99 E5
Clennel Av HEBB NE31.............................84 C3
Clent Wy LGB/KIL NE12.............................48 D3
Clephan St DUN/TMV NE11......................97 E1
Clervaux Ter JRW NE32............................86 B2
Cleveland Av WD/WHPE/BLK DH2.........153 D6
   NSHW NE29.......................................54 B5
Cleveland Ct SSH NE33............................71 D4
Cleveland Crs NSHW NE29.......................54 C6
Cleveland Dr WASHS NE38....................138 A3

Cleveland Gdns LGB/HTN NE7.................64 C2
   WLSD/HOW NE28.............................69 D3
Cleveland Ms DUN/TMV NE11.................97 F1
Cleveland Pl PLEE/EAS SR8...................208 A2
Cleveland Rd MLFD/PNYW SR4.............148 E2
Cleveland St SSH NE33............................71 F2
Cleveland Ter NSHW * NE29....................54 B6
Cleveland Vw
   CLDN/WHIT/ROK SR6.....................109 D4
Clickemin PONT/DH NE20........................28 C4
Clifford Rd BYK/HTN/WLK NE6................82 C1
Cliffords Fort TYNE/NSHE NE30..............55 E6
Clifford St BLAY NE21..............................76 B5
   BYK/HTN/WLK NE6............................82 A2
   CLS/BIR/GTL DH3............................166 B1
   MLFD/PNYW SR4............................125 F6
Clifford Ter CLS/BIR/GTL DH3................166 B1
Cliff Rd ASHBK/HED/RY SR2..................162 C2
Cliff Rw WBAY NE26.................................41 E6
Cliffside HAR/WTLS NE34.........................90 B2
Clifton Av HAR/WTLS NE34......................89 D1
   WLSD/HOW NE28.............................67 D4
Cliftonbourne Av
   CLDN/WHIT/ROK SR6.....................109 D6
Clifton Cl RYTON NE40............................75 D4
Clifton Ct GOS/KPK NE3..........................45 F5
Clifton Gdns BLYTH NE24........................16 C2
   LWF/SPW/WRK NE9..........................99 E3
   NSHW NE29.......................................70 A3
Clifton Gv MONK NE25.............................40 A4
Clifton Rd CLDN/WHIT/ROK SR6...........127 D1
   CRAM NE23.......................................22 B3
   ELS/FEN NE4.....................................79 D3
Clifton Sq PLEE/EAS SR8.......................208 C1
Clifton Ter LGB/KIL NE12..........................49 F5
   SSH NE33...88 B1
   WBAY NE26.......................................41 D5
Cliftonville Av ELS/FEN NE4.....................79 D3
Cliftonville Gdns WBAY NE26...................40 C4
Clinton Pl GOS/KPK NE3...........................47 D2
Clipsham Cl LGB/KIL NE12.......................49 D6
Clipstone Av BYK/HTN/WLK NE6.............83 D5
Clipstone Cl BW/LEM/TK/HW NE15.........57 E4
Clive St HAR/WTLS NE34..........................87 F4
   NSHW NE29.......................................71 D1
Clockburn Lonnen
   WICK/BNPF NE16..............................94 C5
Clockburnsyde Cl
   WICK/BNPF NE16..............................95 D5
Clockmill Rd GATE NE8............................97 F1
Clockstand Cl
   CLDN/WHIT/ROK SR6.....................127 D2
Clockwell St SWCK/CAS SR5..................125 E3
Cloister Av HAR/WTLS NE34.....................87 F3
Cloister Garth LGB/HTN NE7.....................64 B1
The Cloisters ASHBK/HED/RY NE7........144 C2
   LGB/HTN NE7.....................................64 B1
Cloister Wk JRW NE32.............................86 B1
Closeburn St SUNDSW SR3...................161 D2
Closefield Gv MONK NE25........................40 A6
Close St MLFD/PNYW SR4.......................125 F5
   SWCK/CAS* SR5.............................126 A3
The Close BLAY NE21...............................93 F1
   CLDN/WHIT/ROK SR6.....................107 E1
   CRAM NE23.......................................36 B1
   HLH DH5..171 E2
   PONT/DH NE20.................................28 A5
   WD/WHPE/BLK NE5............................60 A4
   WICK/BNPF NE16............................112 B5
Cloth Market CNUT NE1.............................2 D4
Clousden Dr LGB/KIL NE12......................50 A3
Clousden Gra LGB/KIL NE12....................50 A3
Clovelly Av ELS/FEN NE4..........................79 D3
Clovelly Gdns BDLGTN NE22.....................7 E4
   WBAY NE26.......................................40 C4
Clovelly Pl JRW NE32...............................87 D3
Clovelly Rd SWCK/CAS SR5...................123 E1
Clover Av BLAY NE21................................94 B4
   FELL NE10...82 A6
Cloverdale BDLGTN NE22...........................7 D3
Cloverdale Gdns LGB/HTN NE7...............50 A3
   WICK/BNPF NE16..............................96 A5
Cloverfield Av GOS/KPK NE3....................46 B6
Cloverhill Av HEBB NE31..........................84 C5
Cloverhill Cl CRAM NE23..........................34 C1
Clover Laid BDN/LAN/SAC DH7..............202 C5
Clowes Ter STLY/ANP DH9......................146 B4
Club La DHAM DH1.................................193 F3
Clumber St ELS/FEN NE4..........................79 E5
Clumber St North ELS/FEN NE4...............79 F4
Clyde Av HEBB NE31.................................85 D5
Clydedale Av LGB/KIL NE12......................49 E5
Clydesdale Av HLS DH4..........................157 D1
Clydesdale Garth DHAM DH1..................180 C4
Clydesdale Mt BYK/HTN/WLK NE6...........82 B3
Clydesdale Rd BYK/HTN/WLK NE6...........82 B3
Clydesdale St HLH DH5..........................185 F2
Clyde St GATE NE8...................................99 F2
Clyvedon Ri HAR/WTLS NE34...................89 F5
Coach La DIN/WO NE13............................32 A6
   LGB/HTN NE7.....................................65 E1
   NSHW NE29.......................................70 C1

Coach Open WLSD/HOW NE28................69 D5
Coach Rd BW/LEM/TK/HW NE15............57 E4
   DUN/TMV NE11.................................98 A5
   WASHN NE37...................................120 B2
   WLSD/HOW NE28.............................67 E5
Coach Road Gn FELL NE10......................82 B6
Coalbank Rd HLH DH5............................185 E2
Coaley La HLS DH4.................................157 E5
Coalford La RDHAMSE DH6....................184 A6
Coalford Rd RDHAMSE DH6...................197 E4
Coalway Dr WICK/BNPF NE16..................96 A2
Coalway La WICK/BNPF NE16...................96 A2
Coalway La North
   WICK/BNPF NE16..............................96 A1
Coanwood Dr CRAM NE23.......................22 A3
Coanwood Gdns DUN/TMV NE11............98 A5
Coanwood Rd
   BW/LEM/TK/HW NE15.......................78 A2
Coanwood Wy WICK/BNPF NE16...........114 A1
Coast Rd BYK/HTN/WLK NE6...................65 E4
   HAR/WTLS NE34...............................90 C1
   NSHW NE29.......................................53 F6
   SSH NE33...72 B5
   WLSD/HOW NE28.............................67 F2
Coates Cl STLY/ANP DH9.......................148 C2
Coatsworth Ct GATE NE8..........................81 D6
Coatsworth Rd GATE NE8.........................81 D6
Cobalt Cl BW/LEM/TK/HW NE15..............59 E6
Cobbett Crs HAR/WTLS NE34..................88 A5
Cobden Rd CRAM NE23............................22 B4
Cobden St GATE NE8................................99 F1
   WLSD/HOW NE28.............................66 C4
Cobden Ter GATE NE8..............................99 F1
Cobham Pl BYK/HTN/WLK NE6................83 F4
Cobham Sq SWCK/CAS SR5..................126 A2
Coble Dene NSHW NE29..........................70 A4
Coble Dene Rd NSHW NE29.....................70 A4
Coble Landing SSH NE33.........................71 D3
Coburg St BLYTH NE24............................11 E5
   GATE NE8..81 E6
   TYNE/NSHE NE30.............................55 F5
Cochrane Ct ELS/FEN * NE4.....................79 D3
Cochrane Park Av LGB/HTN NE7.............65 E4
Cochrane St ELS/FEN NE4........................79 D3
Cochran St BLAY * NE21...........................76 B5
Cockburn Ter NSHW NE29........................69 F3
Cocken La CLS/BIR/GTL DH3..................168 A4
   DHAM DH1......................................182 A1
Cocken Rd CLS/BIR/GTL DH3.................180 C1
   DHAM DH1......................................182 B1
Cockermouth Rd SWCK/CAS SR5.........123 E1
Colbeck Av WICK/BNPF NE16..................96 A1
Colbeck Ter TYNE/NSHE NE30.................55 F5
Colbourne Av CRAM NE23........................13 D5
Colbourne Crs
   CRAM (off Nelson Pk) NE23..............13 D5
Colbury Ct CRAM NE23............................13 F5
Colby Ct ELS/FEN NE4..............................80 A4
Colchester St HAR/WTLS NE34................87 E4
Colchester Ter MLFD/PNYW SR4...........143 E1
Coldbeck Ct CRAM NE23..........................22 B3
Coldingham Ct
   BDN/LAN/SAC DH7.........................178 A1
Coldingham Gdns
   WD/WHPE/BLK NE5............................61 F4
Coldside Gdns WD/WHPE/BLK NE5.........59 D4
Coldstream CLSW/PEL DH2....................135 E4
Coldstream Av SWCK/CAS SR5..............126 A2
Coldstream Cl HLS DH4..........................157 D3
Coldstream Dr BLAY NE21........................93 F2
Coldstream Gdns
   WLSD/HOW NE28.............................68 D3
Coldstream Rd
   BW/LEM/TK/HW NE15.......................78 A2
Coldstream Wy NSHW NE29.....................53 E4
Coldwell Cl RDHAMSE DH6....................187 D5
Coldwell La FELL NE10...........................100 B3
Coldwell Park Av FELL NE10...................100 B3
Coldwell Park Dr FELL NE10...................100 B3
Coldwell St FELL NE10............................100 C2
Coldwell Ter FELL NE10..........................100 B3
Colebridge Cl WD/WHPE/BLK NE5..........61 E3
Colebrooke CLS/BIR/GTL DH3................136 C4
Cole Gdns FELL NE10.............................101 E3
Colegate FELL NE10...............................101 E3
Colegate West FELL NE10......................101 D3
Colepeth FELL NE10...............................101 D3
Coleridge Av LWF/SPW/WRK NE9............99 D6
   SSH NE33...72 A5
Coleridge Rd SWCK/CAS SR5................124 A2
Coleridge Sq HEBB NE31..........................85 D2
Coley Hill Cl WD/WHPE/BLK NE5............59 E2
Coley Ter CLDN/WHIT/ROK SR6............127 D1
Colgrove Wy GOS/KPK NE3......................62 B1
Colima Av SWCK/CAS SR5.....................124 B3
Colin Pl BYK/HTN/WLK NE6.....................66 C6
Colin Ter ASHBK/HED/RY SR2................162 B2
College Burn Rd SUNDSW SR3..............160 A3
College Cl FELL NE10.............................100 C4
College Dr SSH NE33................................72 A6
College La CNUT NE1.................................3 E1
   LGB/HTN NE1....................................49 E6
College Rd HEBB NE31.............................84 C5
College St CNUT NE1..................................3 E1
College Vw SWCK/CAS SR5...................126 B3

Collier Cl *BW/LEM/TK/HW* NE15..........**57** F5
Collierley La *STLY/ANP* DH9..........**128** B5
Colliery La *ELS/FEN* NE4..........**80** A3
  HLH DH5..........**186** A2
Colliery Rd *DUN/TMV* NE11..........**79** E6
Collin Av *HAR/WTLS* NE34..........**90** A3
Colling Av *SEA/MUR* SR7..........**175** F3
Collingwood Av *WLSD/HOW* NE28..........**67** D2
Collingwood Dr *HLS* DH4..........**156** C2
Collingwood Man *NSHW* NE29..........**71** D2
Collingwood Gdns *FELL* NE10..........**82** C6
Collingwood Rd *MONK* NE25..........**38** C5
Collingwood St *CNUT* NE1..........**2** D5
  *FELL** NE10..........**100** C1
  HEBB NE31..........**85** F2
  HLH DH5..........**171** F4
  SSH NE33..........**71** E6
  SWCK/CAS SR5..........**126** A2
Collingwood Ter *BLYTH* NE24..........**11** D5
Collingwood Vw *NSHW* NE29..........**70** B1
Collywell Bay Rd *WBAY* NE26..........**26** C2
Collywell Ct *WBAY* NE26..........**26** C2
Colman Av *HAR/WTLS* NE34..........**87** F3
Colnbrook Cl *GOS/KPK* NE3..........**45** F5
Colombo Rd *SWCK/CAS* SR5..........**123** C5
Colpitts Ter *DHAM* DH1..........**194** A5
Colston Ri *PLEE/EAS* SR8..........**208** B1
Colston St *ELS/FEN* NE4..........**78** C3
Colston Wy *MONK* NE25..........**39** F3
Coltere Av *BOL* NE36..........**107** D3
Colton Gdns *LWF/SPW/WRK* NE9..........**117** F1
Coltpark *WD/WHPE/BLK * NE5..........**60** B5
Coltsfoot Gdns *FELL* NE10..........**100** B5
Coltspool *DUN/TMV* NE11..........**116** C6
Columba St *SWCK/CAS* SR5..........**126** A2
Columba Wk *GOS/KPK* NE3..........**63** F1
Columbia Gra *GOS/KPK* NE3..........**62** A1
Columbia Ter *BLYTH* NE24..........**11** D5
Colville Ct *STLY/ANP* DH9..........**119** D6
Colwell Pl *WD/WHPE/BLK* NE5..........**78** A1
Colwell Rd *NSHW* NE29..........**54** B3
  SMOOR NE27..........**52** B2
Colwyne Pl *WD/WHPE/BLK* NE5..........**61** D4
Combe Dr *BW/LEM/TK/HW* NE15..........**76** A1
Comet Rw *LGB/KIL* NE12..........**49** E2
Comet Sq *SUNDSW* SR3..........**160** C1
Comical Cnr *SSH* NE33..........**71** D2
Comma Ct *DUN/TMV* NE11..........**98** F3
Commercial Rd
  ASHBK/HED/RY SR2..........**145** E2
  BYK/HTN/WLK NE6..........**82** B3
  *GOS/KPK** NE3..........**64** A1
  JRW NE32..........**69** E6
  SSH NE33..........**71** D5
Commercial St *BLAY* NE21..........**94** A1
Commissioners' Whf *NSHW* NE29..........**70** B4
Compton Av *HAR/WTLS* NE34..........**88** C1
Compton Rd *NSHW* NE29..........**70** B1
Concorde Wy *JRW* NE32..........**86** A2
Condercum Ct
  BW/LEM/TK/HW NE15..........**78** B3
Condercum Rd *ELS/FEN* NE4..........**78** C3
Cone St *SSH* NE33..........**71** D4
Congburn Bank
  BDN/LAN/SAC DH7..........**164** C1
Conhope La *BW/LEM/TK/HW* NE15..........**78** C3
Conifer Cl *DHAM* DH1..........**195** F3
Conifer Ct
  RYTON (off Lead Rd) NE40..........**92** A1
Coniscliffe Av *GOS/KPK* NE3..........**62** B3
Coniscliffe Pl
  CLDN/WHIT/ROK SR6..........**127** D3
Coniscliffe Rd *STLY/ANP* DH9..........**147** F5
Conishead Dr *RDHAMSE* DH6..........**187** E4
Coniston *CLS/BIR/GTL* DH3..........**136** C5
  FELL NE10..........**101** F2
Coniston Av *HEBB* NE31..........**85** E3
  HLH DH5..........**186** B4
  JES NE2..........**4** B1
  SWCK/CAS SR5..........**108** B6
  WICK/BNPF NE16..........**96** C5
Coniston Cl *DHAM* DH1..........**197** D2
  LGB/KIL NE12..........**49** E1
  PLEE/EAS SR8..........**209** D2
Coniston Crs *BLAY* NE21..........**94** A2
Coniston Dr *BDN/LAN/SAC* DH7..........**164** A6
  JRW NE32..........**86** C5
Coniston Gdns
  LWF/SPW/WRK NE9..........**100** A5
Coniston Pl *LWF/SPW/WRK* NE9..........**100** A5
Coniston Rd *BLYTH* NE24..........**9** E3
  TYNE/NSHE NE30..........**54** B2
  WLSD/HOW NE28..........**68** B2
Connaught Cl *HLS* DH4..........**157** E3
Connaught Ter *JRW* NE32..........**86** A2
Conningsby Cl *GOS/KPK* NE3..........**47** F4
Consett Rd *DUN/TMV* NE11..........**97** E5
Constable Cl *RYTON* NE40..........**74** B4
  STLY/ANP DH9..........**124** B6
Constable Gdns *HAR/WTLS* NE34..........**88** B5
Constance St *CLSW/PEL* DH2..........**152** A1
Content St *BLAY* NE21..........**94** B1
Convent Rd *ELS/FEN* NE4..........**78** C1
Conway Cl *BDLGTN* NE22..........**6** C3
  RYTON NE40..........**74** C5

Conway Dr *LGB/HTN* NE7..........**64** C2
Conway Gdns *SUNDSW* SR3..........**159** E1
  WLSD/HOW NE28..........**66** C2
Conway Gv *WBAY* NE26..........**26** A1
Conway Pl *CLSW/PEL* DH2..........**135** E6
Conway Rd *SWCK/CAS* SR5..........**123** E2
Conway Sq *LWF/SPW/WRK* NE9..........**99** F2
  SWCK/CAS SR5..........**123** E2
Conyers Av *CLSW/PEL* DH2..........**153** D3
Conyers Crs *PLEE/EAS* SR8..........**201** D5
Conyers Gdns *CLSW/PEL* DH2..........**153** D3
Conyers Pl *CLSW/PEL* DH2..........**153** D3
Conyers Rd *BYK/HTN/WLK* NE6..........**82** A2
  CLSW/PEL DH2..........**153** D3
Cook Cl *SSH* NE33..........**71** D6
Cook Crs *SEA/MUR* SR7..........**188** C3
Cooke's Wd *BDN/LAN/SAC* DH7..........**192** B6
Cook Gdns *FELL* NE10..........**102** A2
Cookson Cl *ELS/FEN* NE4..........**80** A3
Cookson Pl *STLY/ANP* DH9..........**149** D3
Cookson's La *CNUT* NE1..........**2** C6
Cookson St *ELS/FEN* NE4..........**79** F3
Cookson Ter *CLSW/PEL* DH2..........**153** D5
  SEA/MUR SR7..........**188** C2
Cook Sq *SWCK/CAS* SR5..........**123** F2
Cooks Wd *WASHS* NE38..........**138** C3
Cook Wy *PLEE/EAS* SR8..........**207** D1
Coomassie Rd *BLYTH* NE24..........**11** D5
Coomside *CRAM* NE23..........**22** B4
Co-operative Ter
  MLFD/PNYW SR4..........**143** F1
  STLY/ANP DH9..........**128** B6
Cooper Sq *DHAM* DH1..........**195** E3
Cooper St *CLDN/WHIT/ROK* SR6..........**127** D2
Copeland Ct *DHAM* DH1..........**193** F6
Copland Ter *JES* NE2..........**3** G2
Copley Av *HAR/WTLS* NE34..........**88** B6
Copley Dr *SUNDSW* SR3..........**144** A4
Copperas La
  BW/LEM/TK/HW NE15..........**77** E1
Copperfield *DHAM * DH1..........**204** C1
Coppergate Ct *HEBB* NE31..........**85** E1
Coppice Wy *JES* NE2..........**3** G1
Coppy La *STLY/ANP* DH9..........**132** B3
The Copse *BLAY* NE21..........**77** E6
  WICK/BNPF NE16..........**111** E6
Coquet *WASHS* NE38..........**137** E5
Coquet Av *BLYTH* NE24..........**17** D1
  GOS/KPK NE3..........**47** D6
  HAR/WTLS NE34..........**72** C6
  WBAY NE26..........**40** C5
Coquetdale Av *BYK/HTN/WLK* NE6..........**83** F2
Coquetdale Vls
  CLDN/WHIT/ROK
  (off Roker Baths Rd) SR6..........**127** D2
Coquet Dr *CLSW/PEL* DH2..........**135** D6
Coquet Gdns *STLY/ANP* DH9..........**148** A4
Coquet Gv *BW/LEM/TK/HW* NE15..........**57** F4
Coquet St *CNUT* NE1..........**81** F3
  HEBB NE31..........**84** C2
  JRW NE32..........**85** F3
Coquet Ter *BYK/HTN/WLK* NE6..........**65** D5
  CRAM NE23..........**34** B2
Corbett St *PLEE/EAS* SR8..........**201** E2
Corbiere Cl *SUNDSW* SR3..........**160** A2
Corbitt St *GATE* NE8..........**98** B1
Corbridge Cl *WLSD/HOW* NE28..........**52** A6
Corbridge Rd *BYK/HTN/WLK* NE6..........**82** B2
Corbridge St *BYK/HTN/WLK* NE6..........**82** A2
Corby Gdns *BYK/HTN/WLK* NE6..........**83** C2
Corby Ga *ASHBK/HED/RY* SR2..........**144** C2
Corby Gv *PLEE/EAS* SR8..........**207** F5
Corby Hall Dr *ASHBK/HED/RY* SR2..........**144** C2
Corchester Rd *BDLGTN* NE22..........**7** D2
Corchester Wk *LGB/HTN* NE7..........**65** D2
Corinthian Sq *SWCK/CAS* SR5..........**123** F2
Cork St *SUND* SR1..........**5** K2
Cormorant Dr *BLYTH* NE24..........**17** E2
Cormbank Ct *SUNDSW* SR3..........**160** C3
Corndean *WASHS* NE38..........**139** F2
Cornel Rd *LGB/HTN* NE7..........**65** D3
Corney St *SSH* NE33..........**88** A1
The Cornfields *HEBB* NE31..........**85** D2
Cornforth Cl *FELL* NE10..........**102** B4
Cornhill Av *GOS/KPK* NE3..........**46** A5
Cornhill Crs *NSHW* NE29..........**53** F5
Cornhill Rd *CRAM* NE23..........**22** A2
  SWCK/CAS SR5..........**126** A2
Corn Mill Dr *HLH* DH5..........**170** C4
Cornmoor Gdns *WICK/BNPF* NE16..........**96** A5
Cornmoor Rd *WICK/BNPF* NE16..........**96** A4
Cornthwaite Dr
  CLDN/WHIT/ROK SR6..........**109** D1
Cornwalls Sq *SSH* NE33..........**71** D5
Cornwallis St *SSH* NE33..........**71** E3
Cornwall Rd *HEBB* NE31..........**85** E5
Cornwall St *PLEE/EAS* SR8..........**201** E2
Cornwell Crs *BDLGTN* NE22..........**7** E4
Cornwell Ct *BDLGTN* NE22..........**8** A4
Coronation Av
  ASHBK/HED/RY SR2..........**162** B2
  DHAM DH1..........**196** C2
Coronation Bungalows
  GOS/KPK (off Church Rd) NE3..........**63** F1

Coronation Cl *SUND* SR1..........**5** E2
Coronation Gn *HLH* DH5..........**186** C4
Coronation Rd
  WD/WHPE/BLK NE5..........**59** D3
  WICK/BNPF NE16..........**114** A2
Coronation Sq *RDHAMSE* DH6..........**188** A5
Coronation St *CLS/BIR/GTL* DH3..........**153** F6
  NSHW NE29..........**70** C2
  SSH NE33..........**71** D4
  SUND SR1..........**5** E2
  WLSD/HOW NE28..........**67** E4
Coronation Ter *MLFD/PNYW* SR4..........**124** A6
Corporation Rd
  ASHBK/HED/RY SR2..........**145** E2
Corporation St *ELS/FEN* NE4..........**2** A4
Corriedale Cl *DHAM * DH1..........**180** B5
Corrofell Gdns *FELL* NE10..........**83** D6
Corry Ct *MLFD/PNYW* SR4..........**143** D2
Corsair *WD/WHPE/BLK* NE5..........**60** B5
Corsenside *WD/WHPE/BLK* NE5..........**60** B5
Corstorphine Town *SSH* NE33..........**71** D6
Cortina Av *MLFD/PNYW* SR4..........**142** C2
Cossack Ter *MLFD/PNYW* SR4..........**125** D5
Cosserat Pl *HEBB* NE31..........**84** C1
Cosser St *BLYTH * NE24..........**16** A2
Coston Dr *SSH* NE33..........**71** E3
Cosyn St *BYK/HTN/WLK* NE6..........**81** F3
Cotehill Rd *WD/WHPE/BLK* NE5..........**61** D5
Cotemede *FELL* NE10..........**101** F5
Cotfield Wk *GATE* NE8..........**98** C1
The Cotgarth *FELL* NE10..........**101** E5
Cotherstone Ct *SUNDSW* SR3..........**144** A4
Cotherstone Rd *DHAM* DH1..........**180** C6
Cotman Gdns *HAR/WTLS* NE34..........**88** C6
Cotsford La *PLEE/EAS* SR8..........**209** F2
Cotswold Av *LGB/KIL* NE12..........**49** D3
Cotswold Cl *WASHS* NE38..........**138** A2
Cotswold Dr *MONK* NE25..........**38** A3
Cotswold Gdns *DUN/TMV* NE11..........**97** F3
  LGB/HTN NE7..........**64** C3
Cotswold La *BOLCOL* NE35..........**87** D6
Cotswold Pl *PLEE/EAS* SR8..........**208** A1
Cotswold Rd *NSHW* NE29..........**54** A2
  SWCK/CAS SR5..........**123** E2
Cotswold Sq *SWCK/CAS* SR5..........**123** F1
Cotswold Ter *STLY/ANP* DH9..........**148** C3
Cottage La *WD/WHPE/BLK* NE5..........**61** F5
Cottages Rd *SEA/MUR* SR7..........**176** C4
Cottenham Chare *ELS/FEN* NE4..........**80** A3
Cottenham St *ELS/FEN* NE4..........**80** A3
Cotterdale *WLSD/HOW* NE28..........**66** B1
Cotterdale Av *GATE * NE8..........**99** E2
Cotter Riggs Pl
  WD/WHPE/BLK NE5..........**59** D4
Cottersdale Gdns
  WD/WHPE/BLK NE5..........**59** D3
Cottingham Cl *PLEE/EAS* SR8..........**208** A1
Cottingwood Gdns *ELS/FEN * NE4..........**80** A2
Cottingwood Gn *ELS/FEN* NE4..........**16** A3
Cottonwood *HLS* DH4..........**156** B2
  SUNDSW SR3..........**160** A3
Coulthards La *GATE* NE8..........**81** F5
Coulthards Pl *GATE* NE8..........**81** F4
Coulton Dr *BOL* NE36..........**106** C3
Council Av *HLS* DH4..........**157** D2
Counden Rd *WD/WHPE/BLK* NE5..........**60** A3
Countess Av *WBAY* NE26..........**40** C5
Countess Cl *SEA/MUR* SR7..........**176** B2
Countess Dr
  BW/LEM/TK/HW NE15..........**77** F1
Coupland Gv *JRW* NE32..........**85** F5
Courtfield Rd *BYK/HTN/WLK* NE6..........**66** B6
Court La *DHAM* DH1..........**194** C5
Courtney Ct *GOS/KPK* NE3..........**45** C5
Courtney Dr *SUNDSW* SR3..........**143** E6
Court Rd *BDLGTN* NE22..........**7** E3
Court St *PLEE/EAS* SR8..........**201** E2
The Court *WICK/BNPF* NE16..........**96** B4
The Courtyard *STLY/ANP* DH9..........**130** B6
Cousin St *SUND* SR1..........**5** F2
Coutts Rd *BYK/HTN/WLK* NE6..........**66** A6
Coventry Gdns *ELS/FEN* NE4..........**79** D4
  NSHW NE29..........**70** A2
Coventry Rd *DHAM* DH1..........**180** C5
Coverdale *FELL* NE10..........**101** F4
  WLSD/HOW NE28..........**66** B1
Coverdale Av *BLYTH* NE24..........**9** F5
Coverley Rd *SWCK/CAS* SR5..........**123** F1
The Covers *LGB/KIL* NE12..........**50** A6
The Cove *HLS* DH4..........**157** D2
Cowan Cl *BLAY* NE21..........**75** F4
Cowans Av *LGB/KIL* NE12..........**35** E6
Cowan Ter *ASHBK/HED/RY* SR2..........**4** B4
Cowdray Ct *GOS/KPK* NE3..........**45** C5
Cowdray Rd *SWCK/CAS* SR5..........**124** A2
Cowell Gv *ROWG* NE39..........**110** B2
Cowell St *PLEE/EAS* SR8..........**209** E1
Cowen Gdns *LWF/SPW/WRK* NE9..........**117** F3
Cowen Rd *BLAY* NE21..........**76** C5
Cowen St *BYK/HTN/WLK* NE6..........**81** F2
Cowley Pl *BLYTH* NE24..........**10** A4
Cowley Rd *BLYTH* NE24..........**10** A3
Cowley St *RDHAMSE* DH6..........**206** C2
Cowpath Gdns *FELL* NE10..........**101** F1
Cowpen Hall Rd *BLYTH* NE24..........**9** F4

Cowpen Rd *BLYTH* NE24 ....9 E4
Coxfoot Cl *HAR/WTLS* NE34 ....88 B3
Coxgreen Rd *HLS* DH4 ....139 F6
Coxlodge Rd *GOS/KPK* NE3 ....62 C1
Coxlodge Ter *GOS/KPK* NE3 ....62 C1
Coxon St *ASHBK/HED/RY* SR2 ....5 E4
  FELL NE10 ....84 A6
Coxon Ter *FELL* * NE10 ....100 B1
Cradock Av *HEBB* NE31 ....84 C4
Craggyknowe *WASHN* NE37 ....119 E6
Craghall Dene *JES* NE2 ....64 A2
Craghall Dene Av *JES* NE2 ....64 A2
Craghead La *STLY/ANP* DH9 ....150 A5
Cragleas *WICK/BNPF* NE16 ....129 F2
Cragside *BDN/LAN/SAC* DH7 ....178 A4
  CLSW/PEL DH2 ....152 C4
  CRAM NE23 ....22 A4
  HAR/WTLS NE34 ....90 A3
  LGB/HTN NE7 ....65 D3
  WBAY NE26 ....40 A3
Cragside Av *NSHW* NE29 ....53 F4
Cragside Ct *STLY/ANP* DH9 ....146 B5
Cragside Gdns *DUN/TMV* NE11 ....97 F5
  LGB/KIL NE12 ....36 B6
  WLSD/HOW NE28 ....68 B3
Cragside Rd *WASHN* NE37 ....119 F5
Cragston Av *WD/WHPE/BLK* NE5 ....61 E3
Cragston Ct *WD/WHPE/BLK* NE5 ....61 E4
Cragton Gdns *BLYTH* NE24 ....10 A5
Craigavon Rd *SWCK/CAS* SR5 ....124 A3
Craighill *HLS* DH4 ....156 C2
Craigmillar Av *WD/WHPE/BLK* NE5 ....61 E3
Craigmillar Cl *WD/WHPE/BLK* NE5 ....61 D3
Craigmill Pk *BLYTH* NE24 ....9 F4
Craigshaw Rd *SWCK/CAS* SR5 ....123 E1
Craig Ter *PLEE/EAS* SR8 ....200 A3
Craigwell Dr *SUNDSW* SR3 ....160 C4
Craik Av *HAR/WTLS* NE34 ....88 A3
Crake Wy *WASHS* NE38 ....137 E4
Cramer St *GATE* NE8 ....99 E1
Cramlington Rd *SWCK/CAS* SR5 ......123 E3
Cramlington Sq *SWCK/CAS* SR5 ......123 E2
Cramlington Ter *BLYTH* NE24 ....16 B2
Cramond Ct *LWF/SPW/WRK* NE9 ....117 D1
Cramond Wy *CRAM* NE23 ....22 A4
Cranberry Rd *SWCK/CAS* SR5 ....123 F2
Cranberry Sq *SWCK/CAS* SR5 ....123 F2
Cranborne *SUNDSW* SR3 ....159 F2
Cranbourne Gv *TYNE/NSHE* NE30 ......55 D1
Cranbrook Av *GOS/KPK* NE3 ....47 E5
Cranbrook Ct *GOS/KPK* NE3 ....46 A5
Cranbrook Pl
  BW/LEM/TK/HW NE15 ....78 A4
Cranbrook Rd
  BW/LEM/TK/HW NE15 ....78 A4
Craneswater Av *WBAY* NE26 ....40 B1
Cranfield Pl *BW/LEM/TK/HW* NE15 ....76 B1
Cranford St *HAR/WTLS* NE34 ....88 B2
Cranford Ter *MLFD/PNYW* SR4 ....143 F1
Cranham Ct *LGB/KIL* NE12 ....36 B6
Cranleigh Av *DIN/WO* NE13 ....45 D5
Cranleigh Pl *MONK* NE25 ....39 F3
Cranleigh Rd *SWCK/CAS* SR5 ....123 F2
Cranshaw Pl *CRAM* NE23 ....22 B3
Crantock Rd *GOS/KPK* NE3 ....62 B1
Cranwell Ct *GOS/KPK* NE3 ....45 E5
Cranwell Dr *DIN/WO* NE13 ....33 D4
Craster Av *HAR/WTLS* NE34 ....73 D6
  LGB/KIL NE12 ....50 B3
  SMOOR NE27 ....52 A1
Craster Cl *BLYTH* NE24 ....10 B5
  CLSW/PEL DH2 ....165 E1
  MONK NE25 ....39 F1
Craster Gdns *WLSD/HOW* NE28 ....68 B3
Craster Rd *NSHW* NE29 ....53 F4
Craster Sq *GOS/KPK* NE3 ....46 C6
Craster Ter *LGB/HTN* NE7 ....65 D4
Craven Ct *CLDN/WHIT/ROK* SR6 ......127 E3
Crawford Av *PLEE/EAS* SR8 ....200 C6
Crawford Ct *RDHAMSE* DH6 ....197 E5
Crawford St *SUNDSW* SR3 ....160 B2
Crawford Pl *MONK* NE25 ....40 A6
Crawford Pl *BLYTH* NE24 ....10 C3
Crawford Ter *BYK/HTN/WLK* NE6 ......83 E3
Crawhall Rd *CNUT* NE1 ....3 H3
Crawlaw Rd *PLEE/EAS* SR8 ....200 C1
Crawley Av *HEBB* NE31 ....84 C5
Crawley Gdns *WICK/BNPF* NE16 ....96 B3
Crawley Rd *WLSD/HOW* NE28 ....67 D5
Crawley Sq *HEBB* NE31 ....84 C5
Craythorne Gdns
  BYK/HTN/WLK NE6 ....65 E4
Creeverlea *WASHS* NE38 ....138 B3
Creighton Av *GOS/KPK* NE3 ....62 A3
Creland Wy *WD/WHPE/BLK* NE5 ....61 D3
Crescent Cl *RDHAMSE* DH6 ....197 E5
The Crescent *BDN/LAN/SAC* DH7 .....178 A3
  BW/LEM/TK/HW NE15 ....57 F4
  CLDN/WHIT/ROK SR6 ....107 E2
  CLSW/PEL DH2 ....173 D5
  CLSW/PEL DH2 ....165 F3
  CRAM NE23 ....36 B3
  DHAM DH1 ....193 F3
  DIN/WO NE13 ....45 D6

HAR/WTLS NE34 ....89 E4
HLS DH4 ....156 C3
HLS DH4 ....157 F4
HLS DH4 ....183 E2
JRW NE32 ....85 F4
LGB/HTN NE7 ....65 D1
PLEE/EAS SR8 ....201 D1
RDHAMSE DH6 ....197 E5
ROWG NE39 ....111 E2
RYTON NE40 ....74 C3
STLY/ANP DH9 ....130 C6
SUNDSW SR3 ....143 F5
TYNE/NSHE NE30 ....55 E4
WICK/BNPF NE16 ....96 B4
WLSD/HOW NE28 ....67 D3
Crescent Wy North *LGB/KIL* NE12 ....50 A4
Crescent Wy South *LGB/KIL* NE12 ....50 A4
Cressbourne Av
  CLDN/WHIT/ROK SR6 ....109 D6
Cresswell Av *LGB/KIL* NE12 ....50 A5
  NSHW NE29 ....54 B5
  PLEE/EAS SR8 ....209 F2
  WBAY NE26 ....26 B2
Cresswell Cl *BLAY* NE21 ....93 E2
  MONK NE25 ....54 A1
Cresswell Dr *BLYTH* NE24 ....16 A1
  GOS/KPK NE3 ....46 A5
Cresswell Rd *WLSD/HOW* NE28 ....66 C5
Cresswell St *BYK/HTN/WLK* NE6 ......82 C1
Cresswell Ter *ASHBK/HED/RY* SR2 .....4 B5
The Crest *BDLGTN* NE22 ....7 D3
  DIN/WO NE13 ....31 D3
  WBAY NE26 ....26 C4
Crichton Av *CLS/BIR/GTL* DH3 ......166 C1
Cricklewood Dr *HLS* DH4 ....157 D1
Cricklewood Rd *SWCK/CAS* SR5 ......123 E2
Criddle St *GATE* NE8 ....81 F4
Crieff Gv *JRW* NE32 ....86 C5
Crieff Sq *SWCK/CAS* SR5 ....123 E2
Crigdon Hl *WD/WHPE/BLK* NE5 ....60 B5
Crighton *WASHS* NE38 ....137 F1
Crimdon Gv *HLS* DH4 ....170 B3
Crindledykes *WASHS* NE38 ....139 D4
Cripps Av *FELL* NE10 ....102 A2
Croft Av *LGB/KIL* NE12 ....50 A5
  WLSD/HOW NE28 ....67 E4
Croft Cl *RYTON* NE40 ....74 C4
Croftdale Rd *BLAY* NE21 ....76 A6
Crofter Cl *CRAM* NE23 ....34 C1
Crofthead Dr *CRAM* NE23 ....22 A4
Crofton St *BLYTH* NE24 ....11 D5
  HAR/WTLS NE34 ....88 B2
Crofton Wy *BW/LEM/TK/HW* NE15 ......76 A1
Croft Rigg *BDN/LAN/SAC* DH7 ....202 C5
Croft Rd *BLYTH* NE24 ....11 D5
Croftside Av
  CLDN/WHIT/ROK SR6 ....109 E2
Croft St *CNUT* NE1 ....3 E4
Croftsway *ELS/FEN* NE4 ....79 E4
Croft Ter *JRW* NE32 ....86 A2
  STLY/ANP DH9 ....146 C4
The Croft *GOS/KPK* NE3 ....62 C2
  LGB/KIL NE12 ....36 A6
Cromarty *CLSW/PEL* DH2 ....135 E4
Cromarty St *CLDN/WHIT/ROK* SR6 ....126 C2
Cromdale Pl *WD/WHPE/BLK* NE5 ....61 D5
Cromer Av *LWF/SPW/WRK* NE9 ....117 E1
Cromer Gdns *WBAY* NE26 ....40 C4
Crompton Rd *BYK/HTN/WLK* NE6 ....65 D5
Cromwell Av *BLAY* NE21 ....76 A4
Cromwell Ct *BLAY* NE21 ....75 F4
  FELL NE10 ....84 B6
Cromwell Rd *FELL* NE10 ....84 A6
  WICK/BNPF NE16 ....96 B2
Cromwell St *GATE* NE8 ....99 F1
  MLFD/PNYW SR4 ....125 F5
Cromwell Ter *GATE* NE8 ....98 C1
  NSHW NE29 ....54 B6
Crondall St *SSH* NE33 ....88 C1
Cronin Av *HAR/WTLS* NE34 ....87 F4
Crookham Wy *CRAM* NE23 ....22 B4
Cropthorne *FELL* NE10 ....102 A4
Cross Av *WLSD/HOW* NE28 ....66 B2
Crossbank Rd *WD/WHPE/BLK* NE5 ......61 F3
Crossbrook Rd
  WD/WHPE/BLK NE5 ....61 F4
Crossby Ct *ASHBK/HED/RY* SR2 ....5 C5
Crossfield *BDN/LAN/SAC* DH7 ....178 B2
Crossfield Pk *FELL* NE10 ....100 B4
Crossfield Ter *BYK/HTN/WLK* NE6 ....83 F4
Crossgate *DHAM* DH1 ....194 A5
  SSH NE33 ....71 D4
Crossgate Moor Gdns *DHAM* DH1 .....193 E4
Crossgate Peth *DHAM* DH1 ....193 F5
Crossgate Rd *HLH* DH5 ....185 F2
Crosshill Rd *BW/LEM/TK/HW* NE15 ....78 A4
Cross Keys La *LWF/SPW/WRK* NE9 .....99 E5
Cross La *BDN/LAN/SAC* DH7 ....164 B6
  DUN/TMV NE11 ....78 C6
  DUN/TMV NE11 ....115 F1
  WICK/BNPF NE16 ....96 B2
Croslaw *WD/WHPE/BLK* NE5 ....60 D5
Crosslea Av *SUNDSW* SR3 ....144 A3
Crossley Ter *ELS/FEN* NE4 ....79 E2
  LGB/KIL NE12 ....50 B3

Cross Morpeth St *JES* NE2 ....63 D6
Cross Pde *ELS/FEN* NE4 ....80 A4
Cross Pl *SUND* SR1 ....5 E2
Cross Rigg Cl *HLS* DH4 ....156 B1
Cross Rw *GATE* NE8 ....100 A1
Cross St *BYK/HTN/WLK* NE6 ....81 F3
  CNUT NE1 ....2 B4
  GATE NE8 ....99 E1
  HLS DH4 ....169 F2
  HLS DH4 ....170 C1
Cross Ter *ROWG* NE39 ....110 C3
Cross Vale Rd
  ASHBK/HED/RY SR2 ....144 B2
Cross Villa Pl No 4 *ELS/FEN* * NE4 .80 A3
Cross Villa Pl No 5 *ELS/FEN* * NE4 .80 A3
Crossway *HAR/WTLS* NE34 ....89 F3
  JES NE2 ....64 A3
  LWF/SPW/WRK NE9 ....100 A3
  TYNE/NSHE NE30 ....55 E4
Crossways *BOL* NE36 ....107 D3
  SUNDSW SR3 ....160 B1
The Crossway
  BW/LEM/TK/HW NE15 ....76 C1
The Cross Wy *GOS/KPK* NE3 ....62 B2
Croudace Rw *FELL* NE10 ....100 C2
Crow Bank *WLSD/HOW* NE28 ....67 E4
Crowhall La *FELL* NE10 ....100 C2
Crow Hall Rd *CRAM* NE23 ....13 E5
Crow La *SUNDSW* SR3 ....159 D1
Crowley Av *WICK/BNPF* NE16 ....96 B3
Crowley Gdns *BLAY* NE21 ....76 B6
Crowley Rd *WICK/BNPF* NE16 ....95 F1
Crowley Vls *WICK/BNPF* * NE16 ......95 F1
Crown Rd *SWCK/CAS* SR5 ....125 F4
Crown St *BLYTH* NE24 ....11 E5
Crowther Rd *WASHS* NE38 ....137 E1
Crowtree Rd *SUND* SR1 ....4 B2
Croxdale Gdns *FELL* NE10 ....83 F6
Croxdale Ter *FELL* * NE10 ....102 A3
Croydon Rd *ELS/FEN* NE4 ....79 F2
Crozier St *SWCK/CAS* SR5 ....126 B3
Cruddas Pk
  ELS/FEN
  (off Westmorland Rd) NE4 ....79 F4
Crudwell Cl *BOLCOL* NE35 ....87 D6
Crummock Av
  CLDN/WHIT/ROK SR6 ....108 B6
Crummock Rd *WD/WHPE/BLK* NE5 ....61 D6
Crumstone Ct *LGB/KIL* NE12 ....36 A6
Cuba St *ASHBK/HED/RY* SR2 ....145 D2
Cuillin Cl *WASHS* NE38 ....138 A3
Culford St *BYK/HTN/WLK* NE6 ....82 A6
Cullercoats Rd *SWCK/CAS* SR5 ......123 E3
Cullercoats St
  BYK/HTN/WLK * NE6 ....83 D3
Culloden Ter *PLEE/EAS* SR8 ....201 E3
Culloden Wk *LGB/KIL* NE12 ....35 F6
Cumberland Av *BDLGTN* NE22 ....7 D3
Cumberland Pl *CLS/BIR/GTL* DH3 ....136 C5
  HAR/WTLS NE34 ....90 A1
Cumberland Rd *NSHW* NE29 ....53 D5
  SUNDSW SR3 ....143 F6
Cumberland St *SUND* SR1 ....4 C1
  WLSD/HOW NE28 ....67 E4
  WLSD/HOW NE28 ....67 E4
Cumberland Wk *WASHN* NE37 ....120 C2
Cumbrian Av
  CLDN/WHIT/ROK SR6 ....108 B5
Cumbrian Gdns *DUN/TMV* NE11 ....97 F4
Cumbrian Wy *PLEE/EAS* SR8 ....209 D2
Cumbria Pl *STLY/ANP* DH9 ....148 C1
Cumbria Wk *ELS/FEN* * NE4 ....79 F3
Cummings Av *RDHAMSE* DH6 ....197 E4
Cummings St *BLYTH* * NE24 ....11 D4
Cunningham Pl *DHAM* DH1 ....195 E3
Curlew Cl *LGB/KIL* NE12 ....48 C5
  RYTON NE40 ....75 D4
  WASHS NE38 ....137 F4
Curlew Rd *JRW* NE32 ....69 E6
Curlew Wy *BLYTH* NE24 ....17 D2
Curren Gdns *FELL* NE10 ....84 A5
Curtis Rd *ELS/FEN* NE4 ....79 E1
Curzon Pl *WD/WHPE/BLK* NE5 ....61 D4
Curzon Rd West *WLSD/HOW* NE28 ......67 D5
Curzon St *GATE* NE8 ....98 C2
Cushat Cl *BYK/HTN/WLK* NE6 ....82 B3
Cushy Cow La *RYTON* NE40 ....74 C4
Cut Bank *CNUT* NE1 ....81 F3
Cuthbert Av *DHAM* DH1 ....195 F5
Cuthbert Cl *DHAM* DH1 ....196 A5
Cuthbert Ct *JRW* NE32 ....87 D2
Cuthbertson Cl
  CLDN/WHIT/ROK SR6 ....109 D5
Cuthbert St *GATE* NE8 ....80 C6
  WICK/BNPF NE16 ....113 F3
Cygnet Cl *WD/WHPE/BLK* NE5 ....59 F2
Cyncopa Wy *WD/WHPE/BLK* NE5 ....61 F6
Cypress Av *ELS/FEN* NE4 ....61 F6
Cypress Ct *BDN/LAN/SAC* DH7 ....203 D5
Cypress Crs *BLYTH* NE24 ....11 D5
  DUN/TMV NE11 ....97 E2
Cypress Dr *BLYTH* NE24 ....11 D5
Cypress Gdns *BLYTH* NE24 ....11 D5

Cypress Gv *DHAM* DH1 ....**195** F3
   RYTON NE40 ....**74** B2
Cypress Rd *BLAY* NE21 ....**76** B6
   LWF/SPW/WRK NE9 ....**118** C2
Cypress Sq *SUNDSW* SR3 ....**143** F6
Cyprus Gdns *LWF/SPW/WRK* NE9 ......**99** F4

D

Dachet Rd *MONK* NE25 ....**39** E3
Dacre Rd *CLDN/WHIT/ROK* SR6 ......**108** C6
Dacre St *SSH* NE33 ....**71** E6
Dahlia Ct *MLFD/PNYW* SR4 ....**126** A5
Dahlia Pl *ELS/FEN* NE4 ....**61** F5
Dahlia Wy *HEBB* NE31 ....**85** D4
Dainton Cl *HLS* DH4 ....**157** E4
Dairy La *HLS* DH4 ....**170** C2
Dalegarth *WASHN* NE37 ....**120** A6
Dalegarth Cl
   CLDN/WHIT/ROK SR6 ....**108** B5
Dale Rd *MONK* NE25 ....**39** F6
Daleside *BDN/LAN/SAC* DH7 ....**164** B6
Dale St *BLYTH* NE24 ....**11** D3
   SSH NE33 ....**71** F3
Dale Ter *CLDN/WHIT/ROK* SR6 .....**127** D1
Dale Top *MONK* NE25.........................**38** A1
Dalla St *MLFD/PNYW* SR4 ....**123** F5
Dalmahoy *WASHN* NE37 ....**120** C1
Dalmatia Ter *BLYTH* NE24 ....**11** D6
Dalston Pl *BLYTH* NE24 ....**17** D2
Dalton Av *SEA/MUR* SR7 ....**176** A3
Dalton Cl *CRAM* NE23 ....**22** A2
Dalton Ct *WLSD/HOW* NE28 ....**66** B1
Dalton Cts *BYK/HTN/WLK* NE6 ....**82** A2
Dalton Pl
   MLFD/PNYW
   (off St. Marks Rd) SR4 ....**126** A6
   WD/WHPE/BLK NE5 ....**59** E3
Daltons La *SSH* NE33 ....**71** D4
Dalton St *BYK/HTN/WLK* NE6 ....**82** A2
Dame Dorothy Crs
   CLDN/WHIT/ROK * SR6 ....**127** D3
Dame Dorothy St
   CLDN/WHIT/ROK SR6 ....**126** C4
Dame Flora Robson Av
   HAR/WTLS NE34 ....**87** E4
Danby Gdns *BYK/HTN/WLK* NE6 .....**65** F5
Danby Cl *SUNDSW* SR3 ....**161** D2
   WASHS NE38 ....**137** E6
Danville Rd *CLDN/WHIT/ROK* NE9 ..**109** D6
Daphne Crs *SEA/MUR* SR7 ....**176** B5
D'arcy Cl *SUND* SR1 ....**5** F3
D'arcy St *SEA/MUR* SR7 ....**175** D6
Darden Cl *LGB/KIL* NE12 ....**36** B6
Darden Lough *WD/WHPE/BLK* NE5...**60** B5
Darien Av *CLDN/WHIT/ROK* SR6 ...**108** C5
Darley Ct *CLSW/PEL* DH2 ....**165** F5
Darley Pl *BW/LEM/TK/HW* NE15 ......**77** F3
Darlington Rd *DHAM* DH1 ....**193** F6
Darnell Pl *ELS/FEN* NE4 ....**80** A2
Darras Ct *SSH* NE33 ....**71** F5
Darras Dr *NSHW* NE29 ....**53** E5
Darrell St *DIN/WO* NE13 ....**32** C4
Dartford Rd *CLDN/WHIT/ROK* SR6 ..**108** C6
   SSH NE33 ....**72** B4
Dartmouth Av
   LWF/SPW/WRK NE9 ....**117** E1
Dartmouth Cl *SEA/MUR* SR7 ....**175** F4
Dart Rd *PLEE/EAS* SR8 ....**208** B3
Darvall Cl *MONK* NE25 ....**39** F3
Darwin Crs *GOS/KPK* NE3 ....**62** B3
Darwin St *SWCK/CAS* SR5 ....**125** E3
Daryl Cl *BLAY* NE21 ....**93** F1
Daryl Wy *FELL* NE10 ....**102** C3
Davenport Dr *GOS/KPK* NE3 ....**47** D5
David Gdns *CLDN/WHIT/ROK* SR6 ..**127** E1
Davidson Rd *FELL* NE10 ....**84** A6
Davidson St *FELL* NE10 ....**100** C2
David St *WLSD/HOW* NE28 ....**67** D5
Davies Hall
   HEBB (off Ellison St) NE31 ....**84** C1
Davison Av *SUNDSW* SR3 ....**161** D1
   WBAY NE26 ....**40** B4
Davison Crs *SEA/MUR* SR7 ....**174** A6
Davison St *BLYTH* * NE24 ....**11** D4
   BOLCOL NE35 ....**105** D1
   BW/LEM/TK/HW NE15 ....**48** A6
Davis Ter *PLEE/EAS* SR8.................**200** C3
Davis Wk *PLEE/EAS* SR8 ....**201** D6
Davy Bank *WLSD/HOW* NE28 ....**67** F5
Davy Dr *PLEE/EAS* SR8 ....**199** E6
Dawdon Crs *SEA/MUR* SR7 ....**176** C4
Dawlish Cl *SEA/MUR* SR7 ....**175** F4
Dawlish Gdns
   LWF/SPW/WRK NE9 ....**117** E1
Dawlish Pl *WD/WHPE/BLK* NE5 ....**59** E3
Dawson Sq *TYNE/NSHE* NE30 ....**55** F5
Dawson Ter *MLFD/PNYW* SR4 ....**123** F5
Daylesford Dr *LGB/HTN* NE7 ....**64** B2
Daylesford Rd *CRAM* NE23 ....**13** F5
Dayshield *WD/WHPE/BLK* NE5.........**60** B5
Deacon Cl *WD/WHPE/BLK* NE5 ....**59** D4

Deacon Ct *LGB/KIL* NE12 ....**48** C5
Deaconsfield Cl *SUNDSW* SR3 ....**160** B3
Deal Cl *BLYTH* NE24 ....**17** D2
Dean Cl *PLEE/EAS* SR8 ....**209** E3
Deanery St *BDLGTN* NE22 ....**7** D3
Deanham Gdns
   WD/WHPE/BLK NE5 ....**61** E6
Dean Rd *SSH* NE33 ....**71** F6
Deans Cl *WICK/BNPF* NE16 ....**96** A3
Deansfield Cl *SUNDSW* SR3 ....**160** B3
Dean St *CNUT* NE1 ....**3** E4
   LWF/SPW/WRK NE9 ....**99** E5
Dean Ter *SSH* NE33 ....**71** F3
   SWCK/CAS SR5 ....**125** E3
Dean View Dr *BLYTH* NE24 ....**10** A4
Dearham Gv *CRAM* NE23 ....**13** F4
Debdon Gdns *BYK/HTN/WLK* NE6 ...**65** C5
Debdon Pl *CRAM* NE23 ....**22** A2
Deckham Ter *GATE* NE8 ....**99** F2
Deepbrook Rd
   WD/WHPE/BLK NE5 ....**61** C5
Deepdale *WLSD/HOW* NE28 ....**66** B3
Deepdale Cl *WICK/BNPF* NE16 ....**95** E6
Deepdale Crs *WD/WHPE/BLK* NE5 ..**61** F4
Deepdale Gdns *LGB/KIL* NE12 ....**49** E1
Deepdale Rd *TYNE/NSHE* NE30 ......**55** D2
Deepdale St *HLH* DH5 ....**185** F3
Deepdene Gv
   CLDN/WHIT/ROK SR6 ....**108** C5
Deepdene Rd
   CLDN/WHIT/ROK SR6 ....**108** C5
Deerbolt Pl *LGB/KIL* NE12 ....**49** E5
Deer Bush *WD/WHPE/BLK* NE5 ......**60** B5
Deerness Ct
   BDN/LAN/SAC
   (off Station Av) DH7 ....**203** C4
Deerness Hts *BDN/LAN/SAC* DH7...**203** B3
Deerness Rd *ASHBK/HED/RY* SR2 ....**5** F5
Dee Rd *HEBB* NE31 ....**85** D5
Deer Park Wy *BLAY* NE21 ....**95** D1
Dees Av *WLSD/HOW* NE28...............**67** D3
Dee St *JRW* NE32 ....**86** B1
Defender Ct *SWCK/CAS* SR5 ....**124** B4
Defoe Av *HAR/WTLS* NE34 ....**88** A3
De Grey St *ELS/FEN* NE4 ....**79** F5
Deighton Wk *WD/WHPE/BLK* NE5....**60** B5
Delacour Rd *BLAY* NE21 ....**76** B5
Delamere Ct *SUNDSW* * SR3 ....**160** C2
Delamere Crs *CRAM* NE23...............**13** F4
Delamere Rd *GOS/KPK* NE3 ....**62** B1
Delaval Av *NSHW* NE29 ....**54** A6
Delaval Ct *BDLGTN* NE22 ....**8** D2
   SSH NE33 ....**71** F5
Delaval Cts *BLYTH* NE24 ....**16** A2
Delavale Cl *PLEE/EAS* SR8 ....**209** E3
Delaval Gdns
   BW/LEM/TK/HW NE15 ....**78** A4
   BW/LEM/TK/HW NE15 ....**78** A4
   LGB/KIL NE12 ....**49** F4
   WBAY NE26 ....**41** E6
Delaval Rd *BLYTH* NE24 ....**16** A2
   GOS/KPK NE3 ....**62** C2
Dellfield Dr *MLFD/PNYW* SR4 ....**141** F2
The Dell *HLS* DH4 ....**157** F5
Delta Bank Rd *DUN/TMV* NE11 ....**78** B5
Demesne Dr *BDLGTN* NE22 ....**7** E4
Dempsey Rd *DIN/WO* NE13 ....**33** D5
Denbigh Av *CLDN/WHIT/ROK* SR6 ..**108** C6
   WLSD/HOW NE28 ....**68** C2
Denby Cl *CRAM* NE23 ....**13** F4
Dene Av *BW/LEM/TK/HW* NE15 ....**76** C2
   DIN/WO NE13.................................**32** C4
   GOS/KPK NE3 ....**62** C2
   HLH DH5 ....**171** F2
   LGB/KIL NE12 ....**48** C2
   PLEE/EAS SR8 ....**201** D1
   ROWG NE39 ....**110** C3
Denebank *MONK* NE25 ....**40** A5
Dene Bank Av *PLEE/EAS* SR8 ....**209** F2
Dene Bank Vw *GOS/KPK* NE3 ....**62** A3
Dene Cl *LGB/HTN* NE7 ....**64** C4
   RYTON NE40 ....**74** C3
Dene Ct *BDN/LAN/SAC* DH7...........**178** A3
   CLS/BIR/GTL DH3.......................**129** D6
   WASHS NE38 ....**120** B6
Dene Crs *GOS/KPK* NE3 ....**64** A2
   ROWG NE39 ....**110** C3
   RYTON NE40 ....**74** C3
   WBAY NE26 ....**40** B4
   WLSD/HOW NE28 ....**67** F3
Dene Dr *DHAM* DH1 ....**196** C1
Deneford *LWF/SPW/WRK* NE9 ....**117** F3
Dene Gdns *FELL* NE10 ....**102** A1
   HLH DH5 ....**171** F1
Dene Gv *CRAM* NE23 ....**23** F6
   GOS/KPK NE3 ....**64** A2
Deneholm *MONK* NE25 ....**40** A4
   WLSD/HOW NE28 ....**67** F3
Dene House Rd *SEA/MUR* SR7 ......**176** B2
Dene La *CLDN/WHIT/ROK* SR6 ......**108** C5
   CLDN/WHIT/ROK SR6 ....**108** B3
Dene Pk *SWCK/CAS* SR5.................**124** B2

Dene Rd *BLAY* NE21 ....**76** B5
   ROWG NE39 ....**110** C3
   SEA/MUR SR7 ....**176** A5
   SWCK/CAS SR5 ....**124** B3
   TYNE/NSHE NE30 ....**55** E4
Deneside *BDN/LAN/SAC* DH7.........**164** B6
   BDN/LAN/SAC DH7 ....**178** A4
   CRAM NE23 ....**23** F6
   DUN/TMV NE11 ....**97** E4
   WD/WHPE/BLK NE5 ....**60** B2
Deneside Av *LWF/SPW/WRK* NE9 ...**99** D6
Deneside Ct *JES* NE2 ....**64** C6
Dene St *HLH* DH5 ....**171** F4
   MLFD/PNYW SR4 ....**125** E5
   PLEE/EAS SR8 ....**209** F1
   SUNDSW SR3 ....**143** F5
Dene Ter *JRW* NE32 ....**85** F4
   SEA/MUR SR7 ....**176** C2
The Dene *CLSW/PEL* DH2 ....**166** A2
   HLS DH4 ....**183** F1
   MONK NE25 ....**40** A5
Dene Vw *BDLGTN* NE22 ....**8** B3
   GOS/KPK NE3 ....**64** A2
Dene View Ct
   BLYTH (off Dene View Dr) NE24 ...**10** A5
Dene View Crs *MLFD/PNYW* SR4 ...**124** A6
Dene Vw East *BDLGTN* NE22 ....**8** B4
Dene Vw West *BDLGTN* NE22 ....**8** A4
Dene Vls *PLEE/EAS* SR8 ....**209** F2
Deneway *ROWG* NE39 ....**93** F6
Dene Wy *SEA/MUR* SR7 ....**176** B2
Denewell Av *LGB/HTN* NE7 ....**64** C3
   LWF/SPW/WRK NE9 ....**99** E5
Denewood *LGB/KIL* NE12 ....**50** A2
Denham Av *CLDN/WHIT/ROK* SR6 ..**108** C6
Denham Dr *MONK* NE25 ....**24** C6
Denham Gv *BLAY* NE21 ....**93** E2
Denhill Pk *BW/LEM/TK/HW* NE15 ....**78** C2
Denholm Av *CRAM* NE23 ....**13** F4
Denmark Ct *BYK/HTN/WLK* * NE6 ...**82** B1
Denmark St *BYK/HTN/WLK* NE6.......**82** A1
   GATE NE8 ....**81** E6
Denshaw Cl *CRAM* NE23 ....**13** F4
Dentdale *HLS* DH4 ....**156** A1
Denton Av *BW/LEM/TK/HW* NE15 ....**76** C2
   NSHW NE29 ....**53** E6
Denton Gdns *BW/LEM/TK/HW* NE15..**78** B3
Denton Ga *WD/WHPE/BLK* NE5 ....**60** C3
Denton Gv *WD/WHPE/BLK* NE5 ....**60** C3
Denton Rd *BW/LEM/TK/HW* NE15 ....**77** E3
Denton Vw *BLAY* NE21 ....**76** A6
Dent St *BLYTH* NE24 ....**11** E6
   CLDN/WHIT/ROK SR6 ....**108** C6
Denver Gdns *BYK/HTN/WLK* NE6 ....**83** D5
Denway Gv *WBAY* NE26 ....**26** A1
Denwick Cl *CLSW/PEL* DH2 ....**165** F2
Denwick Ter *TYNE/NSHE* NE30 ....**55** E5
Depot Rd *BYK/HTN/WLK* NE6 ....**82** B1
Deptford Rd *GATE* NE8 ....**81** F4
   MLFD/PNYW SR4 ....**126** A5
Deptford Ter *MLFD/PNYW* SR4 ......**125** F4
Derby Ct *ELS/FEN* NE4 ....**80** A2
Derby Crs *HEBB* NE31 ....**84** C3
Derby Gdns *WLSD/HOW* NE28 ....**66** C3
Derby Rd *STLY/ANP* DH9 ....**148** A3
Derbyshire Dr *DHAM* DH1 ....**196** C4
Derby St *ASHBK/HED/RY* SR2 ....**4** A4
   ELS/FEN NE4 ....**80** A2
   JRW NE32 ....**86** B1
   SSH NE33 ....**71** F4
Derby Ter *SSH* NE33 ....**71** F4
Dereham Cl *WBAY* NE26 ....**26** C3
Dereham Ct *WD/WHPE/BLK* NE5.....**61** D2
Dereham Rd *WBAY* NE26 ....**26** C4
Dereham Wy *NSHW* NE29 ....**53** D4
Derry Av *CLDN/WHIT/ROK* SR6 .....**109** D6
Derwent Av *DUN/TMV* NE11 ....**98** C5
   *HEBB** NE31 ....**85** D5
   ROWG NE39 ....**111** D3
Derwent Cl *BDN/LAN/SAC* DH7 .....**178** A1
   SEA/MUR SR7 ....**176** B2
Derwent Crs *WICK/BNPF* NE16 ....**95** F2
Derwentdale Gdns *LGB/HTN* NE7 ...**65** D3
Derwent Gdns *WLSD/HOW* NE28.....**68** C2
Derwenthaugh Marina *BLAY* NE21 ...**77** F5
Derwenthaugh Rd *BLAY* NE21 ....**77** F5
Derwent Rd *PLEE/EAS* SR8 ....**209** D1
   TYNE/NSHE NE30 ....**55** D2
   WBAY NE26 ....**26** A2
Derwentside
   WICK/BNPF
   (off Woodhouse La) NE16 ....**95** F2
Derwent St *HLH* DH5 ....**186** A2
   SUND SR1 ....**4** B4
Derwent Ter *STLY/ANP* DH9 ....**146** A5
Derwent Vw *BLAY* NE21 ....**95** D1
Derwent Wk *WICK/BNPF* NE16 ....**95** E2
Derwentwater Ct *GATE* * NE8 ....**98** C1
Derwentwater Rd *GATE* NE8 ....**97** F2
Derwent Wy *BLAY* NE21 ....**95** D1
   LGB/KIL NE12 ....**49** E1
Deuchar St *JES* NE2 ....**64** C6
Devon Crs *CLS/BIR/GTL* DH3..........**118** A6
Devon Dr *SUNDSW* SR3 ....**143** F6
Devon Gdns *HAR/WTLS* NE34 ....**90** A1

LWF/SPW/WRK* NE9 ....99 E3
Devonport HLS DH4 ....157 E5
Devon Rd HEBB NE31 ....85 E5
    NSHW NE29 ....53 F3
Devonshire Dr SMOOR NE27 ....51 E3
Devonshire Gdns
    WLSD/HOW NE28 ....66 B5
Devonshire PI JES NE2 ....64 B5
Devonshire Rd DHAM DH1 ....196 B4
Devonshire St SSH NE33 ....88 A1
    SWCK/CAS SR5 ....126 B3
Devonshire Ter JES NE2 ....80 C1
Devon St HLS DH4 ....157 F2
Devonworth PI BLYTH NE24...................9 E5
Dewberry Ct BLYTH NE24 ....16 B2
Dewley CRAM NE23 ....22 A3
Dewley PI WD/WHPE/BLK NE5 ....60 A3
Dewley Rd WD/WHPE/BLK NE5 ....60 C5
Dewsgreen CRAM NE23 ....22 A3
Dexter Wy FELL NE10 ....100 B2
Deyncourt DHAM DH1 ....204 C3
Diamond Ct GOS/KPK NE3 ....61 E1
Diamond St WLSD/HOW NE28 ....67 D4
Diamond Ter DHAM DH1 ....194 B3
Diana St ELS/FEN NE4 ....80 A3
Dibley St BYK/HTN/WLK * NE6 ....82 A3
Dibley St BYK/HTN/WLK * NE6 ....82 A3
Dickens Av HAR/WTLS NE34 ....88 A5
    WICK/BNPF NE16 ....95 F2
Dickens St HLS DH4 ....170 C2
    SWCK/CAS SR5 ....125 E3
Dickens Wynd DHAM DH1 ....204 C1
Didcot Av NSHW NE29 ....70 A1
Didcot Wy BOL NE36 ....105 E3
    BOLCOL NE35 ....105 E3
Dillon St JRW NE32 ....85 F3
Dilston Av MONK NE25 ....41 D6
Dilston CI PLEE/EAS SR8 ....208 A3
    SMOOR NE27 ....52 B2
    WASHS NE38 ....137 F2
Dilston Dr WD/WHPE/BLK NE5 ....60 A3
Dilston Gdns MLFD/PNYW SR4 ....143 E1
Dilston Rd DHAM DH1 ....180 C6
    ELS/FEN NE4 ....79 F2
Dilston Ter JRW NE32 ....86 A5
Dimbula Gdns LGB/HTN NE7 ....65 F4
Dinsdale Av WLSD/HOW NE28 ....67 E1
Dinsdale Dr DHAM DH1 ....196 C3
Dinsdale PI JES NE2 ....81 E1
Dinsdale Rd CLDN/WHIT/ROK SR6 ..127 E3
    JES NE2 ....81 E1
Dinsdale St ASHBK/HED/RY SR2 ....162 B3
Dinsdale St South
    ASHBK/HED/RY SR2 ....162 B2
Dinting CI PLEE/EAS SR8 ....208 A3
Dipe La BOL NE36 ....105 F4
Dipton Gdns SUNDSW SR3 ....144 A4
Dipton Gv CRAM NE23 ....22 A2
Dipton Rd MONK NE25 ....39 F3
Dipwood Rd ROWG NE39 ....110 C3
Dipwood Wy ROWG NE39 ....110 C4
Disraeli St BLYTH NE24 ....10 C4
    HLS DH4 ....170 A2
Dissington PI WD/WHPE/BLK NE5......61 E6
    WICK/BNPF NE16 ....95 F5
Ditchburn Ter MLFD/PNYW SR4........125 E4
Dixon Est RDHAMSE DH6 ....206 B3
Dixon Estate Bungalows
    RDHAMSE DH6 ....206 B4
Dixon PI DUN/TMV NE11 ....97 E2
Dixon Rd HLH DH5 ....170 C4
Dixon's Sq CLDN/WHIT/ROK SR6 ......126 C3
Dixon St GATE NE8 ....98 B1
    SSH NE33 ....71 E5
Dobson CI ELS/FEN NE4 ....80 A3
Dobson Crs BYK/HTN/WLK NE6............82 B4
Dobson Ter SEA/MUR SR7 ....188 B1
Dockendale La WICK/BNPF NE16 ......96 B3
Dock Rd NSHW NE29 ....70 C2
Dock Rd South NSHW NE29 ....70 C3
Dock St WLSD/HOW NE28 ....127 D4
Dockwray CI TYNE/NSHE NE30 ....71 D1
Dockwray Sq TYNE/NSHE NE30..........71 D1
Doddfell CI WASHN NE37 ....119 F6
Doddington
    BW/LEM/TK/HW NE15 ....76 A1
Doddington Dr CRAM NE23 ....21 F2
Dodds Farm
    GOS/KPK
    (off Princes Meadow) NE3 ....62 C3
Dolphin Ct ELS/FEN * NE4 ....78 C3
Dolphin Quay
    NSHW (off Clive St) NE8 ....71 D1
    TYNE/NSHE (off Liddell St) NE30....71 D1
Dolphin St ELS/FEN NE4 ....78 C3
Dominies CI ROWG NE39 ....111 E3
Dominion Rd BDN/LAN/SAC DH7 ......203 D5
Donald Av RDHAMSE DH6 ....187 D4
Donald St GOS/KPK NE3 ....61 F1
Doncaster Rd JES NE2 ....81 E1
Don Dixon Dr JRW NE32 ....104 A1
Donerston Gv PLEE/EAS SR8 ....207 F5
Don Gdns BOL NE36 ....105 E3
Donkin Rd WASHN NE37 ....119 E5

Donkin Ter TYNE/NSHE NE30 ....55 E5
Donnington CI SWCK/CAS SR5 ....123 F3
Donnington St GOS/KPK NE3................64 B2
Donnini PI DHAM DH1 ....195 D2
Donnison Gdns SUND SR1 ....5 F2
Donridge WASHN NE37 ....120 A3
Don Rd JRW NE32 ....86 C1
Don St DUN/TMV NE11 ....98 B6
Donvale Rd WASHN NE37 ....119 F3
Don Vw BOL NE36 ....105 E3
Dorcas Av BW/LEM/TK/HW NE15 ......78 B3
Dorchester CI WD/WHPE/BLK NE5 ....59 D3
Dorchester Ct MONK NE25 ....24 B2
Dorchester Gdns
    LWF/SPW/WRK NE9 ....117 E2
Doreen Av SEA/MUR SR7 ....175 E4
Doric Rd BDN/LAN/SAC DH7 ....202 B1
Dorking Av NSHW NE29 ....70 A2
Dorking CI BLYTH NE24 ....17 D2
Dorking Rd CLDN/WHIT/ROK SR6 ....108 C6
Dorlonco Vls BDN/LAN/SAC DH7 ......203 B3
Dormand Dr PLEE/EAS SR8 ....208 B5
Dornoch Crs FELL NE10 ....101 D4
Dorrington Rd GOS/KPK NE3 ....46 A6
Dorset Av CLDN/WHIT/ROK SR6 ......109 D6
    CLS/BIR/GTL DH3 ....136 B5
    HAR/WTLS NE34 ....90 A1
    HEBB NE31 ....85 E3
    WLSD/HOW NE28 ....66 C4
Dorset Gv NSHW NE29 ....53 F3
Dorset La SUNDSW SR3 ....161 D1
Dorset Rd BW/LEM/TK/HW NE15 ......77 E2
    GATE NE8 ....81 F4
Dorset St HLH DH5 ....186 B4
Double Rw MONK NE25 ....24 A3
Douglas Av HAR/WTLS NE34 ....88 B4
Douglas Ct STLY/ANP DH9 ....146 A5
Douglas Gdns DUN/TMV NE11..............97 F3
Douglas Rd CLDN/WHIT/ROK SR6 ....109 D6
Douglass St WLSD/HOW NE28 ....66 C4
Douglas St WLSD/HOW NE28 ....68 C5
Douglas Ter ELS/FEN NE4 ....80 A3
    HLS DH4 ....140 A6
Douglas Vls DHAM DH1 ....195 D4
Douglas Wy
    CNUT (off Eldon Sq) NE1 ....2 C2
Doulting CI LGB/KIL NE12 ....49 D6
Douro Ter ASHBK/HED/RY SR2..............4 C5
Dove Av JRW NE32 ....86 B5
Dove CI BDN/LAN/SAC DH7 ....202 C5
Dovecote CI MONK NE25 ....39 E4
Dovecote Rd LGB/KIL NE12 ....50 A5
Dovedale Av BLYTH NE24........................9 F5
Dovedale Gdns LGB/HTN NE7 ....64 C3
    LWF/SPW/WRK NE9 ....99 F6
Dovedale Rd
    CLDN/WHIT/ROK SR6 ....108 B5
Dover CI BDLGTN NE22 ....9 E3
    WD/WHPE/BLK NE5 ....59 E3
Dovercourt Rd BYK/HTN/WLK NE6 ....83 F4
Dowling Av MONK NE25 ....40 B6
Downe CI BLYTH NE24 ....17 D2
Downend Rd WD/WHPE/BLK NE5 ......59 F3
Downfield WASHN NE37 ....120 C1
Downham WD/WHPE/BLK NE5 ....60 B5
Downham Ct SSH NE33 ....71 E5
Downhill La BOL NE36 ....105 D6
    WASHN NE37 ....104 C6
Downs La HLH DH5 ....172 A5
Downs Pit La HLH DH5 ....172 C5
Downswood LGB/KIL NE12 ....50 B1
Dowsey Rd RDHAMSE DH6 ....197 E4
Dowson Sq SEA/MUR SR7 ....187 F1
Doxford Av HLH DH5 ....171 E4
Doxford Dr PLEE/EAS SR8 ....207 E2
Doxford Gdns WD/WHPE/BLK NE5 ....60 B5
Doxford Park Wy SUNDSW SR3 ....160 A2
Doxford PI CRAM NE23 ....22 A3
Doxford Ter HLH DH5 ....171 E4
Dragon La DHAM DH1 ....196 A4
Drake CI SSH NE33 ....71 D6
Drayton Rd CLDN/WHIT/ROK SR6 ....108 C6
    GOS/KPK NE3 ....61 G3
Drivecote FELL NE10 ....101 D2
The Drive CLS/BIR/GTL DH3 ....136 C5
    FELL NE10 ....101 D2
    GOS/KPK NE3 ....63 E3
    LGB/HTN NE7 ....65 D2
    LWF/SPW/WRK NE9 ....99 E4
    TYNE/NSHE NE30 ....55 F4
    WASHN NE37 ....120 B3
    WD/WHPE/BLK NE5 ....60 B6
    WICK/BNPF NE16 ....96 B4
    WLSD/HOW NE28 ....67 D4
Dronfield CLSW/PEL DH2 ....165 E1
Drove Rd BW/LEM/TK/HW NE15 ....57 D3
Drummond Crs HAR/WTLS NE34 ....87 E3
Drummond Rd GOS/KPK NE3 ....62 A6
Drummond Ter TYNE/NSHE NE30 ......55 D5
Drumoyne CI SUNDSW SR3 ....159 D2
Drumoyne Gdns MONK NE25................53 F1
Drum Rd CLSW/PEL DH2 ....136 A6
Drumsheugh PI
    WD/WHPE/BLK NE5 ....61 D4
Druridge Av CLDN/WHIT/ROK SR6 ....108 C5

Druridge Crs BLYTH NE24 ....16 A1
    HAR/WTLS NE34 ....73 D6
Druridge Dr BLYTH NE24 ....16 A1
    WD/WHPE/BLK NE5 ....61 F5
Drury La NSHW NE29 ....53 E5
    SUND SR1 ....5 E2
Drybeck Ct CRAM NE23 ....14 C6
    ELS/FEN* NE4 ....80 A3
Drybeck Sq SUNDSW SR3 ....161 D2
Drybeck Wk CRAM NE23 ....14 C6
Dryborough St MLFD/PNYW SR4 ....126 A5
Dryburgh WASHS NE38 ....138 B1
Dryburgh CI NSHW NE29 ....54 A4
Dryburn HI DHAM DH1 ....193 F2
Dryburn Rd DHAM DH1 ....193 F1
Dryden CI HAR/WTLS NE34 ....88 A6
    STLY/ANP DH9 ....148 C2
Dryden Rd LWF/SPW/WRK NE9 ....99 E3
Dryden St SWCK/CAS SR5 ....125 F2
Drysdale CI DIN/WO NE13 ....32 C4
Drysdale Crs DIN/WO NE13 ....32 C4
Dubmire Cottages HLS DH4 ....169 E2
Dubmire Ct HLS DH4 ....169 F2
Duchess Crs JRW NE32 ....86 A5
Duchess Crs East JRW NE32 ....86 A5
Duchess Dr BW/LEM/TK/HW NE15 ....77 F1
Duchess St WBAY NE26 ....40 C5
Duckpool La WICK/BNPF NE16 ....96 B2
Duddon CI PLEE/EAS SR8 ....209 D2
Duddon PI LWF/SPW/WRK NE9 ....100 A6
Dudley Av CLDN/WHIT/ROK SR6 ......108 C5
Dudley Dr CRAM NE23 ....34 C2
Dudley Gdns SUNDSW SR3 ....161 D1
Dudley La CRAM NE23 ....21 F5
    DIN/WO NE13 ....33 E2
Dugdale Rd GOS/KPK NE3 ....61 F1
Duke's Av HEBB NE31 ....84 C4
Dukes Dr GOS/KPK NE3 ....47 D3
Dukesfield CRAM NE23 ....22 A2
Dukes Meadow DIN/WO NE13 ....44 A4
Duke St FELL NE10 ....101 F1
    MLFD/PNYW SR4 ....125 F6
    SEA/MUR SR7 ....176 A2
    WBAY NE26 ....40 C5
Duke St North
    CLDN/WHIT/ROK SR6 ....126 C2
Dukes Wk
    WBAY (off Northern Prom) NE26 ....40 C3
Dukesway DUN/TMV NE11 ....98 A5
Duke Wk GATE NE8 ....98 B1
Dulverton CI WD/WHPE/BLK NE5 ......59 E3
Dulverton Av WD/WHPE/BLK NE33 ....88 C1
Dumfries Crs JRW NE32 ....87 D4
Dunbar CI WD/WHPE/BLK NE5..............59 E3
Dunbar St MLFD/PNYW SR4 ....143 E1
Dunblane Crs WD/WHPE/BLK NE5 ......60 B6
Dunblane Dr BLYTH NE24 ....17 D2
Dunblane Rd
    CLDN/WHIT/ROK SR6 ....109 D6
Dunbreck Gv MLFD/PNYW SR4 ....143 F2
Duncan St BYK/HTN/WLK NE6 ....83 F2
    MLFD/PNYW SR4 ....125 E5
Duncombe Crs STLY/ANP DH9 ....131 E6
Duncow La DHAM DH1 ....194 B5
Dun Cow Wy SUND SR1 ....4 B2
Dundas CI CLDN/WHIT/ROK SR6 ......126 C4
Dundas Wy FELL NE10 ....100 B3
Dundee CI WD/WHPE/BLK NE5 ....59 E3
Dundee Ct JRW NE32 ....87 D5
Dundrennan WASHS NE38 ....138 B3
Dunedin CI
    STLY/ANP (off Kyo Rd) DH9 ....146 B3
Dunelm ASHBK/HED/RY SR2................144 A2
Dunelm Ct
    DHAM (off South St) DH1 ....194 B5
Dunelm Dr BOL NE36 ....106 A3
    HLS DH4 ....170 B2
Dunelm PI RDHAMSE DH6 ....206 C2
Dunelm Rd HLH DH5 ....171 E6
Dunelm South
    ASHBK/HED/RY SR2 ....144 A2
Dunelm St SSH NE33 ....71 F4
Dunelm Wk PLEE/EAS SR8 ....208 C1
Dunford Gdns WD/WHPE/BLK NE5 ....59 F2
Dunholm CI HLH DH5 ....171 D3
Dunholme CI DHAM DH1 ....194 A1
Dunholme Rd ELS/FEN NE4 ....79 E3
Dunira CI JES NE2 ....64 B4
Dunkeld CI BLYTH NE24 ....17 D2
Dunkirk Av HLH DH5 ....171 E3
Dunlin CI RYTON NE40 ....75 D4
Dunlin Dr BLYTH NE24 ....17 D2
    WASHS NE38 ....137 E3
Dunlop CI LGB/HTN NE7 ....65 E2
Dunlop Crs HAR/WTLS NE34 ....89 F2
Dunmoor CI GOS/KPK NE3 ....62 C2
Dunmore Av
    CLDN/WHIT/ROK SR6 ....109 D5
Dunmorlie St BYK/HTN/WLK NE6 ......82 C3
Dunn Av SUNDSW SR3 ....143 F5
Dunning St SUND SR1 ....4 B1
Dunnlynn CI SUNDSW SR3 ....160 A2
Dunnock Dr WASHS NE38 ....137 E4

WICK/BNPF NE16.................................**113** F1
Dunn Rd *PLEE/EAS* SR8.................**208** C1
Dunn's Ter *JES* NE2.............................**63** D6
Dunn St *ELS/FEN* NE4........................**80** A5
Dunn Ter *BYK/HTN/WLK* NE6............**82** A2
Dunnykirk Av *GOS/KPK* NE3...............**61** F1
Dunsdale Av *CRAM* NE23....................**14** C6
Dunsdale Rd *MONK* NE25....................**25** D6
Dunsgreen *PONT/DH* NE20.................**28** A5
Dunsley Gdns *DIN/WO* NE13...............**31** D3
Dunsmuir Gv *GATE* NE8.......................**99** D2
Dunstable Pl *WD/WHPE/BLK* NE5......**59** D3
Dunstanburgh *BDLGTN* NE22.................**6** C3
Dunstanburgh Cl *BDLGTN* NE22.
BYK/HTN/WLK NE6.............................**82** C3
WASHS NE38......................................**138** A2
Dunstanburgh Rd
BYK/HTN/WLK NE6.............................**82** C3
Dunstan Cl *CLSW/PEL* DH2................**165** F1
Dunston Bank *DUN/TMV* NE11............**97** D3
Dunston Pl *BLYTH* NE24......................**10** A5
Dunston Rd *DUN/TMV* NE11................**97** E1
Dunvegan *CLS/BIR/GTL* DH3..............**137** D4
Dunvegan Av *CLSW/PEL* DH2..............**166** A1
Durant Rd *CNUT* NE1..............................**3** E2
Durban St *BLYTH* NE24.......................**10** C3
Durham Av *PLEE/EAS* SR8...................**201** E4
WASHN NE37.....................................**120** A4
Durham Cl *BDLGTN* NE22......................**6** C2
Durham Dr *BOLCOL* NE35...................**104** A2
JRW NE32...**86** A6
Durham Gdns *BDN/LAN/SAC* DH7.....**178** A3
Durham Gv *JRW* NE32..........................**86** A6
Durham La *PLEE/EAS* SR8..................**199** E3
RDHAMSE DH6..................................**198** A5
Durham Pl *CLS/BIR/GTL* DH3..............**136** B5
GATE NE8..**99** F1
Durham Rd *ASHBK/HED/RY* SR2.......**126** A6
BDN/LAN/SAC DH7............................**178** B2
CLS/BIR/GTL DH3..............................**136** B1
CLS/BIR/GTL DH3..............................**166** B1
CRAM NE23...**14** B5
GATE NE8..**99** E1
HLH DH5...**158** B5
HLH DH5...**170** C3
HLS DH4...**171** D1
LWF/SPW/WRK NE9...........................**99** E6
STLY/ANP DH9...................................**146** C5
SUNDSW DH3.....................................**143** F3
Durham St *ELS/FEN* NE4.....................**79** E4
FELL NE10..**101** E1
HLS DH4...**169** F2
SEA/MUR SR7....................................**176** A2
WLSD/HOW NE28................................**67** E4
Durham St West *WLSD/HOW* NE28.....**67** E4
Durham Ter *SUNDSW* SR3.................**143** F5
Durham Wy *PLEE/EAS* SR8................**208** A5
Duxfield Rd *LGB/HTN* NE7....................**65** D3
Dwyer Crs *ASHBK/HED/RY* SR2........**162** B2
Dyer Sq *SWCK/CAS* SR5.....................**126** A2
Dykefield Av *GOS/KPK* NE3..................**46** A3
Dyke Heads La *RYTON* NE40................**74** A6
Dykelands Rd
CLDN/WHIT/ROK SR6........................**108** C3
Dykelands Wy *HAR/WTLS* NE34...........**87** F3
Dykenook Cl *WICK/BNPF* NE16.............**95** F6
Dykes Wy *FELL* NE10.........................**100** C5
Dymock Ct *WD/WHPE/BLK* NE5............**61** D1

E

Eaglescliffe Dr *LGB/HTN* NE7.............**65** F3
Eaglesdene *HLH* DH5..........................**171** F6
Eagle St *DUN/TMV* NE11......................**98** A4
Ealing Ct *DIN/WO* NE13.......................**45** D6
Ealing Dr *TYNE/NSHE* NE30................**55** E3
Eardulph Av *CLS/BIR/GTL* DH3...........**153** F5
Earl Grey Wy *NSHW* NE29...................**70** B3
Earlington Ct *LGB/KIL* NE12................**50** A3
Earl's Dr *BW/LEM/TK/HW* NE15...........**77** F1
LWF/SPW/WRK NE9............................**99** E6
Earl's Gdns *BLYTH* NE24......................**10** B4
Earls Gn *HLH* DH5...............................**184** C1
Earl St *MLFD/PNYW* SR4....................**126** A6
SEA/MUR SR7....................................**175** F2
STLY/ANP DH9...................................**146** A3
Earlsway *DUN/TMV* NE11.....................**98** B3
Earlswood Av *LWF/SPW/WRK* NE9......**99** E6
Earlswood Gv *BLYTH* NE24...................**16** C3
Earnshaw Wy *MONK* NE25....................**39** F3
Earsdon Cl *WD/WHPE/BLK* NE5...........**60** C4
Earsdon Rd *GOS/KPK* NE3....................**62** A3
HLH DH5...**171** E2
MONK NE25...**39** F6
SMOOR NE27.......................................**38** B6
Earsdon Vw *SMOOR* NE27....................**38** B6
Easby Cl *GOS/KPK* NE3.........................**47** F4
Easby Rd *WASHS* NE38......................**138** C2
Easdale Av *GOS/KPK* NE3.....................**47** E3
Easedale *WBAY* NE26...........................**26** B2
Easedale Gdns
LWF/SPW/WRK NE9............................**99** F6

Easington Av *CRAM* NE23......................**14** B4
LWF/SPW/WRK NE9...........................**118** B1
Easington St *PLEE/EAS* SR8...............**200** C2
SWCK/CAS SR5..................................**126** B4
Easington St North *SWCK/CAS* SR5...**126** B4
East Acre *BLAY* NE21...........................**76** C6
East Acres *DIN/WO* NE13......................**31** D2
East Atherton St *DHAM* DH1...............**194** A5
East Av *HAR/WTLS* NE34......................**89** F2
LGB/KIL NE12.....................................**49** F6
WASHS NE38.....................................**138** B5
East Back Pde *ASHBK/HED/RY* SR2......**5** H5
East Bailey *LGB/KIL* NE12.....................**50** A1
East Boldon Rd
CLDN/WHIT/ROK SR6........................**107** D2
Eastbourne Av *BYK/HTN/WLK* NE6.......**83** F1
GATE NE8..**99** D2
Eastbourne Gdns
BYK/HTN/WLK NE6..............................**83** F1
WBAY NE26..**40** B4
Eastbourne Gv *SSH* NE33....................**71** F3
Eastburn Gdns *FELL* NE10.................**102** A1
Eastcheap *BYK/HTN/WLK* NE6.............**65** E5
East Cleft Rd *ASHBK/HED/RY* SR2.....**126** A6
Eastcliffe Av *GOS/KPK* NE3...................**62** C3
East Cl *HAR/WTLS* NE34........................**89** F2
Eastcombe Cl *BOLCOL* NE35................**87** D6
Eastcote Ter *BYK/HTN/WLK* NE6..........**83** E5
East Crs *BDLGTN* NE22...........................**8** C2
East Cross St *SUND* SR1.........................**4** D1
Eastdene Rd *SEA/MUR* SR7.................**175** E3
Eastdene Wy *PLEE/EAS* SR8...............**209** E3
East Dr *BLYTH* NE24..............................**16** B2
CLDN/WHIT/ROK SR6........................**107** D2
East End *WBAY* NE26.............................**27** D4
Easten Gdns *FELL* NE10......................**100** C1
Eastern Av *DUN/TMV* NE11...................**98** C6
LGB/KIL (off Station Rd North) NE12.......**49** F4
Eastern Wy *WD/WHPE/BLK* NE5............**61** F4
East Farm Ct *WICK/BNPF* NE16...........**114** B1
Eastfield *PLEE/EAS* SR8......................**209** F3
Eastfield Av *BYK/HTN/WLK* NE6............**66** C6
MONK NE25...**39** F6
Eastfield Rd *HAR/WTLS* NE34...............**72** B5
LGB/KIL NE12......................................**49** E6
East Flds *CLDN/WHIT/ROK* SR6..........**109** E2
Eastfield St *MLFD/PNYW* SR4.............**143** E1
Eastfield Ter *LGB/KIL* NE12.................**49** F6
East Forest Hall Rd *LGB/KIL* NE12.......**50** A1
East Front *JES* NE2...............................**64** A6
Eastgarth *WD/WHPE/BLK* NE5..............**60** C1
Eastgate Gdns *ELS/FEN* NE4.................**81** E5
East George Potts St *SSH* NE33..........**71** F5
East George St *TYNE/NSHE* NE30.........**55** E6
East Gra *MONK* NE25.............................**25** E6
SWCK/CAS SR5..................................**126** B1
East Grange Ct *PLEE/EAS* * SR8.........**200** A3
East Gn *RDHAMSE* DH6.......................**206** C2
East Gv *MLFD/PNYW* SR4....................**142** A1
East Hill Rd *GATE* NE8........................**100** A1
East Holborn *SSH* NE33........................**71** D4
Eastlands *BLAY* NE21............................**94** A1
LGB/HTN NE7......................................**64** C3
East Lea *BLAY* NE21..............................**94** B2
Eastlea Crs *SEA/MUR* SR7..................**175** F3
Eastlea Rd *SEA/MUR* SR7....................**175** E3
Eastleigh Cl *BOLCOL* NE35.................**105** D2
East Moffett St *SSH* NE33......................**71** F5
East Moor Rd *MLFD/PNYW* SR4...........**125** E5
East Park Gdns *BLAY* NE21...................**94** B1
East Park Rd *LWF/SPW/WRK* NE9.........**99** F1
East Park Vw *BLYTH* NE24....................**11** E5
East Percy St *TYNE/NSHE* NE30............**55** E6
East Riggs *BDLGTN* NE22........................**7** F1
East Stevenson St *SSH* NE33................**71** F5
East Stoneycroft *LGB/KIL* NE12............**50** A2
East St *CLDN/WHIT/ROK* SR6..............**109** E2
CLSW/PEL DH2..................................**150** C3
GATE NE8..**81** E5
RDHAMSE DH6..................................**206** C2
SSH NE33..**71** E3
STLY/ANP DH9...................................**149** D1
East Thorp *WD/WHPE/BLK* NE5.............**60** B1
East Vw *CLDN/WHIT/ROK* SR6............**127** D1
HEBB NE31..**71** G6
PLEE/EAS SR8..................................**191** D4
STLY/ANP (off Flint Hl) DH9..................**129** D5
SWCK/CAS SR5..................................**124** B3
WICK/BNPF NE16...............................**111** F6
East View Ter *WICK/BNPF* NE16............**96** A2
East Vines *SUND* SR1.............................**5** G1
Eastward Gn *MONK* NE25......................**39** F6
Eastway *HAR/WTLS* NE34......................**90** A3
Eastwood *BDN/LAN/SAC* DH7..............**178** B2
Eastwood Av *BLYTH* NE24......................**16** C3
Eastwood Cl *CRAM* NE23......................**35** E5
Eastwood Gdns *FELL* NE10.................**100** B4
GOS/KPK NE3......................................**62** B2
LWF/SPW/WRK NE9............................**99** F1
Eastwood Pl *CRAM* NE23......................**14** B4
Eaton Pl *ELS/FEN* NE4..........................**79** E3
Eavers Ct *HAR/WTLS* NE34...................**88** B3
Ebba Wk *GOS/KPK* NE3.........................**63** F1

Ebchester Ct *GOS/KPK* NE3..................**61** E1
Ebchester St *HAR/WTLS* NE34..............**87** F3
Ebdon La *CLDN/WHIT/ROK* SR6..........**108** C6
Ebor St *BYK/HTN/WLK* NE6....................**65** E6
HAR/WTLS NE34..................................**87** F4
Eccleston Cl *SMOOR* NE27....................**37** E6
Eccleston Rd *SSH* NE33.........................**72** A4
Ecgfrid Ter *JRW* NE32...........................**86** B3
Eddison Rd *WASHS* NE38....................**139** E2
Eddleston Av *GOS/KPK* NE3...................**62** C3
Eddrington Gv
WD/WHPE/BLK NE5.............................**59** E3
Ede Av *DUN/TMV* NE11..........................**97** E2
HAR/WTLS NE34..................................**90** A2
Eden Av *WICK/BNPF* NE16...................**111** F6
Edenbridge Crs *LGB/KIL* NE12..............**49** D5
Eden Cl *WD/WHPE/BLK* NE5..................**59** E4
Edendale Av *BLYTH* NE24......................**10** A4
BYK/HTN/WLK NE6..............................**83** F2
Edendale Ter *GATE* NE8.........................**99** E2
PLEE/EAS * SR8................................**209** E2
Edenfield *STLY/ANP* DH9.....................**150** C1
Edenhill Rd *PLEE/EAS* SR8.................**209** D1
Eden House Rd *MLFD/PNYW* SR4........**144** A1
Eden La *PLEE/EAS* SR8........................**200** C6
Eden Pl *TYNE/NSHE* NE30.....................**54** C3
Eden Rd *DHAM* DH1.............................**180** B6
Eden St *PLEE/EAS* SR8........................**209** F1
WLSD/HOW NE28.................................**67** D5
Eden St West *SUND* SR1..........................**4** A2
Eden Ter *MLFD/PNYW* SR4...................**144** A1
Eden V *MLFD/PNYW* SR4......................**144** A1
Eden Vw *RDHAMSE* DH6......................**206** C2
Edgar St *GOS/KPK* NE3..........................**64** B1
Edgecote *WASHN* NE37.......................**121** E4
Edge Ct *DHAM* DH1..............................**195** E4
Edgefield Av *GOS/KPK* NE3....................**62** B1
Edgefield Dr *CRAM* NE23......................**14** B4
Edge Mt *LGB/KIL* NE12...........................**35** F6
Edgeware Wk *ELS/FEN* * NE4................**79** E5
Edgewood Av *BDLGTN* NE22...................**8** B3
Edgeworth Cl *BOLCOL* NE35..................**87** D6
Edgeworth Crs
CLDN/WHIT/ROK SR6........................**126** C2
Edgmond Ct *ASHBK/HED/RY* SR2.......**145** D6
Edgware Rd *GATE* NE8...........................**99** F2
Edhill Av *HAR/WTLS* NE34.....................**87** E3
Edinburgh Ct *DIN/WO* * NE13................**45** F4
Edinburgh Dr *BDLGTN* NE22...................**6** C2
Edinburgh Rd *JRW* NE32........................**87** D4
Edington Gv *TYNE/NSHE* NE30...............**54** C3
Edington Rd *TYNE/NSHE* NE30...............**54** C3
Edison Gdns *GATE* NE8.........................**99** D3
Edison St *SEA/MUR* SR7......................**188** B1
Edith Av *BLAY* NE21...............................**76** B6
Edith St *ASHBK/HED/RY* SR2...............**145** D2
JRW NE32...**85** F1
SEA/MUR SR7....................................**177** D5
SWCK/CAS SR5..................................**126** A2
TYNE/NSHE NE30................................**55** E4
Edith Ter *WICK/BNPF* * NE16................**95** F3
Edlingham Cl *GOS/KPK* NE3...................**64** B2
Edlingham Ct *HLH* * DH5.....................**171** E2
Edlingham Rd *DHAM* DH1....................**194** B1
Edmondsley La
BDN/LAN/SAC DH7............................**164** A5
Edmund Pl *LWF/SPW/WRK* NE9............**99** E5
Edna Ter *WD/WHPE/BLK* NE5.................**60** C3
Edward Av *PLEE/EAS* SR8....................**209** E1
Edward Burdis St *SWCK/CAS* SR5.......**126** A2
Edward Cain Ct *PLEE/EAS* SR8............**209** F1
Edward Pl *ELS/FEN* * NE4......................**80** A3
Edward Rd *BDLGTN* * NE22.....................**8** C2
CLS/BIR/GTL DH3...............................**136** A1
WLSD/HOW NE28.................................**68** B3
Edwardson Rd
BDN/LAN/SAC DH7............................**203** F5
Edwards Rd *WBAY* NE26........................**41** D4
Edward St *BLYTH* NE24..........................**10** C4
DHAM DH1..**195** E4
GOS/KPK NE3......................................**63** E1
HEBB NE31..**84** B1
HLH DH5...**171** F6
STLY/ANP DH9...................................**149** E6
SUNDSW SR3.....................................**160** C1
Edward's Wk *CNUT* NE1..........................**2** F1
Edwin Gv *WLSD/HOW* NE28...................**68** C3
Edwins Av *LGB/KIL* NE12.......................**50** A4
Edwin's Av South *LGB/KIL* NE12...........**50** A4
Edwin St *BYK/HTN/WLK* * NE6................**82** A2
HLH DH5...**171** D1
MLFD/PNYW SR4...............................**125** D5
Egerton Rd *HAR/WTLS* NE34.................**88** B2
Egerton St *ASHBK/HED/RY* SR2.............**5** L3
BW/LEM/TK/HW NE15...........................**78** B4
Eggleston Cl *CLS/BIR/GTL* DH3...........**168** A4
DHAM DH1..**181** D6
Eggleston Dr *SUNDSW* SR3.................**143** F4
Egham Rd *WD/WHPE/BLK* NE5...............**59** E4
Eglesfield Rd *SSH* NE33........................**71** E6
Eglinton St *SWCK/CAS* SR5.................**126** B3
Eglinton St North *SWCK/CAS* SR5.......**126** B3
Egremont Dr *LWF/SPW/WRK* NE9.........**99** F1
Egremont Gdns
LWF/SPW/WRK NE9............................**99** F4

Egremont Gv *PLEE/EAS* SR8 ....207 F5
Egremont Pl *WBAY* NE26 ....41 D6
Eider Cl *BLYTH* NE24 ....17 D3
Eighteenth Av *BLYTH* NE24 ....16 B1
Eighth Av *BLYTH* NE24 ....10 C6
　BYK/HTN/WLK NE6 ....65 E6
　CLSW/PEL DH2 ....153 D5
Eighth St *PLEE/EAS* SR8 ....209 F1
Eighton Ter *LWF/SPW/WRK* NE9 ....118 C1
Eishort Wy *LGB/KIL* NE12 ....49 D6
Eland Cl *GOS/KPK* NE3 ....61 F1
Eland Edge *PONT/DH* NE20 ....28 B4
Eland La *PONT/DH* NE20 ....28 B3
Elberfeld Ct *JRW* NE32 ....86 A2
Elder Cl *BDN/LAN/SAC* DH7 ....192 A5
Elder Gv *HAR/WTLS* NE34 ....89 E4
　LWF/SPW/WRK NE9 ....99 E5
Elderwood Gdns *DUN/TMV* NE11 ......98 A5
Eldon Ct
　CNUT (off Percy St) NE1 ....2 C2
Eldon Gdns *CNUT* * NE1 ....2 C2
Eldon La *CNUT* NE1 ....2 C2
Eldon Pl *BW/LEM/TK/HW* NE15 ....76 C1
Eldon Rd *BW/LEM/TK/HW* NE15 ....76 C1
Eldon Sq *CNUT* NE1 ....2 D2
Eldon St *GATE* NE8 ....81 F5
　MLFD/PNYW SR4 ....125 F6
　SSH NE33 ....71 D5
　WLSD/HOW NE28 ....68 C4
Eldon Wy
　CNUT (off Eldon Sq) NE1 ....2 C2
Eleanor St *SSH* NE33 ....71 F3
　TYNE/NSHE NE30 ....41 E6
Eleanor Ter *WD/WHPE/BLK* NE16 ......95 F3
Elemore La *HLH* DH5 ....186 A4
　RDHAMSE DH6 ....185 D6
Elemore Vw *RDHAMSE* DH6 ....187 D5
Elenbel Av *BDLGTN* NE22 ....8 B3
Eleventh Av *BLYTH* NE24 ....11 D6
Eleventh St *PLEE/EAS* SR8 ....209 E1
Elford Cl *MONK* NE25 ....39 F5
Elfordleigh *HLS* DH4 ....157 E4
Elgar Av *WD/WHPE/BLK* NE5 ....59 E4
Elgar Cl *STLY/ANP* DH9 ....148 C3
Elgin Av *SEA/MUR* SR7 ....175 E3
　WLSD/HOW NE28 ....68 B2
Elgin Cl *NSHW* NE29 ....53 E4
Elgin Ct *FELL* NE10 ....84 A6
Elgin Gdns *BYK/HTN/WLK* NE6 ....83 C2
Elgin Gv *STLY/ANP* DH9 ....149 D2
Elgin Rd *LWF/SPW/WRK* NE9 ....100 A3
Elgin St *JRW* NE32 ....87 D4
Elgy Rd *GOS/KPK* NE3 ....63 D3
Elisabeth Av *CLS/BIR/GTL* DH3 ....118 A6
Elizabeth Ct *LGB/KIL* NE12 ....50 C4
Elizabeth Crs *CRAM* NE23 ....34 C2
Elizabeth Diamond Gdns
　SSH NE33 ....71 D6
Elizabeth Dr *LGB/KIL* NE12 ....50 C4
Elizabeth Rd *WLSD/HOW* NE28 ....68 C3
Elizabeth St *BYK/HTN/WLK* NE6 ....81 F2
　HLH DH5 ....171 D1
　SSH* NE33 ....71 F4
　SWCK/CAS SR5 ....124 A3
　SWCK/CAS SR5 ....126 B1
Elizabeth Way
　SSH NE33 ....71 D6
Elizabeth Av *CLS/BIR/GTL* DH3 ....118 A6
Ell-Dene Crs *FELL* NE10 ....101 D5
Ellerbeck Cl *FELL* NE10 ....100 B2
Ellersmere Gdns *TYNE/NSHE* NE30 ...55 D2
Ellerton Wy *CRAM* NE23 ....14 B4
　FELL NE10 ....100 B2
Ellesmere *HLS* DH4 ....155 F5
Ellesmere Av *BYK/HTN/WLK* NE6 .....83 D1
　WD/WHPE/BLK NE5 ....60 C4
Ellesmere Ct *ASHBK/HED/RY* SR2 ...145 D5
Ellesmere Dr *SEA/MUR* SR7 ....175 E3
Ellesmere Rd *ELS/FEN* NE4 ....79 D3
Ellington Cl *ASHBK/HED/RY* SR2 .....162 B3
　BW/LEM/TK/HW NE15 ....76 A1
Elliot Cl *HLS* DH4 ....157 D1
Elliot Rd *FELL* NE10 ....100 A1
Elliott Dr *FELL* NE10 ....100 A1
Elliott Gdns *WLSD/HOW* NE28 ....66 C6
Elliott Rd *FELL* * NE10 ....82 A6
　PLEE/EAS SR8 ....208 C1
Elliott St *BLYTH* NE24 ....16 A2
Elliott Ter *ELS/FEN* NE4 ....79 E3
Ellis Leazes *DHAM* DH1 ....195 D4
Ellison Main Gdns *FELL* NE10 ....101 D1
Ellison Pl *CNUT* NE1 ....3 E2
　JRW NE32 ....69 D6
　LWF/SPW/WRK NE9 ....99 E6
Ellison Rd *DUN/TMV* NE11 ....97 F2
　PLEE/EAS SR8 ....209 D1
Ellison St *GATE* NE8 ....81 E5
　HEBB NE31 ....84 C2
　JRW NE32 ....86 A1
Ellison Vls *GATE* NE8 ....99 F1
Ellis Rd *SWCK/CAS* SR5 ....125 F1
Ellis Sq *SWCK/CAS* SR5 ....126 A1
Ellwood Gdns *LWF/SPW/WRK* NE9 ...99 E2
Elm Av *BDN/LAN/SAC* DH7 ....203 D5
　CLSW/PEL DH2 ....151 E2
　DIN/WO NE13 ....31 D3
　DUN/TMV NE11 ....97 E3

　HAR/WTLS NE34 ....89 E4
　WICK/BNPF NE16 ....96 B2
Elm Cl *CRAM* NE23 ....14 B4
Elm Ct *WICK/BNPF* NE16 ....96 A5
Elm Crs *CLSW/PEL* DH2 ....179 E1
Elm Croft Rd *LGB/KIL* NE12 ....50 A5
Elm Dr *BDLGTN* NE22 ....7 E5
　CLDN/WHIT/ROK SR6 ....109 F1
Elmfield Av *DHAM* DH1 ....196 A3
Elmfield Cl *SUNDSW* SR3 ....159 D2
Elmfield Gdns *WLSD/HOW* NE28 ....66 B2
Elmfield Gv *GOS/KPK* NE3 ....63 D3
Elmfield Pk *GOS/KPK* NE3 ....63 D3
Elmfield Rd *BW/LEM/TK/HW* NE15 ....58 A4
　GOS/KPK NE3 ....63 D3
　HEBB NE31 ....85 E4
Elmfield Ter *FELL* * NE10 ....101 F1
　HEBB NE31 ....85 E4
Elm Gv *BDN/LAN/SAC* DH7 ....192 A5
　GOS/KPK NE3 ....88 B5
　HAR/WTLS NE34 ....89 E4
　LGB/KIL NE12 ....49 F3
　WICK/BNPF NE16 ....111 E6
Elm Rd *BLAY* NE21 ....76 C6
　NSHW NE29 ....53 D5
　PONT/DH NE20 ....28 C5
Elmsford Gv *LGB/KIL* NE12 ....49 E6
Elmsleigh Gdns
　CLDN/WHIT/ROK SR6 ....89 F5
The Elms *ASHBK/HED/RY* SR2 ....4 C6
　GOS/KPK (off Elmfield Rd) NE3 ....63 D3
　HLH DH5 ....186 C3
Elm St *CLS/BIR/GTL* DH3 ....153 E5
　DUN/TMV NE11 ....98 A4
　JRW NE32 ....85 F1
　STLY/ANP DH9 ....147 F4
　WICK/BNPF NE16 ....114 A2
Elm St West *WICK/BNPF* NE16 ....114 A2
Elms West *ASHBK/HED/RY* SR2 ....4 C6
Elm Ter *STLY/ANP* DH9 ....146 A4
Elmtree Ct *SEA/MUR* SR7 ....176 B5
Elmtree Gdns *MONK* NE25 ....54 A1
Elmtree Gv *GOS/KPK* NE3 ....63 D2
Elm Trees *BLYTH* NE24 ....10 C6
Elmway *CLSW/PEL* DH2 ....152 C3
Elmwood *BW/LEM/TK/HW* NE15 ....59 E6
Elmwood Av *DIN/WO* NE13 ....33 D5
　SWCK/CAS SR5 ....125 E1
Elmwood Crs *BYK/HTN/WLK* NE6 ......66 B5
Elmwood Dr *PONT/DH* NE20 ....28 A3
Elmwood Gdns *DUN/TMV* NE11 ....98 A4
Elmwood Rd *MONK* NE25 ....40 A6
Elmwood St *ASHBK/HED/RY* SR2 .....144 A1
　HLS DH4 ....169 D1
Elrick Cl *WD/WHPE/BLK* NE5 ....59 E4
Elrington Gdns
　WD/WHPE/BLK NE5 ....61 D6
Elsdon Av *MONK* NE25 ....24 C5
Elsdonburn Rd *SUNDSW* SR3 ....160 A3
Elsdon Cl *BLYTH* NE24 ....10 B5
　PLEE/EAS SR8 ....208 B5
Elsdon Ct *WICK/BNPF* NE16 ....95 F5
Elsdon Gdns *LGB/KIL* NE12 ....50 B4
Elsdon Gdns *DUN/TMV* NE11 ....97 E2
Elsdon Ms
　HEBB (off High Lane Rw) NE31 ....85 E1
Elsdon Pl *NSHW* NE29 ....70 C2
Elsdon Rd *DHAM* DH1 ....180 C6
　GOS/KPK NE3 ....63 E1
　WICK/BNPF NE16 ....95 F4
Elsdon St *NSHW* * NE29 ....70 C2
Elsdon Ter *NSHW* NE29 ....69 F3
Elsing Cl *WD/WHPE/BLK* NE5 ....61 D2
Elstob Pl *BYK/HTN/WLK* NE6 ....83 D4
　SUNDSW SR3 ....143 F4
Elston Cl *WD/WHPE/BLK* NE5 ....59 E4
Elstree Ct *DIN/WO* NE13 ....45 D5
Elstree Gdns *BLYTH* NE24 ....16 C3
Elswick East Ter *ELS/FEN* NE4 ....80 A4
Elswick Rd *ELS/FEN* NE4 ....79 D4
Elswick Rw *ELS/FEN* NE4 ....80 A3
Elswick St *ELS/FEN* NE4 ....80 A3
Elswick Wy *HAR/WTLS* NE34 ....87 F2
Elterwater Rd *CLSW/PEL* DH2 ....166 A1
Elton St East *WLSD/HOW* NE28 ....67 D5
Elton St West *WLSD/HOW* NE28 ....66 C5
Eltringham Cl *WLSD/HOW* NE28 ....66 C5
Elvaston Rd *RYTON* NE40 ....74 B2
Elvet Br *DHAM* DH1 ....194 B5
Elvet Cl *BYK/HTN/WLK* * NE6 ....82 B1
　DIN/WO NE13 ....32 C4
Elvet Ct *BYK/HTN/WLK* NE6 ....82 B1
Elvet Crs *DHAM* DH1 ....194 C5
Elvet Gn *CLSW/PEL* DH2 ....153 E6
　HLH DH5 ....185 D1
Elvet Hill Rd *DHAM* DH1 ....205 E1
Elvet Wy *BYK/HTN/WLK* * NE6 ....82 B1
Elvington St
　CLDN/WHIT/ROK SR6 ....127 D1
Elwin Cl *WBAY* NE26 ....26 C3
Elwin Pl *CLSW/PEL* DH2 ....152 A2
Elwin Ter *ASHBK/HED/RY* SR2 ....4 A4
Elwyn Cl *WBAY* NE26 ....26 C3
Ely Cl *LGB/KIL* NE12 ....65 F2

Ely Rd *DHAM* DH1 ....180 C3
Elysium La *GATE* NE8 ....98 C1
Ely St *GATE* NE8 ....99 D1
Embankment Rd *SEA/MUR* SR7 ....176 A1
　SEA/MUR SR7 ....177 D4
Embassy Gdns
　BW/LEM/TK/HW NE15 ....78 A2
Emblehope *WASHN* NE37 ....119 F6
Emblehope Dr *GOS/KPK* NE3 ....62 C2
Embleton Av *GOS/KPK* NE3 ....46 C6
　HAR/WTLS NE34 ....73 D6
　WLSD/HOW NE28 ....68 A1
Embleton Cl *DHAM* DH1 ....180 C5
Embleton Crs *NSHW* NE29 ....53 E4
Embleton Dr *BLYTH* NE24 ....16 B1
　CLSW/PEL DH2 ....165 C2
Embleton Gdns *FELL* NE10 ....100 C1
　WD/WHPE/BLK NE5 ....61 F5
Embleton Rd *FELL* NE10 ....84 A6
　NSHW NE29 ....53 E4
Embleton St *SEA/MUR* SR7 ....176 C5
Emden Rd *GOS/KPK* NE3 ....46 A6
Emerson Chambers
　CNUT (off Blackett St) NE1 ....2 D3
Emily St *BYK/HTN/WLK* NE6 ....83 D2
　GATE NE8 ....100 A1
Emlyn Rd *HAR/WTLS* NE34 ....88 B2
Emma Ct *ASHBK/HED/RY* SR2 ....5 F5
Emmbrook Cl *HLH* DH5 ....170 C6
Emmerson Pl *SMOOR* NE27 ....52 A1
Emperor Wy *SUNDSW* SR3 ....159 D3
Empress Rd *BYK/HTN/WLK* NE6 ....84 A4
Empress St *SWCK/CAS* SR5 ....126 B3
Emsworth Rd *SWCK/CAS* SR5 ....125 F1
Enderby Rd *MLFD/PNYW* SR4 ....126 A5
Enfield Av *WICK/BNPF* NE16 ....96 A1
Enfield Gdns *WICK/BNPF* NE16 ....96 A5
Enfield Rd *LWF/SPW/WRK* NE9 ....99 E3
　SEA/MUR SR7 ....175 E3
Enfield St *MLFD/PNYW* SR4 ....125 C3
Engine Inn Rd *WLSD/HOW* NE28 ....68 B2
Engine La *LWF/SPW/WRK* NE9 ....99 E6
Englefield Cl *GOS/KPK* NE3 ....45 F5
Englemann Wy *SUNDSW* SR3 ....160 A4
Enid Av *CLDN/WHIT/ROK* SR6 ....126 C1
Enid St *DIN/WO* NE13 ....32 C6
Ennerdale *ASHBK/HED/RY* SR2 ....144 B2
　CLS/BIR/GTL DH3 ....136 C4
　FELL NE10 ....101 F2
Ennerdale Cl *DHAM* DH1 ....197 D3
　SEA/MUR SR7 ....175 E3
Ennerdale Crs *BLAY* NE21 ....94 A2
　HLS DH4 ....139 F6
Ennerdale Gdns
　LWF/SPW/WRK NE9 ....99 F5
　WLSD/HOW NE28 ....68 C2
Ennerdale Rd *BLYTH* NE24 ....9 E3
　BYK/HTN/WLK NE6 ....83 E2
　TYNE/NSHE NE30 ....54 C2
Ennerdale St *HLH* DH5 ....185 D2
Enslin St *BYK/HTN/WLK* NE6 ....83 E5
Enterprise Ct
　CRAM (off Crosland Pk) NE23 ....13 E5
　SEA/MUR SR7 ....162 A6
Enterprise House
　DUN/TMV (off Kingsway) NE11 ....98 C6
Epping Cl *SEA/MUR* SR7 ....175 E4
Eppleton Hall Cl *SEA/MUR* SR7 ....175 D2
Eppleton Rw *HLH* DH5 ....172 A6
Epsom Cl *NSHW* NE29 ....70 B2
Epsom Ct *GOS/KPK* NE3 ....45 E5
Epsom Wy *BLYTH* NE24 ....16 C3
Epwell Gv *CRAM* NE23 ....14 B4
Epworth *STLY/ANP* DH9 ....130 B6
Epworth Gv *GATE* NE8 ....98 C1
Equitable St *WLSD/HOW* NE28 ....67 D4
Erick St *CNUT* NE1 ....3 E3
Erith Ter *MLFD/PNYW* SR4 ....125 E6
Ernest Pl *DHAM* DH1 ....195 F4
Ernest St *ASHBK/HED/RY* SR2 ....145 D2
　BOLCOL NE35 ....117 F3
　CLSW/PEL DH2 ....152 A1
Ernest Ter *STLY/ANP* DH9 ....131 E6
Ernwill Av *SWCK/CAS* SR5 ....124 C3
Errington Dr *STLY/ANP* DH9 ....130 B6
Errington Ter *LGB/KIL* NE12 ....50 A5
Errol Pl *CLS/BIR/GTL* DH3 ....136 C4
Erskine Rd *SSH* NE33 ....71 F4
Erskine Wy *SSH* NE33 ....72 A4
Escallond Dr *SEA/MUR* SR7 ....175 E4
Esdale *ASHBK/HED/RY* SR2 ....162 A2
Esher Ct *GOS/KPK* NE3 ....45 E5
Esher Gdns *BLYTH* NE24 ....16 C3
Eshmere Crs *WD/WHPE/BLK* NE5 ......59 E4
Eshott Cl *GOS/KPK* NE3 ....46 C6
　WD/WHPE/BLK NE5 ....60 C5
Eskdale *CLS/BIR/GTL* DH3 ....137 D5
　HLS DH4 ....139 F6
Eskdale Av *BLYTH* NE24 ....9 F4
　WLSD/HOW NE28 ....67 E2
Eskdale Cl *SEA/MUR* SR7 ....175 E3
Eskdale Ct *HAR/WTLS* NE34 ....88 B2
Eskdale Dr *JRW* NE32 ....86 B3
Eskdale Gdns *LWF/SPW/WRK* NE9 ....99 F6
Eskdale Rd *CLDN/WHIT/ROK* SR6 ....109 E4

Eskdale St *HAR/WTLS* * NE34 ....88 B3
  HLH DH5 ....185 E2
Eskdale Ter *JES* NE2 ....64 A6
  WBAY NE26 ....41 E6
Eskdale Wk *PLEE/EAS* SR8 ....209 D2
Esk St *LWF/SPW/WRK* NE9 ....100 A3
Eslington Ct *GATE* NE8 ....98 A2
Eslington Rd *JES* NE2 ....81 E1
Eslington Ter *JES* NE2 ....64 A6
Esmaralda Gdns *CRAM* NE23 ....36 B1
Esplanade *WBAY* NE26 ....41 E6
Esplanade Ms *ASHBK/HED/RY* SR2 ....4 C5
The Esplanade *ASHBK/HED/RY* SR2 ...4 C6
Esplanade West
  ASHBK/HED/RY SR2 ....4 C6
Espley Cl *LGB/KIL* NE12 ....50 C4
Espley Ct *GOS/KPK* NE3 ....46 A5
Essen Wy *SUNDSW* SR3 ....144 A3
Essex Cl *ELS/FEN* NE4 ....80 A5
Essex Crs *SEA/MUR* SR7 ....175 E3
Essex Dr *WASHN* NE37 ....120 C3
Essex Gdns *HAR/WTLS* NE34 ....90 B1
  LWF/SPW/WRK NE9 ....99 E3
  WLSD/HOW NE28 ....68 A3
Essex Gv *SUNDSW* SR3 ....143 F6
Essex Pl *PLEE/EAS* SR8 ....200 B6
Essington Wy *PLEE/EAS* SR8 ....200 B5
Esst Vw *HLH* DH5 ....186 C3
Esther Campbell Ct
  JES (off Richardson Rd) NE2 ....80 B1
Esther Sq *WASHS* NE38 ....139 D2
Esthwaite Av *CLSW/PEL* DH2 ....166 A1
Eston Ct *BLYTH* NE24 ....10 A4
  WLSD/HOW NE28 ....66 B1
Eston Gv *SWCK/CAS* SR5 ....126 F1
Estuary Wy *MLFD/PNYW* SR4 ....124 A5
Etal Av *MONK* NE25 ....41 D6
  NSHW NE29 ....69 F2
Etal Ct *NSHW* NE29 ....54 C6
Etal Crs *JRW* NE32 ....86 C4
  SMOOR NE27 ....52 B1
Etal La *WD/WHPE/BLK* NE5 ....60 C3
Etal Pl *GOS/KPK* NE3 ....46 C5
Etal Rd *BLYTH* NE24 ....16 A3
Etal Wy *WD/WHPE/BLK* NE5 ....61 D2
Ethel Av *ASHBK/HED/RY* SR2 ....162 C2
  BLAY NE21 ....76 B6
Ethel St *CRAM* NE23 ....34 C4
  ELS/FEN NE4 ....78 C4
Ethel Ter *HAR/WTLS* NE34 ....88 A3
  SWCK/CAS SR5 ....124 A3
Etherley Cl *DHAM* DH1 ....180 C5
Etherley Rd *BYK/HTN/WLK* NE6 ....82 C1
Etherstone Av *LGB/HTN* NE7 ....65 E4
Eton Cl *CRAM* NE23 ....14 B4
Eton Sq *HEBB* NE31 ....85 E2
Ettrick Cl *LGB/KIL* NE12 ....35 E6
Ettrick Gdns *GATE* NE8 ....100 A2
  MLFD/PNYW SR4 ....143 D2
Ettrick Gv *MLFD/PNYW* SR4 ....143 E2
  SUNDSW SR3 ....143 E3
Ettrick Rd *JRW* NE32 ....85 E5
European Wy *MLFD/PNYW* SR4 ......124 C4
Euryalus Ct *SSH* NE33 ....72 B5
Eustace Av *NSHW* NE29 ....70 A1
Evanlade *FELL* NE10 ....102 A4
Evenwood Gdns
  LWF/SPW/WRK NE9 ....100 A3
Everard St *CRAM* NE23 ....14 A3
Everest Gv *BOL* NE36 ....106 A4
Eversleigh Pl
  BW/LEM/TK/HW NE15 ....58 A4
Eversley Pl *BYK/HTN/WLK* * NE6 ....82 A1
  WLSD/HOW NE28 ....68 B3
Everton Dr *SEA/MUR* SR7 ....175 E3
Everton La *SWCK/CAS* SR5 ....125 F1
Evesham *MLFD/PNYW* SR4 ....123 F6
Evesham Av *WBAY* NE26 ....40 B4
Evesham Cl *BOLCOL* NE35 ....105 E1
Evesham Garth *GOS/KPK* NE3 ....62 A3
Evesham Rd *SEA/MUR* SR7 ....175 E3
Evistones Gdns
  BYK/HTN/WLK NE6 ....83 D5
Evistones Rd *LWF/SPW/WRK* NE9 .....99 F4
Ewart Crs *HAR/WTLS* NE34 ....87 D4
Ewbank Av *ELS/FEN* NE4 ....79 D1
Ewehurst Crs *STLY/ANP* DH9 ....129 E3
Ewehurst Pde *STLY/ANP* DH9 ....129 D5
Ewehurst Rd *STLY/ANP* DH9 ....129 E3
  WICK/BNPF NE16 ....129 E4
Ewen Ct *NSHW* NE29 ....53 E6
Ewesley *WASHS* NE38 ....137 F6
Ewesley Cl *WD/WHPE/BLK* NE5 ....60 B1
Ewesley Gdns *DIN/WO* NE13 ....33 D4
Ewesley Rd *MLFD/PNYW* SR4 ....143 E1
Ewing Rd *MLFD/PNYW* SR4 ....143 F1
Exebly Cl *GOS/KPK* NE3 ....47 F4
Exeter Av *SEA/MUR* SR7 ....176 A3
Exeter Cl *CLS/BIR/GTL* DH3 ....167 F4
Exeter Rd *WLSD/HOW* NE28 ....66 C1
Exeter St *BYK/HTN/WLK* NE6 ....83 F4
  GATE NE8 ....99 D1

MLFD/PNYW SR4 ....125 E5
Exmouth Cl *SEA/MUR* * SR7 ....175 F4
Exmouth Rd *NSHW* NE29 ....69 E1
Exmouth Sq *SWCK/CAS* SR5 ....125 F1
Extension Rd *SUND* SR1 ....5 H3
Eyemouth La *SWCK/CAS* SR5 ....125 F1
Eyemouth Rd *NSHW* NE29 ....69 E1
Eyre St *STLY/ANP* DH9 ....147 F3

F

Faber Rd *SWCK/CAS* SR5 ....125 F1
Factory Rd *BLAY* NE21 ....76 C4
Fairbairn Rd *PLEE/EAS* SR8 ....200 C6
Fairburn Av *HLH* DH5 ....171 D4
  LGB/HTN NE7 ....65 E2
Faircloud Clough *PLEE/EAS* SR8 ...208 A3
Fairdale Av *LGB/HTN* NE7 ....65 E2
Fairfield *CLSW/PEL* DH2 ....151 F1
  LGB/KIL NE12 ....48 B6
  STLY/ANP DH9 ....146 B3
Fairfield Av *BLYTH* NE24 ....16 C2
  WICK/BNPF NE16 ....95 F5
Fairfield Cl *DUN/TMV* NE11 ....97 E3
Fairfield Dr *CLDN/WHIT/ROK* SR6 .....91 D6
  MONK NE25 ....39 E6
  TYNE/NSHE NE30 ....55 D2
Fairfield Gn *MONK* NE25 ....39 E6
Fairfield Rd *JES* NE2 ....63 F5
Fairfield Ter *FELL* * NE10 ....101 F1
Fairfields *RYTON* NE40 ....74 A4
Fair Gn *MONK* NE25 ....39 E6
Fairgreen Cl *SUNDSW* SR3 ....160 B3
Fairhaven *LWF/SPW/WRK* NE9 ....119 E2
Fairhaven Av *BYK/HTN/WLK* NE6 ......83 F2
Fairhill Cl *LGB/HTN* NE7 ....65 E3
Fairholme Av *HAR/WTLS* NE34 ....89 D2
Fairholme Rd *SUNDSW* SR3 ....144 B3
Fairholm Rd *ELS/FEN* NE4 ....79 D3
Fairlands East
  CLDN/WHIT/ROK SR6 ....126 C2
Fairlands West *SWCK/CAS* SR5 .....126 C2
Fairlawn Gdns *MLFD/PNYW* SR4 .....143 D2
Fairles St *SSH* NE33 ....71 F2
Fairmead Wy *MLFD/PNYW* SR4 ......141 F1
Fairmile Dr *SUNDSW* SR3 ....160 C3
Fairmont Wy *LGB/HTN* NE7 ....65 E1
Fairney Cl *PONT/DH* NE20 ....28 B4
Fairney Edge *PONT/DH* NE20 ....28 B4
Fairport Ter *PLEE/EAS* SR8 ....201 E3
Fairspring *WD/WHPE/BLK* NE5 ....60 C1
Fairview Av *HAR/WTLS* NE34 ....89 E1
Fairview Gn *LGB/HTN* NE7 ....65 E3
Fairview Ter *STLY/ANP* DH9 ....146 A5
Fairville Cl *CRAM* NE23 ....14 A4
Fairville Crs *LGB/HTN* NE7 ....65 E2
Fairway Cl *GOS/KPK* NE3 ....47 D4
Fairways *MONK* NE25 ....39 E5
  SUNDSW SR3 ....161 D1
Fairways Av *LGB/HTN* NE7 ....65 E1
The Fairways *BOL* * NE36 ....105 F3
  BOL NE36 ....106 B3
  STLY/ANP DH9 ....147 F6
The Fairway *BLAY* NE21 ....75 F4
  GOS/KPK NE3 ....47 D4
  WASHN NE37 ....120 C1
Falconer's Ct *CNUT* NE1 ....2 C4
Falconar St *JES* NE2 ....3 F2
Falcon Cl *LGB/KIL* NE12 ....48 C5
Falcon Wy *HAR/WTLS* NE34 ....88 A4
Faldonside *BYK/HTN/WLK* NE6 ....65 F4
Falkirk *LGB/KIL* NE12 ....35 F6
Falkland Av *GOS/KPK* NE3 ....62 B3
  HEBB NE31 ....85 D2
Falkland Rd *MLFD/PNYW* SR4 ....125 D6
Falla Park Crs *FELL* NE10 ....100 B3
Falla Park Rd *FELL* NE10 ....100 B3
Fallodon Av *GOS/KPK* NE3 ....46 B4
Fallodon Gdns
  WD/WHPE/BLK NE5 ....61 F4
Fallodon Rd *NSHW* NE29 ....69 F1
Fallowfeld *FELL* NE10 ....101 F3
Fallowfield Av *GOS/KPK* NE3 ....46 B6
Fallowfield Wy *WASHS* NE38 ....138 C3
Fallow Park Av *BLYTH* NE24 ....10 B6
Fallow Rd *HAR/WTLS* NE34 ....90 C2
Fallsway *DHAM* DH1 ....196 C1
Falmouth Cl *SEA/MUR* SR7 ....175 F4
Falmouth Dr *JRW* NE32 ....86 C3
Falmouth Rd *BYK/HTN/WLK* NE6 ......82 A1
  MLFD/PNYW SR4 ....125 D5
  NSHW NE29 ....53 F3
  NSHW NE29 ....69 F1
Falmouth Sq *MLFD/PNYW* SR4 ......125 D6
Falsgrave Pl *WICK/BNPF* NE16 ....95 E5
Falstaff Rd *NSHW* NE29 ....53 F6
Falstone *FELL* NE10 ....101 E1
  WASHS NE38 ....116 C3
Falstone Av *BW/LEM/TK/HW* NE15 ...60 A6
  HAR/WTLS NE34 ....89 D2
Falstone Cl *LGB/KIL* NE12 ....50 C4

Falstone Dr *CLSW/PEL* DH2 ....165 E1
Falstone Sq *GOS/KPK* NE3 ....46 C6
Falston Rd *BLYTH* NE24 ....16 B1
Faraday Cl *WASHS* NE38 ....140 A1
Faraday Gv *GATE* NE8 ....98 C3
  MLFD/PNYW SR4 ....125 D6
Faraday Rd *PLEE/EAS* SR8 ....201 D5
Fareham Gv *BOLCOL* NE35 ....104 C2
Farlam Av *TYNE/NSHE* NE30 ....54 C3
Farlam Rd *WD/WHPE/BLK* NE5 ....61 D6
Farleigh Ct *NSHW* NE29 ....53 D4
Farm Cl *WASHN* NE37 ....120 A3
  WICK/BNPF NE16 ....114 A2
Farm Ct *BLAY* NE21 ....77 E6
Farmer Crs *SEA/MUR* SR7 ....188 A1
Farm Hill Rd *CLDN/WHIT/ROK* SR6 ...89 F6
Farm Rd *DHAM* DH1 ....205 F3
Farn St *SWCK/CAS* SR5 ....126 A3
Farnborough Cl *CRAM* NE23 ....14 A6
Farnborough Dr *SUNDSW* SR3 ....144 A6
Farn Ct *DIN/WO* NE13 ....149 E1
Farndale Av *WLSD/HOW* NE28 ....66 B3
Farndale Av *CLDN/WHIT/ROK* SR6 ..109 E4
Farndale Cl *BLAY* NE21 ....93 E2
  DIN/WO NE13 ....31 D3
Farndale Rd *ELS/FEN* NE4 ....79 D3
Farne Av *GOS/KPK* NE3 ....46 C4
  HAR/WTLS NE34 ....90 A1
Farne Rd *LGB/KIL* NE12 ....50 A4
  SMOOR NE27 ....52 B1
Farne Ter *BYK/HTN/WLK* NE6 ....83 D2
Farnham Cl *DHAM* DH1 ....194 B1
Farnham Gv *BLYTH* NE24 ....16 C2
Farnham Ldg
  LGB/KIL (off Bardsey Pl) NE12 ....49 D5
Farnham Rd *DHAM* DH1 ....180 B6
  HAR/WTLS NE34 ....88 B2
Farnham St *BW/LEM/TK/HW* NE15 ...76 C2
Farnham Ter *MLFD/PNYW* SR4 ....143 E1
Farnley Hey Rd *DHAM* DH1 ....193 F5
Farnley Mt *DHAM* DH1 ....193 F5
Farnley Rdg *DHAM* DH1 ....193 F5
Farnley Rd *BYK/HTN/WLK* NE6 ....65 E5
Farnon Rd *GOS/KPK* NE3 ....62 C1
Farquhar St *JES* NE2 ....64 B6
Farrier Cl *WASHS* NE38 ....139 D4
Farringdon Rd *TYNE/NSHE* NE30 .....54 C2
Farrington Rw *MLFD/PNYW* SR4 ....126 A4
  SUND SR1 ....126 A5
Farrington Sq *SUNDSW* SR3 ....142 B6
Farrow Dr *CLDN/WHIT/ROK* SR6 ....109 D1
The Farthings *WASHN* NE37 ....120 A2
Fatfield Pk *WASHS* NE38 ....138 C5
Fatfield Rd *WASHS* NE38 ....139 D2
Faversham Ct *GOS/KPK* NE3 ....45 F5
Faversham Pl *CRAM* NE23 ....14 A6
Fawcett St *SUND* SR1 ....4 C2
Fawcett Wy *SSH* NE33 ....71 E3
Fawdon Cl *GOS/KPK* NE3 ....46 A4
Fawdon La *GOS/KPK* NE3 ....45 F5
Fawdon Park Rd *GOS/KPK* NE3 ....46 A5
Fawdon Pl *NSHW* NE29 ....53 E6
Fawney Cl *BOLCOL* NE35 ....105 D1
Fawn Rd *MLFD/PNYW* SR4 ....124 B6
Feather Bed La
  ASHBK/HED/RY SR2 ....162 C2
Featherstone Gv *BDLGTN* NE22 ....6 C2
  JRW NE32 ....85 F5
Featherstone Rd *DHAM* DH1 ....194 C1
Featherstone St
  CLDN/WHIT/ROK SR6 ....127 C1
Federation Sq *SEA/MUR* SR7 ....188 B2
Federation Wy *DUN/TMV* NE11 ....97 D1
Fee Ter *ASHBK/HED/RY* SR2 ....162 A2
Feetham Av *LGB/KIL* NE12 ....50 B4
Felixstowe Dr *LGB/HTN* NE7 ....65 E3
Fell Bank *CLS/BIR/GTL* DH3 ....136 C2
Fell Cl *CLS/BIR/GTL* DH3 ....137 D3
  WICK/BNPF NE16 ....114 A2
Felldyke *FELL* NE10 ....101 E5
Fellgate Av *JRW* NE32 ....104 B3
Fellgate Gdns *FELL* NE10 ....102 B2
Felling Dene Gdns *FELL* NE10 ....101 D1
Felling Ga *FELL* NE10 ....100 B1
Felling House Gdns *FELL* NE10 ....82 C6
Felling Vw *BYK/HTN/WLK* NE6 ....83 E5
Fellmere Av *FELL* NE10 ....101 E3
Fell Rd *CLSW/PEL* DH2 ....152 A5
  LWF/SPW/WRK NE9 ....119 E3
  SWCK/CAS SR5 ....124 C5
Fellside *HAR/WTLS* NE34 ....90 A3
Fellside Av *WICK/BNPF* NE16 ....114 A1
Fellside Ct *WICK/BNPF* NE16 ....95 F3
Fellside Gdns *DHAM* DH1 ....196 B2
Fellside Rd *WICK/BNPF* NE16 ....95 E5
The Fell Side *GOS/KPK* NE3 ....62 B2
Fells Rd *DUN/TMV* NE11 ....98 C3
The Fell Wy *WD/WHPE/BLK* NE5 ......59 F5
Felsham Sq *MLFD/PNYW* SR4 ....125 D6
Felstead Crs *MLFD/PNYW* SR4 ......124 C5
Felstead Pl *BLYTH* NE24 ....16 C2
Felstead Sq *MLFD/PNYW* SR4 ....124 C6

Felton Av GOS/KPK NE3 ......46 C6
  HAR/WTLS NE34 ......89 F2
  MONK NE25 ......41 D6
Felton Cl SMOOR NE27 ......52 B1
Felton Crs GATE NE8 ......99 D3
Felton Dr LGB/KIL NE12 ......50 B3
Felton Gn BYK/HTN/WLK * NE6 ......82 B2
Felton Wk BYK/HTN/WLK NE6 ......82 B2
Fencer Ct GOS/KPK NE3 ......47 E4
Fence Rd CLS/BIR/GTL DH3 ......156 A2
Fenham Cha ELS/FEN NE4 ......61 F6
Fenham Hall Dr ELS/FEN NE4 ......61 F6
Fenham Rd ELS/FEN NE4 ......79 E2
Fenkle St CNUT NE1 ......2 B3
Fennel Gv HAR/WTLS NE34 ......89 D5
Fenning Pl BYK/HTN/WLK * NE6 ......82 B4
Fenside Rd ASHBK/HED/RY SR2 ......145 E6
Fenton Cl CLSW/PEL DH2 ......165 F1
Fenton Sq MLFD/PNYW SR4 ......124 B6
Fenton Ter HLS DH4 ......157 F2
Fenton Well La CLS/BIR/GTL DH3 ......167 D3
Fenwick Av BLYTH NE24 ......16 C1
  HAR/WTLS NE34 ......87 F3
Fenwick Cl CLSW/PEL DH2 ......165 E1
  HLS DH4 ......140 A6
  JES NE2 ......64 B5
Fenwick Rw SEA/MUR SR7 ......177 D4
Fenwick St HLS DH4 ......140 A6
Fenwick Ter
  NSHW (off Preston Rd) NE29 ......54 C5
Ferens Cl DHAM DH1 ......194 C3
Ferens Pk DHAM DH1 ......194 C3
Ferguson Crs DIN/WO NE13 ......32 C6
Ferguson's La
  BW/LEM/TK/HW NE15 ......77 F2
Ferguson St ASHBK/HED/RY SR2 ......5 H4
Fern Av CLDN/WHIT/ROK SR6 ......91 E6
  CRAM NE23 ......14 A4
  GOS/KPK NE3 ......46 B5
  JES NE2 ......64 A5
  NSHW NE29 ......69 F2
  SWCK/CAS SR5 ......125 F2
Fern Crs SEA/MUR SR7 ......176 B6
Ferndale Av BOL NE36 ......106 C3
  GOS/KPK NE3 ......47 F3
  WLSD/HOW NE28 ......67 E4
Ferndale Cl BLYTH NE24 ......9 F5
Ferndale Gv BOL NE36 ......106 C3
Ferndale La BOL NE36 ......106 C3
Ferndale Rd HLS DH4 ......139 F6
Ferndale Ter MLFD/PNYW SR4 ......125 D4
Fern Dene
  WLSD/HOW
  (off Simonside Av) NE28 ......68 A2
Ferndene Crs MLFD/PNYW SR4 ......125 E6
Ferndene Gv LGB/HTN NE7 ......65 D3
Fern Dene Rd GATE NE8 ......99 D2
Ferndown Ct FELL * NE10 ......102 A3
  RYTON NE40 ......74 C4
Fern Dr CLDN/WHIT/ROK SR6 ......107 E1
  CRAM NE23 ......34 C2
Fernhill Av WICK/BNPF NE16 ......95 F3
Fernlea Cl WASHS NE38 ......139 D4
Fernley Vls CRAM NE23 ......22 C2
Fern Rd BDN/LAN/SAC DH7 ......178 C1
Fernsway SUNDSW SR3 ......144 A3
Fernville Rd GOS/KPK NE3 ......63 D3
Fernville St MLFD/PNYW SR4 ......144 A3
Fernwood Av GOS/KPK NE3 ......47 F6
Fernwood Cl SUNDSW * SR3 ......160 C3
Fernwood Rd
  BW/LEM/TK/HW NE15 ......76 C2
  JES NE2 ......64 A6
Ferrand Dr HLS DH4 ......170 C2
Ferriby Cl GOS/KPK NE3 ......47 F4
Ferrisdale Wy GOS/KPK NE3 ......46 B5
Ferryboat La SWCK/CAS SR5 ......123 E3
Ferrydene Av GOS/KPK NE3 ......62 B2
Ferry Ms NSHW NE29 ......71 D2
Ferry St JRW NE32 ......69 D6
  SSH NE33 ......71 D3
Festival Park Dr DUN/TMV NE11 ......98 A3
Festival Wy DUN/TMV NE11 ......97 F1
Fetcham Ct GOS/KPK NE3 ......45 E5
Field Cl JES NE2 ......3 H2
Field Fare Ct WICK/BNPF NE16 ......130 B1
Fieldhouse La DHAM DH1 ......193 F3
Field House Rd GATE NE8 ......99 D3
Field House Ter DHAM DH1 ......194 A3
Fielding Ct WD/WHPE/BLK NE5 ......60 C2
Fielding Pl LWF/SPW/WRK NE9 ......100 A2
Field La FELL NE10 ......101 E2
Fieldside CLDN/WHIT/ROK SR6 ......109 D1
  CLSW/PEL DH2 ......152 A1
  HLH DH5 ......184 B1
Field Sq MLFD/PNYW SR4 ......124 B6
Field St FELL NE10 ......100 C1
  GOS/KPK NE3 ......64 A1
Field Ter JRW NE32 ......86 A3
Fieldway BOLCOL NE35 ......104 B2
  JRW NE32 ......104 C1
Fife Av JRW NE32 ......87 D5

Fife St GATE NE8 ......99 F1
  SEA/MUR SR7 ......188 C2
Fifteenth Av BLYTH NE24 ......10 C6
Fifth Av BYK/HTN/WLK NE6 ......82 B1
  DUN/TMV NE11 ......98 C5
Fifth St PLEE/EAS SR8 ......209 F1
Filby Dr DHAM DH1 ......196 C1
Filey Cl CRAM NE23 ......14 A6
Filton Cl CRAM NE23 ......14 A6
Finchale WASHS NE38 ......138 B3
Finchale Av DHAM DH1 ......181 E4
Finchale Cl ASHBK/HED/RY SR2 ......5 F5
  DUN/TMV NE11 ......97 E4
  HLS DH4 ......170 C2
Finchale Gdns
  BW/LEM/TK/HW NE15 ......57 F3
Finchale Rd DHAM DH1 ......180 C4
  DHAM DH1 ......193 F1
  HEBB NE31 ......85 D5
Finchale Ter BYK/HTN/WLK * NE6 ......82 C4
  JRW NE32 ......86 C4
  HLS DH4 ......183 D2
Finchale Vw DHAM DH1 ......180 A5
Finchdale Cl NSHW NE29 ......70 B2
Finchley Crs BYK/HTN/WLK NE6 ......66 C6
Findon Av BDN/LAN/SAC DH7 ......178 A3
Findon Gv NSHW NE29 ......70 A2
Findon Hl BDN/LAN/SAC DH7 ......178 B2
Fines Pk STLY/ANP DH9 ......146 B4
Finney Ter DHAM * DH1 ......194 C4
Finsbury Av BYK/HTN/WLK NE6 ......83 D2
Finsbury St SWCK/CAS SR5 ......126 B3
Finsmere Av WD/WHPE/BLK NE5 ......61 D5
Finsmere Pl WD/WHPE/BLK NE5 ......61 D5
Finstock Ct LGB/HTN NE7 ......64 B2
Fir Av BDN/LAN/SAC DH7 ......203 D5
  DHAM DH1 ......195 F5
Firbank Av TYNE/NSHE NE30 ......55 D2
Firbanks JRW NE32 ......104 C1
Firfield Rd WD/WHPE/BLK NE5 ......61 F4
Fir Gv HAR/WTLS NE34 ......89 E3
Fir Pk BDN/LAN/SAC DH7 ......192 A4
First Av BLYTH NE24 ......10 C6
  BYK/HTN/WLK NE6 ......82 B1
  CLSW/PEL DH2 ......136 A6
  DUN/TMV NE11 ......98 B4
  NSHW NE29 ......69 D2
The Firs GOS/KPK NE3 ......63 D2
Fir St JRW NE32 ......85 F1
First St GATE NE8 ......98 C1
  PLEE/EAS SR8 ......209 F1
Firth Sq MLFD/PNYW SR4 ......124 C5
Firtree Av BYK/HTN/WLK NE6 ......66 C5
  LGB/KIL NE12 ......49 F3
  WASHS NE38 ......138 B5
Fir Tree Cl DHAM * DH1 ......195 F2
Firtree Crs LGB/KIL NE12 ......49 E3
Firtree Gdns MONK NE25 ......54 B1
Firtree Rd WICK/BNPF NE16 ......95 F4
Firtrees CLSW/PEL DH2 ......153 D3
  FELL NE10 ......101 D5
Firtrees Av WLSD/HOW NE28 ......69 D3
Firwood Gdns DUN/TMV NE11 ......98 A5
Fisher La CRAM NE23 ......12 B6
  DIN/WO NE13 ......20 A5
Fisher Rd SMOOR NE27 ......37 D4
Fisher St BYK/HTN/WLK NE6 ......84 A1
  WLSD/HOW NE28 ......84 A1
Fisherwell Rd FELL NE10 ......83 F6
Fish Market CNUT NE1 ......2 C3
Fish Quay TYNE/NSHE NE30 ......71 E1
Fitzpatrick Pl SSH NE33 ......72 A4
Fitzsimmons Av WLSD/HOW NE28 ......67 D3
Flagg Ct SSH NE33 ......71 F3
Flambard Rd DHAM DH1 ......194 A1
Flassburn Rd DHAM DH1 ......193 F3
Flass St DHAM DH1 ......194 A4
Flaunden Cl HAR/WTLS NE34 ......90 A3
Flaxby Cl GOS/KPK NE3 ......47 F4
Flax Sq MLFD/PNYW SR4 ......124 B5
Fleet St SUND SR1 ......15 F5
Fleming Ct GATE NE8 ......80 B6
Fleming Gdns FELL NE10 ......100 B3
Fleming Pl PLEE/EAS SR8 ......208 C2
Fletcher Crs HLS DH4 ......158 A2
Flexbury Gdns
  BW/LEM/TK/HW NE15 ......77 D1
  FELL NE10 ......100 B2
  LWF/SPW/WRK NE9 ......117 F2
Flint Hill Bank STLY/ANP DH9 ......129 D5
Flodden LGB/KIL NE12 ......35 F6
Flodden Cl CLSW/PEL DH2 ......165 E1
Flodden Rd MLFD/PNYW SR4 ......124 C6
Flodden St BYK/HTN/WLK NE6 ......82 C5
Floral Dene MLFD/PNYW SR4 ......123 F6
Flora St BYK/HTN/WLK * NE6 ......82 A2
Florence Av LWF/SPW/WRK NE9 ......99 F4
Florence Crs SWCK/CAS SR5 ......125 E2
Florence St BLAY NE21 ......94 A1
Florida St MLFD/PNYW SR4 ......125 E4
Flotterton Gdns
  WD/WHPE/BLK NE5 ......78 B1
The Fold MONK NE25 ......40 A5
  SUNDSW SR3 ......161 D3
  WICK/BNPF NE16 ......111 F5

Folldon Av CLDN/WHIT/ROK SR6 ......126 C1
Follingsby Av FELL NE10 ......103 D4
Follingsby Cl FELL NE10 ......102 B3
Follingsby La FELL NE10 ......103 D5
Follingsby Wy FELL NE10 ......102 C4
Folly La RYTON NE40 ......74 A6
Folly Ter DHAM DH1 ......179 F5
The Folly BOL NE36 ......105 F3
Fontaine Rd SUND SR1 ......4 A1
Fontburn Ct NSHW NE29 ......70 A2
  SWCK/CAS SR5 ......107 E6
Fontburn Pl LGB/HTN NE7 ......64 C1
Fontburn Rd MONK NE25 ......24 C5
Fontburn Ter TYNE/NSHE NE30 ......55 D6
Fonteyn Pl CRAM NE23 ......14 A4
  STLY/ANP DH9 ......149 D3
Fontwell Dr GATE NE8 ......98 C3
Forbeck Rd MLFD/PNYW SR4 ......124 C6
Forber Av HAR/WTLS NE34 ......90 A2
Ford Av MLFD/PNYW SR4 ......123 F6
  NSHW NE29 ......69 F2
Ford Crs JRW NE32 ......86 A5
  MLFD/PNYW SR4 ......123 F6
  SMOOR NE27 ......52 A1
Ford Dr BLYTH NE24 ......10 B5
Fordenbridge Crs
  MLFD/PNYW SR4 ......124 C6
Fordenbridge Rd
  MLFD/PNYW SR4 ......124 C6
Fordenbridge Sq
  MLFD/PNYW SR4 ......125 D6
Fordfield Rd MLFD/PNYW SR4 ......124 B6
Ford Gv GOS/KPK NE3 ......47 D5
Fordhall Dr MLFD/PNYW SR4 ......125 D6
Fordham Rd DHAM DH1 ......194 B1
Fordham Sq MLFD/PNYW SR4 ......125 D6
Fordland Pl MLFD/PNYW SR4 ......125 E6
Ford Ov MLFD/PNYW SR4 ......124 A5
Ford Rd DHAM DH1 ......180 C5
Ford St BYK/HTN/WLK NE6 ......81 F3
  GATE NE8 ......100 A1
Ford Ter WLSD/HOW NE28 ......68 A4
Ford Vw CRAM NE23 ......34 C1
Forest Av LGB/KIL NE12 ......50 A4
Forest Dr WASHS NE38 ......137 E6
Forest Hall Rd LGB/KIL NE12 ......50 A3
Fore St JES NE2 ......64 C6
Forest Rd BW/LEM/TK/HW NE15 ......78 A4
  MLFD/PNYW SR4 ......124 C5
  SSH NE33 ......71 E4
Forest Vw BDN/LAN/SAC DH7 ......202 B5
Forest Wy CRAM NE23 ......36 B1
Forfar St SWCK/CAS SR5 ......126 C2
Forge La CLS/BIR/GTL DH3 ......155 D5
Forge Rd DUN/TMV NE11 ......97 F2
Forres Ct STLY/ANP DH9 ......149 D2
Forres Pl CRAM NE23 ......14 A6
Forrest Rd WLSD/HOW NE28 ......66 C5
Forster Av BDLGTN NE22 ......11 F5
  HAR/WTLS NE34 ......89 D1
  RDHAMSE DH6 ......197 E4
Forster Ct
  LWF/SPW/WRK
  (off Durham Rd) NE9 ......99 E6
Forster St BLYTH NE24 ......11 E5
  CLDN/WHIT/ROK SR6 ......127 D3
Forsyth Rd JES NE2 ......63 F5
Forth Banks CNUT NE1 ......2 C5
Forth Cl PLEE/EAS SR8 ......208 C3
Forth Ct HAR/WTLS NE34 ......88 B3
Forth Pl CNUT NE1 ......2 B5
Forth St CNUT NE1 ......2 B6
Fortrose Av SUNDSW SR3 ......143 F3
Fort Sq SSH NE33 ......71 F2
Fort St SSH NE33 ......71 F2
Forum Ct BDLGTN NE22 ......7 E3
The Forum BW/LEM/TK/HW NE15 ......77 E1
Forum Wy CRAM NE23 ......21 E1
Fossdyke FELL NE10 ......101 E5
Fossefeld FELL NE10 ......101 F3
Fosse Law BW/LEM/TK/HW NE15 ......58 A5
Fosse Ter LWF/SPW/WRK NE9 ......100 A4
Fossway BYK/HTN/WLK NE6 ......83 E1
Foster St BYK/HTN/WLK NE6 ......84 A3
Foundry Ct BYK/HTN/WLK * NE6 ......82 B4
Foundry La BYK/HTN/WLK NE6 ......81 F2
Foundry Rd SEA/MUR SR7 ......177 D3
Fountain Cl BDLGTN NE22 ......7 E3
Fountain Gv HAR/WTLS NE34 ......72 B6
Fountain Head Bank WBAY NE26 ......26 A2
Fountain La BLAY NE21 ......76 A4
Fountain Rw JES NE2 ......80 A1
Fountains Cl DUN/TMV NE11 ......97 E4
  WASHS NE38 ......138 C2
Fountains Crs HEBB NE31 ......85 D5
  HLS DH4 ......157 E6
Fountain Vw
  GATE (off Armstrong St) NE8 ......98 C3
Fouracres Rd WD/WHPE/BLK NE5 ......62 A4
Four Lane Ends HLH DH5 ......186 A2
Fourstones WD/WHPE/BLK NE5 ......60 C4
Fourstones Cl GOS/KPK NE3 ......61 F1
Fourstones Rd MLFD/PNYW SR4 ......125 D5
Fourth Av BLYTH NE24 ......10 C6

BYK/HTN/WLK NE6 ....82 B1
CLSW/PEL DH2..........................153 D5
DUN/TMV NE11 ....98 B5
Fourth St GATE NE8.......................98 C1
PLEE/EAS SR8 ....209 F1
Fowberry Crs ELS/FEN NE4 ....79 D1
Fowberry Rd
BW/LEM/TK/HW NE15 ....77 E4
Fowler Cl HLS DH4 ....157 E4
Fowler Gdns DUN/TMV * NE11 ....97 E1
Fowler St NE33 ....71 E3
Fox & Hounds La
BW/LEM/TK/HW NE15 ....78 B2
Fox & Hounds Rd
WD/WHPE/BLK NE5 ....78 B1
Fox Av HAR/WTLS NE34..................87 E4
Foxcover La SUNDSW SR3 ....159 D1
Foxcover Rd MLFD/PNYW SR4 ....141 E4
Foxglove Cl BLYTH NE24.................16 B2
Foxglove Ct HAR/WTLS NE34...........87 F4
Foxhills Cl WASHS NE38 ....139 E4
Foxhills Covert WICK/BNPF NE16 .....95 D5
The Foxhills WICK/BNPF NE16 ....95 D4
Foxhunters Rd MONK NE25 ....54 B1
Foxlair Cl SUNDSW SR3 ....160 C4
Fox Lea Wk CRAM NE23 ....36 A1
Foxley WASHN NE37 ....121 D4
Foxley Cl LGB/KIL NE12 ....36 B6
Fox St ASHBK/HED/RY SR2 ....144 A1
FELL NE10..................................100 B1
SEA/MUR SR7.............................176 C4
Foxton Av GOS/KPK NE3 ....46 B5
TYNE/NSHE NE30 ....55 D1
Foxton Cl NSHW NE29 ....70 A3
Foxton Hall WASHN NE37 ....120 C1
Foxton Wy FELL NE10 ....84 A6
Foyle St SUND SR1 ....4 D5
Framlington Pl JES NE2 ....80 E1
Framwelgate DHAM * DH1 ....194 B4
Framwelgate Br DHAM * DH1 ....194 B5
Framwelgate Peth DHAM DH1 ....194 A3
Framwelgate Waterside
DHAM DH1 ....194 B4
Frances St BLAY NE21 ....75 F6
Francis St CLDN/WHIT/ROK SR6.....126 C2
Frank Av SEA/MUR SR7..................176 A3
Frankham St WD/WHPE/BLK NE5......60 B4
Frankland Dr MONK NE25 ....54 A1
Frankland La DHAM DH1 ....194 B3
Frankland Rd DHAM DH1 ....194 A4
Franklin St MLFD/PNYW SR4 ....125 F5
SSH NE33 ....71 E3
Franklyn Av WBAY NE26 ....26 A1
Franklyn Rd PLEE/EAS SR8............208 A1
Frank Pl NSHW NE29 ....54 C6
Frank St DHAM DH1......................195 F4
SWCK/CAS SR5 ....126 A2
WLSD/HOW NE28 ....67 D5
Fraser Cl SSH NE33.......................71 D6
Frazer Ter RDHAMSE DH6 ....187 E1
Freda St SWCK/CAS SR5 ....125 E3
Frederick Gdns FELL * NE10 ....101 F1
Frederick Rd SUND SR1 ....4 D2
Frederick St MLFD/PNYW SR4 ....123 F6
SEA/MUR SR7.............................176 C3
SSH NE33 ....71 E4
SUND SR1 ....4 D2
Frederick Ter RDHAMSE DH6 ....187 E6
Freeman Rd GOS/KPK NE3 ....64 B2
LGB/HTN NE7 ....64 B2
Freemans Pl DHAM DH1 ....194 B4
Freesia Gra WASHS NE38 ....139 D3
Freezemoor Rd HLS DH4 ....157 F2
Fremantle Rd HAR/WTLS NE34 ....90 A3
Frenchman's Wy HAR/WTLS NE34 .....90 A1
French St BLYTH NE24....................11 D4
Frensham WASHS NE38.................139 F2
Frensham Wy BDN/LAN/SAC DH7 ...203 D4
Frenton Cl WD/WHPE/BLK NE5 ....59 E4
Friarage Av CLDN/WHIT/ROK NE26..126 C1
Friar Rd MLFD/PNYW SR4 ....124 C6
Friars CNUT NE1 ....2 B4
Friars Dene Rd FELL NE10 ....82 A6
Friarsfield Cl SUNDSW SR3 ....160 A3
Friarside BDN/LAN/SAC DH7..........178 A4
Friarside Crs ROWG NE39 ....110 C3
Friarside Gdns WICK/BNPF NE16 ......95 F4
WICK/BNPF NE16.........................111 E3
Friarside Rd ELS/FEN NE4...............62 A6
Friar Sq MLFD/PNYW SR4 ....124 C6
Friars' Rw DHAM DH1 ....195 E3
Friars St CNUT NE1 ....2 B4
Friar St RDHAMSE DH6 ....206 C2
Friars Wy WD/WHPE/BLK NE5 ....61 E6
Friar Wy JRW NE32 ....86 B1
Friary Gdns FELL NE10 ....100 B1
Frobisher Cl SUNDSW SR3 ....160 B3
Frobisher St HEBB NE31..................85 E2
Frome Gdns LWF/SPW/WRK NE9 ...117 D2
Frome Pl CRAM NE23 ....14 A6
Frome Sq MLFD/PNYW SR4 ....124 B6
Front Rd BDN/LAN/SAC DH7 ....178 A1
Front St BDN/LAN/SAC DH7 ....178 A1
BDN/LAN/SAC DH7 ....204 A2
BLAY NE21 ....94 A1

BLYTH NE24..................................8 C5
BOL NE36 ....106 B3
BOLCOL NE35 ....105 D1
CLDN/WHIT/ROK SR6 ....107 F1
CLDN/WHIT/ROK SR6 ....109 D2
CLS/BIR/GTL DH3 ....153 E5
CLS/BIR/GTL DH3 ....167 F3
CLSW/PEL DH2............................151 E3
CLSW/PEL DH2............................151 F1
CRAM NE23 ....23 E6
CRAM NE23 ....35 D1
CRAM NE23 ....36 C1
DHAM DH1 ....179 F6
DHAM DH1 ....195 F5
DIN/WO NE13................................31 D3
DIN/WO NE13................................33 D1
HLH DH5 ....171 F6
HLH DH5 ....185 D3
HLS DH4 ....157 F5
HLS DH4 ....169 F2
LGB/HTN NE7 ....65 E1
LGB/KIL NE12 ....35 D5
MONK NE25 ....38 C5
MONK NE25 ....40 A6
NSHW NE29 ....54 B4
NSHW NE29 ....70 A1
RDHAMSE DH6 ....183 F6
RDHAMSE DH6 ....187 D4
STLY/ANP DH9 ....130 C2
STLY/ANP DH9 ....130 A4
STLY/ANP DH9 ....148 A2
STLY/ANP DH9 ....149 E5
TYNE/NSHE NE30 ....55 F5
TYNE/NSHE NE30 ....55 E1
WASHN NE37 ....120 C4
WICK/BNPF NE16.........................95 F3
WICK/BNPF NE16.........................111 D6
WICK/BNPF NE16.........................111 F6
WICK/BNPF NE16.........................129 F2
Front St East BDLGTN NE22 ....7 F4
Frosteday Gdns STLY/ANP DH9 ......146 B4
Frosterley Cl CLS/BIR/GTL DH3 ......168 A3
DHAM DH1 ....180 C5
HLH DH5 ....186 C3
Frosterley Gdns SUNDSW SR3 ....144 A4
Frosterley Pl ELS/FEN NE4...............80 A4
Froude Av HAR/WTLS NE34 ....88 A5
Fuchia Gdns HEBB NE31..................85 D5
Fuchsia Pl WD/WHPE/BLK NE5 ....61 E4
Fulbrook Rd GOS/KPK NE3 ....62 B1
Fullerton Pl LWF/SPW/WRK NE9 ....99 F2
Fulmar Dr BLYTH NE24 ....17 D1
WASHS NE38 ....137 E3
Fulmar Wk CLDN/WHIT/ROK SR6.....91 E6
Fulwell Av HAR/WTLS NE34 ....90 A1
Fulwell Ct CLDN/WHIT/ROK SR6.....126 C1
Fulwell Gn WD/WHPE/BLK NE5 ....61 D5
Fulwell Rd CLDN/WHIT/ROK SR6 ....126 C1
PLEE/EAS SR8 ....209 E3
Furnace Bank BDLGTN NE22 ....8 C3
Furness Cl PLEE/EAS SR8 ....208 A1
Furrowfield FELL * NE10 ....100 B4
Furzefield Rd GOS/KPK NE3 ....63 D2
Fylingdale Dr SUNDSW SR3 ....161 E1
Fyndoune Wy BDN/LAN/SAC DH7 ...178 A3
Fynes Cl PLEE/EAS SR8 ....200 C6
Fynway BDN/LAN/SAC DH7 ....178 B2

G

The Gables DIN/WO NE13 ....45 D6
Gadwall Rd HLS DH4 ....170 A4
Gainers Ter WLSD/HOW NE28...........67 E4
Gainford CLSW/PEL DH2 ....152 C5
Gainsborough Av HAR/WTLS NE34 ...88 C5
WASHS NE38 ....139 D2
Gainsborough Cl MONK NE25 ....39 D3
Gainsborough Crs HLS DH4 ....156 B3
LWF/SPW/WRK NE9 ....100 A3
Gainsborough Gv ELS/FEN * NE4 .....79 E2
Gainsborough Pl CRAM NE23............22 A5
Gainsborough Rd
MLFD/PNYW SR4 ....142 B4
STLY/ANP DH9 ....148 B3
Gainsbro Gv ELS/FEN NE4...............79 E2
Gairloch Cl CRAM NE23 ....14 A5
Gairloch Dr CLSW/PEL DH2 ....152 B1
WASHS NE38 ....137 F3
Gairloch Rd MLFD/PNYW SR4 ....142 B3
Galashiels Gv HLS DH4 ....157 D3
Galashiels Rd MLFD/PNYW SR4 .....142 A3
Galashiels Sq MLFD/PNYW SR4 .....142 A3
Gale St STLY/ANP DH9 ....147 F3
Galfrid Cl SEA/MUR SR7.................175 D4
Gallalaw Ter GOS/KPK NE3 ....64 B1
The Galleria
WICK/BNPF
(off Metrocentre) NE16 ....78 B6
The Galleries
WASHS
(off Washington Centre) NE38..........138 B1
Galley's Gill Rd SUND SR1 ....4 B1

Galloping Green Rd
LWF/SPW/WRK NE9 ....118 C2
Galloway Rd PLEE/EAS SR8 ....208 C1
Gallowgate CNUT NE1 ....2 B3
ELS/FEN NE4 ....2 A2
Galsworthy Rd HAR/WTLS NE34 ....87 F5
MLFD/PNYW SR4 ....142 B3
Galway Rd MLFD/PNYW SR4 ....142 A3
Gambia Rd MLFD/PNYW SR4 ....142 A4
Gambia Sq MLFD/PNYW SR4 ....142 A4
Ganton Av CRAM NE23 ....22 A4
Ganton Cl HAR/WTLS NE34.............89 E5
Ganton Ct WASHN NE37 ....120 B2
Garasdale Cl BLYTH NE24 ....16 C2
Garden Cl DIN/WO NE13 ....33 D2
Garden Cft LGB/KIL NE12 ....50 A4
Garden Dr HEBB NE31.....................84 C4
Gardener St ELS/FEN NE4 ....75 F5
Garden La SSH NE33 ....71 E4
Garden Pk WLSD/HOW NE28 ....68 B2
Garden Pl HLS DH4 ....157 D1
SUND SR1 ....4 B2
The Gardens CLSW/PEL DH2..........153 D5
MONK NE25 ....40 B6
Garden St HLS DH4 ....157 F5
Garden Ter MONK NE25...................38 C5
Garden Wk
WICK/BNPF
(off Metrocentre) NE16 ....96 B1
Gardiner Rd MLFD/PNYW SR4 ....141 F3
Gardiner Sq MLFD/PNYW SR4 ....142 A3
Gardner Pk NSHW NE29 ....70 B1
Gardner Pl NSHW NE29 ....70 C1
Garesfield Gdns ROWG * NE39 ....111 D1
Garesfield La BLAY NE21 ....93 E3
Gareston Cl BLYTH NE24 ....10 A5
Garfield St MLFD/PNYW SR4 ....125 E5
Garforth Cl CRAM NE23...................21 F4
Garleigh Cl LGB/KIL NE12 ....50 B1
Garmondsway
BYK/HTN/WLK * NE6.....................82 B3
Garner Cl WD/WHPE/BLK NE5 ....59 F3
Garnet St MLFD/PNYW SR4 ....125 E5
Garrick Cl NSHW NE29 ....53 E5
Garrick St SSH NE33 ....71 E6
Garrigill WASHS NE38 ....139 E5
Garsdale Av WASHN NE37 ....120 B4
Garsdale Rd WBAY NE26 ....40 A4
Garside Av CLS/BIR/GTL DH3 ....136 B1
Garside Gv PLEE/EAS SR8 ....200 A6
Garsin Cl LGB/HTN NE7 ....66 A3
Garth Cornfield PLEE/EAS SR8 ....209 E3
Garth Crs BLAY NE21 ....94 A1
HAR/WTLS NE34 ....72 C5
Garth Farm Rd BLAY NE21 ....94 A1
Garthfield Crs WD/WHPE/BLK NE5 ...60 C4
Garth Heads CNUT NE1 ....3 G4
Garth Six LGB/KIL NE12 ....49 E1
Garth Sixteen LGB/KIL NE12 ....35 F6
The Garth
BLAY (off Front St) NE21 ....94 A1
GOS/KPK NE3 ....62 B2
WD/WHPE/BLK NE5 ....60 A6
Garth Thirteen LGB/KIL NE12 ....35 F6
Garth Thirty Three LGB/KIL NE12 .....49 E1
Garth Thirty Two LGB/KIL NE12 ....50 A1
Garth Twelve LGB/KIL NE12 ....35 E6
Garth Twenty LGB/KIL NE12 ....50 A1
Garth Twenty Five LGB/KIL NE12 .....50 B1
Garth Twenty Four LGB/KIL NE12 .....50 A1
Garth Twenty Seven LGB/KIL NE12...50 B1
Garth Twenty Two LGB/KIL NE12 .....50 A1
Gartland Rd MLFD/PNYW SR4 ....141 F3
Garvey Vls LWF/SPW/WRK NE9 ......100 B4
Garwood St SSH NE33 ....71 D6
Gaskell Av HAR/WTLS NE34............88 A5
Gas La BLAY NE21 ....76 B4
Gas Works Bridge Rd
DUN/TMV NE11 ....97 F1
Gas Works Rd SEA/MUR SR7 ....177 D4
Gatacre St BLYTH NE24 ....11 D4
Gateley Av BLYTH NE24...................16 C2
Gatesgarth LWF/SPW/WRK NE9 ....99 F5
Gatesgarth Gv
CLDN/WHIT/ROK SR6 ....108 B5
Gateshead Hwy GATE NE8...............81 E6
Gateshead Rd WICK/BNPF NE16 ....114 B1
Gatwick Ct GOS/KPK NE3 ....45 E5
Gatwick Rd MLFD/PNYW SR4 ....142 A3
Gaughan Cl BYK/HTN/WLK * NE6......83 E5
Gayfield Ter PLEE/EAS SR8 ....201 E3
Gayhurst Crs SUNDSW SR3 ....160 C2
Gayton Rd WASHN NE37 ....121 D3
Geddes Rd MLFD/PNYW SR4 ....142 A3
Gelt Crs HLH DH5 ....186 A2
General Graham St
MLFD/PNYW SR4 ....143 E1
General Havelock Rd
MLFD/PNYW SR4 ....125 D6
The General's Wd WASHS NE38 ......138 B6
Geneva Rd MLFD/PNYW SR4 ....142 A3
Genister Pl ELS/FEN NE4.................61 F6
Geoffrey Av DHAM DH1..................193 F6
Geoffrey St CLDN/WHIT/ROK SR6 ...109 E1
Geoffrey Ter STLY/ANP DH9 ....147 F3

George Pit La CLS/BIR/GTL DH3........168 B4
George Rd BDLGTN * NE22 ....8 C2
  WLSD/HOW NE28 ....67 D6
George Scott St SSH NE33 ....71 F2
George Smith Gdns FELL NE10 ....82 C6
George Sq TYNE/NSHE NE30 ....55 D6
Georges Rd ELS/FEN NE4 ....79 E4
George Stephenson Wy
  NSHW NE29 ....70 B3
George St ASHBK/HED/RY SR2 ......162 C2
  BLAY NE21 ....76 C5
  BLYTH NE24 ....11 D6
  CLS/BIR/GTL DH3 ....136 A2
  CLS/BIR/GTL DH3 ....153 F6
  DHAM DH1 ....193 F5
  ELS/FEN NE4 ....2 A6
  FELL NE10 ....101 E1
  GOS/KPK NE3 ....62 C1
  HLH DH5 ....171 F5
  RDHAMSE DH6 ....197 E5
  SEA/MUR SR7 ....188 B2
  TYNE/NSHE NE30 ....55 D6
  WD/WHPE/BLK NE5 ....58 B4
  WICK/BNPF NE16 ....95 F3
  WLSD/HOW NE28 ....69 D5
George St North
  CLDN/WHIT/ROK SR6 ....126 C4
Georgian Cl LGB/KIL NE12 ....49 D3
  MLFD/PNYW SR4 ....143 F2
Gerald St ELS/FEN NE4 ....78 C4
  HAR/WTLS NE34 ....88 B5
Gerrard Cl CRAM NE23..................22 A4
  WBAY NE26 ....40 A1
Gerrard Rd MLFD/PNYW SR4 ....142 A3
  WBAY NE26 ....40 A1
Gertrude St HLS DH4 ....157 F6
Ghyll Field Rd DHAM DH1 ....194 A1
Gibside CLSW/PEL DH2 ....152 C5
Gibside Cl STLY/ANP DH9 ....149 D1
Gibside Ct DUN/TMV NE11 ....97 E4
Gibside Gdns
  BW/LEM/TK/HW NE15 ....78 A2
Gibside Vw BLAY NE21....................94 A2
Gibside Way WICK/BNPF NE16 ....78 A6
Gibson Ct BOLCOL NE35 ....105 E2
Gibson St CNUT NE1......................3 H3
  WLSD/HOW NE28 ....68 A2
Gifford Sq MLFD/PNYW SR4 ....142 A3
Gilbert Rd MLFD/PNYW SR4 ....142 A3
  PLEE/EAS SR8 ....208 B1
Gilbert St SSH * NE33 ....71 E6
Gilderdale HLS DH4 ....139 D6
Gilderdale Wy CRAM NE23 ....21 F5
Gilesgate DHAM DH1 ....194 C4
Gilesgate Ct DHAM DH1 ....194 C4
Gilesgate Rd HLH DH5 ....186 A2
Gilhurst Gra SUND SR1 ....126 A6
Gillas La HLH DH5 ....171 F3
Gillas La East HLH DH5 ....171 E3
Gillas La West HLH DH5 ....171 D4
Gill Burn ROWG NE39 ....111 D1
Gillies St BYK/HTN/WLK NE6 ....82 C2
Gillingham Rd MLFD/PNYW SR4 .....142 B3
Gill Rd SUND SR1 ....4 B1
Gill Side Gv CLDN/WHIT/ROK SR6...127 D2
Gill St ELS/FEN NE4 ....79 D3
Gilmore Cl WD/WHPE/BLK NE5 ......59 F3
Gilpin St HLS DH4 ....170 C2
Gilsland Av WLSD/HOW NE28 ....68 B3
Gilsland Gv CRAM NE23 ....14 A5
Gilsland St MLFD/PNYW SR4 ....125 F5
Gilwell Wy GOS/KPK NE3................47 D3
Girtin Rd HAR/WTLS NE34 ....88 C6
Girton Cl PLEE/EAS SR8 ....208 A3
Girvan Cl STLY/ANP DH9 ....149 D2
Gisburn Ct CRAM NE23 ....14 A5
Gishford Wy WD/WHPE/BLK NE5 ....59 E3
Givens St CLDN/WHIT/ROK SR6 .....127 D2
Gladeley Wy WICK/BNPF NE16 ....113 F2
The Glade JRW NE32 ....104 A1
  WD/WHPE/BLK NE5 ....58 C4
Gladstonbury Pl LGB/KIL NE12 ......49 E6
Gladstone Pl JES NE2 ....81 D1
Gladstone St BLYTH NE24 ....10 C4
  BW/LEM/TK/HW NE15 ....76 B2
  CLDN/WHIT/ROK SR6 ....126 C3
  HEBB NE31 ....85 E2
  HLS DH4 ....170 A2
  STLY/ANP DH9 ....147 F3
  STLY/ANP DH9 ....149 E1
  WLSD/HOW NE28 ....69 D5
Gladstone Ter JES NE2 ....81 D1
Gladstone Ter West GATE NE8 ....99 D1
Gladwyn Rd MLFD/PNYW SR4 ....142 A4
Glaholm Rd MLFD/PNYW SR4 ....5 G4
Glaisdale Dr CLDN/WHIT/ROK SR6 ..109 D4
Glaisdale Rd LGB/HTN NE7 ....64 C1
Glamis Av GOS/KPK NE3 ....47 E2
  MLFD/PNYW SR4 ....142 B2
Glamis Ct HAR/WTLS NE34 ....89 E5
Glamis Crs ROWG NE39 ....93 F6
Glamis Vls CLS/BIR/GTL DH3 ....118 B6
Glanmore Rd MLFD/PNYW SR4 ......142 A3
Glantlees WD/WHPE/BLK NE5 ....60 C4
Glanton Av MONK NE25 ....24 B5

Glanton Cl BYK/HTN/WLK NE6 ....82 B3
  CLSW/PEL DH2............................152 C6
Glanton Ct DUN/TMV * NE11 ....97 F1
Glanton Rd NSHW NE29 ....53 F5
Glanton Sq MLFD/PNYW SR4 ....142 B3
Glanton Wynd GOS/KPK NE3 ....47 D5
Glanville Cl DUN/TMV NE11 ....98 A3
Glanville Rd SUNDSW SR3 ....159 F3
Glasbury Av MLFD/PNYW SR4 ....142 B2
Glasgow Rd JRW NE32 ....87 D5
Glasshouse St BYK/HTN/WLK NE6 ...82 B5
Glastonbury WASHS NE38...............138 C2
Glastonbury Gv JES NE2 ....64 B4
Glazebury Wy CRAM NE23 ....14 A5
Gleaston Ct PLEE/EAS SR8 ....208 A5
Glebe Av LGB/KIL NE12 ....49 F5
  WICK/BNPF NE16 ....96 A3
Glebe Cl WD/WHPE/BLK NE5 ....59 F3
Glebe Crs LGB/KIL NE12 ....49 F3
  WASHS NE38 ....121 D6
Glebe Ms BDLGTN NE22 ....7 D3
Glebe Ri WICK/BNPF NE16 ....95 F3
Glebe Rd BDLGTN NE22 ....7 E3
  LGB/KIL NE12 ....49 F3
Glebeside BDN/LAN/SAC DH7 ....178 A4
  HLH (off Church Rd) DH5 ....171 F5
Glebe St ELS/FEN NE4 ....78 C2
Glebe Ter DUN/TMV * NE11 ....97 E2
  LGB/KIL NE12 ....49 F3
Glebe Vw SEA/MUR SR7 ....175 D6
Glebe Vls LGB/KIL NE12 ....49 E3
Glebe Wk WICK/BNPF NE16 ....96 A3
Glenallen Gdns TYNE/NSHE NE30 ....55 E3
Glen Barr CLSW/PEL DH2 ....153 D4
Glenbrooke Ter
  LWF/SPW/WRK NE9 ....99 E6
Glenburn Cl WASHS NE38 ....137 E3
Glencarron Cl WASHS NE38 ....137 F2
Glen Cl ROWG NE39 ....111 D1
Glencoe Av CLSW/PEL DH2 ....153 D4
  CRAM NE23 ....22 A5
Glencoe Rd MLFD/PNYW SR4 ....142 A4
Glencourse BOL NE36 ....107 D3
Glendale Av BLYTH NE24 ....9 D4
  GOS/KPK NE3 ....62 C2
  NSHW NE29 ....54 A6
  WBAY NE26 ....40 C3
  WICK/BNPF NE16 ....95 F4
  WLSD/HOW NE28 ....67 D2
Glendale Cl BLAY NE21 ....93 E2
  SUNDSW SR3 ....159 E2
  WD/WHPE/BLK NE5 ....59 F2
Glendale Gdns
  LWF/SPW/WRK NE9 ....100 A5
Glendale Gv NSHW NE29 ....54 B6
Glendale Rd SMOOR NE27 ....52 C1
Glendale Ter BYK/HTN/WLK NE6 ......82 B2
Glendford Pl BLYTH NE24 ....16 C2
Glendower Av NSHW NE29 ....53 F6
Glendyn Cl LGB/HTN NE7 ....64 C5
Gleneagle Cl WD/WHPE/BLK NE5 ....59 F3
Gleneagles SSH NE33 ....72 A5
Gleneagles Cl LGB/HTN NE7 ....65 E1
Gleneagles Dr WASHN NE37 ....120 A2
Gleneagles Rd LWF/SPW/WRK NE9..117 D1
  MLFD/PNYW SR4 ....142 A4
Gleneagles Sq MLFD/PNYW SR4 .....142 A4
Glenesk Gdns
  ASHBK/HED/RY SR2 ....144 B4
Glenesk Rd ASHBK/HED/RY SR2.....144 B3
Glenfield Av CRAM NE23 ....14 A5
Glenfield Rd LGB/KIL NE12 ....49 D5
Glengarvan Cl WASHS NE38 ....137 F3
Glenhurst Dr WD/WHPE/BLK NE5 ....59 E6
  WICK/BNPF NE16 ....95 E6
Glenhurst Gv HAR/WTLS NE34 ....89 E2
Glenhurst Rd PLEE/EAS SR8 ....200 C2
Glenkerry Cl WASHS NE38 ....137 F3
Glenleigh Dr MLFD/PNYW SR4 ....142 B3
Glen Luce Dr ASHBK/HED/RY SR2 ...145 E4
Glenluce Dr CRAM NE23 ....21 F5
Glenmoor HEBB NE31 ....84 C1
Glenmore Av CLSW/PEL DH2 ....153 D4
Glenmuir Av CRAM NE23 ....21 F5
Glenorrin Cl WASHS NE38 ....137 F3
Glen Pth ASHBK/HED/RY SR2 ....144 C3
Glenridge Av BYK/HTN/WLK NE6 .....65 D5
Glenroy Gdns CLSW/PEL DH2 ....153 D4
Glenshiel Cl WASHS NE38 ....137 F3
Glen St HEBB NE31 ....84 C3
Glen Ter CLSW/PEL DH2 ....152 C4
The Glen ASHBK/HED/RY SR2 ....144 C3
Glenthorn Rd JES NE2 ....64 A4
Glenuce CLS/BIR/GTL DH3 ....137 D5
Gloria Av MONK NE25 ....24 C2
Gloucester Av
  CLDN/WHIT/ROK SR6 ....109 D6
Gloucester Cl CLS/BIR/GTL DH3 .....167 F4
Gloucester Ct DIN/WO NE13 ....45 E4
Gloucester Pl HAR/WTLS NE34 ....89 F3
  PLEE/EAS SR8 ....208 A1
Gloucester Rd ELS/FEN NE4 ....79 F3
  NSHW NE29 ....53 D5
Gloucestershire Dr DHAM DH1 ......196 B3

Gloucester Ter ELS/FEN NE4 ....79 F4
Gloucester Wy ELS/FEN NE4 ....80 A4
Glover Rd MLFD/PNYW SR4 ....142 A4
  WASHN NE37 ....121 E4
Glynfellis FELL NE10......................101 E5
Glynwood Gdns
  LWF/SPW/WRK NE9 ....99 F5
Goalmouth Cl
  CLDN/WHIT/ROK SR6 ....127 D2
Goathland Av LGB/KIL NE12 ....49 E5
Goathland Cl SUNDSW SR3 ....161 E1
Goathland Dr SUNDSW SR3 ....161 D1
Godfrey Rd MLFD/PNYW SR4 ....141 F3
Goldcrest Rd WASHS NE38 ....137 E3
Goldlynn Dr SUNDSW SR3 ....159 F2
Goldsbrough Ct
  JES (off Richardson Rd) NE2 ....80 B1
Goldsmith Rd MLFD/PNYW SR4 .....142 A4
Goldspink La JES NE2 ....81 E1
Goldstone
  LWF/SPW/WRK
  (off Pimlico Ct) NE9 ....99 E6
Goldthorpe Cl CRAM NE23 ....14 A5
Golf Course Rd HLS DH4 ....156 B4
Gompertz Gdns HAR/WTLS NE33 .....71 D6
Goodrich Cl HLS DH4 ....157 E4
Good St STLY/ANP DH9 ....131 D6
Goodwood CL LGB/KIL NE12 ....50 A1
Goodwood Av GATE NE8 ....98 B2
Goodwood Cl WD/WHPE/BLK NE5 ....59 F3
Goodwood Rd MLFD/PNYW SR4 .....141 F3
Goodyear Crs DHAM DH1 ....195 F5
Goole Rd MLFD/PNYW SR4 ....142 B3
Gordon Av GOS/KPK NE3 ....63 E2
  SWCK/CAS SR5 ....123 F4
Gordon Ct FELL * NE10 ....100 C1
Gordon Dr BOL NE36 ....106 C3
Gordon Rd BYK/HTN/WLK * NE6 ......82 A3
  HAR/WTLS NE34 ....88 B2
  MLFD/PNYW SR4 ....141 F4
Gordon Sq BYK/HTN/WLK NE6 ....82 A3
  WBAY NE26 ....41 E6
Gordon St GATE NE8 ....80 C6
  SSH NE33 ....71 E6
Gordon Ter SWCK/CAS SR5 ....125 F4
Gorleston Wy SUNDSW SR3 ....160 B4
Gorse Av HAR/WTLS NE34 ....89 F3
Gorsedale Gv DHAM DH1 ....196 C3
Gorsedene Rd WBAY NE26 ....40 B1
Gorse Rd ASHBK/HED/RY SR2 ....162 C2
Gort Pl DHAM DH1 ....195 E5
Goschen St BLYTH NE24 ....10 C4
  GATE NE8 ....98 C2
  SWCK/CAS SR5 ....125 F2
Gosforth Av HAR/WTLS NE34 ....88 B5
Gosforth Park Wy LGB/KIL NE12 .....48 B5
Gosforth St CLDN/WHIT/ROK SR6 ...127 D3
  JES NE2 ....3 G1
Gosforth Ter ELS/FEN NE10 ....101 E1
Gosport Wy BLYTH NE24 ....16 C2
Gossington WASHS NE38 ....139 F1
Goswick Av LGB/HTN NE7 ....65 D4
Goswick Dr GOS/KPK NE3 ....46 B4
Goundry Av ASHBK/HED/RY SR2 ....162 C2
Gowanburn CRAM NE23 ....21 F5
  WASHS NE38 ....139 D4
Gowan Ter JES NE2 ....64 B5
Gower Rd SWCK/CAS SR5 ....125 F2
Gower St BYK/HTN/WLK NE6 ....83 F4
Gower Wk FELL NE10 ....100 B2
Gowland Av ELS/FEN NE4 ....79 D1
Gowland Sq SEA/MUR SR7 ....188 A1
Gracefield Cl WD/WHPE/BLK NE5 ....59 F5
Grace Gdns WLSD/HOW NE28 ....66 C2
Grace St BYK/HTN/WLK NE6 ....82 B5
  DUN/TMV NE11 ....97 E2
Grafton Cl BYK/HTN/WLK * NE6 ....82 A3
Grafton Rd WBAY NE26 ....41 E6
Grafton St BYK/HTN/WLK * NE6 ....82 A3
  MLFD/PNYW SR4 ....125 F5
Graham Av WICK/BNPF NE16 ....95 F3
Graham Ct BDN/LAN/SAC DH7 ....178 B3
Graham Park Rd GOS/KPK NE3 ....63 E3
Grahamsley St GATE NE8 ....81 E6
Graham St SSH NE33 ....71 F6
The Graham Wy SEA/MUR SR7 ....175 F4
Grainger Ar CNUT * NE1 ....2 D3
Grainger Market CNUT * NE1 ....2 C3
Grainger Park Rd ELS/FEN NE4 ....79 E4
Grainger St CNUT * NE1 ....2 C4
Graingerville North
  ELS/FEN (off Westgate Rd) NE4 ....79 F3
Graingerville South
  ELS/FEN (off Westgate Rd) NE4 ....79 F3
Grampian Cl STLY/ANP DH9 ....146 A5
Grampian Dr PLEE/EAS SR8 ....208 A3
Grampian Gv BOL NE36 ....106 A3
Grampian Pl LGB/KIL NE12 ....49 D3
Granby Cl SUNDSW SR3 ....144 A3
  WICK/BNPF NE16 ....114 A1
Grand Pde TYNE/NSHE NE30 ....55 F4
Grandstand Rd JES NE2 ....62 C6
Grange Av BDLGTN NE22....................8 C1
  HLS DH4 ....169 F1

LGB/KIL NE12 ....50 A6
PLEE/EAS SR8 ....200 A3
SMOOR NE27 ....38 B6
Grange CI BLYTH NE24 ....16 C2
  MONK NE25 ....39 F6
  PLEE/EAS SR8 ....200 B6
  TYNE/NSHE NE30 ....55 D2
  WLSD/HOW NE28 ....67 E4
Grange Ct FELL NE10 ....101 F3
Grange Crs ASHBK/HED/RY SR2 ....4 C5
  FELL NE10 ....101 F3
  RYTON NE40 ....74 B4
Grange Dr RYTON NE40 ....74 B4
Grange Est DUN/TMV NE11 ....116 B6
Grange Farm Dr WICK/BNPF NE16 ...95 F5
Grange La WICK/BNPF NE16 ....95 F5
Grange Lonnen RYTON NE40 ....74 A3
Grangemere CI
  ASHBK/HED/RY SR2 ....145 E4
Grange Nook WICK/BNPF NE16 ....95 F5
Grange Pk MONK NE25 ....53 E1
Grange Park Av BDLGTN NE22 ....8 C1
  SWCK/CAS SR5 ....126 B1
Grange PI JRW NE32 ....86 A1
Grange Rd BW/LEM/TK/HW NE15 .....58 A6
  DHAM DH1 ....196 B2
  ELS/FEN NE4 ....78 C2
  FELL NE10 ....101 F3
  GOS/KPK NE3 ....47 E5
  JRW NE32 ....86 A1
  PONT/DH NE20 ....28 A3
  RYTON NE40 ....74 B3
  STLY/ANP DH9 ....147 F2
  SWCK/CAS SR5 ....123 F5
Grange Rd West JRW NE32 ....85 F1
Grange St CLSW/PEL DH2 ....152 A2
Grange St South
  ASHBK/HED/RY SR2 ....145 E4
Grange Ter BOL NE36 ....106 C3
  CLSW/PEL DH2 ....151 E4
  LWF/SPW/WRK NE9 ....99 F2
  SWCK/CAS SR5 ....126 A2
The Grange
  BOL (off Front St) NE36 ....106 C3
  STLY/ANP DH9 ....130 B6
Grange Vw HLH DH5 ....170 C5
  HLS DH4 ....157 F5
  RYTON NE40 ....74 B4
  SWCK/CAS SR5 ....126 B1
Grantham Av SEA/MUR SR7 ....176 A4
Grantham Dr LWF/SPW/WRK NE9 ....99 D6
Grantham PI CRAM NE23 ....21 F5
Grantham Rd
  CLDN/WHIT/ROK SR6 ....127 D2
  JES NE2 ....81 E1
Grantham St BLYTH NE24 ....11 E6
Grant St JRW NE32 ....85 F1
  PLEE/EAS SR8 ....209 F1
Granville Av LGB/KIL NE12 ....50 A3
  WBAY NE26 ....26 C3
Granville Ct JES NE2 ....64 A6
Granville Crs LGB/KIL NE12 ....50 A6
Granville Dr HLS DH4 ....157 E3
  LGB/KIL NE12 ....50 A4
  WD/WHPE/BLK NE5 ....59 F3
Granville Gdns JES NE2 ....64 C6
Granville Rd GOS/KPK NE3 ....47 E5
  JES NE2 ....64 A6
  PLEE/EAS SR8 ....209 E3
Granville St GATE NE8 ....99 E1
  MLFD/PNYW SR4 ....194 A5
Grape La DHAM DH1 ....196 A5
Grasmere CLDN/WHIT/ROK SR6 .....107 F1
Grasmere Av BYK/HTN/WLK NE6 .....83 D3
  FELL NE10 ....101 E2
  HLH DH5 ....186 B4
  JRW NE32 ....86 C5
Grasmere CI LGB/KIL NE12 ....49 E1
Grasmere Crs BLAY NE21 ....94 A2
  SWCK/CAS SR5 ....126 B1
  WBAY NE26 ....40 B3
Grasmere Gdns HAR/WTLS NE34 .....89 D2
Grasmere PI GOS/KPK NE3 ....47 D5
Grasmere Rd CLSW/PEL DH2 ....166 A1
  HEBB NE31 ....85 E3
  PLEE/EAS SR8 ....209 D1
  WICK/BNPF NE16 ....96 B3
  WLSD/HOW NE28 ....66 C5
Grasmere St GATE NE8 ....99 D1
Grasmere St West GATE NE8 ....99 D1
Grasmere Ter
  NSHW (off Hawkeys La) NE29 ....54 B4
  RDHAMSE DH6 ....188 A5
  SEA/MUR SR7 ....188 C2
Grasmoor PI
  BW/LEM/TK/HW NE15 ....76 A1
Grassdale DHAM DH1 ....196 C3
Grasshome Mdw SUNDSW SR3 ......144 A4
Grassholm PI LGB/KIL NE12 ....48 C5
Grassington Dr CRAM NE23 ....21 F4
Grasslees WASHS NE38 ....137 E6
Grassmere Ter STLY/ANP DH9 ....147 F4
Grasswell Dr WD/WHPE/BLK NE5 .....61 F3
Gravel Wks HLH DH5 ....171 D1

Gravesend Rd MLFD/PNYW * SR4 ....142 A4
Gravesend Sq MLFD/PNYW SR4......142 B4
Gray Av DHAM DH1 ....193 F1
  DIN/WO NE13 ....33 E3
  RDHAMSE DH6 ....197 E4
  SEA/MUR SR7 ....188 B1
Grayling Ct SUNDSW SR3 ....159 E3
Grayling Rd DUN/TMV NE11 ....98 A3
Gray Rd ASHBK/HED/RY SR2 ....5 H5
Grays Cross SUND SR1 ....5 F2
Grays Ter BOLCOL NE35 ....105 D1
Graystones FELL NE10 ....102 A3
Gray St BLYTH NE24 ....11 D3
Graythwaite CLSW/PEL DH2 ....152 B5
Greathead St SSH NE33 ....88 A1
Great Lime Rd DIN/WO NE13 ....34 C5
  LGB/KIL NE12 ....49 E3
Great North Forest Trail
  HAR/WTLS NE34 ....90 C1
Great North Rd GOS/KPK NE3 ....47 E5
Grebe CI BLYTH NE24 ....17 D1
Greely Rd WD/WHPE/BLK NE5 ....60 B4
Greenacres CLSW/PEL DH2 ....151 F1
Green Av HLS DH4 ....157 F4
Greenbank BLAY NE21 ....76 B6
  JRW NE32 ....86 A1
Greenbank Dr MLFD/PNYW SR4 .....141 F1
Greenbourne Gdns FELL NE10 ....100 B3
Green CI TYNE/NSHE NE30 ....55 D3
Green Crs CRAM NE23 ....34 A2
Greencroft RDHAMSE DH6 ....188 A5
Greencroft Av BYK/HTN/WLK NE6 ...66 C6
Greendale CI BLYTH NE24 ....9 F4
Greendale Gdns HLH DH5 ....185 E2
Greenfield Av WD/WHPE/BLK NE5 ...60 C4
Greenfield PI ELS/FEN NE4 ....2 A1
Greenfield Rd DIN/WO NE13 ....47 D3
  GOS/KPK NE3 ....47 D3
Greenfields
  CLSW/PEL (off Ross) DH2 ....135 F4
Greenfield Ter FELL * NE10 ....101 E1
  STLY/ANP DH9 ....146 B4
Greenfinch CI WASHS NE38 ....137 E2
Greenford DUN/TMV NE11 ....116 C6
Greenford La DUN/TMV NE11 ....117 D5
Greenford Rd BYK/HTN/WLK NE6 ....83 E5
Greenhaugh LGB/KIL NE12 ....49 D3
Greenhead LGB/KIL NE12 ....35 E5
Greenhills LGB/KIL NE12 ....35 E5
Greenhill Vw WD/WHPE/BLK NE5 .....62 A4
Green Hill Wk HAR/WTLS NE34.........90 B2
Greenholme CI CRAM NE23 ....14 A5
Greenhow CI ASHBK/HED/RY SR2 ...162 B3
Greenlands STLY/ANP DH9 ....147 F4
Greenlands Ct MONK NE25 ....24 C4
Green La BOL NE36 ....106 C4
  DHAM DH1 ....195 C4
  DIN/WO NE13 ....44 B4
  FELL NE10 ....82 C6
  FELL NE10 ....101 F1
  HAR/WTLS NE34 ....88 A4
  LGB/KIL NE12 ....50 A1
  SEA/MUR SR7 ....173 D1
Green Lane Gdns FELL NE10 ....82 B6
Greenlaw WD/WHPE/BLK NE5 ....60 A6
Greenlaw Rd CRAM NE23 ....21 F5
Green Lea BDN/LAN/SAC DH7 ....178 D5
Greenlea NSHW NE29 ....53 D3
Greenlea CI MLFD/PNYW SR4 ....142 B3
Greenlee Dr LGB/HTN NE7 ....65 F3
Greenmarket CNUT * NE1 ....2 C3
Greenock Rd MLFD/PNYW SR4 ......142 A4
Green Pk WLSD/HOW NE28 ....66 A3
Greenrigg Gdns SUNDSW SR3 ....144 A3
Green's Bank STLY/ANP DH9 ....150 C1
Greenshields Rd
  MLFD/PNYW SR4 ....142 A4
Greenside Av PLEE/EAS SR8 ....209 E1
  WLSD/HOW NE28 ....68 B3
Greenside Crs
  BW/LEM/TK/HW NE15 ....77 F1
Green's PI SSH NE33 ....71 E2
Green St SEA/MUR SR7 ....176 C3
  SUND SR1 ....4 C2
Green Ter SUND SR1 ....4 B3
The Green BW/LEM/TK/HW NE15 .....58 B5
  FELL NE10 ....101 D4
  GOS/KPK NE3 ....62 B3
  HLH DH5 ....171 E1
  MONK NE25 ....40 A4
  PLEE/EAS SR8 ....207 F4
  PONT/DH NE20 ....28 B2
  SWCK/CAS SR5 .... F4
Greentree La STLY/ANP DH9...........146 A3
Greenway ELS/FEN NE4 ....61 F6
  WD/WHPE/BLK NE5 ....59 E2
The Greenway MLFD/PNYW SR4 .....142 B2
Greenwell CI BLAY NE21 ....93 F1
Greenwich Ri GATE NE8 ....81 F4
Greenwood LGB/KIL NE12 ....50 B3
Greenwood Av BDLGTN NE22 ....8 C1
  BYK/HTN/WLK NE6 ....66 C5
  HLS DH4 ....170 B4
Greenwood Gdns DUN/TMV NE11 ....97 F5
  FELL NE10 ....100 C1

Greenwood Rd MLFD/PNYW SR4 ....142 A3
Greetlands Rd
  ASHBK/HED/RY SR2 ....144 B3
Gregson St BDN/LAN/SAC DH7 ....178 B1
Gregson Ter SEA/MUR SR7 ....175 E1
Grenada CI WBAY NE26 ....40 B2
Grenada Dr WBAY NE26 ....40 B2
Grenada PI WBAY NE26 ....40 B2
Grenfell Sq PLEE/EAS SR8 ....142 A4
Grenville Ct
  CRAM (off Megstone Av) NE23 ....21 F3
Grenville Dr GOS/KPK NE3 ....47 D3
Grenville Wy WBAY NE26 ....40 A3
Gresford St SSH NE33 ....88 B2
Gresham St CRAM NE23 ....22 A4
Gresley Rd PLEE/EAS SR8 ....207 F2
Greta Gdns SSH NE33 ....71 F6
Greta Ter MLFD/PNYW SR4 ....143 F1
Gretna Dr HAR/WTLS NE34 ....87 E5
Gretna Rd BW/LEM/TK/HW NE15 ....78 A1
Gretton PI LGB/HTN NE7 ....64 C3
Grey Av CRAM NE23 ....21 F5
Greybourne Gdns
  ASHBK/HED/RY SR2 ....144 B4
Greyfriars La LGB/KIL NE12 ....48 C6
Greystead CI WD/WHPE/BLK NE5 ....59 F3
Greystead Rd MONK NE25 ....39 D5
Greystoke Av ASHBK/HED/RY SR2 ..144 B4
  JES NE2 ....81 F1
  WICK/BNPF NE16 ....96 A4
Greystoke Gdns
  ASHBK/HED/RY SR2 ....144 B3
  JES NE2 ....64 C6
  LWF/SPW/WRK NE9 ....118 A2
  WICK/BNPF NE16 ....96 A5
Greystoke Pk GOS/KPK NE3 ....47 D4
Greystoke Wk WICK/BNPF NE16 ......96 A4
Grey St CNUT NE1 ....2 D3
  DIN/WO NE13 ....32 C4
  HLS DH4 ....170 C1
  TYNE/NSHE NE30 ....55 D6
  WLSD/HOW NE28 ....67 E4
Greywood Av ELS/FEN NE4 ....79 D1
Grieves' Rw CRAM NE23 ....34 C2
Grieve St BLYTH NE24 ....10 C3
Grimsby St BLYTH NE24 ....11 D6
Grindon Av MLFD/PNYW SR4 ....142 A1
Grindon CI CRAM NE23 ....21 F5
  MONK NE25 ....54 A2
Grindon Ct MLFD/PNYW SR4 ....142 B3
Grindon Gdns MLFD/PNYW SR4 .....142 B3
Grindon La MLFD/PNYW SR4 ....142 A1
  SUNDSW SR3 ....142 C3
Grindon Pk MLFD/PNYW SR4 ....142 B3
Grindon Ter MLFD/PNYW SR4 ....143 F1
Grinstead CI HAR/WTLS NE34 ....89 E1
Grinstead Wy DHAM DH1 ....196 C1
Grisedale Gdns
  LWF/SPW/WRK NE9 ....99 F6
Grisedale Rd PLEE/EAS SR8 ....209 D2
Grizedale WASHN NE37 ....120 A6
Grizedale Ct CLDN/WHIT/ROK SR6 ..108 B4
Groat Market CNUT NE1 ....2 D4
Grosvenor Av JES NE2 ....64 B5
  WICK/BNPF NE16 ....96 A2
Grosvenor CI CRAM NE23 ....21 F5
Grosvenor Ct WD/WHPE/BLK NE5 ...59 F3
Grosvenor Crs HEBB NE31 ....85 E5
Grosvenor Dr
  CLDN/WHIT/ROK SR6 ....107 F2
  HAR/WTLS NE34 ....72 B6
  MONK NE25 ....40 C6
Grosvenor Gdns HAR/WTLS NE34 ....89 E2
  JES NE2 ....64 C6
  WLSD/HOW NE28 ....68 C3
Grosvenor PI JES NE2 ....64 B5
  NSHW NE29 ....54 B4
Grosvenor Rd HAR/WTLS NE34 ....72 A6
  JES NE2 ....64 B5
Grosvenor St SWCK/CAS SR5 ....125 E2
Grosvenor Wy WD/WHPE/BLK NE5 ..59 F4
Grotto Gdns HAR/WTLS NE34 ....90 C1
Grotto Rd HAR/WTLS NE34 ....90 C2
Grove Av GOS/KPK NE3 ....63 E2
Grove Ct RDHAMSE DH6 ....206 B3
Grove Rd BDN/LAN/SAC DH7 ....203 D5
  BW/LEM/TK/HW NE15 ....99 F4
  LWF/SPW/WRK NE9 ....99 F4
Grove St DHAM DH1 ....194 A6
Grove Ter BDN/LAN/SAC DH7 ....204 A2
The Grove ASHBK/HED/RY SR2 ....144 C2
  ASHBK/HED/RY SR2 ....162 B1
  DHAM DH1 ....193 F3
  GOS/KPK NE3 ....63 F2
  HLH DH5 ....171 D4
  JES NE2 ....64 B4
  JRW NE32 ....104 A1
  LGB/KIL NE12 ....49 F6
  MONK NE25 ....40 B6
  PLEE/EAS SR8 ....199 F2
  ROWG NE39 ....111 E3
  SWCK/CAS SR5 ....124 A3
  WD/WHPE/BLK NE5 ....59 F5
  WICK/BNPF NE16 ....96 B4
Guardians Ct PONT/DH NE20 ....28 B3

Guelder Rd LGB/HTN NE7 ....65 E3
Guernsey Rd MLFD/PNYW SR4 ....142 A4
Guernsey Sq MLFD/PNYW SR4 .....142 A4
Guildford Pl BYK/HTN/WLK NE6 ....82 A1
Guildford St ASHBK/HED/RY SR2 ...145 E2
Guillemot Cl BLYTH NE24 ....17 D1
Guisborough Dr NSHW NE29 ....53 D4
Guisborough St MLFD/PNYW SR4 ...143 E1
Gullane WASHN NE37 ....120 C1
Gullane Cl FELL NE10 ....84 B6
 STLY/ANP DH9 ....149 D2
Gunnerston Gv GOS/KPK NE3 ....61 F1
Gunnerton Cl CRAM NE23 ....22 A4
Gunnerton Pl NSHW NE29 ....53 F5
Gunn St DUN/TMV NE11 ....97 F2
Gut Rd WLSD/HOW NE28 ....68 B4
Guyzance Av GOS/KPK NE3 ....46 C6

Hall Vw CLDN/WHIT/ROK SR6 ....109 E2
Hall Wks PLEE/EAS SR8 ....199 F3
Halstead Rd SSH NE33 ....71 F5
Halstead Sq MLFD/PNYW SR4 ....142 C1
Halterburn Cl GOS/KPK NE3 ....63 D2
Halton Rd DHAM DH1 ....194 C1
Hamar Cl NSHW NE29 ....69 E2
Hambard Wy WASHS NE38 ....138 C2
Hambledon Av TYNE/NSHE NE30 .....54 C1
Hambledon Cl BOLCOL NE35 ....104 C2
Hambledon Gdns LGB/HTN NE7 ....64 C3
Hambledon Pl PLEE/EAS SR8 ....207 F3
Hambledon St BLYTH NE24 ....10 C4
Hambleton Dr SEA/MUR SR7 ....176 A3
Hambleton Rd WASHS NE38 ....138 A3
Hamilton Ct GATE NE8 ....99 F2
 RDHAMSE DH6 ....206 D2
Hamilton Crs ELS/FEN NE4 ....80 A2
 NSHW NE29 ....53 E4
Hamilton Dr WBAY NE26 ....40 A2
Hamilton Pl ELS/FEN NE4 ....80 A2
Hamilton St ELS/FEN NE4 ....80 A2
Hamilton Ter BDN/LAN/SAC DH7 ...164 A4
 BOL NE36 ....105 F3
Hammer Square Bank
 STLY/ANP DH9 ....133 E5
Hampden Rd
 CLDN/WHIT/ROK SR6 ....127 D2
Hampden St SSH NE33 ....71 E6
Hampshire Ct ELS/FEN NE4 ....79 F6
Hampshire Pl WASHN NE37 ....120 C3
Hampshire Rd DHAM DH1 ....180 C6
Hampshire Wy HAR/WTLS * NE34 ....90 B1
Hampstead Cl BLYTH NE24 ....16 B3
Hampstead Rd ELS/FEN NE4 ....79 D5
 MLFD/PNYW SR4 ....142 C2
Hampton Cl CRAM NE23 ....142 C2
Hampton Ct CLS/BIR/GTL DH3 ......153 F1
 WICK/BNPF
 (off Coalway La North) NE16 ....96 A1
Hampton Dr FELL NE10 ....100 C1
Hampton Rd TYNE/NSHE NE30 ....54 C2
Hamsterley Cl CLS/BIR/GTL DH3 ...168 A1
Hamsterley St SUNDSW * SR3 ....160 C2
Hamsterley Crs
 BW/LEM/TK/HW NE15 ....76 A1
 DHAM DH1 ....180 C6
 LWF/SPW/WRK NE9 ....118 B1
Hamsterley Dr LGB/KIL NE12 ....35 E6
Hamsterley Gdns STLY/ANP DH9 ...146 B4
Hanby Gdns SUNDSW SR3 ....143 F3
Hancock St CNUT NE1 ....80 C1
Handel St MLFD/PNYW SR4 ....125 F5
 SSH NE33 ....71 F4
Handley St PLEE/EAS SR8 ....209 E1
Handy Dr DUN/TMV NE11 ....78 C6
Hangmans La HLH DH5 ....160 A5
Hanlon Ct JRW NE32 ....85 E1
Hannington Pl
 BYK/HTN/WLK * NE6 ....81 F2
Hannington St BYK/HTN/WLK NE6 ...81 F2
Hanover Ct CRAM NE23 ....35 D1
 DHAM DH1 ....194 A5
Hanover Dr BLAY NE21 ....93 F1
Hanover Pl CRAM NE23 ....13 F5
 MLFD/PNYW SR4 ....126 A4
Hanover Sq CNUT NE1 ....2 D6
Harbottle Av GOS/KPK NE3 ....46 C6
 SMOOR NE27 ....52 B2
Harbottle Ct BYK/HTN/WLK NE6 .....82 B4
Harbottle Crs JRW NE32 ....86 A6
Harbour Dr SSH NE33 ....71 F1
The Harbour HLS DH4 ....157 D2
Harbour Vw CLDN/WHIT/ROK SR6 ...127 E3
 SSH NE33 ....71 F1
Harbour Wk SEA/MUR SR7 ....176 B2
Harcourt Rd ASHBK/HED/RY SR2 ...144 C5
Harcourt St LWF/SPW/WRK * NE9 ...99 F5
Hardgate Rd ASHBK/HED/RY SR2 ..145 D5
Hardie Av WICK/BNPF NE16 ....95 F2
Hardie Dr BOL NE36 ....105 F3
Hardwick Ct GATE NE8 ....99 F1
Hardwick Pl GOS/KPK NE3 ....62 C3
Hardwick Ri CLDN/WHIT/ROK SR6 ...127 D4
Hardwick St PLEE/EAS SR8 ....209 F3
Hardyards Ct HAR/WTLS NE34 ....88 B3
Hardy Av HAR/WTLS NE34 ....88 A5
Hardy Ct TYNE/NSHE * NE30 ....55 D6
Hardy Gv WLSD/HOW NE28 ....66 C1
Hardy Sq SWCK/CAS SR5 ....125 F1
Harebell Rd LWF/SPW/WRK NE9 ...100 B6
Harehills Av WD/WHPE/BLK NE5 .....61 F3
Harelaw Gv WD/WHPE/BLK NE5 .....59 F5
Hareside CRAM NE23 ....21 F3
Harewood Cl WICK/BNPF NE16 ....95 F6
Harewood Crs MONK NE25 ....39 D6
Harewood Dr BDLGTN NE22 ....8 B2
Harewood Gdns SUNDSW SR3 ......143 F3
Harewood Rd GOS/KPK NE3 ....47 E6
Hareydene WD/WHPE/BLK NE5 ....60 B1
Hargill Dr WASHS NE38 ....137 F5
Hargrave Ct BLYTH NE24 ....10 B6
Harland Wy WASHS NE38 ....138 C1
Harle Cl WD/WHPE/BLK NE5 ....60 A5

Harlequin Ldg FELL NE10 ....100 C2
Harle Rd SMOOR NE27 ....37 F6
Harleston Wy FELL NE10 ....101 D4
Harle St WLSD/HOW NE28 ....67 D4
Harley Ter GOS/KPK NE3 ....63 F1
Harlow Av GOS/KPK NE3 ....46 B5
 SMOOR NE27 ....51 F1
Harlow Green La
 LWF/SPW/WRK NE9 ....117 F2
Harlow Pl LGB/HTN NE7 ....65 D3
Harlow St MLFD/PNYW SR4 ....126 A6
Harnham Av NSHW NE29 ....69 E1
Harnham Gdns
 WD/WHPE/BLK NE5 ....61 E6
Harnham Gv CRAM NE23 ....21 F3
Harold Sq ASHBK/HED/RY SR2 ....5 E6
Harold St JRW NE32 ....86 B1
Harperley Dr SUNDSW SR3 ....144 A4
Harperley Gdns STLY/ANP DH9 .....146 A3
Harperley La STLY/ANP DH9 ....147 D1
Harperley Rd STLY/ANP DH9 ....146 B3
Harper St BLYTH NE24 ....10 C5
Harras Bank CLS/BIR/GTL DH3 .....136 B3
Harraton Ter
 CLS/BIR/GTL
 (off Durham Rd) DH3 ....136 B3
Harriet Pl BYK/HTN/WLK * NE6 ....82 B1
Harriet St BLAY NE21 ....76 B6
 BYK/HTN/WLK NE6 ....82 C2
Harrington St WLSD/HOW NE28 ......67 D4
Harriot Dr LGB/KIL NE12 ....48 C2
Harrison Cl PLEE/EAS SR8 ....209 D3
Harrison Gdns GATE NE8 ....98 C3
Harrison Garth RDHAMSE DH6 ......197 E4
Harrison Pl JES NE2 ....81 D1
Harrison Rd WLSD/HOW NE28 ....68 C3
Harrogate St ASHBK/HED/RY SR2 ....5 E5
Harrogate Ter SEA/MUR SR7 ....188 B1
Harrow Gdns DIN/WO NE13 ....33 E5
Harrow Sq MLFD/PNYW SR4 ....142 C1
Hartburn FELL NE10 ....101 F5
Hartburn Dr WD/WHPE/BLK NE5 .....59 F3
Hartburn Pl ELS/FEN NE4 ....79 F6
Hartburn Rd TYNE/NSHE NE30 ....54 B3
Hartburn Wk GOS/KPK NE3 ....61 F1
Hartford Bank CRAM NE23 ....12 B2
Hartford Br BDLGTN NE22 ....12 B2
Hartford Ct BDLGTN NE22 ....7 D4
Hartford Crs BDLGTN NE22 ....12 B1
Hartford Dr BDLGTN NE22 ....12 B1
Hartford Rd BDLGTN NE22 ....6 C6
 GOS/KPK NE3 ....47 F5
 HAR/WTLS NE34 ....87 F3
 MLFD/PNYW SR4 ....142 C1
Hartford St BYK/HTN/WLK NE6 ....82 B1
Hartforth Crs FELL NE10 ....102 A1
Harthope Av SWCK/CAS SR5 ....124 B1
Harthope Cl WASHS NE38 ....137 E6
Harthope Dr NSHW NE29 ....70 A3
Hartington Rd TYNE/NSHE NE30 .....54 C3
Hartington St
 CLDN/WHIT/ROK SR6 ....127 D2
 ELS/FEN NE4 ....79 D2
 GATE NE8 ....99 E1
Hartington Ter SSH NE33 ....71 F6
Hartland Dr CLS/BIR/GTL DH3 ......136 C4
Hartlands BDLGTN NE22 ....7 D4
Hartleigh Pl CNUT NE1 ....10 A5
Hartlepool Av PLEE/EAS SR8 ....201 E6
Hartley Av WBAY NE26 ....40 A5
Hartleyburn Av HEBB NE31 ....84 C5
Hartley La MONK NE25 ....39 D4
Hartley St MONK NE25 ....24 B5
 SUND SR1 ....5 G1
Hartley Ter BLYTH NE24 ....16 B2
Hartoft Cl HLS DH4 ....157 F4
Harton Gv HAR/WTLS NE34 ....89 D1
Harton House Rd HAR/WTLS NE34 ...89 F1
Harton House Rd East
 HAR/WTLS 89 F1
Harton La HAR/WTLS NE34 ....88 B3
Harton Ri HAR/WTLS NE34 ....89 E1
Hartside BW/LEM/TK/HW NE15 ......76 B1
 CLS/BIR/GTL DH3 ....136 C5
Hartside Crs BLAY NE21 ....93 E2
 CRAM NE23 ....13 F4
 SMOOR NE27 ....37 F6
Hartside Gdns HLH DH5 ....186 B3
 JES NE2 ....64 B5
Hartside Pl GOS/KPK NE3 ....47 E3
Hartside Vw DHAM DH1 ....179 F5
Hart Sq MLFD/PNYW SR4 ....142 C1
Hart Ter CLDN/WHIT/ROK SR6 ......109 E4
Harvard Rd GOS/KPK NE3 ....62 A1
Harvest Cl SUNDSW SR3 ....160 B3
Harvey Cl PLEE/EAS SR8 ....208 C1
 WASHS NE38 ....137 E1
Harvey Combe LGB/KIL NE12 ....49 D1
Harvey Crs FELL NE10 ....102 A2
Harwick Ct STLY/ANP DH9 ....149 E2
Harwood Cl CRAM NE23 ....21 F3
 WASHS NE38 ....137 F5
Harwood Dr LGB/KIL NE12 ....50 B1
Hascombe Cl MONK NE25 ....39 F4
Haslemere Dr SUNDSW SR3 ....143 F3

Hackworth Rd PLEE/EAS SR8 ....199 E5
Hackworth Wy NSHW NE29 ....70 B3
Haddington Rd MONK NE25 ....39 E3
Haddon Cl MONK NE25 ....39 D5
Haddon Gn MONK NE25 ....39 D5
Haddricksmill Rd GOS/KPK NE3 ......64 A2
Hadleigh Rd MLFD/PNYW SR4 ......142 C1
Hadrian Av CLS/BIR/GTL DH5 ....153 F3
Hadrian Ct
 LGB/KIL
 (off Garth Thirtythree) NE12 ....49 F1
Hadrian Gdns BLAY NE21 ....94 C1
Hadrian Pl BW/LEM/TK/HW NE15 ...57 F4
 LWF/SPW/WRK NE9 ....100 A3
Hadrian Rd BLYTH NE24 ....16 B3
 ELS/FEN NE4 ....79 D2
 JRW NE32 ....86 C4
 WLSD/HOW NE28 ....67 E5
Hadrians Ct DUN/TMV NE11 ....98 C6
Hadrian St DHAM DH1 ....195 F5
Hadstone Pl WD/WHPE/BLK NE5 ....61 E5
Haggerston Cl
 WD/WHPE/BLK NE5 ....61 D2
Haggerston Ct
 WD/WHPE/BLK NE5 ....61 D2
Haggerston Crs
 WD/WHPE/BLK NE5 ....61 D2
Haggerstone Dr SWCK/CAS SR5 ...123 F4
Haggerston Ter JRW NE32 ....87 D4
Haggie Av WLSD/HOW NE28 ....67 F3
Haig Av WLSD/HOW NE28 ....40 B6
Haig Crs BW/LEM/TK/HW NE15 ......77 F2
 DHAM DH1 ....195 F5
Haigh Ter DHAM DH1 ....195 F5
Haig Rd BDLGTN NE22 ....8 A4
Haig St DUN/TMV * NE11 ....97 F2
Hailsham Av LGB/KIL NE12 ....49 E5
Haininghead WASHS NE38 ....139 D4
Hainingwood Ter FELL NE10 ....84 A6
Haldane Ct JES NE2 ....64 A6
Haldane Ter JES NE2 ....64 A6
Haldon Pl PLEE/EAS SR8 ....208 A3
Hale Ri PLEE/EAS SR8 ....208 C2
Halewood Av GOS/KPK NE3 ....62 C3
Half Fields Rd BLAY NE21 ....94 A1
Half Moon La GATE * NE8 ....81 D5
Halfway House La
 ASHBK/HED/RY SR2 ....145 F3
Halidon Rd ASHBK/HED/RY SR2 ...144 C5
Halidon Sq ASHBK/HED/RY SR2 ...144 C5
Halifax Pl DUN/TMV NE11 ....97 D1
Halifax Rd DUN/TMV NE11 ....97 D1
Halkirk Wy CRAM NE23 ....13 F5
Hallam Rd PLEE/EAS SR8 ....208 C1
Hall Cl HLS DH4 ....183 F2
 SEA/MUR SR7 ....174 C2
Hall Dene Wy SEA/MUR SR7 ....162 A6
Hall Dr LGB/KIL NE12 ....35 D5
Halleypike Cl LGB/HTN NE7 ....65 D5
Hall Farm Rd SUNDSW SR3 ....160 B3
Hallfield Cl SUNDSW SR3 ....160 C3
Hallfield Dr PLEE/EAS SR8 ....199 F3
Hall Gdns BOL NE36 ....105 F3
 FELL NE10 ....100 C3
Hallgarth Rd BLAY NE21 ....76 A6
Hallgarth St DHAM DH1 ....194 C6
 RDHAMSE DH6 ....197 E4
The Hallgarth DHAM DH1 ....194 C6
Hallgarth Vw DHAM DH1 ....194 C6
Hallgarth Vlls RDHAMSE DH6 ....197 F5
Hall Gn BLYTH NE24 ....10 A5
Halling Cl BYK/HTN/WLK NE6 ....83 F4
Hallington Dr MONK NE25 ....24 C5
Halliwell St HLS DH4 ....170 C1
Hall La HLH DH5 ....171 D3
 HLS DH4 ....183 F2
Hallow Dr BW/LEM/TK/HW NE15 ....57 F5
Hall Pk BLAY NE21 ....75 F4
Hall Rd HEBB NE31 ....85 D3
 WASHN NE37 ....121 D4
Hallside Rd BLYTH NE24 ....10 A6
Hall Ter FELL * NE10 ....84 A6

Hassop Wy *BDLGTN* NE22 ....7 E2
Hastings Av *DHAM* DH1 ....204 C1
　GOS/KPK NE3 ....45 F5
　LGB/KIL NE12 ....49 F5
　WBAY NE26 ....26 A1
　WBAY NE26 ....40 B2
Hastings Ct *BDLGTN* NE22 ....8 B2
Hastings Dr *TYNE/NSHE* NE30 ....55 E4
Hastings Gdns *MONK* NE25 ....24 C2
Hastings St *ASHBK/HED/RY* SR2 ....145 D2
　CRAM NE23 ....22 B3
Hastings Ter *ASHBK/HED/RY* SR2 ......145 E3
　CRAM NE23 ....14 C4
　MONK NE25 ....24 C1
Haswell Cl *FELL* NE10 ....102 C3
Haswell Gdns *TYNE/NSHE* NE30.........54 C6
Hatfield Av *HEBB* NE31 ....85 E2
Hatfield Cl *DHAM* DH1 ....179 F6
Hatfield Dr *CRAM* NE23 ....23 E6
Hatfield Gdns *MONK* NE25 ....39 D6
　SUNDSW SR3 ....143 F3
Hatfield Pl *PLEE/EAS* SR8 ....209 D3
Hatfield Sq *SSH* NE33 ....71 F3
Hathaway Gdns *SUNDSW* SR3 ....143 F3
Hatherton Av *TYNE/NSHE* NE30 ....55 F5
Hathery La *BLYTH* NE24 ....8 C5
Haugh La *RYTON* NE40 ....75 D2
Haughton Crs *JRW* NE32 ....86 A6
　WD/WHPE/BLK NE5 ....60 A3
Haughton Ter *BLYTH* NE24 ....11 D5
Hautmont Rd *HEBB* NE31 ....85 E4
Hauxley *LGB/KIL* NE12 ....35 F5
Hauxley Dr *CLSW/PEL* DH2 ....165 E2
　CRAM NE23 ....13 F4
　GOS/KPK NE3 ....46 A5
Hauxley Gdns *WD/WHPE/BLK* NE5 .....61 F4
Havanna *LGB/KIL* NE12 ....35 F6
Havannah Crs *DIN/WO* NE13 ....31 D4
Havannah Rd *WASHN* NE37 ....120 A5
Havant Gdns *DIN/WO* NE13 ....33 D3
Havelock Cl *GATE* NE8 ....81 D6
Havelock Crs *BDLGTN* NE22 ....9 E1
Havelock Pl *ELS/FEN* NE4 ....80 A3
Havelock Rd *SMOOR* NE27 ....51 F1
Havelock St *SSH* NE33 ....71 D5
　SUND SR1 ....5 F1
Havelock Ter *ASHBK/HED/RY* SR2 .....144 A1
　GATE NE8 ....81 D6
　JRW NE32 ....86 A3
Haven Ct *BLYTH* NE24 ....10 B6
　DHAM DH1 ....180 B4
The Haven *HLS* DH4 ....157 D2
　NSHW NE29 ....70 C3
Havercroft *FELL* NE10 ....102 A3
Haverley Dr *SEA/MUR* SR7 ....175 D2
Haversham Pk *SWCK/CAS* SR5 ....168 B5
Haversham Rd *LGB/HTN* NE7 ....64 C1
Hawarden Crs *MLFD/PNYW* SR4 ....143 F1
Hawes Av *CLSW/PEL* DH2 ....166 B1
Hawes Ct *CLDN/WHIT/ROK* SR6 ....108 B5
Hawes Rd *PLEE/EAS* SR8........................208 C1
Haweswater Cl *HAR/WTLS* NE34 ....88 C2
Hawick Ct *STLY/ANP* DH9 ....149 D2
Hawick Crs *BYK/HTN/WLK* NE6 ....82 A4
Hawkey's La *NSHW* NE29 ....54 B6
Hawkhill Cl *CLSW/PEL* DH2 ....165 F2
Hawkhurst *WASHS* NE38 ....139 E4
Hawkins Ct *SUNDSW* SR3 ....160 B2
Hawksbury *WICK/BNPF* NE16 ....95 F2
Hawkshead Cl *DIN/WO* NE13 ....45 F5
Hawkshead Pl
　LWF/SPW/WRK NE9 ....100 A5
Hawksley *WD/WHPE/BLK* NE5 ....60 B4
Hawks Rd *GATE* NE8 ....3 C6
Hawks St *GATE* NE8 ....81 F4
Hawkwell Ri
　BW/LEM/TK/HW NE15 ....57 F5
Hawsker Cl *SUNDSW* SR3 ....161 E1
Hawthorn Av *DIN/WO* NE13 ....32 C5
　SUNDSW SR3 ....144 A6
Hawthorn Cl *CLSW/PEL* DH2 ....179 E1
　WICK/BNPF NE16 ....96 A5
Hawthorn Cottages
　RDHAMSE DH6 ....188 A5
Hawthorn Crs *DHAM* DH1 ....195 F3
Hawthorn Dr *DUN/TMV* NE11 ....97 E2
　JRW NE32 ....86 C6
Hawthorne Av *HAR/WTLS* NE34 ....89 E4
　HEBB NE31 ....85 E2
Hawthorne Cl *SEA/MUR* SR7 ....188 C4
Hawthorne Rd *RDHAMSE* DH6 ....11 C6
Hawthorne Ter *RDHAMSE* DH6 ....206 B2
Hawthorn Gdns *FELL* * NE10 ....100 C1
　GOS/KPK NE3 ....62 B2
　NSHW NE29 ....54 B5
　WBAY NE26 ....40 B5
Hawthorn Pk *BDN/LAN/SAC* DH7 ......203 D4
Hawthorn Pl *ELS/FEN* NE4 ....79 F5
　LGB/KIL * NE12 ....35 E6
Hawthorn Rd *BLAY* NE21 ....76 B6
　DHAM DH1 ....196 C1
　GOS/KPK NE3 ....63 E2
Hawthorn Rd West *GOS/KPK* NE3 ....63 E2
The Hawthorns *BOL* NE36 ....106 C3
　ELS/FEN (off Park Rd) NE4 ....79 F5

STLY/ANP DH9 ....146 B3
Hawthorn St *JRW* NE32 ....85 F1
　MLFD/PNYW SR4 ....125 F6
　PLEE/EAS SR8 ....200 C1
Hawthorn Ter
　CLDN/WHIT/ROK SR6 ....109 D4
　DHAM DH1 ....194 A5
　ELS/FEN NE4 ....79 F4
　WD/WHPE/BLK NE5 ....58 C4
Hawthorn Vls *CRAM* NE23 ....22 B2
Hawthorn Wk *ELS/FEN* NE4 ....80 C6
Haydock Dr *FELL* NE10 ....102 A3
Haydon *WASHS* NE38 ....139 D5
Haydon Pl *WD/WHPE/BLK* NE5 ....60 C6
Haydon Sq *MLFD/PNYW* SR4 ....142 C1
Hayes Wk *DIN/WO* NE13 ....33 D4
Hayfield La *WICK/BNPF* NE16 ....96 A4
Hayhole Rd *NSHW* NE29 ....70 A4
Hayleazes Rd
　BW/LEM/TK/HW NE15 ....77 E1
Haymarket *CNUT* * NE1 ....2 D1
The Haynyng *FELL* NE10 ....101 D3
The Hayricks *STLY/ANP* DH9 ....130 C2
Hay St *SWCK/CAS* SR5 ....126 B4
Hayton Av *HAR/WTLS* NE34 ....89 F3
Hayton Cl *CRAM* NE23 ....22 B1
Hayton Rd *TYNE/NSHE* NE30 ....54 B3
Hazard La *HLH* DH5 ....185 D1
Hazel Av *BDN/LAN/SAC* DH7 ....202 C5
　NSHW NE29 ....70 C3
　SUNDSW SR3 ....144 A6
Hazeldene *MONK* NE25 ....39 F5
Hazeldene Av *GOS/KPK* NE3 ....61 E2
Hazeldene Ct *TYNE/NSHE* NE30 ....55 E5
Hazeley Gv *GOS/KPK* NE3 ....61 F1
Hazelmere Av *BDLGTN* NE22 ....7 D3
Hazelmere Crs *CRAM* NE23 ....14 B6
Hazelmere Dene *CRAM* NE23 ....36 A1
Hazelmoor *HEBB* NE31 ....84 C1
Hazel Rd *BLAY* NE21 ....76 C6
　GATE NE8 ....98 B2
Hazel St *JRW* NE32 ....85 F1
Hazel Ter *RDHAMSE* DH6 ....206 B2
　STLY/ANP DH9 ....149 D5
Hazelwood *LGB/KIL* NE12 ....50 B1
Hazelwood Av *JES* NE2 ....64 A4
　SWCK/CAS SR5 ....125 E2
Hazelwood Cl
　LWF/SPW/WRK NE9 ....118 C2
Hazelwood Ter *WLSD/HOW* NE28 ....68 C4
Hazledene Ter *MLFD/PNYW* SR4 ....125 E6
Hazlitt Av *HAR/WTLS* NE34 ....88 A5
Hazlitt Pl *CRAM* NE23 ....36 A1
Hazel Leigh *CLS/BIR/GTL* DH3 ....167 F3

Heaton Pl *BYK/HTN/WLK* NE6 ....82 A2
Heaton Rd *BYK/HTN/WLK* NE6 ....65 D5
Heaton Ter *BYK/HTN/WLK* NE6 ....81 F2
　NSHW NE29 ....54 A6
Heaton Wk *BYK/HTN/WLK* * NE6 ....82 A2
Heaviside Pl *DHAM* DH1 ....195 D4
Heber St *ELS/FEN* NE4 ....2 A3
Hebron Wy *CRAM* NE23 ....21 F5
Hector St *SMOOR* NE27 ....38 B6
Heddon Banks
　BW/LEM/TK/HW NE15 ....56 A5
Heddon Cl *GOS/KPK* NE3 ....46 C6
Heddon Gv *BLAY* NE21 ....76 A6
Heddon Vw *HAR/WTLS* NE34 ....88 A2
Hedge Cl *DUN/TMV* NE11 ....98 A3
Hedgefield Ct
　BLAY (off Stella Rd) NE21 ....75 E3
Hedgefield Gv *BLYTH* NE24 ....16 B3
Hedgefield Vw *CRAM* NE23 ....34 C1
Hedgehope Rd
　WD/WHPE/BLK NE5 ....60 C2
Hedgelea *RYTON* NE40 ....74 A3
Hedgelea Rd *HLH* DH5 ....184 B1
Hedgeley Rd *HEBB* NE31 ....85 D2
　NSHW NE29 ....53 F5
　WD/WHPE/BLK NE5 ....60 A6
Hedgeley Ter *BYK/HTN/WLK* NE6 ....83 E2
　GOS/KPK NE3 ....63 E1
Hedley Cl *SSH* NE33 ....71 E2
Hedley La *WICK/BNPF* NE16 ....114 B6
Hedley Pl *WLSD/HOW* NE28 ....67 D5
Hedley Rd *MONK* NE25 ....25 D6
　NSHW NE29 ....70 B5
Hedley St *GATE* NE8 ....81 E3
　GOS/KPK NE3 ....63 E1
　SSH NE33 ....71 E2
Hedley Ter *ASHBK/HED/RY* SR2 ....162 C2
　GOS/KPK NE3 ....63 E1
Hedworth Av *HAR/WTLS* NE34 ....87 E4
Hedworth Ct *SUND* SR1 ....5 F3
Hedworth La *BOLCOL* NE35 ....104 C1
　JRW NE32 ....86 C6
Hedworth Ter *SUND* SR1 ....5 F5
Heighley St *BW/LEM/TK/HW* NE15 ......77 E3
Helen St *BLAY* NE21 ....75 F6
　CLDN/WHIT/ROK SR6 ....109 D6
Helford Rd *PLEE/EAS* SR8 ....208 B4
Hellvellyn Ct *STLY/ANP* DH9 ....146 B5
Helmdon *WASHN* NE37 ....121 D4
Helmsdale Av *FELL* NE10 ....100 C1
Helmsdale Rd *MLFD/PNYW* SR4 ....142 C1
Helmsley Cl *HLS* DH4 ....156 C2
Helmsley Ct *SWCK/CAS* SR5 ....125 D1
Helmsley Dr *WLSD/HOW* NE28 ....68 B4
Helmsley Rd *DHAM* DH1 ....180 B5
　JES NE2 ....81 E1
Helston Ct *BW/LEM/TK/HW* NE15 ....76 A1
Helvellyn Av *WASHS* NE38 ....137 F3
Helvellyn Rd *ASHBK/HED/RY* SR2 .....144 C4
Hemlington Cl
　ASHBK/HED/RY SR2 ....162 B3
Hemmel Cts *BDN/LAN/SAC* DH7 ....203 E3
Hemming St *ASHBK/HED/RY* SR2 ......145 E4
Hemsley Rd *HAR/WTLS* NE34 ....72 B5
Henderson Av *WICK/BNPF* NE16 ....95 F2
Henderson Gdns *FELL* NE10 ....102 A3
Henderson Rd *HAR/WTLS* NE34 ....87 E3
　MLFD/PNYW SR4 ....143 E1
　WLSD/HOW NE28 ....67 D3
Hendersyde Cl
　WD/WHPE/BLK NE5 ....61 D3
Hendon Burn Av
　ASHBK/HED/RY SR2 ....5 F6
Hendon Cl *NSHW* NE29 ....70 C3
　SUND SR1 ....5 F5
Hendon Gdns *JRW* NE32 ....86 C6
Hendon Rd *LWF/SPW/WRK* NE9 ....100 A2
　SUND SR1 ....5 F2
Hendon Rd East *SUND* SR1 ....5 H3
Hendon St *SUND* SR1 ....5 G4
Hendon Valley Ct
　ASHBK/HED/RY SR2 ....145 D2
Hendon Valley Rd
　ASHBK/HED/RY SR2 ....5 E6
Henley Av *CLSW/PEL* DH2 ....152 A5
Henley Cl *CRAM* NE23 ....22 C1
Henley Gdns *WLSD/HOW* NE28 ....69 D2
Henley Rd *MLFD/PNYW* SR4 ....142 C1
　TYNE/NSHE NE30 ....55 D3
Henley Wy *BOLCOL* NE35 ....105 D2
Henlow Rd *BW/LEM/TK/HW* NE15 ....76 B1
Henry Nelson St *SSH* NE33 ....71 F2
Henry Robson Wy *SSH* NE33 ....71 E4
Henry Sq *JES* NE2 ....81 E1
Henry St *GOS/KPK* NE3 ....63 E1
　HLH DH5 ....171 F4
　HLH DH5 ....171 D1
　NSHW NE29 ....70 C1
　SEA/MUR SR7 ....176 C2
　SSH NE33 ....71 F2
Henry St East *ASHBK/HED/RY* SR2 ....5 G4
Hensby Ct *WD/WHPE/BLK* NE5 ....61 D2
Henshaw Gv *MONK* NE25 ....25 E6
Henshaw Pl *WD/WHPE/BLK* NE5 ....77 F1
Henshelwood Ter *JES* NE2 ....64 A5
Henson Cl *WASHS* NE38 ....138 C2

Hepburn Gdns FELL NE10 ...100 B1
Hepburn Gv SWCK/CAS SR5 ...123 E3
Hepple Ct BLYTH NE24 ...10 B6
Hepple Wy GOS/KPK NE3 ...46 C6
Hepscott Dr MONK NE25 ...39 F4
Hepscott Ter HAR/WTLS NE28 ...88 C3
Herbert St NE8 ...99 F1
Herd Cl BLAY NE21 ...93 F1
Herd House La BLAY NE21 ...75 E6
Herdinghill WASHN NE37 ...119 E6
Herdlaw CRAM NE23 ...22 C1
Hereford Ct ASHBK/HED/RY SR2 ...144 C5
  DIN/WO NE13... ...45 F4
Hereford Rd ASHBK/HED/RY SR2 ...144 C5
Herefordshire Dr DHAM DH1 ...196 B3
Hereford Sq ASHBK/HED/RY SR2 ...144 C5
Hermiston MONK NE25 ...40 A5
Hermitage Gdns CLSW/PEL DH2 ...166 A1
Heron Cl BLYTH NE24 ...17 D3
  WASHS NE38 ...137 F4
Heron Dr SSH NE33 ...71 E2
Heron Pl LGB/KIL NE12 ...48 C5
Herrick St WD/WHPE/BLK NE5 ...60 C3
Herring Gull Cl BLYTH NE24 ...17 D3
Herrington Rd HLS DH4 ...158 B2
  SUNDSW SR3 ...159 D1
Hersham Cl DIN/WO * NE13 ...45 F4
  GOS/KPK NE3 ...45 F5
Hertford LWF/SPW/WRK NE9 ...117 F2
Hertford Av HAR/WTLS NE34 ...90 A1
Hertford Cl MONK NE25 ...39 E4
Hertford Crs HLH DH5 ...171 E6
Hertford Gv CRAM NE23 ...22 B1
Herton Cl PLEE/EAS SR8 ...208 B3
Hesket Ct GOS/KPK NE3 ...46 A5
Hesleden Rd RHTLP TS27 ...209 F6
Hesledon Wk SEA/MUR SR7 ...175 D6
Hesleyside Dr WD/WHPE/BLK NE5 ...61 D6
Hesleyside Rd MONK NE25 ...39 D5
Hester Av MONK NE25 ...24 C2
Hetton Rd HLS DH4 ...171 D3
Heugh Hl LWF/SPW/WRK NE9 ...119 F2
Hewitson Ter FELL NE10 ...100 B3
Hewitt Av ASHBK/HED/RY SR2 ...145 D6
Hewley Crs BW/LEM/TK/HW NE15 ...57 F5
Heworth Burn Crs FELL NE10 ...101 D1
Heworth Dene Gdns FELL * NE10 ...101 D1
Heworth Gv WASHN NE37 ...120 B4
Heworth Rd WASHN NE37 ...120 C2
Heworth Wy FELL NE10 ...101 F2
Hewson Pl LWF/SPW/WRK NE9 ...100 A4
Hexham WASHS NE38 ...137 F2
Hexham Av BYK/HTN/WLK NE6 ...83 E3
  CRAM NE23 ...22 C1
  HEBB NE31 ...85 D6
  SEA/MUR SR7 ...175 F4
Hexham Cl NSHW NE29 ...53 E5
Hexham Ct DUN/TMV NE11 ...97 E4
Hexham Dr STLY/ANP DH9 ...146 B3
Hexham Old Rd RYTON NE40 ...75 F4
Hexham Rd BLAY NE21 ...95 F1
  BW/LEM/TK/HW NE15 ...57 F4
  MLFD/PNYW SR4 ...142 C2
  WICK/BNPF NE16 ...95 F1
Hextol Gdns
  BW/LEM/TK/HW NE15 ...77 E1
Heybrook Av NSHW NE29 ...54 B4
Heyburn Gdns
  BW/LEM/TK/HW NE15 ...78 C3
Hibernian Rd JRW NE32 ...86 A1
Hibernia Rd BYK/HTN/WLK NE6 ...83 F4
Hickling Ct WD/WHPE/BLK NE5 ...61 D2
Hickstead Ct WLSD/HOW NE28 ...52 A5
Hickstead Gv CRAM NE23 ...22 C1
Hiddleston Av LGB/HTN NE7 ...65 D1
Higham Pl CNUT NE1 ...3 E2
High Back Cl JRW NE32 ...85 F4
High Barnes Ter MLFD/PNYW SR4 ...143 F1
High Br CNUT NE1 ...3 D4
Highbury FELL NE10 ...101 D2
  JES NE2 ...63 F4
  MONK NE25 ...40 A5
Highbury Av LWF/SPW/WRK NE9 ...119 F2
Highbury Cl LWF/SPW/WRK NE9 ...119 F2
Highbury NSHW NE29 ...70 B1
High Carr Cl DHAM DH1 ...194 A1
High Chare CLS/BIR/GTL DH3 ...153 E5
Highcliffe Gdns GATE NE8 ...99 F1
High Cft CLDN/WHIT/ROK SR6 ...109 E1
  WASHN NE37 ...120 A3
High Croft Cl HEBB NE31 ...84 C4
Highcroft Dr CLDN/WHIT/ROK SR6 ...109 D1
Highcross Rd TYNE/NSHE NE30 ...54 C1
High Dene LGB/HTN NE7 ...64 C5
Highfield BDN/LAN/SAC DH7 ...178 B1
  WICK/BNPF NE16 ...114 A1
Highfield Cl WD/WHPE/BLK NE5 ...60 B3
Highfield Ct FELL NE10 ...101 D3
Highfield Crs CLS/BIR/GTL DH3 ...153 E3
Highfield Dr HAR/WTLS NE34 ...72 B6
  HLS DH4 ...170 A3
Highfield Gra HLS DH4 ...170 A3
Highfield Pl DIN/WO NE13 ...32 C5
Highfield Ri CLS/BIR/GTL DH3 ...153 E3
Highfield Rd GATE NE8 ...99 F1
  HAR/WTLS NE34 ...72 B6
  HLS DH4 ...156 C2
  ROWG NE39 ...110 B3
  WD/WHPE/BLK NE5 ...60 B4
Highfield Ter BW/LEM/TK/HW NE6 ...83 E4
High Flatworth NSHW NE29 ...69 D1
High Friars
  CNUT (off Eldon Sq) NE1 ...2 C3
Highgate Gdns JRW NE32 ...86 C6
Highgate Rd MLFD/PNYW SR4 ...142 C1
The High Ga GOS/KPK NE3 ...46 C6
Highgreen Cha WICK/BNPF NE16 ...95 F6
High Gv ELS/FEN NE4 ...79 F3
  RYTON NE40 ...74 C4
Highgrove WD/WHPE/BLK NE5 ...59 F4
Highheath WASHN NE37 ...119 F6
High Heworth La FELL NE10 ...101 C2
High Horse Cl ROWG NE39 ...93 F6
High Horse Close Wd ROWG NE39 ...93 F6
High House Gdns FELL NE10 ...101 D1
Highland Rd WD/WHPE/BLK NE5 ...61 F3
High La HLS DH4 ...158 B4
  FELL NE10 ...101 E3
High Lane Rw HEBB NE31 ...68 B6
High Laws GOS/KPK NE3 ...64 D2
High Level Br GATE NE8 ...3 D6
High Meadow HAR/WTLS NE34 ...72 B6
High Mdw BDN/LAN/SAC DH7 ...202 C3
High Moor Pl HAR/WTLS NE34 ...88 B3
High Pasture WASHS NE38 ...139 D5
High Rdg DIN/WO NE13 ...33 D5
The High Rd HAR/WTLS NE34 ...89 E2
High Rw BW/LEM/TK/HW NE15 ...76 B2
High Sandgrove
  CLDN/WHIT/ROK SR6 ...107 F1
Highside Dr SUNDSW SR3 ...143 F3
Highstead Av CRAM NE23 ...13 F5
High St BDN/LAN/SAC DH7 ...204 A3
  BLYTH NE24 ...10 C5
  BW/LEM/TK/HW NE15 ...75 E1
  DHAM DH1 ...196 B2
  FELL NE10 ...100 C2
  GATE NE8 ...3 G7
  GOS/KPK NE3 ...63 E1
  HLH DH5 ...186 B3
  JRW NE32 ...86 B1
  MLFD/PNYW SR4 ...123 F6
  RDHAMSE DH6 ...184 A6
  STLY/ANP DH9 ...148 B1
High St East SUND SR1 ...5 F1
  WLSD/HOW NE28 ...67 E5
High St South Back
  BDN/LAN/SAC DH7 ...204 A3
High St West BYK/HTN/WLK NE6 ...66 C5
  SUND SR1 ...4 B3
High Swinburne Pl ELS/FEN * NE4 ...80 A3
Hightree Cl SUNDSW SR3 ...160 B3
High Vw WD/WHPE/BLK NE5 ...60 B5
High Vw North WLSD/HOW NE28 ...67 D2
Highwell Gdns FELL * NE10 ...101 D1
Highwell La WD/WHPE/BLK NE5 ...60 A5
High West St GATE NE8 ...81 D5
Highwood Rd
  BW/LEM/TK/HW NE15 ...77 E1
High Wood Ter DHAM DH1 ...194 C6
High Wood Vw DHAM DH1 ...194 C6
Highworth Dr LGB/HTN NE7 ...65 F3
  LWF/SPW/WRK NE9 ...119 E2
Hilda Av DHAM DH1 ...195 F2
Hilda Cl DHAM DH1 ...196 A5
Hilda Pk CLSW/PEL DH2 ...153 D3
Hilda St CLDN/WHIT/ROK SR6 ...126 C1
  GATE NE8 ...98 C1
  STLY/ANP DH9 ...146 A3
Hilden Gdns LGB/HTN NE7 ...65 E4
Hillary Av LGB/KIL NE12 ...50 A4
Hillary Pl WD/WHPE/BLK NE5 ...60 C3
Hill Av CRAM NE23 ...23 F6
Hill Crs SEA/MUR SR7 ...177 D5
  SEA/MUR SR7 ...177 D5
Hill Crest BDN/LAN/SAC DH7 ...178 B2
  WICK/BNPF NE16 ...112 A6
Hillcrest DHAM DH1 ...194 C4
  HAR/WTLS NE34 ...90 A4
  JRW NE32 ...86 B6
  MONK NE25 ...40 A5
  SUNDSW SR3 ...159 D1
Hillcrest Dr DUN/TMV NE11 ...97 D3
Hill Crest Gdns JES * NE2 ...64 A2
Hillcroft LWF/SPW/WRK NE9 ...99 F4
Hill Dyke LWF/SPW/WRK NE9 ...118 B2
Hillfield MONK NE25 ...39 F5
Hillfield Gdns SUNDSW SR3 ...144 A3
Hillfield St GATE NE8 ...81 D6
Hillgate GATE NE8 ...3 F6
Hill Head Dr WD/WHPE/BLK NE5 ...59 F5
Hillhead Gdns DUN/TMV NE11 ...97 F4
Hillhead La WICK/BNPF NE16 ...112 C3
Hillhead Pkwy
  WD/WHPE/BLK NE5 ...59 E3
Hill Head Rd WD/WHPE/BLK NE5 ...59 F4
Hillheads Rd MONK NE25 ...40 A5
Hillhead Wy WD/WHPE/BLK NE5 ...60 A3
Hill House Rd
  BW/LEM/TK/HW NE15 ...57 D4

Hillingdon Gv MLFD/PNYW SR4 ...141 F4
Hill La HLS DH4 ...140 B5
Hillmeads CLSW/PEL DH2 ...165 E6
Hill Park Rd JRW NE32 ...86 B3
Hill Ri WASHS NE38 ...121 D6
Hillrise Crs SEA/MUR SR7 ...174 C2
Hillsden Rd MONK NE25 ...39 F3
Hillside BDN/LAN/SAC DH7 ...178 A3
  BLAY NE21 ...76 A6
  BOL NE36 ...105 F3
  CLS/BIR/GTL DH3 ...136 C2
  CLS/BIR/GTL DH3 ...153 E4
  DUN/TMV NE11 ...97 D3
  HAR/WTLS NE34 ...90 A4
  SUNDSW SR3 ...144 B3
Hillside Av BW/LEM/TK/HW NE15 ...77 E1
Hillside Cl ROWG NE39 ...111 D1
Hillside Crs BW/LEM/TK/HW NE15 ...77 F1
Hillside Dr CLDN/WHIT/ROK SR6 ...109 D1
Hillside Gdns STLY/ANP DH9 ...131 F6
  SUNDSW SR3 ...144 B3
Hillside Pl LWF/SPW/WRK NE9 ...99 F4
Hillside Vw HLS DH4 ...171 D1
Hillsleigh Rd WD/WHPE/BLK NE5 ...61 F3
Hills St GATE NE8 ...81 D5
Hill St JRW NE32 ...85 F1
  SSH NE33 ...71 D5
  SUNDSW SR3 ...160 C1
Hillsview Av GOS/KPK NE3 ...62 B1
Hill Ter HLS DH4 ...158 A2
Hillthorne Cl WASHS NE38 ...139 E2
Hill Top BLAY NE21 ...94 A1
  CLS/BIR/GTL DH3 ...136 C2
  STLY/ANP DH9 ...149 D1
Hill Top Av LWF/SPW/WRK NE9 ...99 F5
Hill Top Gdns LWF/SPW/WRK NE9 ...99 F5
Hilltop Gdns SUNDSW SR3 ...161 E1
Hillview SUNDSW SR3 ...159 D1
Hillview Crs HLS DH4 ...157 F5
Hill View Gdns SUNDSW SR3 ...144 B3
Hillview Gv HLS DH4 ...157 F5
Hill View Rd ASHBK/HED/RY SR2 ...145 D4
Hillview Rd HLS DH4 ...157 F5
Hill View Sq ASHBK/HED/RY SR2 ...144 C5
Hilton Av WD/WHPE/BLK NE5 ...61 D4
Hilton Cl CRAM NE23 ...13 F4
Hilton Dr PLEE/EAS SR8 ...208 C3
Hindley Gdns ELS/FEN NE4 ...78 C1
Hindmarch Dr BOL NE36 ...105 F3
Hind St SUND SR1 ...4 A3
Hinkley Cl SUNDSW SR3 ...160 C2
Hipsburn Dr SUNDSW SR3 ...143 F3
Hiram Dr BOL NE36 ...106 C3
Histon Wy WD/WHPE/BLK NE5 ...61 D3
Hither Gn JRW NE32 ...86 C6
Hobart WBAY NE26 ...40 B3
Hobart Av HAR/WTLS NE34 ...87 E4
Hodgkin Park Crs
  BW/LEM/TK/HW NE15 ...78 B3
Hodgkin Park Rd
  BW/LEM/TK/HW NE15 ...78 B3
Hodgson's Rd BLYTH NE24 ...10 C4
Hodkin Gdns LWF/SPW/WRK NE9 ...100 A4
Hogarth Dr WASHS NE38 ...139 D3
Hogarth Rd HAR/WTLS NE34 ...88 B6
Holbein Rd HAR/WTLS NE34 ...88 A5
Holborn Pl WD/WHPE/BLK * NE5 ...60 B5
Holborn Rd MLFD/PNYW SR4 ...142 C2
Holborn Sq MLFD/PNYW SR4 ...142 C2
Holburn Cl RYTON NE40 ...74 C3
Holburn Ct BDN/LAN/SAC DH7 ...192 A5
  RYTON NE40 ...74 C2
Holburn Crs RYTON NE40 ...75 D3
Holburn Gdns RYTON NE40 ...75 D3
Holburn La RYTON NE40 ...74 C3
Holburn Wk RYTON NE40 ...74 C3
Holburn Wy RYTON NE40 ...74 C3
Holden Pl WD/WHPE/BLK NE5 ...61 F4
Holder House La HAR/WTLS NE34 ...89 D5
Holderness Rd BYK/HTN/WLK NE6 ...68 C3
  WLSD/HOW NE28 ...68 C3
Hole La WICK/BNPF NE16 ...95 E6
Holeyn Rd BW/LEM/TK/HW NE15 ...57 E5
Holland Dr JES NE2 ...80 A1
Holland Pk
  JES (off Holland Dr) NE2 ...80 A1
  WLSD/HOW NE28 ...66 A3
Holland Park Dr JRW NE32 ...86 C6
The Hollies
  RYTON (off King Edward Rd) NE40 ...75 D4
Hollinghill Rd MONK NE25 ...25 D6
Hollings Crs WLSD/HOW NE28 ...67 D2
Hollingside La DHAM DH1 ...205 E2
Hollington Av LGB/KIL NE12 ...49 D3
Hollinhill ROWG NE39 ...93 F5
Hollinhill La ROWG NE39 ...93 E6
Hollinside Cl WICK/BNPF NE16 ...95 F5
Hollinside Gdns
  BW/LEM/TK/HW NE15 ...78 A2
Hollinside Rd MLFD/PNYW SR4 ...142 C2
  WICK/BNPF NE16 ...78 A6
Hollinside Sq MLFD/PNYW SR4 ...142 B1
Hollinside Ter ROWG NE39 ...110 C2
Hollowdene HLH DH5 ...185 F1
Holly Av BLAY NE21 ...94 B4

CLDN/WHIT/ROK SR6 ....109 E2
DUN/TMV NE11 ....97 E3
GOS/KPK NE3 ....46 B6
HAR/WTLS NE34 ....89 F3
HLH DH5 ....171 D2
JES NE2 ....64 A5
LGB/KIL NE12 ....49 F3
MONK NE25 ....39 D5
RYTON NE40 ....74 B2
SUNDSW SR3 ....144 A6
WBAY NE26 ....40 C5
WLSD/HOW NE28 ....67 E5
Holly Av West JES * NE2 ....64 A5
Hollybush Rd FELL NE10 ....100 B2
Hollycarrside Rd
    ASHBK/HED/RY SR2 ....145 D6
Holly Crs BDN/LAN/SAC DH7 ....178 B2
Hollydene DUN/TMV NE11 ....116 C6
    ROWG NE39 ....111 E2
Holly Hvn HLH DH5 ....170 C6
Holly Hl FELL NE10 ....100 C2
Holly Hill Gdns STLY/ANP DH9 ....148 B4
Holly Hill Gdns East
    STLY/ANP DH9 ....148 C3
Holly Hill Gdns West
    STLY/ANP DH9 ....148 B4
Hollyhock HEBB NE31 ....85 D5
Hollymount Sq BDLGTN NE22 ....7 E4
Holly Pk BDN/LAN/SAC DH7 ....203 D4
Holly Park Vw FELL NE10 ....100 C2
Holly Rd NSHW NE29 ....54 B5
The Hollys CLS/BIR/GTL DH3 ....118 A5
Holly St DHAM DH1 ....194 A5
    JRW NE32 ....85 F1
Holly Vw FELL NE10 ....100 B2
Hollywell Cl BDN/LAN/SAC DH7 ....192 A5
Hollywell Ct DIN/WO NE13 ....44 B4
Hollywell Rd NSHW NE29 ....53 F6
Hollywood Av GOS/KPK NE3 ....47 F6
    SWCK/CAS SR5 ....125 E2
Hollywood Crs GOS/KPK NE3 ....47 F6
Hollywood Gdns DUN/TMV NE11 ....98 A5
Holme Av BYK/HTN/WLK NE6 ....66 B5
    WICK/BNPF NE16 ....96 A3
Holme Gdns SUNDSW SR3 ....144 A3
    WLSD/HOW NE28 ....68 C4
Holme Ri WICK/BNPF NE16 ....96 A3
Holmesdale Rd
    WD/WHPE/BLK NE5 ....61 F5
Holmeside SUND SR1 ....4 C3
Holmewood Dr ROWG NE39 ....110 C4
Holmfield Av HAR/WTLS NE34 ....89 D1
Holm Gn MONK NE25 ....39 F6
Holmhill La CLS/BIR/GTL DH3 ....166 B3
    PLEE/EAS SR8 ....200 C1
Holmland BW/LEM/TK/HW NE15 ....78 B4
Holmlands MONK NE25 ....40 A5
Holmlands Pk North
    ASHBK/HED/RY SR2 ....144 B2
Holmlands Pk South
    ASHBK/HED/RY SR2 ....144 B2
Holmside PI BYK/HTN/WLK NE6 ....82 A1
Holmwood Av MONK NE25 ....39 F6
Holmwood Gv JES NE2 ....63 F4
Holwick Cl WASHS NE38 ....137 F4
Holyfields SMOOR NE27 ....51 F2
Holy Jesus Bungalows JES NE2 ....63 D6
Holylake Sq MLFD/PNYW SR4 ....142 C1
Holyoake Gdns CLS/BIR/GTL DH3 ....136 B2
    LWF/SPW/WRK NE9 ....99 E2
Holyoake St CLSW/PEL DH2 ....151 E2
Holystone Av GOS/KPK NE3 ....47 D6
    MONK NE25 ....41 D6
Holystone Cl BLYTH NE24 ....16 B1
    HLS DH4 ....157 D6
Holystone Ct
    GATE (off Fourth St) NE8 ....98 C1
Holystone Dr LGB/HTN NE7 ....64 C3
Holystone Dr SMOOR NE27 ....51 E2
Holystone Gdns NSHW NE29 ....53 F5
Holystone Gra LGB/KIL NE12 ....51 E3
Holystone St HEBB NE31 ....84 C1
Holywell Av BYK/HTN/WLK NE6 ....83 D5
    MONK NE25 ....25 E6
    WBAY NE26 ....40 A4
Holywell Cl ELS/FEN NE4 ....80 A5
    MONK NE25 ....25 E6
Holywell Dene Rd MONK NE25 ....38 B1
Home Av LWF/SPW/WRK NE9 ....99 E6
Home Pk WLSD/HOW NE28 ....66 A3
Homestall Cl HAR/WTLS NE34 ....88 C3
Honeycomb Cl SUNDSW SR3 ....160 B3
Honeycrook Dr LGB/HTN NE7 ....66 A3
Honeysuckle Av HAR/WTLS NE34 ....88 A4
Honeysuckle Cl SUNDSW SR3 ....160 C3
Honister Av JES NE2 ....64 C1
Honister Cl BW/LEM/TK/HW NE15 ....76 C1
Honister Dr SWCK/CAS SR5 ....126 B1
Honister PI BW/LEM/TK/HW NE15 ....76 C1
Honister Rd TYNE/NSHE NE30 ....55 D2
Honister Wy BLYTH NE24 ....16 B3
Honiton Cl HLS DH4 ....157 E4
Honiton Ct WD/WHPE/BLK NE5 ....45 D6
Honiton Wy NSHW NE29 ....53 D4

Hood Cl SWCK/CAS SR5 ....126 B3
Hood St CNUT NE1 ....2 D3
    WICK/BNPF NE16 ....95 F1
Hooper Ter RDHAMSE DH6 ....206 B2
Hopedene FELL NE10 ....101 F5
Hope Shield WASHS NE38 ....137 E5
Hope St HAR/WTLS NE34 ....88 A3
    JRW NE32 ....86 B1
    RDHAMSE DH6 ....197 E5
Hope Vw ASHBK/HED/RY SR2 ....162 B1
Hopgarth Gdns CLS/BIR/GTL DH3 ....153 F4
Hopkins Ct MLFD/PNYW SR4 ....125 E5
Hopper PI GATE NE8 ....81 E5
Hopper Rd FELL NE10 ....100 B3
Hopper St GATE NE8 ....81 E5
    SSH NE33 ....70 B1
    WLSD/HOW NE28 ....67 D4
Horatio St CLDN/WHIT/ROK SR6 ....127 D3
    CNUT NE1 ....81 F3
Hornbeam PI ELS/FEN NE4 ....80 A5
Horncliffe Gdns WICK/BNPF NE16 ....96 B2
Horncliffe PI
    BW/LEM/TK/HW NE15 ....57 D4
Hornsea Cl DIN/WO NE13 ....32 C5
Hornsey Ter HLH DH5 ....186 A3
Horse Crofts BLAY NE21 ....76 B5
Horsham Gdns SUNDSW SR3 ....143 F5
Horsham Gv NSHW NE29 ....70 A2
Horsley Av SMOOR NE27 ....52 B2
Horsley Ct GOS/KPK NE3 ....46 A6
Horsley Gdns DUN/TMV NE11 ....97 F2
    MONK NE25 ....25 E6
Horsley Gv SUNDSW SR3 ....143 F3
Horsley Hill Rd SSH NE33 ....72 A5
Horsley Hill Sq HAR/WTLS NE34 ....90 A1
Horsley Rd LGB/HTN NE7 ....65 D5
    WASHS NE38 ....121 F6
Horsley Ter BYK/HTN/WLK NE6 ....83 E5
    TYNE/NSHE NE30 ....55 F4
Horsley V HAR/WTLS NE34 ....89 E1
Horton Av BDLGTN NE22 ....7 E4
    HAR/WTLS NE34 ....88 C5
    SMOOR NE27 ....52 B2
Horton Crs DIN/WO NE13 ....31 D3
Hortondale Gv BLYTH NE24 ....10 A5
Horton Dr CRAM NE23 ....13 F5
Horton PI BLYTH NE24 ....16 A2
Horton Rd BLYTH NE24 ....8 B6
Horwood Av WD/WHPE/BLK NE5 ....59 F4
Hospital Dr HEBB NE31 ....84 C4
Hospital La BW/LEM/TK/HW NE15 ....76 A1
Hotch Pudding PI
    WD/WHPE/BLK NE5 ....60 B6
Hotspur Av BDLGTN NE22 ....7 E4
    HAR/WTLS NE34 ....89 D1
    MONK NE25 ....40 C6
Hotspur Rd WLSD/HOW NE28 ....66 C1
Hotspur St BYK/HTN/WLK NE6 ....81 F1
    TYNE/NSHE NE30 ....55 F4
Hotspur Wy
    CNUT (off Eldon Sq) NE1 ....2 C3
Houghton Av TYNE/NSHE NE30 ....55 D1
    WD/WHPE/BLK NE5 ....61 F3
Houghton Cut HLH DH5 ....171 D1
Houghton Rd HLH DH5 ....171 E4
    HLS DH4 ....157 F5
Houghton La MLFD/PNYW SR4 ....125 F6
Houlet Garth BYK/HTN/WLK * NE6 ....82 B3
Houlskye Cl SUNDSW SR3 ....161 E1
Hoults Est
    BYK/HTN/WLK
    (off Walker Rd) NE6 ....82 A3
Houndelee PI WD/WHPE/BLK NE5 ....61 E5
Hounslow Gdns JRW NE32 ....86 C6
House Ter WASHN NE37 ....120 C4
Houston Ct ELS/FEN NE4 ....80 A5
Houxty Rd MONK NE25 ....39 D5
Hovingham Ct PLEE/EAS SR8 ....209 D3
Hovingham Gdns SUNDSW SR3 ....143 F5
Howard Cl LGB/KIL NE12 ....51 E3
Howard Ct TYNE/NSHE * NE30 ....71 D1
Howardian Cl WASHS NE38 ....138 A3
Howard St CNUT NE1 ....3 H3
    FELL NE10 ....100 B4
    GATE NE8 ....100 A1
    JRW NE32 ....86 B1
    SWCK/CAS SR5 ....126 C3
    TYNE/NSHE NE30 ....55 D6
Howard Ter
    TYNE/NSHE (off Albion Rd) NE30 ....55 D6
Howarth St MLFD/PNYW SR4 ....125 D5
Howat Av WD/WHPE/BLK NE5 ....62 A5
Howdene Rd
    BW/LEM/TK/HW NE15 ....77 E2
Howdon La WLSD/HOW NE28 ....68 C3
Howdon Rd NSHW NE29 ....70 C2
    WLSD/HOW NE28 ....69 E4
Howe Sq MLFD/PNYW SR4 ....142 B1
Howe St GATE NE8 ....100 A1
    HEBB NE31 ....85 F2
Howick Av GOS/KPK NE3 ....46 C5
Howick Pk CLDN/WHIT/ROK * SR6 ....126 C4
Howletch La PLEE/EAS SR8 ....208 B2
Howlett Hall Rd
    BW/LEM/TK/HW NE15 ....77 E2

Howley Av SWCK/CAS SR5 ....124 B2
Hownam Cl GOS/KPK * NE3 ....62 C2
Hoy Crs SEA/MUR SR7 ....175 E1
Hoylake Av WLSD/HOW NE28 ....65 E1
Hoyle Av ELS/FEN NE4 ....79 D2
Hoyle Fold SUNDSW SR3 ....160 C4
Hubert St BOLCOL NE35 ....105 E2
Huddlestone Ri
    CLDN/WHIT/ROK SR6 ....127 D4
Huddleston Rd BYK/HTN/WLK NE6 ....82 C1
Hudson Av BDLGTN NE22 ....8 A3
    CRAM NE23 ....35 D2
Hudson Rd SUND SR1 ....5 E5
Hudson St GATE NE8 ....81 D5
    HAR/WTLS NE34 ....88 A2
    TYNE/NSHE NE30 ....55 F6
Hudspeth Crs DHAM DH1 ....179 F5
Hugh Gdns ELS/FEN NE4 ....79 D4
Hugh St CLDN/WHIT/ROK SR6 ....127 D1
    WASHS NE38 ....139 E2
    WLSD/HOW NE28 ....67 D5
Hull St ELS/FEN NE4 ....79 E4
Hulme Ct PLEE/EAS SR8 ....208 A3
Hulne Av TYNE/NSHE NE30 ....55 E5
Humber Gdns GATE NE8 ....100 A1
Humber Hl STLY/ANP DH9 ....148 C3
Humbert St JRW NE32 ....86 A2
Humbledon Vw
    ASHBK/HED/RY SR2 ....144 B2
    MLFD/PNYW SR4 ....125 F5
Hume St BYK/HTN/WLK NE6 ....81 F3
    MLFD/PNYW SR4 ....125 F5
Humford Gn BLYTH NE22 ....9 E5
Humford Wy BDLGTN NE22 ....7 F5
Humsford Gv CRAM NE23 ....14 B6
Humshaugh Cl LGB/KIL NE12 ....50 C4
Humshaugh Rd NSHW NE29 ....53 E6
Hunstanton Ct
    LWF/SPW/WRK NE9 ....117 D1
Huntcliffe Av
    CLDN/WHIT/ROK SR6 ....109 D4
Huntcliffe Gdns
    BYK/HTN/WLK NE6 ....65 E5
Hunter Av BLYTH NE24 ....11 E6
Hunter Cl BOL NE36 ....106 C4
Hunter Rd PLEE/EAS SR8 ....207 F1
Hunters Cl NSHW NE29 ....69 F3
    WLSD/HOW NE28 ....67 E4
Hunters Hall Rd MLFD/PNYW SR4 ....143 F1
Hunter's Moor Cl JES NE2 ....62 C6
Hunter's PI JES * NE2 ....63 D6
Hunter's Rd GOS/KPK NE3 ....64 B1
    JES NE2 ....79 F1
Hunters Ter SSH * NE33 ....71 F5
Hunter St HLS DH4 ....156 C3
    SSH NE33 ....71 F5
Hunter Ter ASHBK/HED/RY * SR2 ....145 D2
Huntingdon Cl DIN/WO NE13 ....45 E3
Huntingdon Gdns SUNDSW SR3 ....143 F3
Huntingdon PI TYNE/NSHE NE30 ....55 F5
Huntingdon Rd PLEE/EAS SR8 ....200 B6
Huntingdonshire Dr DHAM DH1 ....196 C2
Huntington Dr CRAM NE23 ....22 B1
Hunt Lea WICK/BNPF NE16 ....95 D5
Huntley Av SEA/MUR SR7 ....188 A1
Huntley Crs BLAY NE21 ....93 F2
Huntley Sq MLFD/PNYW SR4 ....142 C1
Huntly Rd MONK NE25 ....39 E5
Hurst Ter BYK/HTN/WLK NE6 ....83 D2
Hurstwood Rd MLFD/PNYW SR4 ....143 F2
Hurworth Av HAR/WTLS NE34 ....89 F2
Hurworth PI JRW NE32 ....86 A2
Hustledown Gdns STLY/ANP DH9 ....148 B6
Hustledown Rd STLY/ANP DH9 ....148 C6
Hutton Cl HLS DH4 ....170 B2
    WASHS NE38 ....137 E2
Hutton St BOLCOL NE35 ....105 D1
    MLFD/PNYW SR4 ....144 A1
Hutton Ter JES NE2 ....81 D1
    LWF/SPW/WRK NE9 ....99 E6
Huxley Crs GATE NE8 ....98 C3
Hyacinth Ct MLFD/PNYW SR4 ....126 A5
Hyde Pk WLSD/HOW NE28 ....66 B3
Hydepark St GATE NE8 ....98 C2
Hyde St ASHBK/HED/RY SR2 ....145 E3
    SSH NE33 ....71 F4
Hyde Ter GOS/KPK NE3 ....63 F1
Hylton Av HAR/WTLS NE34 ....90 A1
Hylton Bank MLFD/PNYW SR4 ....124 A6
Hylton Castle Rd SWCK/CAS SR5 ....124 A1
Hylton Cl BDLGTN NE22 ....6 C2
Hylton Gra SWCK/CAS SR5 ....123 E1
Hylton La BOL NE36 ....105 F4
    SWCK/CAS SR5 ....123 E2
Hylton Park Rd SWCK/CAS SR5 ....125 D2
Hylton Rd DHAM DH1 ....180 B6
    JRW NE32 ....86 A3
    MLFD/PNYW SR4 ....125 D2
Hylton St GATE NE8 ....100 A1
    HLS DH4 ....157 F1
    MLFD/PNYW SR4 ....125 F1
    NSHW NE29 ....70 C2
Hylton Ter ASHBK/HED/RY SR2 ....162 A1
    FELL* NE10 ....84 A1
    NSHW NE29 ....70 C2

I

Hylton Wk *MLFD/PNYW* SR4 ....141 F1
Hymers Av *HAR/WTLS* NE34.........87 E4
Hyperion Av *HAR/WTLS* NE34.......87 F3

Ilchester St *SEA/MUR* SR7............176 C4
Ilderton Pl *WD/WHPE/BLK* NE5.......60 A6
Ilex St *DUN/TMV* NE11................98 B4
Ilford Av *CRAM* NE23.................13 F5
Ilford Pl *GATE* NE8...................99 F2
Ilford Rd *JES* NE2....................63 F3
  WLSD/HOW NE28....................68 B3
Ilfracombe Av *ELS/FEN* NE4............79 D3
Ilminster Ct *GOS/KPK* NE3.............61 E1
Imeary Gv *SSH* NE33..................71 F5
Imeary St *SSH* NE33..................71 F5
Inchberry Cl *ELS/FEN* NE4.............79 D4
Inchbury Ct *ELS/FEN* NE4.............79 D4
Inchcape Ter *PLEE/EAS* SR8...........201 E3
Inchcliffe Crs *WD/WHPE/BLK* NE5......61 E4
Indigo St *DUN/TMV* NE11..............98 B4
Industrial Rd *WASHN* NE37............121 D5
Industrial St *CLSW/PEL* DH2..........151 E2
Industry Rd *BYK/HTN/WLK* NE6.........65 F4
Ingham Gra *SSH* NE33.................72 A5
Ingham Gv *CRAM* NE23.................13 F5
Ingleby Ter *MLFD/PNYW* SR4..........143 F1
Ingleby Wy *BLYTH* NE24...............16 C3
Inglemere Pl
  BW/LEM/TK/HW NE15................77 F2
Ingleside *WICK/BNPF* NE16............95 E4
Ingleside Rd *NSHW* NE29..............54 B5
Ingleton Ct *MLFD/PNYW* SR4..........143 F1
Ingleton Dr *BW/LEM/TK/HW* NE15......57 D4
Ingleton Gdns *BLYTH* NE24............16 B3
Inglewood Cl *BLYTH* NE24...............9 E5
Inglewood Pl *GOS/KPK* NE3............47 E3
Ingoe Av *GOS/KPK* NE3................46 B5
Ingoe Cl *BLYTH* NE24..................10 B3
Ingoe St *BW/LEM/TK/HW* NE15.........76 B2
  WLSD/HOW NE28....................69 E4
Ingoldsby St *MLFD/PNYW* SR4.........143 D2
Ingram Av *GOS/KPK* NE3...............46 B5
Ingram Cl *CLSW/PEL* DH2.............165 F1
  WLSD/HOW NE28....................68 B1
Ingram Dr *BLYTH* NE24.................10 A5
  WD/WHPE/BLK NE5.................59 F2
Ingram Ter *BYK/HTN/WLK* NE6.........65 F2
Inkerman Rd *WASHN* NE37.............120 C3
Inkerman St *SWCK/CAS* SR5...........125 F3
Inleborough Dr *RYTON* NE40...........74 C4
Innesmoor *HEBB* NE31.................84 C1
Inskip Ter *GATE* NE8..................99 E2
Institute Ter West *CLSW/PEL* DH2.....135 E4
Inverness Rd *JRW* NE32................87 D3
Inverness St
  CLDN/WHIT/ROK SR6................126 C2
Invincible Dr *ELS/FEN* NE4.............79 F5
Iolanthe Crs *BYK/HTN/WLK* NE6........83 D1
Iolanthe Ter *SSH* NE33................72 A4
Iona Pl *BYK/HTN/WLK* NE6.............83 F2
Iona Rd *FELL* NE10...................100 A3
  JRW NE32.........................87 D5
Irene Av *ASHBK/HED/RY* SR2..........145 E4
Iris Crs *CLSW/PEL* DH2...............135 E4
Iris Pl *ELS/FEN* NE4..................78 C1
Iris St *DUN/TMV* NE11.................98 B4
Iroko Ct *DUN/TMV* NE11...............98 B4
Ironside St *HLH* DH5..................171 D1
Irthing Av *BYK/HTN/WLK* NE6..........82 C4
Irton St *GOS/KPK* NE3.................63 E1
Irwin Av *WLSD/HOW* NE28.............67 D3
Isabella Ct *ELS/FEN* NE4..............79 D5
Isabella Rd *BLYTH* NE24................10 B6
Isabella Wk *BW/LEM/TK/HW* NE15.....57 F5
Isis Rd *PLEE/EAS* SR8................208 B3
Islestone
  LWF/SPW/WRK
  (off Pimlico Ct) NE9.................99 E6
Ivanhoe *MONK* NE25...................40 A5
Ivanhoe Crs *ASHBK/HED/RY* SR2......144 A2
Ivanhoe Vw *LWF/SPW/WRK* NE9......118 A2
Iveagh Cl *ELS/FEN* NE4................78 C4
Iveson St *BDN/LAN/SAC* DH7..........178 A1
Ivor St *ASHBK/HED/RY* SR2...........145 F4
Ivy Av *RYTON* NE40....................74 B2
  SEA/MUR SR7......................176 A4
Ivy Cl *ELS/FEN* NE4...................80 A5
Ivy La *LWF/SPW/WRK* NE9.............117 F1
Ivymount Rd *BYK/HTN/WLK* NE6........65 D5
Ivy Rd *BYK/HTN/WLK* NE6..............66 B6
  GOS/KPK NE3......................63 E2
  LGB/KIL NE12......................50 A4
Ivy St *DUN/TMV* NE11..................98 B4
Ivyway *CLSW/PEL* DH2................152 A1
Ixia St *DUN/TMV* NE11................98 B4

J

Jackson Av *PONT/DH* NE20.............28 B3
Jackson St *BYK/HTN/WLK* NE6..........83 E2
  GATE NE8.........................81 E5
  MLFD/PNYW SR4...................143 F1
  TYNE/NSHE NE30..................55 D6
Jackson St West *TYNE/NSHE* NE30....55 D6
Jack's Ter *HAR/WTLS* NE34............88 B3
Jacobins Chare *CNUT* * NE1.............2 B4
Jacques St *MLFD/PNYW* SR4..........125 E5
Jacques Ter *CLSW/PEL* DH2...........153 D5
Jade Cl *BW/LEM/TK/HW* NE15..........59 F1
James Armitage St
  SWCK/CAS SR5....................126 A2
James Mather St *SSH* NE33............71 F2
James St *ELS/FEN* NE4................79 E4
  PLEE/EAS SR8.....................200 C1
  SWCK/CAS SR5....................125 F2
  WD/WHPE/BLK NE5.................59 E1
  WICK/BNPF NE16...................95 F3
James Ter *HLH* DH5..................186 A4
  HLS DH4..........................169 F2
  WLSD/HOW NE28..................67 D5
James Williams St *SUND* SR1...........5 F1
Jane Eyre Ter *GATE* NE8.............100 A1
Jane St *BYK/HTN/WLK* * NE6..........82 B2
Jane Ter *BYK/HTN/WLK* NE6...........83 F3
Janet Sq *BYK/HTN/WLK* NE6..........82 B4
Janet St *BYK/HTN/WLK* NE6...........82 B3
Janus Cl *WD/WHPE/BLK* NE5...........59 E2
Jarrow Rd *HAR/WTLS* NE34.............87 F2
  JRW NE32.........................87 E2
Jarvis Rd *PLEE/EAS* SR8.............200 C6
Jasmin Av *WD/WHPE/BLK* NE5..........59 E2
Jasmine Cl *BYK/HTN/WLK* NE6.........66 A5
Jasmine Crs *SEA/MUR* SR7...........176 B5
Jasper Av *RYTON* NE40................92 A1
  SEA/MUR SR7......................176 A4
Jaycroft Ct
  TYNE/NSHE
  (off Stephenson St) NE30...........71 D1
Jedburgh Cl *GATE* NE8................99 E1
  NSHW NE29........................54 A4
  WD/WHPE/BLK NE5................59 E2
Jedburgh Gdns
  BW/LEM/TK/HW NE15...............78 A2
Jedburgh Rd *HLS* DH4................157 D2
Jedmoor *HEBB* NE31...................84 C1
Jefferson Pl *ELS/FEN* NE4.............80 A2
Jellicoe Rd *BYK/HTN/WLK* NE6.........83 D4
Jenifer Gv *LGB/HTN* NE7...............64 C3
Jenison Av *WD/WHPE/BLK* NE15.......78 B3
Jennifer Av *SWCK/CAS* SR5..........124 A3
Jervis St *HEBB* NE31.................85 E2
Jesmond Dene Rd *JES* NE2.............63 F4
Jesmond Gdns *JES* NE2................64 B5
Jesmond Pk East *LGB/HTN* NE7........65 D4
Jesmond Pk West *LGB/HTN* * NE7.....65 D5
Jesmond Rd *JES* NE2..................64 B6
Jesmond Rd West *JES* NE2............81 D1
Jesmond Ter *WBAY* NE26...............40 C6
Jesmond V *BYK/HTN/WLK* NE6.........81 F1
Jesmond Vale La
  BYK/HTN/WLK NE6..................65 D2
Jesmond Vale Ter
  BYK/HTN/WLK NE6..................65 D6
Jessel St *LWF/SPW/WRK* NE9..........99 E6
Joan Av *ASHBK/HED/RY* SR2..........145 E5
Joannah St *SWCK/CAS* SR5...........126 B1
Joan St *ELS/FEN* NE4.................78 C4
Jobling Av *BLAY* NE21.................75 F6
Joel Ter *FELL* NE10...................84 A6
John Av *RYTON* NE40..................92 A1
John Brown Ct *BDLGTN* * NE22..........7 F3
John Candlish Rd
  MLFD/PNYW SR4...................125 F5
John Clay St *SSH* NE33................71 F5
John Dobson St *CNUT* NE1..............2 D1
John Reid Rd *HAR/WTLS* NE34.........87 E4
Johnson Cl *PLEE/EAS* SR8............200 C6
Johnson St *BW/LEM/TK/HW* NE15......76 B2
  DUN/TMV NE11.....................97 E1
  GATE NE8.........................98 A1
  SSH NE33.........................88 B1
Johnson Ter *STLY/ANP* DH9...........146 C5
Johnston Av *HEBB* NE31...............84 C5
John St *BDN/LAN/SAC* DH7...........178 B1
  BLYTH NE24.......................10 A4
  DHAM DH1.........................194 A5
  FELL NE10........................101 E1
  GATE NE8.........................100 A1
  GOS/KPK NE3......................62 C1
  HLH DH5..........................171 E2
  HLH DH5..........................185 F1
  HLS DH4..........................169 F2
  MLFD/PNYW SR4...................123 F5
  MONK NE25........................38 C5
  PLEE/EAS SR8.....................201 D1
  STLY/ANP DH9.....................147 F4
  STLY/ANP DH9.....................149 E1
  STLY/ANP DH9.....................149 F1

  SUND SR1...........................4 D2
  WBAY NE26.........................41 E6
  WLSD/HOW NE28....................67 D4
John Taylor Ct *SWCK/CAS* SR5.......125 F1
John Williamson St *SSH* NE33..........88 A1
John Wilson Ct *PLEE/EAS* SR8........209 F1
Joicey Gdns *STLY/ANP* DH9...........148 B1
Joicey Rd *LWF/SPW/WRK* NE9..........99 E4
Joicey St *FELL* NE10.................101 F1
Jolliffe St *CLS/BIR/GTL* DH3..........166 C1
Jonadab Rd *FELL* NE10................83 F6
Jonadab St *FELL* NE10................101 F1
Jones St *CLS/BIR/GTL* DH3...........136 A2
Jonquil Cl *WD/WHPE/BLK* NE5..........59 E2
Joseph Cl *ELS/FEN* NE4................79 D4
Joseph Hopper
  CLS/BIR/GTL
  (off Aged Miners Homes) DH3.......118 B5
Joseph St *STLY/ANP* DH9.............148 A3
Jowett Sq *SWCK/CAS* SR5............125 F1
Joyce Cl *FELL* NE10..................102 B2
Joyce Gv *PLEE/EAS* SR8..............207 F5
Joyce Ter *SWCK/CAS* SR5............124 A3
Jubilee Av *LWF/SPW/WRK* NE9........118 B3
Jubilee Cl *BDN/LAN/SAC* DH7.........164 A3
Jubilee Crs *GOS/KPK* NE3.............46 C6
Jubilee Pl *RDHAMSE* DH6.............206 B1
Jubilee Rd *BLYTH* NE24................11 D6
  CNUT NE1...........................3 G3
  GOS/KPK NE3......................62 C1
Jubilee Sq *HLH* DH5..................186 B3
Jubilee Ter *BYK/HTN/WLK* NE6.........82 B2
  WICK/BNPF NE16...................95 F1
Jude Pl *PLEE/EAS* SR8...............200 B6
Judson Rd *PLEE/EAS* SR8............207 E1
Julian Av *BYK/HTN/WLK* NE6..........66 A6
  SSH NE33.........................71 F2
Julian Rd *FELL* NE10.................102 C2
Julian St *SSH* NE33..................71 F2
Juliet Av *NSHW* NE29.................53 F6
Julius Caesar St *SWCK/CAS* SR5......125 F2
June Av *BLAY* NE21...................94 B4
Juniper Cl *ASHBK/HED/RY* * SR2......145 D2
  BLYTH NE24.......................11 D6
  GOS/KPK NE3......................47 E3
Jupiter Ct *PLEE/EAS* SR8............200 B2
Jutland Av *HEBB* NE31................85 D2
Jutland Ter *STLY/ANP* DH9...........130 C6

K

Kalmia St *DUN/TMV* NE11..............98 B5
Kane Gdns *FELL* NE10................100 B4
Katrine Cl *CLSW/PEL* DH2............153 D6
Katrine Ct *SUNDSW* SR3...............60 C3
Kayll Rd *MLFD/PNYW* SR4............125 E6
Kay St *STLY/ANP* DH9................148 B1
Kearsley Cl *MONK* NE25...............24 C5
Kearton Av *WD/WHPE/BLK* NE5.........59 E3
Keats Av *BLYTH* NE24..................16 B1
  BOLCOL NE35......................106 A2
  SWCK/CAS SR5....................125 F2
Keats Cl *STLY/ANP* DH9..............148 C2
Keats Rd *BW/LEM/TK/HW* NE15.........75 F2
Keats Wk *GATE* NE8...................81 F6
Keebledale Av *BYK/HTN/WLK* NE6......83 E1
Keelman's La *MLFD/PNYW* SR4........124 A5
Keelman's Rd *MLFD/PNYW* SR4........124 A5
Keir Hardie Av *FELL* NE10............101 F2
  STLY/ANP DH9....................148 B4
Keir Hardie St *HLS* DH4.............170 A2
Keir Hardie Wy *SWCK/CAS* SR5......126 A3
Keith Cl *ELS/FEN* NE4.................79 D4
Keldane Gdns *ELS/FEN* NE4............79 D3
Kelfield Gv *CRAM* NE23................14 A4
Kelfield Av *LWF/SPW/WRK* NE9.........99 F4
Kelfield Gdns *LWF/SPW/WRK* NE9.....99 F5
Kell Rd *PLEE/EAS* SR8...............209 E2
Kells La *LWF/SPW/WRK* NE9...........99 E5
Kellsway *FELL* NE10..................101 E5
Kell's Wy *ROWG* NE39................111 D3
Kelly Rd *HEBB* NE31..................85 D5
Kelsey Wy *CRAM* NE23.................14 A4
Kelso Cl *WD/WHPE/BLK* NE5...........59 E2
Kelso Dr *NSHW* NE29..................54 A4
Kelso Gdns *BW/LEM/TK/HW* NE15......78 A2
  WLSD/HOW NE28...................68 C2
Kelso Gv *HLS* DH4...................156 C2
Kelso Gv *WD/WHPE/BLK* NE5...........59 E2
Kelso Pl *GATE* NE8...................98 A1
Kelston Wy *WD/WHPE/BLK* NE5.........61 E4
Kelvin Gdns *DUN/TMV* * NE11..........97 E1
Kelvin Gv *CLDN/WHIT/ROK* SR6........107 D1
  CLDN/WHIT/ROK SR6...............127 D2
  GATE NE8.........................98 C2
  HAR/WTLS NE34....................72 B5
  JES NE2..........................81 E1
  NSHW NE29........................54 A4
Kemble Cl *CRAM* NE23.................14 A4
Kemp Rd *PLEE/EAS* SR8..............208 B1
Kempton Gdns *GATE* NE8..............98 B3
Kendal Av *BLYTH* NE24.................10 C6

TYNE/NSHE NE30 ....55 D2
Kendal Cl PLEE/EAS SR8 ....207 F5
Kendal Crs LWF/SPW/WRK NE9 ....100 A5
Kendal Dr BOL NE36 ....106 B3
  CRAM NE23 ....14 B6
Kendale Wk WD/WHPE/BLK NE5 ....60 A3
Kendal Gdns WLSD/HOW NE28 ....68 C1
Kendal Pl BYK/HTN/WLK * NE6 ....82 A2
Kendal St BYK/HTN/WLK * NE6 ....82 A3
Kenilworth LGB/KIL NE12 ....35 F6
  MONK NE25 ....40 B6
Kenilworth Sq SWCK/CAS SR5 ....106 B6
Kenilworth Vw
  LWF/SPW/WRK NE9 ....117 F2
Kenley Rd WD/WHPE/BLK NE5 ....60 C6
Kenmoor Wy WD/WHPE/BLK NE5 ....59 E3
Kenmore Crs RYTON NE40 ....74 A6
Kennersdene TYNE/NSHE NE30 ....55 E4
Kennet Av JRW NE32 ....86 B5
Kennington Gv BYK/HTN/WLK NE6 ....83 D3
Kenny Pl DHAM DH1 ....195 E3
Kensington Av GOS/KPK NE3 ....47 E5
Kensington Ct
  FELL (off Nursery La) NE10 ....100 B2
Kensington Gdns
  TYNE/NSHE NE30 ....55 D6
  WLSD/HOW NE28 ....66 A3
Kensington Gv TYNE/NSHE NE30 ....55 D5
Kensington Ter DUN/TMV * NE11 ....97 E2
  JES NE2 ....80 C1
Kent Av DUN/TMV NE11 ....97 F2
  HEBB NE31 ....84 C3
  WLSD/HOW NE28 ....68 B4
Kentchester Rd SWCK/CAS SR5 ....106 A6
Kent Ct DIN/WO NE13 ....45 F4
Kent Gdns HLH DH5 ....171 E6
Kentmere Av BYK/HTN/WLK NE6 ....83 E2
  CLDN/WHIT/ROK SR6 ....108 B3
Kentmere Cl CRAM NE23 ....23 F6
Kentmere Pl PLEE/EAS SR8 ....209 D2
Kenton Av GOS/KPK NE3 ....62 C3
Kenton Ct SSH NE33 ....71 F5
Kenton Crs GOS/KPK NE3 ....62 B2
Kenton Gv CLDN/WHIT/ROK SR6 ....126 C3
Kenton La GOS/KPK NE3 ....61 F2
  WD/WHPE/BLK NE5 ....62 A3
Kenton Rd GOS/KPK NE3 ....62 C1
  NSHW NE29 ....53 E6
Kent Pl HAR/WTLS NE34 ....89 E2
Kent St JRW NE32 ....85 F2
Kentucky Rd SWCK/CAS SR5 ....105 F6
Kenya Rd SWCK/CAS SR5 ....106 A6
Kepier Ct DHAM DH1 ....194 C4
Kepier Crs DHAM DH1 ....195 F3
Kepier Gdns MLFD/PNYW SR4 ....123 F6
Kepier Hts DHAM DH1 ....194 C4
Kepier Ter DHAM * DH1 ....194 C4
Kepier Vls DHAM * DH1 ....194 C4
Keppel St DUN/TMV NE11 ....97 E1
  SSH NE33 ....71 E3
Kerry Cl BLYTH NE24 ....11 D4
Kerryhill Dr DHAM DH1 ....180 B4
Keston Dr CRAM NE23 ....14 A4
Kestrel Cl WASHS NE38 ....137 F4
Kestrel Ms WICK/BNPF NE16 ....95 F3
Kestrel Pl LGB/KIL NE12 ....49 D5
Kestrel St DUN/TMV NE11 ....98 B4
Kestrel Wy HAR/WTLS NE34 ....88 A4
  NSHW NE29 ....70 C3
Keswick Av CLDN/WHIT/ROK SR6 ....108 B6
Keswick Dr TYNE/NSHE NE30 ....55 D2
Keswick Gdns WLSD/HOW NE28 ....68 C3
Keswick Gv WD/WHPE/BLK NE5 ....60 A3
Keswick Rd PLEE/EAS SR8 ....209 D2
  STLY/ANP DH9 ....147 F4
Keswick St GATE NE8 ....99 D1
Keswick Ter RDHAMSE DH6 ....187 D4
Kettering Pl CRAM NE23 ....14 B6
Kettlewell St TYNE/NSHE NE30 ....55 D6
Ketton Cl LGB/KIL NE12 ....49 D6
Kew Gdns WBAY NE26 ....40 B4
Keyes Gdns JES NE2 ....64 A3
Kibblesworth Bank
  DUN/TMV NE11 ....116 A6
Kidd Av RDHAMSE DH6 ....197 E5
Kidderminster Dr
  WD/WHPE/BLK NE5 ....59 E3
Kidderminster Rd
  SWCK/CAS SR5 ....124 A1
Kidlandlee Gn
  WD/WHPE/BLK NE5 ....60 C2
Kidlandlee Pl WD/WHPE/BLK NE5 ....60 C2
Kielder Av CRAM NE23 ....20 C2
Kielder Cl BLYTH NE24 ....16 A1
  LGB/KIL NE12 ....35 E6
  WD/WHPE/BLK NE5 ....60 C2
Kielder Gdns JRW NE32 ....85 F5
Kielder Pl MONK NE25 ....39 D5
Kielder Rd BW/LEM/TK/HW NE15 ....76 A1
  MONK NE25 ....39 D5
Kielder Ter TYNE/NSHE NE30 ....55 D6
Kielder Wy GOS/KPK NE3 ....47 D5
Kier Hardie Av STLY/ANP DH9 ....148 B3

Kilburn Dr PLEE/EAS SR8 ....201 E5
Kilburne Cl LGB/HTN NE7 ....66 A3
Kilburn Gdns NSHW NE29 ....69 F3
Kildale HLS DH4 ....139 D6
Killin Cl WD/WHPE/BLK NE5 ....59 E2
Killingworth Av SMOOR NE27 ....36 C6
Killingworth Dr LGB/KIL NE12 ....49 D2
  SUNDSW SR3 ....142 C2
Killingworth La LGB/KIL NE12 ....50 C1
Killingworth Pl CNUT NE1 ....2 C2
Killingworth Rd GOS/KPK NE3 ....64 B1
  LGB/KIL NE12 ....34 C6
Killingworth Wy CRAM NE23 ....36 A5
  LGB/KIL NE12 ....34 C6
Kiln Ri WICK/BNPF NE16 ....95 F6
Kilnshaw Pl GOS/KPK NE3 ....47 F3
Kimberley WASHS NE38 ....139 F1
Kimberley Av NSHW NE29 ....54 A6
Kimberley Gdns JES NE2 ....64 C6
Kimberley St BLYTH NE24 ....10 C4
  MLFD/PNYW SR4 ....125 E6
Kingarth Av CLDN/WHIT/ROK SR6 ....109 F1
Kingdom Pl NSHW NE29 ....70 C3
King Edward Bridge Arches
  CNUT NE1 ....80 B5
King Edward Pl GATE NE8 ....100 A1
King Edward Rd
  BYK/HTN/WLK NE6 ....65 D5
  MLFD/PNYW SR4 ....124 A6
  RYTON NE40 ....75 D4
  SEA/MUR SR7 ....176 C4
  TYNE/NSHE NE30 ....55 E4
King Edward St GATE NE8 ....100 A1
Kingfisher Rd LGB/KIL NE12 ....48 C5
Kingfisher Wy BLYTH NE24 ....17 D2
  WLSD/HOW NE28 ....52 C6
King George Av DUN/TMV NE11 ....97 E3
King George Rd GOS/KPK NE3 ....46 A6
  HAR/WTLS NE34 ....89 D1
Kingham Ct LGB/HTN NE7 ....64 B2
King James Hospital Bungalows
  GATE (off Sunderland Rd) NE8 ....100 A1
King James St GATE NE8 ....99 E1
King John St BYK/HTN/WLK NE6 ....65 D6
King John Ter BYK/HTN/WLK NE6 ....65 D6
Kings Av CLDN/WHIT/ROK SR6 ....109 D5
  HEBB NE31 ....85 E3
Kingsbridge LGB/KIL NE12 ....48 B5
Kings Cl GATE NE8 ....100 A1
Kingsdale Av BLYTH NE24 ....9 F5
Kingsdale Rd LGB/KIL NE12 ....48 B5
King's Dr WBAY NE26 ....40 C5
King's Gdns BLYTH NE24 ....10 B3
Kings Gv DHAM DH1 ....204 C1
Kingsland JES NE2 ....64 A6
King's La CLSW/PEL DH2 ....151 F1
Kingsley Av GOS/KPK NE3 ....47 F3
  HAR/WTLS NE34 ....87 F5
  MONK NE25 ....40 B6
Kingsley Cl SWCK/CAS * SR5 ....125 F3
Kingsley Pl BYK/HTN/WLK NE6 ....82 A1
  DUN/TMV* NE11 ....97 E1
  WICK/BNPF NE16 ....96 A2
  WLSD/HOW NE28 ....68 B3
Kingsley Ter ELS/FEN NE4 ....79 F5
Kings Mnr CNUT NE1 ....3 F5
Kings Mdw
  ELS/FEN (off Brunel Ter) NE4 ....79 F5
Kingsmere CLS/BIR/GTL DH3 ....153 E3
Kingsmere Gdns
  BYK/HTN/WLK NE6 ....83 F4
King's Pk MLFD/PNYW SR4 ....125 F5
King's Rd BDLGTN NE22 ....8 C2
  CNUT NE1 ....2 C1
  LGB/KIL NE12 ....49 E3
  WBAY NE26 ....40 B4
Kings Rd North WLSD/HOW NE28 ....67 D2
Kings Rd South WLSD/HOW NE28 ....67 D3
The King's Rd SWCK/CAS SR5 ....125 F2
King's Ter MLFD/PNYW SR4 ....125 E6
Kingston Av BYK/HTN/WLK NE6 ....82 C3
  SEA/MUR SR7 ....176 A4
Kingston Cl WBAY NE26 ....40 B2
Kingston Dr WBAY NE26 ....40 B2
Kingston Gn BYK/HTN/WLK NE6 ....82 C3
Kingston Ms HLS DH4 ....157 E3
Kingston Pk GOS/KPK NE3 ....45 D5
Kingston Park Av GOS/KPK NE3 ....45 E6
Kingston Park Rd DIN/WO NE13 ....45 F1
  GOS/KPK NE3 ....46 B5
Kingston Rd GATE NE8 ....99 F2
Kingston Ter
  CLDN/WHIT/ROK SR6 ....126 C2
King St BLYTH NE24 ....11 D4
  CLDN/WHIT/ROK SR6 ....108 C4
  CLS/BIR/GTL DH3 ....136 A2
  CNUT NE1 ....3 F5
  FELL NE10 ....101 F1
  GATE NE8 ....98 B2
  RDHAMSE DH6 ....197 E5
  RDHAMSE DH6 ....206 A3
  SSH NE33 ....71 E3
  SUND SR1 ....4 C3
  TYNE/NSHE NE30 ....55 D6
Kingsway BLYTH NE24 ....11 D6

ELS/FEN NE4 ....62 A6
HLH DH5 ....171 E2
PONT/DH NE20 ....28 A4
SSH NE33 ....72 B4
TYNE/NSHE NE30 ....55 E4
WICK/BNPF NE16 ....113 F1
Kingsway Av GOS/KPK NE3 ....47 E5
Kingsway North DUN/TMV NE11 ....98 B4
Kingsway Rd SWCK/CAS SR5 ....105 F6
Kingsway South DUN/TMV NE11 ....98 C5
Kingswood Av JES NE2 ....63 F3
Kingswood Cl BOLCOL NE35 ....105 D1
Kingswood Gv MLFD/PNYW SR4 ....141 E4
Kingswood Rd CRAM NE23 ....14 B6
King Ter STLY/ANP DH9 ....147 F3
Kinlett WASHS NE38 ....139 F1
Kinley Rd DHAM DH1 ....196 C5
Kinloch Ct CLSW/PEL DH2 ....166 A1
Kinloss Sq CRAM NE23 ....14 B6
Kinnaird Av BW/LEM/TK/HW NE15 ....77 F2
Kinross Ct FELL NE10 ....84 A5
Kinross Dr GOS/KPK NE3 ....62 A1
  STLY/ANP DH9 ....149 D2
Kinver Dr WD/WHPE/BLK NE5 ....59 E3
Kiphill Ct STLY/ANP DH9 ....131 F6
Kipling Av BOLCOL NE35 ....106 A2
  HEBB NE31 ....85 E2
  WICK/BNPF NE16 ....96 A2
Kipling Cl STLY/ANP DH9 ....148 C2
Kipling Ct WICK/BNPF NE16 ....96 A2
Kipling St SWCK/CAS SR5 ....125 F3
Kipling Wk GATE NE8 ....81 F6
Kira Dr DHAM DH1 ....180 B4
Kirby Av DHAM DH1 ....193 F1
Kirby Cl HAR/WTLS NE34 ....87 E4
Kirkbride Pl CRAM NE23 ....14 B6
Kirkdale Gn ELS/FEN NE4 ....80 A4
Kirkdale St HLH DH5 ....185 E2
Kirkfield Gdns STLY/ANP DH9 ....146 A3
Kirkham Av GOS/KPK NE3 ....45 E5
Kirkham Rd DHAM DH1 ....180 C6
Kirkheaton Pl WD/WHPE/BLK NE5 ....61 E6
Kirkland Hl PLEE/EAS SR8 ....208 C1
Kirklands CRAM NE23 ....35 E5
Kirkland Wk SMOOR NE27 ....52 A1
Kirklea Rd HLH DH5 ....171 E2
Kirkleatham Gdns
  BYK/HTN/WLK NE6 ....65 F4
Kirkley Av HAR/WTLS NE34 ....89 F2
Kirkley Cl GOS/KPK NE3 ....47 D6
Kirkley Dr PONT/DH NE20 ....28 A2
Kirkley Ldg
  GOS/KPK (off Park Av) NE3 ....47 D6
Kirkley Rd SMOOR NE27 ....52 B2
Kirklinton Rd TYNE/NSHE NE30 ....54 C2
Kirknewton Cl HLH DH5 ....171 E2
Kirkside HLS DH4 ....158 A2
Kirkston Av BW/LEM/TK/HW NE15 ....76 C4
Kirkstone CLS/BIR/GTL DH3 ....136 C4
Kirkstone Av JRW NE32 ....86 C5
  PLEE/EAS SR8 ....209 D2
  SWCK/CAS SR5 ....126 B1
  TYNE/NSHE NE30 ....54 C2
Kirkstone Cl HLH DH5 ....171 E2
Kirkstone Dr DHAM DH1 ....196 B2
Kirkstone Gdns LGB/HTN NE7 ....64 C3
Kirkstone Rd FELL NE10 ....101 E1
Kirk St BYK/HTN/WLK NE6 ....82 B3
Kirk Vw HLS DH4 ....157 F4
Kirkwall Cl SWCK/CAS SR5 ....123 F3
Kirkwood CRAM NE23 ....35 E1
Kirkwood Av MLFD/PNYW SR4 ....141 F4
Kirkwood Cl CRAM NE23 ....23 F6
Kirkwood Dr GOS/KPK NE3 ....62 B1
Kirkwood Gdns FELL NE10 ....102 A1
Kirton Av ELS/FEN NE4 ....79 D2
Kirton Park Ter NSHW NE29 ....54 C1
Kirton Wy CRAM NE23 ....14 B6
Kismet St SWCK/CAS SR5 ....106 B4
Kitchener Rd CLDN/WHIT/ROK SR6 ....91 D7
Kitchener St LWF/SPW/WRK NE9 ....99 F1
  MLFD/PNYW SR4 ....143 E2
Kitchener Ter
  ASHBK/HED/RY SR2 ....145 E3
  JRW NE32 ....86 A3
  TYNE/NSHE NE30 ....55 E4
Kitching Rd PLEE/EAS SR8 ....199 F2
Kittiwake Cl BLYTH NE24 ....17 D2
  NSHW NE29 ....52 C1
Kittiwake Dr WASHS NE38 ....137 E2
Kittiwake St DUN/TMV NE11 ....98 B3
Kitty Brewster Rd BLYTH NE24 ....9 E3
Knaresborough Cl BDLGTN NE22 ....9 F4
Knaresborough Rd SEA/MUR SR7 ....188 B3
Knaresdale CLS/BIR/GTL DH3 ....136 C4
Knarsdale Av NSHW NE29 ....53 F4
Knarsdale Pl WD/WHPE/BLK NE5 ....60 A3
Kneller St STLY/ANP DH9 ....148 B6
Knightsbridge GOS/KPK NE3 ....47 E1
  SUNDSW SR3 ....143 D5
Knightside Gdns DUN/TMV NE11 ....97 E3
Knivestone Ct LGB/KIL NE12 ....36 A4
Knobbyends La BLAY NE21 ....93 E2
Knoll Ri DUN/TMV NE11 ....97 E3
Knollside Cl SUNDSW SR3 ....160 B3

The Knoll *ASHBK/HED/RY* * SR2 ....**144** A1
Knott Memorial Flats
TYNE/NSHE NE30 ....**55** F5
Knott Pl *BW/LEM/TK/HW* NE15 ......**77** F3
Knoulberry Rd *WASHN* NE37 ....**119** F6
Knoulberry Rd *WASHN* NE37 ....**119** F6
Knowledge Hl *BLAY* NE21 ....**94** A1
Knowle Pl *LGB/KIL* NE12 ....**65** D1
Knowsley Ct *WD/WHPE/BLK* NE5 ....**61** D1
Knox Ct *BDLGTN* NE22 ....**8** C2
Knox Rd *BDLGTN* NE22 ....**8** A4
Knox Sq *SWCK/CAS* SR5 ....**125** F1
Kristin Av *JRW* NE32 ....**86** D4
Kyffin Vw *HAR/WTLS* NE34 ....**90** A3
Kyle Cl *ELS/FEN* NE4 ....**80** A4
Kyle Rd *GATE* NE8 ....**98** B2
Kyloe Av *MONK* NE25 ....**24** C6
Kyloe Cl *GOS/KPK* NE3 ....**46** A5
Kyloe Pl *WD/WHPE/BLK* NE5 ....**60** C3
Kyloe Vls *WD/WHPE/BLK* NE5 ....**60** C3
Kyo Heugh Rd *STLY/ANP* DH9 ....**146** C3
Kyo La *STLY/ANP* DH9 ....**147** D3
Kyo Rd *STLY/ANP* DH9 ....**146** B3

L

Laburnam Pk *BDN/LAN/SAC* DH7 ....**202** B5
Laburnam Rd
CLDN/WHIT/ROK SR6 ....**126** C1
Laburnam Ter *STLY/ANP* DH9 ....**146** A3
Laburnum Av *BLYTH* NE24 ....**10** C4
BYK/HTN/WLK NE6 ....**66** B6
DHAM DH1 ....**194** A4
FELL NE10 ....**101** F3
WLSD/HOW NE28 ....**67** D4
Laburnum Ct *LGB/KIL* NE12 ....**35** E6
Laburnum Crs *DUN/TMV* NE11 ....**116** B6
SEA/MUR SR7 ....**176** B6
JRW NE32 ....**85** F4
Laburnum Gdns *FELL* * NE10 ....**100** C1
JRW NE32 ....**85** F4
Laburnum Gv
CLDN/WHIT/ROK SR6 ....**107** F1
HAR/WTLS NE34 ....**89** F3
HEBB NE31 ....**85** D5
SWCK/CAS SR5 ....**123** F4
WICK/BNPF NE16 ....**95** F3
WICK/BNPF NE16 ....**114** A1
Laburnum Rd *BLAY* NE21 ....**76** B6
CLDN/WHIT/ROK SR6 ....**126** C1
Lacebark *HLS* DH4 ....**156** B2
SUNDSW SR3 ....**160** A4
Ladock Cl *ASHBK/HED/RY* SR2 .....**145** D6
Lady Anne Rd *RDHAMSE* DH6 ....**197** E4
Ladybank *WD/WHPE/BLK* NE5 ....**59** D3
Ladyhaugh Dr *WICK/BNPF* NE16 .....**95** F6
Ladykirk Rd *ELS/FEN* NE4 ....**79** D3
Ladykirk Wy *CRAM* NE23 ....**21** D2
Ladysmith St *STLY/ANP* DH9 ....**148** C3
Ladysmith St *SSH* NE33 ....**71** F4
Lady's Piece La *RDHAMSE* DH6 .....**183** F6
Lady's Wk *SSH* NE33 ....**71** E2
Ladywell Rd *BLAY* NE21 ....**76** B6
Ladywood Pk *HLS* DH4 ....**139** E6
Laet St *NSHW* NE29 ....**71** D1
Laindon Av *CLDN/WHIT/ROK* SR6 ..**108** C6
Laing Gv *WLSD/HOW* NE28 ....**68** C3
Laith Rd *GOS/KPK* NE3 ....**62** A1
Lake Ap *BLAY* NE21 ....**95** D1
Lake Av *HAR/WTLS* NE34 ....**90** A4
Lake Ct *SUNDSW* SR3 ....**160** C2
Lakeland Dr *PLEE/EAS* SR8 ....**209** D1
Lake Rd *HLS* DH4 ....**171** D2
Lakeside *BLAY* NE21 ....**95** E1
HAR/WTLS NE34 ....**90** C2
Lake Vw *HEBB* NE31 ....**84** C4
Laleham Ct *GOS/KPK* NE3 ....**45** F5
Lambden Cl *NSHW* NE29 ....**70** A3
Lambert Rd *WASHN* NE37 ....**119** E5
Lambeth Pl *GATE* NE8 ....**99** F2
Lambley Av *TYNE/NSHE* NE30 ....**55** D2
Lambley Cl *WICK/BNPF* NE16 ....**113** E2
Lambley Crs *HEBB* NE31 ....**84** C5
Lambourn Av *LGB/KIL* NE12 ....**49** E5
NSHW NE29 ....**69** F2
Lambourne Ct *HLS* DH4 ....**156** A5
Lambourne Rd
ASHBK/HED/RY SR2 ....**144** B3
Lamb St *BYK/HTN/WLK* NE6 ....**83** F3
Lambton Av *WICK/BNPF* NE16 ....**96** B2
Lambton Ct *PLEE/EAS* SR8 ....**208** B5
SUNDSW SR3 ....**159** E1
WASHN NE38 ....**137** D6
Lambton Dr *HLS* DH4 ....**185** F2
Lambton Rd *HEBB* NE31 ....**85** E1
JES NE2 ....**64** A6
Lambton St *DHAM* DH1 ....**194** A4
GATE NE8 ....**81** E5
SUND SR1 ....**4** D1
Lambton Ter *JRW* NE32 ....**86** A5
Lambton Wk *DHAM* DH1 ....**194** A4
Lampeter Cl *WD/WHPE/BLK* NE5 ....**61** D1
Lamport St *HEBB* NE31 ....**84** B1

Lampton Ct *BDLGTN* NE22 ....**8** B2
Lanark Cl *NSHW* NE29 ....**53** E4
Lanark Dr *JRW* NE32 ....**87** D5
Lancashire Dr *DHAM* DH1 ....**196** C5
Lancaster Ct *GOS/KPK* NE3 ....**45** F5
Lancaster Dr *WLSD/HOW* NE28 ....**51** F5
Lancaster Hl *PLEE/EAS* SR8 ....**200** A6
Lancaster Rd *DUN/TMV* NE11 ....**97** D1
Lancaster St *ELS/FEN* NE4 ....**80** A3
Lancaster Ter *CLS/BIR/GTL* DH3 ....**153** F6
Lancastrian Rd *CRAM* NE23 ....**21** E2
Lancefield Av *BYK/HTN/WLK* NE6 ...**83** E4
Lancet Ct *GATE* NE8 ....**81** E6
Lanchester Av
LWF/SPW/WRK NE9 ....**118** C1
Lanchester Cl *FELL* NE10 ....**102** B4
Lanchester Gn *BDLGTN* NE22 ....**7** E2
Lanchester Pk *WASHS* NE38 ....**139** D4
Lancing Ct *GOS/KPK* NE3 ....**45** E5
Landseer Cl *STLY/ANP* DH9 ....**148** B2
Landseer Gdns *HAR/WTLS* NE34 ....**88** C6
LWF/SPW/WRK NE9 ....**100** A2
Lane Cnr *HAR/WTLS* NE34 ....**88** B3
Lanercost *WASHS* NE38 ....**138** B1
Lanercost Av *BLAY* NE21 ....**76** A6
Lanercost Dr *WD/WHPE/BLK* NE5 ...**61** D6
Lanercost Gdns
BW/LEM/TK/HW NE15 ....**57** F3
FELL NE10 ....**100** B4
Lanercost Rd *NSHW* NE29 ....**70** A1
Langdale *MONK* NE25 ....**40** A5
Langdale Cl *LGB/KIL* NE12 ....**48** C6
Langdale Crs *DHAM* DH1 ....**196** B1
Langdale Dr *CRAM* NE23 ....**21** D2
Langdale Gdns *BYK/HTN/WLK* NE6 ..**83** F2
WLSD/HOW NE28 ....**68** C2
Langdale Pl *PLEE/EAS* * SR8 ....**209** D2
WLSD/HOW NE28 ....**68** C2
Langdale Rd *HLS* DH4 ....**139** F6
LWF/SPW/WRK NE9 ....**99** F5
Langdale St *HLH* DH5 ....**185** E2
Langdale Wy *BOL* NE36 ....**106** B2
Langdon Cl *NSHW* NE29 ....**54** B3
Langdon Gdns *STLY/ANP* DH9 ......**146** A3
Langdon Rd *WD/WHPE/BLK* NE5 .....**59** F4
Langford Dr *BOLCOL* NE35 ....**87** D6
Langham Rd
BW/LEM/TK/HW NE15 ....**77** E3
Langholm Rd *BOL* NE36 ....**106** C2
GOS/KPK NE3 ....**47** D5
Langhorn Cl *BYK/HTN/WLK* NE6 .....**82** A2
Langhurst *ASHBK/HED/RY* SR2 .....**145** D6
Langleeford Rd
WD/WHPE/BLK NE5 ....**60** C3
Langley Av *BLYTH* NE24 ....**10** A4
FELL NE10 ....**101** E2
MONK NE25 ....**53** F1
SMOOR NE27 ....**52** C2
Langley Cl *WASHS* NE38 ....**138** A2
Langley Crs *BDN/LAN/SAC* DH7 .....**203** F3
Langley Gv *PLEE/EAS* SR8 ....**207** F4
Langley Rd *BYK/HTN/WLK* NE6 ....**83** E2
DHAM DH1 ....**180** B6
NSHW NE29 ....**53** F6
SUNDSW SR3 ....**144** A4
WD/WHPE/BLK NE5 ....**60** B6
Langley St *HLS* DH4 ....**157** F2
Langley Tarn *NSHW* NE29 ....**70** C2
Langley Ter *JRW* NE32 ....**86** A5
STLY/ANP DH9 ....**146** C4
Langport Rd *ASHBK/HED/RY* SR2 ..**144** D5
Langton Cl *MLFD/PNYW* * SR4 ....**126** A6
Langton Ct *CRAM* NE23 ....**14** B4
Langton St *GATE* * NE8 ....**99** F1
Langton Ter *LGB/HTN* NE7 ....**65** D5
Lanivet Cl *ASHBK/HED/RY* SR2 ......**145** E6
Lannerwood *NSHW* * NE29 ....**70** C2
Lansbury Cl *CLS/BIR/GTL* DH3 ......**118** A6
Lansbury Ct *CLS/BIR/GTL* DH3 ......**118** A6
SEA/MUR SR7 ....**188** B1
Lansbury Gdns *FELL* NE10 ....**101** F2
Lansbury Rd *WICK/BNPF* NE16 ....**96** C3
Lansbury Wy *SWCK/CAS* SR5 ....**124** A3
Lansdowne *ASHBK/HED/RY* SR2 ...**162** A1
Lansdowne Gdns *JES* NE2 ....**64** C6
Lansdowne Rd *LGB/KIL* NE12 ....**49** F4
Lansdowne St *MLFD/PNYW* SR4 ...**126** A5
Lansdowne Ter *NSHW* NE29 ....**54** B6
Lansdowne Ter West *NSHW* NE29 ...**54** A6
Lanthwaite Rd
LWF/SPW/WRK NE9 ....**99** F5
Lanton St *HLS* DH4 ....**157** F2
Lapford Dr *CRAM* NE23 ....**14** B5
Lapwing Cl *BLYTH* NE24 ....**17** D2
WASHS NE38 ....**137** E3
Lapwing Ct *WICK/BNPF* NE16 ....**130** B1
L'arbre Crs *WICK/BNPF* NE16 ....**95** E3
Larch Av *CLDN/WHIT/ROK* SR6 ......**109** F1
HAR/WTLS NE34 ....**89** F3
HLS DH4 ....**170** C1
Larch Cl *LWF/SPW/WRK* NE9 ....**118** C2
Larches Rd *DHAM* DH1 ....**193** F3
The Larches
ELS/FEN (off Park Rd) NE4 ....**79** F5
WICK/BNPF NE16 ....**112** A5

Larch Rd *BLAY* NE21 ....**76** C5
Larch Ter *STLY/ANP* DH9 ....**129** F5
Larchwood *WASHS* NE38 ....**138** A5
Larchwood Av *BYK/HTN/WLK* NE6 ...**66** A6
DIN/WO NE13 ....**33** E5
GOS/KPK NE3 ....**46** B5
Larchwood Gdns *DUN/TMV* NE11 ...**98** A5
Larchwood Gv
ASHBK/HED/RY SR2 ....**144** B4
Larkfield Crs *HLS* DH4 ....**156** C5
Larkfield Rd *ASHBK/HED/RY* SR2 ..**144** B3
Lark Rise Cl *LGB/HTN* * NE7 ....**65** F3
Larkspur Cl *STLY/ANP* DH9 ....**130** C6
Larkspur Rd *WICK/BNPF* NE16 ....**95** F4
Larkspur Ter *JES* NE2 ....**64** F5
Larne Crs *LWF/SPW/WRK* NE9 ....**99** F5
Larriston Pl *CRAM* NE23 ....**21** E2
Lartington Cl *CLS/BIR/GTL* DH3 ....**168** A4
Lartington Gdns *GOS/KPK* NE3 ....**64** B1
Larwood Cl *CLS/BIR/GTL* DH3 ....**167** D1
Larwood Ct *STLY/ANP* DH9 ....**146** A5
Lascelles Av *HAR/WTLS* NE34 ....**89** D3
Laski Gdns *FELL* NE10 ....**102** A2
Latimer St *TYNE/NSHE* NE30 ....**55** F4
Lauderdale Av *WLSD/HOW* NE28 ....**67** D2
Launceston Cl *DIN/WO* NE13 ....**45** F4
Launceston Dr *SUNDSW* SR3 ....**159** E1
Laura St *SUND* SR1 ....**4** D4
Laurel Av *DHAM* DH1 ....**195** F4
GOS/KPK NE3 ....**46** C6
LGB/KIL NE12 ....**50** B3
SEA/MUR SR7 ....**176** A3
Laurel Ct *CLSW/PEL* DH2 ....**153** D3
TYNE/NSHE NE30 ....**71** D1
Laurel Crs *BYK/HTN/WLK* NE6 ....**66** B5
STLY/ANP DH9 ....**146** A3
Laurel Gv *ASHBK/HED/RY* SR2 ......**144** B4
Laurel Rd *BLAY* NE21 ....**76** C6
Laurel St *BW/LEM/TK/HW* NE15 .....**57** F3
WLSD/HOW NE28 ....**67** E5
Laurelwood Gdns *DUN/TMV* NE11 ...**98** A4
Laurens Ct *WASHN* NE37 ....**120** C4
Lavender Gdns
BDN/LAN/SAC DH7 ....**178** C1
JES NE2 ....**63** F5
Lavender Gv *SWCK/CAS* SR5 ....**123** F4
Lavender La *HAR/WTLS* NE34 ....**88** A3
Lavender Rd *WICK/BNPF* NE16 ....**95** F4
Lavender Rw *LWF/SPW/WRK* NE9 ...**100** A5
Laverick La
FELL (off Newcastle Rd) NE10 ....**103** E3
Laverock Ct *BYK/HTN/WLK* NE6 ....**82** B3
Laverock Hall Rd *BLYTH* NE24 ....**15** F3
Laverock Pl *BLYTH* NE24 ....**16** A3
GOS/KPK NE3 ....**61** F1
Lavington Rd *HAR/WTLS* NE34 ....**72** A6
Lawe Rd *SSH* NE33 ....**71** F2
Lawmill Wy *WD/WHPE/BLK* NE5 ......**61** D4
Lawn Dr *BOL* NE36 ....**105** E4
Lawnside *SEA/MUR* SR7 ....**175** F4
The Lawns *HLH* DH5 ....**186** B3
SEA/MUR SR7 ....**175** F4
Lawnswood *HLH* DH5 ....**171** E3
Lawrence Av *BLAY* NE21 ....**76** B5
HAR/WTLS NE34 ....**88** C3
Lawrence Ct *BLAY* NE21 ....**76** B5
Lawrence Hill Ct *FELL* NE10 ....**102** A4
Lawrence St *SUND* SR1 ....**5** F3
Lawson Av *JRW* NE32 ....**86** B6
Lawson Crs *CLDN/WHIT/ROK* SR6 ..**108** C6
Lawson St *NSHW* NE29 ....**70** C2
WLSD/HOW NE28 ....**67** E5
Lawson Ter *DHAM* DH1 ....**194** A4
ELS/FEN NE4 ....**79** D4
HLH DH5 ....**186** A3
Laws St *CLDN/WHIT/ROK* SR6 ....**108** C6
Laxford Ct *SUNDSW* SR3 ....**160** B3
Layburn Gdns *HAR/WTLS* * NE34 ....**87** F4
Layburn Gdns
BW/LEM/TK/HW NE15 ....**60** A6
Layburn Pl *PLEE/EAS* SR8 ....**208** A1
Layfield Rd *GOS/KPK* NE3 ....**47** E3
Laygate *SSH* NE33 ....**71** E6
Laygate Pl *SSH* NE33 ....**71** E5
Laygate St *SSH* NE33 ....**71** D5
Lea Av *JRW* NE32 ....**86** B4
Leabank *BW/LEM/TK/HW* NE15 ....**59** F6
Leafield Crs *HAR/WTLS* NE34 ....**72** C6
Lea Gn *CLS/BIR/GTL* DH3 ....**137** D5
Leagreen Ct *GOS/KPK* NE3 ....**46** B6
Leaholme Crs *BLYTH* NE24 ....**10** B6
Lealholm Rd *LGB/HTN* NE7 ....**64** C1
Leam Gdns *FELL* NE10 ....**102** B2
Leamington St *MLFD/PNYW* SR4 ...**126** A6
Leam La *FELL* NE10 ....**101** F5
LWF/SPW/WRK NE9 ....**101** E6
Leamside *FELL* NE10 ....**101** E4
JRW NE32 ....**86** B4
Leander Av *CLS/BIR/GTL* DH3 ....**153** F1
Leander Dr *BOLCOL* NE35 ....**105** D2
Leaplish *WASHS* NE38 ....**139** E4
Lea Riggs *HLS* DH4 ....**183** F2
The Leas *HLH* DH4 ....**157** F3
Leazes Ct *DHAM* DH1 ....**194** C4
Leazes Crs *CNUT* NE1 ....**2** B2

Leazes La *CNUT* NE1 ....2 C2
  DHAM DH1 ....194 C4
Leazes Park Rd *CNUT* NE1 ....2 B2
Leazes Pkwy
  BW/LEM/TK/HW NE15 ....57 E5
Leazes Pl *DHAM* DH1 ....194 C4
Leazes Ri *PLEE/EAS* SR8 ....209 E2
Leazes Rd *DHAM* DH1 ....194 B4
Leazes Ter *CNUT* NE1 ....2 B1
The Leazes *HAR/WTLS* NE34 ....89 E2
  SUND SR1 ....126 A6
Leazes Vw *ROWG* NE39 ....110 C3
Lecondale *FELL* NE10 ....101 E5
Ledbury Rd *ASHBK/HED/RY* SR2 ....144 C3
Leech Ct *PLEE/EAS* SR8 ....201 E2
Leechmere Rd
  ASHBK/HED/RY SR2 ....144 B4
Leechmere Wy
  ASHBK/HED/RY SR2 ....145 D6
Lee Cl *WASHS* NE38 ....140 A1
Leeds St *CLDN/WHIT/ROK* SR6 ....126 C2
Leeholme *HLH* DH5 ....171 E3
Leeholme Ct *STLY/ANP* DH9 ....146 C5
Leeming Gdns
  LWF/SPW/WRK NE9 ....100 A4
Leesfield Dr *BDN/LAN/SAC* DH7 ....203 E5
Leesfield Gdns
  BDN/LAN/SAC DH7 ....203 D5
Leesfield Rd *BDN/LAN/SAC* DH7 ....203 D5
Lees St *STLY/ANP* DH9 ....148 B1
Lee St *CLDN/WHIT/ROK* SR6 ....108 C6
  SWCK/CAS SR5 ....126 A3
Legg Av *BDLGTN* NE22 ....9 D1
Legges Dr *DIN/WO* NE13 ....18 C2
Legion Gv *BW/LEM/TK/HW* NE15 ....77 E1
Legion Rd *BW/LEM/TK/HW* NE15 ....77 E1
Leicester Cl *WLSD/HOW* NE28 ....66 C1
Leicestershire Dr *DHAM* DH1 ....196 C3
Leicester St *BYK/HTN/WLK* NE6 ....83 D5
Leighton Av *ASHBK/HED/RY* SR2 ....144 C4
Leighton St *BYK/HTN/WLK* NE6 ....81 F2
  SSH NE33 ....72 A4
Leith Ct *HAR/WTLS* NE34 ....88 B3
Leith Gdns *STLY/ANP* DH9 ....130 C3
Lemington Gdns
  WD/WHPE/BLK NE5 ....78 B1
Lemington Rd
  BW/LEM/TK/HW NE15 ....75 F1
Lemon St *SSH* NE33 ....88 A2
Lena Av *MONK* NE25 ....30 A6
Lenin St *STLY/ANP* DH9 ....148 C3
Leominster Rd
  ASHBK/HED/RY SR2 ....144 C4
Leopold St *JRW* NE32 ....86 A2
Lesbury Av *SMOOR* NE27 ....52 A1
  WLSD/HOW NE28 ....68 B3
Lesbury Cha *GOS/KPK* NE3 ....47 D6
Lesbury Cl *CLSW/PEL* DH2 ....165 E1
Lesbury Rd *BYK/HTN/WLK* NE6 ....65 D5
Lesbury St *BW/LEM/TK/HW* NE15 ....76 C2
  WLSD/HOW NE28 ....68 B3
Leslie Av *HEBB* NE31 ....85 D3
Leslie Crs *GOS/KPK* NE3 ....63 E3
Leven Av *CLSW/PEL* DH2 ....166 A1
Levens Wk *CRAM* NE23 ....21 E1
Levisham Cl *SUNDSW* SR3 ....161 E1
Lewis Crs *ASHBK/HED/RY* SR2 ....5 G6
Lewis Dr *ELS/FEN* NE4 ....79 E2
Lexington Ct *BDN/LAN/SAC* DH7 ....202 C5
Leybourne Av *LGB/KIL* NE12 ....49 F3
Leyburn Cl *CLSW/PEL* DH2 ....134 E5
  HLH DH4 ....170 B1
Leyburn Dr *LGB/HTN* NE7 ....64 C3
Leyburn Gv *HLS* DH4 ....170 B1
Leyburn Pl *CLS/BIR/GTL* DH3 ....118 A6
Leyfield Cl *SUNDSW* SR3 ....160 C3
Leyton Pl *GATE* NE8 ....99 F2
Liburn Cl *BOL* NE36 ....106 A2
Lichfield Av *BYK/HTN/WLK* NE6 ....83 D4
Lichfield Cl *CLS/BIR/GTL* DH3 ....167 F4
  GOS/KPK NE3 ....47 E3
Lichfield Rd *SWCK/CAS* SR5 ....125 F1
Lidcombe Cl *SUNDSW* SR3 ....161 D1
Liddell St *CLDN/WHIT/ROK* SR6 ....126 C4
  NSHW NE29 ....71 D1
Liddell Ter *GATE* NE8 ....98 C2
Liddle Av *RDHAMSE* DH6 ....197 E4
Liddle Cl *PLEE/EAS* SR8 ....200 A6
Liddle Ct *ELS/FEN* NE4 ....79 E3
Liddle Rd *ELS/FEN* NE4 ....79 E3
Lieven St *DIN/WO* NE13 ....32 C6
Liffey Rd *HEBB* NE31 ....85 D5
Lightbourne Rd
  BYK/HTN/WLK NE6 ....83 F2
Lightwood Av
  BW/LEM/TK/HW NE15 ....77 F4
Lilac Av *BDN/LAN/SAC* DH7 ....178 D1
  BLYTH NE24 ....10 C4
  CLDN/WHIT/ROK SR6 ....91 E5
  DHAM DH1 ....194 A1
  HAR/WTLS NE34 ....89 E3
  LGB/KIL NE12 ....50 B4
  SUNDSW SR3 ....144 A6
Lilac Cl *WD/WHPE/BLK* NE5 ....59 D2
Lilac Crs *WICK/BNPF* NE16 ....111 F6

Lilac Gdns *LWF/SPW/WRK* NE9 ....99 E4
  WICK/BNPF NE16 ....95 F4
Lilac Gv *CLSW/PEL* DH2 ....152 C3
Lilac Pk *BDN/LAN/SAC* DH7 ....192 A5
Lilac Rd *BYK/HTN/WLK* NE6 ....66 C5
Lilac Sq *HLS* DH4 ....156 A5
Lilac St *MLFD/PNYW* SR4 ....123 F6
Lilac Ter *RDHAMSE* DH6 ....206 B2
Lilburn Cl *BYK/HTN/WLK* NE6 ....82 B4
  CLSW/PEL DH2 ....165 F2
Lilburne Cl *SUND* SR1 ....5 F2
Lilburn Gdns *GOS/KPK* NE3 ....64 B2
Lilburn Pl *SWCK/CAS* SR5 ....125 F3
Lilburn Rd *SMOOR* NE27 ....52 A2
Lilburn St *NSHW* NE29 ....70 B1
Lilian Av *ASHBK/HED/RY* SR2 ....145 D6
  WLSD/HOW NE28 ....66 C5
Lilley Gv *SWCK/CAS* SR5 ....124 A3
Lily Av *BDLGTN* NE22 ....64 A5
Lily Bank *WLSD/HOW* NE28 ....67 D4
Lily Crs *CLDN/WHIT/ROK* SR6 ....91 E5
  JES NE2 ....64 A5
Lily Gdns *STLY/ANP* DH9 ....129 D6
Lily St *MLFD/PNYW* SR4 ....15 C6
Lily Ter *WD/WHPE/BLK* NE5 ....60 C3
Lilywhite Ter *HLH* DH5 ....186 A5
Lime Av *HLS* DH4 ....170 B2
Limecragg Av *DHAM* DH1 ....196 A3
Limecroft *JRW* NE32 ....104 B1
Lime Gv *RYTON* NE40 ....74 B3
Limekiln Ct *WLSD/HOW* NE28 ....67 F4
Limekiln Rd *WLSD/HOW* NE28 ....67 F4
Lime Pk *BDN/LAN/SAC* DH7 ....203 D4
The Limes *ASHBK/HED/RY* SR2 ....144 C2
  HLS DH4 ....140 A6
Lime St *BLAY* NE21 ....94 C1
  CNUT NE1 ....81 F3
  MLFD/PNYW SR4 ....126 A5
  STLY/ANP DH9 ....147 F5
Limetrees Gdns
  LWF/SPW/WRK NE9 ....99 E3
Limewood Ct *JES* NE2 ....63 G5
Limewood Gv *DIN/WO* NE13 ....33 D5
Linacre Cl *DIN/WO* NE13 ....45 D6
Linacre Ct *PLEE/EAS* SR8 ....208 A3
Linbridge Dr *WD/WHPE/BLK* NE5 ....60 A5
Linburn *WASHS* NE38 ....137 F5
Lincoln Av *SUNDSW* SR3 ....143 F6
  WLSD/HOW NE28 ....66 C3
Lincoln Gn *GOS/KPK* NE3 ....47 D3
Lincoln Rd *CRAM* NE23 ....14 B5
  DHAM DH1 ....180 C5
  HAR/WTLS NE34 ....90 A1
Lincolnshire Cl *DHAM* DH1 ....196 B3
Lincoln St *GATE* NE8 ....99 D1
  MLFD/PNYW SR4 ....125 E5
Lincrest Ct
  WD/WHPE/BLK
  (off Linhope Rd) NE5 ....60 B4
Lindale Av *WICK/BNPF* NE16 ....95 F5
Lindale Rd *ELS/FEN* NE4 ....62 A6
Lindean Pl *CRAM* NE23 ....21 E2
Linden Av *ELS/FEN* NE4 ....78 C1
  GOS/KPK NE3 ....63 E2
Linden Gdns *ASHBK/HED/RY* SR2 ....144 B3
Linden Gv *DUN/TMV* NE11 ....97 E2
  HLS DH4 ....170 C2
Linden Pk *BDN/LAN/SAC* DH7 ....203 D4
Linden Rd *ASHBK/HED/RY* SR2 ....144 B3
  BLAY NE21 ....76 C6
  GOS/KPK NE3 ....63 E2
  LGB/KIL NE12 ....49 F5
  MONK NE25 ....31 D5
Lindfield Av *WD/WHPE/BLK* NE5 ....61 D5
Lindisfarne *PLEE/EAS* SR8 ....208 B4
  WASHS NE38 ....138 B2
Lindisfarne Cl *CLS/BIR/GTL* DH3 ....155 F5
Lindisfarne Cl *HLS* DH4 ....170 A1
  JES NE2 ....64 B3
  WD/WHPE/BLK NE5 ....60 B5
Lindisfarne Ct *JRW* NE32 ....87 E2
Lindisfarne Dr *GATE* NE8 ....87 E2
Lindisfarne Pl *WLSD/HOW* NE28 ....67 F3
Lindisfarne Recess *JRW* NE32 ....86 C4
Lindisfarne Rd *DHAM* DH1 ....194 C1
  HEBB NE31 ....85 D5
  JES NE2 ....64 B3
Lindisfarne Ter *TYNE/NSHE* NE30 ....54 C5
Lindom Av *CLS/BIR/GTL* DH3 ....153 E3
Lindon Rd *STLY/ANP* DH9 ....148 A3
Lindrick Ct *FELL* NE10 ....102 B3
Lindsay Av *BLYTH* NE24 ....10 B4
Lindsay Cl *ASHBK/HED/RY* SR2 ....5 E5
Lindsay Rd *ASHBK/HED/RY* SR2 ....5 F5
Lindsay St *HLH* DH5 ....172 A4
Lindsey Cl *CRAM* NE23 ....21 D2
Lindum Rd *LWF/SPW/WRK* NE9 ....99 E2
Lingdale *DHAM* DH1 ....195 F5
Lingdale Av *CLDN/WHIT/ROK* SR6 ....109 D4
Lingey Gdns *FELL* NE10 ....102 B2
Lingey La *FELL* NE10 ....102 A3
Lingfield *HLH* DH5 ....171 E4
Lingholme *CLSW/PEL* DH2 ....152 C4
Lingmell *WASHN* NE37 ....120 A6

Lingshaw *FELL* NE10 ....102 A3
Linhope Av *GOS/KPK* NE3 ....46 B5
Linhope Rd *WD/WHPE/BLK* NE5 ....60 B4
Link Av *BDLGTN* NE22 ....6 C3
Link Rd *WD/WHPE/BLK* NE5 ....62 A4
Links Av *TYNE/NSHE* NE30 ....55 E2
  WBAY NE26 ....40 B3
Links Gn *GOS/KPK* NE3 ....47 F6
Links Rd *BLYTH* NE24 ....17 E2
  TYNE/NSHE NE30 ....55 E2
The Links *DHAM* DH1 ....196 C2
  WBAY NE26 ....26 B2
  WBAY NE26 ....40 B1
Links Vw *BLYTH* NE24 ....16 B2
Linkway *JRW* NE32 ....104 C1
Linley Hl *WICK/BNPF* NE16 ....95 D6
Linnel Dr *BW/LEM/TK/HW* NE15 ....77 F1
Linnet Gv *SWCK/CAS* SR5 ....124 B3
Linskell *ASHBK/HED/RY* SR2 ....146 D6
Linskill Pl *TYNE/NSHE* NE30 ....55 D5
Linskill St *TYNE/NSHE* NE30 ....71 D1
Linskill Ter *TYNE/NSHE* NE30 ....55 D6
Linslade Wk *CRAM* NE23 ....21 E2
Lintfort *CLS/BIR/GTL* DH3 ....153 F1
Linthorpe Rd *GOS/KPK* NE3 ....47 E5
  TYNE/NSHE NE30 ....55 D3
Linton Rd *LWF/SPW/WRK* NE9 ....117 E1
  WBAY NE26 ....40 A1
Lintzford Gdns
  BW/LEM/TK/HW NE15 ....77 D1
  ROWG NE39 ....110 C4
Lintzford La *ROWG* NE39 ....110 A4
Lintz Green La *ROWG* NE39 ....110 B5
Lintz La *WICK/BNPF* NE16 ....128 C2
Lintz Ter *WICK/BNPF* NE16 ....111 E6
Linum Pl *ELS/FEN* NE4 ....62 A6
Linwood Pl *GOS/KPK* NE3 ....47 E3
Lion Wk *NSHW* NE29 ....70 B3
Lisa Av *MLFD/PNYW* SR4 ....141 F1
Lisburn Ter *MLFD/PNYW* SR4 ....125 F5
Lisle Gv *WLSD/HOW* NE28 ....68 C3
Lisle Rd *HAR/WTLS* NE34 ....89 E1
Lisle St *WLSD/HOW* NE28 ....67 D4
Lismore Av *SSH* NE33 ....88 B1
Lismore Pl *BW/LEM/TK/HW* NE15 ....78 B2
Lismore Ter *DUN/TMV* NE11 ....97 E1
Lister Cl *HLH* DH5 ....170 C4
Lister Rd *PLEE/EAS* SR8 ....199 F6
Litchfield La *BLAY* NE21 ....94 A1
Litchfield Rd *DHAM* DH1 ....180 C4
Little Bedford St *NSHW* NE29 ....71 D1
Littlebridge Ct *DHAM* DH1 ....179 F6
Littleburn Cl *HLS* DH4 ....170 B1
Littleburn La *BDN/LAN/SAC* DH7 ....204 A3
Littleburn Rd *BDN/LAN/SAC* DH7 ....204 A4
Little Dene
  JES (off Lodore Rd) NE2 ....63 F3
Littledene *LWF/SPW/WRK* NE9 ....99 E3
Little Eden *PLEE/EAS* SR8 ....208 C1
Little Villiers St *SUND* SR1 ....4 D2
Little Wy *BW/LEM/TK/HW* NE15 ....78 A4
Littondale *WLSD/HOW* NE28 ....66 B2
Livingstone Pl *SSH* NE33 ....71 E2
Livingstone Rd *SUND* SR1 ....4 A2
Livingstone St *SSH* NE33 ....71 F2
Livingstone Vw
  TYNE/NSHE NE30 ....55 E5
Lizard La *CLDN/WHIT/ROK* SR6 ....91 E6
  HAR/WTLS NE34 ....90 C2
Lloyd Av *HLH* DH5 ....170 B6
Lloyd Ct *DUN/TMV* NE11 ....79 D6
Lobban Av *HEBB* NE31 ....84 C5
Lobelia Av *FELL* NE10 ....82 A6
Lobelia Cl *WD/WHPE/BLK* NE5 ....59 E3
Lobley Gdns *DUN/TMV* NE11 ....97 F4
Lobley Hill Rd *DUN/TMV* NE11 ....97 F4
Lobleyhill Rd *WICK/BNPF* NE16 ....112 C4
Lochcraig Pl *CRAM* NE23 ....21 E2
Lochmaben Ter *SWCK/CAS* SR5 ....126 C2
Lockerbie Cl *NSHW* NE29 ....53 D5
Lockerbie Rd *CRAM* NE23 ....21 E2
Locksley Cl *NSHW* NE29 ....53 D5
Locomotion Wy *LGB/KIL* NE12 ....35 D5
  NSHW NE29 ....70 C3
Lodgeside Meadow
  SUNDSW SR3 ....161 D3
The Lodges Rd
  LWF/SPW/WRK NE9 ....117 D1
Lodore Gv *JRW* NE32 ....86 C5
Lodore Rd *JES* NE2 ....63 F3
Logan Rd *BYK/HTN/WLK* NE6 ....66 B5
Logan St *HLH* DH5 ....185 F1
Lola St *DIN/WO* NE13 ....32 B5
Lombard Dr *CLS/BIR/GTL* DH3 ....153 E1
Lombard St *SUND* SR1 ....5 F2
Lomond Ct *SUNDSW* SR3 ....160 C2
Lomond Pl *CLSW/PEL* DH2 ....166 A1
London Av *WASHN* NE37 ....120 A3
Londonderry Av *DHAM* DH1 ....195 F5
Londonderry St *SEA/MUR* SR7 ....177 D5
  SUNDSW SR3 ....160 C1
Londonderry Ter *SUNDSW* SR3 ....161 D1
Longacre *HLS* DH4 ....170 B2
  WASHS NE38 ....139 D5
Long Acres *DHAM* DH1 ....195 D3

Long Bank *CLS/BIR/GTL* DH3 ....**118** B5
LWF/SPW/WRK NE9 ....**118** B3
Longborough Ct *LGB/HTN* NE7 ......**64** A2
Long Burn Dr *CLSW/PEL* DH2 ......**152** B6
Long Dl *CLSW/PEL* DH2 ....**152** B6
Longdean Cl *HEBB* NE31 ....**84** B3
Longdean Pk *CLS/BIR/GTL* DH3 ....**153** E2
Longfield Rd
CLDN/WHIT/ROK SR6 ....**126** C1
Longfield Ter *BYK/HTN/WLK* NE6 ....**83** E4
Long Gair *BLAY* NE21 ....**93** F2
Long Garth *DHAM* DH1 ....**193** E2
Long Headlam *BYK/HTN/WLK* NE6 ....**82** B2
Longhirst *FELL* NE10 ....**101** F3
LGB/KIL NE12 ....**35** F6
WD/WHPE/BLK NE5 ....**60** D4
Longhirst Dr *DIN/WO* NE13 ....**53** D5
Longlands Dr *HLH* DH5 ....**171** D3
Longleat Gdns *SSH* NE33 ....**71** F3
Longley St *ELS/FEN* NE4 ....**79** F2
Longmeadows *SUNDSW* SR3 ....**159** E2
Longnewton St *SEA/MUR* SR7 ......**176** C5
Longniddry *WASHN* NE37 ....**120** B3
Longniddry Ct
LWF/SPW/WRK NE9 ....**117** D1
Longridge Av *LGB/HTN* NE7 ....**65** F3
WASHS NE38 ....**137** F4
Longridge Dr *WBAY* NE26 ....**40** A3
Long Ridge Rd *RYTON* NE40 ....**74** B6
Longridge Sq *ASHBK/HED/RY* SR2 ..**144** C4
Longridge Wy *CRAM* NE23 ....**21** E2
STKFD/GP NE62 ....**7** F1
Longrigg *FELL* NE10 ....**101** F3
Long Rigg *WICK/BNPF* NE16 ....**95** F1
Longrigg Rd *WICK/BNPF* NE16 ......**95** F1
Long Rw *NSH* NE33 ....**71** D3
Longrigg Av *BLYTH* NE24 ....**9** D4
Longshank La *CLS/BIR/GTL* DH3 ....**117** F6
Longston Av *TYNE/NSHE* NE30 ......**55** D1
Longstone
LWF/SPW/WRK
(off Pimlico) NE9 ....**99** E6
Longstone Ct *LGB/KIL* NE12 ....**36** A6
Longstone Sq *WD/WHPE/BLK* NE5 ....**59** F5
Longwood Cl *WICK/BNPF* NE16 ....**114** A1
Lonnen Av *ELS/FEN* NE4 ....**78** C1
Lonnen Dr *WICK/BNPF* NE16 ....**95** F2
The Lonnen *HAR/WTLS* NE34 ....**90** A4
Lonsdale *CLS/BIR/GTL* DH3 ....**137** D5
Lonsdale Av *CLDN/WHIT/ROK* SR6 ..**109** D4
Lonsdale Ct
JES (off West Jesmond Av) NE2 ....**64** A4
Lonsdale Gdns *WLSD/HOW* NE28 ....**68** C2
Lonsdale Rd *CLDN/WHIT/ROK* SR6 ..**127** D2
Lonsdale Ter *JES* NE2 ....**64** A4
Loraine Ter *BW/LEM/TK/HW* NE15 ....**76** B2
Lord Byrons Wk *SEA/MUR* SR7 ......**175** E1
Lordenshaw *WD/WHPE/BLK* NE5 ......**60** B2
Lord Nelson St *HAR/WTLS* NE34 ......**88** A2
Lord St *SEA/MUR* SR7 ....**176** C4
SSH NE33 ....**72** A5
SUNDSW SR3 ....**161** D1
Lorimers Cl *PLEE/EAS* SR8 ....**208** A4
Lorne St *HLH* DH5 ....**186** A4
Lorne Ter *ASHBK/HED/RY* SR2 ....**4** B6
Lorrain Rd *HAR/WTLS* NE34 ....**88** C6
Lorton Av *TYNE/NSHE* NE30 ....**54** C2
Lorton Rd *LWF/SPW/WRK* NE9 ......**99** F6
Losh Ter *BYK/HTN/WLK* NE6 ....**83** E3
Lossiemouth Rd *NSHW* NE29 ....**69** D1
Lothian Ct *WD/WHPE/BLK* NE5 ......**61** D3
Lotus Cl *WD/WHPE/BLK* NE5 ....**59** D3
Lotus Pl *ELS/FEN* NE4 ....**78** C1
Loudon St *HAR/WTLS* NE34 ....**88** B3
Loughborough Av
ASHBK/HED/RY SR2 ....**144** B3
Loughrigg Av *CRAM* NE23 ....**21** D2
Louie Ter *LWF/SPW/WRK* NE9 ....**99** F5
Louis Av *CLDN/WHIT/ROK* SR6 ......**126** C1
Loup St *BLAY* NE21 ....**76** B5
Lovaine Av *MONK* NE25 ....**40** C6
NSHW NE29 ....**70** C1
Lovaine Pl *NSHW* NE29 ....**70** C1
Lovaine Pl West *NSHW* NE29 ....**70** B1
Lovaine Rw *TYNE/NSHE* NE30 ......**55** F4
Lovaine St *BW/LEM/TK/HW* NE15 ....**58** A6
CLSW/PEL DH2 ....**151** E2
Lovaine Ter *NSHW* NE29 ....**54** C6
Love Av *CRAM* NE23 ....**35** D3
Love La *CNUT* NE1 ....**3** G4
Loveless Gdns *FELL* NE10 ....**102** A3
Lovett Wk *GATE* NE8 ....**80** B6
Lowbiggin *WD/WHPE/BLK* NE5 ......**44** A6
Low Chare *CLS/BIR/GTL* DH3 ....**153** F5
Low Church St *STLY/ANP* DH9 ......**146** B3
Lowdham Av *NSHW* NE29 ....**70** A2
Lowdon Ct
JES (off Richardson Rd) NE2 ......**80** B1
Low Downs Rd *HLH* DH5 ....**171** F4
Lower Dundas St
CLDN/WHIT/ROK SR6 ....**126** C4
Lower Rudyerd St *NSHW* NE29 ....**70** C1
Lowerson Av *HLS* DH4 ....**156** C3
Lowery La *STLY/ANP* DH9 ....**149** F6
Lowe's Barn Bank *DHAM* DH1 ......**204** B1

Lowes Ct *DHAM* DH1 ....**193** F6
Lowes Fall *DHAM* DH1 ....**193** F6
Lowes Rd *DHAM* DH1 ....**204** C1
Loweswater Av *HLH* DH5 ....**186** B4
Loweswater Cl *BLYTH* NE24 ....**9** E3
Loweswater Rd
WD/WHPE/BLK NE5 ....**61** D6
Loweswood Cl *LGB/HTN* NE7 ....**64** C5
Lowes Wynd *DHAM* DH1 ....**193** F6
Lowfield Ter *BYK/HTN/WLK* NE6 ......**83** E4
Lowfield Wk *WICK/BNPF* NE16 ......**95** F3
Low Flatts Rd *CLSW/PEL* DH2 ......**153** D2
Low Fold *BYK/HTN/WLK* NE6 ....**81** F2
Low Friar St *CNUT* NE1 ....**2** C4
Lowgate *BW/LEM/TK/HW* NE15 ......**57** F5
Low Gosforth Ct *GOS/KPK* NE3 ......**47** F3
Low Haugh *PONT/DH* NE20 ....**28** B3
Low Heyworth La *FELL* NE10 ......**101** E1
Lowhills Rd *PLEE/EAS* SR8 ....**200** A6
Lowland Cl *SUNDSW* SR3 ....**160** C3
Lowland Rd *BDN/LAN/SAC* DH7 ....**203** D4
Low La *HAR/WTLS* NE34 ....**88** B4
Low Meadow
CLDN/WHIT/ROK SR6 ....**107** F1
Lownds Ter *BYK/HTN/WLK* NE6 ......**83** D2
Low Quay *BLYTH* NE24 ....**11** E5
Lowrey's La *LWF/SPW/WRK* NE9 ....**99** E5
Low Rw *PLEE/EAS* SR8 ....**200** A2
SUND SR1 ....**4** A3
Lowry Gdns *HAR/WTLS* NE34 ....**88** C6
Lowry Rd *CLDN/WHIT/ROK* SR6 ....**109** D5
Low Station Rd *HLS* DH4 ....**183** D2
Low St *SUND* SR1 ....**5** F1
Lowther Cl *PLEE/EAS* SR8 ....**208** C1
Lowther Ct *PLEE/EAS* SR8 ....**208** A6
Lowthian Crs *BYK/HTN/WLK* NE6 ....**83** D3
Low Well Gdns *FELL* * NE10 ....**101** D1
Low West Av *ROWG* NE39 ....**110** B3
Lucknow St *SUND* SR1 ....**5** C1
Lucock St *HAR/WTLS* NE34 ....**88** A3
Ludlow Av *NSHW* NE29 ....**54** A4
Ludlow Ct *GOS/KPK* NE3 ....**46** A5
Ludlow Dr *MONK* NE25 ....**39** D6
Ludlow Rd *ASHBK/HED/RY* SR2 ....**144** C4
Luffness Dr *HAR/WTLS* NE34 ....**89** E5
Luke Crs *SEA/MUR* SR7 ....**188** A1
Luke's La *HEBB* NE31 ....**85** E6
Lulsgate *SWCK/CAS* SR5 ....**123** F3
Lulworth Av *JRW* NE32 ....**86** C3
Lulworth Ct *SUNDSW* SR3 ....**159** E1
Lulworth Gdns
ASHBK/HED/RY SR2 ....**144** B3
Lumley Av *HAR/WTLS* NE34 ....**90** A2
WICK/BNPF NE16 ....**96** A1
Lumley Cl *WASHS* NE38 ....**137** F3
Lumley Ct *BDLGTN* NE22 ....**8** B2
HEBB NE31 ....**68** B6
SUNDSW SR3 ....**159** E1
Lumley Dr *PLEE/EAS* SR8 ....**208** C3
Lumley Gdns *GATE* NE8 ....**100** A1
Lumley New Rd *CLS/BIR/GTL* DH3 ..**154** B6
Lumley Rd *DHAM* DH1 ....**180** B5
Lumley St *HLS* DH4 ....**157** F6
MLFD/PNYW SR4 ....**125** F6
Lumley Ter *CLS/BIR/GTL* DH3 ......**153** F6
JRW NE32 ....**86** A5
Lumley Wk *DUN/TMV* NE11 ....**97** F1
Lumsden Sq *SEA/MUR* SR7 ....**188** A1
Lund Av *DHAM* DH1 ....**179** F6
Lunedale Av *CLDN/WHIT/ROK* SR6 ..**108** B5
Lunedale Dr *CLS/BIR/GTL* DH3 ......**168** A4
Lunesdale St *HLH* DH5 ....**185** F2
Lupin Cl *WD/WHPE/BLK* NE5 ......**59** E2
Luss Av *JRW* NE32 ....**87** D5
Lutterworth Cl *LGB/KIL* NE12 ......**49** D6
Lutterworth Dr *LGB/KIL* NE12 ......**48** C6
Lutterworth Rd
ASHBK/HED/RY SR2 ....**144** B3
LGB/KIL NE12 ....**65** D1
Luxembourg Rd
MLFD/PNYW SR4 ....**124** C4
Lychgate Ct *GATE* * NE8 ....**81** E5
Lydbury Cl *CRAM* NE23 ....**14** B5
Lydcott *WASHS* NE38 ....**140** A3
Lydford Ct *HLS* DH4 ....**157** E5
WD/WHPE/BLK NE5 ....**45** E6
Lydford Wy *CLS/BIR/GTL* DH3 ......**136** C3
Lyncroft Rd *NSHW* NE29 ....**54** A6
Lyndale *CRAM* NE23 ....**14** B5
Lyndhurst Av *CLS/BIR/GTL* DH3 ....**153** E2
JES NE2 ....**63** F4
LWF/SPW/WRK NE9 ....**99** E6
Lyndhurst Cl *BLAY* NE21 ....**93** F2
Lyndhurst Crs *LWF/SPW/WRK* NE9 ..**99** F6
Lyndhurst Dr *DHAM* DH1 ....**193** D5
LWF/SPW/WRK NE9 ....**99** F6
Lyndhurst Gdns *JES* NE2 ....**63** F4
Lyndhurst Gv *LWF/SPW/WRK* NE9 ..**99** F6
Lyndhurst Rd *LGB/KIL* NE12 ....**49** E2
STLY/ANP DH9 ....**147** F2
Lyndhurst St *SSH* NE33 ....**71** F4
Lyndhurst Ter *MLFD/PNYW* SR4 ....**125** D4
Lyndon Cl *BOL* NE36 ....**106** A3
Lyndon Dr *BOL* NE36 ....**106** A3
Lyndon Gv *BOL* NE36 ....**106** A3

Lyndon Wk *BLYTH* NE24 ....**9** E4
Lyne Cl *CLSW/PEL* DH2 ....**135** E6
Lyne's Dr *BDN/LAN/SAC* DH7 ......**203** F3
Lynfield *WBAY* NE26 ....**40** A2
Lynfield Ct *WD/WHPE/BLK* NE5 ......**61** D3
Lynfield Pl *WD/WHPE/BLK* NE5 ......**61** D3
Lynford Gdns *ASHBK/HED/RY* SR2 ..**144** B3
Lynholm Gv *LGB/KIL* NE12 ....**49** F5
Lynmouth Pl *LGB/HTN* NE7 ....**65** D3
Lynmouth Rd *NSHW* NE29 ....**69** E1
Lynndale Av *BLYTH* NE24 ....**9** F5
Lynnholme Gdns
LWF/SPW/WRK NE9 ....**99** F2
Lynn Rd *NSHW* NE29 ....**53** F5
WBAY NE26 ....**66** C5
Lynn St *BLYTH* NE24 ....**10** C5
Lynnwood Av *ELS/FEN* NE4 ....**79** E3
Lyntgrove *ASHBK/HED/RY* SR2 ....**145** E6
Lynthorpe *ASHBK/HED/RY* SR2 ....**145** E6
Lyn-Thorpe Gv
CLDN/WHIT/ROK SR6 ....**109** D6
Lynton Av *JRW* NE32 ....**87** D5
Lynton Ct *HLS* DH4 ....**157** E5
Lynton Pl *WD/WHPE/BLK* NE5 ......**61** D3
Lynton Wy *WD/WHPE/BLK* NE5 ......**61** D3
Lynwood Av *BLAY* NE21 ....**76** B5
MLFD/PNYW SR4 ....**141** F4
Lyons Av *HLH* DH5 ....**186** A2
Lyons La *HLH* DH5 ....**186** B3
Lyon St *HEBB* NE31 ....**84** C2
Lyric Cl *NSHW* NE29 ....**53** D4
Lysdon Av *MONK* NE25 ....**24** C2
Lyster Cl *SEA/MUR* SR7 ....**175** D1
Lytchfield *FELL* * NE10 ....**102** A3
Lytham Cl *CRAM* NE23 ....**21** D2
WASHN NE37 ....**120** B2
WLSD/HOW NE28 ....**52** A5
Lytham Dr *MONK* NE25 ....**39** F5
Lytham Gra *HLS* DH4 ....**156** C4
Lytham Gn *FELL* * NE10 ....**84** A6
Lytham Pl *BYK/HTN/WLK* NE6 ......**83** D3
Lythe Wy *LGB/KIL* NE12 ....**49** E6

M

Mabel St *BLAY* NE21 ....**76** B5
Macadam St *GATE* NE8 ....**98** C3
Mackintosh Ct *DHAM* DH1 ....**195** E4
Maclynn Cl *SUNDSW* SR3 ....**160** A2
Macmerry Cl *SWCK/CAS* SR5 ......**123** E4
Macmillan Gdns *FELL* NE10 ....**101** F2
Maddison Ct *SUND* SR1 ....**5** G1
Maddison St *BLYTH* NE24 ....**11** D4
Maddox Rd *LGB/KIL* NE12 ....**49** F6
Madeira Av *WBAY* NE26 ....**40** B3
Madeira Cl *WD/WHPE/BLK* NE5 ......**59** E2
Madeira Ter *SSH* NE33 ....**72** B3
Madras St *HAR/WTLS* NE34 ....**87** F4
Mafeking Pl *NSHW* NE29 ....**53** D3
Mafeking St *BYK/HTN/WLK* NE6 ......**83** E5
LWF/SPW/WRK NE9 ....**99** F2
MLFD/PNYW SR4 ....**125** E6
Magdalene Av *DHAM* DH1 ....**196** B2
Magdalene Ct *DHAM* DH1 ....**195** D4
Magdalene Hts *DHAM* DH1 ....**195** D4
Magdalene St *DHAM* DH1 ....**195** D4
Magdalene Pl *MLFD/PNYW* SR4 ....**125** E5
Magenta Crs *WD/WHPE/BLK* NE5 ..**59** E2
Magnolia Cl *ELS/FEN* NE4 ....**78** C1
Maiden Law *HLS* DH4 ....**169** F3
Maiden St *ELS/FEN* NE4 ....**80** A5
Maidstone Cl *SUNDSW* SR3 ....**159** F2
Main Crs *WLSD/HOW* NE28 ....**66** B2
Main Rd *DIN/WO* NE13 ....**31** D3
DIN/WO NE13 ....**35** D5
RYTON NE40 ....**74** A3
Mainsforth Ter
ASHBK/HED/RY SR2 ....**5** G6
Mainsforth Ter West
ASHBK/HED/RY SR2 ....**145** D2
Mains Park Rd *CLS/BIR/GTL* DH3 ..**153** F2
Mainstone Cl *CRAM* NE23 ....**21** F2
Main St *PONT/DH* NE20 ....**28** A4
Main St North *CRAM* NE23 ....**36** A2
Makendon St *HEBB* NE31 ....**85** D1
Malaburn Wy *SWCK/CAS* SR5 ......**125** F3
Malaga Cl *WD/WHPE/BLK* NE5 ......**59** D2
Malaya Dr *BYK/HTN/WLK* NE6 ......**83** F3
Malcolm St *BYK/HTN/WLK* NE6 ......**83** F1
Malden Cl *CRAM* NE23 ....**21** E2
Maling Pk *MLFD/PNYW* SR4 ....**124** A5
Malings Cl *SUND* SR1 ....**5** G3
Maling St *BYK/HTN/WLK* NE6 ....**81** F3
Mallard Cl *WASHS* NE38 ....**137** E3
Mallard Ldg *FELL* * NE10 ....**100** C3
Mallard Wy *BLYTH* NE24 ....**17** E3
HLS DH4 ....**170** A4
WLSD/HOW NE28 ....**52** C6
Mallowburn Crs *GOS/KPK* NE3 ......**61** E2
Malmo Cl *NSHW* NE29 ....**69** D1
Malone Gdns *CLS/BIR/GTL* DH3 ....**118** C6
Malory Pl *GATE* NE8 ....**81** E6

Maltby CI WASHS NE38 ....138 C2
Malton CI BLYTH NE24 ....10 A5
  BW/LEM/TK/HW NE15 ....77 D2
Malton Crs NSHW NE29 ....70 A2
Malton Gdns WLSD/HOW NE28 ....67 D5
Malvern CI PLEE/EAS SR8 ....208 A3
Malvern Ct BW/LEM/TK/HW NE15....76 A1
  DUN/TMV NE11 ....97 F4
Malvern Crs SEA/MUR SR7 ....175 F3
Malvern Gdns
  CLDN/WHIT/ROK SR6 ....127 D1
  DUN/TMV NE11 ....97 F3
Malvern Rd NSHW NE29 ....54 A4
  WASHS NE38 ....138 A3
  WBAY NE26 ....26 C3
  WLSD/HOW NE28 ....68 B3
Malvern St SSH NE33 ....88 B1
Malvern Ter STLY/ANP DH9 ....148 C3
Malvins Close Rd BLYTH NE24 ....10 B5
Malvins Rd BLYTH NE24 ....10 A4
Mandale Crs TYNE/NSHE NE30.........54 C1
Mandarin CI WD/WHPE/BLK NE5 ......59 D2
Mandarin Ldg FELL * NE10 ....100 C2
Mandarin Wy WASHS NE38 ....122 B6
Mandela CI STLY/ANP DH9 ....147 F3
  SUND SR1 ....5 C3
Mandela Wy DUN/TMV NE11 ....78 B5
Mandeville WASHN NE37 ....121 D4
Manet Gdns HAR/WTLS NE34 ....88 C4
Mangrove CI WD/WHPE/BLK NE5 ....59 D2
Manila St ASHBK/HED/RY SR2 ....145 D2
Manisty Ter PLEE/EAS SR8 ....21 F5
Mann Crs SEA/MUR SR7 ....174 C6
Manningford CI CRAM NE23 ....21 F3
Manningford Dr SUNDSW SR3 ....160 A3
Manor Av LGB/HTN NE7 ....65 E1
Manor Chare CNUT NE1 ....3 F4
Manor CI GOS/KPK NE3 ....63 F2
Manor Ct SSH NE33 ....72 A5
Manor Dr LGB/HTN NE7 ....65 E1
  STLY/ANP DH9 ....146 B3
Manorfields LGB/KIL NE12 ....49 F6
Manor Gdns FELL NE10 ....102 B2
  LGB/HTN NE7 ....65 E1
Manor Gv BW/LEM/TK/HW NE15.....75 F1
  HLS DH4 ....158 B1
  LGB/HTN NE7 ....65 E1
Manor Hall CI SEA/MUR SR7 ....175 D2
Manor House CI
  BYK/HTN/WLK * NE6.......................82 B3
Manor House Rd JES NE2 ....64 B5
Manor PI LGB/HTN NE7 ....65 E1
Manor Rd LGB/HTN NE7 ....65 E2
  STLY/ANP* DH9 ....148 B3
  TYNE/NSHE NE30 ....55 F4
  WASHN NE37 ....120 C4
Manor Ter BLAY NE21 ....94 B3
Manor Vw WASHN NE37 ....120 C4
Manor Vw East WASHN NE37 ....121 D4
Manor Wk LGB/HTN NE7 ....65 E1
Manor Wy PLEE/EAS SR8 ....209 D2
Manorway TYNE/NSHE NE30 ....55 F4
Mansell PI PLEE/EAS SR8 ....209 D1
Mansfield Ct BOL NE36 ....105 F3
Mansfield Crs
  CLDN/WHIT/ROK SR6 ....127 D1
Mansfield PI ELS/FEN NE4 ....80 A3
Mansfield St ELS/FEN NE4 ....80 A3
Manston CI SUNDSW SR3 ....159 F3
Manx Sq SWCK/CAS SR5 ....126 A1
Maple Av DHAM DH1 ....195 F4
  DUN/TMV NE11 ....97 F3
  MONK NE25 ....54 B1
  SUNDSW SR3 ....144 A6
  WICK/BNPF NE16 ....111 E6
Maplebeck CI SUNDSW SR3 ....159 F3
Maple CI BW/LEM/TK/HW NE15 ......77 D2
  MONK NE25 ....24 C2
Maple Crs BLYTH NE24 ....9 E4
  SEA/MUR SR7 ....176 B6
Mapledene Rd GOS/KPK NE3 ....46 B6
Maple Gv CLDN/WHIT/ROK SR6 ....109 E1
  FELL NE10 ....101 D2
  GATE NE8 ....99 D3
  HAR/WTLS NE34 ....89 E3
  STLY/ANP DH9 ....147 F5
Maple Pk BDN/LAN/SAC DH7 ....192 A5
Maple Rd BLAY NE21 ....76 B6
Maple Rw WICK/BNPF NE16 ....78 A6
Maple St ELS/FEN NE4 ....80 A4
  JRW NE32 ....85 F1
  STLY/ANP DH9 ....147 F3
Maple Ter HLS DH4 ....156 C3
Maplewood BYK/HTN/WLK NE6.......66 A6
  CLSW/PEL DH2 ....125 E5
Maplewood Av SWCK/CAS SR5........125 E1
Maplewood St HLS DH4 ....169 D1
Mapperley Dr
  BW/LEM/TK/HW NE15 ....77 D1
Marblet Ct DUN/TMV NE11 ....98 A3
Marbury CI SUNDSW SR3.....................159 F2
March Rd CRAM NE23 ....35 D3

Marcia Av CLDN/WHIT/ROK SR6 .....126 C1
Marconi Wy WICK/BNPF NE16 ....96 A1
Marcross CI WD/WHPE/BLK NE5 ......59 D4
Marcross Dr SUNDSW SR3..................159 F3
Mardale WASHN NE37 ....120 A5
Mardale Gdns
  LWF/SPW/WRK NE9 ....117 F1
Mardale Rd WD/WHPE/BLK NE5 ....61 D5
Mardale St HLH DH5 ....185 F2
Marden Av TYNE/NSHE NE30 ....55 E1
Marden Ct WBAY NE26 ....26 A1
Marden Crs WBAY NE26 ....41 E1
Marden Rd South MONK NE25.............40 C6
Marden Ter TYNE/NSHE NE30 ....55 E1
Mareburn Crs FELL NE10 ....101 D2
Maree CI SUNDSW SR3 ....160 A3
Margaret Alice St
  MLFD/PNYW SR4 ....125 D5
Margaret Dr LGB/KIL NE12 ....50 C4
Margaret Gv HAR/WTLS NE34 ....87 F2
Margaret Rd WBAY NE26 ....41 E6
Margaret St ASHBK/HED/RY SR2 .....145 E4
Margaret Ter ROWG NE39 ....110 B3
Margery La DHAM DH1 ....194 A6
Marguerite Ct MLFD/PNYW SR4 ....126 A5
Marian Ct GATE NE8 ....98 C1
Marian Dr FELL NE10 ....84 A6
Marian Wy HAR/WTLS NE34 ....89 E5
Maria St ELS/FEN NE4 ....79 D4
  SEA/MUR SR7 ....176 C3
  SUNDSW SR3 ....160 C1
Marie Curie Dr ELS/FEN NE4...............79 E4
Marigold Av FELL NE10 ....82 A6
Marigold Ct MLFD/PNYW SR4 ....126 A5
Marigold Crs HLS DH4 ....158 A5
Marigold Wk HAR/WTLS NE34 ....88 A3
Marina Av CLDN/WHIT/ROK SR6 ....108 B6
Marina Ct CLDN/WHIT/ROK SR6 .....126 C1
Marina Dr MONK NE25 ....39 D6
  SSH NE33 ....72 A3
Marina Gv CLDN/WHIT/ROK SR6 ....126 C1
Marina Ter CLDN/WHIT/ROK SR6 ....109 E1
Marina Vw HEBB NE31 ....85 F6
  WLSD/HOW NE28 ....68 B4
Marine Ap SSH NE33 ....72 A4
Marine Av WBAY NE26............................40 C4
Marine Dr ASHBK/HED/RY SR2 ....145 E6
  HEBB NE31 ....85 F5
  JRW NE32 ....85 F6
Marine Gdns WBAY NE26 ....40 C5
Mariners Cottages SSH NE33 ....72 A3
Mariners' La TYNE/NSHE NE30...........55 E5
Mariners Point TYNE/NSHE NE30 .....55 F5
Mariner Sq SUND SR1 ....127 E4
Mariners Whf
  CNUT (off Quayside) NE1 ....81 F3
Marine Ter BLYTH NE24 ....10 C5
Marine Wk CLDN/WHIT/ROK SR6 ....127 E2
Marion St ASHBK/HED/RY SR2 ....145 D4
Maritime Crs PLEE/EAS SR8 ....201 E3
Maritime St SUND * SR1 ....4 C3
Maritime Ter SUND SR1 ....4 B3
Marius Av BW/LEM/TK/HW NE15......56 B4
Mariville East
  ASHBK/HED/RY SR2 ....162 C3
Mariville West
  ASHBK/HED/RY SR2 ....162 C3
Market La CNUT NE1 ....2 D4
  WICK/BNPF NE16...............................95 F1
Market PI DHAM * DH1 ....194 B4
  HLH DH5 ....171 E2
  SSH NE33 ....71 E3
Market Sq JRW NE32 ....86 A1
  SUND SR1 ....4 C2
Market St CNUT NE1 ....2 D3
  CRAM NE23 ....34 C2
  HLH DH5 ....172 A5
Market Wy DUN/TMV NE11 ....98 C4
Markham Av
  CLDN/WHIT/ROK SR6 ....109 F2
Markham St ASHBK/HED/RY SR2.....145 E4
Markington Dr
  ASHBK/HED/RY SR2 ....162 B2
Markle Gv HLH DH5 ....170 C5
Mark Ri HLH DH5 ....171 F5
Mark's La HLS DH4 ....169 E6
Marlboro Av WICK/BNPF NE16...........96 B6
Marlborough Ap GOS/KPK NE3 ....47 E5
Marlborough Av GOS/KPK NE3 ....47 D6
Marlborough Ct GOS/KPK NE3 ....45 F5
  HLH DH5 ....171 D4
Marlborough Crs CNUT NE1 ....2 B5
Marlborough Rd
  MLFD/PNYW SR4 ....141 E3
  WASHN NE37 ....121 D3
Marlborough St North SSH NE33 ....71 F6
Marlborough St South SSH NE33 ......71 F6
Marleen Av BYK/HTN/WLK NE6 ....65 E6
Marleen Ct BYK/HTN/WLK NE6 ....65 E6
Marley Crs SWCK/CAS SR5.................125 E1
Marlfield Ct WD/WHPE/BLK NE5 ......61 D3
Marlow Dr SUNDSW SR3 ....159 F3
Marlowe Gdns GATE NE8 ....99 E1
Marlowe PI HLH DH5 ....171 D3
Marlow PI LGB/KIL NE12 ....49 E6

Marlow St BLYTH NE24 ....10 C5
Marmion Rd BYK/HTN/WLK NE6 ....66 B6
Marmion Ter MONK NE25 ....40 B5
Marne St HLS DH4 ....157 D2
Marondale Av BYK/HTN/WLK NE6 ....66 B5
Marquis Av WD/WHPE/BLK NE5 ....59 E1
Marr Rd HEBB NE31 ....85 E3
Marsden Av CLDN/WHIT/ROK SR6 ....91 E6
Marsden CI HLS DH4 ....170 B2
Marsden Gv LWF/SPW/WRK NE9 ....118 C1
Marsden La HAR/WTLS NE34 ....90 A1
  WD/WHPE/BLK NE5 ....60 C3
Marsden Rd CLDN/WHIT/ROK SR6...107 E2
  HAR/WTLS NE34 ....89 E1
Marshall St CLDN/WHIT/ROK SR6....108 C6
Marshall Ter DHAM DH1 ....195 F4
Marsham CI BW/LEM/TK/HW NE15...77 F2
  CLDN/WHIT/ROK SR6 ....89 F6
Marsham Rd WD/WHPE/BLK * NE5...60 A3
Marsh Ct DUN/TMV NE11 ....98 A3
Marske Ter BYK/HTN/WLK NE6 ....83 D2
Marston LGB/KIL NE12...........................35 F6
Martello Gdns LGB/HTN NE7 ....65 F4
Martin Ct WASHS NE38 ....137 E4
Martindale Av
  CLDN/WHIT/ROK SR6 ....108 B5
Martindale Pk HLH DH5 ....171 D3
Martin Rd WLSD/HOW NE28 ....68 B4
Marwell Dr WASHN NE37....................121 D2
Marwood Gv PLEE/EAS SR8 ....208 B3
Maryhill CI ELS/FEN NE4 ....79 D4
Mary Magdalene Bungalows
  JES (off Claremont Rd) NE2 ....63 D6
Mary's PI BYK/HTN/WLK NE6 ....84 A2
Mary St BLAY NE21 ....75 F6
  BLAY NE21 ....76 B5
  SEA/MUR SR7 ....177 D3
  SUND SR1 ....4 B4
  SUNDSW SR3 ....143 F6
Mary Ter WD/WHPE/BLK NE5..............60 A4
Masefield Av WICK/BNPF NE16 ....96 A1
Masefield CI STLY/ANP DH9 ....149 D1
Masefield Dr HAR/WTLS NE34 ....87 F6
Masefield PI GATE NE8 ....81 E6
Maslin Gv PLEE/EAS SR8 ....207 F5
Mason Rd WLSD/HOW NE28 ....66 C2
Mason St BYK/HTN/WLK NE6 ....82 B3
Mast La TYNE/NSHE NE30 ....55 D1
Matamba Ter MLFD/PNYW SR4 ....126 A6
Matanzas St ASHBK/HED/RY SR2 ....145 D3
Matfen CI AV SMOOR NE27 ....52 B1
Matfen CI BLYTH NE24............................10 B5
  BW/LEM/TK/HW NE15 ....77 D2
Matfen Dr SUNDSW SR3 ....159 F2
Matfen Gdns WLSD/HOW NE28 ....68 B1
Matfen PI ELS/FEN NE4 ....79 D2
  GOS/KPK NE3 ....46 C6
Mather Rd ELS/FEN NE4 ....80 A4
Matlock Gdns WD/WHPE/BLK NE5....60 B3
Matlock Rd JRW NE32 ....86 B3
Matlock St SUND SR1...............................4 C1
Matterdale Rd PLEE/EAS SR8 ....209 E2
Matthew Bank JES NE2 ....64 A3
Matthew CI BYK/HTN/WLK NE6 ....82 A2
Matthew Rd BLYTH NE24 ....17 E1
Matthew St BYK/HTN/WLK * NE6 ......82 A2
Maudlin PI WD/WHPE/BLK NE5 ....61 F5
Maudlin St HLH DH5...............................172 A4
Mauds La SUND SR1 ....5 F2
Maud St BW/LEM/TK/HW NE15 ....76 B2
  CLDN/WHIT/ROK SR6 ....109 D6
Maughan St BLYTH NE24 ....11 E5
Maureen Ter SEA/MUR SR7 ....176 B3
Maurice Rd WLSD/HOW NE28 ....67 D6
Mautland St HLS DH4 ....171 D1
Mavin St DHAM DH1 ....194 C6
Maxton CI SUNDSW * SR3 ....159 F3
Maxwell SSH NE33 ....71 E4
Maxwell St GATE NE8 ....98 C3
  MLFD/PNYW SR4 ....125 E5
  SSH NE33 ....71 E4
May Av BLAY NE21 ....94 B3
  RYTON NE40 ....74 B2
Maydown CI SWCK/CAS SR5 ....123 E4
Mayfair Gdns GATE NE8 ....99 F2
  HAR/WTLS NE34 ....89 D1
  PONT/DH NE20 ....28 B4
Mayfair Rd JES NE2 ....63 F4
Mayfield WICK/BNPF NE16 ....96 A5
Mayfield Av BW/LEM/TK/HW NE15 ...58 A5
  CRAM NE23 ....22 B2
Mayfield Ct CLDN/WHIT/ROK SR6 ...126 C1
Mayfield Dr CLDN/WHIT/ROK SR6 ...108 A1
Mayfield Gdns
  BW/LEM/TK/HW * NE15 ....58 A5
  JRW NE32 ....85 F2
  WLSD/HOW NE28 ....66 B3
Mayfield Gv MLFD/PNYW SR4 ....141 F4
Mayfield PI DIN/WO NE13 ....32 C5
Mayfield Rd GOS/KPK NE3 ....63 D2
  MLFD/PNYW SR4 ....123 E6
Mayfield Ter WD/WHPE/BLK NE5 ......62 A5

May Gv CLDN/WHIT/ROK SR6 ....91 E5
May Lea BDN/LAN/SAC DH7 ....178 A3
Maynard's Rw DHAM DH1 ....195 E4
Mayo Dr SUNDSW SR3 ....160 A3
Mayoral Wy DUN/TMV NE11 ....116 C2
Mayorswell Cl DHAM DH1 ....194 C4
Mayorswell Fld DHAM * DH1 ....194 C4
Mayorswell St DHAM DH1 ....194 C4
Maypole Cl SWCK/CAS SR5 ....126 A3
May St BLAY NE21 ....94 A1
  CLS/BIR/GTL DH3 ....136 B1
  DHAM DH1 ....194 A5
  MLFD/PNYW SR4 ....126 A5
  SSH NE33 ....71 F5
Mayswood Rd
  CLDN/WHIT/ROK SR6 ....126 C1
Maythorne Dr RDHAMSE DH6 ....188 A6
Maywood Cl GOS/KPK NE3 ....62 A2
McAnany Av HAR/WTLS NE34 ....88 C3
McClaren Wy HLS DH4 ....158 B1
McCracken Cl GOS/KPK NE3 ....47 E4
McCracken Dr DIN/WO NE13 ....33 E3
McCutcheon Ct
  BYK/HTN/WLK NE6 ....83 D4
McErlane Sq FELL NE10 ....101 F1
McEwan Gdns ELS/FEN NE4 ....79 E3
McGuiness Av PLEE/EAS SR8 ....201 D5
McIntyre Rd HEBB NE31 ....85 E1
McKendrick Vls
  WD/WHPE/BLK NE5 ....61 F5
McNally Pl DHAM DH1 ....195 E4
McNamara Ct
  WLSD/HOW
  (off Mcnamara Rd) NE28 ....68 B3
McNamara Rd WLSD/HOW NE28 ....68 A3
Meacham Wy WICK/BNPF NE16.......95 F5
Mead Av LGB/KIL NE12 ....50 A4
Mead Crs LGB/KIL NE12 ....50 A4
Meadowbank CRAM NE23 ....34 C2
Meadowbrook Dr FELL NE10 ....102 B3
Meadow Cl BLAY NE21 ....93 E1
  CRAM NE23 ....25 E6
  HLH DH5 ....171 E3
  LGB/KIL* NE12 ....49 D6
  RYTON NE40 ....74 C3
Meadow Ct BDLGTN NE22 ....7 D3
  PONT/DH NE20 ....28 A5
Meadowdale Crs BDLGTN NE22 ....6 C3
  WD/WHPE/BLK NE5 ....61 F3
Meadow Dr CLSW/PEL DH2 ....152 B6
  DIN/WO NE13 ....33 E3
  SUNDSW SR3 ....159 D3
Meadowfield MONK NE25 ....39 F5
  PONT/DH NE20 ....28 A3
Meadowfield Av
  GOS/KPK NE3 ....46 C6
Meadowfield Dr
  CLDN/WHIT/ROK SR6 ....107 F1
Meadowfield Gdns
  BYK/HTN/WLK NE6 ....66 C5
Meadowfield Rd GOS/KPK NE3 ....63 D2
Meadowfield Wy STLY/ANP DH9 ....130 B6
Meadow Gdns SUNDSW SR3 ....144 A3
Meadow Gra HLS DH4 ....156 A6
Meadow Gv MLFD/PNYW SR4 ....141 F1
Meadow La DUN/TMV * NE11 ....97 E1
Meadow Laws HAR/WTLS NE34 ....89 F4
Meadow Ri LWF/SPW/WRK NE9 ....100 B5
  WD/WHPE/BLK NE5 ....61 D2
Meadow Rd BW/LEM/TK/HW NE15.......76 C1
  MONK NE25 ....39 F6
  WBAY NE26 ....26 A2
  WLSD/HOW NE28 ....68 B5
Meadowside ASHBK/HED/RY SR2 ....144 A2
Meadows La HLS DH4 ....170 A6
The Meadows GOS/KPK NE3 ....46 B6
  HLS DH4 ....156 A4
  HLS DH4 ....183 F1
  RYTON NE40 ....74 C3
  WICK/BNPF NE16 ....129 F2
Meadow St HLH DH5 ....170 B6
Meadowsweet Cl BLYTH NE24 ....16 B2
Meadow V ASHBK/HED/RY SR2 ....144 B2
Meadow Vw
  BOLCOL (off Foxhomes) NE35.......104 C3
  MONK NE25 ....24 C2
  STLY/ANP DH9 ....128 C5
  SUNDSW SR3 ....159 D3
Meadow Well Wy NSHW NE29 ....70 A2
Mead Wk BYK/HTN/WLK NE6 ....83 E2
Mead Wy LGB/KIL NE12 ....50 B4
Meadway Dr LGB/KIL NE12 ....50 B5
Means Dr CRAM NE23 ....35 D5
Medburn Av TYNE/NSHE NE30.......55 E2
Medburn Rd
  BW/LEM/TK/HW NE15 ....76 A1
  MONK NE25 ....25 D6
Medham Cl FELL NE10 ....101 D4
Medina Cl SUNDSW SR3 ....160 A3
Mediterranean Village
  WICK/BNPF
  (off Metrocentre) NE16 ....78 B6
Medlar Cl HLS DH4 ....156 B3
Medomsley Gdns
  LWF/SPW/WRK NE9 ....101 D6

Medomsly St MLFD/PNYW SR4 ....125 F5
Medway JRW NE32 ....86 B6
Medway Av HEBB NE31 ....85 D5
Medway Ct PLEE/EAS SR8 ....208 B4
Medway Crs GATE NE8 ....100 A2
Medway Gdns MLFD/PNYW SR4 ....142 C2
  TYNE/NSHE NE30 ....54 C5
Medway Pl CRAM NE23 ....14 B5
Megstone
  LWF/SPW/WRK
  (off Pimlico Ct) NE9 ....99 E6
Megstone Av CRAM NE23 ....21 F3
Megstone Ct LGB/KIL NE12 ....36 A6
Melbeck Dr CLSW/PEL DH2 ....135 D4
Melbourne Ct GATE * NE8 ....81 D5
Melbourne Crs MONK NE25 ....54 A1
Melbourne Gdns HAR/WTLS NE34 ....87 E5
Melbourne Pl MLFD/PNYW SR4 ....143 D2
Melbourne St CNUT NE1 ....3 F4
Melbury MONK NE25 ....39 E4
Melbury Ct CLDN/WHIT/ROK SR6 ....126 C1
Melbury Rd LGB/HTN NE7 ....64 C5
Melbury St SEA/MUR SR7 ....176 C5
Meldon Av GOS/KPK NE3 ....46 B5
  HAR/WTLS NE34 ....89 D2
  RDHAMSE DH6 ....197 F5
Meldon Gdns DUN/TMV NE11 ....97 F5
Meldon Rd MLFD/PNYW SR4 ....125 D5
Meldon St WLSD/HOW NE28 ....69 E5
Meldon Ter BYK/HTN/WLK NE6 ....65 D6
Meldon Wy BLAY NE21 ....93 E2
  STLY/ANP DH9 ....147 D4
Melgarve Dr SUNDSW SR3 ....160 A3
Melkington Ct WD/WHPE/BLK NE5.......61 D3
Melkridge Pl CRAM NE23 ....21 E3
Mellendean Ct WD/WHPE/BLK NE5.......61 D3
Melling Rd CRAM NE23 ....21 E3
Melmerby Cl GOS/KPK NE3 ....47 F5
Melness Rd DIN/WO NE13 ....32 C5
Melock Ct
  DIN/WO (off Melness Rd) NE13.......32 C5
Melrose WASHS NE38 ....138 C3
Melrose Av BDLGTN NE22 ....8 C3
  HEBB NE31 ....85 D5
  SEA/MUR SR7 ....187 F2
  SMOOR NE27 ....37 E5
  SMOOR NE27 ....37 E1
  TYNE/NSHE NE30 ....54 C2
Melrose Cl BW/LEM/TK/HW NE15 ....77 D2
  GOS/KPK NE3 ....47 D2
Melrose Ct BDLGTN NE22 ....8 C2
Melrose Crs SEA/MUR SR7 ....175 E2
Melrose Gdns
  CLDN/WHIT/ROK SR6 ....127 D1
  WLSD/HOW NE28 ....68 C3
Melrose Gv JRW NE32 ....87 D4
Melsonby Ct SUNDSW SR3.......159 F3
Meltham Ct WD/WHPE/BLK NE5 ....58 C4
Meltham Dr SUNDSW SR3 ....160 A3
Melton Av BYK/HTN/WLK NE6 ....83 E3
Melton Crs WBAY NE26 ....26 C3
Melton Dr MONK NE25 ....24 C2
Melvaig Cl SUNDSW SR3 ....160 A3
Melville Av BLYTH NE24 ....16 C1
Melville Gdns MONK NE25 ....39 E6
Melville Gv LGB/HTN NE7 ....64 C3
Melville St CLS/BIR/GTL DH3 ....153 E6
Melvin Pl WD/WHPE/BLK NE5 ....61 D4
Melvyn Gdns
  CLDN/WHIT/ROK SR6 ....127 D1
Membury Ct WLSD/HOW NE28 ....68 B3
Memorial Av SUNDSW SR3.......160 A3
Mendip Av CLSW/PEL DH2 ....153 D6
Mendip Cl PLEE/EAS SR8 ....208 A2
Mendip Dr WASHS NE38 ....138 A3
Mendip Gdns DUN/TMV NE11 ....98 A4
Mendip Ter STLY/ANP DH9 ....148 C3
Mendip Wy LGB/KIL NE12 ....48 B6
Menvill Pl SUND SR1 ....5 F3
Mercantile Rd HLS DH4 ....170 B3
Merchants Whf
  BYK/HTN/WLK * NE6 ....82 B4
Mercia Wy BW/LEM/TK/HW NE15 ....77 D3
Meredith Gdns GATE * NE8 ....99 E1
Mere Dr DHAM DH1 ....180 A5
Mere Knolls Rd
  CLDN/WHIT/ROK SR6 ....109 D5
Meresyde FELL NE10 ....101 F3
Merevale Cl WASHN NE37 ....121 D2
Merganser Ldg FELL * NE10 ....100 C2
Meridan Wy LGB/HTN NE7 ....65 F3
Merlay Dr DIN/WO NE13 ....31 D4
Merle Gdns BYK/HTN/WLK * NE6 ....82 B3
Merle Ter MLFD/PNYW SR4 ....125 E4
Merlin Cl FELL * NE10 ....100 C1
Merlin Crs WLSD/HOW NE28 ....68 B3
Merlin Dr CLS/BIR/GTL DH3 ....153 F1
Merlin Pl LGB/KIL NE12 ....48 C5
Merlin Wy SMOOR NE27 ....52 C3
Merrington Cl SUNDSW SR3 ....159 F3
Merrion Cl SUNDSW SR3 ....159 F2
Merryfield Gdns
  CLDN/WHIT/ROK SR6 ....127 D1
Mersey Pl GATE NE8 ....100 A1
Mersey Rd GATE NE8 ....100 A2

HEBB NE31 ....85 D5
Merton Ct ELS/FEN NE4 ....78 C4
Merton Rd BYK/HTN/WLK NE6 ....83 E4
  PONT/DH NE20 ....28 A4
Merton Sq BLYTH NE24 ....11 D4
Metcalfe Crs SEA/MUR SR7 ....188 A3
Methuen St LWF/SPW/WRK NE9 ....99 F2
Methven Wy CRAM NE23 ....14 B4
The Mews BLAY NE21 ....77 D6
  CNUT* NE1 ....2 C2
  FELL NE10 ....102 A2
  HLS DH4 ....169 F3
  SUNDSW SR3 ....159 D1
  TYNE/NSHE NE30 ....54 C6
Michaelgate BYK/HTN/WLK NE6 ....82 B2
Mickle Ct WASHN NE37 ....119 F6
Mickleton Cl CLS/BIR/GTL DH3 ....168 A3
Mickleton Gdns SUNDSW SR3 ....144 A4
Middle Cl WASHS NE38 ....138 A5
Middle Dr DIN/WO NE13 ....44 B3
Middle Engine La SMOOR NE27 ....52 C5
Middlefield CLSW/PEL DH2 ....152 A1
Middlegarth WD/WHPE/BLK NE5 ....61 F4
Middle Ga WD/WHPE/BLK NE5 ....59 F5
Middle Gn MONK NE25 ....39 E6
Middleham Ct CLSW/PEL DH2 ....135 C5
Middleham Ct SWCK/CAS SR5 ....125 D1
Middleham Rd DHAM 180 C5
Middles Rd STLY/ANP DH9 ....148 C5
Middle St BYK/HTN/WLK NE6 ....83 E2
  SUND* 4 B2
  TYNE/NSHE NE30 ....55 F5
Middle St East BYK/HTN/WLK NE6 ....83 F2
Middleton Av ELS/FEN NE4 ....79 D2
  ROWG NE39 ....111 E3
Middleton Cl SEA/MUR SR7 ....175 D1
Middleton St BLYTH NE24 ....11 D5
Middlewood Pk ELS/FEN NE4 ....62 A6
Midfield Dr CLDN/WHIT/ROK SR6.......127 D2
Midgley Dr SUNDSW SR5 ....160 A3
Midhill Cl BDN/LAN/SAC DH7 ....203 D3
Midhurst Av HAR/WTLS NE34 ....72 B6
Midhurst Cl SUNDSW SR3 ....159 F2
Midhurst Rd LGB/KIL NE12 ....49 F5
Midmoor Rd MLFD/PNYW SR4 ....125 D5
Midsomer Cl SUNDSW SR3 ....159 F3
Midway BYK/HTN/WLK NE6 ....83 E2
Milbanke Cl CLSW/PEL DH2 ....135 E5
Milbank Ter RDHAMSE DH6.......206 C3
Milburn Dr BW/LEM/TK/HW NE15.......78 A2
Milbank Ter RDHAMSE DH6.......206 C3
Mildmay Rd JES NE2 ....63 F4
Milecastle Ct WD/WHPE/BLK NE5 ....59 F4
Mile End Rd SSH NE33 ....71 F4
Milfield Av SMOOR NE27 ....52 B1
  WLSD/HOW NE28 ....67 E2
Milford Gdns GOS/KPK NE3 ....47 D3
Milford Rd BW/LEM/TK/HW NE15 ....78 B3
Military Rd TYNE/NSHE NE30 ....55 D6
Milk Market CNUT NE1 ....3 G4
Millais Gdns HAR/WTLS NE34 ....88 B6
Millbank
  SSH (off Station Rd) NE33 ....71 E4
Mill Bank SWCK/CAS SR5 ....108 C5
Millbank Pl BDLGTN NE22 ....8 A4
Millbank Rd BDLGTN NE22 ....8 A3
  BYK/HTN/WLK NE6 ....83 F4
Millbeck Gv HLH DH5 ....170 C4
Millbrook NSHW NE29 ....70 A1
Millbrook Rd CRAM NE23 ....14 B5
Millburngate DHAM DH1.......194 B5
Millburn St MLFD/PNYW SR4 ....125 A5
Mill Cl NSHW NE29 ....70 A1
Mill Ct HLS DH4 ....156 A6
Mill Crs HEBB NE31 ....84 B5
Milldale SEA/MUR SR7 ....175 E2
Milldale Av BLYTH NE24 ....9 F5
Mill Dam SSH NE33 ....71 D4
Mildene Av TYNE/NSHE NE30 ....55 E4
Mill Dene Vw JRW NE32 ....86 A3
Mill Dyke Cl MONK NE25 ....39 E4
Millenium Wy SWCK/CAS SR5 ....126 B4
Miller Gdns CLSW/PEL DH2 ....151 F4
Millers Dene
  (off Shields Rd) NE6 ....66 B6
Millers Hl HLS DH4 ....157 E2
Miller's La WICK/BNPF NE16 ....96 A1
Millers Rd BYK/HTN/WLK NE6 ....82 B1
Miller St GATE NE8 ....98 C2
Miller Ter SUNDSW SR3 ....143 F6
Millfield BDLGTN NE22 ....7 F5
  WBAY NE26 ....26 C3
Millfield Av GOS/KPK NE3 ....62 A3
Millfield Cl BW/LEM/TK/HW NE15 ....58 B6
  CLSW/PEL DH2.......165 F1
Millfield Ct BDLGTN NE22 ....7 F4
Millfield East BDLGTN NE22 ....7 F4
Millfield Gdns BLYTH NE24 ....10 C3
  FELL NE10.......100 B2
  TYNE/NSHE NE30 ....55 E4
Millfield Gv TYNE/NSHE NE30.......55 E4
Millfield La BW/LEM/TK/HW NE15.......58 B6
Millfield North BDLGTN NE22 ....7 F4
Millfield Rd WICK/BNPF NE16.......96 A4
Millfield South BDLGTN NE22 ....7 F5

Millfield West *BDLGTN* NE22................7 F4
Millford *FELL* NE10.............................101 F5
Mill Gv *HAR/WTLS* NE34.....................90 A4
  TYNE/NSHE NE30.............................55 E4
Millgrove Vw *GOS/KPK* NE3................62 B3
Mill Hl *HLH* DH5...............................170 C4
  PLEE/EAS SR8...............................199 E6
Mill Hill Rd *SUNDSW* SR3..................160 B2
  WD/WHPE/BLK NE5..........................60 B6
Mill House Ct *DHAM* DH1..................195 F4
Milling Ct *GATE* NE8...........................80 B6
Mill La *BLAY* NE21.............................94 A3
  BW/LEM/TK/HW NE15.........................56 B3
  CLDN/WHIT/ROK SR6.........................91 E5
  CLSW/PEL DH2................................166 A6
  CRAM NE23.....................................35 E1
  DHAM DH1....................................195 F3
  ELS/FEN NE4....................................79 F3
  HEBB NE31......................................84 C6
  NSHW NE29.....................................71 D2
  RDHAMSE DH6...............................197 E5
  STLY/ANP DH9...............................134 C4
Milne Ct *BDLGTN* NE22.........................7 E3
Millom Ct *PLEE/EAS* SR8....................207 F5
Millom Pl *LWF/SPW/WRK* NE9............100 A5
Mill Pit *HLS* DH4..............................157 D2
Mill Ri *GOS/KPK* NE3..........................64 A2
Mill Rd *BDN/LAN/SAC* DH7................204 A3
  GATE NE8..3 H6
  SEA/MUR SR7.................................175 E2
Mills Gdns *WLSD/HOW* NE28................67 D3
Mill St *MLFD/PNYW* SR4....................126 A6
Millthorp Cl *ASHBK/HED/RY* SR2........145 E5
Mill Vw *BOL* NE36............................105 F3
  FELL NE10......................................100 B1
Mill View Av *CLDN/WHIT/ROK* SR6....126 C1
Millview Dr *TYNE/NSHE* NE30..............55 E4
Millway *LWF/SPW/WRK* NE9................99 F3
  WBAY NE26.....................................26 C3
Milner Crs *BLAY* NE21.........................93 F1
Milner St *SSH* NE33.............................72 A4
Milne Wy *GOS/KPK* NE3......................46 B6
Milrig Cl *SUNDSW* SR3......................160 A3
Milsted Cl *SUNDSW* SR3.....................159 F3
Milsted Ct *WD/WHPE/BLK* NE5............58 C4
Milton Av *HEBB* NE31..........................85 D2
  HLH DH5......................................171 D3
Milton Cl *JES* NE2..............................81 E1
  SEA/MUR SR7................................176 A3
  STLY/ANP DH9..............................149 D2
Milton Gn *JES* NE2.............................81 E1
Milton Gv *NSHW* NE29........................54 B6
  RDHAMSE DH6..............................206 C2
Milton Pl *JES* NE2...............................81 E1
  LWF/SPW/WRK NE9........................119 D3
  NSHW NE29....................................54 B6
Milton Rd *WICK/BNPF* NE16................96 A2
Milton Sq *GATE* NE8............................81 E6
Milton St *JRW* NE32 *..........................69 D6
  MLFD/PNYW SR4...........................125 F5
  SSH NE33.......................................71 F5
Milton Ter *NSHW* NE29.......................54 B6
Milvain Av *ELS/FEN* NE4.....................79 E1
Milvain Cl *GATE* NE8...........................99 E1
Milvain St *GATE* NE8...........................99 E1
Milverton Ct *GOS/KPK* NE3..................45 E6
Mimosa Dr *HEBB* NE31.........................85 D2
Mimosa Pl *ELS/FEN* NE4.......................61 F6
Mindrum Ter *BYK/HTN/WLK* NE6..........83 E4
  NSHW NE29.....................................69 F2
Mindrum Wy *MONK* NE25......................24 C5
Minehead Gdns *SUNDSW* SR3.............143 F6
Minerva Cl *WD/WHPE/BLK* NE5............59 E2
Mingary Cl *HLH* DH5.........................170 B6
Minorca Cl *SUND* SR1............................5 F4
Minorca Pl *GOS/KPK* NE3.....................62 B3
Minskip Cl *SUNDSW* SR3....................159 F3
Minster Ct *GATE* NE8..........................81 E5
Minster Gv *WD/WHPE/BLK* NE5............59 D1
Minster Pde *JRW* NE32.........................86 B1
Minting Pl *CRAM* NE23........................21 E2
Minton Ct *NSHW* NE29.........................70 B2
Minton La *NSHW* NE29.........................70 B2
Minton Sq *MLFD/PNYW* SR4...............125 D5
Mirk La *GATE* NE8.................................5 F6
Mirlaw Rd *CRAM* NE23.........................21 F1
Mistletoe Rd *JES* NE2..........................64 A5
Mistletoe St *DHAM* DH1.....................194 A5
Mitcham Crs *LGB/HTN* NE7..................65 D3
Mitchell Av *JES* NE2............................64 A4
  MONK NE25....................................39 F6
Mitchell Cl *PLEE/EAS* SR8..................200 A6
Mitchell Gdns *HAR/WTLS* NE34............89 E1
Mitchell St *BYK/HTN/WLK* NE6............84 A3
  DHAM DH1....................................194 A4
  STLY/ANP DH9...............................147 F4
Mitford Av *BLYTH* NE24.......................10 B6
  MONK NE25....................................24 B5
Mitford Cl *WASHS* NE38......................138 A2
Mitford Ct *PLEE/EAS* SR8....................208 C4
Mitford Dr *RDHAMSE* DH6...................197 F4
  WD/WHPE/BLK NE5...........................60 A3
Mitford Gdns *DUN/TMV* NE11..............97 F5
  WLSD/HOW NE28...............................68 B1
Mitford Pl *GOS/KPK* NE3......................46 C6

Mitford Rd *HAR/WTLS* NE34................89 D2
Mitford St *CLDN/WHIT/ROK* SR6.........109 D6
  WLSD/HOW NE28.............................69 E4
Mitford Ter *JRW* NE32..........................86 A6
Mithra Wy *DIN/WO* NE13......................31 D4
Mithras Gdns
  BW/LEM/TK/HW NE15.........................56 A4
Mitre Pl *SSH* NE33...............................71 D6
Moat Gdns *FELL* NE10........................102 B2
Moatside Ms
  DHAM (off Saddler St) DH1................194 B5
Modder St *BYK/HTN/WLK* NE6..............83 E5
Moffat Av *JRW* NE32............................87 D4
Moffat Cl *NSHW* NE29..........................53 E4
Moffatt Vls
  SSH (off Imeary St) NE33....................71 F5
Moine Gdns *CLDN/WHIT/ROK* SR6.......127 D1
Molineux Cl *BYK/HTN/WLK* NE6............82 A2
Molineux Ct *BYK/HTN/WLK* NE6............82 A2
Molineux St *BYK/HTN/WLK* NE6............82 A2
Monarch Rd *ELS/FEN* NE4....................79 F5
Monarch Wy *SUNDSW* SR3..................159 E5
Mona St *STLY/ANP* DH9......................148 B1
Moncreiff Ter *PLEE/EAS* SR8................200 B2
Monday Crs *ELS/FEN* NE4.....................80 A2
Monday St *ELS/FEN* NE4......................80 A2
Money Slack *DHAM* DH1.....................205 D3
Monkchester Gn
  BYK/HTN/WLK NE6...........................83 D3
Monkchester Rd
  BYK/HTN/WLK NE6...........................83 D3
Monk Ct *GATE* NE8..............................81 E6
  PLEE/EAS SR8................................208 A5
Monkdale Av *BLYTH* NE24......................9 F6
Monkhouse Av *TYNE/NSHE* NE30..........54 C3
Monkridge *WBAY* NE26.........................40 A3
  WD/WHPE/BLK NE5...........................59 D6
Monkridge Gdns *DUN/TMV* NE11..........97 E3
Monks Av *MONK* NE25..........................53 F1
Monks' Crs *DHAM* DH1.......................195 E3
Monkseaton Dr *MONK* NE25..................39 E5
Monkseaton Rd *MONK* NE25..................39 D5
Monksfeld *FELL* NE10..........................101 D3
Monksfield Cl *SUNDSW* SR3................160 B3
Monkside
  BYK/HTN/WLK
  (off Rothbury Ter) NE6...........................65 F5
Monkside Cl *WASHS* NE38...................137 F4
Monks Park Wy *LGB/KIL* NE12.............48 C6
Monks Rd *MONK* NE25...........................53 E1
Monkstone Av *TYNE/NSHE* NE30...........55 E4
Monkstone Crs *TYNE/NSHE* NE30...........55 E4
Monk St *CLDN/WHIT/ROK* SR6.............126 C3
Monksway *JRW* NE32.............................87 D2
Monks Wy *TYNE/NSHE* NE30..................55 E3
Monks Wd *NSHW* NE29..........................54 A4
Monkswood Sq *SUNDSW* SR3..............161 D2
Monkton *FELL* NE10.............................101 E4
Monkton Av *HAR/WTLS* NE34................87 E4
Monkton La *HEBB* NE31.........................85 D6
  JRW NE32.......................................85 E4
Monkton Rd *JRW* NE32..........................86 A1
Monkton Ter *JRW* NE32.........................86 A2
Monmouth Gdns
  WLSD/HOW NE28.............................68 C2
Monroe Pl *WD/WHPE/BLK* NE5.............61 F4
Mons Av *HEBB* NE31.............................85 D3
Montagu Av *GOS/KPK* NE3....................62 C4
Montagu Ct *GOS/KPK* NE3.....................62 C4
Montague Ct
  LWF/SPW/WRK
  (off Lindum Rd) NE9.............................99 E2
Montague St
  BW/LEM/TK/HW NE15.........................76 C2
  CLDN/WHIT/ROK SR6.......................126 C1
Monterey *SUNDSW* SR3.......................160 A3
  WASHN NE37.................................120 C3
Montfalcon Cl *PLEE/EAS* SR8...............208 B2
Montford Cl *SUNDSW* * SR3.................159 F3
Montgomery Rd *DHAM* DH1.................195 E3
Montpellier Pl *GOS/KPK* NE3.................62 B3
Montpellier Ter
  ASHBK/HED/RY SR2.........................145 D2
Montrose Cl *MONK* NE25.......................24 C2
Montrose Crs
  LWF/SPW/WRK NE9.........................100 A3
Montrose Dr *FELL* NE10.......................102 B3
Montrose Gdns *SUNDSW* SR3..............143 F3
Monument Ml *CNUT* NE1.........................2 D3
Monument Vw
  BDN/LAN/SAC (off Brookside) DH7...164 B6
  HLS DH4..139 F6
Moor Cl *NSHW* NE29.............................53 E4
  SUND SR1...5 G2
Moor Ct *CLDN/WHIT/ROK* SR6.............109 D2
  JES (off Westfield) NE2........................63 D4
Moor Crs *DHAM* DH1...........................195 F3
  GOS/KPK NE3..................................63 E3
Moor Crest Ter *NSHW* * NE29................54 B4
Moorcroft Cl
  BW/LEM/TK/HW NE15.........................76 C1
Moorcroft Rd
  BW/LEM/TK/HW NE15.........................77 D1
Moordale Av *BLYTH* NE24.......................9 F6

Moore Av *DUN/TMV* * NE11.................97 E2
  HAR/WTLS NE34..............................89 D2
Moore Crs South *HLH* DH5..................171 D3
Moor Edge *BDN/LAN/SAC* DH7.............203 D5
Moor Edge Rd *SMOOR* NE27..................38 A6
Moor End
  GOS/KPK (off High St) NE3................63 E3
Moore St *GATE* NE8..............................99 F1
  STLY/ANP DH9...............................148 A3
Moore Street Vls *GATE* NE8..................99 F1
Moorfield *JES* NE2...............................63 F3
Moorfield Gdns
  CLDN/WHIT/ROK SR6.......................107 F2
Moorfoot Av *CLSW/PEL* DH2.................153 E6
Moorfoot Gdns *DUN/TMV* NE11............97 F3
Moorhead *WD/WHPE/BLK* NE5..............62 A5
Moorhill *DUN/TMV* NE11.....................116 B6
Moorhouse Cl *HAR/WTLS* * NE34..........88 C3
Moorhouses Rd *NSHW* NE29..................53 E4
The Moorings *BYK/HTN/WLK* * NE6.......82 B4
Moorland Av *BDLGTN* NE22.....................9 D1
Moorland Ct *BDLGTN* NE22......................9 D1
Moorland Crs *BDLGTN* NE22....................9 D1
  BYK/HTN/WLK NE6...........................83 D1
Moorland Dr *BDLGTN* NE22.....................9 D2
Moorlands *DHAM* DH1.........................195 F4
  JRW NE32......................................104 C1
The Moorlands *STLY/ANP* DH9.............129 D5
Moorland Vls *BDLGTN* NE22.....................9 D1
Moorland Wy *CRAM* NE23.....................13 D5
Moor La *BOL* NE36..............................107 D2
  CLDN/WHIT/ROK SR6.......................108 B2
  HAR/WTLS NE34..............................89 D2
  WD/WHPE/BLK NE5...........................61 F2
Moor La East *HAR/WTLS* NE34..............89 E2
Moormill La *DUN/TMV* NE11................117 D6
Moor Park Ct *NSHW* NE29.....................53 E5
Moor Park Rd *NSHW* NE29.....................53 D5
Moor Pl *GOS/KPK* NE3..........................63 E3
Moor Rd North *GOS/KPK* NE3................63 F2
Moor Rd South *JES* NE2.........................63 F3
Moorsburn Dr *HLS* DH4.......................170 B1
Moors Cl *HLS* DH4..............................170 A2
Moorsfield *HLS* DH4............................170 A2
Moorside
  LGB/KIL (off Great Lime Rd) NE12.......49 D2
  WASHN NE37..................................120 A5
Moorside North *ELS/FEN* NE4................62 A5
Moorside Rd *SUNDSW* SR3...................159 F3
Moorside South *ELS/FEN* NE4................79 E1
Moorsley Rd *HLH* DH5.........................184 B4
Moor St *SUND* SR1.................................5 F2
Moor Ter *SUND* SR1...............................5 G3
Moorvale La *WD/WHPE/BLK* NE5..........62 A4
Moor Vw *CLDN/WHIT/ROK* SR6.............109 D2
  LGB/KIL NE12.................................35 E6
Moorview Crs *WD/WHPE/BLK* NE5........62 A4
Moor View Ter *STLY/ANP* DH9..............146 A5
Moorway *WASHN* NE37.........................120 A6
Moorway Dr
  BW/LEM/TK/HW NE15.........................77 D1
Moralee Cl *LGB/HTN* NE7......................65 F3
Moran St *CLDN/WHIT/ROK* SR6............108 C6
Moray Cl *CLS/BIR/GTL* DH3..................136 C5
  PLEE/EAS SR8................................208 B3
Moray St *CLDN/WHIT/ROK* SR6............126 C2
Morcott Gdns *NSHW* NE29.....................70 A2
Morden St *CNUT* NE1..............................2 C2
Mordey Cl *ASHBK/HED/RY* SR2................5 F1
Moreland Rd *HAR/WTLS* NE34...............88 C5
Moreland St *CLDN/WHIT/ROK* SR6.......126 C2
Morgan St *SWCK/CAS* SR5...................126 A2
Morgans Wy *BLAY* NE21........................75 F6
Morland Av *WASHS* NE38.....................139 D3
Morland Gdns
  LWF/SPW/WRK NE9.........................100 A3
Morley Ct *BYK/HTN/WLK* NE6................82 B1
Morley Hill Rd *WD/WHPE/BLK* NE5........60 B6
Morley Ter *FELL* NE10..........................100 B2
  HLS DH4.......................................169 F2
Morningside *BDN/LAN/SAC* DH7...........164 B6
  WASHS NE38..................................137 D6
Mornington Av *GOS/KPK* NE3................62 B3
Morpeth Av *DIN/WO* NE13.....................33 E3
  HAR/WTLS NE34..............................89 D1
  JRW NE32.......................................86 A3
Morpeth Cl *WASHS* NE38......................137 F2
Morpeth Dr *SUNDSW* SR3....................159 F2
Morpeth St *JES* NE2.............................63 D6
  PLEE/EAS SR8................................201 E6
Morpeth Ter *NSHW* NE29.......................69 F2
Morris Av *HAR/WTLS* NE34...................88 A5
Morris Crs *BOLCOL* NE35.....................105 F2
Morris Gdns *FELL* NE10.......................102 A2
Morrison St *GATE* NE8...........................80 B6
Morris Rd *WICK/BNPF* NE16..................96 A2
Morris St *CLS/BIR/GTL* DH3..................136 A2
Morston Dr *BW/LEM/TK/HW* NE15.........77 D2
Mortimer Av *NSHW* NE29......................53 F6
  WD/WHPE/BLK NE5...........................60 C3
Mortimer Cha *CRAM* NE23.....................14 A3
Mortimer Rd *HAR/WTLS* NE34...............89 D1
  SSH NE33.......................................71 F6
Mortimer St *MLFD/PNYW* SR4.............125 E5
Morton Cl *WASHS* NE38.......................138 C2

Morton Sq *PLEE/EAS* SR8 ....208 B1
Morton St *BYK/HTN/WLK* NE6 ......82 C2
SSH* NE33 ....71 E2
Morton Wk *SSH* NE33 ....71 E2
Morval Cl *SUNDSW* SR3 ....159 F3
Morven Dr *FELL* NE10 ....102 A1
Morwick Cl *CRAM* NE23 ....21 E3
Morwick Pl *WD/WHPE/BLK* NE5 .....61 F3
Morwick Rd *NSHW* NE29 ....53 F4
Mosley St *CNUT* NE1 ....2 D4
Moss Bank *LWF/SPW/WRK* NE9 .....118 A1
Moss Cl *BW/LEM/TK/HW* NE15 ......59 E6
Mossdale *DHAM* DH1 ....196 C2
Moss Side *LWF/SPW/WRK* NE9 .....118 A1
Mossway *CLSW/PEL* DH2 ....151 F1
Motcombe Wy *CRAM* NE23 ....14 B4
Moulton Pl *WD/WHPE/BLK* NE5 .....61 E6
Mountbatten Av *HEBB* NE31 ....85 D4
Mount Cl *LGB/KIL* NE12 ....35 F6
MLFD/PNYW SR4 ....124 A6
MONK NE25 ....53 F1
Mountfield Gdns *GOS/KPK* NE3 ......52 A2
Mountford Rd *MONK* NE25 ....24 C1
Mount Gv *DUN/TMV* NE11 ....97 F3
MLFD/PNYW SR4 ....143 F2
Mount Joy Crs *DHAM* DH1 ....194 C6
Mount La *LWF/SPW/WRK* NE9 ......119 D4
Mount Pleasant *BLAY* * NE21 ....94 A1
CLS/BIR/GTL DH3 ....136 B1
HLH DH5 ....171 E2
STLY/ANP DH9 ....129 D5
SWCK/CAS SR5 ....125 F3
Mount Pleasant Ct
BW/LEM/TK/HW NE15 ....57 F4
Mount Pleasant Gdns *GATE* NE8 .....99 F1
Mount Rd *CLS/BIR/GTL* DH3 ....136 C1
LWF/SPW/WRK NE9 ....119 D4
MLFD/PNYW SR4 ....143 E2
Mountside Gdns *DUN/TMV* NE11 .....97 E5
Mount Stewart St *SEA/MUR* SR7 ...176 C5
Mount Ter *SSH* NE33 ....71 E4
The Mount *BW/LEM/TK/HW* NE15 ...57 F4
RYTON NE40 ....74 B3
Mount Vw *WICK/BNPF* NE16 ....96 A2
Mourne Gdns *DUN/TMV* NE11 ....97 F4
Moutter Cl *PLEE/EAS* SR8 ....201 D6
Mowbray Cl *ASHBK/HED/RY* SR2 ......4 D6
Mowbray Rd *ASHBK/HED/RY* SR2 ....5 E6
LGB/KIL NE12 ....49 F4
NSHW NE29 ....53 F6
SSH NE33 ....71 E5
Mowbray St *BYK/HTN/WLK* NE6 ......81 F2
DHAM DH1 ....194 A4
Mowlam Dr *STLY/ANP* DH9 ....148 C5
Mozart St *SSH* NE33 ....71 F4
Muirfield *MONK* NE25 ....39 F5
SSH NE33 ....72 B5
Muirfield Dr *FELL* NE10 ....100 C4
WASHN NE37 ....120 B2
Muirfield Rd *LGB/HTN* NE7 ....65 E1
Mulben Cl *ELS/FEN* NE4 ....79 D4
Mulberry Gdns *FELL* NE10 ....82 B6
Mulberry Gv *WICK/BNPF* NE16 .....129 F2
Mulberry Pl *ELS/FEN* NE4 ....80 A5
Mulberry St *FELL* NE10 ....100 B1
Mulcaster Gdns *WLSD/HOW* NE28 ..66 C3
Mulgrave Dr
CLDN/WHIT/ROK SR6 ....127 D4
Mulgrave Ter *GATE* NE8 ....81 D5
Mulgrave Vls *GATE* NE8 ....81 D5
Mullen Dr *RYTON* NE40 ....74 B4
Mullen Gdns *WLSD/HOW* NE28 ......66 C2
Mullen Rd *WLSD/HOW* NE28 ....66 C2
Mull Gv *JRW* NE32 ....87 D5
Muncaster Ms *PLEE/EAS* SR8 ......207 F1
Mundella Ter *BYK/HTN/WLK* NE6 ....82 A1
Mundell St *STLY/ANP* DH9 ....147 F4
Mundle Av *BLAY* NE21 ....94 B4
Mundles La *BOL* NE36 ....106 B3
Munslow Rd *SUNDSW* SR3 ....142 B6
Muriel St *STLY/ANP* DH9 ....148 A5
Murphy Gv *ASHBK/HED/RY* SR2 ....162 A1
Murray Av *HLS* DH4 ....169 F1
Murrayfield *CRAM* NE23 ....23 E6
Murrayfield Dr
BDN/LAN/SAC DH7 ....202 C5
Murrayfield Rd
BDN/LAN/SAC DH7 ....61 F3
Murrayfields *SMOOR* NE27 ....71 F3
Murray Gdns *DUN/TMV* NE11 ....97 F3
Murray Rd *CLSW/PEL* DH2 ....153 D5
WLSD/HOW NE28 ....68 D3
Murray St *BLAY* NE21 ....76 B5
PLEE/EAS SR8 ....209 F3
Murston Av *CRAM* NE23 ....14 B4
Murton La *HLH* DH5 ....186 C3
NSHW NE29 ....53 E4
Murton St *SUND* SR1 ....5 E4
Muscott Gv *BW/LEM/TK/HW* NE15 ..77 F2
Musgrave Gdns *DHAM* DH1 ....195 F4
Musgrave Rd *LWF/SPW/WRK* NE9 ..96 A2
Musgrave Ter *BYK/HTN/WLK* NE6 ...83 D2
Muswell Hl *BW/LEM/TK/HW* NE15 ...77 F3
Mutual St *WLSD/HOW* NE28 ....67 D4
Mylord Crs *LGB/KIL* NE12 ....35 D5

Myrella Crs *ASHBK/HED/RY* SR2 ...144 B4
Myreside Pl *LGB/KIL* NE12 ....49 D5
Myrtle Av *CLDN/WHIT/ROK* SR6 ....109 E1
DUN/TMV NE11 ....97 E3
Myrtle Crs *LGB/KIL* NE12 ....49 F3
Myrtle Gv *HAR/WTLS* NE34 ....89 E4
JES NE2 ....64 A4
LWF/SPW/WRK NE9 ....99 E6
SUNDSW SR3 ....161 D1
WLSD/HOW NE28 ....67 F5
Myrtle Rd *BLAY* NE21 ....94 B1
Myrtles *CLSW/PEL* DH2 ....153 D3

N

Nafferton Pl *WD/WHPE/BLK* NE5 ....61 E6
Nailsworth Cl *BOLCOL* NE35 ....87 D6
Nairn Cl *CLS/BIR/GTL* DH3 ....136 C4
WASHN NE37 ....120 B2
Nairn Rd *CRAM* NE23 ....22 A1
Nairn St *JRW* NE32 ....87 D5
Naisbitt Av *PLEE/EAS* SR8 ....201 D6
Nansen Cl *WD/WHPE/BLK* * NE5 .....60 B4
Napier Rd *SEA/MUR* SR7 ....175 F2
WICK/BNPF NE16 ....95 F1
Napier St *HAR/WTLS* NE34 ....88 A2
JES NE2 ....3 C1
JRW NE32 ....86 A1
Napier Wy *NSHW* NE29 ....77 D6
Narvik Wy *NSHW* NE29 ....69 D1
Nash Av *HAR/WTLS* NE34 ....88 C5
Naters St *WBAY* NE26 ....41 E6
Natley Av *BOL* NE36 ....107 D5
Navenby Cl *GOS/KPK* NE3 ....47 F4
Naworth Av *TYNE/NSHE* NE30 ....54 C3
Naworth Ct *PLEE/EAS* SR8 ....208 A5
Naworth Dr *WD/WHPE/BLK* NE5 ....60 A3
Naworth Ter *JRW* NE32 ....86 C2
Nawton Av *SWCK/CAS* SR5 ....126 B2
Nayland Rd *CRAM* NE23 ....21 F1
Naylor Av *BLAY* NE21 ....94 C4
Naylor Pl *WBAY* NE26 ....26 C1
Neale St *CLDN/WHIT/ROK* SR6 .....126 C1
Nearlane Cl *DIN/WO* NE13 ....33 E2
Neasdon Crs *TYNE/NSHE* NE30 .....55 D3
Neasham Rd *SEA/MUR* SR7 ....175 F1
Nedderton Cl *WD/WHPE/BLK* NE5 ..59 D2
Needham Pl *CRAM* NE23 ....22 A1
Neill Dr *WICK/BNPF* NE16 ....114 A2
Neilson Rd *FELL* NE10 ....82 A5
Neil St *HLH* DH5 ....186 B3
Nelson Av *CRAM* NE23 ....13 D6
GOS/KPK NE3 ....62 C1
SSH NE33 ....72 A3
Nelson Cl *ASHBK/HED/RY* SR2 ....5 E5
PLEE/EAS SR8 ....201 F6
Nelson Crs *NSHW* NE29 ....69 F3
Nelson Dr *CRAM* NE23 ....13 D6
Nelson Rd *BYK/HTN/WLK* NE6 ....84 A4
CRAM NE23 ....13 D5
MONK NE25 ....39 D5
Nelson St *ASHBK/HED/RY* SR2 .....162 B1
CLS/BIR/GTL DH3 ....153 E6
CNUT NE1 ....2 C3
DUN/TMV NE11 ....97 E1
GATE NE8 ....81 E5
HLH DH5 ....185 F1
SEA/MUR SR7 ....176 A2
SSH NE33 ....71 E3
WASHS NE38 ....139 D2
Nelson Ter *NSHW* NE29 ....69 F3
Nelson Wy *CRAM* NE23 ....12 C4
Nenthead Cl *CLS/BIR/GTL* DH3 .....168 A3
Neptune Rd *BW/LEM/TK/HW* NE15 ..76 C2
WLSD/HOW NE28 ....67 D6
Nesbit Rd *PLEE/EAS* SR8 ....209 D3
Nesburn Rd *MLFD/PNYW* SR4 ......143 F2
Nesham Pl *HLH* DH5 ....171 D2
Nesham Ter *SUND* * SR1 ....5 C1
Ness Ct *BLAY* NE21 ....82 C6
Nest Rd *FELL* NE10 ....82 C6
Netherburn Rd *SWCK/CAS* SR5 ....126 B2
Netherby Dr *WD/WHPE/BLK* NE5 ...61 E6
Netherdale *BDLGTN* NE22 ....6 C3
Nether Farm Rd *FELL* NE10 ....101 E1
Nether Riggs *BDLGTN* NE22 ....7 E4
Netherton Cl *LGB/KIL* NE12 ....35 E5
Netherton Av *NSHW* NE29 ....53 F5
Netherton Cl *CLSW/PEL* DH2 ....152 B6
Netherton Gdns *DIN/WO* NE13 ....33 D4
Netherton Gv *NSHW* NE29 ....53 F5
Netherton La *BDLGTN* NE22 ....6 B1
Netherwitton Rd *SWCK/CAS* SR5 ...126 B2
Nettles La *SUNDSW* SR3 ....161 D2
Nevilledale Ter *DHAM* * DH1 ....194 A5
Neville Dene *DHAM* DH1 ....193 E5
Neville Rd *BW/LEM/TK/HW* NE15 ...76 C1
MLFD/PNYW SR4 ....125 E5
PLEE/EAS SR8 ....208 B1
Neville's Cross Bank *DHAM* DH1 ...193 E6
Neville's Cross Rd *HEBB* NE31 ....85 E3
Neville Sq *DHAM* DH1 ....204 C1

Neville St *CNUT* NE1 ....2 B5
DHAM DH1 ....194 B5
Nevinson Av *HAR/WTLS* NE34 ....5 C5
Nevis Cl *WBAY* NE26 ....39 F2
Nevis Gv *BOL* NE36 ....106 A3
Newacres Rd *STLY/ANP* DH9 ....148 A6
Newark Cl *PLEE/EAS* SR8 ....208 B1
Newark Crs *SEA/MUR* SR7 ....175 F2
Newark Dr *CLDN/WHIT/ROK* SR6 ..109 E2
Newark Sq *NSHW* NE29 ....70 B2
Newarth Cl *BW/LEM/TK/HW* NE15 ..76 C1
Newbiggin La
WD/WHPE/BLK * NE5 ....60 B3
Newbold Av *SWCK/CAS* SR5 ....126 B2
Newbold St *BYK/HTN/WLK* NE6 ......82 C3
Newbolt Ct *GATE* NE8 ....81 F6
Newbottle La *HLS* DH4 ....169 E3
Newbottle St *HLS* DH4 ....157 F6
Newbridge Av *SWCK/CAS* SR5 ......126 B2
Newbridge Bank
CLS/BIR/GTL DH3 ....154 A3
Newbridge Banks *CLSW/PEL* DH2 .150 C4
New Bridge St *CNUT* NE1 ....3 F2
New Bridge St West *CNUT* * NE1 ......3 E2
Newbrough Crs *JES* NE2 ....64 A4
Newburgh Av *MONK* NE25 ....24 B6
Newburn Av *SWCK/CAS* SR5 ....126 B2
Newburn Bridge Rd *BLAY* NE21 ......75 D2
Newburn Ct *SSH* NE33 ....71 F5
Newburn Crs *HLS* DH4 ....170 C1
Newburn Rd
BW/LEM/TK/HW NE15 ....58 A5
STLY/ANP DH9 ....131 F6
Newbury *LGB/KIL* NE12 ....35 F6
Newbury Av *GATE* NE8 ....98 C2
Newbury Cl *BW/LEM/TK/HW* NE15 ..76 C1
Newbury St *SSH* NE33 ....88 C1
SWCK/CAS SR5 ....126 B1
Newby Cl *BDLGTN* NE22 ....8 B1
Newby Pl *LWF/SPW/WRK* NE9 ......100 A6
Newcastle Av *PLEE/EAS* SR8 ....201 E6
Newcastle Bank
CLS/BIR/GTL DH3 ....118 A5
Newcastle Rd *BLYTH* NE24 ....16 B2
BOL NE36 ....103 F3
CLS/BIR/GTL DH3 ....118 B6
CLS/BIR/GTL DH3 ....153 E3
DHAM DH1 ....193 E5
HAR/WTLS NE34 ....87 E3
SWCK/CAS SR5 ....107 F5
Newcastle St *NSHW* NE29 ....70 C1
New Dr *SEA/MUR* SR7 ....176 A1
New Durham Rd
ASHBK/HED/RY SR2 ....126 A6
STLY/ANP DH9 ....146 C5
New Elvet *DHAM* DH1 ....194 C5
Newfield Wk *WICK/BNPF* * NE16 .....96 A4
New Front *STLY/ANP* DH9 ....146 B4
New Front St *STLY/ANP* DH9 ....130 C5
Newgate Ml
CNUT (off Eldon Sq) NE1 ....2 C3
Newgate St *CNUT* NE1 ....2 C3
New George St *SSH* NE33 ....71 E6
New Grange Ter *CLSW/PEL* DH2 ...151 F4
New Green St *SSH* NE33 ....71 E5
Newham Av *DIN/WO* NE13 ....32 C6
Newhaven Av *SWCK/CAS* SR5 ......126 B2
Newington Ct *SWCK/CAS* SR5 ......126 B2
Newington Rd *BYK/HTN/WLK* NE6 ..81 F2
JES NE2 ....81 E1
Newland Ct *HAR/WTLS* NE34 ....88 B3
Newlands Av *BLYTH* NE24 ....16 C1
GOS/KPK NE3 ....47 E3
MONK NE25 ....53 F1
SUNDSW SR3 ....144 A3
Newlands Pl *BLYTH* NE24 ....16 C1
Newlands Rd *BLYTH* NE24 ....16 C1
DHAM DH1 ....196 B2
JES NE2 ....63 F3
Newlands Rd East *SEA/MUR* SR7 ..176 A2
Newlands Rd West *SEA/MUR* SR7 .175 F1
Newlyn Crs *NSHW* NE29 ....70 A1
Newlyn Dr *CRAM* NE23 ....10 A6
JRW NE32 ....86 C2
Newlyn Rd *GOS/KPK* NE3 ....62 A1
Newman Pl *GATE* NE8 ....99 F2
Newman Ter *GATE* NE8 ....99 F2
Newmarch St *JRW* NE32 ....85 F1
Newmarket Wk *SSH* NE33 ....71 F4
New Mills *ELS/FEN* NE4 ....80 A1
Newminster Cl *HLS* DH4 ....157 D6
Newport Gv *SUNDSW* SR3 ....143 F6
New Quay *NSHW* NE29 ....71 D2
Newquay Gdns
LWF/SPW/WRK NE9 ....117 E2
Newriggs *WASHS* NE38 ....139 D4
New Rd *BOLCOL* NE35 ....105 F2
DUN/TMV NE11 ....98 A4
FELL NE10 ....102 B5
STLY/ANP DH9 ....150 B1
WICK/BNPF NE16 ....111 F5
Newsham Cl *WD/WHPE/BLK* NE5 ...59 D2
Newsham Rd *BLYTH* NE24 ....16 B1
Newstead Ct *WASHS* NE38 ....138 B1
Newstead Rd *HLS* DH4 ....157 E6

Newsteads Cl *MONK* NE25 ....**39** F5
Newsteads Dr *MONK* NE25 ....**39** E5
Newstead Sq *SUNDSW* SR3..............**160** C2
New Strangford Rd
  SEA/MUR SR7...............................**176** B3
New St *DHAM* DH1 ....**194** A5
  MLFD/PNYW SR4 ....**123** F6
Newton Av *TYNE/NSHE* NE30.............**55** D1
  WLSD/HOW NE28 ....**68** B3
Newton Cl *BW/LEM/TK/HW* NE15 ......**77** D1
Newton Dr *DHAM* DH1 ....**194** A1
Newton Gv *HAR/WTLS* NE34...............**87** F3
Newton Pl *LGB/HTN* NE7 ....**65** D4
Newton Rd *LGB/HTN* NE7 ....**64** C3
Newton St *DUN/TMV* NE11..................**97** E1
  GATE NE8 ....**98** C2
New Vis
  JES (off Hunters Rd) NE2 ....**63** D6
New York Rd *NSHW* NE29 ....**53** D3
  SMOOR NE27......................................**52** A1
New York Wy *SMOOR* NE27.................**52** C4
Nicholas Av *CLDN/WHIT/ROK* SR6 ...**109** E2
Nicholas St *HLH* DH5 ....**172** A5
Nichol Cl *ELS/FEN* * NE4 ....**78** C3
Nicholson Cl *SUND* SR1 ....**5** F3
Nicholson Ter *LGB/KIL* NE12 ....**50** C3
Nichol St *ELS/FEN* NE4 ....**78** C3
Nickleby Chare *DHAM* DH1 ....**205** D1
Nidderdale Av *HLH* DH5 ....**185** E2
Nidderdale Cl *BLYTH* NE24 ....**9** F4
Nidsdale Av *BYK/HTN/WLK* NE6.........**83** F1
Nightingale Cl *MLFD/PNYW* SR4 .....**141** F2
Nightingale Pl *STLY/ANP* DH9 ....**149** D3
Nile Cl *HAR/WTLS* NE34 ....**141** F2
Nile Ct *GATE* NE8..................................**99** F1
Nile St *NSHW* NE29 ....**70** C1
  SSH NE33 ....**71** D4
  SUND SR1 ....**5** E2
Nilverton Av *ASHBK/HED/RY* SR2 ...**144** C3
Nimbus Ct *SUNDSW* SR3 ....**160** C2
Nine Lands *HLS* DH4...........................**170** B2
Ninth Av *BLYTH* NE24 ....**10** C6
  BYK/HTN/WLK NE6 ....**65** E6
  CLSW/PEL DH2..................................**153** D5
Ninth St *PLEE/EAS* SR8 ....**209** F1
Nissan Wy *WASHN* NE37 ....**122** A5
Nixon St *GATE* NE8 ....**81** F4
Nixon Ter *BLYTH* NE24 ....**11** E6
Noble's Bank Rd
  ASHBK/HED/RY SR2 ....**5** C5
Noble St *ASHBK/HED/RY* SR2 ....**5** G6
  ELS/FEN NE4 ....**79** E1
  FELL NE10...**100** C1
  PLEE/EAS SR8 ....**200** C1
Noble Ter *ASHBK/HED/RY* SR2 ....**5** G6
Noel Av *BLAY* NE21 ....**94** B4
Noel St *STLY/ANP* DH9 ....**148** C1
Noel Ter *BLAY* NE21 ....**94** C3
  GATE (off Sunderland Rd) NE8........**100** B1
Noirmont Wy *SUNDSW* SR3 ....**160** A2
Nookside *MLFD/PNYW* SR4 ....**142** C2
Nookside St *MLFD/PNYW* SR4 ....**142** B2
The Nook *NSHW* NE29 ....**70** B1
Nora St *HAR/WTLS* NE34 ....**88** B3
  MLFD/PNYW SR4...............................**143** F2
Norbury Gv *BYK/HTN/WLK* NE6 ....**82** C3
Nordale Wy *BLYTH* NE24 ....**9** F4
Norfolk Av *CLS/BIR/GTL* DH3 ....**136** B5
  SUNDSW SR3 ....**143** E6
Norfolk Cl *SEA/MUR* SR7 ....**175** F1
Norfolk Dr *WASHN* NE37 ....**120** C2
Norfolk Gdns *WLSD/HOW* NE28 ....**68** A3
Norfolk Rd *GATE* NE8...........................**81** F4
  HAR/WTLS NE34................................**90** B1
Norfolk Sq *BYK/HTN/WLK* NE6 ....**82** A2
Norfolk St *SUND* SR1 ....**4** D3
  TYNE/NSHE NE30..............................**55** D6
Norfolk Wk *PLEE/EAS* SR8 ....**200** B6
Norfolk Wy *BW/LEM/TK/HW* NE15 ....**77** D1
Norham Av *HAR/WTLS* NE34.................**72** C6
Norham Av North *HAR/WTLS* NE34....**72** C6
Norham Av South *HAR/WTLS* NE34....**72** C6
Norham Cl *BLYTH* NE24 ....**10** B5
  DIN/WO NE13....................................**32** C5
Norham Ct *HLS* DH4............................**168** C1
Norham Dr *PLEE/EAS* SR8 ....**208** A5
  WD/WHPE/BLK NE5 ....**60** A3
Norham Pl *JES* NE2 ....**64** C3
Norham Rd *DHAM* DH1 ....**180** B5
  GOS/KPK NE3 ....**47** D6
  MONK NE25 ....**40** B3
  NSHW NE29 ....**69** E1
Norham Rd North *NSHW* NE29 ....**53** D4
Norham Ter *JRW* NE32 ....**86** A4
Norhurst *WICK/BNPF* NE16 ....**95** D5
Norland Rd *BW/LEM/TK/HW* NE15 ....**77** E3
Norley Av *SWCK/CAS* SR5 ....**126** B2
Norma Crs *WBAY* NE26 ....**41** E6
Norman Av *SUNDSW* SR3 ....**161** D1
Normanby Cl *SEA/MUR* SR7 ....**175** F1
Normanby Ct
  CLDN/WHIT/ROK SR6 ....**127** C3
Normandy Crs *HLH* DH5 ....**171** E2
Norman Rd *ROWG* NE39 ....**111** D3
Norman Ter *WLSD/HOW* NE28 ....**69** D4

Normanton Ter *ELS/FEN* NE4..............**79** F3
Normount Rd *ELS/FEN* NE4 ....**79** D3
Northampton Rd *PLEE/EAS* SR8 ....**200** B6
Northamptonshire Dr *DHAM* DH1....**196** C3
North Ap *CLSW/PEL* DH2...................**153** D4
North Av *GOS/KPK* NE3 ....**63** D2
  HAR/WTLS NE34................................**89** D2
  LGB/KIL NE12 ....**49** F6
  PLEE/EAS SR8 ....**209** E1
  WD/WHPE/BLK NE5 ....**60** B4
North Bailey *DHAM* DH1 ....**194** B5
Northbourne Rd *HEBB* NE31 ....**85** F2
Northbourne St *ELS/FEN* NE4 ....**79** E4
  GATE NE8 ....**99** E2
North Brancepeth Cl
  BDN/LAN/SAC DH7 ....**204** A2
North Bridge St *SWCK/CAS* SR5 ....**126** C4
North Burns *CLS/BIR/GTL* DH3 ....**153** E4
North Church St *TYNE/NSHE* NE30 ....**55** D6
North Cliff
  CLDN/WHIT/ROK
  (off Roker Ter) SR6............................**127** E1
North Cl *BYK/HTN/WLK* NE6 ....**82** B1
  HAR/WTLS NE34................................**89** D2
  RYTON NE40......................................**74** B5
Northcote *WICK/BNPF* NE16 ....**95** F5
Northcote Av *SUND* SR1 ....**5** E4
  WD/WHPE/BLK NE5 ....**59** E5
Northcote St *ELS/FEN* NE4 ....**79** F3
  SSH NE33 ....**71** F6
North Crs *PLEE/EAS* SR8 ....**200** B3
  WASHS NE38 ....**138** A5
North Cft *LGB/KIL* NE12.......................**50** A5
North Cross St *GOS/KPK* NE3 ....**63** E1
Northdene *CLS/BIR/GTL* DH3 ....**118** B6
North Dr *CLDN/WHIT/ROK* SR6.........**107** D1
  CLS/BIR/GTL DH3............................**153** F1
  HEBB NE31 ....**84** B3
North Durham St *SUND* SR1 ....**5** F2
North Eastern Ct *SUND/TMV* * NE11...**97** D2
North End *BDN/LAN/SAC* DH7 ....**202** C3
  DHAM DH1 ....**194** A3
Northern Wy *SWCK/CAS* SR5 ....**125** F2
North Farm Av *MLFD/PNYW* SR4.......**142** A4
North Farm Rd *HEBB* NE31 ....**84** C2
Northfield Cl *WICK/BNPF* NE16 ....**95** E5
Northfield Dr *LGB/KIL* NE12 ....**49** D2
  MLFD/PNYW SR4 ....**142** A4
Northfield Gdns *HAR/WTLS* NE34 ....**72** B6
Northfield Rd *GOS/KPK* NE3 ....**63** D2
  SSH NE33 ....**72** B5
Northgate *LGB/KIL* NE12......................**35** F6
North Gra *PONT/DH* NE20.....................**28** A2
North Gv *CLDN/WHIT/ROK* SR6 ....**127** D1
  RYTON NE40......................................**74** C3
North Guards
  CLDN/WHIT/ROK SR6 ....**109** D2
North Hall Rd *MLFD/PNYW* SR4.........**142** C2
North Hvn *SEA/MUR* SR7 ....**176** A2
North Hylton St *SWCK/CAS* SR5 ....**125** F2
North Jesmond Av *JES* NE2 ....**64** A4
North King St *TYNE/NSHE* NE30 ....**55** D6
Northlands *BLAY* NE21 ....**94** A1
North La *BOL* NE36.............................**106** B3
  HLH DH5 ....**172** C5
Northlea *BW/LEM/TK/HW* * NE15 ......**60** A4
Northlea Rd *SEA/MUR* SR7 ....**175** F1
North Mason Ldg *DIN/WO* NE13 ....**30** C2
North Milburn St
  MLFD/PNYW SR4.............................**126** A5
North Moor Ct *SUNDSW* SR3 ....**143** D5
North Moor La *SUNDSW* SR3 ....**143** D5
Northmoor Rd *BYK/HTN/WLK* NE6 ......**66** A6
North Moor Rd *SUNDSW* SR3 ....**143** D5
Northolt Av *CRAM* NE23 ....**22** A1
North Pde *WBAY* NE26 ....**41** D5
North Railway St *SEA/MUR* * SR7 ......**176** C3
North Ravensworth St
  MLFD/PNYW SR4.............................**126** A5
North Rdg *BDLGTN* NE22 ....**6** C3
  MONK NE25 ....**39** E5
North Rd *BOL* NE36 ....**106** B3
  BOLCOL NE35...................................**105** D1
  CLS/BIR/GTL DH3............................**153** E1
  DHAM DH1 ....**194** A3
  HLH DH5 ....**171** D5
  NSHW NE29 ....**54** B4
  PONT/DH NE20..................................**28** A2
  STLY/ANP DH9 ....**129** D6
  WLSD/HOW NE28 ....**67** D4
North Rd Head *DHAM* * DH1 ....**194** A4
Northside Pl *MONK* NE25 ....**25** D6
North St *BLAY* NE21 ....**75** F6
  CLDN/WHIT/ROK SR6 ....**107** F1
  CNUT NE1 ....**170** C5
  HLH DH5 ....**170** C5
  HLS DH4 ....**157** F4
  JRW NE32 ....**86** A1
  SSH NE33 ....**71** G3
  SUNDSW SR3 ....**143** F6
  SWCK/CAS SR5 ....**126** B3
North Ter *JES* NE2 ....**80** B1
  SEA/MUR SR7...................................**176** C2
  SUNDSW SR3 ....**143** F6
  WLSD/HOW NE28 ....**68** A4

Northumberland Av *BDLGTN* NE22 ....**7** D3
  GOS/KPK NE3 ....**62** C2
  LGB/KIL NE12 ....**49** F5
Northumberland Dock
  NSHW (off Hayhole Rd) NE29 ....**70** A5
Northumberland Dock Rd *WLSD/HOW*
  NE28 ....**69** E5
Northumberland Gdns *JES* * NE2 ....**64** C6
  WD/WHPE/BLK NE5 ....**59** D3
Northumberland Pl
  PLEE/EAS SR8 ....**200** A6
  TYNE/NSHE * NE30............................**54** C6
Northumberland Rd
  BW/LEM/TK/HW NE15 ....**76** B2
  CNUT NE1 ....**2** D2
  RYTON NE40......................................**74** B2
Northumberland Sq
  TYNE/NSHE NE30 ....**54** C6
Northumberland St *CNUT* NE1 ....**2** D2
  GATE NE8 ....**98** B1
  PLEE/EAS SR8 ....**201** E6
  TYNE/NSHE NE30 ....**55** D6
  WLSD/HOW NE28 ....**67** E4
Northumberland Ter
  BYK/HTN/WLK NE6............................**82** A2
  TYNE/NSHE NE30 ....**55** F5
Northumberland Village Homes
  WBAY
  (off Norham Rd) NE26 ....**40** B5
Northumberland Vis
  WLSD/HOW NE28 ....**68** A4
Northumberland Wy
  WASHN NE37 ....**120** C2
  WASHS NE38 ....**139** D3
Northumbria Rd *CRAM* NE23 ....**14** B6
Northumbrian Wy *LGB/KIL* NE12 ....**49** E2
  NSHW NE29 ....**70** C5
Northumbria Pl *STLY/ANP* DH9 ....**148** C1
North Vw *BYK/HTN/WLK* NE6...............**82** A2
  CLDN/WHIT/ROK SR6 ....**126** C1
  DHAM DH1 ....**195** E4
  DIN/WO NE13.....................................**31** D3
  HAR/WTLS NE34................................**72** B6
  HLH DH5 ....**186** C3
  JRW NE32 ....**86** A3
  LGB/KIL NE12 ....**49** F4
  SWCK/CAS SR5 ....**124** B3
  WBAY NE26 ....**41** E6
  WICK/BNPF NE16...............................**95** F5
  WLSD/HOW NE28 ....**67** E4
North View Ter *GATE* * NE8 ....**100** B1
North Walbottle Rd
  WD/WHPE/BLK NE5 ....**58** C3
Northway *BW/LEM/TK/HW* NE15 ....**57** F3
  LWF/SPW/WRK NE9 ....**100** A3
Northwood Ct *SWCK/CAS* SR5 ....**126** B2
Northwood Rd *SEA/MUR* SR7 ....**176** A2
Norton Av *SEA/MUR* SR7 ....**175** F1
Norton Cl *CLSW/PEL* DH2 ....**165** E1
Norton Rd *SWCK/CAS* SR5 ....**125** F1
Norton Wy *BW/LEM/TK/HW* NE15 ......**77** D2
Norway Av *MLFD/PNYW* SR4 ....**143** D2
Norwich Av *DIN/WO* NE13 ....**33** D5
Norwich Cl *CLS/BIR/GTL* DH3 ....**167** F3
Norwich Rd *DHAM* DH1 ....**180** C5
Norwood Av *BYK/HTN/WLK* NE6 ....**65** D5
  GOS/KPK NE3 ....**47** E2
Norwood Gdns
  LWF/SPW/WRK NE9 ....**99** F2
Norwood Rd
  BW/LEM/TK/HW NE15 ....**59** F6
  DUN/TMV NE11...................................**98** A3
Nottingham Pl *PLEE/EAS* SR8 ....**200** A6
Nottinghamshire Rd *DHAM* DH1.......**196** B3
Nuneaton Wy *WD/WHPE/BLK* NE5 ......**59** D2
Nuns La *CNUT* NE1 ....**2** C4
  GATE NE8 ....**81** E5
Nuns Moor Crs *ELS/FEN* NE4 ....**79** D1
Nuns Moor Rd *ELS/FEN* NE4...............**79** D1
Nuns' Rw *DHAM* DH1 ....**195** E3
Nuns St *CNUT* NE1 ....**2** C3
Nunwick Gdns *NSHW* NE29 ....**53** E6
Nunwick Wy *LGB/HTN* NE7 ....**65** F3
Nursery Cl *SUNDSW* SR3 ....**143** F4
Nursery Gdns *PLEE/EAS* SR8 ....**200** A3
Nursery La *CLDN/WHIT/ROK* SR6 ......**107** F1
  FELL NE10...**100** B3
Nursery Rd *SUNDSW* SR3 ....**143** F4
Nutley Pl *BW/LEM/TK/HW* NE15 ....**77** F3
Nye Dene *SWCK/CAS* SR5 ....**124** A3

O

Oakapple Cl *BDLGTN* NE22 ....**7** E3
Oak Av *DHAM* DH1 ....**195** F3
  DIN/WO NE13......................................**31** E3
  DUN/TMV NE11...................................**97** E3
  HAR/WTLS NE34................................**89** F3
Oak Crs *CLDN/WHIT/ROK* SR6 ....**109** F1
  CLSW/PEL DH2..................................**179** F1
Oakdale *BDLGTN* NE22............................**6** A4
Oakdale Cl *BW/LEM/TK/HW* NE15 ......**76** C2

Oakenshaw *BW/LEM/TK/HW* NE15.....76 C2
Oakerside Dr *PLEE/EAS* SR8 ....208 B4
Oakes Pl *ELS/FEN* NE4................80 A3
Oakey Rd *STLY/ANP* DH9 ....131 E5
Oakfield Av *WICK/BNPF* NE16 ....96 A4
Oakfield Cl *SUNDSW* SR3 ....159 E4
  WICK/BNPF NE16...................96 A4
Oakfield Dr *LGB/KIL* NE12 ....50 B1
  WICK/BNPF NE16...................96 A4
Oakfield Gdns
  BW/LEM/TK/HW NE15 ....78 C3
  WLSD/HOW NE28 ....66 B3
Oakfield Gra *DIN/WO* NE13...........31 D3
Oakfield North *RYTON* NE40 ....74 A3
Oakfield Rd *DUN/TMV* NE11 ....97 F4
  GOS/KPK NE3.......................63 D3
  WICK/BNPF NE16...................95 E5
Oakfields *WICK/BNPF* NE16 ....112 A5
Oakfield Ter *FELL* NE10..............101 F1
  GOS/KPK NE3.......................63 D2
Oakfield Wy *CRAM* NE23 ....36 B1
Oakgreen Flats
  BDN/LAN/SAC DH7 ....203 D4
Oak Gv *WLSD/HOW* NE28 ....67 F4
Oakham Av *WICK/BNPF* NE16 ....95 E4
Oakham Dr *DHAM* DH1 ....196 C1
Oakleigh Gdns
  CLDN/WHIT/ROK SR6 ....89 D2
Oakley Cl *CRAM* NE23 ....35 D2
Oakley Dr *CRAM* NE23 ....22 B1
Oakmere Cl *HLS* DH4 ....157 D2
Oakridge *WICK/BNPF* NE16..........95 E4
Oak Rd *NSHW* NE29 ....52 C5
  PLEE/EAS SR8 ....200 C3
Oak Sq *GATE* NE8.....................98 B1
The Oaks *ASHBK/HED/RY* SR2 ....5 E6
  RYTON NE40.........................92 A1
Oak St *HLS* DH4......................169 D1
  JRW NE32............................85 F1
  SUND SR1.............................5 H3
Oak Ter *CLSW/PEL* DH2 ....151 E1
  SEA/MUR SR7.......................188 B1
  STLY/ANP DH9......................146 A3
  STLY/ANP DH9......................149 D5
Oaktree Av *WLSD/HOW* NE28........66 C5
Oaktree Gdns *MONK* NE25 ....54 A1
Oakway Ct *BDN/LAN/SAC* DH7 .....204 A4
Oakwellgate *GATE* NE8 ....3 G6
Oakwood *FELL* NE10 ....101 D5
  HEBB NE31..........................84 B1
  RDHAMSE DH6 ....188 A6
Oakwood Av *DIN/WO* NE13...........33 E5
  LWF/SPW/WRK NE9 ....117 F1
Oakwood Cl *LWF/SPW/WRK* NE9..119 E2
Oakwood Gdns *DUN/TMV* NE11 .....98 A5
Oakwood Pl *WD/WHPE/BLK* NE5 ....61 E5
Oakwood St *ASHBK/HED/RY* SR2 ..144 A1
Oates St *MLFD/PNYW* SR4 ....125 F6
Oatlands Rd *MLFD/PNYW* SR4 ......143 D2
Oatlands Wy *DHAM* DH1 ....180 B4
Oban Av *WLSD/HOW* NE28 ....68 B2
Oban Gdns *BYK/HTN/WLK* NE6 ......82 B3
Oban St *GATE* NE8 ....100 B1
  JRW NE32............................87 D5
Oban Ter *FELL* NE10 ....100 B1
Obelisk La *DHAM* DH1 ....194 A4
Ocean Rd *ASHBK/HED/RY* SR2 .....145 E4
  SSH NE33..............................71 E3
Ocean Vw *BLYH* NE24................162 B1
  WBAY NE26...........................41 D5
Ochiltree Ct *WBAY* NE26.............26 C2
Octavia Ct *BDLGTN* NE22 ....7 D2
Octavia Wy *WLSD/HOW* NE28 ....68 A2
Octavian Wy *DUN/TMV* NE11.......116 B1
Offerton Cl *MLFD/PNYW* SR4 ......123 E6
Offerton La *MLFD/PNYW* SR4 ......123 D6
Offerton St *MLFD/PNYW* SR4 ......125 F6
Office Pl *HLH* DH5...................185 F1
Office Rw
  RDHAMSE (off Front St) DH6 .....206 C1
Office St *PLEE/EAS* SR8 ....201 E2
Ogden St *MLFD/PNYW* SR4 ....125 F6
Ogle Av *DIN/WO* NE13................32 C6
Ogle Dr *BLYH* NE24....................10 B6
Ogle Gv *JRW* NE32....................85 F5
O'Hanlon Crs *WLSD/HOW* NE28 ....66 A2
Oil Mill Rd *BYK/HTN/WLK* NE6 .....84 A1
Okehampton Dr *HLS* DH4 ....157 E4
Okehampton Sq *SWCK/CAS* SR5 ..125 F1
Old Coronation St *SSH* NE33 ....71 E4
Old Course Rd
  CLDN/WHIT/ROK SR6 ....107 F2
Old Durham Rd
  LWF/SPW/WRK NE9 ....100 A5

Old Elvet *DHAM* DH1 ....194 C5
Old Farm Ct *WICK/BNPF* NE16 .....114 A2
Oldfield Rd *BYK/HTN/WLK* NE6 .....83 E1
Old Fold Rd *FELL* NE10................82 A6
  GATE NE8............................100 A1
Old George Yd *CNUT* * NE1...........2 D4
Old Mill La *CLS/BIR/GTL* DH3......167 E4
Old Mill Rd *ASHBK/HED/RY* SR2 .....5 H5
  SWCK/CAS SR5 ....125 F1
Oldstead Gdns *MLFD/PNYW* SR4 ..143 D2
Old Vicarage Wk
  BYK/HTN/WLK * NE6...............82 B2
Old Well La *BLAY* NE21................94 A1
Olive Gdns *LWF/SPW/WRK* NE9 .....99 F4
Olive Pl *ELS/FEN* NE4..................78 C1
Oliver Pl *DHAM* DH1 ....204 C1
Oliver St *BW/LEM/TK/HW* NE15 ....78 A3
  SEA/MUR SR7.......................176 A2
  STLY/ANP DH9......................148 A3
Olive St *CLSW/PEL* DH2 ....165 D1
  SSH NE33..............................88 A2
  SUND SR1..............................4 B4
Ollerton Dr *BW/LEM/TK/HW* NE15 ..57 D4
Ollerton Gdns *FELL* NE10...........100 B3
Olney Cl *CRAM* NE23 ....22 C1
O'Neil Dr *PLEE/EAS* SR8 ....208 C3
Ongar Wy *LGB/KIL* NE12 ....49 D5
Onslow Gdns *LWF/SPW/WRK* NE9...99 E5
Onslow St *MLFD/PNYW* SR4 ....125 E1
The Open *CNUT* * NE1 ....2 C2
Orange Gv *CRAM* NE23 ....35 D1
  WICK/BNPF NE16...................96 B3
Orchard Av *ROWG* NE39 ....110 C3
Orchard Cl *HAR/WTLS* NE34..........88 A3
  LGB/KIL NE12........................50 B3
  ROWG NE39.........................110 C4
  STLY/ANP DH9......................150 C4
Orchard Ct *RYTON* NE40..............74 B3
Orchard Dene *ROWG* NE39 ....110 C3
Orchard Dr *DHAM* DH1 ....195 D3
Orchard Gdns
  CLDN/WHIT/ROK SR6 ....109 D2
  CLS/BIR/GTL DH3..................166 B1
  LWF/SPW/WRK NE9 ....99 F6
  WLSD/HOW NE28 ....66 C3
Orchard-Leigh
  BW/LEM/TK/HW NE15 ....76 C2
Orchard Pk *CLS/BIR/GTL* DH3......136 B2
Orchard Pl *JES* NE2 ....64 B3
Orchard Priory *DHAM* DH1..........194 A5
Orchard Rd *ROWG* NE39 ....110 C3
  WICK/BNPF NE16...................96 B3
The Orchards *BLYH* NE24............10 A4
Orchard St *CLS/BIR/GTL* DH3......136 C5
  CLSW/PEL DH2.....................152 A1
  CNUT NE1..............................2 D5
  MLFD/PNYW SR4 ....125 E5
Orchard Ter *CLS/BIR/GTL* DH3.....166 B1
The Orchard
  BW/LEM/TK/HW NE15 ....76 C2
  CLS/BIR/GTL
  (off Picktree La) DH3.................153 F4
  DHAM DH1 ....180 A4
  NSHW
  (off South Preston Gv) NE29 ....70 C1
  WICK/BNPF NE16...................96 B3
Ord Ct *ELS/FEN* NE4..................78 C1
Orde Av *WLSD/HOW* NE28...........68 A3
Ordley Cl *BW/LEM/TK/HW* NE15 ...77 D2
Ord St *ELS/FEN* NE4..................80 A5
Oriel Cl *CLDN/WHIT/ROK* SR6 .....126 C3
Orkney Dr *ASHBK/HED/RY* SR2 ...144 C6
Orlando Rd *NSHW* NE29 ....53 F6
Ormesby Rd
  CLDN/WHIT/ROK SR6 ....126 C1
Ormiscraig *BW/LEM/TK/HW* NE15 ..77 D2
Ormiston St *BW/LEM/TK/HW* NE15 .77 D2
Ormonde Av
  BW/LEM/TK/HW NE15 ....77 F2
Ormonde St *JRW* NE32...............86 A1
  MLFD/PNYW SR4 ....143 E1
Ormskirk Gv *CRAM* NE23 ....14 A3
Ormston St *CRAM* NE23 ....23 D3
Orpen Av *HAR/WTLS* NE34............88 B5
Orpington Av *BYK/HTN/WLK* NE6 ...83 D1
Orpington Rd *CRAM* NE23 ....22 B1
Orr Av *SUNDSW* SR3.................161 D2
Orton Cl *ELS/FEN* * NE4..............78 A1
Orwell Cl *HAR/WTLS* NE34............88 A6
  PLEE/EAS SR8 ....208 A4
Orwell Gdns *STLY/ANP* DH9 ....148 A4
Osbaldeston Gdns *GOS/KPK* NE3....63 E3
Osborne Av *JES* NE2 ....64 A6
  SSH NE33..............................71 F5
Osborne Ct *BDLGTN* NE22 ....8 B2
Osborne Gdns *NSHW* NE29 ....54 C5
  WBAY NE26...........................40 B5
Osborne Rd *JES* NE2 ....64 A6
  SWCK/CAS SR5 ....123 F5
Osborne St *CLDN/WHIT/ROK* SR6 ..126 C2
  SSH NE33..............................72 A5
Osborne Ter *GATE* NE8................98 C1
  JES NE2...............................81 D1
Osborne Vls *JES* NE2 ....64 A6

Oslo Cl *NSHW* NE29...................69 D3
Osman Cl *ASHBK/HED/RY* SR2 ....5 E5
Osprey Dr *BLYH* NE24.................17 D2
  NSHW NE29..........................52 C6
Osprey Wy *HAR/WTLS* NE34.........87 F4
Oswald Cl *DHAM* DH1 ....195 F5
Oswald Ct *DHAM* DH1 ....194 C6
Oswald Rd *HLH* DH5.................171 F5
Oswald St *HAR/WTLS* NE34........125 F5
Oswald Ter *ASHBK/HED/RY* SR2 ..145 E4
  GATE NE8.............................98 C1
  PLEE/EAS SR8 ....200 C2
Oswald Ter South *SWCK/CAS* SR5 .124 B3
Oswald Wk *GOS/KPK* NE3.............64 A1
Oswestry Pl *CRAM* NE23 ....22 B1
Oswin Av *LGB/KIL* NE12 ....50 A3
Oswin Ct *LGB/KIL* NE12 ....50 A3
Oswin Ter *NSHW* NE29................69 F1
Otley Cl *CRAM* NE23 ....22 C1
Otterburn Av *MONK* NE25 ....39 D6
Otterburn Cl *LGB/KIL* NE12 ....50 B4
Otterburn Ct
  GATE (off Fourth St) NE8...........98 C1
Otterburn Crs *HLS* DH4 ....170 B1
Otterburn Gdns *DUN/TMV* NE11 ...97 F3
  HAR/WTLS NE34....................99 D2
  LWF/SPW/WRK NE9 ....99 D6
  WICK/BNPF NE16...................96 A3
Otterburn Gv *BLYH* NE24............10 A6
Otterburn Rd *NSHW* NE29 ....54 B5
Otterburn Ter *JES* NE2 ....64 A5
Otterburn Vls *JES* * NE2 ....64 A5
Otterburn Vls South *JES* * NE2 .....64 A6
Ottercap Cl *BW/LEM/TK/HW* NE15 ..76 C2
Otterington *WASHS* NE38 ....139 F2
Ottershaw *BW/LEM/TK/HW* NE15 ..77 D2
Otto Ter *ASHBK/HED/RY* SR2 ......144 A1
Ottovale Crs *BLAY* NE21...............93 F1
Ottringham Cl
  BW/LEM/TK/HW NE15 ....76 C2
Oulton Cl *CRAM* NE23 ....22 C1
Ousby Ct *DIN/WO* NE13...............45 F5
Ouseburn Cl *ASHBK/HED/RY* SR2 .145 E5
Ouseburn Rd *BYK/HTN/WLK* NE6 ...65 D5
  CNUT NE1.............................81 F2
Ouselaw *DUN/TMV* NE11 ....116 C3
Ouse St *CNUT* NE1 ....81 F3
Ouslaw La *DUN/TMV* NE11 ....116 A6
Ousterley Ter *STLY/ANP* DH9 ......149 D6
Ouston Cl *FELL* NE10 ....102 B3
Ouston La *CLSW/PEL* DH2 ....152 B1
Ouston St *BW/LEM/TK/HW* NE15 ...77 E3
Outram St *HLH* DH5..................171 D1
Oval Park Vw *FELL* NE10............100 C3
The Oval *BDLGTN* NE22 ....8 B3
  BLYH NE24...........................16 A3
  BYK/HTN/WLK NE6 ....83 D5
  CLSW/PEL DH2.....................135 E4
  CLSW/PEL DH2.....................166 A3
  DIN/WO NE13.........................44 B4
  HLS DH4.............................170 B2
  LGB/KIL NE12........................49 F6
Overdene *BW/LEM/TK/HW* NE15....77 E1
  SEA/MUR SR7.......................175 E5
Overfield Rd *GOS/KPK* NE3..........62 B1
Overhill Ter *GATE* NE8 ....98 C1
Overton Cl *BW/LEM/TK/HW* NE15 ..76 C2
Overton Rd *NSHW* NE29 ....54 A4
Ovingham Cl *WASHS* NE38 ....139 E1
Ovingham Gdns *DIN/WO* NE13 .....33 E5
Ovington Gv *WD/WHPE/BLK* NE5 ...61 E6
Owen Brannigan Dr *CRAM* NE23 ...35 D3
Owen Ct
  JES (off Richardson Rd) NE2 ......80 B1
Owen Dr *BOL* NE36...................106 A2
Owengate *DHAM* DH1 ....194 B5
Owen St *HAR/WTLS* NE34............88 A3
Owlet Cl *BLAY* NE21...................94 A4
Oxbridge St *ASHBK/HED/RY* SR2 .145 E4
Oxclose Rd *WASHS* NE38 ....139 D2
Oxford Av *CRAM* NE23................22 B1
  SSH NE33..............................71 F6
  WASHN NE37.......................120 A4
  WLSD/HOW NE28 ....66 C3
Oxford Cl *SUNDSW* SR3 ....143 E6
Oxford Crs *HEBB* NE31...............85 E2
Oxford Pl *CLS/BIR/GTL* DH3........136 B5
Oxfordshire Dr *DHAM* DH1 ....196 B3
Oxford Sq *MLFD/PNYW* SR4 ....125 D5
Oxford St *BLYH* NE24..................11 E5
  CNUT NE1..............................3 E2
  MLFD/PNYW SR4 ....125 D5
  SEA/MUR SR7.......................175 F3
  SSH NE33..............................71 F6
  TYNE/NSHE NE30..................55 F5
  WBAY NE26...........................41 D5
Oxford Ter *GATE* * NE8................99 D1
Oxnam Crs *CRAM* NE23 ....80 A1
Oxted Cl *CRAM* NE23 ....22 C1
Oxted Pl *BYK/HTN/WLK* NE6.........83 D5
Oyston St *SSH* NE33.................71 E4
Ozanan Cl *CRAM* NE23...............35 D3

P

Pacific Hall *SEA/MUR* SR7 ....175 D2
Packham Rd *MLFD/PNYW* SR4 ....142 B1
Paddock Cl *CLDN/WHIT/ROK* SR6 .....107 D1
  HLS DH4 ....156 B3
Paddock Hl *PONT/DH* NE20 ....28 B3
Paddock La *SUNDSW* SR3 ....161 E1
The Paddock *BLYTH* NE24...................10 B5
  BW/LEM/TK/HW NE15 ....58 B5
  CRAM NE23 ....22 C2
  DIN/WO NE13..................................44 B4
  FELL NE10.....................................101 E4
  HLS DH4 ....158 B1
  LGB/KIL
  (off Garth Thirtytwo) NE12..............50 A1
  STLY/ANP DH9 ....130 B6
Pader Cl *DIN/WO* NE13 ....33 D5
Padgate Rd *MLFD/PNYW* SR4 ....142 B1
Padstow Cl *ASHBK/HED/RY* SR2 ....145 E6
Padstow Rd *NSHW* NE29 ....70 A2
Page Av *HAR/WTLS* NE34 ....89 D1
Page St *HEBB* NE31 ....85 E1
Paignton Av *ELS/FEN* NE4 ....79 D3
  MONK NE25 ....39 F6
Paignton Sq *SUNDSW* SR3 ....143 D4
Paisley Sq *SUNDSW* SR3 ....143 D4
Palace Buildings
  BOLCOL (off North Rd) NE35........105 E2
Palace Gn *DHAM* DH1 ....194 B5
Palace Rd *BDLGTN* NE22 ....8 C2
Palace St *ELS/FEN* NE4 ....80 A4
Palatine Vw *DHAM* DH1 ....194 A5
Palermo St *MLFD/PNYW* SR4 ....125 D4
Paley St *SUND* SR1 ....4 A2
Palgrove Rd *MLFD/PNYW* SR4 ....142 B1
Palgrove Sq *MLFD/PNYW* SR4 ....142 B1
Pallinsburn Ct *WD/WHPE/BLK* NE5.....61 D3
Pallion New Rd *MLFD/PNYW* SR4 .....125 E4
Pallion Pk *MLFD/PNYW* SR4 ....125 E4
Pallion Rd *MLFD/PNYW* SR4 ....125 E6
Pallion Subway *MLFD/PNYW* SR4 .....125 D4
Palm Av *ELS/FEN* NE4 ....79 F1
  HAR/WTLS NE34 ....89 F5
Palmer Crs *HEBB* NE31 ....85 E2
Palmer Gdns *FELL* NE10 ....102 B2
Palmer Rd *PLEE/EAS* SR8 ....207 F2
  STLY/ANP DH9 ....129 D5
Palmers Garth *DHAM* DH1 ....194 C5
Palmers Gn *LGB/KIL* NE12 ....50 B3
Palmer's Hill Rd
  CLDN/WHIT/ROK SR6 ....126 C4
Palmerston Av *BYK/HTN/WLK* NE6 .....83 D1
Palmerston Rd *MLFD/PNYW* SR4 ....142 A3
Palmerston Wk *GATE* NE8 ....80 B6
Palmer St *JRW* NE32 ....85 F1
  STLY/ANP DH9 ....147 F3
Palm Lea *BDN/LAN/SAC* DH7 ....202 C4
Palmstead Rd *MLFD/PNYW* SR4 ....142 B1
Palmstead Sq *MLFD/PNYW* SR4........142 B1
Palm Ter *STLY/ANP* DH9 ....149 D5
Pan Bank
  SSH (off Commercial Rd) NE33 ....71 D5
Pancras Rd *SUNDSW* SR3 ....143 D4
Pandon *CNUT* NE1 ....3 F3
Pandon Bank *CNUT* NE1 ....3 F3
Pangbourne Cl
  BW/LEM/TK/HW NE15 ....59 E6
Pankhurst Gdns *FELL* NE10 ....101 F2
Pankhurst Pl *STLY/ANP* DH9 ....149 D4
Pann La *SUND* SR1 ....4 C2
Panns Bank *SUND* SR1 ....4 D1
The Parade *ASHBK/HED/RY* SR2 ....5 H4
  BYK/HTN/WLK NE6 ....83 E3
  CLSW/PEL DH2............................151 E2
  WICK/BNPF
  (off Metrocentre) NE16 ....78 B6
Paradise Crs *PLEE/EAS* SR8 ....200 C5
Paradise Rw *CRAM* NE23 ....22 A2
Paradise Yd
  BW/LEM/TK/HW
  (off Scotswood Rd) NE15 ....78 B5
Park Av *BDLGTN* NE22 ....9 D1
  BLAY NE21 ....78 B6
  CLDN/WHIT/ROK SR6 ....127 D1
  GOS/KPK NE3 ....46 B5
  HAR/WTLS NE34 ....89 D1
  SMOOR NE27 ....52 B1
  SUNDSW SR3 ....161 D1
  TYNE/NSHE NE30 ....55 C5
  WBAY NE26 ....40 C5
  WLSD/HOW NE28 ....67 D4
Park Chare *WASHS* NE38 ....138 C1
Park Cl *ELS/FEN* NE4 ....79 F4
  STLY/ANP DH9 ....146 D1
Park Ct *GATE* NE8 ....81 E5
Park Crs *SMOOR* NE27 ....52 B1
  TYNE/NSHE NE30 ....55 D6
Park Crs East *TYNE/NSHE* NE30..........55 C5
Parkdale Ri *WICK/BNPF* NE16 ....95 E3
Park Dr *BLYTH* NE24............................16 A2
  GOS/KPK NE3 ....47 E3
  LGB/KIL NE12 ....50 A4

WICK/BNPF NE16...............................96 B3
Parker Av *GOS/KPK* NE3 ....63 D3
Parker Ct *DUN/TMV* NE11....................79 D6
Park Farm Vls *BLYTH* NE24 ....16 B4
Park Fld *RYTON* NE40 ....74 B3
Park Field Ter *WBAY* NE26 ....26 B2
Park Gdns *WBAY* NE26 ....40 C5
Park Ga *CLDN/WHIT/ROK* SR6............127 D1
Parkgate La *BLAY* NE21 ....94 A2
Park Gv *SMOOR* NE27 ....52 B1
  WASHN NE37 ....120 C3
Parkham Cl *CRAM* NE23 ....14 A5
Parkhead *STLY/ANP* DH9 ....146 A6
Parkhead Gdns *BLAY* NE21 ....94 A2
Park Head Rd *LGB/HTN* NE7 ....64 C3
Parkhouse Av *SWCK/CAS* SR5 ....124 A4
Park House Cl *RDHAMSE* DH6 ....197 E4
Park House Rd *DHAM* DH1 ....204 C1
Parkhurst Rd *MLFD/PNYW* SR4 ....142 A2
Parkin Gdns *FELL* NE10 ....101 D3
Park Lea *SUNDSW* SR3 ....159 D2
Park Lea Rd *CLDN/WHIT/ROK* SR6 ....127 D1
Parkmore Rd *MLFD/PNYW* SR4 ....141 F2
Park Pde *CLDN/WHIT/ROK* SR6 ....127 D2
  WBAY NE26 ....40 C5
Park Pl *CLS/BIR/GTL* DH3 ....153 F3
Park Pl West *ASHBK/HED/RY* SR2 ....4 D5
Park Ri *BW/LEM/TK/HW* NE15 ....76 B1
Park Rd *ASHBK/HED/RY* SR2 ....4 C5
  BDLGTN NE22......................................7 F3
  BW/LEM/TK/HW NE15 ....58 A5
  ELS/FEN NE4 ....79 F4
  FELL NE10.......................................82 B6
  GATE NE8 ....81 A6
  HEBB NE31 ....85 D3
  JRW NE32 ....85 F2
  MONK NE25 ....24 B5
  PLEE/EAS SR8 ....201 E6
  ROWG NE39 ....110 C2
  SMOOR NE27 ....52 B1
  STLY/ANP DH9 ....147 F3
  WBAY NE26 ....40 C4
  WLSD/HOW NE28 ....67 D4
Park Rd Central *CLS/BIR/GTL* DH3......153 F5
Park Rd North *CLS/BIR/GTL* DH3 ....153 F4
Park Rd South *CLS/BIR/GTL* DH3 ....153 F6
Park Rw *FELL* NE10 ....100 C2
  SWCK/CAS SR5 ....125 F2
Parkshiel *HAR/WTLS* NE34 ....89 E4
Parkside *BDLGTN* NE22 ....8 B1
  BDN/LAN/SAC DH7 ....178 B1
  BW/LEM/TK/HW NE15 ....58 A5
  DHAM DH1 ....194 A4
  DUN/TMV NE11 ....97 E2
  HEBB NE31 ....84 B4
  STLY/ANP DH9 ....130 B5
  TYNE/NSHE NE30 ....55 F3
  WLSD/HOW NE28 ....67 F3
Parkside Av *BLAY* NE21 ....94 A1
  LGB/HTN NE7 ....65 D1
Parkside Crs *SEA/MUR* SR7 ....176 B5
  TYNE/NSHE NE30 ....55 F4
The Parks *CLS/BIR/GTL* DH3 ....167 D1
Parkstone Cl *MLFD/PNYW* SR4 ....141 F4
Park St South *SWCK/CAS* SR5 ....124 B3
Park Ter *BDLGTN* NE22 ....8 B1
  DUN/TMV NE11 ....97 D2
  JES NE2 ....80 C1
  PLEE/EAS SR8 ....209 F2
  SWCK/CAS SR5 ....125 E2
  TYNE/NSHE NE30 ....55 E6
  WICK/BNPF NE16............................95 F1
  WLSD/HOW NE28 ....111 F6
Park Vw *BLAY* NE21 ....94 B2
  BLYTH NE24 ....11 E5
  BYK/HTN/WLK NE6 ....83 F3
  CLSW/PEL DH2..............................165 E6
  CRAM (off Burradon Rd) NE23 ....35 D4
  HLH DH5 ....185 F1
  JRW NE32 ....86 A4
  LGB/KIL NE12 ....49 F4
  MONK NE25 ....24 C5
  WBAY NE26 ....40 C5
  WICK/BNPF NE16..........................112 A6
  WLSD/HOW NE28 ....67 D4
Parkville *BYK/HTN/WLK* NE6 ....81 F1
Parkway *GOS/KPK* NE3 ....45 E6
  WASHS NE38 ....138 B1
  WICK/BNPF NE16............................95 D5
Parmeter St *STLY/ANP* DH9 ....148 A4

Parmontley St
  BW/LEM/TK/HW NE15 ....77 E3
Parnell St *HLS* DH4 ....170 A2
Parry Dr *CLDN/WHIT/ROK* SR6 ....109 D1
Parson's Av *BYK/HTN/WLK* NE6 ....83 E5
Parsons Gdns *DUN/TMV* * NE11 ....97 E1
Parsons Rd *PLEE/EAS* SR8 ....200 C5
  WASHN NE37 ....120 A5
Partick Rd *MLFD/PNYW* SR4 ....142 A4
Partick Sq *MLFD/PNYW* SR4 ....142 A2
Partnership Ct *SEA/MUR* SR7 ....162 A6
Partridge Cl *WASHS* NE38 ....137 E3
Passfield Wy *PLEE/EAS* SR8 ....207 F4
Paston Rd *MONK* NE25 ....24 C6
The Pastures *BLYTH* NE24 ....16 C2
Pathside *BLAY* NE21 ....82 A6
Patience Av *DIN/WO* NE13 ....33 E2
Patina Cl *BW/LEM/TK/HW* NE15 ....59 E6
Paton Rd *SUNDSW* SR3 ....143 E4
Paton Sq *SUNDSW* SR3 ....143 E4
Patrick Crs *RDHAMSE* DH6 ....187 D4
Patterdale Cl *BOL* NE36......................106 B3
  DHAM DH1 ....193 E1
Patterdale Gdns *LGB/HTN* NE7 ....65 D3
Patterdale Gv *SWCK/CAS* SR5............108 B6
Patterdale Rd *BLYTH* NE24 ....9 F4
Patterdale Ter *GATE* NE8 ....99 E2
Patterson St *BLAY* NE21 ....77 D4
Pattinson Gdns *FELL* NE10 ....82 B6
  LWF/SPW/WRK NE9 ....100 A3
Pattinson Rd *WASHS* NE38 ....122 A6
Pauline Av *CLDN/WHIT/ROK* SR6 ......126 C1
Pauline Gdns
  BW/LEM/TK/HW NE15 ....77 F1
Pauls Gn *HLH* DH5 ....171 F4
Paulsway *JRW* NE32 ....87 D2
The Pavilion *WICK/BNPF* NE16............95 E1
Paxford Cl *LGB/HTN* NE7 ....64 B1
Paxton Ter *MLFD/PNYW* SR4 ....125 F5
Peacock Ct *DUN/TMV* NE11 ....98 A3
Peacock St West
  MLFD/PNYW SR4 ....125 E6
Pea Flatts La *CLS/BIR/GTL* DH3 ....168 B3
Peareth Ct *GATE* * NE8 ....81 E5
Peareth Gv *CLDN/WHIT/ROK* SR6 .....127 D1
Peareth Hall Rd
  LWF/SPW/WRK NE9 ....119 E3
  WASHN NE37 ....120 A2
Peareth Rd *CLDN/WHIT/ROK* SR6 ......109 D6
Pear Lea *BDN/LAN/SAC* DH7 ....202 C4
Pearl Rd *SUNDSW* SR3 ....143 E4
Pearson Pl *JRW* NE32 ....69 E6
  TYNE/NSHE NE30 ....55 D6
Pearson St *SSH* NE33 ....71 F2
  STLY/ANP DH9 ....131 E6
Peart Cl *RDHAMSE* DH6 ....197 F5
Peartree Gdns
  BYK/HTN/WLK NE6 ....66 B5
Peary Cl *WD/WHPE/BLK* NE5 ....60 B4
Pease Av *BW/LEM/TK/HW* NE15 ....78 B2
Peasemoor Rd *MLFD/PNYW* SR4.......142 A1
Pease Rd *PLEE/EAS* SR8 ....199 E6
Pecket Cl *BLYTH* NE24 ....15 F4
Peebles Cl *NSHW* NE29 ....53 D4
Peebles Rd *SUNDSW* SR3 ....143 D4
Peel Av *DHAM* DH1 ....196 A3
Peel La *CNUT* NE1 ....2 D1
Peel St *ASHBK/HED/RY* SR2 ....5 E5
Peggy's Wicket *STLY/ANP* DH9 ....133 E2
Pegwood Rd *MLFD/PNYW* SR4 ....142 B1
Pelaw Av *CLSW/PEL* DH2 ....153 D3
  STLY/ANP DH9 ....131 F6
Pelaw Bank *CLS/BIR/GTL* DH3 ....153 E4
Pelaw Crs *CLSW/PEL* DH2 ....153 D3
Pelaw Grange Ct
  CLS/BIR/GTL DH3 ....136 B6
Pelaw Leazes La *DHAM* DH1 ....194 C4
Pelaw Pl *CLSW/PEL* DH2 ....153 D3
Pelaw Rd *CLSW/PEL* DH2 ....153 D3
Pelaw Sq *CLSW/PEL* DH2 ....153 D3
  MLFD/PNYW SR4...........................124 B5
Pelaw Wy *FELL* NE10 ....101 F2
Peldon Cl *LGB/HTN* NE7 ....64 B1
Pelham Ct *GOS/KPK* NE3 ....46 A5
Peltondale Av *BLYTH* NE24 ....9 F5
Pelton Fell Rd *CLSW/PEL* DH2 ....152 C4
Pelton La *CLSW/PEL* DH2 ....151 D3
  CLSW/PEL DH2..............................152 B2
Pelton Ms *CLSW/PEL* DH2 ....151 E2
Pelton Rd *MLFD/PNYW* SR4 ....142 B2
Pemberton Bank *HLH* DH5 ....186 A3
Pemberton Ct *SWCK/CAS* SR5 ....126 A5
Pemberton Gdns *SUNDSW* SR3 ....144 A3
Pemberton St *HLH* DH5 ....171 F6
Pembroke Av *CLS/BIR/GTL* DH3 ....136 C5
  SUNDSW SR3 ....160 C2
Pembroke Ct *GOS/KPK* NE3 ....45 F5
Pembroke Gdns *WLSD/HOW* NE28 .....68 C2
Pembroke Pl *PLEE/EAS* SR8 ....200 A6
Pembroke Ter *SSH* NE33 ....88 B1
Pembrooke Av *BYK/HTN/WLK* NE6 ......66 A6
Pendeford *WASHS* NE38 ....139 F2
Pendle Cl *WASHS* NE38 ....138 A3
Pendleton Dr *CRAM* NE23.....................13 F5

Pendower Wy
BW/LEM/TK/HW NE15 ....**78** B2
Penfold CI *LGB/HTN* * NE7 ....**65** E2
Penhale Dr *ASHBK/HED/RY* SR2 ...**162** B1
Penhill CI *CLSW/PEL* DH2 ....**135** D5
Penistone Rd *MLFD/PNYW* SR4 .....**141** F3
Penman PI *NSHW* NE29 ....**70** C2
Penman Sq *MLFD/PNYW* SR4 ....**141** F3
Penman St *NSHW* NE29 ....**70** C2
Pennant Sq *MLFD/PNYW* SR4 ....**124** B6
Pennine Ct *STLY/ANP* DH9 ....**146** B5
Pennine Dr *PLEE/EAS* SR8 ....**208** A2
Pennine Gdns *DUN/TMV* NE11 ....**97** F3
    STLY/ANP DH9 ....**148** C3
Pennine Gv *BOL* NE36 ....**106** A3
Pennine Wy *LGB/KIL* NE12 ....**48** C6
Penn Sq *MLFD/PNYW* SR4 ....**124** B6
Penn St *ELS/FEN* NE4 ....**80** A5
Pennycross Rd *MLFD/PNYW* SR4 ...**141** F3
Pennycross Sq *MLFD/PNYW* SR4 ...**141** F1
Pennyfine CI *NSHW* NE29 ....**54** B4
Pennyfine Rd *WICK/BNPF* NE16 .....**114** B1
Pennygate Sq *MLFD/PNYW* SR4 .....**141** F1
Pennygreen Sq *MLFD/PNYW* SR4 ...**141** F1
Pennymore Sq *MLFD/PNYW* SR4 ....**141** F1
Pennywell Rd *MLFD/PNYW* SR4 ......**142** B2
Penrith Av *TYNE/NSHE* NE30 ....**54** C2
Penrith Gdns *LWF/SPW/WRK* NE9 ..**100** A6
Penrith Rd *HEBB* NE31 ....**85** E4
    SWCK/CAS SR5 ....**108** B6
Penryn Av *SEA/MUR* SR7 ....**188** C1
Penryn Wy *BDN/LAN/SAC* DH7 ....**203** E4
Pensford Ct *GOS/KPK* NE3 ....**61** E1
Penshaw Gn *WD/WHPE/BLK* NE5 ...**61** F3
Penshaw La *HLS* DH4 ....**140** A6
Penshaw Vw *BDN/LAN/SAC* DH7 ...**178** C2
    FELL NE10 ....**102** B2
    HEBB NE31 ....**84** C4
    JRW NE32 ....**86** A4
Penshaw Wy *CLS/BIR/GTL* DH3 .....**137** D2
Pensher St *MLFD/PNYW* SR4 ....**125** F6
Pensher St East *FELL* NE10 ....**100** B1
Pentland CI *CRAM* NE23 ....**14** A5
    NSHW NE29 ....**54** B3
    PLEE/EAS SR8 ....**207** F3
    WASHS NE38 ....**138** A3
Pentland Gdns *DUN/TMV* NE11 ......**97** F3
Pentland Gv *LGB/KIL* NE12 ....**49** D3
Pentlands Ter *SUNDSW* * SR3 ....**148** C3
Pentridge CI *CRAM* NE23 ....**22** B1
Penwood Rd *MLFD/PNYW* SR4 ....**142** B1
Pen-y-Ghent Wy *WASHN* NE37 .....**119** F6
Penzance Bungs *SEA/MUR* SR7 ....**174** C6
Penzance Rd *MLFD/PNYW* SR4 ......**142** A2
Peppercorn Ct *CNUT* * NE1 ....**3** F5
Percival St *MLFD/PNYW* SR4 ....**125** E5
Percy Av *WBAY* NE26 ....**40** B5
Percy Ct *NSHW* NE29 ....**69** F3
Percy Crs *NSHW* NE29 ....**69** F3
Percy Gdns *DUN/TMV* NE11 ....**97** F3
    LGB/KIL NE12 ....**49** F4
    MONK NE25 ....**40** C6
Percy La *DHAM* DH1 ....**193** F2
Percy Pk *TYNE/NSHE* NE30 ....**55** F4
Percy Park Rd *TYNE/NSHE* NE30 ...**55** F4
Percy Rd *WBAY* NE26 ....**41** D5
Percy Scott St *HAR/WTLS* NE34 .....**88** B5
Percy Sq *DHAM* DH1 ....**204** C1
Percy St *BLYTH* NE24 ....**11** E4
    BW/LEM/TK/HW NE15 ....**76** B2
    CNUT NE1 ....**2** C2
    CRAM NE23 ....**22** B3
    HLH DH5 ....**172** A6
    JRW NE32 ....**86** B1
    LGB/KIL NE12 ....**50** B3
    SSH NE33 ....**71** F4
    TYNE/NSHE NE30 ....**55** F5
    WLSD/HOW NE28 ....**67** H3
Percy St South *BLYTH* NE24 ....**11** E5
Percy Ter *ASHBK/HED/RY* * SR2 ...**145** D2
    DHAM DH1 ....**193** F5
    MONK NE25 ....**40** A5
Percy Ter South
    ASHBK/HED/RY SR2 ....**145** D3
Percy Wy *BW/LEM/TK/HW* NE15 ...**58** E2
Peregrine PI *LGB/KIL* NE12 ....**48** C5
Perivale Rd *MLFD/PNYW* SR4 ....**142** A2
Perrycrofts *SUNDSW* SR5 ....**160** C4
Perry St *GATE* NE8 ....**99** E2
Perth Av *JRW* NE32 ....**86** C5
Perth CI *NSHW* NE29 ....**53** E4
    WLSD/HOW NE28 ....**68** B2
Perth Ct *SUNDSW* SR3 ....**143** D5
Perth Gdns *WLSD/HOW* NE28 ....**68** B2
Perth Rd *SUNDSW* SR3 ....**143** D5
Perth Sq *SUNDSW* SR3 ....**143** E4
Pesspool La *RDHAMSE* DH6 ....**198** A2
Peterborough CI *GATE* * NE8 ....**81** D6
Peterborough Rd *DHAM* DH1 ....**181** D6
    GATE NE8 ....**81** D6
Peter's Bank *STLY/ANP* DH9 ....**146** C1
Petersfield Rd *MLFD/PNYW* SR4 ....**142** A2
Petersham Rd *MLFD/PNYW* SR4 .....**124** B6
Petherton Ct *GOS/KPK* NE3 ....**45** E6
Peth Gn *HLH* DH5 ....**186** A1

Peth La *RYTON* NE40 ....**74** C2
Petrel CI *SSH* NE33 ....**71** E2
Petrel Wy *BLYTH* NE24 ....**17** E2
Petteril *WASHS* NE38 ....**137** F5
Petworth CI *SSH* NE33 ....**71** F3
Pevensey CI *NSHW* NE29 ....**54** B3
Philadelphia La *HLS* DH4 ....**157** E3
Philiphaugh *WLSD/HOW* NE28 ......**67** D6
Philip PI *ELS/FEN* NE4 ....**79** D2
Philipson St *BYK/HTN/WLK* NE6 ....**83** E2
Philip Sq *SUNDSW* SR3 ....**143** D4
Phillips Av *WICK/BNPF* NE16 ....**95** F2
Phoenix Cha *NSHW* NE29 ....**53** D4
Phoenix House
    SUND (off Union St) SR1 ....**4** C2
Phoenix Rd *MLFD/PNYW* SR4 ....**124** B6
    WASHS NE38 ....**119** D6
Phoenix Wy *HLS* DH4 ....**170** B3
Piccadilly *SUNDSW* SR3 ....**143** D6
Picherwell *FELL* NE10 ....**100** C3
Pickard St *PLEE/EAS* SR8 ....**209** D1
Pickard St *MLFD/PNYW* SR4 ....**125** F5
Pickering Rd *MLFD/PNYW* SR4 ......**141** F3
Pickering Sq *MLFD/PNYW* SR4 ......**142** A3
Pickhurst Rd *MLFD/PNYW* SR4 ......**142** A3
Pickhurst Sq *MLFD/PNYW* SR4 ......**142** A3
Picktree La *CLS/BIR/GTL* DH3 ....**153** F4
    WASHS NE38 ....**137** D6
Picktree Ldg *CLS/BIR/GTL* DH3 ......**136** C6
Pickwick CI *DHAM* DH1 ....**205** D1
Pier Pde *SSH* NE33 ....**72** A2
Pier Vw *CLDN/WHIT/ROK* SR6 ......**106** A1
Pikestone CI *WASHS* NE38 ....**137** F3
Pilgrim CI *SWCK/CAS* SR5 ....**126** B3
Pilgrim St *CNUT* NE1 ....**2** D5
Pilgrims' Wy *JRW* NE32 ....**87** D2
Pilgrimsway *JRW* NE32 ....**87** D2
    LWF/SPW/WRK NE9 ....**99** F3
Pilton Rd *WD/WHPE/BLK* NE5 ....**60** B3
Pimlico *DHAM* DH1 ....**194** B6
Pimlico Rd *HLH* DH5 ....**186** A3
    MLFD/PNYW SR4 ....**142** A2
Pine Av *DHAM* DH1 ....**195** F5
    DIN/WO NE13 ....**31** E3
    GOS/KPK NE3 ....**46** B5
    HAR/WTLS NE34 ....**89** F3
    WICK/BNPF NE16 ....**111** E6
Pinedale Dr *RDHAMSE* DH6 ....**187** E5
Pine Lea *BDN/LAN/SAC* DH7 ....**202** C4
Pine Pk *BDN/LAN/SAC* DH7 ....**192** A5
Pine Rd *BLAY* NE21 ....**76** B6
The Pines
    ELS/FEN (off Park Rd) NE4 ....**79** F5
    RYTON NE40 ....**92** A1
Pine St *CLS/BIR/GTL* DH3 ....**136** B3
    CLSW/PEL DH2 ....**150** C3
    JRW NE32 ....**85** F2
    MLFD/PNYW SR4 ....**125** E5
    STLY/ANP DH9 ....**147** E4
Pinesway *SUNDSW* SR3 ....**144** A3
Pinetree Centre
    CLS/BIR/GTL
    (off Durham Rd) DH3 ....**136** B3
Pinetree Gdns *MONK* NE25 ....**54** A1
Pinetree Wy *WICK/BNPF* NE16 ....**78** A6
Pinewood *HEBB* NE31 ....**84** B1
Pinewood Av *CRAM* NE23 ....**14** A5
    DIN/WO NE13 ....**33** E5
    GOS/KPK NE3 ....**33** E5
    WASHS NE38 ....**138** B5
Pinewood CI *BYK/HTN/WLK* NE6 ...**66** A5
    DIN/WO NE13 ....**45** D6
Pinewood Gdns *DUN/TMV* NE11 ....**97** F5
Pinewood Rd *SWCK/CAS* SR5 ....**125** E2
Pinewood Sq *SWCK/CAS* SR5 ....**125** E2
Pinewood St *HLS* DH4 ....**169** D1
Pinewood Vls *HAR/WTLS* NE34 ......**89** F2
Pink La *CNUT* * NE1 ....**2** C5
Pinner PI *BYK/HTN/WLK* NE6 ....**83** D4
Pinner Rd *MLFD/PNYW* SR4 ....**142** B1
Pintail Ct
    HAR/WTLS (off Clive St) NE34 ....**87** F4
Pipershaw *WASHN* NE37 ....**119** E6
Pipe Track La *ELS/FEN* NE4 ....**78** C4
Pipewellgate *GATE* NE8 ....**80** C5
Pitcairn Rd *MLFD/PNYW* SR4 ....**142** B1
Pithouse La *HLS* DH4 ....**183** D1
Pit La *DHAM* DH1 ....**180** B4
Pittington La *DHAM* DH1 ....**197** D1
Pittington Rd *HLH* DH5 ....**183** F4
Pitt St *ELS/FEN* NE4 ....**80** A2
Plains Rd *SUNDSW* SR3 ....**143** E4
Plaistow Sq *MLFD/PNYW* SR4 ....**124** B6
Plaistow Wy *CRAM* NE23 ....**14** A5
Planesway *FELL* NE10 ....**101** D5
Planet PI *LGB/KIL* NE12 ....**49** E2
Planetree Av *ELS/FEN* NE4 ....**61** F6
Plane Tree Ct *SUNDSW* * SR3 ....**160** A2
Plantation Av *WICK/BNPF* NE16 .....**95** F2
Plantation Gv *FELL* NE10 ....**84** A6
Plantation Rd *MLFD/PNYW* SR4 .....**125** D5
Plantation Sq *MLFD/PNYW* SR4 .....**125** D5
Plantation St *WLSD/HOW* NE28 .....**67** D6
The Plantation
    LWF/SPW/WRK NE9 ....**99** F5

Plantation Vw *STLY/ANP* DH9 ....**150** B2
Plantation Wk *RDHAMSE* DH6 ....**187** E5
Plawsworth Gdns
    LWF/SPW/WRK NE9 ....**118** B1
Plawsworth Rd
    BDN/LAN/SAC DH7 ....**178** B1
Plenmeller PI *WICK/BNPF* NE16 ....**113** F1
Plessey Av *BLYTH* NE24 ....**11** D6
Plessey Crs *MONK* NE25 ....**41** D6
Plessey Gdns *NSHW* NE29 ....**69** F1
Plessey Rd *BLYTH* NE24 ....**16** A2
Plessey Ter *LGB/HTN* NE7 ....**65** D4
Plough Rd *SUNDSW* SR3 ....**160** B3
Plover CI *BLYTH* NE24 ....**17** D2
Plover Dr *WICK/BNPF* NE16 ....**130** B3
Plover Ldg
    CLS/BIR/GTL
    (off Durham Rd) DH3 ....**118** B6
Plunkett Rd *STLY/ANP* DH9 ....**129** D5
Plunkett Ter *CLSW/PEL* DH2 ....**151** F4
Plymouth CI *SEA/MUR* SR7 ....**175** E4
Plymouth Sq *SUNDSW* SR3 ....**143** D4
Point Pleasant Ter
    WLSD/HOW NE28 ....**68** A4
Polden CI *PLEE/EAS* SR8 ....**207** F3
Polden Crs *NSHW* NE29 ....**54** A2
Polebrook Rd *MLFD/PNYW* SR4 .....**124** B6
Polgrade Ct
    HLS (off Wynyard St) DH4 ....**169** F2
Pollard St *SSH* NE33 ....**71** F2
Polmuir Rd *SUNDSW* SR3 ....**143** D4
Polmuir Sq *SUNDSW* * SR3 ....**143** D4
Polpero CI *CLSW/PEL* DH2 ....**136** C3
Polperro CI *ASHBK/HED/RY* SR2 ...**162** B1
Polton Sq *MLFD/PNYW* SR4 ....**124** B6
Polwarth Crs *GOS/KPK* NE3 ....**47** E3
Polwarth Dr *GOS/KPK* NE3 ....**47** E3
Polwarth Rd *GOS/KPK* NE3 ....**47** E3
Polworth Sq *SUNDSW* SR3 ....**143** E4
Pontefract Rd *MLFD/PNYW* SR4 .....**142** A3
Ponteland CI *NSHW* NE29 ....**53** E5
    WASHS NE38 ....**137** E5
Ponteland Rd
    BW/LEM/TK/HW NE15 ....**57** F2
    DIN/WO NE13 ....**44** C5
    ELS/FEN NE4 ....**62** C6
    PONT/DH NE20 ....**28** C4
    WD/WHPE/BLK NE5 ....**45** D6
Ponthaugh *ROWG* NE39 ....**111** E1
Pontop Sq *MLFD/PNYW* SR4 ....**124** B6
Pontop St *HLH* DH5 ....**186** B3
Pontop Vw *ROWG* NE39 ....**110** C2
Pont Vw *PONT/DH* NE20 ....**28** B3
Poole CI *CRAM* NE23 ....**22** B1
Poole Rd *MLFD/PNYW* SR4 ....**124** B6
Pooley CI *WD/WHPE/BLK* NE5 ....**61** D5
Pooley Rd *WD/WHPE/BLK* NE5 ....**61** D5
Poplar Av *BLYTH* NE24 ....**10** C3
    BYK/HTN/WLK * NE6 ....**66** B5
    DIN/WO NE13 ....**31** E3
    WICK/BNPF NE16 ....**111** E6
Poplar Crs *CLS/BIR/GTL* DH3 ....**136** A1
    DUN/TMV NE11 ....**97** E3
    GATE NE8 ....**81** D6
Poplar Dr *CLDN/WHIT/ROK* SR6 ....**109** E1
    DHAM DH1 ....**195** F3
Poplar Gv *ASHBK/HED/RY* SR2 .....**145** D6
    BDLGTN NE22 ....**8** A3
    HAR/WTLS NE34 ....**89** E3
Poplar Lea *BDN/LAN/SAC* DH7 .....**202** C4
Poplar Rd *BLAY* NE21 ....**94** B1
    DHAM DH1 ....**196** C2
The Poplars
    ELS/FEN (off De Grey St) NE4 ....**79** F5
    GOS/KPK NE3 ....**63** E3
    HLH DH5 ....**186** B3
    SWCK/CAS SR5 ....**125** E2
Poplar St *CLS/BIR/GTL* DH3 ....**153** E5
    STLY/ANP DH9 ....**147** E4
Popplewell Gdns
    LWF/SPW/WRK NE9 ....**99** F6
Popplewell Ter *NSHW* NE29 ....**54** C4
The Populars *HLS* DH4 ....**140** A6
The Porchesters *CRAM* NE23 ....**22** B1
Porchester Dr *CRAM* NE23 ....**22** B1
Porlock Ct *CRAM* NE23 ....**13** F5
Porlock Rd *JRW* NE32 ....**86** C3
Portadown Rd *MLFD/PNYW* SR4 ....**142** A3
Portberry St *SSH* NE33 ....**71** D6
Portberry Wy *SSH* NE33 ....**71** D5
Porchester Gv *BOLCOL* NE35 ....**105** D2
Porchester Rd *MLFD/PNYW* SR4 ....**142** B1
Porchester Sq *MLFD/PNYW* SR4 ....**142** B2
Porter Ter *SEA/MUR* SR7 ....**188** B1
Porthcawl Dr *WASHN* NE37 ....**100** B2
Portland Av *SEA/MUR* SR7 ....**175** E3
Portland Gdns *CRAM* NE23 ....**22** B1
    LWF/SPW/WRK NE9 ....**117** D2
    TYNE/NSHE NE30 ....**54** C4
Portland Ms *JES* * NE2 ....**81** E1
Portland Rd
    BW/LEM/TK/HW NE15 ....**58** A4
    JES NE2 ....**81** E1
    SUNDSW SR3 ....**143** E4
Portland Sq *SUNDSW* SR3 ....**143** E3
Portland St *BLYTH* NE24 ....**10** C4

ELS/FEN NE4 ....**79** F4
FELL NE10 ....**101** F1
Portland Ter *JES* NE2 ....**81** D1
Portman Ms *JES* NE2 ....**3** H1
Portman Pl *BYK/HTN/WLK* NE6 .....**83** D5
Portman Sq *MLFD/PNYW* SR4 ......**142** B1
Portmeads Rd *CLS/BIR/GTL* DH3 ...**136** C2
Portobello La
CLDN/WHIT/ROK SR6 ....**126** C3
Portree Sq *SUNDSW* SR3 ....**143** D5
Portrush Cl *WASHN* NE37 ....**120** B2
Portrush Rd *MLFD/PNYW* SR4 ......**124** B6
Portrush Wy *LGB/KIL* NE12 ....**65** E1
Portslade Rd *MLFD/PNYW* SR4 ....**142** A2
Portsmouth Rd *MLFD/PNYW* SR4 ..**142** A1
NSHW NE29 ....**69** F3
Portsmouth Sq *MLFD/PNYW* SR4 ..**142** A2
Portugal Pl *WLSD/HOW* NE28 ....**67** D5
Post Office La *NSHW* NE29 ....**54** C4
Post Office St *BLYTH* NE24 ....**11** E4
Potterhouse La *DHAM* DH1 ....**179** E4
The Potteries *SSH* NE33 ....**72** A5
Potter Pl *STLY/ANP* DH9 ....**149** D3
Potters Bank *DHAM* DH1 ....**205** D1
Potters Cl *DHAM* DH1 ....**204** C1
Potter Sq *SUNDSW* SR3 ....**143** D4
Potter St *JRW* NE32 ....**85** F1
WLSD/HOW NE28 ....**68** C5
Pottersway *LWF/SPW/WRK* NE9 ...**99** F4
Pottery Bank *BYK/HTN/WLK* NE6 ...**83** E5
Pottery La *CNUT* NE1 ....**80** B5
MLFD/PNYW SR4 ....**123** F5
Pottery Yd *HLS* DH4 ....**171** D2
Potto St *BYK/HTN/WLK* NE6 ....**82** B2
Powburn Cl *CLSW/PEL* DH2 ....**165** F1
Powburn Gdns *ELS/FEN* NE4 ....**62** A6
Powis Rd *SUNDSW* SR3 ....**143** E4
Powis Sq *SUNDSW* SR3 ....**143** E4
Powys Pl *ELS/FEN* NE4 ....**79** F2
Poynings Cl *WD/WHPE/BLK* NE5 ....**61** E1
Praetorian Dr *WLSD/HOW* NE28 .....**67** D5
Prebends Fld *DHAM* DH1 ....**195** E2
The Precinct
BLAY (off Wesley Ct) NE21 ....**76** C5
Prefect Pl *LWF/SPW/WRK* NE9 ....**99** F3
Premier Rd *SUNDSW* SR3 ....**143** D4
Prendwick Av *HEBB* NE31 ....**84** C5
Prendwick Cl *CLSW/PEL* DH2 ....**165** F1
Prengarth Av
CLDN/WHIT/ROK SR6 ....**126** C3
Prensgarth Wy *HAR/WTLS* NE34 ....**87** E5
Prescot Rd *MLFD/PNYW* SR4 ....**124** B6
Press La *SUND* SR1 ....**4** D2
Prestbury Av *CRAM* NE23 ....**15** F1
Prestbury Rd *MLFD/PNYW* SR4 .....**141** F2
Prestdale Av *BLYTH* NE24 ....**9** F5
Presthope Rd *MLFD/PNYW* SR4 .....**141** F2
Preston Av *TYNE/NSHE* NE30 ....**54** C5
Preston North Rd *NSHW* NE29 ....**54** B3
Preston Pk *NSHW* NE29 ....**54** B4
Preston Rd *ASHBK/HED/RY* SR2 ....**145** E2
Preston Ter *NSHW* NE29 ....**54** B4
Preston Towers
NSHW (off Preston Rd) NE29 ....**54** C5
Preston Wd *TYNE/NSHE* NE30 ....**54** C3
Prestwick *FELL* NE10 ....**101** D5
Prestwick Av *NSHW* NE29 ....**53** F1
Prestwick Cl *WASHN* NE37 ....**120** B2
Prestwick Dr *FELL* NE10 ....**102** B3
Prestwick Gdns *GOS/KPK* NE3 ....**62** B2
Prestwick Rd *MLFD/PNYW* SR4 .....**124** B6
Pretoria Sq *SUNDSW* SR3 ....**143** D4
Pretoria St *BW/LEM/TK/HW* NE15 ...**77** F4
Price St *HEBB* * NE31 ....**84** B1
Priestfield Cl *SUNDSW* SR3 ....**160** B3
Priestfield Gdns
WICK/BNPF * NE16 ....**111** E6
Priestley Ct *HAR/WTLS* NE34 ....**87** F5
Priestley Gdns *FELL* NE10 ....**102** A2
Priestly Crs *MLFD/PNYW* SR4 ....**126** A4
Priestman Ct *MLFD/PNYW* SR4 .....**124** C6
Primary Gdns *ASHBK/HED/RY* SR2 ....**5** C5
Primate Rd *SUNDSW* SR3 ....**143** D4
Primrose Av *HAR/WTLS* NE34 ....**88** A3
PLEE/EAS SR8 ....**209** E1
Primrose Cl *CRAM* NE23 ....**34** C2
Primrose Crs
CLDN/WHIT/ROK SR6 ....**126** C3
HLS DH4 ....**156** A5
Primrose Gdns *WLSD/HOW* NE28 ....**66** C2
Primrose Hl *LWF/SPW/WRK* NE9 .....**99** F5
Primrose Prec
CLDN/WHIT/ROK SR6 ....**126** C1
Primrose St *MLFD/PNYW* SR4 ....**123** F6
Primrose Ter *CLS/BIR/GTL* DH3 .....**136** C2
JRW NE32 ....**86** B4
Prince Albert Ter *JES* * NE2 ....**3** G2
Prince Consort La *HEBB* NE31 ....**84** C2
Prince Consort Rd *GATE* NE8 ....**81** D6
HEBB NE31 ....**84** B2
JRW NE32 ....**86** B2
Prince Consort Wy *NSHW* NE29 ......**70** C3

Prince Edward Gv
HAR/WTLS NE34 ....**90** B2
Prince Edward Rd
HAR/WTLS NE34 ....**89** D3
Prince Edward Rd East
HAR/WTLS NE34 ....**90** B2
Prince George Av
CLDN/WHIT/ROK SR6 ....**108** C6
Prince of Wales Cl
HAR/WTLS NE34 ....**89** D3
Prince Philip Cl
BW/LEM/TK/HW NE15 ....**78** B3
Prince Rd *WLSD/HOW* NE28 ....**67** D3
Princes Av *CLDN/WHIT/ROK* SR6 ...**109** D5
GOS/KPK NE3 ....**47** D6
Princes Cl *GOS/KPK* NE3 ....**47** D4
Prince's Gdns *BLYTH* NE24 ....**10** B4
CLDN/WHIT/ROK SR6 ....**109** D5
Prince's Meadow *GOS/KPK* NE3 ......**62** C1
Princes Pk *DUN/TMV* NE11 ....**98** A5
Princes Rd *GOS/KPK* NE3 ....**47** D3
Princess Dr *GATE* NE8 ....**97** F2
Princess Louise Rd *BLYTH* NE24 .....**11** D5
Princess Mary Ct *JES* NE2 ....**63** F5
Princess Sq *CNUT* NE1 ....**2** D2
Princess St *ASHBK/HED/RY* SR2 ....**4** B5
FELL NE10 ....**101** F1
WICK/BNPF NE16 ....**114** A2
Princes' St *DHAM* DH1 ....**194** A4
HLS DH4 ....**156** C3
STLY/ANP DH9 ....**146** B3
TYNE/NSHE NE30 ....**55** D5
Prince St *SUND* SR1 ....**4** C2
Princesway *DUN/TMV* NE11 ....**98** B4
Princetown Ter *SUNDSW* SR3 ....**143** D4
Princeway *TYNE/NSHE* NE30 ....**55** F4
Pringle Cl *BDN/LAN/SAC* DH7 ....**202** A1
Pringle Gv *BDN/LAN/SAC* DH7 ......**202** B1
Pringle Pl *BDN/LAN/SAC* DH7 ....**202** B1
Prinn Pl *WICK/BNPF* NE16 ....**114** A2
Priors Cl *DHAM* DH1 ....**193** F4
Prior's Ter *TYNE/NSHE* NE30 ....**55** F5
Priors Wy *WLSD/HOW* NE28 ....**68** A4
Priory Av *MONK* NE25 ....**40** B6
Priory Ct *BDN/LAN/SAC* DH7 ....**178** B2
GATE NE8 ....**81** E5
Priory Flats
DHAM (off Priory Rd) DH1 ....**194** A1
Priory Gra *BLYTH* NE24 ....**10** B4
Priory Gn *BYK/HTN/WLK* NE6 ....**82** A3
Priory Gv *MLFD/PNYW* SR4 ....**143** E1
Priory Pl *BYK/HTN/WLK* NE6 ....**82** B3
DIN/WO NE13 ....**32** C5
Priory Rd *DHAM* DH1 ....**194** A1
JRW NE32 ....**69** E6
Priory Wy *WD/WHPE/BLK* NE5 ....**60** D2
Proctor Sq *SUNDSW* SR3 ....**143** E4
Proctor St *BYK/HTN/WLK* NE6 ....**83** F3
Promenade *ASHBK/HED/RY* SR2 ....**145** F5
SEA/MUR SR7 ....**176** C2
SSH NE33 ....**72** B1
WBAY NE26 ....**40** C4
Prospect Av *MONK* NE25 ....**24** B5
WLSD/HOW NE28 ....**67** D3
Prospect Av North
WLSD/HOW NE28 ....**67** D2
Prospect Ct *ELS/FEN* * NE4 ....**79** F3
Prospect Crs *HLH* DH5 ....**186** B4
Prospect Gdns *BOL* NE36 ....**105** F3
Prospect Pl *ELS/FEN* NE4 ....**79** F3
Prospect Rw *SUND* SR1 ....**5** G1
Prospect Ter *TYNE/NSHE* NE30 ....**55** E6
Prospect Vw *HLS* DH4 ....**183** E2
Providence Ct *DHAM* * DH1 ....**194** C4
Providence Pl *FELL* NE10 ....**100** C2
Providence Rw *DHAM* DH1 ....**194** C4
Provident St *CLSW/PEL* DH2 ....**151** E2
Provost Gdns
BW/LEM/TK/HW NE15 ....**78** C4
Prudhoe Gv *JRW* NE32 ....**85** F5
Prudhoe St *MLFD/PNYW* SR4 ....**125** E5
NSHW NE29 ....**70** C2
Prudhoe Ter *TYNE/NSHE* NE30 ....**55** F4
Pudding Chare *CNUT* NE1 ....**2** D5
Purbeck Gdns *CRAM* NE23 ....**22** B1
Purbeck Rd *LGB/KIL* NE12 ....**49** D6
Purley *WASHS* NE38 ....**139** F2
Purley Cl *WLSD/HOW* NE28 ....**68** B2
Purley Gdns *GOS/KPK* NE3 ....**62** B2
Purley Rd *SUNDSW* SR3 ....**143** D5
Purley Sq *SUNDSW* SR3 ....**143** D4
Putney Sq *MLFD/PNYW* SR4 ....**142** A1
Pykerley Ms
MONK (off Pykerley Rd) NE25 ....**40** A5
Pykerley Rd *MONK* NE25 ....**40** A5

Q

The Quadrant *NSHW* NE29 ....**70** A1
SUND SR1 ....**5** G1
Quality Rw *BYK/HTN/WLK* NE6 ....**82** A3
Quality Row Rd *WICK/BNPF* NE16 ....**95** F1

Quantock Cl *LGB/KIL* NE12 ....**48** C6
NSHW NE29 ....**54** A2
Quantock Pl *PLEE/EAS* SR8 ....**207** F2
Quarry Bank Ct *ELS/FEN* * NE4 ....**3** H6
Quarry Bank *ELS/FEN* NE4 ....**80** A3
Quarry Bank Ct *ELS/FEN* * NE4 ....**80** A3
Quarryfield Rd *GATE* NE8 ....**3** H6
Quarryheads La *DHAM* DH1 ....**194** A6
Quarry House La *DHAM* DH1 ....**193** E5
HLH DH5 ....**170** C6
Quarry La *HAR/WTLS* NE34 ....**89** F3
Quarry Rd
BW/LEM/TK/HW NE15 ....**76** B2
HEBB NE31 ....**85** D3
STLY/ANP DH9 ....**148** B1
SUNDSW SR3 ....**161** D1
Quarry Rw *FELL* NE10 ....**100** C1
Quarry St *SUNDSW* SR3 ....**160** C1
Quay Rd *BLYTH* NE24 ....**11** E4
Quayside *BLYTH* NE24 ....**11** E4
BYK/HTN/WLK NE6 ....**82** A4
CNUT NE1 ....**3** F5
The Quay *HLH* DH5 ....**185** F1
Quay Vw *WLSD/HOW* NE28 ....**68** B4
Queen Alexandra Br
MLFD/PNYW SR4 ....**125** F4
Queen Alexandra Rd
ASHBK/HED/RY SR2 ....**145** D4
NSHW NE29 ....**54** B5
SUNDSW SR3 ....**144** A3
Queen Alexandra Rd West
NSHW NE29 ....**54** A5
Queen Anne Ct *BYK/HTN/WLK* NE6 ...**82** B1
Queen Elizabeth Av
LWF/SPW/WRK NE9 ....**100** A5
Queen Elizabeth Dr *HLH* DH5 ....**186** C4
Queen Elizabeth II Br *CNUT* NE1 .....**80** C5
Queens Av *CLDN/WHIT/ROK* SR6 ...**109** D5
Queensberry St *MLFD/PNYW* SR4 ...**125** A5
Queensbridge *LGB/KIL* NE12 ....**48** B5
Queensbury Dr
WD/WHPE/BLK NE5 ....**59** D4
Queensbury Rd *SEA/MUR* SR7 ....**175** F3
Queen's Ct *BW/LEM/TK/HW* NE15 ....**58** C5
GATE NE8 ....**98** B2
GOS/KPK NE3 ....**47** D2
Queen's Crs *HEBB* NE31 ....**84** C4
MLFD/PNYW SR4 ....**143** F1
WLSD/HOW NE28 ....**66** C3
Queen's Dr *WBAY* NE26 ....**40** C5
WICK/BNPF NE16 ....**96** A5
Queens Gdns *BLYTH* NE24 ....**10** B4
Queens Gv *DHAM* DH1 ....**204** C1
Queensland Av *HAR/WTLS* NE34 .....**87** D4
Queens La *CNUT* * NE1 ....**2** D5
Queensmere *CLS/BIR/GTL* DH3 .....**153** E1
Queen's Rd *BDLGTN* NE22 ....**8** C2
BW/LEM/TK/HW NE15 ....**58** C5
CRAM NE23 ....**35** D1
JES NE2 ....**64** B5
SWCK/CAS SR5 ....**126** A3
WBAY NE26 ....**26** C2
WBAY NE26 ....**40** B4
WD/WHPE/BLK NE5 ....**60** C4
Queen's Ter *JES* NE2 ....**64** B5
WLSD/HOW NE28 ....**67** D4
Queen St *ASHBK/HED/RY* SR2 ....**145** E6
CLSW/PEL DH2 ....**150** C3
CNUT NE1 ....**3** F5
GATE NE8 ....**98** B2
HLH DH5 ....**171** F5
SSH NE33 ....**71** E4
SUND SR1 ....**4** B1
TYNE/NSHE NE30 ....**55** D6
Queen St East *SUND* SR1 ....**5** F1
Queensway *ELS/FEN* NE4 ....**61** F6
GOS/KPK NE3 ....**47** D3
HLH DH5 ....**171** E3
TYNE/NSHE NE30 ....**55** F6
Queensway North *DUN/TMV* NE11 ...**98** B3
Queen Victoria Rd *CNUT* NE1 ....**2** C1
Queen Victoria St *FELL* NE10 ....**101** E1
Quentin Av *GOS/KPK* NE3 ....**61** F1
Quinn Cl *PLEE/EAS* SR8 ....**208** C3
Quilton Cl *WD/WHPE/BLK* NE5 ....**61** D2

R

Rabbit Banks Rd *GATE* NE8 ....**80** C5
Raby Av *PLEE/EAS* SR8 ....**201** D1
Raby Cl *HLS* DH4 ....**169** F1
Raby Crs *BYK/HTN/WLK* NE6 ....**82** B2
Raby Cross *BYK/HTN/WLK* NE6 ....**82** B3
Raby Dr *SUNDSW* SR3 ....**159** E1
Raby Gdns *JRW* NE32 ....**86** A4
WICK/BNPF NE16 ....**111** D6
Raby Rd *DHAM* DH1 ....**180** B5
WASHS NE38 ....**137** E1
Raby St *BYK/HTN/WLK* NE6 ....**82** A2
GATE NE8 ....**99** E2
MLFD/PNYW SR4 ....**126** A6
Raby Wy *BYK/HTN/WLK* NE6 ....**82** B2
Rachel Cl *ASHBK/HED/RY* SR2 ....**161** E1

Rackly Wy *CLDN/WHIT/ROK* SR6 ......109 E2
Radcliffe Cottages
  BW/LEM/TK/HW
  (off Hexham Rd) NE15 ....57 F4
Radcliffe Pl *LGB/KIL* NE12 ....61 F4
Radcliffe Rd *SWCK/CAS* SR5 ....125 D2
Radcliffe St *CLS/BIR/GTL* DH3 ....136 B3
Radlett Rd *SWCK/CAS* SR5 ....124 C2
Radnor Gdns *WLSD/HOW* NE28 ....68 C3
Radnor St *CNUT* NE1 ....3 F1
Radstock Pl *LGB/KIL* NE12 ....49 E5
Rae Av *WLSD/HOW* NE28 ....67 D2
Raeburn Av *WASHS* NE38 ....139 D3
Raeburn Gdns
  LWF/SPW/WRK NE9 ....100 A3
Raeburn Rd *HAR/WTLS* NE34 ....88 C6
  SWCK/CAS SR5 ....124 B1
Raglan *WASHS* NE38 ....137 F1
Raglan Av *ASHBK/HED/RY* SR2 ....145 D3
Raglan Rd *WICK/BNPF* NE16 ....112 A6
Railway Cl *DHAM* DH1 ....197 D5
Railway Rw *SUND* SR1 ....126 A6
Railway St *DUN/TMV* NE11 ....79 E6
  ELS/FEN NE4 ....85 E1
  HEBB NE31 ....85 E3
  HLH DH5 ....185 F1
  HLS DH4 ....157 F6
  JRW NE32 ....85 F1
  STLY/ANP DH9 ....146 C5
  STLY/ANP DH9 ....149 E6
  SUND SR1 ....5 G3
Railway Ter *ELS/FEN* NE4 ....80 A5
  NSHW NE29 ....70 C1
Raine Gv *SUND* SR1 ....5 F4
Rainford Av *ASHBK/HED/RY* SR2 .....145 D3
Rainhill Cl *WASHN* NE37 ....121 D3
Rainhill Rd *WASHN* NE37 ....121 D3
Rainton Cl *FELL* NE10 ....102 B4
Rainton Gv *HLH* DH5 ....171 D4
Rainton St *HLS* DH4 ....140 A6
  MLFD/PNYW SR4 ....125 F6
Rainton Vw *HLS* DH4 ....183 E2
Rake La *NSHW* NE29 ....53 E3
Raleigh Cl *SSH* NE33 ....71 D6
Raleigh Rd *SWCK/CAS* SR5 ....124 C2
Raleigh Sq *SWCK/CAS* SR5 ....124 C2
Ralph Av *ASHBK/HED/RY* SR2 ....145 D6
Ralph St *HEBB* NE31 ....85 E1
Ramilies *ASHBK/HED/RY* SR2 ....161 F2
Ramillies Rd *SWCK/CAS* SR5 ....124 B1
The Ramparts
  BW/LEM/TK/HW NE15 ....60 A6
Ramsay St *BLAY* NE21 ....94 A1
Ramsey Cl *DHAM* DH1 ....195 F4
  PLEE/EAS SR8 ....200 C6
Ramsey St *CLS/BIR/GTL* DH3 ....153 E3
Ramsgate Rd *SWCK/CAS* SR5 ....125 D1
Ramshaw Cl *LGB/HTN* NE7 ....66 A3
Ramside Vw *DHAM* DH1 ....196 C1
Randolph St *JRW* NE32 ....86 B3
Rangoon Rd *SWCK/CAS* SR5 ....124 B1
Ranmere Rd
  BW/LEM/TK/HW NE15 ....77 E3
Ranmore Cl *CRAM* NE23 ....22 A1
Rannoch Av *CLSW/PEL* DH2 ....166 A1
Rannoch Cl *FELL* NE10 ....102 B2
Rannoch Rd *SWCK/CAS* SR5 ....124 B1
Ranson Crs *HAR/WTLS* NE34 ....87 E3
Ranson St *MLFD/PNYW* SR4 ....143 F2
Raphael Av *HAR/WTLS* NE34 ....88 A4
Rathmore Gdns *TYNE/NSHE* NE30 ....54 C4
Ratho Ct *FELL* NE10 ....101 D4
Ravenburn Gdns
  BW/LEM/TK/HW NE15 ....77 E2
Ravenna Rd *SWCK/CAS* SR5 ....124 A1
Ravensbourne Av *BOL* NE36 ....106 C2
Ravenscar Cl *WICK/BNPF* NE16 ....95 D5
Ravenscourt Pl *GATE* * NE8 ....98 C1
Ravenscourt Rd *SWCK/CAS* SR5 ......124 B2
Ravensdale Gv *BLYTH* NE24 ....9 F5
Ravenshill Rd *WD/WHPE/BLK* NE5 ....59 F5
Ravenside Rd *ELS/FEN* NE4 ....62 A6
Ravenside *WASHN* NE37 ....120 A5
Ravenswood Cl *LGB/KIL* NE12 ....50 A4
Ravenswood Gdns
  LWF/SPW/WRK NE9 ....117 E1
Ravenswood Rd
  BYK/HTN/WLK NE6 ....65 E5
  SWCK/CAS SR5 ....124 B1
Ravenswood Sq *SWCK/CAS* SR5 ......124 A1
Ravensworth St *MLFD/PNYW* SR4 ....126 A5
Ravensworth
  ASHBK/HED/RY SR2 ....161 F2
Ravensworth Av *HLS* DH4 ....169 E1
  LWF/SPW/WRK NE9 ....118 B2
Ravensworth Cl *WLSD/HOW* NE28 ......68 B4
Ravensworth Ct *DUN/TMV* NE11 ....97 F2
  GOS/KPK * NE3 ....45 F5
  RDHAMSE DH6 ....187 E5
Ravensworth Rd
  CLS/BIR/GTL DH3 ....136 A1
  DUN/TMV NE11 ....97 F2
Ravensworth St
  MLFD/PNYW * SR4 ....126 A5
  WLSD/HOW NE28 ....68 B4

Ravensworth Ter *DHAM* DH1 ....194 C4
  DUN/TMV NE11 ....97 F2
  ELS/FEN NE4 ....80 A3
  JRW NE32 ....86 A5
  SSH NE33 ....88 B1
Rawdon Rd *SWCK/CAS* SR5 ....125 D1
Rawling Rd *GATE* NE8 ....99 D3
Rawlston Wy *WD/WHPE/BLK* NE5 ......61 E3
Rawmarsh Rd *SWCK/CAS* SR5 ....124 B1
Raydale *SWCK/CAS* SR5 ....125 D1
Raydale Av *WASHN* NE37 ....120 A4
Raylees Gdns *DUN/TMV* NE11 ....97 F3
Rayleigh Dr *DIN/WO* NE13 ....33 D3
Rayleigh Gv *GATE* NE8 ....98 C3
Raynham Cl *CRAM* NE23 ....21 E5
Raynham Ct *SSH* NE33 ....71 E4
Readhead Av *SSH* NE33 ....72 A5
Readhead Dr *BYK/HTN/WLK* NE6 ....83 E4
Readhead Rd *HAR/WTLS* NE34 ....72 A6
Reading Rd *HAR/WTLS* NE34 ....88 C1
  SWCK/CAS SR5 ....124 B1
Reading Sq *SWCK/CAS* SR5 ....124 B1
Rea Pl *GOS/KPK* NE3 ....62 C1
Reasby Gdns *RYTON* NE40 ....74 A3
Reavley Av *BDLGTN* NE22 ....9 D1
Reay Crs *BOLCOL* NE35 ....106 A2
Reay Gdns *WD/WHPE/BLK* NE5 ....60 A2
Reay St *FELL* NE10 ....84 A6
Rectory Bank *BOL* NE36 ....105 E3
Rectory Ct *WICK/BNPF* NE16 ....96 A3
Rectory Dr *JES* NE2 ....64 A2
Rectory Gn *BOL* NE36 ....105 E3
Rectory Gv *GOS/KPK* NE3 ....63 F1
Rectory La *BLAY* NE21 ....94 A1
  WICK/BNPF NE16 ....96 A4
Rectory Pl *GATE* NE8 ....98 C1
Rectory Rd *FELL* NE10 ....100 B3
  GATE NE8 ....99 D1
  GOS/KPK NE3 ....63 F2
  HLH DH5 ....185 F1
Rectory Rd East *FELL* NE10 ....100 C3
Redacre Sq *WICK/BNPF* NE16 ....111 D3
Red Admiral Ct *DUN/TMV* NE11 ....98 A3
Red Barnes *CNUT* NE1 ....3 H5
Red Berry Wy *HAR/WTLS* NE34 ....88 A4
Redburn Cl *HLS* DH4 ....170 B2
Redburn Rd *WD/WHPE/BLK* NE5 ....60 B2
Redby Cl *CLDN/WHIT/ROK* SR6 ....126 C2
Redcar Rd *BYK/HTN/WLK* NE6 ....65 F5
  SWCK/CAS SR5 ....125 D2
  WLSD/HOW NE28 ....68 C3
Redcar Sq *SWCK/CAS* SR5 ....125 D2
Redcliffe Wy *WD/WHPE/BLK* NE5 ....61 D3
Redditch Sq *SWCK/CAS* SR5 ....124 C1
Rede Av *HEBB* NE31 ....84 C2
Redemarsh *FELL* NE10 ....101 E3
Redesdale Av *BLAY* NE21 ....93 E2
  GOS/KPK NE3 ....62 C1
Redesdale Cl *LGB/KIL* NE12 ....49 E4
Redesdale Gdns *DUN/TMV* NE11 ....97 E3
Redesdale Gv *NSHW* NE29 ....53 E6
Redesdale Pl *BLYTH* NE24 ....10 A5
Redesdale Rd *CLSW/PEL* DH2 ....165 F1
  NSHW NE29 ....53 E6
  SWCK/CAS SR5 ....124 B1
Rede St *DUN/TMV* NE11 ....98 B5
  JRW NE32 ....85 F3
Redewater Gdns *WICK/BNPF* NE16 ....95 F4
Redewater Rd *ELS/FEN* NE4 ....62 A6
Redewood Cl *WD/WHPE/BLK* NE5 ......60 C5
Red Firs *BDN/LAN/SAC* DH7 ....203 D4
Redford Pl *LGB/KIL* NE12 ....35 E5
Red Hall Dr *LGB/HTN* NE7 ....65 F3
Redheugh Bridge Rd
  NE4 ....80 B5
Redheugh Ct *GATE* NE8 ....98 A2
Redheugh Rd *MONK* NE25 ....39 D5
Redhill *CLDN/WHIT/ROK* SR6 ....109 D3
Redhill Dr *WICK/BNPF* NE16 ....95 D6
Redhill Rd *SWCK/CAS* SR5 ....124 C1
Redhills La *DHAM* DH1 ....193 F4
Red Hills Ter *DHAM* DH1 ....193 F4
Redhills Wy *HLH* DH5 ....185 F2
Redhouse Cl *BDN/LAN/SAC* DH7 ....178 C2
Red House Dr *MONK* NE25 ....39 E4
Red House Farm *BDLGTN* NE22 ....6 B4
Red House Gdns
  BDLGTN (off Netherton La) NE22 ....6 C4
Red House Rd *HEBB* NE31 ....85 E2
Redland Av *GOS/KPK* NE3 ....45 F6
Red Lion La *WASHN* NE37 ....120 B2
Redmayne Ct *FELL* NE10 ....100 B2
Redmires Ct *CLSW/PEL* DH2 ....135 D5
Redmond Rd *SWCK/CAS* SR5 ....125 D1
Redmond Sq *SWCK/CAS* SR5 ....125 D1
Rednam Pl *WD/WHPE/BLK* NE5 ....61 D4
Red Row Dr *BDLGTN* NE22 ....8 B1
Redruth Gdns
  LWF/SPW/WRK NE9 ....117 D2
Redruth Sq *SWCK/CAS* SR5 ....124 C2
Redshank Cl *WASHS* NE38 ....137 E4
Redshank Dr *BLYTH* NE24 ....17 D2
Redstart Ct
  ROWG (off South Sherburn) NE39 ......110 C3
Red Wk *LGB/HTN* NE7 ....64 C4
Redwell Ct *HAR/WTLS* NE34 ....90 B1

Redwell La *HAR/WTLS* NE34 ....90 C1
Redwing Cl *WASHS* NE38 ....137 E3
Redwood *BDN/LAN/SAC* DH7 ....203 D4
Redwood Cl *HLH* DH5 ....185 E1
  LGB/KIL NE12 ....35 E6
Reed Av *LGB/KIL* NE12 ....35 E5
Reedham Ct *WD/WHPE/BLK* NE5 ....61 D2
Reedling Ct *SWCK/CAS* SR5 ....106 B6
Reedside *RYTON* NE40 ....74 C3
Reedsmouth Pl
  WD/WHPE/BLK NE5 ....61 D6
Reed St *SSH* NE33 ....71 D6
  TYNE/NSHE NE30 ....55 D6
Reedswood Crs *CRAM* NE23 ....22 C3
Reestones Pl *GOS/KPK* NE3 ....61 F1
Reeth Rd *SWCK/CAS* SR5 ....124 C2
Reeth Sq *SWCK/CAS* SR5 ....124 C2
Reeth Wy *BW/LEM/TK/HW* NE15 ....57 E5
Reform Pl
  DHAM (off North Rd) DH1 ....194 B4
Regal Rd *MLFD/PNYW* SR4 ....125 F5
Regency Ct
  JES (off Jesmond Rd) NE2 ....64 B6
  NSHW (off Ritson Cl) NE29 ....54 A5
Regency Dr *SUNDSW* SR3 ....144 A6
  WICK/BNPF NE16 ....95 E4
Regency Gdns *NSHW* NE29 ....54 A5
Regent Av *GOS/KPK* NE3 ....63 D1
Regent Ct *GATE* * NE8 ....81 E6
  SSH NE33 ....71 E5
Regent Dr *WICK/BNPF* NE16 ....95 E6
Regent Farm Rd *GOS/KPK* NE3 ....46 C6
Regent Rd *ASHBK/HED/RY* SR2 ....162 C3
  GOS/KPK NE3 ....63 E1
  JRW NE32 ....86 B2
  WLSD/HOW NE28 ....66 C3
Regents Ct *WLSD/HOW* NE28 ....66 A2
Regents Dr *TYNE/NSHE* NE30 ....55 E4
Regents Pk *WLSD/HOW* NE28 ....66 A3
Regent St *BLYTH* NE24 ....11 D3
  HLH DH5 ....171 F5
  STLY/ANP DH9 ....146 B5
Regent Ter *ASHBK/HED/RY* SR2 ....145 E2
  NSHW NE29 ....54 A5
Reginald St *BOLCOL* NE35 ....105 E2
  GATE NE8 ....100 A1
  MLFD/PNYW SR4 ....125 E5
Regina Sq *SWCK/CAS* SR5 ....124 C1
Reid Av *WLSD/HOW* NE28 ....67 D3
Reid Park Cl *JES* NE2 ....64 B4
Reid Park Rd *JES* NE2 ....64 B4
Reid's La *CRAM* NE23 ....36 A1
Reigate Sq *CRAM* NE23 ....22 A1
Rekendyke La *SSH* NE33 ....71 D5
Relley Cl *BDN/LAN/SAC* DH7 ....192 A5
Relly Pth *DHAM* DH1 ....193 F6
Relton Av *BYK/HTN/WLK* NE6 ....82 C4
Relton Cl *HLS* DH4 ....169 F3
Relton Ter *CLS/BIR/GTL* DH3 ....153 E6
  MONK NE25 ....40 A5
Rembrandt Av *HAR/WTLS* NE34 ....88 B6
Remus Cl *DIN/WO* NE13 ....33 D5
Rendel St *DUN/TMV* NE11 ....97 E1
Rendle Rd *BYK/HTN/WLK* NE6 ....84 A4
Renforth St *DUN/TMV* NE11 ....97 E2
Renfrew Cl *NSHW* NE29 ....53 E4
Renfrew Rd *SWCK/CAS* SR5 ....124 B1
Rennie Rd *SWCK/CAS* SR5 ....124 A1
Rennie Sq *SWCK/CAS* SR5 ....124 A1
Rennington *FELL* NE10 ....101 E5
Rennington Av *TYNE/NSHE* NE30 ....55 E3
Rennington Pl
  WD/WHPE/BLK NE5 ....61 F4
Renny's La *DHAM* DH1 ....195 F4
Renny St *DHAM* DH1 ....195 D4
Renoir Gdns *HAR/WTLS* NE34 ....88 C6
  LGB/KIL NE12 ....49 D2
  WASHS NE38 ....139 D2
Reynolds Av *HAR/WTLS* NE34 ....88 C5
  LGB/KIL NE12 ....49 D2
  WASHS NE38 ....139 D2
Reynolds Cl *STLY/ANP* DH9 ....148 B2
Rheims Ct *MLFD/PNYW* SR4 ....124 C5
Rheydt Av *WLSD/HOW* NE28 ....66 B4
Rhodesia Rd *SWCK/CAS* SR5 ....124 C1
Rhodes St *BYK/HTN/WLK* NE6 ....83 F3
Rhondda Rd *SWCK/CAS* SR5 ....124 A1
Rhuddlan Ct *WD/WHPE/BLK* NE5 ....61 D2
Rhyl Sq *SWCK/CAS* SR5 ....125 D1
Ribbledale Gdns *LGB/HTN* NE7 ....65 D3
Ribble Rd *SWCK/CAS* SR5 ....124 B2
Ribblesdale *HLS* DH4 ....157 D1
  WLSD/HOW NE28 ....66 B2
Ribblesdale Av *BLYTH* NE24 ....9 F4
Richard Av *MLFD/PNYW* SR4 ....143 F2
Richard Browell Rd
  BW/LEM/TK/HW NE15 ....57 F5

Richardson Av *HAR/WTLS* NE34.........87 E4
Richardson Rd *JES* NE2.........80 A1
Richardson St *BYK/HTN/WLK* NE6.........65 E6
  WLSD/HOW NE28.........67 E4
Richardson Ter
  ASHBK/HED/RY SR2.........162 C2
Richard St *BLYTH* NE24.........11 D5
  HLH DH5.........185 F1
Richmond *ASHBK/HED/RY* SR2.........161 E1
Richmond Av *FELL* NE10.........102 B3
  WASHS NE38.........120 C6
  WICK/BNPF NE16.........96 A1
Richmond Cl *BDLGTN* NE22.........7 D2
Richmond Ct *GATE* NE8.........99 E1
  LWF/SPW/WRK (off Kells La) NE9 ....99 E6
Richmond Gdns *WLSD/HOW* NE28 .....68 A3
Richmond Gv *NSHW* NE29.........70 A1
Richmond Ms *GOS/KPK* NE3.........63 D3
Richmond Pk *WLSD/HOW* NE28.........66 A3
Richmond Pl
  CLS/BIR/GTL
  (off Durham Rd) DH3.........136 B4
  HAR/WTLS NE34.........88 B2
Richmond Rd *DHAM* DH1 ....180 C5
Richmond St *SWCK/CAS* SR5.........126 B4
Richmond Ter *FELL* NE10.........100 C2
  GATE NE8.........99 D1
  WBAY NE26.........40 B3
Richmond Wy *CRAM* NE23.........21 E5
Rickgarth *FELL* NE10.........101 E5
Rickleton Av *CLS/BIR/GTL* DH3.........153 F5
Rickleton Wy *WASHS* NE38.........137 E5
Riddell Av *BW/LEM/TK/HW* NE15 .....78 B3
Riddings Rd *SWCK/CAS* SR5.........124 C1
Riddings Sq *SWCK/CAS* SR5.........124 C1
Ridgely Dr *PONT/DH* NE20.........28 C4
Ridge Ter *BDLGTN* NE22.........7 D3
The Ridge *RYTON* NE40.........74 B4
Ridgeway *ASHBK/HED/RY* SR2.........161 E2
  ELS/FEN NE4.........62 A6
  FELL NE10.........102 A4
Ridge Wy *MONK* NE25.........38 A1
Ridgeway Crs *SUNDSW* SR3.........144 A3
The Ridge Wy *GOS/KPK* NE3.........62 B2
The Ridgeway *HAR/WTLS* NE34.........89 E5
Ridgewood Crs *GOS/KPK* NE3.........64 B1
Ridgewood Gdns *GOS/KPK* NE3 ....64 A1
Ridgewood Vls *GOS/KPK* NE3.........64 A1
Riding Hill Rd *STLY/ANP* DH9 ....146 B3
Riding La *DUN/TMV* NE11.........134 A2
Riding Lea *BLAY* NE21.........93 F1
The Ridings *MONK* NE25.........39 E4
The Riding *GOS/KPK* NE3.........62 A3
Ridley Av *ASHBK/HED/RY* SR2.........162 B1
  BLYTH NE24.........11 E5
  WLSD/HOW NE28.........68 C2
Ridley Cl *GOS/KPK* NE3.........46 B4
Ridley Gdns *WICK/BNPF* NE16.........95 F1
Ridley Gv *HAR/WTLS* NE34.........89 F1
Ridley Pl *CNUT* NE1.........2 D1
Ridley St *BLYTH* NE24.........11 E4
  GATE NE8.........98 C2
  STLY/ANP DH9.........148 B1
  SWCK/CAS SR5.........126 A2
Ridley Ter *ASHBK/HED/RY* SR2.........5 C1
  FELL NE10.........101 D2
Ridsdale Av *WD/WHPE/BLK* NE5.........59 F5
Ridsdale Cl *MONK* NE25.........24 B5
  WLSD/HOW NE28.........67 E2
Ridsdale Ct *GATE* NE8.........98 C1
Rievaulx *WASHS* NE38.........138 B3
Riga Sq *SWCK/CAS* SR5.........124 B1
The Riggs *HLH* DH5.........171 E2
Rignall *WASHS* NE38.........139 F1
Riley St *JRW* NE32.........85 F1
Ringlet Cl *DUN/TMV* NE11.........97 F3
Ringmore Ct *ASHBK/HED/RY* SR2 ....144 B4
Ringway *SWCK/CAS* SR5.........123 F4
Ringwood Dr *CRAM* NE23.........22 A1
Ringwood Gn *LGB/KIL* NE12.........49 E5
Ringwood Rd *SWCK/CAS* SR5.........124 C1
Ringwood Sq *SWCK/CAS* SR5.........124 C1
Rink St *BLYTH* NE24.........11 E4
Ripley Av *NSHW* NE29.........70 A2
Ripley Cl *BDLGTN* NE22.........6 C2
Ripley Dr *CRAM* NE23.........21 E5
Ripley Ter *BYK/HTN/WLK* NE6.........83 D2
Ripon Cl *CRAM* NE23.........21 E5
Ripon Ct *BDN/LAN/SAC* DH7.........178 A1
Ripon Gdns *JES* NE2.........64 C6
  WLSD/HOW NE28.........68 A3
Ripon Rd *DHAM* DH1.........180 C4
Ripon St *CLDN/WHIT/ROK* SR6 ....127 D1
  GATE NE8.........99 D1
Ripon Ter *SEA/MUR* SR7.........188 B1
The Rise *BLAY* NE21.........75 F4
  GATE (off Duncan St) NE8 ....100 A1
  GOS/KPK NE3.........62 A2
  WBAY NE26.........26 C4
Rishton Sq *SWCK/CAS* SR5.........124 B1
Ritson Cl *NSHW* NE29.........54 A5
Ritson St *CLDN/WHIT/ROK* SR6 ....109 D6
  STLY/ANP DH9.........148 A2
Riverbank Rd *SWCK/CAS* SR5.........124 C2
Riverdale *SWCK/CAS* SR5.........124 A4

River Dr *SSH* NE33.........71 E2
River La *RYTON* NE40.........74 B2
Rivermead Wy *WASHS* NE38.........139 D5
Riversdale Rd
  GATE (off Askew Rd) NE8.........98 B1
Riversdale Ter
  ASHBK/HED/RY * SR2.........144 A1
Riversdale Wy
  BW/LEM/TK/HW NE15.........76 A2
Riverside *PONT/DH* NE20.........28 A4
Riverside Ct *DUN/TMV* NE11.........97 F1
  SSH NE33.........71 F2
Riverside Pk *MLFD/PNYW* SR4.........124 A5
Riverside Rd *SWCK/CAS* SR5.........125 D2
Riverside Wy *BLAY* NE21.........77 F5
  ROWG NE39.........110 C4
  WICK/BNPF NE16.........77 F5
River Vw *BLAY* NE21.........76 A6
  ELS/FEN NE4.........78 C4
  TYNE/NSHE NE30.........55 E6
River View Cl *BDLGTN* NE22.........8 C3
Roachburn Rd
  WD/WHPE/BLK NE5.........60 A4
Robert Owen Gdns *FELL* NE10.........100 B3
Robertson Rd *SWCK/CAS* SR5.........124 A1
Robertson Sq *SWCK/CAS* SR5.........124 A1
Robert Sq *SEA/MUR* SR7.........177 D4
Roberts St *BW/LEM/TK/HW* NE15 .....77 F4
  SEA/MUR SR7.........177 D4
  SSH NE33.........71 F5
  SUNDSW SR3.........161 D1
Robert Ter *STLY/ANP* DH9.........131 E6
Robert Westall Wy *NSHW* NE29.........70 C3
Robin Ct *HLH* DH5.........184 B1
Robin Gv *SWCK/CAS* SR5.........124 B3
Robin La *HLH* DH5.........184 A2
Robinson Gdns
  CLDN/WHIT/ROK * SR6.........109 E1
  WLSD/HOW NE28.........68 C3
Robinson St *BYK/HTN/WLK* NE6.........82 B2
  SSH NE33.........71 F4
Robinson Ter *ASHBK/HED/RY* SR2....145 E1
Robsheugh Pl *WD/WHPE/BLK* NE5 ....61 E6
Robson Av *PLEE/EAS* SR8.........208 C1
Robson Pl *ASHBK/HED/RY* SR2 ....162 C2
Robson St *BYK/HTN/WLK* NE6.........81 F2
  LWF/SPW/WRK NE9.........99 E5
Rochdale Rd *SWCK/CAS* SR5.........124 C1
Rochdale St *HLH* DH5.........185 F2
  WLSD/HOW NE28.........66 C5
Rochdale Wy *SWCK/CAS* SR5.........124 C1
Roche St *WASHS* NE38.........138 B2
Rochester Gdns *DUN/TMV* NE11 ....97 F2
Rochester Rd *DHAM* DH1.........180 C5
Rochester St *BYK/HTN/WLK* NE6.........83 F3
Rochford Gv *CRAM* NE23.........22 B1
Rochford Rd *SWCK/CAS* SR5.........124 B1
Rockcliffe *SSH* NE33.........72 B5
Rockcliffe Gdns
  BW/LEM/TK/HW NE15.........77 F4
Rockcliffe St *WBAY* NE26.........41 E5
Rockcliffe Wy
  LWF/SPW/WRK NE9.........118 B2
Rocket Wy *LGB/KIL* NE12.........50 B4
Rock Gv *LWF/SPW/WRK* NE9.........99 E5
Rockhope *WASHS* NE38.........137 E6
Rockingham Rd *SWCK/CAS* SR5.........124 B1
Rockingham Sq *SWCK/CAS* SR5.........124 B1
Rock Lodge Rd
  CLDN/WHIT/ROK SR6.........127 D1
Rockmore Rd *BLAY* NE21.........94 B1
Rock Ter *JES* NE2.........3 C1
Rockville *CLDN/WHIT/ROK* SR6 ....109 D6
Rodin Av *HAR/WTLS* NE34.........88 C6
Rodney Cl *ASHBK/HED/RY* * SR2 ....161 E2
  TYNE/NSHE NE30.........55 F5
Rodney St *BYK/HTN/WLK* NE6.........82 A2
Rodney Wy *WBAY* NE26.........39 F3
Rodsley Av *GATE* NE8.........99 D2
Roeburn Wy *GOS/KPK* NE3.........62 B3
Roedean Rd *SWCK/CAS* SR5.........125 D1
Roehedge *FELL* NE10.........102 A4
Rogerley Ter *STLY/ANP* DH9.........146 A3
Rogers Cl *PLEE/EAS* SR8.........209 F2
Rogerson Ter *WD/WHPE/BLK* NE5 .....60 A3
Roger St *BYK/HTN/WLK* NE6.........82 A2
Rokeby Av *BW/LEM/TK/HW* NE15.........76 C2
Rokeby Dr *GOS/KPK* NE3.........62 B2
Rokeby Sq *MLFD/PNYW* SR4.........204 C1
Rokeby St *BW/LEM/TK/HW* NE15 ......76 C2
Rokeby Ter *BYK/HTN/WLK* NE6.........65 E5
Rokeby Vw *LWF/SPW/WRK* NE9 ....117 F2
Roker Av *CLDN/WHIT/ROK* SR6 ....126 C4
  MONK NE25.........54 A1
Roker Baths Rd
  CLDN/WHIT/ROK SR6.........127 D2
Rokerby Av *WICK/BNPF* NE16.........96 B4
Roker Park Rd
  CLDN/WHIT/ROK SR6.........127 D2
Roker Park Ter
  CLDN/WHIT/ROK SR6.........127 E2
Roker Ter *CLDN/WHIT/ROK* SR6 ....127 E1

Roland Burn Wy *ROWG* NE39.........111 D3
Roland Rd *WLSD/HOW* NE28.........68 A4
Rollesby Gv *WD/WHPE/BLK* NE5 ....61 D2
Rolling Mill Rd *JRW* NE32.........68 C6
Romaldskirk Cl *MLFD/PNYW* SR4 ....142 A1
Roman Av *BYK/HTN/WLK* NE6.........83 D2
  CLS/BIR/GTL DH3.........153 F5
Roman Forum
  WICK/BNPF
  (off Metrocentre) NE16.........96 B1
Roman Rd *SSH* NE33.........71 F2
Roman Rd North *SSH* NE33.........71 E2
The Roman Wy
  WD/WHPE/BLK NE5.........59 F5
Romford Cl *CRAM* NE23.........21 F5
Romford Pl *LWF/SPW/WRK* NE9 ....99 F3
Romford St *MLFD/PNYW* SR4.........125 E6
Romilly St *SSH* NE33.........71 F5
Romley Gv *FELL* NE10.........102 C3
Romney Av *ASHBK/HED/RY* SR2 .....145 E3
  HAR/WTLS NE34.........88 C5
  WASHS NE38.........139 D2
Romney Cl *HLS* DH4.........157 E3
Romney Dr *DHAM* DH1.........196 C1
Romney Gdns
  LWF/SPW/WRK NE9.........100 A3
Romsey Cl *CRAM* NE23.........22 A1
Romsey Dr *BOLCOL* NE35.........100 D2
Romsey Gv *BW/LEM/TK/HW* NE15 ....59 E6
Ronald Dr *BW/LEM/TK/HW* NE15 ......77 F2
Ronald Gdns *HEBB* NE31.........84 C4
Ronaldsay Cl *ASHBK/HED/RY* SR2 ...145 D6
Ronald Sq *CLDN/WHIT/ROK* SR6 .....126 C1
Rookery La *BLYTH* NE24.........10 A5
Rookery La *WICK/BNPF* NE16.........95 D6
The Rookery *WICK/BNPF* * NE16 .....111 F6
Rookswood Gdns *ROWG* NE39 ....111 D1
Rookwood Dr *DIN/WO* NE13.........33 C2
Rookwood Rd *WD/WHPE/BLK* NE5....60 C6
Roosevelt Rd *DHAM* DH1.........195 D3
Ropery La *CLS/BIR/GTL* DH3.........153 F6
  CLS/BIR/GTL DH3.........154 C1
  HEBB NE31.........84 C2
  WLSD/HOW NE28.........68 A4
Ropery Rd *GATE* NE8.........98 A1
  MLFD/PNYW SR4.........125 F4
The Ropery *BYK/HTN/WLK* NE6.........82 C4
Ropery Wk *SEA/MUR* SR7.........176 C3
Rosalie Ter *ASHBK/HED/RY* SR2 .....145 D2
Rosalind Av *BDLGTN* NE22.........7 F4
Rosamond Pl *BLYTH* NE24.........11 E5
Rosa St *SSH* NE33.........71 F4
Rose Av *HLS* DH4.........169 E1
  STLY/ANP DH9.........147 F3
  WICK/BNPF NE16.........96 A3
Rosebank Cl *ASHBK/HED/RY* SR2 ...145 D6
Rosebay Rd *BDN/LAN/SAC* DH7 .....204 A4
Roseberry Gra *LGB/KIL* NE12.........50 C3
Roseberry St *STLY/ANP* DH9.........149 F1
Roseberry Vls *CLSW/PEL* DH2 ....151 E3
Rosebery Av *BLYTH* NE24.........10 C5
  GATE NE8.........99 F2
  NSHW NE29.........54 B4
  SSH NE33.........72 A5
Rosebery Crs *JES* NE2.........64 C6
Rosebery Pl *JES* NE2.........64 C6
Rosebery St *SWCK/CAS* SR5.........126 C3
Roseby Rd *PLEE/EAS* SR8.........209 E1
Rose Ct *PLEE/EAS* SR8.........208 A5
Rose Crs *BDN/LAN/SAC* DH7.........178 C1
  CLDN/WHIT/ROK SR6.........91 E6
Rosedale *BDLGTN* NE22.........7 D3
  WLSD/HOW NE28.........66 B2
Rosedale Av *CLDN/WHIT/ROK* SR6...109 D4
Rosedale Ct *WD/WHPE/BLK* NE5 ....59 F5
Rosedale Crs *HLS* DH4.........157 D6
Rosedale Rd *DHAM* DH1.........196 C1
Rosedale St *HLH* DH5.........185 D3
  SUND SR1.........126 A6
Rosedale Ter
  CLDN/WHIT/ROK SR6.........109 D6
  JES NE2.........81 E1
  PLEE/EAS SR8.........209 E1
  TYNE/NSHE NE30.........55 D5
Roseden Ct *LGB/KIL* NE12.........49 E5
Rosedene Vls *CRAM* NE23.........22 C2
Rose Gdns *WLSD/HOW* NE28.........67 D2
Rosehill *WLSD/HOW* NE28.........68 A4
Rosehill Rd *WLSD/HOW* NE28.........68 B4
Rose Hill Wy *WD/WHPE/BLK* NE5 .....61 E5
Rose Lea *BDN/LAN/SAC* DH7.........178 A3
Roselea Av *ASHBK/HED/RY* SR2 .....162 B1
Rosemary La *PLEE/EAS* SR8.........200 A3
Rosemary Rd *SWCK/CAS* SR5.........124 C1
Rosemary Ter *BLYTH* NE24.........11 E6
Rosemount *DHAM* DH1.........180 C4
  MLFD/PNYW SR4.........141 F1
  WD/WHPE/BLK NE5.........60 B4
Rosemount Av *FELL* NE10.........102 A3
Rosemount Cl *WASHN* NE37.........120 B2
Rosemount Ct *BOL* NE36.........106 A3
Rosemount Wy *LGB/HTN* NE7.........65 E1
  MONK NE25.........39 E5
Rose St *GATE* NE8.........80 B6

HEBB NE31 ....84 C3
MLFD/PNYW SR4 ....126 A5
Rose St West *HLS* DH4 ....140 A6
Rose Ter *WD/WHPE/BLK* NE5 ....62 A5
Roseville St *BDLGTN* NE22 ....8 A3
Rosewell Pl *WICK/BNPF* NE16 ....95 F6
Rosewood *LGB/KIL* NE12 ....50 B1
Rosewood Av *GOS/KPK* NE3 ....47 F6
Rosewood Crs *BYK/HTN/WLK* NE6 ....66 B5
WBAY NE26 ....26 C4
Rosewood Gdns *GOS/KPK* NE3 ....100 A2
LWF/SPW/WRK NE9 ....100 A4
Rosewood Sq *MLFD/PNYW* SR4 ....141 F4
Rosewood Ter *WLSD/HOW* NE28 ....68 C4
Rosewood Av *GOS/KPK* NE3 ....63 E2
Roseworth Crs *GOS/KPK* NE3 ....63 E3
Roseworth Ter *WICK/BNPF* NE16 ....96 A3
Roslin Pk *BDLGTN* NE22........................8 A3
Ross *CLSW/PEL* DH2 ....135 F4
Ross Av *DUN/TMV* NE11 ....97 E1
Rosse Cl *WASHN* NE37 ....120 A4
Rossendale Pl *LGB/KIL* NE12 ....48 B6
Ross Gv *CRAM* NE23 ....21 F5
Ross Lea *HLS* DH4 ....156 C4
Rosslyn Av *ASHBK/HED/RY* SR2 ....162 B1
GOS/KPK NE3 ....62 A1
Rosslyn St *MLFD/PNYW* SR4 ....125 F6
Ross St *SWCK/CAS* SR5 ....126 B3
Ross Wy *GOS/KPK* NE3 ....46 B4
WBAY NE26 ....40 A3
Rosyth Rd *SWCK/CAS* SR5 ....125 D1
Rosyth Sq *SWCK/CAS* SR5 ....125 D1
Rotary Wy *BLYTH* NE24 ....17 D1
NSHW NE29 ....70 A5
Rothay Pl *WD/WHPE/BLK* NE5...............61 E4
Rothbury *ASHBK/HED/RY* SR2 ....161 F2
Rothbury Av *BLYTH* NE24 ....10 A6
FELL NE10......................................101 F1
GOS/KPK NE3 ....47 D6
JRW NE32 ....85 E4
PLEE/EAS SR8 ....201 E6
Rothbury Cl *CLSW/PEL* DH2 ....165 F1
LGB/KIL NE12 ....35 E6
Rothbury Gdns *DUN/TMV* NE11 ....97 F5
WLSD/HOW NE28 ....68 B3
Rothbury Rd *DHAM* DH1 ....180 B5
SWCK/CAS SR5 ....124 C1
Rothbury Ter *BYK/HTN/WLK* NE6 ....65 D6
NSHW NE29 ....69 E2
Rotherfield Cl *CRAM* NE23 ....22 A1
Rotherfield Gdns
LWF/SPW/WRK NE9 ....117 F2
Rotherfield Rd *SWCK/CAS* SR5 ....124 B1
Rotherfield Sq *SWCK/CAS* SR5 ....124 B1
Rotherham Cl *HLH* DH5 ....170 C4
Rotherham Rd *SWCK/CAS* SR5 ....124 B1
Rothley *WASHS* NE38...........................139 E4
Rothley Av *WD/WHPE/BLK* NE5.............78 B1
Rothley Cl *GOS/KPK* NE3 ....63 F1
Rothley Ct *SWCK/CAS* SR5 ....107 E6
Rothley Gdns *TYNE/NSHE* NE30 ....54 C2
Rothley Gv *MONK* NE25 ....24 B5
Rothley Wy *WBAY* NE26 ....40 A3
Rothsay *CLSW/PEL* DH2 ....135 E5
Rothwell Rd *GOS/KPK* NE3 ....63 E1
SWCK/CAS SR5 ....124 B1
Roundhill Av *WD/WHPE/BLK* NE5 ....61 E4
Roundstone Cl *LGB/KIL* NE12 ....65 F2
The Roundway *LGB/KIL* NE12 ....49 D6
Rowan Av *WASHS* NE38 ....38 B5
Rowanberry Rd *LGB/KIL* NE12 ....49 D6
Rowan Cl *BDLGTN* NE22 ....7 E2
MLFD/PNYW SR4 ....142 A1
Rowan Dr *BLYTH* NE24 ....10 C6
Rowan Dr *DHAM* DH1 ....181 D4
COS/KPK NE3 ....46 A6
HLH DH5 ....171 E6
PONT/DH NE20 ....28 A3
Rowan Lea *BDN/LAN/SAC* DH7 ....203 D4
Rowan Tree Av *DHAM* DH1 ....195 F2
Rowantree Rd *BYK/HTN/WLK* NE6 ....66 C5
Rowanwood Gdns
DUN/TMV NE11 ....97 F5
Rowell Cl *SUNDSW* SR3 ....161 E2
Rowes Ms *BYK/HTN/WLK* NE6 ....82 B4
Rowlandson Crs *FELL* NE10 ....100 C3
Rowlandson Ter *FELL* * NE10 ....100 C2
Rowland Sq *SEA/MUR* SR7 ....188 A1
Rowley Cl *BDN/LAN/SAC* DH7 ....202 A1
Rowley Dr *BDN/LAN/SAC* DH7 ....192 A5
Rowley St *BLYTH* NE24 ....11 D5
Rowntree Wy *NSHW* NE29 ....70 C3
Rowsley Rd *JRW* NE32 ....86 B3
Roxburgh Cl *BLAY* NE21 ....93 F2
Roxburgh Pl *BYK/HTN/WLK* NE6 ....82 A1
Roxburgh St
CLDN/WHIT/ROK SR6 ....126 C2
Roxburgh Ter *WBAY* NE26 ....40 C5
Roxby Gdns *NSHW* NE29 ....70 A1
Royal Crs *ELS/FEN* NE4 ....62 A6
Royal Rd *STLY/ANP* DH9 ....148 A1
The Royalty *ASHBK/HED/RY* SR2 ....126 A6
Roydon Av *ASHBK/HED/RY* SR2 ....145 D3
Royle St *ASHBK/HED/RY* SR2 ....145 E4

Royston Ter *BYK/HTN/WLK* NE6 ....83 F4
Ruabon Cl *CRAM* NE23 ....21 F5
Rubens Av *HAR/WTLS* NE34 ....88 C5
Ruby St *HLS* DH4 ....157 F6
Rudby Cl *GOS/KPK* NE3 ....47 F4
Rudchester Pl *WD/WHPE/BLK* NE5 ....61 E6
Ruddock Sq *BYK/HTN/WLK* NE6 ....82 B4
Rudyard Av *ASHBK/HED/RY* SR2 ....145 D3
Rudyard Ct *NSHW* NE29 ....71 D1
Rudyerd St *NSHW* NE29 ....70 C1
Rugby Gdns *LWF/SPW/WRK* NE9 ....118 C1
Ruislip Pl *CRAM* NE23 ....21 E5
Ruislip Rd *MLFD/PNYW* SR4 ....124 B5
Runcorn *ASHBK/HED/RY* SR2 ....161 E1
Runcorn Rd *SWCK/CAS* SR5 ....124 B1
Runhead Est *RYTON* NE40 ....74 C3
Runnymede *ASHBK/HED/RY* SR2 ....161 F1
Runnymede Rd *SWCK/CAS* SR5 ....124 C1
WICK/BNPF NE16 ....95 F4
Runnymede Wy *GOS/KPK* NE3 ....62 A2
SWCK/CAS SR5 ....124 C1
Runswick Av *LGB/KIL* NE12 ....48 B6
Runswick Cl *SUNDSW* SR3 ....161 E1
Rupert Sq *SWCK/CAS* SR5 ....125 D1
Rupert St *CLDN/WHIT/ROK* SR6 ....109 E1
Rushall Pl *LGB/KIL* NE12 ....49 D6
Rushey Gill *BDN/LAN/SAC* DH7 ....209 F4
Rushford *ASHBK/HED/RY* SR2 ....161 F1
Rushie Av *BW/LEM/TK/HW* NE15 ....78 B3
Rushley Crs *BLAY* NE21 ....76 B5
Rushsyde Cl *WICK/BNPF* NE16 ....95 D5
Rushton Av *ASHBK/HED/RY* SR2 ....145 D3
Rushyrig *WASHN* NE37 ....119 F6
Ruskin Av *CLSW/PEL* DH2 ....152 A5
DUN/TMV NE11 ....97 E1
HLH DH5 ....170 B4
LGB/KIL NE12 ....49 E3
Ruskin Cl *STLY/ANP* DH9 ....149 D2
Ruskin Crs *HAR/WTLS* NE34 ....88 A5
Ruskin Dr *BOLCOL* NE35 ....105 F2
LGB/HTN NE7 ....66 A4
Ruskin Rd *CLS/BIR/GTL* DH5 ....136 B2
LWF/SPW/WRK NE9 ....100 A3
WICK/BNPF NE16 ....95 F2
Russell Av *HAR/WTLS* NE34 ....89 F2
Russell Ct *GATE* NE8 ....98 B1
Russell Sq *DIN/WO* NE13 ....33 E2
Russell St *JRW* NE32 ....86 B1
NSHW NE29 ....70 C1
SSH NE33 ....71 E3
SUND SR1 ....5 E1
Russell Ter *BDLGTN* NE22 ....7 E4
JES NE2 ....3 G2
Russell Wy
WICK/BNPF
(off Metrocentre) NE16 ....78 B6
Ruswarp Dr *SUNDSW* SR3 ....161 D2
Rutherford Av *SEA/MUR* SR7 ....175 E2
Rutherford Rd *SWCK/CAS* SR5 ....124 A1
WASHN NE37 ....121 D3
Rutherford Sq *SWCK/CAS* SR5 ....124 A1
Rutherford St *BLYTH* NE24 ....11 D6
CNUT NE1 ....2 B4
WLSD/HOW NE28 ....69 D3
Ruthglen Rd *SWCK/CAS* SR5 ....125 D1
Rutland Av *BYK/HTN/WLK* NE6 ....83 F1
SUNDSW SR3 ....160 B1
Rutland Pl *NSHW* NE29 ....54 A6
WASHN NE37 ....120 C2
Rutland Rd *HEBB* NE31 ....85 E5
WLSD/HOW NE28 ....66 C5
Rutland Sq *CLS/BIR/GTL* DH3 ....136 A1
Rutland St *HAR/WTLS* * NE34 ....88 A2
MLFD/PNYW SR4 ....124 A5
Ryal Cl *BLYTH* NE24 ....10 A5
MONK NE25 ....24 C5
Ryal Ter *BYK/HTN/WLK* NE6 ....83 E3
Rydal *FELL* NE10 ....101 F2
Rydal Av *HLH* DH5 ....186 B4
STLY/ANP DH9 ....147 F4
TYNE/NSHE NE30 ....54 C2
Rydal Cl *BDN/LAN/SAC* DH7 ....178 A1
BOL NE36 ....106 B2
LGB/KIL NE12 ....50 B1
Rydal Crs *BLAY* NE21 ....94 A2
PLEE/EAS SR8 ....209 D2
Rydal Gdns *HAR/WTLS* NE34 ....89 D2
Rydal Mt *PLEE/EAS* SR8 ....200 C2
SWCK/CAS SR5 ....123 F4
SWCK/CAS SR5 ....126 B1
Rydal Rd *BW/LEM/TK/HW* NE15 ....59 F6
CLSW/PEL DH2 ....166 A1
GOS/KPK NE3 ....63 F1
Rydal St *GATE* NE8 ....99 D1
Ryde Pl *CRAM* NE23 ....22 A1
Ryde Ter *DUN/TMV* NE11 ....97 F1
Rye Cl *BW/LEM/TK/HW* NE15 ....58 A1
Ryedale *CLDN/WHIT/ROK* SR6 ....109 E3
DHAM DH1 ....196 C3
WLSD/HOW NE28 ....66 B1
Rye Hl *ELS/FEN* NE4 ....80 A4
Ryehill Vw *HLH* DH5 ....170 B6
Ryelands Wy *DHAM* DH1 ....180 B4
Ryemount Rd
ASHBK/HED/RY SR2 ....161 F1

Rye View Rd *ASHBK/HED/RY* SR2 ....145 E6
Ryhope Gdns *LWF/SPW/WRK* NE9 ....118 C1
Ryhope Rd *ASHBK/HED/RY* SR2 ....145 E5
Ryhope St *ASHBK/HED/RY* SR2 ....162 A1
HLH DH5 ....171 E2
Rymers Cl *PLEE/EAS* SR8 ....199 F3
Ryton Cl *SSH* NE33 ....71 F5
Ryton Crs *SEA/MUR* SR7 ....175 F3
STLY/ANP DH9 ....131 E6
Ryton Hall Dr *RYTON* NE40 ....74 B2
Ryton Ter *BYK/HTN/WLK* NE6.................83 E4

S

Sackville Rd *BYK/HTN/WLK* NE6 ....65 E5
SUNDSW SR3 ....143 D3
Sacriston Av *SUNDSW* SR3 ....143 E3
Saddleback *WASHN* NE37 ....120 A4
Saddler St *DHAM* DH1 ....194 B4
Saffron Pl *BYK/HTN/WLK* NE6 ....83 F3
Sage Cl *BW/LEM/TK/HW* NE15 ....59 E6
St Aidan's Av *ASHBK/HED/RY* SR2 ....145 E5
DHAM DH1 ....193 F1
LGB/KIL NE12 ....51 E3
St Aidan's Cl *NSHW* NE29 ....53 F4
St Aidan's Crs *DHAM* DH1 ....193 F4
STLY/ANP DH9 ....146 B5
St Aidan's Rd *SSH* NE33 ....71 F2
WLSD/HOW NE28 ....66 C5
St Aidan's St *GATE* NE8 ....98 C1
St Aidan's Ter *HLS* DH4 ....158 A2
St Alban Cl *CLS/BIR/GTL* DH5 ....168 A3
St Albans Crs *BYK/HTN/WLK* NE6 ....65 F4
St Albans Pl *TYNE/NSHE* NE30 ....55 F5
St Albans St *ASHBK/HED/RY* SR2 ....145 D3
St Alban's Ter *GATE* NE8 ....99 E1
St Albans Vw *SMOOR* NE27 ....52 A2
St Aldwyn Rd *SEA/MUR* SR7 ....176 A2
St Aloysius Vw *HEBB* NE31 ....84 C2
St Andrews *HLS* DH4 ....170 A2
St Andrews Av *WASHN* NE37 ....120 A4
St Andrews Cl *MONK* NE25 ....39 C5
St Andrews Ct *NSHW* NE29 ....54 B4
St Andrew's Dr
LWF/SPW/WRK NE9 ....117 D1
St Andrew's Rd *STLY/ANP* DH9 ....131 E5
St Andrew's Sq *SEA/MUR* SR7 ....175 D6
St Andrew's St *CNUT* NE1 ....2 B3
HEBB NE31 ....84 B1
St Andrew's Ter
CLDN/WHIT/ROK SR6 ....127 D2
St Annes Ct *DHAM* * DH1 ....194 B4
St Ann's Cl *CNUT* NE1 ....81 F3
St Ann's St *CNUT* NE1 ....3 H4
St Ann's Yd
CNUT (off Breamish St) NE1 ....81 F3
St Anselm Crs *NSHW* NE29 ....53 E5
St Anselm Rd *NSHW* NE29 ....53 E5
St Anthony's Rd
BYK/HTN/WLK NE6 ....83 D3
St Anthonys Wk
BYK/HTN/WLK NE6 ....83 E5
St Asaph Cl *LGB/HTN* NE7 ....65 F2
St Aubyn's Wy *STLY/ANP* * DH9 ....149 D1
St Austell Cl *WD/WHPE/BLK* * NE5 ....61 E2
St Austell Gdns
LWF/SPW/WRK NE9 ....117 D1
St Barnabas *HLS* DH4 ....155 F5
St Barnabas Wy
ASHBK/HED/RY SR2 ....5 C6
St Bede's Cl *DHAM* DH1 ....195 F1
St Bede's Dr *GATE* NE8 ....81 E6
St Bedes Pk *ASHBK/HED/RY* SR2 ....4 D5
St Bedes Pl *BLYTH* NE24 ....16 A2
St Bedes Rd *BLYTH* NE24 ....16 A2
St Bedes Ter *ASHBK/HED/RY* SR2 ....4 D5
St Bedes Wk *SMOOR* NE27 ....51 E3
St Bedes Wy *BDN/LAN/SAC* DH7 ....204 A3
St Brandon's Gv
BDN/LAN/SAC DH7 ....202 C4
St Buryan Crs *WD/WHPE/BLK* NE5 ....61 E2
St Catherines Ct *SWCK/CAS* SR5 ....124 C3
St Catherines Gv *JES* * NE2 ....64 B6
St Chad's Crs *SUNDSW* SR3 ....159 D1
St Chad's Rd *SUNDSW* SR3 ....159 D1
St Chad's Vls *BOL* NE36 ....106 C3
St Christopher's Rd *SUNDSW* SR3 ....143 F4
Saint Ct *SUNDSW* SR3 ....160 C3
St Cuthbert Av *CLS/BIR/GTL* DH3 ....153 F5
St Cuthberts Av *DHAM* DH1 ....195 F1
HAR/WTLS NE34 ....72 C6
St Cuthberts Ct *BLYTH* NE24 ....11 E4
GATE NE8 ....80 C6
GOS/KPK (off Coxlodge Rd) NE3 ....62 C1
St Cuthberts Dr
BDN/LAN/SAC DH7 ....178 A1
FELL NE10......................................101 E3
St Cuthberts Pk *WICK/BNPF* NE16........113 F4
St Cuthbert's Pl *GATE* NE8 ....98 C1
St Cuthbert's Rd *GATE* NE8 ....80 C6
HLS DH4 ....157 F5
LGB/KIL NE12 ....51 D3

PLEE/EAS SR8 ....208 C3
WD/WHPE/BLK NE5 ....78 A1
WICK NE16 ....113 F5
WLSD/HOW NE28 ....67 F3
St Cuthbert's Ter
  MLFD/PNYW SR4 ....126 A5
St Cuthberts Wk
  BDN/LAN/SAC DH7 ....204 A3
St Cuthberts Wy *BLAY* NE21 ....76 C5
  RDHAMSE DH6 ....197 E5
  SMOOR NE27 ....51 E3
St David's Wy *WBAY* NE26 ....40 B2
St Edmund's Ct *GATE* * NE8 ....99 F1
St Edmund's Dr *FELL* NE10 ....101 E3
St Edmund's Rd *GATE* NE8 ....99 E1
St Etienne Ct *FELL* * NE10 ....100 C1
St Gabriel's Av *BYK/HTN/WLK* NE6 ......65 D5
  MLFD/PNYW SR4 ....125 E6
St George's Cl *JES* NE2 ....64 A4
St George's Ct *FELL* NE10 ....102 A3
St Georges Est
  WASHS NE38 ....138 B5
St George's Pl
  BW/LEM/TK/HW NE15 ....77 D3
St George's Rd
  BW/LEM/TK/HW NE15 ....76 C5
  TYNE/NSHE NE30 ....55 D1
St George's Ter *BOL* NE36 ....106 C3
  BW/LEM/TK/HW NE15 ....77 D3
  CLDN/WHIT/ROK SR6 ....127 E2
  JES NE2 ....64 A4
St George's Wy *ASHBK/HED/RY* SR2 ....4 C5
St Giles Cl *DHAM* DH1 ....195 E4
St Godric's Cl *DHAM* DH1 ....180 B5
St Godric's Dr *HLS* DH4 ....183 F2
St Helen's Crs *LWF/SPW/WRK* NE9 .....99 D5
St Heliers Wy *STLY/ANP* DH9 ....149 D1
St Hilda's Av *WLSD/HOW* NE28 ....68 A3
St Hilda St *SSH* NE33 ....71 E4
St Hilds Ct *DHAM* DH1 ....195 F4
St Hild's La *DHAM* * DH1 ....195 D4
St Ignatius Cl *ASHBK/HED/RY* SR2 ....5 F6
St Ives Wy *WD/WHPE/BLK* NE5 ....61 D2
St James Bvd *CNUT* * NE1 ....2 B3
St James Ct *GATE* NE8 ....100 A1
St James' Crs
  BW/LEM/TK/HW NE15 ....78 C4
St James Gdns
  BW/LEM/TK/HW * NE15 ....78 C3
St James' Rd
  BW/LEM/TK/HW NE15 ....78 C3
  GATE NE8 ....81 F6
St James Sq *GATE* NE8 ....81 F6
St James' St *CNUT* NE1 ....2 B2
  GOS/KPK NE3 ....63 F1
St James' Ter *NSHW* NE29 ....127 E4
St John's *SUND* SR1 ....127 E4
St John's Av *HEBB* NE31 ....84 C3
St John's Cl *WBAY* NE26 ....40 B2
St Johns Ct *ELS/FEN* * NE4 ....79 D4
St John's Crs *BDLGTN* NE22 ....8 C1
St John's Gn *NSHW* NE29 ....69 F3
St John's Pl *BDLGTN* NE22 ....8 C1
  CLS/BIR/GTL DH3 ....136 B2
  FELL NE10 ....100 C2
  WBAY NE26 ....40 B2
St John's Rd *BDLGTN* NE22 ....8 C2
  BDN/LAN/SAC DH7 ....204 A3
  DHAM DH1 ....193 F5
  ELS/FEN NE4 ....79 D4
St John's St *NSHW* NE29 ....69 F3
St John's Ter *BOL* NE36 ....107 D3
  JRW NE32 ....86 A1
  NSHW NE29 ....69 F3
St John St *CNUT* NE1 ....2 C4
St Johns V *MLFD/PNYW* SR4 ....141 F2
St Johns Wk *ELS/FEN* NE4 ....79 D4
  NSHW NE29 ....69 F3
Saint Joseph's Cl *DHAM* DH1 ....195 F4
St Josephs Ct
  CLS/BIR/GTL (off Mount Rd) DH3 ....136 B1
  HEBB NE31 ....84 C5
St Joseph's Wy *JRW* NE32 ....104 A1
St Jude's Ter *SSH* NE33 ....71 E5
St Julien Gdns *LGB/HTN* NE7 ....65 F4
  WLSD/HOW NE28 ....69 D3
St Lawrence Rd
  BYK/HTN/WLK NE6 ....82 A4
St Lawrence Sq
  BYK/HTN/WLK NE6 ....82 A3
St Leonard St
  ASHBK/HED/RY SR2 ....145 D2
St Lucia Cl *ASHBK/HED/RY* SR2 ....5 E6
  WBAY NE26 ....40 A2
St Luke's Rd *MLFD/PNYW* SR4 ....124 B5
St Luke's St *NSHW* NE29 ....69 F3
St Luke's Ter *MLFD/PNYW* SR4 ....125 E5
St Margaret's Av *SWCK/CAS* SR5 ....123 F3
St Margaret's Ct *DHAM* DH1 ....194 A5
St Margaret's Dr *STLY/ANP* DH9 ....130 B3
St Margarets Garth *DHAM* * DH1 ....194 A5
St Margarets Ms *DHAM* DH1 ....194 A5

St Margaret's Rd
  BW/LEM/TK/HW NE15 ....78 A4
St Margarets Av *LGB/KIL* NE12 ....49 F6
St Mark's Cl *BYK/HTN/WLK* NE6 ....82 B1
St Marks Crs *MLFD/PNYW* SR4 ....126 A6
St Mark's Rd *MLFD/PNYW* SR4 ....126 A6
St Mark's Rd North
  MLFD/PNYW SR4 ....125 F5
St Mark's Ter *MLFD/PNYW* SR4 ....126 A6
St Mark's Wy *SSH* NE33 ....71 E5
St Martin's Cl *WBAY* NE26 ....40 A3
St Mary's Av *HAR/WTLS* NE34 ....89 E2
  WBAY NE26 ....40 B3
St Marys Cl *CLSW/PEL* DH2 ....153 D6
  PLEE/EAS SR8 ....199 F3
St Marys Ct *GATE* NE8 ....81 E6
St Mary's Dr *BLYTH* NE24 ....16 A1
  HLS DH4 ....183 F2
  RDHAMSE DH6 ....197 E5
St Mary's Gn *WICK/BNPF* * NE16 ....96 A3
St Mary's Pl *BW/LEM/TK/HW* NE15 ......58 A4
  CNUT NE1 ....2 D1
St Mary's Rd *DHAM* DH1 ....196 B2
St Mary's Ter *BOL* NE36 ....106 C3
  FELL * NE10 ....101 E2
St Mary's Wy *SUND* SR1 ....4 B2
St Mary's Wynd *WBAY* NE26 ....27 D4
St Matthews Vw *SUNDSW* SR3 ....160 C1
St Michaels *HLS* DH4 ....170 A2
St Michael's Av *MONK* NE25 ....25 D2
  SSH NE33 ....71 F5
St Michael's Av North *SSH* NE33 ....71 F5
St Michaels Mt *BYK/HTN/WLK* NE6 ....82 B3
St Michael's Rd *BYK/HTN/WLK* NE6 ....82 A3
St Michaels Wy *SUND* SR1 ....4 A2
  WICK/BNPF NE16 ....96 A1
St Monica Gv *DHAM* DH1 ....193 F5
St Nicholas Av *GOS/KPK* NE3 ....63 E2
  SUNDSW SR3 ....144 A3
St Nicholas Chambers *CNUT* * NE1 ....2 D5
St Nicholas Rd *DHAM* DH1 ....193 E2
St Nicholas Rd *BOL* NE36 ....105 F3
St Nicholas' St *CNUT* NE1 ....2 D4
St Omers Rd *DUN/TMV* NE11 ....79 E6
St Oswald Av *BYK/HTN/WLK* NE6 ....83 D1
St Oswalds Av *BYK/HTN/WLK* NE6 ....83 D2
St Oswald's Dr *DHAM* DH1 ....204 C3
St Oswald's Gn *BYK/HTN/WLK* NE6 ....83 D1
St Oswin's Pl *TYNE/NSHE* NE30 ....55 F5
St Oswin's St *SSH* NE33 ....88 C1
St Patricks Cl *FELL* NE10 ....100 C1
St Patricks Wk *FELL* * NE10 ....100 C2
St Pauls Ct
  GATE (off Derwentwater Rd) NE8 ....98 B1
St Pauls Dr *HLS* DH4 ....139 D6
St Paul's Gdns *MONK* NE25 ....40 C6
St Pauls Pl *ELS/FEN* NE4 ....79 F3
St Paul's Rd *JRW* NE32 ....86 B1
St Peter's Av *HAR/WTLS* NE34 ....89 D2
St Peters Ct *BYK/HTN/WLK* NE6 ....82 B2
St Peter's Quayside East
  BYK/HTN/WLK * NE6 ....82 C4
St Peter's Quayside West
  BYK/HTN/WLK * NE6 ....82 B5
St Peter's Rd *BYK/HTN/WLK* NE6 ....82 B4
  WLSD/HOW NE28 ....67 F2
St Peters Vw
  CLDN/WHIT/ROK SR6 ....126 C4
St Peters' Wy
  CLDN/WHIT/ROK SR6 ....127 D4
St Peter's Whf *BYK/HTN/WLK* NE6 ....82 B4
St Philips Cl *ELS/FEN* NE4 ....80 A3
St Philips Wy *ELS/FEN* NE4 ....80 A3
St Ronan's Dr *WBAY* NE26 ....26 A1
St Ronan's Rd *MONK* NE25 ....40 B6
St Ronans Vw
  LWF/SPW/WRK NE9 ....117 F2
St Simon St *HAR/WTLS* NE34 ....87 F4
St Stephen's Cl *MONK* NE25 ....24 A5
St Stephen's Wy *NSHW* NE29 ....69 F4
St Stevens Cl *HLS* DH4 ....139 D6
St Thomas Cl *PLEE/EAS* SR8 ....199 F3
St Thomas' Crs *CNUT* NE1 ....2 C1
St Thomas' St *CNUT* NE1 ....2 C1
  LWF/SPW/WRK NE9 ....99 F5
  SUND SR1 ....4 D2
St Thomas Ter *CNUT* NE1 ....2 C1
St Vincent Ct *GATE* NE8 ....99 F1
St Vincents Cl
  BW/LEM/TK/HW NE15 ....60 A2
St Vincent's Pl *WBAY* NE26 ....40 B2
St Vincent St *ASHBK/HED/RY* SR2 ....5 E5
  GATE NE8 ....99 F1
  SSH NE33 ....72 A5
St Vincent's Wy *WBAY* NE26 ....40 B2
Salcombe Av *JRW* NE32 ....86 C3
Salcombe Cl *SEA/MUR* SR7 ....175 F4
Salcombe Gdns
  LWF/SPW/WRK NE9 ....117 E2
Salem Hl *ASHBK/HED/RY* SR2 ....5 E6
Salem Rd *ASHBK/HED/RY* SR2 ....5 E5
Salem St *ASHBK/HED/RY* SR2 ....5 E5

JRW NE32 ....86 B1
SSH * NE33 ....71 E3
Salem St South *ASHBK/HED/RY* SR2 .....5 E6
Salem Ter *ASHBK/HED/RY* SR2 ....5 E5
Salisbury Av *NSHW* NE29 ....54 B5
Salisbury Cl *CLS/BIR/GTL* DH3 ....167 F4
  CRAM NE23 ....21 D2
Salisbury Gdns *JES* NE2 ....64 C6
Salisbury Pl *SSH* NE33 ....72 A3
Salisbury Rd *DHAM* DH1 ....181 D5
Salisbury St *ASHBK/HED/RY* SR2 ....5 E4
  FELL NE10 ....101 F1
  SSH NE33 ....71 F3
  STLY/ANP DH9 ....147 F3
Salkeld Gdns *LWF/SPW/WRK* NE9 ....99 F2
Salkeld Rd *LWF/SPW/WRK* NE9 ....99 F4
Sallyport Ct *CNUT* NE1 ....3 F4
Salmon St *SSH* NE33 ....71 F2
Saltburn Gdns *WLSD/HOW* NE28 ....69 D3
Saltburn Rd *SUNDSW* SR3 ....143 D3
Saltburn Sq *SUNDSW* SR3 ....143 D3
Salterfen La *ASHBK/HED/RY* SR2 ....145 F6
Salterfen Rd *ASHBK/HED/RY* SR2 ....145 F6
Salters Cl *GOS/KPK* NE3 ....48 A6
Salters' La *GOS/KPK* NE3 ....48 B6
  HLH DH5 ....160 A6
  LGB/KIL NE12 ....48 C3
  RDHAMSE DH6 ....206 B5
  SEA/MUR SR7 ....173 E4
Salters' Rd *GOS/KPK* NE3 ....62 C2
Saltmeadows Rd *GATE* NE8 ....82 A5
Saltwell Rd *GATE* NE8 ....98 C3
Saltwell Rd South
  LWF/SPW/WRK NE9 ....99 D4
Saltwell St *GATE* NE8 ....99 D4
Saltwell Vw *LWF/SPW/WRK* NE9 ....99 D3
Samson Cl *LGB/KIL* NE12 ....49 D2
Sancroft Dr *HLH* DH5 ....171 D3
Sandalwood *HAR/WTLS* NE34 ....88 C5
Sandalwood Sq *MLFD/PNYW* SR4 ....141 F4
Sanderling Cl *RYTON* NE40 ....74 C4
Sanderson Rd *JES* NE2 ....64 A4
Sanderson St *ELS/FEN* NE4 ....79 E5
Sandfield Rd *TYNE/NSHE* NE30 ....55 D1
Sandford Av *CRAM* NE23 ....14 A5
Sandford Ms *DIN/WO* NE13 ....32 B5
Sandgate *CNUT* NE1 ....3 G4
  STLY/ANP DH9 ....147 E4
Sandgrove *CLDN/WHIT/ROK* SR6 ....107 F1
Sandhill *CNUT* NE1 ....3 E5
Sandholm Cl *WLSD/HOW* NE28 ....68 B1
Sandhurst Av *TYNE/NSHE* NE30 ....55 D2
Sandmere Pl
  BW/LEM/TK/HW NE15 ....77 F3
Sandmere Rd
  ASHBK/HED/RY SR2 ....145 D5
Sandoe Gdns
  BW/LEM/TK/HW NE15 ....78 A3
Sandon Cl *SMOOR* NE27 ....37 E5
Sandown *MONK* NE25 ....39 F5
Sandown Cl *SMOOR* NE27 ....37 F1
Sandown Gdns *GATE* NE8 ....98 B3
  SUNDSW SR3 ....143 E6
  WLSD/HOW NE28 ....68 B2
Sandpiper Cl *BLYTH* NE24 ....17 D2
  RYTON NE40 ....74 C4
Sand Point Rd
  CLDN/WHIT/ROK SR6 ....127 E3
Sandray Cl *CLS/BIR/GTL* DH3 ....136 C5
Sandringham Av *LGB/KIL* NE12 ....49 E6
Sandringham Ct
  FELL (off Sheriffs Cl) NE10 ....100 B2
  MONK NE25 ....39 D6
  STLY/ANP DH9 ....146 B3
  WICK/BNPF NE16 ....95 F3
Sandringham Dr *BLYTH* NE24 ....16 C3
Sandringham Gdns *NSHW* NE29 ....54 C5
Sandringham Rd
  CLDN/WHIT/ROK SR6 ....126 C2
  GOS/KPK NE3 ....64 A2
  WD/WHPE/BLK * NE5 ....60 A6
Sandringham Ter
  CLDN/WHIT/ROK SR6 ....127 D2
Sandsay Cl *ASHBK/HED/RY* SR2 ....144 C6
The Sands Flats *DHAM* DH1 ....194 C4
The Sands *WICK/BNPF* NE16 ....95 F1
The Sands *DHAM* DH1 ....194 C3
Sandstone Cl *HAR/WTLS* NE34 ....87 E5
Sandwell Dr *HLS* DH4 ....139 E6
Sandwich Rd *NSHW* NE29 ....54 B3
Sandwich St *BYK/HTN/WLK* NE6 ....83 C5
Sandy Chare
  CLDN/WHIT/ROK SR6 ....109 D2
Sandy Crs *BYK/HTN/WLK* NE6 ....83 D4
Sandyford *CLSW/PEL* DH2 ....151 F1
Sandyford Pk *JES* * NE2 ....64 B6
Sandyford Rd *CNUT* NE1 ....2 D1
  JES NE2 ....81 D1
Sandy La *DIN/WO* NE13 ....31 F4
  GOS/KPK NE3 ....34 A6
  LWF/SPW/WRK NE9 ....118 C3
Sandypath La *WICK/BNPF* NE16 ....111 F5
Sans St South *SUND* * SR1 ....4 D2
Sargent Av *HAR/WTLS* NE34 ....88 C6
Satley Gdns *SUNDSW* SR3 ....144 A4

Saturn CI *PLEE/EAS* SR8 ....200 B2
Saturn St *SEA/MUR* SR7 ....175 F3
Saunton CI *HLS* DH4 ....157 E5
Saville PI *CNUT* NE1 ....3 E2
Saville Rw *CNUT* NE1 ....2 D2
Saville St *SSH* NE33 ....71 F3
  TYNE/NSHE NE30 ....71 D1
Saville St West *NSHW* NE29 ....70 C1
Savory Rd *WLSD/HOW* NE28 ....68 B3
Sawmill La *BDN/LAN/SAC* DH7 ....202 C4
Saxilby Dr *GOS/KPK* NE3 ....47 F4
Saxon CI *CLDN/WHIT/ROK* SR6 ....107 D1
Saxon Crs *SWASH* SR3 ....143 E3
Saxondale Rd *GOS/KPK* NE3 ....62 A1
Saxon Dr *TYNE/NSHE* NE30 ....55 E3
Saxton Gv *DHAM* DH1 ....195 F3
Saxton Gv *LGB/HTN* NE7 ....64 C2
Scafell *CLS/BIR/GTL* DH3 ....136 C4
Scafell CI *BDN/LAN/SAC* DH7 ....209 D2
Scafell Dr *WD/WHPE/BLK* NE5 ....61 F1
Scafell Gdns *DUN/TMV* NE11 ....97 F4
Scalby CI *GOS/KPK* NE3 ....47 F4
Scarborough Ct
  BYK/HTN/WLK NE6 ....82 C2
Scarborough Rd
  BYK/HTN/WLK NE6 ....82 C2
  SUNDSW SR3 ....143 E6
Scardale Wy *DHAM* DH1 ....197 D2
Sceptre Ct *ELS/FEN* * NE4 ....79 F4
Sceptre PI *ELS/FEN* NE4 ....79 F3
Sceptre St *ELS/FEN* NE4 ....79 F3
Schalksmuhle Rd *BDLGTN* NE22 ....7 E3
Schimel St *SWCK/CAS* SR5 ....126 A2
School Ap *HAR/WTLS* NE34 ....89 F2
School Av *DUN/TMV* NE11 ....97 E2
School CI *FELL* NE10 ....100 C4
Schoolhouse La *WICK/BNPF* NE16 ....113 D5
School La *STLY/ANP* DH9 ....147 F4
  WICK/BNPF NE16 ....96 A3
School Loaning *HAR/WTLS* NE34 ....88 A3
School Rd *BDLGTN* NE22 ....8 C1
  HEBB NE31 ....85 D1
  HLH DH5 ....170 B6
  PLEE/EAS SR8 ....201 D2
  SEA/MUR SR7 ....176 C5
  WICK/BNPF NE16 ....95 F3
School Ter *STLY/ANP* DH9 ....147 F3
School Vw *HLH* DH5 ....186 C4
  HLS DH4 ....183 E3
Scorer's La *CLS/BIR/GTL* DH3 ....168 A2
Scorer St *NSHW* NE29 ....70 B1
Scotland Head *BLAY* NE21 ....93 F3
Scotland St *ASHBK/HED/RY* SR2 ....162 C1
Scotswood Rd
  BW/LEM/TK/HW NE15 ....77 F4
  CNUT NE1 ....2 A6
Scotswood Vw *WICK/BNPF* NE16 ....78 B6
Scott Av *CRAM* NE23 ....13 E6
Scott Ct *CLS/BIR/GTL* DH3 ....167 F3
Scott's Ter *HLS* DH5 ....171 F6
Scott St *CRAM* NE23 ....14 A3
  STLY/ANP DH9 ....147 F3
Scripton Gill *BDN/LAN/SAC* DH7 ....202 C4
Scripton Gill Rd
  BDN/LAN/SAC DH7 ....202 B5
Scripton La *BDN/LAN/SAC* DH7 ....202 C6
Scrogg Rd *BYK/HTN/WLK* NE6 ....83 E3
Scruton Av *SUNDSW* SR3 ....143 E4
Seaburn Dr *HLS* DH4 ....170 B2
Seaburn Gdns
  CLDN/WHIT/ROK SR6 ....109 D6
  LWF/SPW/WRK NE9 ....118 C1
Seaburn Gv *WBAY* NE26 ....26 B2
Seaburn HI *CLDN/WHIT/ROK* SR6 ....109 D6
Seaburn Ter *CLDN/WHIT/ROK* SR6 ....109 D6
Seaburn Vw *MONK* NE25 ....24 C2
Seacombe Av *TYNE/NSHE* NE30 ....55 D1
Seacrest Av *TYNE/NSHE* NE30 ....55 D2
Seafield Rd *BLYTH* NE24 ....17 D1
Seafields *CLDN/WHIT/ROK* SR6 ....109 D5
Seafield Ter *SSH* NE33 ....71 F3
Seafield Vw *TYNE/NSHE* NE30 ....55 F4
Seaforth Rd *SUNDSW* SR3 ....143 F3
Seaforth St *BLYTH* NE24 ....11 D4
Seaham Ct *HAR/WTLS* NE34 ....90 A2
Seaham Gdns
  LWF/SPW/WRK NE9 ....118 B2
Seaham Rd *HLH* DH5 ....177 D5
Seaham St *SEA/MUR* SR7 ....177 D5
  SUNDSW SR3 ....160 C1
Sea La *CLDN/WHIT/ROK* SR6 ....109 D6
Sea Rd *CLDN/WHIT/ROK* SR6 ....108 C6
  SSH NE33 ....71 F3
Seascale PI *LWF/SPW/WRK* NE9 ....100 A6
Seaton Av *BLYTH* NE24 ....16 B2
  HLH DH5 ....171 F2
Seaton CI *FELL* NE10 ....102 A4
Seaton Crs *MONK* NE25 ....25 E3
  MONK NE25 ....40 A5
Seaton La *SEA/MUR* SR7 ....175 D1
Seaton Pk *SEA/MUR* SR7 ....175 E2

Seaton PI *BYK/HTN/WLK* NE6 ....83 D5
  DIN/WO NE13 ....32 C4
Seaton Rd *SMOOR* NE27 ....38 C6
  SUNDSW SR3 ....142 C3
Seatonville Crs *MONK* NE25 ....54 A1
Seatonville Rd *MONK* NE25 ....54 A1
Sea Vw *ASHBK/HED/RY* SR2 ....162 C2
  PLEE/EAS SR8 ....200 A3
Sea View Gdns
  CLDN/WHIT/ROK SR6 ....127 D1
  PLEE/EAS SR8 ....200 B2
Sea View Pk *CLDN/WHIT/ROK* SR6 ....108 C2
  CRAM NE23 ....22 C2
Sea View Rd *ASHBK/HED/RY* SR2 ....145 D4
Sea View Rd West
  ASHBK/HED/RY SR2 ....145 D4
Sea View St *ASHBK/HED/RY* SR2 ....145 E4
Sea View Wk *SEA/MUR* SR7 ....175 D6
Sea Wy *SSH* NE33 ....72 A3
Second Av *BLYTH* NE24 ....10 C6
  BYK/HTN/WLK NE6 ....82 B1
  CLSW/PEL DH2 ....136 A6
  CLSW/PEL DH2 ....153 D6
  DUN/TMV NE11 ....98 B4
  NSHW NE29 ....69 D2
Second St *GATE* NE8 ....98 C1
Sedgeletch Rd *HLS* DH4 ....169 F1
Sedgemoor *LGB/KIL* NE12 ....35 F6
Sedgemoor Av
  BW/LEM/TK/HW NE15 ....77 F4
Sedgewick PI *GATE* NE8 ....99 D1
Sedley Rd *WLSD/HOW* NE28 ....67 D5
Sedling Rd *WASHS* NE38 ....138 A4
Sefton Av *BYK/HTN/WLK* NE6 ....65 D5
Sefton Ct *CRAM* NE23 ....14 B5
Sefton Sq *SUNDSW* SR3 ....143 D3
Selborne Gdns *JES* NE2 ....64 C6
Selbourne CI *CRAM* NE23 ....21 D2
Selbourne St *SSH* NE33 ....71 F4
Selby CI *CRAM* NE23 ....14 A5
Selby Gdns *BYK/HTN/WLK* NE6 ....66 B6
  WLSD/HOW NE28 ....67 D3
Selby Sq *SUNDSW* SR3 ....143 D5
Selina PI *CLDN/WHIT/ROK* SR6 ....127 D5
Selkirk Crs *CLS/BIR/GTL* DH3 ....118 B6
Selkirk Gv *CRAM* NE23 ....14 B5
Selkirk Sq *SUNDSW* SR3 ....142 C3
Selkirk St *JRW* NE32 ....87 D5
Selkirk Wy *NSHW* NE29 ....53 E4
Selsdon Av *MLFD/PNYW* SR4 ....141 F4
Selsey CI *FELL* NE10 ....101 D4
Selwood Ct *HAR/WTLS* NE34 ....89 E3
Selwyn Av *MONK* NE25 ....53 F1
Serlby CI *WASHN* NE37 ....120 B3
Seton Av *HAR/WTLS* NE34 ....90 B3
Setting Stones *WASHS* NE38 ....137 F6
Sevenoaks Dr *MLFD/PNYW* SR4 ....141 F3
Seventh Av *BLYTH* NE24 ....10 C6
  BYK/HTN/WLK NE6 ....82 B1
  CLSW/PEL DH2 ....153 D5
Seventh St *PLEE/EAS* SR8 ....209 F1
Severn Av *HEBB* NE31 ....85 D5
Severn CI *PLEE/EAS* SR8 ....208 B4
Severn Dr *JRW* NE32 ....86 B6
Severn Gdns *GATE* NE8 ....100 A2
Severus Rd *ELS/FEN* NE4 ....79 D1
Seymour Ct *DUN/TMV* * NE11 ....97 F1
Seymour Sq *SUNDSW* SR3 ....143 E4
Seymour St *DUN/TMV* NE11 ....97 F1
  NSHW NE29 ....70 C2
Seymour Ter *HLH* DH5 ....186 A3
Shadforth CI *PLEE/EAS* SR8 ....207 F4
Shadon Wy *CLS/BIR/GTL* DH3 ....137 D2
Shaftesbury Av
  ASHBK/HED/RY SR2 ....162 A1
  HAR/WTLS NE34 ....87 D3
  JRW NE32 ....86 C2
  WBAY NE26 ....40 B3
Shaftesbury Crs *SUNDSW* SR3 ....143 E3
  TYNE/NSHE NE30 ....54 C1
Shaftesbury Gv
  BYK/HTN/WLK NE6 ....82 A1
Shaftoe Rd *SUNDSW* SR3 ....143 D4
Shaftoe Sq *SUNDSW* SR3 ....142 C4
Shaftoe Wy *DIN/WO* NE13 ....30 C5
Shafto St *BW/LEM/TK/HW* NE15 ....77 F3
  WLSD/HOW NE28 ....68 A3
Shaftsbury Dr *BDN/LAN/SAC* DH7 ....202 C6
Shaftsbury Wk *GATE* NE8 ....80 B6
Shakespeare Av *HEBB* NE31 ....85 D2
Shakespeare St *HLH* DH5 ....171 D3
  JRW * NE32 ....69 D6
  SEA/MUR SR7 ....176 C3
  SSH NE33 ....71 F5
  SWCK/CAS SR5 ....125 F1
  WLSD/HOW NE28 ....68 B4
Shakespeare Ter
  ASHBK/HED/RY SR2 ....4 A5
Shakespere Ter *CLSW/PEL* DH2 ....152 A5
Shalcombe CI *SUNDSW* SR3 ....160 C2
Shallcross *ASHBK/HED/RY* SR2 ....144 A2
Shalstone *WASHN* NE37 ....121 E3
Shamrock Ct
  BW/LEM/TK/HW NE15 ....59 E6
Shandon Wy *GOS/KPK* NE3 ....62 A1

Shanklin PI *CRAM* NE23 ....21 D2
Shannon CI *SWCK/CAS* SR5 ....123 F3
Shannon Ct *GOS/KPK* NE5 ....45 E5
Shap CI *WASHS* NE38 ....138 C3
Shap La *WD/WHPE/BLK* NE5 ....60 C5
Shap Rd *TYNE/NSHE* NE30 ....55 D1
Sharnford CI *SMOOR* NE27 ....37 F5
Sharon CI *LGB/KIL* NE12 ....49 D3
Sharp Crs *DHAM* DH1 ....195 F3
Sharpendon St *HEBB* * NE31 ....85 D1
Sharpley Dr *SEA/MUR* SR7 ....175 D2
Shaw Av *HAR/WTLS* NE34 ....88 A4
Shawbrow CI *LGB/HTN* NE7 ....66 A3
Shawdon CI *WD/WHPE/BLK* NE5 ....61 D2
Shaw Gdns *FELL* NE10 ....102 A2
Shaw St *SEA/MUR* SR7 ....176 C3
Shaw Wood CI *DHAM* DH1 ....193 F3
Shearlegs Rd *GATE* NE8 ....81 F5
Shearwater *CLDN/WHIT/ROK* SR6 ....91 F5
Shearwater Av *LGB/KIL* NE12 ....48 C5
Shearwater CI *WD/WHPE/BLK* NE5 ....61 D2
Shearwater Wy *BLYTH* NE24 ....17 F2
Sheelin Av *CLSW/PEL* DH2 ....166 B1
Sheen CI *HLS* DH4 ....183 F2
Sheen Ct *WD/WHPE/BLK* NE5 ....61 D1
Sheepfolds North *SWCK/CAS* SR5 ....126 C4
Sheepfolds Rd *SWCK/CAS* SR5 ....126 C4
Sheep HI *WICK/BNPF* NE16 ....112 A6
Sheldon Gv *CRAM* NE23 ....14 A5
  GOS/KPK NE3 ....62 B4
Sheldon Rd *HAR/WTLS* NE34 ....72 B5
Sheldon St *JRW* NE32 ....86 A1
Shelford Gdns
  BW/LEM/TK/HW NE15 ....57 D1
Shellbark *HLS* DH4 ....156 B2
Shelley Av *BOLCOL* NE35 ....105 F2
  HAR/WTLS NE34 ....90 A3
  HLH DH5 ....186 C4
  LWF/SPW/WRK NE9 ....119 D3
Shelley Ct *CLSW/PEL* DH2 ....152 A5
Shelley Gdns *CLSW/PEL* DH2 ....152 B5
Shelley Rd *BW/LEM/TK/HW* NE15 ....75 E1
Shelley St *SEA/MUR* SR7 ....176 C3
Shepherd St *MLFD/PNYW* SR4 ....125 F5
Shepherds Wy *BOL* NE36 ....105 F3
Shepherd Wy *WASHS* NE38 ....139 D4
Sheppard Ter *SWCK/CAS* SR5 ....124 A3
Sheppey Ct *SUNDSW* * SR3 ....160 C2
Shepton Cottages
  WICK/BNPF NE16 ....114 B1
Sheraton *FELL* NE10 ....101 F5
Sheraton St *JES* NE2 ....63 D6
Sherborne Av *NSHW* NE29 ....53 F4
Sherburn Gra North *JRW* NE32 ....85 F3
Sherburn Gra South *JRW* NE32 ....85 F3
Sherburn Gn *ROWG* NE39 ....111 E3
Sherburn Gv *HLS* DH4 ....170 B1
Sherburn Park Dr *ROWG* NE39 ....111 E4
Sherburn Rd *DHAM* DH1 ....195 E4
Sherburn Road Flats *DHAM* DH1 ....195 E4
Sherburn Wy *FELL* NE10 ....102 A3
Sherfield Dr *LGB/HTN* NE7 ....65 E3
Sheridan Dr *STLY/ANP* DH9 ....149 D2
Sheridan Gn *WASHS* NE38 ....137 F5
Sheridan Rd *HAR/WTLS* NE34 ....87 F5
Sheridan St *MLFD/PNYW* SR4 ....125 E5
Sheriff Mt North
  LWF/SPW/WRK NE9 ....99 F3
Sheriffs CI *FELL* NE10 ....100 A2
Sheriff's Moor Av *HLH* DH5 ....186 B4
Sheringham Av *NSHW* NE29 ....53 F5
Sheringham CI *SUNDSW* SR3 ....160 C4
Sheringham Dr *CRAM* NE23 ....21 D2
Sheringham Gdns
  BW/LEM/TK/HW NE15 ....57 D4
Sherringham Av *GOS/KPK* NE3 ....62 A1
Sherwood CI *SMOOR* NE27 ....53 D2
  WASHS NE38 ....138 C2
Sherwood Ct *SUNDSW* * SR3 ....160 C2
Sherwood PI *GOS/KPK* NE3 ....47 E2
Sherwood Vw *WLSD/HOW* NE28 ....66 C2
Shetland Ct *SUNDSW* * SR3 ....160 C2
Shibdon Bank *BLAY* NE21 ....76 C6
Shibdon Crs *BLAY* NE21 ....76 C6
Shibdon Park Vw *BLAY* NE21 ....76 C6
Shibdon Rd *BLAY* NE21 ....76 B5
Shibdon Wy *BLAY* NE21 ....77 E6
Shield Av *WICK/BNPF* NE16 ....96 A1
Shield Ct *JES* * NE2 ....81 E1
Shieldfield La *JES* NE2 ....3 G2
Shield Rd *CLDN/WHIT/ROK* SR6 ....108 B5
Shieldrow La *STLY/ANP* DH9 ....146 C5
Shields Rd *BDLGTN* NE22 ....12 A1
  BYK/HTN/WLK NE6 ....82 A2
  CLDN/WHIT/ROK SR6 ....108 A4
  CLS/BIR/GTL DH3 ....153 F3
  FELL NE10 ....101 F1
  HAR/WTLS NE34 ....89 E5
  MONK NE25 ....54 B2
Shields Rd West
  BYK/HTN/WLK NE6 ....81 F2
Shield St *JES* NE2 ....3 G1
Shiel Gdns *CRAM* NE23 ....21 D2
Shillaw PI *CRAM* NE23 ....35 D5

Shilmore Rd GOS/KPK NE3 ....**62** B1
Shilton Cl HAR/WTLS NE34 ....**89** F3
Shincliffe Av SWCK/CAS SR5 ....**124** B2
Shincliffe Gdns
   LWF/SPW/WRK NE9 ....**118** B1
Shinwell Ter SEA/MUR SR7 ....**188** A1
Shipcote La GATE NE8 ....**99** E2
Shipcote Ter GATE NE8 ....**99** E2
Shipley Av ELS/FEN NE4 ....**79** D2
Shipley Ct GATE NE8 ....**99** E1
Shipley Pl BYK/HTN/WLK NE6 ......**82** A2
Shipley Rd BYK/HTN/WLK NE6 ......**82** B2
Shipley Rd TYNE/NSHE NE30 ....**55** E5
Shipley St BW/LEM/TK/HW NE15 ...**76** B2
Shipley Wk BYK/HTN/WLK NE6 ......**82** A2
Shipton Cl BOLCOL NE35 ....**105** D1
Shire Cha DHAM * DH1 ....**180** C4
Shirlaw Cl WD/WHPE/BLK NE5 ....**60** B2
Shirley Gdns SUNDSW SR3 ....**144** A3
Shirwood Av WICK/BNPF NE16 ......**95** F5
Shop Spouts BLAY NE21 ....**76** B5
Shoreham Ct GOS/KPK NE3 ....**45** E5
Shoreham Sq SUNDSW SR3 ....**143** D3
Shorestone Av TYNE/NSHE NE30 ....**55** D1
Shore St CLDN/WHIT/ROK SR6 .....**126** C3
Short Gv SEA/MUR SR7 ....**187** F1
Shortridge St SSH NE33 ....**71** F3
Shortridge Ter JES NE2 ....**64** B5
Shot Factory La CNUT NE1 ....**80** B5
Shotley Av SWCK/CAS SR5 ....**126** A1
Shotley Gdns LWF/SPW/WRK NE9 ...**99** F3
Shotton Av BLYTH NE24 ....**11** D6
Shotton Bank PLEE/EAS SR8 ....**207** E5
Shotton La CRAM NE23 ....**12** B4
   PLEE/EAS SR8 ....**207** F4
   RDHAMSE DH6 ....**206** C3
Shotton Rd PLEE/EAS SR8 ....**207** D1
   PLEE/EAS SR8 ....**209** E1
Shotton Wy FELL NE10 ....**103** D4
Shrewsbury Cl LGB/KIL NE12 ....**65** F2
   PLEE/EAS SR8 ....**208** A3
Shrewsbury Crs SUNDSW SR3 ......**143** E3
Shrewsbury Dr SMOOR NE27 ....**37** E5
Shrewsbury St DUN/TMV NE11 ......**97** E2
Shrewsbury Ter SSH NE33 ....**88** D1
Shrigley Gdns GOS/KPK NE3 ....**62** B1
Shropshire Dr DHAM DH1 ....**196** B4
Shunner Cl WASHN NE37 ....**119** F6
Sibthorpe St NSHW NE29 ....**71** D1
Side CNUT NE1 ....**3** E5
Side Cliff Rd CLDN/WHIT/ROK SR6 .**126** C1
Sidegate DHAM DH1 ....**194** B4
Sidgate
   CNUT * (off Eldon Sq) NE1 ....**2** C2
Sidlaw Av CLSW/PEL DH2 ....**152** C6
   NSHW NE29 ....**54** B3
Sidmouth Cl HLS DH4 ....**157** E4
   SEA/MUR SR7 ....**175** E4
Sidmouth Rd LWF/SPW/WRK NE9 ...**117** E1
   NSHW NE29 ....**53** E6
Sidney Gv ELS/FEN NE4 ....**79** F2
   GATE NE8 ....**98** C1
Sidney St BLYTH NE24 ....**10** C1
   BOLCOL NE35 ....**105** E2
   NSHW NE29 ....**70** C1
Sidney Ter STLY/ANP DH9 ....**130** C6
Silkey's La NSHW NE29 ....**70** B1
Silksworth Cl SUNDSW SR3 ....**143** E6
Silksworth Gdns
   LWF/SPW/WRK NE9 ....**118** B2
Silksworth Hall Dr SUNDSW SR3 ..**160** B2
Silksworth La SUNDSW SR3 ....**143** E6
Silksworth Rw SUND SR1 ....**4** A2
Silksworth Ter SUNDSW SR3 ....**160** C1
Silksworth Wy SUNDSW SR3 ....**159** F2
Silkwood Cl CRAM NE23 ....**14** A5
Silloth Av WD/WHPE/BLK NE5 ....**60** C6
Silloth Dr WASHN NE37 ....**120** B2
Silloth Pl TYNE/NSHE NE30 ....**55** D2
Silloth Rd SUNDSW SR3 ....**142** C5
Silver Cts BDN/LAN/SAC DH7 ....**203** D4
Silverdale SUNDSW SR3 ....**160** C4
Silverdale Av FELL NE10 ....**102** C3
Silverdale Dr BLAY NE21 ....**93** E1
Silverdale Rd CRAM NE23 ....**14** A5
Silverdale Ter GATE NE8 ....**99** E2
Silverdale Wy HAR/WTLS NE34 ......**87** E5
   WICK/BNPF NE16 ....**95** E6
Silver Fox Wy SMOOR NE27 ....**52** A4
Silverhill Dr WD/WHPE/BLK NE5 ....**77** F1
The Silverlink North SMOOR NE27 ..**52** A3
The Silverlink SMOOR NE27 ....**52** C5
Silver Lonnen WD/WHPE/BLK NE5 ..**61** D6
Silvermere Dr RYTON NE40 ....**74** C4
Silverstone LGB/KIL NE12 ....**50** A1
Silverstone Rd WASHN NE37 ....**121** D4
Silver St DHAM DH1 ....**194** B5
   TYNE/NSHE NE30 ....**55** F5
Silverwood Gdns DUN/TMV NE11 ...**98** A5
Simonburn Av ELS/FEN NE4 ....**62** A6
   NSHW NE29 ....**53** E6
Simon Pl DIN/WO NE13 ....**32** C5
Simonside Av WLSD/HOW NE28 .....**68** B2
Simonside Rd BLAY NE21 ....**94** B1

SUNDSW SR3 ....**142** C3
Simonside Ter BYK/HTN/WLK NE6 ...**65** D6
Simonside Vw JRW NE32 ....**86** B4
Simonside Wy LGB/KIL NE12 ....**36** B6
Simpson St BLYTH NE24 ....**11** D4
   MLFD/PNYW SR4 ....**126** A4
   NSHW NE29 ....**70** A1
   WBAY NE26 ....**41** E6
Simpson Ter JES NE2 ....**3** G2
Sinclair Dr CLS/BIR/GTL DH3 ....**136** C6
Sinclair Gdns MONK NE25 ....**24** C5
Sinderby Cl GOS/KPK NE3 ....**47** F4
Sir Godfrey Thomson Ct
   FELL * NE10 ....**100** B2
Six-Mile Br DIN/WO NE13 ....**33** E2
Sixth Av BLYTH NE24 ....**10** C6
   BYK/HTN/WLK NE6 ....**82** B1
Sixth St PLEE/EAS SR8 ....**209** F1
Skafell Ct STLY/ANP DH9 ....**146** B5
Skaylock Dr WASHS NE38 ....**137** F3
Skelder Av LGB/KIL NE12 ....**49** D6
Skelton Ct PLEE/EAS SR8 ....**46** A4
Skerne Cl PLEE/EAS SR8 ....**208** B4
Skiddaw Cl PLEE/EAS SR8 ....**209** D2
Skiddaw Dr STLY/ANP DH9 ....**146** A5
Skiddaw Dr
   CLDN/WHIT/ROK * SR6 ....**108** B5
Skiddaw Pl LWF/SPW/WRK NE9 ...**100** A6
Skinnerburn Rd ELS/FEN NE4 ....**80** A6
Skipsey Ct NSHW NE29 ....**69** F3
Skipton Cl BDLGTN NE22 ....**22** C5
   CRAM NE23 ....**14** B5
Skirlaw Cl WASHS NE38 ....**138** C2
Ski Vw SUNDSW SR3 ....**143** E6
Skye Ct SUNDSW SR3 ....**160** B2
Skye Gv JRW NE32 ....**87** D1
Slaidburn Rd STLY/ANP DH9 ....**148** B1
Slake Rd JRW NE32 ....**69** F6
Slaley WASHS NE38 ....**139** D5
Slaley Cl FELL NE10 ....**102** B3
Slaley Ct BDLGTN NE22 ....**7** F3
   SUNDSW SR3 ....**160** C2
Slatyford La WD/WHPE/BLK NE5 ....**60** C6
Sledmere Cl PLEE/EAS SR8 ....**208** A3
Sleekburn Av BDLGTN NE22 ....**8** C1
Slingsby Gdns LGB/HTN NE7 ....**65** F3
Sloane Ct JES NE2 ....**81** D1
Smailes La ROWG NE39 ....**110** B2
Smailes St STLY/ANP DH9 ....**148** A3
Smeaton Ct WLSD/HOW NE28 ....**68** C5
Smeaton St WLSD/HOW NE28 ....**68** C5
Smillie Cl PLEE/EAS SR8 ....**208** C1
Smillie Rd PLEE/EAS SR8 ....**201** D5
Smithburn Rd FELL NE10 ....**100** C3
Smithfield DHAM DH1 ....**180** A4
Smith Gv ASHBK/HED/RY SR2 ....**162** A2
Smith St ASHBK/HED/RY SR2 ....**162** B2
   SSH NE33 ....**71** D6
Smith Ter GATE NE8 ....**98** A1
Smithyford LWF/SPW/WRK NE9 ....**117** F3
Smithy La DUN/TMV NE11 ....**117** D3
Smithy St SSH * NE33 ....**71** E3
Smyrna Pl SUND SR1 ....**5** F3
Snipes Dene ROWG NE39 ....**111** D1
Snowdon Ct STLY/ANP DH9 ....**146** A5
Snowdon Gdns DUN/TMV NE11 ......**97** F4
Snowdon Gv BOL NE36 ....**106** A3
Snowdon Pl PLEE/EAS SR8 ....**207** F3
Snowdrop Av PLEE/EAS SR8 ....**209** E1
Soane Gdns HAR/WTLS NE34 ....**88** C5
Softley Pl BW/LEM/TK/HW NE15 .....**77** E1
Solingen Est BLYTH NE24 ....**17** E1
Solway Av TYNE/NSHE NE30 ....**54** C2
Solway Rd HEBB NE31 ....**85** D4
Solway Sq SUNDSW SR3 ....**143** D3
Solway St BYK/HTN/WLK NE6 ....**82** B4
Somerford LWF/SPW/WRK NE9 ....**119** E2
Somersby Dr GOS/KPK NE3 ....**62** A1
Somerset Gdns WLSD/HOW NE28 ...**66** C3
Somerset Gv NSHW NE29 ....**53** F4
Somerset Pl ELS/FEN NE4 ....**79** F3
Somerset Rd HEBB NE31 ....**85** E5
   SUNDSW SR3 ....**142** C3
Somerset Sq SUNDSW SR3 ....**142** C3
Somerset St SUNDSW * SR3 ....**143** F5
Somerton Ct GOS/KPK NE3 ....**45** E6
Sophy St SWCK/CAS SR5 ....**126** A2
Sorley St MLFD/PNYW SR4 ....**125** F6
Sorrel Cl ELS/FEN * NE4 ....**78** C1
Sorrel Gdns HAR/WTLS NE34 ....**89** D5
Soulby Ct DIN/WO NE13 ....**45** F4
Sourmilk Hill La
   LWF/SPW/WRK NE9 ....**99** F4
Souter Rd GOS/KPK NE3 ....**62** C1
Souter Vw CLDN/WHIT/ROK SR6 ...**91** E6
South Ap CLSW/PEL DH2 ....**153** E6
South Av HAR/WTLS NE34 ....**89** E3
South Bailey DHAM DH1 ....**194** B6
South Bend GOS/KPK NE3 ....**47** D3
South Bents Av
   CLDN/WHIT/ROK SR6 ....**109** D4
South Benwell Rd
   BW/LEM/TK/HW NE15 ....**78** B4
Southburn Cl HLS DH4 ....**170** B4

South Burns CLS/BIR/GTL DH3 .....**153** E4
South Cliff
   CLDN/WHIT/ROK
   (off Roker Ter) SR6 ....**127** E2
South Cl HAR/WTLS NE34 ....**89** E3
   HLH DH5 ....**186** C4
   RYTON NE40 ....**74** B4
Southcote WICK/BNPF NE16 ....**95** E5
South Crs BOLCOL NE35 ....**105** E2
   DHAM DH1 ....**194** A3
   SEA/MUR SR7 ....**177** D3
   WASHS NE38 ....**138** A6
South Cft LGB/KIL NE12 ....**50** A5
Southcroft WASHS NE38 ....**138** C5
South Dene HAR/WTLS NE34 ....**88** A3
South Dock SUND SR1 ....**127** F4
South Dr CLDN/WHIT/ROK SR6 .....**107** E1
   DIN/WO NE13 ....**19** D2
   DIN/WO NE13 ....**44** B4
   HEBB NE31 ....**84** B4
South Durham Ct SUND SR1 ....**5** F3
South East Vw PLEE/EAS SR8 ....**209** F1
South Eldon St SSH NE33 ....**88** B1
Southend Av BLYTH NE24 ....**10** B6
Southend Rd LWF/SPW/WRK NE9 ..**100** A5
   SUNDSW SR3 ....**143** D4
Southern Rd BYK/HTN/WLK NE6 ....**83** E4
Southern Wy RYTON NE40 ....**74** B4
Southey St SSH * NE33 ....**71** F3
Southfield CLSW/PEL DH2 ....**152** A1
Southfield Gdns WICK/BNPF NE16 ...**96** B3
Southfield Rd HAR/WTLS NE34 ....**72** B6
   LGB/KIL NE12 ....**49** E6
   WICK/BNPF NE16 ....**96** B5
Southfields CRAM NE23 ....**34** C2
Southfield Wy DHAM DH1 ....**193** F2
South Foreshore SSH NE33 ....**72** B3
Southfork BW/LEM/TK/HW NE15 .....**59** E6
South Frederick St SSH NE33 ....**88** A1
Southgate LGB/KIL NE12 ....**49** F1
South Grange Pk SEA/MUR SR7 ...**162** B6
South Gv RYTON NE40 ....**74** C4
South Hetton Rd HLH DH5 ....**186** C4
South Hill Crs
   ASHBK/HED/RY * SR2 ....**144** A1
South Hill Rd GATE NE8 ....**98** B1
Southhill Rd HAR/WTLS NE34 ....**89** F2
Southlands JRW NE32 ....**104** C1
   LGB/HTN NE7 ....**64** C4
   TYNE/NSHE NE30 ....**55** D4
South La BOL NE36 ....**106** B3
South Lea BDN/LAN/SAC DH7 ....**178** A4
South Market St HLH DH5 ....**172** A6
Southmayne Rd
   MLFD/PNYW SR4 ....**142** C2
Southmead Av
   WD/WHPE/BLK NE5 ....**61** D5
South Mdw STLY/ANP DH9 ....**128** C6
Southmoor Rd BYK/HTN/WLK NE6 ..**83** A4
South Moor Rd STLY/ANP DH9 .....**148** A4
South Nelson Rd CRAM NE23 ....**13** D6
South Newsham Rd BLYTH NE24 .....**16** B3
South Pde FELL NE10 ....**84** A6
   WBAY NE26 ....**41** D5
South Preston Gv NSHW NE29 ....**70** B1
South Preston Ter NSHW * NE29 .....**70** C1
South Railway St SEA/MUR SR7 ....**176** C5
South Rdg GOS/KPK NE3 ....**47** D4
South Riggs BDLGTN NE22 ....**7** F4
South Rd DHAM DH1 ....**205** E2
South Rw GATE NE8 ....**81** F4
South Sherbourne ROWG NE39 ....**111** D2
South Shore Rd GATE NE8 ....**3** H5
South Side PLEE/EAS SR8 ....**200** B3
South St CLSW/PEL DH2 ....**153** D4
   CNUT NE1 ....**2** C6
   DHAM DH1 ....**194** B5
   GATE NE8 ....**99** E1
   GOS/KPK NE3 ....**62** C1
   HLH DH5 ....**170** B6
   HLS DH4 ....**157** F5
   SMOOR NE27 ....**38** C5
   SUND SR1 ....**4** C2
South Ter DHAM DH1 ....**193** F1
   PLEE/EAS SR8 ....**209** E1
   SEA/MUR SR7 ....**177** D3
   SWCK/CAS SR5 ....**126** A3
   WLSD/HOW NE28 ....**68** C4
South Vw BDN/LAN/SAC DH7 ....**203** E5
   BLYTH NE24 ....**16** B3
   CLDN/WHIT/ROK SR6 ....**126** C1
   CLS/BIR/GTL DH3 ....**136** C2
   DHAM DH1 ....**195** E4
   HLH DH5 ....**186** C5
   JRW NE32 ....**85** F2
   RDHAMSE (off Front St) DH6 ....**206** C1
   SEA/MUR SR7 ....**175** E5
   STLY/ANP DH9 ....**130** A4
   WASHS NE38 ....**139** D5
   WD/WHPE/BLK NE5 ....**60** A6
South View Gdns STLY/ANP DH9 ...**146** C5
South View Rd MLFD/PNYW SR4 ....**141** F1
South View Ter HLS DH4 ....**170** A2
   WICK/BNPF NE16 ....**96** A2
South Vw West BYK/HTN/WLK NE6 ..**81** F7

Southward *WBAY* NE26.................**26** C3
Southward Cl *WBAY* NE26 ....**26** C3
Southward Wy *MONK* NE25...............**38** A1
Southway *BW/LEM/TK/HW* NE15 .....**77** D1
  LWF/SPW/WRK NE9 ....**100** A4
  PLEE/EAS SR8 ....**208** B3
Southwick Rd *SWCK/CAS* SR5 ....**126** A2
Southwold Gdns *SUNDSW* SR3 ....**143** E6
Southwold Pl *CRAM* NE23 ....**21** D2
South Woodbine St *SSH* NE33 ....**71** F4
Southwood Gdns *GOS/KPK* NE3 ......**62** B2
Sovereign Ct *ELS/FEN* * NE4...........**79** F4
  JES NE2...**64** B6
Sovereign Pl *ELS/FEN* NE4 ....**79** F4
Spalding Cl *LGB/HTN* NE7 ....**65** E2
Sparkwell Cl *HLS* DH4 ....**157** E4
Spartylea *WASHS* NE38 ....**139** E5
Spa Well Cl *BLAY* NE21....................**94** A2
Spa Well Dr *SWCK/CAS* SR5 ....**124** B2
Spelter Works Rd
  ASHBK/HED/RY SR2.....................**145** E4
Spencer Ct *STLY/ANP* DH9 ....**149** D2
Spencer Ct *BLYTH* NE24...................**10** A3
Spencer Gv *WICK/BNPF* NE16.........**95** F2
Spencer Rd *BLYTH* NE24 ....**10** A3
Spencers Bank *WICK/BNPF* NE16 ....**95** F1
Spencer St *BYK/HTN/WLK* NE6.........**65** E6
  NSHW NE29 ....**70** C1
Spence Ter *NSHW* NE29...................**70** C1
Spenfield Rd *WD/WHPE/BLK* NE5 ....**61** F3
Spenser St *JRW* NE32......................**69** D6
Spen St *STLY/ANP* DH9 ....**148** A3
Spinneyside Gdns *DUN/TMV* NE11 ...**97** E3
Spinney Ter *BYK/HTN/WLK* * NE6 ...**83** E2
The Spinney *CRAM* NE23..................**35** E2
  LGB/HTN (off Newton Pl) NE7..........**65** D4
  WASHS NE38 ....**138** C4
Spire Hollin *PLEE/EAS* SR8 ....**208** B2
Spire Rd *WASHN* NE37 ....**121** E5
Spires La *BYK/HTN/WLK* NE6............**82** B2
Spital Ter *GOS/KPK* NE3..................**63** E1
Split Crow Rd *GATE* NE8 ....**99** F2
Split Level Mwy *JES* NE2..................**81** D1
Spohr Ter *SSH* NE33 ....**71** F5
Spoors Cottages *WICK/BNPF* NE16 ...**95** F4
Spoor St *DUN/TMV* NE11.................**97** F1
Spout La *WASHN* NE37.....................**120** C4
  WASHS NE38 ....**120** C6
Springbank Rd *BYK/HTN/WLK* NE6 ...**81** F1
  JES NE2...**81** F1
  SUNDSW SR3 ....**142** C5
Springbank Sq *SUNDSW* SR3 ....**142** C3
Springbourne *SUND* **54** C6
Springfield Av
  LWF/SPW/WRK NE9 ....**118** B3
Springfield Crs *SEA/MUR* SR7 ....**176** B4
Springfield Gdns
  CLS/BIR/GTL DH3..........................**153** E3
  WLSD/HOW NE28 ....**66** B3
Springfield Gv *MONK* NE25..............**54** A1
Springfield Pk *DHAM* DH1 ....**193** F3
Springfield Pl *LWF/SPW/WRK* NE9 ...**99** F4
Springfield Rd *BLAY* NE21................**76** A6
  HLS DH4..**157** F5
  WD/WHPE/BLK NE5 ....**61** E5
Springfield Ter *FELL* NE10...............**100** B3
  PLEE/EAS SR8 ....**201** F4
Spring Garden Cl *SUND* SR1 ....**5** E2
Spring Garden La *ELS/FEN* NE4 ....**80** A2
Spring Gdns *NSHW* NE29..................**70** B1
Springhill Gdns
  BW/LEM/TK/HW NE15 ....**78** C2
Spring Pk *BDLGTN* NE22 ....**7** F4
Springside *BDN/LAN/SAC* DH7 ....**178** B1
The Springs *CLS/BIR/GTL* DH3 ....**136** C3
Springsyde Cl *WICK/BNPF* NE16 ......**95** D5
Spring Ter *NSHW* NE29 ....**54** C6
Springwell Av *BYK/HTN/WLK* NE6 ...**83** D4
  DHAM DH1 ....**193** F3
  JRW NE32 ....**86** B3
  LWF/SPW/WRK NE9 ....**118** B2
Springwell Rd *DHAM* DH1 ....**193** F3
  JRW NE32 ....**86** A3
  LWF/SPW/WRK NE9 ....**119** D1
  MLFD/PNYW SR4 ....**142** C3
Springwood *HEBB* NE31...................**84** B1
The Square
  WICK/BNPF (off Front St) NE16 ....**96** A3
Squires Gdns *FELL* NE10 ....**100** C3
Stack Garth *BDN/LAN/SAC* DH7 .....**203** E3
Stadium Rd *GATE* NE8.......................**82** A5
Stadium Wy *SWCK/CAS* SR5 ....**126** B4
Stafford Gv *ASHBK/HED/RY* SR2 ....**162** A2
  SWCK/CAS SR5 ....**126** A2
Stafford Pl *PLEE/EAS* SR8 ....**208** A1
Staffordshire Dr *DHAM* DH1............**196** C3
Staffords La *CLDN/WHIT/ROK* SR6 ..**109** E3
Stafford St *SUND* SR1 ....**127** E4
Stafford Vls *LWF/SPW/WRK* NE9 ....**119** E3
Stagshaw *LGB/KIL* NE12 ....**35** E5
Staindrop *FELL* NE10 ....**101** F5
Staindrop Rd *DHAM* DH1 ....**180** C6
Staindrop Ter *STLY/ANP* DH9 ....**146** B4
Staines Rd *BYK/HTN/WLK* NE6.........**82** C4
Stainmore Dr *CLS/BIR/GTL* DH3 .....**168** A4

Stainton Dr *FELL* NE10 ....**100** C2
Stainton Gv *CLDN/WHIT/ROK* SR6 ...**108** B5
Stainton St East *SSH* NE33 ....**71** F5
Stainton Wy *PLEE/EAS* SR8.............**208** B2
Staithes Av *LGB/KIL* NE12 ....**49** E6
Staithes Rd *WASHS* NE38 ....**139** F3
Staithes St *BYK/HTN/WLK* NE6........**84** A2
Staith La *BLAY* NE21 ....**75** F4
Staiths Rd *DUN/TMV* NE11..............**97** F1
Stalks Rd *DIN/WO* NE13 ....**33** D4
Stamford Av *NSHW* NE29 ....**25** D6
  SUNDSW SR3 ....**143** E3
Stamfordham Av *NSHW* NE29 ....**69** F1
Stamfordham Cl
  WLSD/HOW NE28 ....**66** C4
Stamfordham Ms
  WD/WHPE/BLK NE5 ....**61** F5
Stamfordham Rd
  WD/WHPE/BLK NE5 ....**42** B6
Stampley Cl *BLAY* NE21...................**93** F1
Stamps La *SUND* SR1 ....**5** G1
Standfield Gdns *FELL* NE10 ....**102** B2
Standish St *STLY/ANP* DH9 ....**147** F3
Stanelaw Wy *STLY/ANP* DH9 ....**131** E5
Staneway *FELL* NE10 ....**101** D6
Stanfield Ct *LGB/HTN* NE7 ....**66** A3
Stanfield Gdns *FELL* * NE10 ....**102** B2
Stanhope *WASHS* NE38 ....**137** E1
Stanhope Cl *BDN/LAN/SAC* DH7 ....**203** E4
  DHAM DH1 ....**180** C5
  HLS DH4..**170** C3
Stanhope Gdns *STLY/ANP* DH9 .....**146** B4
Stanhope Pde *SSH* NE33 ....**71** F6
Stanhope Rd
  CLDN/WHIT/ROK SR6 ....**109** D6
  HAR/WTLS NE34...........................**88** A3
  JRW NE32 ....**86** C3
  SSH NE33 ....**88** C1
Stanhope St *ELS/FEN* NE4 ....**79** F2
  SSH NE33 ....**71** E3
Stanhope Wy *ELS/FEN* NE4 ....**80** A2
Stanley Cl *RDHAMSE* DH6..............**197** E5
Stanley Gdns *LWF/SPW/WRK* NE9 ...**118** B2
Stanley Gv *BDLGTN* NE22 ....**8** A3
  LGB/HTN NE7 ....**64** C3
Stanley St *BLYTH* NE24 ....**11** E4
  HAR/WTLS NE34...........................**88** A3
  JRW NE32 ....**86** B1
  NSHW NE29 ....**70** C1
  SEA/MUR SR7................................**176** A2
  SWCK/CAS SR5 ....**124** A3
  WLSD/HOW NE28 ....**66** C3
Stanley St West *NSHW* NE29 ....**70** C1
Stanmore Rd *BYK/HTN/WLK* NE6 ....**65** E5
Stannington Av
  BYK/HTN/WLK NE6 ....**82** A1
Stannington Gdns
  ASHBK/HED/RY SR2.....................**144** B4
Stannington Gv
  ASHBK/HED/RY SR2.....................**144** B4
  BYK/HTN/WLK NE6 ....**82** A1
Stannington Pl *BYK/HTN/WLK* NE6...**82** A1
  PONT/DH NE20 ....**28** A2
Stannington Rd *NSHW* NE29 ....**69** E1
Stannington St *BLYTH* NE24 ....**11** E5
Stansfield St
  CLDN/WHIT/ROK SR6 ....**127** D3
Stanstead Cl *SWCK/CAS* SR5 ....**123** F4
Stanton Av *BLYTH* NE24 ....**16** A1
  SSH NE33 ....**89** D1
Stanton Cl *FELL* NE10 ....**102** C3
Stanton Rd *SMOOR* NE27 ....**52** A2
  TYNE/NSHE NE30 ....**54** B3
Stanton St *ELS/FEN* NE4 ....**79** F2
Stanway Dr *LGB/HTN* NE7 ....**64** C3
Stanwick St *TYNE/NSHE* NE30 ....**55** F4
Stapeley Vw *GOS/KPK* NE3 ....**61** F1
Stapleford Cl *WD/WHPE/BLK* NE5 ....**61** D5
Staple Rd *JRW* NE32 ....**86** B1
Stapylton Dr *ASHBK/HED/RY* SR2 ...**144** A2
Starbeck Av *JES* * NE2......................**81** E1
Starbeck Ms *JES* NE2........................**81** E1
Stardale Av *BLYTH* NE24 ....**9** F6
Stargate La *RYTON* NE40 ....**75** D4
Starlight Crs *MONK* NE25 ....**24** B5
Starling Wk *WICK/BNPF* NE16 ....**114** A2
Startforth Cl *CLS/BIR/GTL* DH3 ......**168** A3
Station Ap *BOL* NE36 ....**107** D2
  DHAM DH1 ....**194** A4
  LGB/KIL NE12 ....**49** F6
  SSH NE33 ....**71** E3
Station Av *BDN/LAN/SAC* DH7 ....**203** E4
  HLH DH5 ....**185** F1
Station Bank *DHAM* DH1 ....**194** B4
  RYTON NE40...................................**74** B2
Station Cottages
  GATE (off Elysium La) NE8 ....**98** C2
Station Crs *SEA/MUR* SR7 ....**176** A2
Station Est East *SEA/MUR* SR7 .....**187** F1
Station Est North *SEA/MUR* SR7 ....**187** F1
Station Est South *SEA/MUR* SR7 ....**187** F1
Station Field Rd *STLY/ANP* DH9 .....**131** E5
Station La *CLS/BIR/GTL* DH3 ....**136** A3
  CLSW/PEL DH2...............................**151** F2
  DHAM DH1 ....**195** D4

Station Rd *ASHBK/HED/RY* SR2 ......**162** C1
  BDLGTN NE22 ....**8** A3
  BDN/LAN/SAC DH7 ....**203** E4
  BOLCOL NE35 ....**87** D6
  BW/LEM/TK/HW NE15 ....**56** B4
  BW/LEM/TK/HW NE15 ....**75** E1
  CLS/BIR/GTL DH3..........................**153** E5
  CLSW/PEL DH2...............................**153** E5
  CRAM NE23 ....**21** F1
  CRAM NE23 ....**23** E2
  CRAM NE23 ....**36** B1
  DIN/WO NE13..................................**45** D6
  FELL NE10......................................**84** A6
  GOS/KPK NE3 ....**64** A1
  HEBB NE31 ....**84** C2
  HLH DH5 ....**185** F1
  HLS DH4..**139** E6
  HLS DH4..**156** C2
  HLS DH4..**170** C1
  HLS DH4..**183** E3
  LGB/KIL NE12 ....**35** D6
  LGB/KIL NE12 ....**49** F5
  LWF/SPW/WRK NE9 ....**99** D5
  NSHW NE29 ....**69** F2
  PLEE/EAS SR8 ....**201** E2
  RDHAMSE DH6 ....**183** F5
  RDHAMSE DH6 ....**206** A1
  ROWG NE39 ....**111** E3
  SEA/MUR SR7................................**175** E2
  SEA/MUR SR7................................**187** F1
  SMOOR NE27 ....**51** F1
  SSH NE33 ....**71** E4
  STLY/ANP DH9 ....**133** D6
  STLY/ANP DH9 ....**146** B5
  STLY/ANP DH9 ....**148** B1
  SWCK/CAS SR5 ....**108** B6
  TYNE/NSHE NE30 ....**55** E1
  WASHS NE38 ....**139** E2
  WBAY NE26 ....**41** D6
  WLSD/HOW NE28 ....**66** B1
Station Rd North *LGB/KIL* NE12 ......**49** F4
Station St *BLYTH* NE24 ....**11** D4
  SUND SR1 ....**4** C3
Station Ter *TYNE/NSHE* NE30 ....**55** F5
Station Vw *HLH* DH5 ....**185** F1
Staveley Rd *CLDN/WHIT/ROK* SR6 ...**108** B5
  PLEE/EAS SR8 ....**209** D2
Stavordale St *SEA/MUR* SR7...........**176** C4
Stavordale St West
  SEA/MUR SR7................................**176** C5
Stavordale Ter *LWF/SPW/WRK* NE9 ...**99** F3
Staward Av *MONK* NE25 ....**24** C6
Staward Ter *BYK/HTN/WLK* NE6 .....**83** E4
Staynebrigg *FELL* NE10...................**101** F4
Stead La *BDLGTN* NE22 ....**8** C3
Stead St *WLSD/HOW* NE28 ....**68** C3
Stedham Cl *WASHN* NE37 ....**121** D2
Steep HI *SUNDSW* SR3 ....**142** A6
Stella Bank *BLAY* NE21 ....**75** E3
Stella Gv *BLAY* NE21 ....**75** E4
Stella La *BLAY* NE21........................**75** E4
Stella Rd *BLAY* NE21 ....**75** E3
Stephenson Cl *HLH* DH5 ....**172** A6
Stephenson Ct *TYNE/NSHE* NE30 ...**71** D1
Stephenson Rd
  BYK/HTN/WLK NE6 ....**65** D5
  PLEE/EAS SR8 ....**200** B5
  WASHN NE37 ....**121** D2
Stephenson St *GATE* NE8 ....**98** C2
Stephenson St *SEA/MUR* SR7 ....**188** B1
  SEA/MUR SR7................................**188** B1
  TYNE/NSHE NE30 ....**71** D1
  WLSD/HOW NE28 ....**69** D5
Stephenson Ter
  BW/LEM/TK/HW
  (off Hexham Rd) NE15 ....**57** F2
  FELL NE10......................................**100** C3
Stephenson Wy *BLAY* NE21 ....**94** A2
Stephens Rd *SEA/MUR* SR7 ....**188** A1
Stephen St *BLYTH* NE24 ....**11** D4
  BYK/HTN/WLK NE6 ....**81** F2
Stepney La *CNUT* NE1 ....**3** G3
Stepney Rd *JES* NE2...........................**3** H1
Sterling Cottages *FELL* NE10 ....**100** B3
Sterling St *MLFD/PNYW* SR4...........**125** F6
Steward Crs *HAR/WTLS* NE34..........**90** A1
Stewart Av *ASHBK/HED/RY* SR2......**162** A2
Stewart Dr *BOL* NE36 ....**106** A3
Stewart St *MLFD/PNYW* SR4 ....**125** F6
  PLEE/EAS SR8 ....**200** C2
  SEA/MUR SR7................................**177** D4
  SUNDSW SR3 ....**160** C1
Stileford *FELL* NE10 ....**101** F3
Stirling Av *JRW* NE32 ....**87** D4
  ROWG NE39 ....**111** D3
Stirling Cl *WASHS* NE38 ....**139** E2
Stirling Dr *BDLGTN* NE22 ....**8** B2
  NSHW NE29 ....**53** E4
Stirling La *ROWG* NE39 ....**111** D3
St Leonards Ct *PLEE/EAS* SR8 ....**208** A3
St Michaels Wy *SUND* SR1.................**4** A3
Stobart St *BDN/LAN/SAC* DH7 ....**164** A3
  SWCK/CAS SR5 ....**126** B4
Stockholm Cl *NSHW* NE29................**69** D1
Stockley Av *SWCK/CAS* SR5............**124** B2

Stockley Ct BDN/LAN/SAC DH7 ......192 B5
Stockley Rd WASHS NE38 ....121 E6
Stocksfield Av WD/WHPE/BLK NE5..78 B1
Stockton Rd ASHBK/HED/RY SR2 ......4 B5
  ASHBK/HED/RY SR2 ....162 B3
  DHAM DH1 ....194 B6
  NSHW NE29 ....70 B3
  PLEE/EAS SR8 ....162 B4
  SEA/MUR SR7 ....162 B6
  SUND SR1 ....4 B4
Stockton St SEA/MUR SR7 ....176 A2
Stockwell Gn BYK/HTN/WLK NE6 .....66 B6
Stoddart St HAR/WTLS NE34 ....88 B2
  JES NE2 ....3 H1
Stoker Av HAR/WTLS NE34 ....87 E4
Stokesley Gv LGB/HTN NE7 ....64 C3
Stone Br DHAM DH1 ....204 B6
Stone Cellar Rd WASHN NE37 ....120 A2
Stonechat PI LGB/KIL NE12 ....48 C5
Stonecroft Gdns LGB/HTN NE7 ......65 F3
Stonefold CI WD/WHPE/BLK NE5 .....61 D3
Stonehills
  FELL (off Shields Rd) NE10......102 A1
Stoneleigh Av LGB/KIL NE12........48 C5
Stoneleigh CI HLS DH4 ....170 B1
Stone Rw CLSW/PEL DH2 ....150 C3
Stonesdale HLS DH4 ....139 D6
Stone St FELL NE10 ....100 B4
Stoneygate Gdns FELL NE10 ....101 D1
Stoneygate La FELL NE10 ....83 D6
Stoneyhurst Av
  BW/LEM/TK/HW NE15 ....78 A3
Stoneyhurst Rd GOS/KPK NE3 ....64 A2
Stoney La LWF/SPW/WRK NE9 ....119 E3
  SWCK/CAS SR5 ....125 F3
Stoneylea Rd WD/WHPE/BLK NE5 ....60 B6
Stony La STLY/ANP DH9 ....133 F6
Store St BW/LEM/TK/HW NE15 ....76 B2
Storey La BLAY NE21 ....75 F4
Stormont St NSHW NE29 ....70 B3
Stotfold CI SEA/MUR SR7 ....175 D2
Stothard St JRW NE32 ....86 B1
Stotts Rd BYK/HTN/WLK NE6 ....66 C6
Stowell Gn CNUT NE1 ....2 B4
Stowell Ter FELL NE10 ....101 D2
The Stow LGB/KIL NE12 ....64 C1
Straker St JRW NE32 ....86 C2
Straker Ter HAR/WTLS NE34 ....88 A5
The Strand WASHS NE38 ....143 D6
Strangford Rd SEA/MUR SR7 ....176 A3
Strangways St SEA/MUR SR7 ....176 C4
Stranton Ter
  CLDN/WHIT/ROK SR6 ....126 C2
Stratfield St MLFD/PNYW SR4 ......125 D5
Stratford Av ASHBK/HED/RY SR2 ....145 D3
Stratford CI DHAM DH1 ....21 D1
  LGB/KIL NE12 ....50 A1
Stratford Gdns LWF/SPW/WRK NE9 ..99 E4
Stratford Rd BYK/HTN/WLK NE6 .....81 F1
Stratford Grove Ter
  BYK/HTN/WLK * NE6 ....81 F1
Stratford Gv West
  BYK/HTN/WLK NE6 ....81 F1
Stratford Rd BYK/HTN/WLK NE6 ....81 F1
Stratford Vls BYK/HTN/WLK NE6 ...81 F1
Strathearn Wy GOS/KPK NE3 ....46 B5
Strathmore Av ROWG NE39 ....111 D3
Strathmore CI STLY/ANP DH9 ......149 D1
Strathmore Crs ELS/FEN NE4 ......79 D3
Strathmore Rd GOS/KPK NE3 ....47 E5
  LWF/SPW/WRK NE9 ....100 A3
  ROWG NE39 ....110 C3
  SUNDSW SR3 ....143 D4
Strathmore Sq SUNDSW SR3 ....143 D4
Stratton CI ASHBK/HED/RY SR2 ....145 F6
Stratus Ct SUNDSW SR3 ....160 C2
Strawberry Gdns
  WLSD/HOW NE28 ....66 C2
Strawberry La CNUT NE1 ....2 B2
Strawberry PI CNUT NE1 ....2 B3
Street Gate Pk WICK/BNPF NE16....114 B1
Stretton CI HLS DH4 ....169 F3
Stretton Wy SMOOR NE27 ....37 E5
Stridingedge WASHN NE37 ....119 F6
Stuart Ct GOS/KPK NE3 ....45 D6
Stuart Gdns BW/LEM/TK/HW NE15 ...57 E4
Stuart Ter FELL * NE10 ....100 C1
Stubbs Av WICK/BNPF NE16 ....95 F2
Studdon Wk GOS/KPK NE3 ....61 F1
Studland CI NSHW NE29 ....54 B3
Studley Gdns LWF/SPW/WRK NE9 ....99 E5
  MONK NE25 ....40 C6
Studley Ter ELS/FEN NE4 ....79 E1
Studley Vls LGB/KIL NE12 ....50 A5
Sturdee Gdns JES NE2 ....64 A3
Styford Gdns
  BW/LEM/TK/HW NE15 ....77 D1
Success Rd HLS DH4 ....157 D3
Sudbury Wy CRAM NE23 ....21 D1
Suddick St SWCK/CAS SR5 ....126 A3
Suez St TYNE/NSHE NE30 ....55 D5
Suffolk Gdns HAR/WTLS NE34 ......90 B1
  WLSD/HOW NE28 ....68 A2
Suffolk PI CLS/BIR/GTL DH3 ......136 C5
  GATE NE8 ....81 F4

Suffolk Rd HEBB NE31 ....85 E5
Suffolk St ASHBK/HED/RY SR2 .....5 F6
  JRW NE32 ....86 A2
Suffolk Wk PLEE/EAS SR8 ....200 B6
Suffolk Wy DHAM DH1 ....180 C4
Sugley Dr BW/LEM/TK/HW NE15 .....76 C2
Sugley St BW/LEM/TK/HW NE15 .....76 C2
Sulgrave Rd WASHN NE37 ....121 E3
Sullivan Wk HEBB NE31 ....85 D3
Summerfield STLY/ANP DH9 ....150 C2
Summerfield Rd
  LWF/SPW/WRK NE9 ....99 E3
Summerhill ASHBK/HED/RY SR2 .....126 A6
  BLAY NE21 ....76 A5
  JRW NE32 ....104 C1
  SUNDSW SR3 ....159 D1
Summerhill Av GOS/KPK NE3 ....47 F5
Summerhill Rd HAR/WTLS NE34 .....89 E1
Summerhill St ELS/FEN NE4 ....80 A4
Summerhill Ter CNUT NE1 ....2 A5
Summerhouse Farm HLH DH5........170 C5
Summerson St HLH DH5 ....172 A6
Summer St HLH DH5 ....172 B6
Summerville DHAM DH1 ....194 A5
Sunbury Av JES NE2 ....64 A4
Sunderland Av PLEE/EAS SR8 .....201 E6
Sunderland Hwy WASHS NE38.......119 E6
Sunderland Rd BOL NE36 ....107 D3
  CLDN/WHIT/ROK SR6 ....108 A2
  DHAM DH1 ....195 E4
  GATE NE8 ....100 A1
  HAR/WTLS NE34 ....89 D1
  HLS DH4 ....158 A5
  PLEE/EAS SR8 ....201 E4
  SSH NE33 ....71 F6
  SWCK/CAS SR5 ....125 F3
Sunderland Road Vls FELL * NE10..101 E2
Sunderland St CNUT NE1 ....2 B5
  HLH DH5 ....171 D1
  HLS DH4 ....171 D2
Sundew Rd LWF/SPW/WRK NE9 .....100 B5
Sundridge Dr FELL NE10 ....102 B3
Sunholme Dr WLSD/HOW NE28 .....66 C1
Sunlea Av TYNE/NSHE NE30.......55 E2
Sunnidale WICK/BNPF NE16 ......95 D5
Sunnilaws HAR/WTLS NE34 ....89 F4
Sunningdale MONK NE25 ....39 F6
  SSH* NE33 ....72 A5
Sunningdale Av
  BYK/HTN/WLK NE6 ....83 F2
  WLSD/HOW NE28 ....67 E4
Sunningdale CI FELL NE10 ......100 C3
Sunningdale Dr WASHN NE37 .....120 B1
Sunningdale Rd SUNDSW SR3 .....142 C3
Sunnirise HAR/WTLS NE34 ....89 F4
Sunniside MLFD/PNYW SR4 ....123 F6
  NSHW NE29 ....69 F4
Sunniside Dr HAR/WTLS NE34 ....89 F4
Sunniside Gdns
  BW/LEM/TK/HW NE15 ....78 A2
Sunniside La CLDN/WHIT/ROK SR6..90 A6
Sunniside Rd WICK/BNPF NE16 ...96 A5
Sunniside Ter
  CLDN/WHIT/ROK SR6 ....89 F6
Sunnybank Av
  BW/LEM/TK/HW NE15 ....78 C3
Sunny Blunts PLEE/EAS SR8......208 B4
Sunnybrow SUNDSW SR3 ....143 E6
Sunnycrest Av BYK/HTN/WLK NE6..83 E2
Sunny Ter STLY/ANP DH9 ....148 A1
Sunnyway WD/WHPE/BLK NE5 ....61 D2
Sunrise La HLS DH4 ....170 C1
Surrey Av SUNDSW SR3 ....160 C2
Surrey PI ELS/FEN NE4 ....79 F3
  HLS DH4 ....157 E2
Surrey Rd HEBB NE31 ....85 E5
  NSHW NE29 ....53 F6
Surrey St HLS DH4 ....157 E2
  JRW NE32 ....85 F2
Surtees Dr DHAM DH1 ....193 F4
Surtees Rd PLEE/EAS SR8 ....209 F3
Sussex Gdns WLSD/HOW NE28 ....68 A3
Sussex PI WASHN NE37 ....120 C3
Sussex St BLYTH NE24 ....11 E4
  JRW NE32 ....86 A2
Sutherland Av ELS/FEN NE4......79 D1
Sutherland Ct HAR/WTLS NE34 ...88 C6
Sutherland Gra HLS DH4 ....157 F2
Sutherland Gv RDHAMSE DH6 ....206 B1
Sutherland St DHAM DH1 ....195 F5
Sutherland St
  CLDN/WHIT/ROK SR6 ....126 C2
  GATE* NE8 ....99 E1
  SEA/MUR SR7 ....176 A2
Sutton CI HLS DH4 ....156 C2
Sutton Ct WLSD/HOW NE28 .....66 B1
The Sutton Est
  JES (off Barrack Rd) NE2 .....80 A2
Sutton PI
  MLFD/PNYW
  (off Midmoor Rd) SR4.........125 D5
Sutton St BYK/HTN/WLK NE6 ....66 A6

DHAM DH1 ....194 A4
Sutton Wy HAR/WTLS NE34 ....90 A3
Swainby CI GOS/KPK NE3 ....47 F4
Swaledale CLDN/WHIT/ROK SR6 ....109 E3
  WLSD/HOW NE28 ....66 B1
Swaledale Av BLYTH NE24 ....11 F5
Swaledale CI HLH DH5 ....185 D3
Swaledale Crs HLS DH4 ....139 F6
Swaledale Gdns LGB/HTN NE7 .....65 D3
  MLFD/PNYW SR4 ....143 E1
The Swallows WLSD/HOW NE28 .....52 A5
Swallow Tail Ct HAR/WTLS NE34...88 A4
Swallow Tail Dr DUN/TMV NE11 ...98 A3
Swalwell Bank WICK/BNPF NE16...95 F1
Swan Av WLSD/HOW * NE28.........67 F3
Swan Ct DUN/TMV NE11 ....97 F1
Swan Dr DUN/TMV NE11 ....97 F1
Swan Rd BYK/HTN/WLK NE6 ....68 A4
  PLEE/EAS SR8 ....207 E3
  WASHS NE38 ....139 E5
Swan St GATE NE8 ....81 D5
  STLY/ANP DH9 ....146 A5
  SWCK/CAS SR5 ....126 B3
Swanton CI WD/WHPE/BLK NE5 ....61 D2
Swards Rd FELL NE10 ....101 D3
Swarland Av LGB/HTN NE7 ....65 D1
Swarland Rd MONK NE25 ....24 C6
Swarth CI WASHN NE37 ....119 F6
Sweetbriar Wy WASHN NE38 ......16 B2
Sweethope Av BLYTH NE24 ....10 C4
Swiftden Dr MLFD/PNYW SR4 ....141 F2
Swinbourne Gdns WBAY NE26 ....40 B4
Swinbourne Ter JRW NE32 ......86 A5
Swinburne PI GATE NE8 ....81 D5
Swinburne St GATE NE8 ....81 D5
  JRW NE32 ....87 D2
Swinburn Rd MONK NE25 ....24 C6
Swindale Dr LGB/KIL NE12 .....49 E1
Swindon Rd SUNDSW SR3 ....142 C3
Swindon Sq SUNDSW SR3 ....143 D3
Swindon St HEBB NE31 ....84 C2
Swindon Ter BYK/HTN/WLK NE6 ..65 D5
Swing Br CNUT NE1 ....3 E5
Swinhoe Gdns DIN/WO NE13 .....33 D3
Swinhope WASHS NE38 ....137 F6
Swinley Gdns
  BW/LEM/TK/HW NE15 ....77 E2
Swinside Dr DHAM DH1 ....196 B2
The Swirle CNUT NE1 ....3 H4
Sycamore Av BLYTH NE24 ....10 C3
  DIN/WO NE13..................31 E3
  HAR/WTLS NE34 ....89 E4
  MONK NE25 ....40 B6
Sycamore CI JES NE2 ....64 A4
Sycamore Dr SWCK/CAS SR5 .....126 A1
Sycamore Gv FELL NE10 ....101 D2
  LWF/SPW/WRK NE9 ....119 E3
Sycamore Rd BLAY NE21 ....76 B6
  CLDN/WHIT/ROK SR6 ....109 E1
  CLSW/PEL DH2 ....179 E1
The Sycamores
  ASHBK/HED/RY SR2 ....145 D3
  ELS/FEN (off Park Rd) NE4 ...79 F5
  WICK/BNPF NE16...............130 B1
Sycamore St
  BW/LEM/TK/HW NE15 ....57 F3
  WLSD/HOW NE28 ....67 E5
Sydenham Ter MLFD/PNYW SR4 ...143 F1
  SSH NE33 ....71 F3
Sydney Ct GATE * NE8 ....81 D5
Sydney Gdns HAR/WTLS NE34 ....87 E5
Sydney Gv WLSD/HOW NE28 .....66 C1
Sydney St HLS DH4 ....156 A6
  STLY/ANP DH9 ....150 C1
Syke Rd WICK/BNPF NE16 ......111 E6
Sylverton Gdns SSH NE33 ......72 A5
Sylvia Ter STLY/ANP DH9 .....131 E6
Symington Gdns SUNDSW SR3 ...143 E6
Syon St TYNE/NSHE NE30 ......55 F4
Syron WICK/BNPF NE16 ....95 E4
Syston CI HLS DH4 ....169 F3

T

Taberna CI BW/LEM/TK/HW NE15 ...56 A4
Tadcaster Rd SUNDSW SR3 ....142 B5
Tadema Rd SSH NE33 ....72 B4
Talbot CI WASHS NE38 ....138 C2
Talbot Gv WD/WHPE/BLK NE5 ....60 B6
Talbot Rd CLDN/WHIT/ROK SR6 ..127 D1
  HAR/WTLS NE34 ....88 B2
Talgarth WASHS NE38 ....140 A1
Talisman CI RDHAMSE DH6 ......197 E5
Talley Ct WASHS NE38 ....138 D1
Tamar CI NSHW NE29 ....53 E4
  PLEE/EAS SR8 ....208 B3
Tamar St HLH DH5 ....186 B4
Tamerton Dr CLS/BIR/GTL DH3 ..136 C4
Tamerton St MLFD/PNYW SR4 ....125 D4
Tamworth Rd ELS/FEN NE4 ......79 F2
Tamworth Sq SUNDSW SR3 ......142 B5

Tanbark *HLS* DH4 ....156 B2
Tanfield Gdns *HAR/WTLS* NE34 ....90 A2
Tanfield Pl *LWF/SPW/WRK* NE9 ....118 B2
Tanfield Rd *BW/LEM/TK/HW* NE15 ....77 F2
  LWF/SPW/WRK NE9 ....118 B2
  SUNDSW SR3 ....142 C5
Tanfield St *MLFD/PNYW* SR4 ....125 D5
Tangmere Cl *CRAM* NE23 ....22 B1
Tankerville Pl *JES* NE2 ....64 A5
Tankerville Ter *JES* NE2 ....64 A5
Tanmeads *CLSW/PEL* DH2 ....165 E6
Tanners' Bank *TYNE/NSHE* NE30 ......55 E6
Tantobie Rd *BW/LEM/TK/HW* NE15...77 F2
Tarlton Crs *FELL* NE10 ....100 B2
Tarn Dr *PLEE/EAS* SR8 ....209 D2
Tarn Rd *ASHBK/HED/RY* SR2 ....145 E6
Tarragon Wy *HAR/WTLS* NE34 ....88 C5
Tarrington Cl *WLSD/HOW* NE28 ....68 B2
Tarset Rd *MONK* NE25 ....39 D5
Tarset St *CNUT* NE1 ....81 F3
Tasmania Rd *HAR/WTLS* NE34 ....87 E5
Tasman Rd *SUNDSW* SR3 ....142 B6
Tate St *BLYTH* NE24 ....11 E4
Tatham St *SUND* SR1 ....5 E3
Tatham Street Back *SUND* SR1 ....5 E3
Tattersall *ASHBK/HED/RY* SR2 ....144 A2
Taunton Av *JRW* NE32 ....87 D3
  NSHW NE29 ....53 F3
Taunton Cl *WLSD/HOW* NE28 ....68 B1
Taunton Pl *CRAM* NE23 ....14 A6
Taunton Rd *SUNDSW* SR3 ....142 C5
Tavistock Ct *HLS* DH4 ....157 E5
Tavistock Pl *JRW* NE32 ....86 C3
  SUND SR1 ....4 D3
Tavistock Rd *JES* NE2 ....64 A4
Tavistock Sq *SUNDSW* SR3 ....143 F6
Taylor Av *BDN/LAN/SAC* DH7 ....192 A3
  DIN/WO NE13 ....33 E4
  ROWG NE39 ....111 E3
Taylor Gdns *FELL* NE10 ....101 F1
  WBAY NE26 ....26 C2
Taylor St *BLYTH* NE24 ....9 F4
  SSH NE33 ....88 A1
  STLY/ANP DH9 ....146 A3
Taynton Gv *CRAM* NE23 ....23 E6
Tay Rd *SUNDSW* SR3 ....142 B4
Tay St *HLH* DH5 ....186 B4
Teal Av *BLYTH* NE24 ....17 E2
Teal Cl *WASHS* NE38 ....137 E3
Team St *GATE* NE8 ....98 A1
Teasdale St *ASHBK/HED/RY* SR2 ....5 G6
Tebay Dr *WD/WHPE/BLK* NE5 ....60 B6
Teddington Cl *DIN/WO* NE13 ....45 D5
Teddington Sq *SUNDSW* SR3 ....142 B4
Tedham Rd *BW/LEM/TK/HW* NE15 ...76 B1
Tees Cl *PLEE/EAS* SR8 ....208 B4
Tees Ct *HAR/WTLS* NE34 ....88 C5
Tees Crs *STLY/ANP* DH9 ....148 B3
Teesdale Av *HLS* DH4 ....139 F6
Teesdale Gdns *LGB/HTN* NE7 ....65 D3
Teesdale Gv *LGB/KIL* NE12 ....49 E5
Teesdale Pl *BLYTH* NE24 ....9 E4
Tees Rd *HEBB* NE31 ....85 D5
Tees St *HLH* DH5 ....186 C4
  PLEE/EAS SR8 ....209 F1
  SEA/MUR SR7...................................176 C2
Teign Cl *PLEE/EAS* SR8 ....208 B3
Teindland Cl *ELS/FEN* NE4 ....79 D4
Tel-el-Kebir Rd
  ASHBK/HED/RY SR2 ....145 D2
Telford Cl *SMOOR* NE27 ....37 E5
Telford Ct *WLSD/HOW* NE28 ....69 D4
Telford Rd *SUNDSW* SR3 ....142 C4
Telford St *GATE* NE8 ....98 C3
  WLSD/HOW NE28 ....69 E4
Tempest St *BLAY* NE21 ....75 F4
  SUNDSW SR3 ....160 C1
Temple Gn *GATE* NE8 ....98 B4
  HAR/WTLS NE34 ....89 D3
Temple Park Rd *HAR/WTLS* NE34 ......88 C2
Temple St *CNUT* NE1 ....2 B5
  FELL NE10 ....100 C1
  SSH NE33 ....88 A1
Temple St West *SSH* NE33 ....71 D6
Temple Town *SSH* NE33 ....71 D6
Tenbury Crs *LGB/KIL* NE12 ....49 E5
  NSHW NE29 ....54 A3
Tenby Rd *SUNDSW* SR3 ....142 B6
Tenby Sq *CRAM* NE23 ....14 B6
Ten Flds *HLH* DH5 ....185 E1
Tennant St *HAR/WTLS* NE34 ....87 F3
  HEBB NE31 ....85 E2
Tennyson Av *BOLCOL* NE35 ....106 A2
  HEBB NE31 ....85 E2
Tennyson Ct *GATE* NE8 ....81 F6
Tennyson Crs *WICK/BNPF* NE16 ....95 F3
Tennyson Rd *CLSW/PEL* DH2 ....152 A5
Tennyson St *SWCK/CAS* SR5 ....125 F2
Tennyson Ter *NSHW* NE29 ....70 C2
Tenter Garth
  BW/LEM/TK/HW
  (off Hexham Rd) NE15 ....57 E4
Tenter Ter *DHAM* DH1 ....194 B4
Tenth Av *BLYTH* NE24 ....16 C1
  BYK/HTN/WLK NE6 ....65 E6
  DUN/TMV NE11 ....116 C3

Tenth Av West *DUN/TMV* NE11 ....116 B2
Tenth St *PLEE/EAS* SR8 ....209 F1
Tern Cl *BLYTH* NE24 ....17 E2
Terrace Pl *CNUT* NE1 ....2 B2
The Terrace
  RDHAMSE (off Front St) DH6 ....206 C1
Terrier Cl *BDLGTN* NE22 ....8 B3
Territorial La *DHAM* DH1 ....194 C5
Tetford Pl *LGB/KIL* NE12 ....49 E5
Teviot *WASHS* NE38 ....137 F5
Teviotdale Gdns *LGB/HTN* NE7 ....65 D3
Teviot St *GATE* NE8 ....98 C3
  HLH DH5 ....186 B4
Teviot Wy *JRW* NE32 ....85 F3
Tewkesbury *LGB/KIL* NE12 ....35 F6
Tewkesbury Rd
  BW/LEM/TK/HW NE15 ....76 B1
Thackeray Rd *SUNDSW* SR3 ....142 C4
Thames Av *JRW* NE32 ....86 B5
Thames Crs *HLH* DH4 ....169 F2
  STLY/ANP DH9 ....148 B4
Thames Gdns *WLSD/HOW* NE28 ....67 D5
Thames Rd *HEBB* NE31 ....85 E4
  PLEE/EAS SR8 ....208 B3
  SUNDSW SR3 ....142 B6
Thames St *GATE* NE8 ....99 F2
  HLH DH5 ....186 B4
Thanet Rd *SUNDSW* SR3 ....142 C5
Tharsis Rd *HEBB* NE31........................84 C3
Thatcher Cl *WICK/BNPF* NE16 ....95 F5
Theatre Pl *NSHW* NE29 ....70 C1
Thelma St *MLFD/PNYW* SR4 ....126 A6
Theme Rd *SUNDSW* SR3 ....142 B6
Theresa St *BLAY* NE21 ....76 B5
The Tyne Tunnel (Pedestrian)
  WLSD/HOW NE28 ....69 D5
Third Av *BLYTH* NE24 ....10 C6
  BYK/HTN/WLK NE6 ....82 B1
  CLSW/PEL DH2 ....153 D1
  CLSW/PEL DH2 ....153 D5
  DUN/TMV NE11 ....98 C4
  NSHW NE29 ....69 D1
Third St *PLEE/EAS* SR8 ....209 F1
Thirkeld Pl *HLS* DH4 ....156 C1
Thirlington Cl *WD/WHPE/BLK* NE5 ...61 D3
Thirlmere *CLSW/PEL* DH2 ....137 D4
  CLS/BIR/GTL DH3 ....137 D4
  FELL NE10 ....101 F2
Thirlmere Av *CLSW/PEL* DH2 ....166 A1
  HLH DH5 ....186 B4
  TYNE/NSHE NE30 ....54 C2
Thirlmere Cl *LGB/KIL* NE12 ....50 B1
Thirlmere Ct *HEBB* NE31.....................85 E3
Thirlmere Crs *BLAY* NE21 ....94 A2
  HLS DH4 ....157 D2
Thirlmere Rd *PLEE/EAS* SR8 ....209 D1
  WD/WHPE/BLK NE5 ....61 D5
Thirlmoor *WASHN* NE37 ....119 F6
Thirlwell Gv *JRW* NE32 ....85 F5
Thirlwell Rd *GATE* NE8 ....81 F5
Thirsk Rd *SUNDSW* SR3 ....142 C4
Thirston Dr *CRAM* NE23 ....22 B2
Thirston Pl *NSHW* NE29 ....53 F5
Thirston Wy *GOS/KPK* NE3 ....61 F1
Thistlecroft *HLH* DH5 ....171 D3
Thistledon Av *WICK/BNPF* NE16 ......95 E5
Thistle Rd *BDN/LAN/SAC* DH7 ....204 B4
  SUNDSW SR3 ....142 B5
Thistley Cl *BYK/HTN/WLK* NE6 ....66 A6
Thistley Gn *FELL* NE10 ....102 A1
Thomas Hawksley Pk
  SUNDSW SR3 ....143 F3
Thomas St *ASHBK/HED/RY* SR2 ......162 B3
  LWF/SPW/WRK NE9 ....118 C3
  PLEE/EAS SR8 ....201 D1
  SSH NE33 ....71 E3
  STLY/ANP DH9 ....149 F5
  WICK/BNPF NE16 ....95 F3
Thomas St North
  CLDN/WHIT/ROK SR6 ....126 C4
Thomas St South
  ASHBK/HED/RY SR2 ....162 B2
  SWCK/CAS SR5 ....125 F5
Thompson Av *LGB/KIL* NE12 ....35 E6
Thompson Crs *SWCK/CAS* SR5 ....124 A3
Thompson Gdns *WLSD/HOW* NE28 ...67 D4
Thompson Pl *FELL* NE10 ....100 C2
Thompson Rd *SWCK/CAS* SR5 ....126 B2
Thompson St *BLYTH* NE24 ....11 D3
  HAR/WTLS NE34 ....88 A3
  PLEE/EAS SR8 ....201 F6
Thorburn St *CLDN/WHIT/ROK* SR6 ..108 C6
Thornbank Cl *SUNDSW* SR3 ....160 C4
Thornbridge *WASHS* NE38 ....139 F1
Thornbury Av *CRAM* NE23 ....23 E6
Thornbury Cl *BOLCOL* NE35 ....105 D1
  DIN/WO NE13 ....45 D6
Thornbury Dr *MONK* NE25 ....39 D4
Thornbury St *MLFD/PNYW* SR4 ....125 F5
Thorncliffe Pl *NSHW* NE29 ....70 A1
Thorn Cl *DIN/WO* NE13 ....32 C5
Thorndale Pl *BLYTH* NE24 ....9 E1
Thorndale Rd
  BW/LEM/TK/HW NE15 ....77 E3

DHAM DH1 ....196 C3
  SUNDSW SR3 ....142 B5
Thorne Av *FELL* NE10 ....102 A2
Thorne Brake *FELL* NE10 ....101 F3
Thorne Rd *SUNDSW* SR3 ....142 B5
Thornes Cl *PLEE/EAS* SR8 ....209 E3
Thorne Sq *SUNDSW* SR3 ....142 B5
Thorne Ter *BYK/HTN/WLK* NE6 ....83 D1
Thorneyburn Cl *HLS* DH4 ....157 D6
Thorneyburn Wy *BLYTH* NE24 ....10 A5
Thorney Close Rd *SUNDSW* SR3......142 C5
Thorneyford Pl *PONT/DH* NE20 ....28 A3
Thorneyholme Ter *STLY/ANP* DH9...148 A3
Thornfield Gv
  ASHBK/HED/RY SR2 ....145 D4
Thornfield Pl *ROWG* NE39 ....111 D1
Thornfield Rd *GOS/KPK* NE3 ....63 D2
Thorngill *WASHN* NE37 ....120 A6
Thornhaugh Av *WICK/BNPF* NE16.....95 E4
Thornhill Cl *DUN/TMV* NE11 ....97 F2
  MONK NE25 ....24 C6
Thornhill Crs *ASHBK/HED/RY* SR2 .....4 A4
Thornhill Gdns
  ASHBK/HED/RY SR2 ....144 B2
Thornhill Pk *ASHBK/HED/RY* SR2.......4 B5
  PONT/DH NE20 ....28 A3
Thornhill Reach *SEA/MUR* SR7.........176 A2
Thornhill Rd *LGB/KIL* NE12 ....49 F6
  PONT/DH NE20 ....28 A3
  RDHAMSE DH6 ....206 B2
Thornhill St *HLS* DH4 ....170 C2
Thornhill Ter *ASHBK/HED/RY* SR2 .....4 A5
Thornholme Av *HAR/WTLS* NE34 ......90 A2
Thornholme Rd
  ASHBK/HED/RY SR2 ....144 A1
Thornhope Cl *WASHS* NE38 ....121 E6
Thorniea Gdns
  LWF/SPW/WRK NE9 ....99 E4
Thornleigh Gdns
  CLDN/WHIT/ROK SR6 ....89 F6
Thornleigh Rd *JES* NE2 ....64 A5
Thornley Av *CRAM* NE23 ....22 B5
  FELL NE10 ....102 A4
Thornley Cl *BDN/LAN/SAC* DH7 ....192 A5
  WICK/BNPF NE16 ....95 F6
Thornley La *BLAY* NE21 ....93 F4
  ROWG NE39 ....111 F6
Thornley Rd *WD/WHPE/BLK* NE5 ......60 A5
Thornley Vw *ROWG* NE39 ....111 E2
Thornton Cl *HLS* DH4 ....156 C1
Thornton Ct
  CNUT (off Forth Pl) NE1 ....2 B5
  WASHS NE38 ....138 B1
Thornton Crs *BLAY* NE21 ....76 B5
Thornton Lea *CLSW/PEL* DH2...........151 F1
Thornton St *CNUT* NE1 ....2 B5
Thorntree Av *DIN/WO* NE13 ....33 D1
Thorn Tree Dr *BDLGTN* NE22 ....7 E2
Thorntree Dr
  BW/LEM/TK/HW NE15 ....77 F1
  MONK NE25 ....39 D6
Thorntree Ter *STLY/ANP* DH9 ....149 D1
Thorntree Wy *BLYTH* NE24 ....9 E5
Thornwood Gdns *DUN/TMV* NE11 .....98 A5
Thornygarth *FELL* NE10 ....101 D3
Thorp Cl *BLYTH* NE24 ....16 A1
Thorpe Cl *ELS/FEN* NE4 ....79 F2
Thorpe Dr *RYTON* NE40 ....74 C3
Thorpeness Rd *SUNDSW* SR3 ....142 B5
Thorpe Rd *PLEE/EAS* SR8 ....200 A3
Thorpe St *PLEE/EAS* SR8 ....201 D1
  PLEE/EAS SR8 ....209 F1
Threap Gdns *WLSD/HOW* NE28 ....68 A2
Three Rivers Ct *BOL* NE36 ....105 F3
Threlkeld Gv
  CLDN/WHIT/ROK SR6 ....108 B5
Thrift St *NSHW* NE29 ....70 C2
Thristley Gdns
  ASHBK/HED/RY SR2 ....144 B3
Throckley Wy *HAR/WTLS* NE34 ....88 C5
Thropton Av *BLYTH* NE24 ....16 B1
  LGB/HTN NE7 ....65 D1
Thropton Cl *FELL* NE10 ....102 B3
Thropton Crs *GOS/KPK* NE3 ....47 D6
Thropton Pl *NSHW* NE29 ....53 F5
Thropton Ter *LGB/HTN* NE7 ....65 D4
Thrush Gv *SWCK/CAS* SR5 ....124 B3
Thurleston *HLS* DH4 ....157 E4
Thursby Av *TYNE/NSHE* NE30...........55 D2
Thurso Cl *SUNDSW* SR3 ....142 A5
Tiberius Cl *WLSD/HOW* NE28 ....67 D5
Tilbeck Sq *SUNDSW* SR3 ....160 C2
Tilbury Cl *HLS* DH4 ....157 E3
Tilbury Gdns *SUNDSW* SR3 ....142 B6
Tilbury Gv *MONK* NE25 ....54 C1
Tilbury Rd *SUNDSW* SR3 ....142 B6
Tileshed La *BOL* NE36 ....106 B1
Till Av *BLAY* NE21 ....76 A6
Tilley Rd *WASHS* NE38 ....137 E1
Tillmouth Av *MONK* NE25 ....24 C6
Tillmouth Gdns *ELS/FEN* NE4 ....78 B2
Tillmouth Park Rd
  BW/LEM/TK/HW NE15 ....57 F5
Till St *BYK/HTN/WLK* NE6 ....82 B4

Tilson Wy GOS/KPK NE3 ....46 B6
Timber Beach Rd SWCK/CAS SR5....124 C3
Timber Rd PLEE/EAS SR8 ....201 F5
Times Sq
 CNUT (off Scotswood Rd) NE1 ....2 B6
Timlin Gdns WLSD/HOW NE28 ....69 D3
Tindal Cl ELS/FEN NE4 ....80 A3
Tindale Av CRAM NE23 ....22 B2
Tindale Dr WICK/BNPF NE16................95 F4
Tindal St ELS/FEN NE4........................80 A3
Tintagel Cl CRAM NE23 ....14 A6
 SUND SR1 ....142 A5
Tintagel Dr SEA/MUR SR7 ....176 B2
Tintern WASHS NE38 ....138 B3
Tintern Cl HLS DH4 ....157 E6
Tintern Crs BYK/HTN/WLK NE6 ....82 A1
 NSHW NE29 ....53 F4
Tintern St GATE NE8............................98 C2
Tiree Cl BDN/LAN/SAC DH7 ....203 E3
Tiree Ct SUNDSW * SR3 ....160 C2
Tirril Pl WD/WHPE/BLK NE5 ....60 C5
Titan Rd BYK/HTN/WLK NE6 ....83 F2
Titchfield Rd WASHS NE38 ....138 B3
Titian Av HAR/WTLS NE34 ....88 B6
Titlington Gv HEBB NE31 ....84 C5
Tiverton Av ELS/FEN NE4 ....79 D3
 NSHW NE29 ....53 E3
Tiverton Cl HLS DH4 ....157 E4
 WLSD/HOW NE28 ....68 B1
Tiverton Gdns
 LWF/SPW/WRK NE9 ....117 E1
Tiverton Pl CRAM NE23 ....14 A6
Tiverton Sq SUNDSW SR3 ....142 B5
Toberty Gdns FELL NE10....................102 A2
Toft Crs SEA/MUR SR7 ....188 D1
Togstone Pl WD/WHPE/BLK NE5 ......61 E5
Toll Bar Rd ASHBK/HED/RY SR2 ....144 C5
Toll Bridge Rd BLAY NE21 ....77 E3
Tollerton Dr SWCK/CAS SR5 ....123 E3
Tollgate Flds HLS DH4 ....183 E5
Toll House Rd DHAM DH1 ....193 E4
Tolls Cl MONK NE25 ....39 C5
Toll Sq TYNE/NSHE NE30 ....55 E6
Tomlea Av BDLGTN NE22 ....8 C3
Tonbridge Av NSHW NE29 ....70 A1
Toner Av HEBB NE31 ....84 C5
Topaz St SEA/MUR SR7 ....175 F3
Topcliff CLDN/WHIT/ROK SR6 ....127 D4
Torcross Wy CRAM NE23 ....14 A6
Toronto Rd SUNDSW SR3 ....142 C4
Toronto Sq SUNDSW SR3....................142 C4
Torquay Gdns
 LWF/SPW/WRK NE9 ....117 E1
Torquay Rd SUNDSW SR3 ....142 C4
Torrens Rd SUNDSW SR3 ....142 C4
Torrington Cl HLS DH4 ....157 E4
Torver Cl DIN/WO NE13........................32 C5
Torver Crs CLDN/WHIT/ROK SR6 ....108 B5
Torver Pl LWF/SPW/WRK NE9 ....100 A6
Torver Wy TYNE/NSHE NE30 ....54 B2
Tosson Pl NSHW NE29 ....69 F1
Tosson Ter BYK/HTN/WLK NE6 ....65 E5
Totnes Dr CRAM NE23 ....14 A6
Toward Rd ASHBK/HED/RY SR2 ....5 E5
 SUND SR1 ....4 D4
Toward St BYK/HTN/WLK NE6 ....82 A2
Tower Ct DUN/TMV * NE11 ....97 F1
Tower Gdns RYTON NE40 ....74 B3
Tower Pl ASHBK/HED/RY SR2 ....5 F6
Tower Rd STLY/ANP DH9 ....146 A6
 WASHN NE37 ....121 D5
Towers Av JES NE2..............................64 A3
Towers Cl BDLGTN NE22 ....7 F4
Towers Pl HAR/WTLS NE34 ....87 D3
Tower St ASHBK/HED/RY SR2 ....5 G6
 CNUT NE1 ....3 F4
 PLEE/EAS SR8 ....201 E1
Tower St West
 ASHBK/HED/RY SR2 ....145 D2
The Towne Ga
 BW/LEM/TK/HW NE15 ....56 A4
Townend Ct HAR/WTLS NE34 ....88 B4
Townfield Gdns
 BW/LEM/TK/HW NE15 ....58 B6
Townley Flds ROWG NE39 ....111 E2
Townley Rd ROWG NE39 ....110 C2
Townsend Rd SUNDSW SR3 ....142 B6
Townsville Av MONK NE25 ....53 F1
Towton LGB/KIL NE12 ....35 F6
Toynbee WASHS NE38 ....139 F1
Tracey Av BOL NE36..............................106 A2
Trafalgar Rd WASHN NE37................121 D3
Trafalgar Sq SUND SR1 ....5 G2
Trafalgar St CNUT NE1 ....3 F5
Trafford LWF/SPW/WRK NE9 ....117 F2
Trafford Rd SWCK/CAS SR5..............125 F3
Trafford Wk WD/WHPE/BLK NE5......60 A3
Trajan Av SSH NE33 ....71 F2
Trajan St SSH NE33..............................71 F2
Tranwell Cl GOS/KPK NE3 ....46 B4
Tranwell Dr MONK NE25 ....25 D6
Travers St HLS DH4 ....157 E2
Treby St MLFD/PNYW SR4..................125 F5
Tredegar Cl WD/WHPE/BLK NE5 ......61 D2
Treecone Cl SUNDSW SR3 ....160 C3

Treen Crs SEA/MUR SR7 ....188 C1
Trefoil Rd STLY/ANP DH9..................130 C6
Tregoney Av SEA/MUR SR7 ....188 C1
Treherne Rd JES NE2............................63 F3
Trent Av HEBB NE31 ....85 D5
Trent Dr JRW NE32................................68 B4
Trent Gdns GATE NE8........................100 A2
Trentham Av LGB/HTN NE7................65 D1
Trenton Av WASHS NE38 ....120 C6
Trent Rd SUNDSW SR3 ....142 B5
Trent St HLH DH5 ....186 B4
Trevarren Dr ASHBK/HED/RY SR2 ..145 E6
Trevelyan Av BDLGTN NE22 ....8 A3
 BLYTH NE24 ....10 B6
Trevelyan Cl SUNDSW SR3 ....142 A5
Trevelyan Pl PLEE/EAS SR8 ....60 C3
Trevelyan Pl PLEE/EAS SR8................208 A3
Trevethick St GATE NE8......................98 C2
Trevone Pl CRAM NE23 ....23 F6
Trevone Sq SEA/MUR SR7 ....188 C1
Trevor Gv CLDN/WHIT/ROK SR6 ....107 F2
Trevor Ter TYNE/NSHE NE30..............54 C5
Trewhitt Rd BYK/HTN/WLK NE6 ....65 E6
Tribune Pl LWF/SPW/WRK NE9 ......100 A4
Trident Rd SUNDSW SR3 ....160 C1
Trimdon St MLFD/PNYW SR4 ....126 A5
Trinity Buildings TYNE/NSHE NE30 ..71 E1
Trinity Chare
 CNUT (off Quayside) NE1 ....3 F5
Trinity Cl NSHW NE29 ....70 C2
Trinity Ct GATE NE8..............................81 E5
Trinity Ctyd BYK/HTN/WLK * NE6 ..82 C4
Trinity Gv CRAM NE23 ....23 F6
Trinity Pk HLS DH4 ....157 D3
Trinity Sq NSHW NE29 ....70 C2
Trinity Sq GATE * NE8..........................81 E5
 SUND SR1 ....5 F2
Trinity St NSHW NE29 ....70 C2
 SWCK/CAS SR5 ....125 E2
Trinity Wk SSH NE33............................71 D5
Trojan Av BYK/HTN/WLK NE6 ....83 D1
Tromso Cl NSHW NE29..........................69 D1
Trool Ct SUNDSW SR3 ....160 C3
Troon Cl WASHN NE37 ....120 B2
Trotter Gv BDLGTN NE22 ....8 B5
Trotter Ter ASHBK/HED/RY SR2 ......162 B2
Troutbeck Av BYK/HTN/WLK NE6 ....83 E3
Troutbeck Rd
 CLDN/WHIT/ROK SR6 ....108 B5
Troutbeck Wy HAR/WTLS NE34 ....87 E5
 PLEE/EAS SR8 ....209 D1
Troutdale Pl LGB/KIL NE12 ....48 B6
Trout's La DHAM DH1 ....178 C5
Trowbridge Wy GOS/KPK NE3 ....62 B1
Truro Av SEA/MUR SR7 ....174 C6
Truro Gv NSHW NE29 ....53 F4
Truro Rd SUNDSW SR3 ....142 C5
Tuart St CLS/BIR/GTL DH3 ....153 E5
Tudor Av NSHW NE29 ....54 A6
Tudor Ct RDHAMSE DH6 ....206 C2
Tudor Dr STLY/ANP DH9 ....130 C3
Tudor Gra PLEE/EAS SR8 ....199 F3
Tudor Gv SUNDSW SR3 ....143 E3
Tudor Rd CLS/BIR/GTL DH3 ....153 F3
 SSH NE33 ....71 E4
Tudor Wk GOS/KPK NE3 ....45 F5
Tudor Wy GOS/KPK NE3 ....45 E5
 WD/WHPE/BLK NE5 ....61 D1
Tudor Wynd BYK/HTN/WLK NE6 ......65 F5
Tulip St GATE NE8..............................100 A1
Tumulus Av BYK/HTN/WLK NE6 ......66 C6
Tunbridge Rd SUNDSW SR3 ....142 C4
Tundry Wy BLAY NE21..........................77 E4
Tuneside FELL NE10............................102 A3
Tunis Rd SUNDSW SR3 ....142 C4
Tunstall Av BYK/HTN/WLK NE6 ....82 C2
 HAR/WTLS NE34..................................90 A2
Tunstall Bank SUNDSW SR3 ....161 E1
Tunstall Hill Cl
 ASHBK/HED/RY SR2 ....144 C5
Tunstall Pk ASHBK/HED/RY SR2 ....144 B2
Tunstall Rd ASHBK/HED/RY SR2........4 B4
 SUNDSW SR3 ....144 A5
Tunstall Ter ASHBK/HED/RY SR2 ......4 B4
Tunstall Ter West
 ASHBK/HED/RY SR2 ....4 A4
Tunstall V ASHBK/HED/RY SR2 ......144 B2
Tunstall Vw SUNDSW SR3 ....144 A6
Tunstall Village Gn SUNDSW SR3 ..161 E1
Tunstall Village Rd SUNDSW SR3 ..161 D1
Tunstall Vs SUNDSW SR3 ....161 D1
Turbinia Gdns LGB/HTN NE7..............65 E4
Turfside FELL * NE10 ....102 A3
Turnberry CLSW/PEL DH2 ....135 E4
 MONK NE25 ....39 C5
 SSH NE33..72 A5
Turnberry Cl WASHN NE37 ....120 B2
Turnberry Wy GOS/KPK * NE3 ....48 A6
Turnbull Cl DHAM DH1 ....195 F4
Turner Av HAR/WTLS NE34................88 C5
Turner Cl RYTON NE40 ....74 C4
Turner Crs GOS/KPK NE3 ....62 C1
Turner St SMOOR NE27 ....52 A3
Turnham Rd SUNDSW SR3 ....142 B5

Turn Pk
 CLS/BIR/GTL (off Station Rd) DH3....153 E5
Turnstone Dr WASHS NE38 ....137 E3
Turret Rd BW/LEM/TK/HW NE15 ......77 E1
Tuscan Cl BDN/LAN/SAC DH7 ....202 A1
Tuscan Rd SUNDSW SR3 ....142 B5
Tweed Cl ASHBK/HED/RY SR2..........145 E6
 CLSW/PEL DH2....................................135 E6
 PLEE/EAS SR8 ....208 B3
Tweed Gv BW/LEM/TK/HW NE15......76 B1
Tweed St ELS/FEN NE4 ....79 E3
 HEBB NE31 ....84 C2
 HLH DH5 ....186 B4
 JRW NE32 ....83 F3
 WASHS NE38 ....139 D2
Tweed Ter STLY/ANP DH9 ....148 B3
Tweedy St BYK/HTN/WLK NE6 ....83 E3
Twelfth Av BLYTH NE24........................10 C6
 CLSW/PEL DH2....................................153 D4
Twelfth St PLEE/EAS SR8 ....209 E1
Twentieth Av BLYTH NE24 ....16 B1
Twentyfifth Av BLYTH NE24 ....16 C1
Twentyfirst Av BLYTH NE24 ....16 B1
Twentysixth Av BLYTH NE24 ....16 B1
Twentythird Av BLYTH NE24 ....16 B1
Twickenham Ct CRAM NE23 ....23 E6
Twickenham Rd SUNDSW SR3 ......142 B4
Twizell La STLY/ANP DH9..................150 A3
Twizell Pl PONT/DH NE20 ....28 A3
Twizell St BLYTH * NE24......................11 E6
Twyford Cl CRAM NE23 ....14 A6
Tyldesley Sq SUNDSW SR3 ....142 B5
Tyndal Gdns DUN/TMV * NE11..........97 E1
Tyne Ap JRW NE32................................68 C2
Tynebank BLAY NE21............................76 A6
Tyne Br GATE NE8....................................3 F5
Tynedale Av WBAY NE26 ....40 B4
 WLSD/HOW NE28 ....67 D2
Tynedale Cl HLS DH4 ....157 D1
Tynedale Dr BLYTH NE24......................9 F5
Tynedale Rd HAR/WTLS NE34............72 A6
Tynedale St HLH DH5 ....185 D3
Tynedale Ter LGB/KIL NE12................49 F6
Tyne Gdns WASHN NE37 ....120 C3
Tynegate Prec
 GATE (off Sunderland Rd) NE8..........81 E6
Tyne Main Rd FELL NE10 ....82 B5
Tynemouth Cl
 BYK/HTN/WLK * NE6 ....82 A2
Tynemouth Ct
 BYK/HTN/WLK * NE6..........................82 B1
Tynemouth Pl MONK NE25 ....40 B6
 TYNE/NSHE NE30 ....55 F5
Tynemouth Rd BYK/HTN/WLK NE6 ..82 A2
 JRW NE32 ....85 F6
 TYNE/NSHE NE30 ....55 E6
 WLSD/HOW NE28 ....68 B4
Tynemouth Sq SUNDSW SR3 ....142 C5
Tynemouth Ter TYNE/NSHE NE30 ..55 F5
Tynemouth Wy
 BYK/HTN/WLK * NE6..........................82 B1
Tyne Rd STLY/ANP DH9 ....148 A3
Tyne Rd East GATE NE8 ....80 B6
 STLY/ANP DH9....................................148 A3
Tyneside Rd ELS/FEN NE4....................80 A5
Tyne St BLAY NE21 ....94 A1
 CNUT NE1 ....81 F3
 FELL NE10 ....83 D6
 HLH DH5 ....186 B4
 JRW NE32 ....69 D6
 SEA/MUR* SR7 ....176 C3
 TYNE/NSHE NE30 ....71 D1
Tyne Ter HAR/WTLS NE34 ....88 A3
Tynevale Av BLAY NE21 ....94 A1
Tyne Vw BW/LEM/TK/HW NE15......76 B2
 HEBB NE31 ....84 B2
Tyne View Av WICK/BNPF NE16........96 B2
Tyne View Gdns FELL NE10................101 E1
Tyneview Pk
 DUN/TMV (off Whitley Rd) NE11........98 C4
Tyne View Ter WLSD/HOW NE28 ......69 D5
Tyne-wear Trail DUN/TMV NE11 ......96 C1
Tyne Wear Trail WICK/BNPF NE16 ..96 C5

U

Ugly La CLSW/PEL DH2 ....165 E6
Uldale Ct GOS/KPK NE3 ....46 A5
Ullerdale Cl DHAM DH1 ....197 D2
Ullswater Av HLH DH5 ....186 B4
 JRW NE32 ....86 C5
Ullswater Cl BLYTH NE24......................9 D4
Ullswater Crs BLAY NE21 ....94 A2
Ullswater Dr LGB/KIL NE12 ....50 B4
Ullswater Gdns HAR/WTLS NE34 ......88 C5
Ullswater Gv SWCK/CAS SR5 ....108 B6
Ullswater Rd CLSW/PEL DH2 ....166 A1
Ullswater Wy WD/WHPE/BLK NE5 ..61 D5
Ulverstone Ter BYK/HTN/WLK NE6 ..83 D1
Ulverston Gdns LWF/SPW/WRK
 NE9..118 A1

Underhill
LWF/SPW/WRK (off Kells La) NE9 ......**99** F4
Underhill Rd
CLDN/WHIT/ROK SR6 ....**107** E2
Underwood Gv *CRAM NE23* **13** F5
Union Aly *SSH NE33* **71** E3
Union Hall Rd
BW/LEM/TK/HW NE15 ....**59** E6
Union La *CLSW/PEL DH2* **166** A3
SUND SR1 ....**5** F1
Union Quay *TYNE/NSHE NE30* **71** E1
Union Rd *BYK/HTN/WLK NE6* **82** B2
TYNE/NSHE NE30 ....**55** E6
Union Stairs *TYNE/NSHE NE30* **71** D1
Union St *BLYTH NE24* **11** D4
HLH DH5 ....**171** F6
JES NE2 ....**3** H2
JRW NE32 ....**69** D6
MLFD/PNYW SR4 ....**123** F6
NSHW NE29 ....**71** D1
SSH NE33 ....**88** A2
SUND SR1 ....**4** C2
WLSD/HOW NE28 ....**67** D6
Unity Ter *STLY/ANP DH9* **130** A4
STLY/ANP DH9 ....**146** A1
University Prec
MLFD/PNYW SR4
(off Chester Rd) SR4 ....**126** A6
Uplands *MONK NE25* **39** F5
The Uplands *CLS/BIR/GTL DH3*......**136** C1
GOS/KPK NE3..**62** B2
Uplands Wy *LWF/SPW/WRK NE9*....**119** E2
Upper Camden St
TYNE/NSHE NE30 ....**54** C6
Upper Elsdon St *NSHW NE29* **70** C2
Upper Market Sq *SUND SR1*..............**4** C3
Upper Norfolk St
TYNE/NSHE NE30 ....**55** D6
Upper Pearson St
TYNE/NSHE NE30 ....**55** D6
Upper Prec
BLAY (off Wesley Ct) NE21 ....**76** C5
Upper Queen St *TYNE/NSHE NE30*...**55** D6
Upper Walworth Wy *SUND SR1*..........**4** B2
Upton St *GATE NE8* **98** D1
Urfa Ter *SSH NE33* **71** F2
Urswick Ct *WD/WHPE/BLK NE5* **61** D1
Urwin St *HLH DH5* **186** A1
Ushaw Rd *HEBB NE31* **85** D1
Usher Av *RDHAMSE DH6* **197** E4
Usher St *SWCK/CAS SR5* **126** A3
Usk Av *JRW NE32* **86** B5
Usworth Cottages
SWCK/CAS
(off Washington Rd) SR5 ....**122** C1
Usworth Station Rd *WASHN NE37* ...**121** D4
Uxbridge Ter *FELL NE10* **100** C1

V

Valebrooke Av
ASHBK/HED/RY SR2 ....**144** B2
Valebrooke Gdns
ASHBK/HED/RY SR2 ....**4** B6
Valehead *MONK NE25* **39** F5
Valentia Av *BYK/HTN/WLK NE6* **83** D1
Valeria Cl *WLSD/HOW NE28* **51** F6
Valerian Av *BW/LEM/TK/HW NE15* ...**56** B4
Valeside *BW/LEM/TK/HW NE15* **57** E4
DHAM DH1 ....**194** A4
Vale St *HLH DH5* **186** A4
MLFD/PNYW SR4 ....**144** A1
Vale Wk *JES NE2* **81** F1
Valley Crs *BLAY NE21*........................**75** F6
Valley Dr *LWF/SPW/WRK NE9*..........**99** F3
WICK/BNPF NE16 ....**95** F3
Valley Forge *WASHS NE38* **120** C6
Valley Gdns *LWF/SPW/WRK NE9* **99** F3
MONK NE25 ....**39** F5
WLSD/HOW NE28 ....**67** F3
Valley Rd *CLSW/PEL DH2*................**152** A4
MONK NE25 ....**25** E6
Valley Vw *BDN/LAN/SAC DH7* **178** A2
BDN/LAN/SAC DH7 ....**192** A5
BW/LEM/TK/HW NE15 ....**76** B3
CLS/BIR/GTL DH3 ....**118** A5
JES NE2 ....**64** B5
JRW NE32 ....**86** A4
ROWG NE39 ....**110** C2
WASHS NE38 ....**139** D5
WICK/BNPF NE16 ....**111** E5
Vallum Rd *BW/LEM/TK/HW NE15* **58** A4
BYK/HTN/WLK NE6 ....**83** D2
Vanburgh Ct *MONK NE25* **24** C6
Vanceuver Dr *LGB/HTN NE7* **65** F4
Vane St *PLEE/EAS SR8* **201** D2
SUNDSW SR3 ....**160** C1
Vane Ter *ASHBK/HED/RY SR2*............**5** H5
Van Mildert Cl *PLEE/EAS SR8* **208** A4
Vardy Ter *HLS DH4* **158** A1

Vauxhall Rd *BYK/HTN/WLK NE6*.......**66** C6
Vedra St *SWCK/CAS SR5* **126** A3
Velville Ct *WD/WHPE/BLK NE5*.........**45** D6
Ventnor Av *ELS/FEN NE4* **79** E3
Ventnor Crs *LWF/SPW/WRK NE9* **99** D4
Ventnor Gdns *LWF/SPW/WRK NE9* ...**99** D4
WBAY NE26 ....**40** C4
Verdun Av *NSHW NE31*......................**85** D2
Vermont *WASHN NE37* **120** C4
Verne Rd *NSHW NE29* **69** F1
Vernon Cl *SSH NE33* **71** D6
Vernon Dr *MONK NE25* **40** A6
Vernon St *WASHN NE37*..................**120** C4
Veryan Gdns *SUNDSW SR3* **144** A3
Vespasian St *SSH NE33* **71** F2
Viador *CLS/BIR/GTL DH3*................**153** E4
Viaduct St *WLSD/HOW NE28* **68** A4
Vicarage Cl *CLSW/PEL DH2* **152** A1
SUNDSW SR3 ....**160** B1
Vicarage Ct *FELL NE10* **101** E2
Vicarage Flats *BDN/LAN/SAC DH7*...**203** D4
Vicarage La *MLFD/PNYW SR4* **123** F6
Vicarage Rd *SUNDSW SR3*.............**160** C1
Vicarage St *NSHW NE29* **70** C1
Vicarsholme Cl *SUNDSW SR3* **160** A3
Vicars' La *LGB/HTN NE7* **64** C1
Vicars Wy *LGB/KIL NE12* **48** A4
Victoria Av *ASHBK/HED/RY SR2* **145** D4
BDN/LAN/SAC DH7 ....**203** E4
FELL NE10...**100** B2
LGB/KIL NE12 ....**49** F5
MLFD/PNYW SR4 ....**124** A6
WLSD/HOW NE28 ....**67** D4
Victoria Av West
ASHBK/HED/RY SR2 ....**145** D4
Victoria Ct *GATE * NE8*.....................**98** B1
Victoria Crs *NSHW NE29* **70** B2
Victoria Ms *BLYTH NE24* **10** C6
JES NE2...**64** C6
Victoria Pl
SUND (off Murton St) SR1 ....**5** E4
SSH NE33 ....**71** E5
WASHN NE37 ....**120** C4
Victoria Rd *GATE NE8* **98** B2
SSH NE33 ....**71** E5
WASHN NE37 ....**120** C4
Victoria Rd East *HEBB NE31*............**85** E2
Victoria Rd West *FELL NE10*.............**84** B6
HEBB NE31 ....**84** B6
Victoria Sq *FELL * NE10* **100** C2
Victoria Ter *DHAM * DH1* **194** A4
JRW NE32 ....**85** F2
WBAY NE26 ....**41** D5
Victor St *CLDN/WHIT/ROK SR6* **127** D3
CLS/BIR/GTL DH3 ....**153** E5
Victory St East *MLFD/PNYW SR4* ...**125** D5
Victory St West *HLH DH5* **172** A6
Victory Wy *SUNDSW SR3* **159** E3
Viewforth Dr *SWCK/CAS SR5* **126** B1
Viewforth Rd
ASHBK/HED/RY SR2 ....**162** B3
Viewforth Ter *SWCK/CAS SR5*........**126** A1
View La *STLY/ANP DH9*....................**148** B1
View Pk *MONK NE25* **24** C5
Vigo La *CLS/BIR/GTL DH3* **154** A2
WASHS NE38 ....**137** E6
Village Centre *WASHS NE38* **138** C2
Village Ct *WBAY NE26* **40** B5
Village East *RYTON NE40* **74** B2
Village Farm
BW/LEM/TK/HW NE15 ....**58** C5
Village Hts *GATE NE8* **81** D6
Village La *WASHS NE38* **120** C6
Village Pl *BYK/HTN/WLK * NE6*........**82** B3
Village Rd *CRAM NE23* **22** B2
The Village *ASHBK/HED/RY SR2*....**162** C2
Villa Pl *GATE NE8* **99** D1
The Villas *STLY/ANP DH9* **146** A5
Villa Vw *LWF/SPW/WRK NE9* **99** F4
Villette Brook St
ASHBK/HED/RY SR2 ....**145** D2
Villette Pth *ASHBK/HED/RY SR2* **145** D2
Villette Rd *ASHBK/HED/RY SR2* **145** D2
Villiers St *SUND SR1* **5** E2
Villiers St South *SUND SR1* **5** E2
Vimy Av *HEBB NE31* **85** D2
Vincent St *PLEE/EAS SR8* **201** D2
Vincent Ter *STLY/ANP DH9* **146** C5
Vine Cl *GATE NE8* **98** B1
Vine La *CNUT NE1* **2** D1
Vine Pl *HLS DH4* **171** D2
SUND SR1 ....**4** D3
Vine St *SSH NE33* **88** B2
WLSD/HOW NE28 ....**67** E5
Viola Crs *BDN/LAN/SAC DH7* **178** B2
CLSW/PEL DH2 ....**135** E4
Viola St *WASHN NE37*......................**120** C4
Viola Ter *WICK/BNPF * NE16*.............**96** A3

Violet Cl *ELS/FEN NE4* **78** C4
Violet St *HLS DH4* **170** C2
MLFD/PNYW SR4 ....**123** F6
MLFD/PNYW SR4 ....**126** A5
Viscount Rd *SUNDSW SR3*.............**160** C1
Vivian Crs *CLSW/PEL DH2* **153** E6
Vivian St *CLDN/WHIT/ROK SR6* **126** C1
Vivian Sq *CLDN/WHIT/ROK SR6* **126** C1
Voltage Ter *HLS DH4* **157** F4
Vulcan Pl *BDLGTN NE22*......................**7** F4

W

Waddington St *DHAM DH1* **194** A4
Wadsley Sq *ASHBK/HED/RY SR2* **145** D3
Wagon Wy *WLSD/HOW NE28* **67** F4
Wagonway Rd *HEBB NE31* **84** C1
Wagtail Cl *BLAY NE21*.........................**94** B2
Wagtail La *STLY/ANP DH9* **149** E6
Wagtail Ter *STLY/ANP DH9* **149** E6
Wakefield Av *HAR/WTLS NE34* **90** A3
Wakenshaw Rd *DHAM DH1* **195** E3
Walbottle Rd
BW/LEM/TK/HW NE15 ....**58** B5
Walden Cl *CLSW/PEL DH2* **134** C5
Waldo St *NSHW NE29* **70** C1
Waldridge La *CLSW/PEL DH2* **152** B6
Waldridge Rd *CLSW/PEL DH2*.........**153** D1
Waldron Sq *ASHBK/HED/RY SR2* ...**145** D3
Walkerburn *CRAM NE23* **22** A5
Walkergate *DHAM DH1* **194** B4
Walker Gv *BYK/HTN/WLK NE6* **66** B6
Walker Pl *TYNE/NSHE * NE30* **55** E6
Walker Riverside
BYK/HTN/WLK
(off Wincomblee Rd) NE6 ....**84** A4
Walker Rd *BYK/HTN/WLK NE6* **82** B4
Walker Ter *GATE * NE8* **81** D6
Wallace Av *WICK/BNPF NE16* **96** B2
Wallace Gdns *LWF/SPW/WRK NE9*...**101** D6
Wallace St *DUN/TMV NE11* **97** F1
HLH DH4 ....**170** C2
JES NE2...**80** A1
SWCK/CAS SR5 ....**126** B3
Wallflower Av *PLEE/EAS SR8* **209** E1
Wallingford Av
ASHBK/HED/RY SR2 ....**145** D4
Wallington Av *DIN/WO NE13* **32** C4
TYNE/NSHE NE30 ....**54** C3
Wallington Cl *BDLGTN NE22* **8** B2
Wallington Ct *MONK NE25* **24** C5
Wallington Dr
BW/LEM/TK/HW NE15 ....**60** A6
Wallington Gv *SSH NE33* **71** F3
Wallis St *HLS DH4* **140** A6
SSH NE33 ....**71** E3
Wallridge Dr *MONK NE25* **38** A1
Wallsend Rd *NSHW NE29* **69** F2
WLSD/HOW NE28 ....**69** E3
Wall St *GOS/KPK * NE3* **62** C1
Wall Ter *BYK/HTN/WLK NE6* **83** E1
Walnut Gdns *GATE NE8*.....................**98** B2
Walnut Pl *GOS/KPK NE3* **62** B3
Walpole Cl *MLFD/PNYW SR4* **125** E6
Walpole St *BYK/HTN/WLK NE6* **66** A6
Walsham Cl *BLYTH NE24* **16** A1
Walsh Av *HEBB NE31*.........................**85** D1
Walsingham *WASHS NE38*...............**138** B3
Walter St *JRW NE32* **69** D6
Walter Ter *ELS/FEN NE4* **79** F2
HLH DH5 ....**186** A3
Walter Thomas St *SWCK/CAS SR5* ...**125** E2
Waltham *WASHS NE38*.....................**138** C2
Waltham Cl *WLSD/HOW NE28* **66** B3
Waltham Pl *WD/WHPE/BLK NE5* **61** D4
Walton Av *BLYTH NE24* **10** B4
NSHW NE29 ....**54** B5
SWAR NE37 ....**175** E4
Walton La *STLY/ANP DH9*.................**148** C3
Walton La *SUND SR1* **5** F1
Walton Pk *NSHW NE29* **54** B5
Walton Rd *WASHS NE38* **140** A1
WD/WHPE/BLK NE5 ....**60** C5
Walwick Av *NSHW NE29* **53** F6
Walwick Rd *MONK NE25* **39** D5
Walworth Av *HAR/WTLS NE34* **90** A3
Walworth Gv *JRW NE32* **86** A5
Wandsworth Rd
BYK/HTN/WLK NE6 ....**82** A1
Wanbeck *WASHS NE38* **137** F5
Wanless Ter *DHAM DH1*..................**194** C4
Wanley St *BLYTH NE24* **11** D4
Wanlock Cl *CRAM NE23* **22** A5
Wanny Rd *BDLGTN NE22* **8** A4
Wansbeck Av *BLYTH NE24* **11** D6
STLY/ANP DH9 ....**148** B3
TYNE/NSHE NE30 ....**55** E1
Wansbeck Cl *CLSW/PEL DH2* **135** E6
WICK/BNPF NE16 ....**113** F1
Wansbeck Gv *MONK NE25* **24** C2
Wansbeck Rd *CRAM NE23* **34** B2
JRW NE32...**85** F3

Wansbeck Rd North
  GOS/KPK NE3 ....46 C5
Wansbeck Rd South
  GOS/KPK NE3 ....46 C6
Wansfell Av WD/WHPE/BLK NE5 ....61 F3
Wansford Av WD/WHPE/BLK NE5 ....61 D5
Wantage Av NSHW NE29 ....69 F2
Wantage Rd DHAM DH1 ....196 C1
Wantage St SSH NE33 ....88 C1
Wapping St SUND SR1 ....71 D2
Warbeck Cl WD/WHPE/BLK NE5 ....45 D6
Warburton Crs
  LWF/SPW/WRK NE9 ....99 F2
Warcop Ct GOS/KPK NE3 ....46 A5
Ward Ct ASHBK/HED/RY SR2 ....5 F6
Warden Law La SUNDSW SR3 ....160 A2
Wardill Gdns LWF/SPW/WRK NE9 ......100 A3
Wardle Av SSH NE33 ....72 A5
Wardle Dr CRAM NE23 ....35 D2
Wardle Gdns FELL NE10 ....101 D3
Wardle Rd GOS/KPK NE3 ....64 A1
  STLY/ANP DH9 ....148 A5
Wardley Ct FELL NE10 ....102 C2
Wardley Dr FELL NE10 ....102 C2
Wardley La FELL NE10 ....102 A3
Warenford Cl CRAM NE23 ....22 B4
Warenford Pl WD/WHPE/BLK NE5 ....78 B1
Warenmill Cl
  BW/LEM/TK/HW NE15 ....76 A1
Warennes St MLFD/PNYW SR4 ....125 D5
Warenton Pl NSHW NE29 ....53 D3
Waring Av WBAY NE26 ....26 A1
Waring Ter SEA/MUR SR7 ....175 E4
Wark Av NSHW NE29 ....53 E6
  SMOOR NE27 ....38 B6
Wark Crs JRW NE32 ....86 A6
Warkdale Av BLYTH NE24 ....9 F5
Warkworth Av BLYTH NE24 ....17 D1
  HAR/WTLS NE34 ....90 A1
  WLSD/HOW NE28 ....67 E2
Warkworth Cl WASHS NE38 ....138 A2
Warkworth Crs GOS/KPK NE3 ....47 D6
  SEA/MUR SR7 ....175 D3
Warkworth Dr CLSW/PEL DH2 ....165 F1
  DIN/WO NE13 ....33 E3
Warkworth Gdns FELL NE10 ....100 B3
Warkworth Rd DHAM DH1 ....180 B5
Warkworth St
  BW/LEM/TK/HW NE15 ....76 B2
  BYK/HTN/WLK NE6 ....82 B2
  JRW NE32 ....86 A5
  TYNE/NSHE NE30 ....55 F4
Warnham Av ASHBK/HED/RY SR2 ....145 D4
Warnhead Rd BDLGTN NE22 ....8 A3
Warren Av BYK/HTN/WLK NE6 ....66 C6
Warren Cl HLS DH4 ....157 E4
Warrenmoor FELL NE10 ....101 F3
Warren Sq SUND SR1 ....127 E4
Warren St PLEE/EAS SR8 ....209 F1
Warrington Rd ELS/FEN NE4 ....79 F4
  GOS/KPK NE3 ....46 A6
Warton Ter BYK/HTN/WLK NE6 ....65 E6
Warwick Av WICK/BNPF NE16 ....95 F5
Warwick Cl CRAM NE23 ....36 A1
  WICK/BNPF NE16 ....16 ...
Warwick Ct DHAM DH1 ....204 C1
  GATE NE8 ....81 E6
  GOS/KPK NE3 ....45 F5
Warwick Dr HLH DH5 ....171 D4
  SUNDSW SR3 ....159 E1
  WASHN NE37 ....120 C2
  WICK/BNPF NE16 ....96 A5
Warwick Hall Wk LGB/HTN NE7 ....65 F4
Warwick Pl PLEE/EAS SR8 ....200 A6
Warwick Rd HAR/WTLS NE34 ....88 C1
  HEBB NE31 ....85 E5
  WD/WHPE/BLK NE5 ....60 A6
  WLSD/HOW NE28 ....67 D5
Warwickshire Dr DHAM DH1 ....196 B4
Warwick St BLYTH NE24 ....16 A2
  GATE NE8 ....81 E6
  JES NE2 ....81 E1
  SWCK/CAS SR5 ....125 F3
Warwick Ter SUNDSW SR3 ....143 F6
Wasdale Cl CRAM NE23 ....22 A5
  PLEE/EAS SR8 ....209 D2
Wasdale Ct CLDN/WHIT/ROK SR6 ....108 B5
Wasdale Rd WD/WHPE/BLK NE5 ....61 D6
Washington Hwy HLS DH4 ....156 A1
  WASHN NE38 ....119 F4
  WASHS NE38 ....138 B4
Washington Rd SWCK/CAS SR5 ....123 E1
Washington St MLFD/PNYW SR4 ....125 E6
Washingwell La WICK/BNPF NE16 ....96 C3
Washingwell Pk WICK/BNPF NE16 ....96 B4
Waskdale Crs BLAY NE21 ....94 C3
Waskerley Cl WICK/BNPF NE16 ....113 F1
Waskerley Dr RDHAMSE DH6 ....206 A1
Waskerley Rd WASHS NE38 ....139 E1
Watch House La NSHW NE29 ....70 C3
Watcombe Cl WASHN NE37 ....121 E2
Waterbeach Pl
  WD/WHPE/BLK NE5 ....60 C4
Waterbeck Cl CRAM NE23 ....22 A5

Waterbury Rd GOS/KPK NE3 ....47 D3
Waterford Cl HLH DH5 ....170 C1
  WBAY NE26 ....26 C2
Waterford Pk DIN/WO NE13 ....32 B4
Waterloo Pl NSHW NE29 ....54 C6
  SUND SR1 ....4 C3
Waterloo Rd BLYTH NE24 ....11 D5
  MONK NE25 ....38 C5
  WASHN NE37 ....121 D3
Waterloo Sq SSH NE33 ....71 E3
Waterloo St BLAY NE21 ....93 F1
  CNUT NE1 ....2 B5
Waterloo V SSH * NE33 ....71 E3
Waterlow Cl SWCK/CAS SR5 ....107 E6
Watermill RYTON NE40 ....74 C3
Watermill La FELL NE10 ....101 D2
Water Rw BW/LEM/TK/HW NE15 ....75 D1
Waterside Dr DUN/TMV NE11 ....79 D6
Waterside Elvet DHAM DH1 ....194 C5
Waterside Pk HEBB NE31 ....84 B2
Waterson Crs BDN/LAN/SAC DH7 ....178 A3
Water St BDN/LAN/SAC DH7 ....178 B1
  ELS/FEN NE4 ....80 A5
Waterville Pl NSHW * NE29 ....70 C1
Waterville Rd NSHW NE29 ....69 F2
Waterville Ter NSHW * NE29 ....70 C1
Waterworks Rd SUND SR1 ....126 A6
Watford Cl SWCK/CAS SR5 ....107 E6
Watkin Crs SEA/MUR SR7 ....188 B1
Watling Av SEA/MUR SR7 ....175 E4
Watling Pl LWF/SPW/WRK NE9 ....100 A4
Watling St HAR/WTLS NE34 ....90 A3
Watson Av HAR/WTLS NE34 ....90 A3
Watson Cl SEA/MUR SR7 ....175 E4
Watson Gdns WLSD/HOW NE28 ....68 C3
Watson Pl HAR/WTLS NE34 ....90 A3
Watson St JRW NE32 ....69 E6
  STLY/ANP DH9 ....131 E6
  WICK/BNPF NE16 ....112 A6
Watt's Rd WBAY NE26 ....40 C4
Watts St SEA/MUR SR7 ....188 B1
Watt St GATE NE8 ....8 C3
Wavendon Crs MLFD/PNYW SR4 ....142 C2
Waveney Gdns STLY/ANP DH9 ....148 A4
Waveney Rd PLEE/EAS SR8 ....208 A4
Waverdale Av BYK/HTN/WLK NE6 ....83 F1
Waverdale Wy SSH NE33 ....88 A2
Waverley Av BDLGTN NE22 ....8 B2
  MONK NE25 ....40 B6
Waverley Cl BLAY NE21 ....93 E2
  RDHAMSE DH6 ....206 A1
Waverley Crs
  BW/LEM/TK/HW NE15 ....76 C1
Waverley Dr BDLGTN NE22 ....8 B2
Waverley Rd ELS/FEN NE4 ....80 A4
  LWF/SPW/WRK NE9 ....117 F2
Waverley Ter MLFD/PNYW SR4 ....125 D5
Waverton Cl CRAM NE23 ....22 A5
Wawn St SSH NE33 ....71 F5
Wayfarer Rd SWCK/CAS SR5 ....125 F3
Wayland Sq ASHBK/HED/RY SR2 ....145 D5
Wayman St SWCK/CAS SR5 ....126 B3
Wayside ASHBK/HED/RY SR2 ....144 A2
  BW/LEM/TK/HW NE15 ....78 A3
Wealcroft FELL NE10 ....101 E4
Wear Ct HAR/WTLS NE34 ....88 B3
Weardale Av BLYTH NE24 ....9 E4
  BYK/HTN/WLK NE6 ....83 F1
  CLDN/WHIT/ROK SR6 ....109 D3
  LGB/KIL NE12 ....49 F4
  WASHN NE37 ....120 B4
  WLSD/HOW NE28 ....67 D3
Weardale Crs HLS DH4 ....157 D1
Weardale St HLH DH5 ....185 D1
Weardale Ter STLY/ANP DH9 ....146 C5
Wearfield SWCK/CAS SR5 ....125 D3
Wear Ldg CLS/BIR/GTL DH3 ....153 E1
Wearmouth Av SWCK/CAS SR5 ....126 B2
Wearmouth Br SUND SR1 ....4 C1
Wearmouth Dr SWCK/CAS SR5 ....126 B2
Wearmouth St
  CLDN/WHIT/ROK SR6 ....126 C3
Wear Rd HEBB NE31 ....85 D4
  STLY/ANP DH9 ....148 B3
Wearside Dr DHAM DH1 ....194 C3
Wear St HLH DH5 ....185 F1
  HLS DH4 ....169 F3
  JRW NE32 ....86 A1
  MLFD/PNYW SR4 ....123 F5
  SEA/MUR* SR7 ....176 C3
  SUND SR1 ....5 G3
  SWCK/CAS SR5 ....125 F3
Wear Vw DHAM DH1 ....194 C4
Weathercock La
  LWF/SPW/WRK NE9 ....99 E5
Weatherside BLAY NE21 ....94 A1
Webb Av SEA/MUR SR7 ....174 B6
  SEA/MUR SR7 ....175 D3
Webb Gdns FELL NE10 ....101 F2
Webb Sq PLEE/EAS SR8 ....201 D5
Wedgewood Cottages
  BW/LEM/TK/HW NE15 ....76 C2
Wedgwood Rd SEA/MUR SR7 ....175 D4
Wedmore Rd WD/WHPE/BLK NE5 ....59 F4
Weetman St SSH NE33 ....71 D5

Weetslade Crs CRAM NE23 ....34 C3
Weetslade Rd CRAM NE23 ....34 C3
Weetwood Rd CRAM NE23 ....22 B4
Weidner Rd BW/LEM/TK/HW NE15 ....78 C3
Welbeck Gn BYK/HTN/WLK NE6 ....82 C3
Welbeck Rd BYK/HTN/WLK NE6 ....83 E2
Weldon Av ASHBK/HED/RY SR2 ....145 D4
Weldon Crs LGB/HTN NE7 ....65 D4
Weldon Pl NSHW NE29 ....53 F4
Weldon Rd CRAM NE23 ....23 D3
  LGB/KIL NE12 ....49 D6
Weldon Ter CLS/BIR/GTL DH3 ....153 F6
Weldon Wy GOS/KPK NE3 ....47 D6
Welfare Cl PLEE/EAS SR8 ....201 D2
Welfare Rd HLH DH5 ....171 F6
Welford Av GOS/KPK NE3 ....46 C2
Welland Cl PLEE/EAS SR8 ....208 B2
Welland La CLDN/WHIT/ROK SR6 ....109 D1
Wellands Cl CLDN/WHIT/ROK SR6 ....109 D1
Wellands Ct CLDN/WHIT/ROK SR6 ....109 D1
Wellands Dr CLDN/WHIT/ROK SR6 ....109 D1
Well Bank Rd WASHN NE37 ....120 A4
Wellburn Pk JES NE2 ....64 C5
Wellburn Rd WASHN NE37 ....120 A3
Well Close Wk WICK/BNPF NE16 ....95 F4
Wellesley St JRW NE32 ....86 A3
Wellfield Cl PLEE/EAS SR8 ....157 E5
Wellfield La WD/WHPE/BLK NE5 ....60 C4
Wellfield Rd ELS/FEN NE4 ....78 C3
  ROWG NE39 ....110 B2
  SEA/MUR SR7 ....188 A1
Wellfield Ter FELL NE10 ....100 B3
  FELL* NE10 ....102 A1
Wellington Av MONK NE25 ....38 C5
Wellington Ct FELL * NE10 ....100 B2
  GOS/KPK NE3 ....45 F5
Wellington Dr SSH NE33 ....71 E2
Wellington La MLFD/PNYW SR4 ....126 A4
Wellington Rd DUN/TMV NE11 ....96 C1
Wellington St BLYTH * NE24 ....11 E5
  ELS/FEN NE4 ....2 A1
  FELL NE10 ....100 B2
  HEBB NE31 ....84 C3
Well La SMOOR NE27 ....53 D2
Wellmere Rd ASHBK/HED/RY SR2 ....145 E5
Well Ridge Cl MONK NE25 ....39 E4
Well Ridge Pk MONK NE25 ....39 E4
Wells Cl LGB/KIL NE12 ....65 F2
Wells Crs SEA/MUR SR7 ....175 E5
Wells Gdns LWF/SPW/WRK NE9 ....117 E2
Wells Gv HAR/WTLS NE34 ....89 F1
Wellshede FELL NE10 ....102 A3
Well St MLFD/PNYW SR4 ....125 E5
Welsh Ter STLY/ANP DH9 ....146 C5
Welwyn Cl SWCK/CAS SR5 ....123 F4
  WLSD/HOW NE28 ....66 B2
Wembley Av MONK NE25 ....40 A6
Wembley Rd SWCK/CAS SR5 ....125 E6
Wendover Cl SWCK/CAS SR5 ....107 D6
Wendover Wy SWCK/CAS SR5 ....107 D6
Wenham Sq ASHBK/HED/RY SR2 ....144 A2
Wenlock Cl WASHS NE38 ....138 B2
Wenlock Dr NSHW NE29 ....54 A4
Wenlock Rd HAR/WTLS NE34 ....87 F3
Wensley Cl CLSW/PEL DH2 ....135 D5
Wensleydale WLSD/HOW NE28 ....66 B3
Wensleydale Av HLS DH4 ....156 C1
  WASHN NE37 ....120 B4
Wens Leydale Dr LGB/KIL NE12 ....49 F4
Wensleydale Ter BLYTH NE24 ....11 E5
Wentworth SSH NE33 ....72 A5
Wentworth Cl FELL NE10 ....100 C3
Wentworth Dr WASHN NE37 ....120 B2
Wentworth Gdns MONK NE25 ....39 E5
Wentworth Gra
  GOS/KPK (off the Gv) NE3 ....63 F2
Wentworth Pl ELS/FEN NE4 ....80 A4
Wentworth Ter MLFD/PNYW SR4 ....126 A4
Werhale Gn FELL NE10 ....100 B2
Wesley Ct FELL NE10 ....100 B3
  STLY/ANP DH9 ....146 B2
Wesley Dr LGB/KIL NE12 ....51 D3
Wesley St LWF/SPW/WRK NE9 ....99 E5
Wesley Ter STLY/ANP DH9 ....146 B6
Wesley Wy BW/LEM/TK/HW NE15 ....57 F4
  LGB/KIL NE12 ....51 D3
  SEA/MUR SR7 ....175 E3
Wessex Cl SWCK/CAS SR5 ....107 E6
Wessington Wy SWCK/CAS SR5 ....125 D3
Westacre Gdns
  WD/WHPE/BLK NE5 ....78 B1
West Acres DIN/WO NE13 ....31 D7
Westacres Av WICK/BNPF NE16 ....96 A4
Westacres Crs
  BW/LEM/TK/HW NE15 ....78 B1
West Av CLDN/WHIT/ROK SR6 ....109 D3
  GOS/KPK NE3 ....63 F2
  HAR/WTLS NE34 ....89 D2
  NSHW NE29 ....69 F1
  PLEE/EAS SR8 ....201 D3
  ROWG NE39 ....110 C3
  SEA/MUR SR7 ....188 B3
  WASHS NE38 ....138 A1
  WD/WHPE/BLK NE5 ....60 B3

West Bailey *LGB/KIL* NE12........................**35** F6
Westbourne Av
  BYK/HTN/WLK NE6.........................**66** B6
  GATE NE8...**99** D2
  GOS/KPK NE3......................................**47** E5
Westbourne Dr *HLS* DH4......................**156** C2
Westbourne Rd *SUND* SR1..................**126** A6
West Bridge St *BLYTH* NE24...................**10** C1
Westburn Gdns *WLSD/HOW* NE28......**66** B2
Westburn Ter
  CLDN/WHIT/ROK SR6.....................**127** D2
Westbury Av *BYK/HTN/WLK* NE6.......**66** B6
Westbury Rd *NSHW* NE29......................**54** B3
Westbury St *MLFD/PNYW* SR4...........**126** A5
Westcliff Cl *PLEE/EAS* SR8.....................**199** F3
Westcliffe Rd
  CLDN/WHIT/ROK SR6.....................**109** E6
Westcliffe Wy *HAR/WTLS* NE34.........**87** E5
West Clifton *LGB/KIL* NE12.....................**35** E6
West Copperas
  BW/LEM/TK/HW NE15.....................**77** D1
Westcott Av *SSH* NE33..........................**72** A5
Westcott Dr *DHAM* DH1.......................**193** F1
Westcott Rd *HAR/WTLS* NE34...............**88** B3
  PLEE/EAS SR8....................................**208** C1
West Ct
  DHAM (off Elvet Hill Rd) DH1.........**205** E1
West Crs *FELL* NE10...............................**102** D2
Westcroft *CLDN/WHIT/ROK* SR6.......**109** D1
Westcroft Rd *LGB/KIL* NE12..................**50** A4
West Dene Dr *TYNE/NSHE* NE30.........**54** C4
West Denton Cl
  BW/LEM/TK/HW NE15.....................**59** F6
West Denton Rd
  BW/LEM/TK/HW NE15.....................**59** F6
West Denton Wy
  WD/WHPE/BLK NE5..........................**59** F4
West Dr
  BLYTH NE24...**16** B2
  CLDN/WHIT/ROK SR6.....................**107** D1
  CLSW/PEL DH2...................................**152** D6
West End Front St *BDLGTN* * NE22.......**7** E4
Westerdale *HLS* DH4.............................**139** D6
  WLSD/HOW NE28..............................**66** B2
Westerdale Pl
  BYK/HTN/WLK NE6.........................**84** A2
Westerham Cl *SWCK/CAS* SR5...........**107** E6
Westerhope Gdns
  WD/WHPE/BLK NE5..........................**61** F5
Westerhope Homes
  WD/WHPE/BLK
  (off Hillhead Rd) NE5.........................**60** A3
Westerhope Rd *WASHS* NE38............**139** E1
Westerkirk *CRAM* NE23...........................**22** A4
Western Ap *SSH* NE33............................**71** E5
Western Av *ELS/FEN* NE4.......................**79** E3
  MONK NE25...**24** A5
  SSH NE33..**59** F5
Western Dr *ELS/FEN* NE4.......................**79** F2
Western Hwy *WASHS* NE38.................**137** F4
Western Hl *ASHBK/HED/RY* SR2.......**162** A1
  MLFD/PNYW SR4..............................**144** A1
Westernmoor *WASHN* NE37................**119** E6
Western Rd *JRW* NE32.............................**85** F1
  WLSD/HOW NE28..............................**68** B4
Western Ter *BOL* NE36..........................**105** F3
  CRAM NE23...**34** B2
Western Wy *BLAY* NE21..........................**77** D6
  RYTON NE40.......................................**74** B4
  WBAY NE26...**40** B2
West Farm
  BOL (off North Rd) NE36..................**106** B3
West Farm Av *LGB/KIL* NE12.................**48** B6
West Farm Ct *CRAM* * NE23...................**22** A1
West Farm Rd *BYK/HTN/WLK* NE6.....**83** D1
  CLDN/WHIT/ROK SR6.....................**108** A3
  WLSD/HOW NE28..............................**68** A3
West Farm Wynd *LGB/KIL* NE12.........**64** B1
Westfield *GOS/KPK* NE3..........................**63** D4
Westfield Av *DIN/WO* NE13....................**32** C4
  GOS/KPK NE3......................................**63** E3
  MONK NE25...**39** F6
Westfield Ct
  JRW (off Borough Rd) NE32............**86** A2
  MLFD/PNYW SR4..............................**143** D2
  WLSD/HOW NE28..............................**67** D3
Westfield Dr *GOS/KPK* NE3....................**63** D3
Westfield Gv *GOS/KPK* NE3....................**63** D3
  MLFD/PNYW SR4..............................**143** D2
Westfield La *RYTON* NE40......................**74** A2
Westfield Pk *WLSD/HOW* NE28............**66** C4
Westfield Rd
  BW/LEM/TK/HW NE15.....................**78** D3
Westfields *STLY/ANP* DH9...................**148** A3
Westfield Ter *GATE* NE8..........................**99** D2
Westgarth *WD/WHPE/BLK* NE5............**60** A2
Westgarth Gv *RDHAMSE* DH6.............**206** A1
Westgate Av *SUNDSW* SR3...................**143** F6
Westgate Cl *MONK* NE25.......................**39** E4
Westgate Gv *SUNDSW* SR3..................**143** F6
Westgate Hill Ter *CNUT* NE1...................**2** A5
Westgate Rd *CNUT* NE1...........................**2** A4
  ELS/FEN NE4.......................................**79** D2
West George Potts St *SSH* NE33........**71** E5
West Gra *SWCK/CAS* SR5......................**126** B1

West Gv *MLFD/PNYW* SR4.................**142** A1
Westheath Av
  ASHBK/HED/RY SR2.......................**145** D4
West High Horse Cl *ROWG* NE39........**93** E6
West Hl *MLFD/PNYW* SR4...................**143** D2
Westhills *STLY/ANP* DH9.......................**129** F4
Westhills Cl *BDN/LAN/SAC* DH7.......**164** A5
West Holborn *SSH* NE33.........................**71** D5
Westholme Gdns
  BW/LEM/TK/HW NE15.....................**78** C2
Westhope Cl *HAR/WTLS* NE34.............**89** F1
Westhope Rd *HAR/WTLS* NE34............**89** F1
West Jesmond Av *JES* NE2.....................**64** A4
Westlands *BW/LEM/TK/HW* NE15.......**59** E5
  JRW NE32...**104** C3
  LGB/HTN NE7.......................................**64** C3
  TYNE/NSHE NE30...............................**55** D3
  WBAY NE26...**26** A2
West La *BLAY* NE21.................................**93** F2
  CLS/BIR/GTL DH3...............................**153** E6
  LGB/KIL NE12..**48** C6
  WICK/BNPF NE16...............................**112** B3
West Lawn *ASHBK/HED/RY* SR2........**144** B2
West Lawson St *NSHW* NE29.................**70** C2
West Lea *BLAY* NE21................................**94** B2
Westleigh Ct *MLFD/PNYW* SR4..........**125** E6
Westleigh Rd *HLS* DH4..........................**157** E4
Westley Av *WBAY* NE26..........................**40** A1
Westley Cl *WBAY* NE26............................**40** A1
Westloch Rd *CRAM* NE23.......................**22** A5
Westmacott St
  BW/LEM/TK/HW NE15.....................**58** A6
West Mdw
  WD/WHPE/BLK NE5..........................**59** F2
West Meadows Dr
  CLDN/WHIT/ROK SR6.....................**107** F2
West Meadows Rd
  CLDN/WHIT/ROK SR6.....................**107** F2
Westminster Av *NSHW* NE29.................**53** D4
Westminster Crs *HEBB* NE31.................**85** D6
Westminster Dr *DUN/TMV* * NE11.......**97** E4
Westminster St *GATE* NE8.......................**98** C2
Westminster Wy *LGB/KIL* NE12.............**49** D3
West Moffett St *SSH* * NE33...................**71** F5
West Moor Dr
  CLDN/WHIT/ROK SR6.....................**107** F3
Westmoor Dr *LGB/KIL* NE12...................**49** D3
Westmoor Rd *MLFD/PNYW* SR4........**124** C5
Westmoreland St
  WLSD/HOW NE28..............................**67** E4
Westmorland Av *BDLGTN* NE22............**7** D3
  WASHN NE37....................................**120** C2
  WLSD/HOW NE28..............................**69** D5
Westmorland Gdns
  LWF/SPW/WRK NE9...........................**99** E5
Westmorland Ri *PLEE/EAS* SR8.........**200** A6
Westmorland Rd *CNUT* NE1....................**2** A5
  ELS/FEN NE4.......................................**79** E4
  HAR/WTLS NE34................................**90** B1
  NSHW NE29...**53** D5
Westmorland Wy *CRAM* NE23..............**21** E2
West Mt *MLFD/PNYW* SR4..................**143** D1
Westoe Av *SSH* NE33..............................**72** A5
Westoe Dr *SSH* NE33...............................**72** A5
Westoe Rd *SSH* NE33...............................**71** F4
Westoe Village *SSH* NE33......................**72** A6
Weston Av *WICK/BNPF* NE16.................**95** F5
Weston Vw *PLEE/EAS* SR8....................**208** B1
West Ousterley Rd
  STLY/ANP DH9.................................**148** C2
Westover Gdns
  LWF/SPW/WRK NE9...........................**99** E3
West Pde *ELS/FEN* NE4............................**80** A4
  HEBB NE31..**84** C4
West Pk *DUN/TMV* NE11.........................**97** D1
  SUNDSW SR3...................................**159** D2
West Park Gdns *BLAY* NE21...................**94** B3
West Park Rd
  CLDN/WHIT/ROK SR6.....................**107** E4
  LWF/SPW/WRK NE9...........................**99** D3
  SSH NE33..**71** E6
West Park Vw *CRAM* NE23.....................**34** B2
West Pastures *BOL* NE36......................**104** B5
West Percy Rd *NSHW* NE29....................**70** A2
West Percy St *NSHW* NE29......................**70** C1
Westport Cl *SWCK/CAS* SR5................**107** E6
West Quay Rd *SWCK/CAS* SR5...........**125** E3
West Riggs *BDLGTN* NE22........................**7** E4
The West Rig *GOS/KPK* NE3.....................**62** A2
West Rd *BDLGTN* NE22.............................**8** C2
  STLY/ANP DH9.................................**129** F5
West Salisbury St *BLYTH* NE24............**10** C4
West St *SMOOR* NE27..............................**51** F3
West Stainton St *SSH* * NE33.................**71** F5
West Stevenson St *SSH* NE33..............**71** F5
West Stoneycroft *LGB/KIL* NE12..........**50** A2
West St *CLS/BIR/GTL* DH3....................**136** B2
  CLSW/PEL DH2.................................**150** C3
  GATE NE8...**81** D5
  HEBB NE31..**85** D1
  RDHAMSE DH6..................................**206** B2
  SEA/MUR SR7....................................**176** C3
  STLY/ANP DH9..................................**130** C6
  SUND SR1...**4** B2

  SUNDSW SR3....................................**143** F6
  WICK/BNPF NE16...............................**95** F3
  WLSD/HOW NE28..............................**66** C4
West Sunniside *SUND* SR1.......................**4** D2
West Ter *DHAM* * DH1...........................**194** A4
  WBAY NE26...**26** C2
West Thorns Wk *WICK/BNPF* NE16.....**95** F4
West Thorp *WD/WHPE/BLK* NE5..........**60** B1
West Vallum
  BW/LEM/TK/HW NE15.....................**77** E1
West Vw *BDLGTN* NE22.............................**8** B1
  BDN/LAN/SAC DH7..........................**203** E5
  BLAY NE21...**76** B3
  BW/LEM/TK/HW NE15.....................**76** B2
  CLDN/WHIT/ROK SR6.....................**126** C1
  DHAM DH1..**195** D4
  DUN/TMV NE11.................................**116** C6
  ELS/FEN NE4.......................................**79** E4
  HLS DH4...**157** D4
  LGB/KIL NE12..**49** D4
  STLY/ANP (off Catchwell Rd) DH9...**128** C6
  SWCK/CAS SR5................................**105** D4
  WICK/BNPF NE16.............................**111** F6
West View Ter *DUN/TMV* NE11.............**79** D6
West Walls *CNUT* NE1...............................**2** B4
West Walpole St *SSH* NE33.....................**71** D5
Westward Cl *WD/WHPE/BLK* NE5.........**60** A3
Westward Pl *WASHS* NE38..................**138** A5
West Wy *DUN/TMV* NE11........................**97** F2
  SSH NE33..**88** B1
Westway *BLAY* NE21................................**76** A6
  BW/LEM/TK/HW NE15.....................**57** F3
  PLEE/EAS SR8....................................**208** B3
West Wear St *SUND* SR1............................**4** C1
Westwell Ct *LGB/HTN* NE7.....................**64** B2
West Wellington St *NSHW* NE29...........**70** C1
Westwood Av *BYK/HTN/WLK* NE6.......**65** D5
Westwood Gdns *GOS/KPK* NE3.............**62** A2
Westwood Rd *GOS/KPK* NE3...................**47** E5
West Wynd *LGB/KIL* NE12.......................**49** F1
Wetheral Gdns
  LWF/SPW/WRK NE9.........................**117** F1
Wetheral Ter *BYK/HTN/WLK* NE6........**83** E4
Wetherburn Av *SEA/MUR* SR7............**188** A1
Wetherby Gv *GATE* NE8...........................**98** C3
Wetherby Rd *ASHBK/HED/RY* SR2.....**145** F5
Wettondale Av *BLYTH* NE24.....................**9** F5
Weybourne Sq
  ASHBK/HED/RY SR2.......................**145** D4
Weyhill Av *NSHW* NE29...........................**69** F2
Weymouth Dr *SEA/MUR* SR7...............**175** F4
Weymouth Gdns
  LWF/SPW/WRK NE9.........................**117** E2
Whaggs La *WICK/BNPF* NE16................**96** A4
Whalton Av *GOS/KPK* NE3......................**46** C6
Whalton Cl *FELL* NE10...........................**102** B3
  RDHAMSE DH6..................................**197** F5
Whalton Ct *HAR/WTLS* NE34.................**89** D2
Wharfdale Pl *BYK/HTN/WLK* NE6........**83** F2
Wharfedale *HLS* DH4.............................**139** F6
  WLSD/HOW NE28..............................**66** B1
Wharfedale Av *WASHN* NE37..............**120** A4
Wharfedale Dr *SSH* NE33.......................**88** B3
Wharfedale Gdns *BLYTH* NE24................**9** F4
Wharmlands Rd
  BW/LEM/TK/HW NE15.....................**77** E1
Wharncliffe St *SUND* SR1.....................**126** A6
Wharrier St *BYK/HTN/WLK* NE6...........**83** E4
Wharton St *BLYTH* NE24.........................**16** B1
  SSH NE33..**71** F4
Wheatall Dr *CLDN/WHIT/ROK* SR6......**91** E5
Wheatfield Gv *LGB/KIL* NE12..................**49** D5
Wheatfield Rd *WD/WHPE/BLK* NE5......**60** B3
Wheatley Gdns *BOL* NE36....................**105** F3
Wheatleywell La
  CLS/BIR/GTL DH3.............................**166** B5
Wheatridge *MONK* NE25.........................**24** A4
Wheatsheaf Ct
  CLDN/WHIT/ROK SR6.....................**127** E3
Whernside Pl *CRAM* NE23......................**22** A5
Whernside Wk *RYTON* NE40...................**74** C4
Whickham Av *DUN/TMV* NE11...............**97** E2
Whickham Bank *WICK/BNPF* NE16......**95** F5
Whickham Cl *HLS* DH4...........................**170** B2
Whickham Gdns
  BYK/HTN/WLK NE6.........................**82** B3
Whickham Hwy *DUN/TMV* NE11...........**97** D3
  WICK/BNPF NE16...............................**96** C3
Whickham Ldg *WICK/BNPF* NE16.........**96** B3
Whickham Pk *WICK/BNPF* NE16...........**96** B3
Whickham Rd *HEBB* NE31......................**84** C3
Whickham St
  CLDN/WHIT/ROK SR6.....................**127** D3
Whickham St East
  CLDN/WHIT/ROK SR6.....................**127** D3
Whickham Vw
  BW/LEM/TK/HW NE15.....................**77** F2
  LWF/SPW/WRK NE9...........................**99** F5
Whickhope *WASHS* NE38......................**139** D4
Whinbrooke *FELL* NE10.........................**101** F4
Whinbush Pl
  BW/LEM/TK/HW NE15.....................**77** F3
Whinfell Cl *CRAM* NE23...........................**22** B5

Whinfield Av *RDHAMSE* DH6 ....206 B2
Whinfield Ter *ROWG* NE39 ....110 C2
Whinfield Wy *ROWG* NE39 ....110 B3
Whinlatter Gdns
   LWF/SPW/WRK NE9 ....99 F6
Whinmoor Pl *WD/WHPE/BLK* NE5.....62 A5
Whinney La *DIN/WO* NE21 ....93 F2
Whinneyfield Rd
   BYK/HTN/WLK NE6 ....66 B6
Whinney Hi *DHAM* DH1 ....194 C6
Whinshaw *FELL* NE10 ....101 E3
Whinside *STLY/ANP* DH9 ....148 A1
Whinstone Ms
   LGB/KIL (off Station Rd) NE12 .....49 F6
Whistler Gdns *HAR/WTLS* NE34 .....88 C5
Whitbay Crs *LGB/KIL* NE12 ....49 E6
Whitbeck Rd *WD/WHPE/BLK* NE5 .....60 C5
Whitbourne Cl *WASHN* NE37 ....121 D2
Whitburn Bents Rd
   CLDN/WHIT/ROK SR6 ....109 E3
Whitburn Gdns
   LWF/SPW/WRK NE9 ....118 C1
Whitburn Pl *CRAM* NE23 ....22 A5
Whitburn Rd
   CLDN/WHIT/ROK SR6 ....107 E2
   CLDN/WHIT/ROK SR6 ....109 E6
Whitburn Rd East
   CLDN/WHIT/ROK SR6 ....108 A1
Whitburn St
   CLDN/WHIT/ROK SR6 ....126 C4
Whitburn Ter *BOL* NE36 ....106 C3
   CLDN/WHIT/ROK SR6 ....108 C6
Whitby Av *CLDN/WHIT/ROK* SR6 .....109 E4
Whitby Cl *GATE* NE8 ....99 F3
Whitby Dr *WASHS* NE38 ....138 C3
Whitby Gdns *WLSD/HOW* NE28 .....68 A2
Whitby St *TYNE/NSHE* NE30 ....55 D6
Whitchurch Cl *BOLCOL* NE35 ....105 D1
   SWCK/CAS SR5 ....107 E6
Whitchurch Rd *SWCK/CAS* SR5 .....107 E6
Whitebark *SUNDSW* SR3 ....160 A4
Whitebridge Cl *GOS/KPK* NE3 ....47 E4
Whitebridge Pk *GOS/KPK* NE3 ....47 E4
Whitebridge Pk *GOS/KPK* NE3 ....47 F5
White Cedars *BDN/LAN/SAC* DH7 .....202 D3
Whitecliff Cl *NSHW* NE29 ....54 B4
Whitecroft Rd *LGB/KIL* NE12 ....48 C2
Whitecross Wy
   CNUT (off Eldon Sq) NE1 ....2 C2
Whitefield Crs *HLS* DH4 ....156 C1
Whitefield Gv *FELL* NE10 ....100 C2
Whitefield Ter *BYK/HTN/WLK* NE6.....65 F5
Whiteford Pl *CRAM* NE23 ....23 F6
Whitefriars Wy *LGB/KIL* NE12 ....64 C1
White Gates Dr * DH5 ....186 A2
Whitegates Rd *RDHAMSE* DH6 ....197 F3
Whitehall Rd
   BW/LEM/TK/HW NE15 ....58 B4
   GATE NE8 ....99 D1
Whitehall St *SSH* NE33 ....88 B2
Whitehead St *SSH* NE33 ....88 A1
Whitehill *FELL* NE10 ....101 E5
Whitehill Crs *CLSW/PEL* DH2 ....152 A4
Whitehill Dr *FELL* NE10 ....100 E4
Whitehill Hall Gdns
   CLSW/PEL DH2 ....152 C4
Whitehill Rd *CRAM* NE23 ....13 F5
White Hill Rd *HLH* DH5 ....186 B4
Whitehorn Crs
   WD/WHPE/BLK NE5 ....61 F4
White Horse Vw *HAR/WTLS* NE34 .....90 B2
Whitehouse Crs
   LWF/SPW/WRK NE9 ....101 D6
Whitehouse La *NSHW* NE29 ....53 F4
White House Pl *ASHBK/HED/RY* SR2 ....5 C4
White House Rd
   ASHBK/HED/RY SR2 ....5 E4
Whitehouse Rd
   BW/LEM/TK/HW NE15 ....78 A4
White House Wy *FELL* NE10 ....101 D5
Whitehouse Wy *PLEE/EAS* SR8 .....207 D2
   RDHAMSE DH6 ....207 E4
Whitelaw Pl *CRAM* NE23 ....22 B4
White Lea Cl *PLEE/EAS* SR8 ....209 E3
Whiteleas Wy *HAR/WTLS* NE34 ....88 C5
Whitelees Ct *GOS/KPK* NE3 ....46 A5
White Le Head Gdns
   STLY/ANP DH9 ....129 F4
Whiteley Rd *BLAY* NE21 ....77 D3
Whitemere Cl
   ASHBK/HED/RY SR2 ....145 D4
White Mere Gdns *FELL* NE10 ....102 B3
Whiteoak Av *DHAM* DH1 ....196 A3
White Oaks *FELL* NE10 ....101 D5
White Rocks Gv
   CLDN/WHIT/ROK SR6 ....91 G5
Whitesmocks *DHAM* DH1 ....193 F2
Whitesmocks Av *DHAM* DH1 ....193 E5
White St *BYK/HTN/WLK* NE6.........84 A3
Whitewell La *RYTON* NE40 ....74 B3
Whitewell Rd *BLAY* NE21 ....76 B6
Whitfield Dr *LGB/KIL* NE12 ....49 E6
Whitfield Rd
   BW/LEM/TK/HW NE15 ....77 E3

LGB/KIL NE12 ....49 F4
MONK NE25 ....24 C5
Whitgrave Rd *WD/WHPE/BLK* NE5 ....61 F3
Whithorn Ct *BLYTH* NE24 ....10 B5
Whitley Rd *LGB/KIL* NE12 ....50 A6
   MONK NE25 ....38 C5
Whitmore Rd *BLAY* NE21 ....76 B5
Whittingham Ct *GATE* NE8 ....98 C1
Whittingham Rd *TYNE/NSHE* NE30....55 E2
   WD/WHPE/BLK NE5 ....60 B2
Whittington Gv
   WD/WHPE/BLK NE5 ....78 B1
Whittleburn *FELL* NE10 ....101 E5
Whitton Av *BLYTH* NE24 ....16 A1
Whitton Gdns *NSHW* NE29 ....53 F5
Whitton Pl *LGB/HTN* NE7 ....64 C2
   MONK NE25 ....24 C5
Whittonstall *WASHS* NE38 ....139 E5
Whitton Wy *GOS/KPK* NE3 ....47 D6
Whitwell Ct *DHAM* DH1 ....195 F3
Whitworth Cl *BYK/HTN/WLK* NE6 .....83 F3
   GATE NE8 ....98 C3
Whitworth Rd *PLEE/EAS* SR8 ....207 E2
   WASHN NE37 ....119 E5
Whorlton Pl *WD/WHPE/BLK* NE5.....60 A3
Whyndyke *FELL* NE10 ....101 D5
Whytrigg Cl *MONK* NE25 ....24 A4
Widdrington Av *HAR/WTLS* NE34 .....73 D5
Widdrington Gdns *DIN/WO* NE13 .....33 E4
Widdrington Rd *BLAY* NE21 ....76 B6
Widdrington Ter
   NSHW (off West Percy St) NE29 .....70 C1
Widnes Pl *LGB/KIL* NE12 ....49 E5
Wigeon Cl *WASHS* NE38 ....137 E4
Wigmore Av *BYK/HTN/WLK* NE6 .....83 D4
Wilber Ct *MLFD/PNYW* SR4 ....125 E5
Wilberforce St *JRW* NE32 ....86 B1
   WLSD/HOW NE28 ....67 D6
Wilberforce Wk *GATE* NE8 ....80 B6
Wilber St *MLFD/PNYW* SR4 ....125 E5
Wilbury Pl *WD/WHPE/BLK* NE5 .....61 F4
Wilden Ct *SUNDSW* SR3 ....144 A4
Wilden Rd *WASHS* NE38 ....139 E3
Wildshaw Cl *CRAM* NE23 ....22 B5
Wilfred St *BOLCOL* NE35 ....105 E3
   BYK/HTN/WLK NE6 ....81 F2
   CLS/BIR/GTL DH3 ....125 E5
   MLFD/PNYW SR4 ....125 D5
Wilfrid St *CLS/BIR/GTL* DH3 ....136 B3
Wilkes Cl *WD/WHPE/BLK* * NE5 .....60 B4
Wilkinson Av *HEBB* NE31 ....84 C5
Wilkinson Rd *PLEE/EAS* SR8 ....201 D5
Wilkinson Ter
   ASHBK/HED/RY SR2 ....162 A2
Wilkwood Cl *CRAM* NE23 ....22 B4
Willans Buildings *DHAM* DH1 .....195 E4
Willerby Dr *GOS/KPK* NE3 ....47 F4
Willerby Gv *PLEE/EAS* SR8 ....208 A1
William Armstrong Dr
   ELS/FEN NE4 ....79 D5
William Cl *LGB/KIL* NE12 ....50 C4
William Morris Av *ROWG* NE39.....110 A2
William Pl *DHAM* DH1 ....195 E4
Williams Cl *SEA/MUR* SR7 ....188 B1
Williams Ter *ASHBK/HED/RY* SR2....162 A2
William St *BLYTH* NE24 ....11 D5
   FELL NE10 ....100 C1
   GOS/KPK NE3 ....64 A1
   HEBB NE31 ....84 C1
   NSHW NE29 ....70 C1
   SUND SR1 ....4 D1
   WICK/BNPF NE16 ....95 F3
William St West *HEBB* NE31 ....84 C2
   NSHW NE29 ....70 C1
Willington Ter *WLSD/HOW* NE28 .....68 A3
Willis St *HLH* DH5 ....171 F5
Willmore St *MLFD/PNYW* SR4.........125 E5
Willoughby Dr *WBAY* NE26 ....40 A3
Willoughby Rd *NSHW* NE29 ....53 F5
Willow Av *BLYTH* NE24 ....10 C3
   DUN/TMV NE11 ....97 E2
   ELS/FEN NE4 ....61 F6
Willowbank Gdns *JES* NE2 ....64 A3
Willow Bank Rd
   ASHBK/HED/RY SR2 ....144 B3
Willow Cl *BDN/LAN/SAC* DH7 ....203 D4
   WICK/BNPF (off Whaggs La) NE16 ....96 A4
Willow Ct *RYTON* NE40 ....74 C2
Willow Crs *BLYTH* NE24 ....16 B2
   HLH DH5 ....186 C3
Willowdene *LGB/KIL* NE12 ....50 A3
Willowfield Av *GOS/KPK* NE3 ....46 B4
Willow Gdns *LGB/KIL* NE12 ....35 E6
Willow Gra *JRW* NE32 ....85 F1
Willow Gv *FELL* * NE10 ....100 C2
   HAR/WTLS NE34 ....89 E3
   WLSD/HOW NE28 ....67 F4
Willow Pl *PONT/DH* NE20 ....28 A6
Willow Rd *BLAY* NE21 ....76 C6
   HLS DH4 ....170 B2

Willows Cl *DIN/WO* NE13.........32 C5
The Willows *BW/LEM/TK/HW* NE15....57 F5
   DHAM DH1 ....196 C1
   ELS/FEN (off Clumber St) NE4 .....79 F5
   WASHS NE38 ....139 E2
Willowtree Av *DHAM* DH1 ....195 F2
Willow Vw *WICK/BNPF* NE16 ....111 F6
Wilmington Cl *WD/WHPE/BLK* NE5....45 D6
Wilson Av *CLS/BIR/GTL* DH3 ....136 B1
Wilson Crs *DHAM* DH1 ....195 F3
Wilson Dr *BOLCOL* NE35 ....106 A2
Wilson Gdns *GOS/KPK* NE3 ....63 D3
Wilson Pl *PLEE/EAS* SR8 ....200 C6
Wilson's La *LWF/SPW/WRK* NE9 .....99 E5
Wilson St *DUN/TMV* NE11 ....97 E2
   MLFD/PNYW SR4 ....125 F5
   SSH NE33 ....71 E5
   WLSD/HOW NE28 ....67 D4
Wilson St North *SWCK/CAS* SR5 .....126 B4
Wilson Ter *LGB/KIL* NE12 ....49 F3
   SUNDSW SR3 ....143 F6
Wilsway *BW/LEM/TK/HW* NE15.......57 E4
Wilton Av *BYK/HTN/WLK* NE6 ....83 D3
Wilton Cl *CRAM* NE23 ....22 B5
   MONK NE25 ....39 D5
Wilton Dr *MONK* NE25 ....39 D6
Wilton Gdns North *BOLCOL* NE35 .....87 D6
Wilton Gdns South *BOLCOL* NE35 .....96 D1
Wiltshire Cl *DHAM* DH1 ....196 B3
   SWCK/CAS SR5 ....107 D6
Wiltshire Dr *WLSD/HOW* NE28.........66 B1
Wiltshire Gdns *WLSD/HOW* NE28.....66 B3
Wiltshire Pl *WASHN* NE37 ....120 C2
Wiltshire Rd *SWCK/CAS* SR5 ....125 E1
Wimbledon Cl *SWCK/CAS* SR5.......125 E1
Wimborne Cl *BOLCOL* NE35 ....105 D2
Wimborne Av *MLFD/PNYW* SR4 .....143 D2
Wimbourne Gn
   WD/WHPE/BLK NE5 ....60 B3
Wimple Cl *WASHN* NE37 ....121 D2
Wimslow Cl *WLSD/HOW* NE28 ....66 B3
Winalot Av *ASHBK/HED/RY* SR2 .....145 D4
Wincanton Pl *NSHW* NE29 ....70 A2
Winchcombe Pl *LGB/HTN* NE7 ....64 C3
Winchester Av *BLYTH* NE24 ....11 D5
Winchester Cl *CLS/BIR/GTL* DH3 .....167 F3
Winchester Ct *JRW* NE32 ....104 A1
   MLFD/PNYW SR4 ....125 E5
Winchester Dr *BDN/LAN/SAC* DH7 ....202 C6
   PLEE/EAS SR8 ....207 E3
Winchester Rd *DHAM* DH1 ....181 D5
Winchester St *SSH* NE33 ....71 F3
Winchester Wk *DIN/WO* NE13 ....33 D1
Winchester Wy *BDLGTN* NE22 ....7 E2
Wincomblee Rd
   BYK/HTN/WLK NE6 ....84 A5
Windburgh Dr *CRAM* NE23 ....22 A5
Windermere
   CLDN/WHIT/ROK SR6 ....107 F1
Windermere Av *CLSW/PEL* DH2 .....166 B1
   FELL NE10 ....101 E2
   HLH DH5 ....186 B4
Windermere Cl *CRAM* NE23 ....22 A5
Windermere Crs *BLAY* NE21 ....94 A2
   HAR/WTLS NE34 ....89 D3
   HEBB NE31 ....85 E3
   HLS DH4 ....170 D1
   JRW NE32 ....86 C5
Windermere Gdns
   WICK/BNPF NE16.........96 B3
Windermere Rd *RDHAMSE* DH6 .....188 A4
   SEA/MUR SR7 ....175 D3
   WD/WHPE/BLK NE5 ....61 D6
Windermere St
   ASHBK/HED/RY SR2 ....145 E4
   STLY/ANP DH9 ....147 F3
Windermere Ter *NSHW* NE29 ....54 B6
Windhill Rd *BYK/HTN/WLK* NE6 .....83 F5
The Winding *DIN/WO* NE13 ....31 D3
Windlass Ct *HAR/WTLS* NE34 ....88 B3
Windlass La *WASHN* NE37 ....120 B5
Windmill Ct *JES* NE2 ....63 D6
Windmill Gv *BLYTH* NE24.........9 F4
Windmill Hl *DHAM* DH1 ....205 D1
   SSH NE33 ....71 D5
Windmill Sq *SWCK/CAS* SR5 ....108 B6
Windmill Wy *GATE* NE8 ....81 D6
   HEBB NE31 ....68 A6
Winds La *SEA/MUR* SR7 ....188 A4
Winds Lonnen Est *SEA/MUR* SR7....187 F1
Windsor Av *GATE* NE8 ....99 D2
Windsor Cl *WICK/BNPF* NE16 ....95 F6
Windsor Cottages
   WLSD/HOW NE28 ....68 C2
Windsor Ct *BDLGTN* NE22 ....7 E4
   CRAM NE23 ....13 F5
   FELL (off Sheriffs Cl) NE10 ....100 B2
   GOS/KPK NE3 ....46 A5
Windsor Crs *HEBB* NE31 ....85 E2
   HLH DH5 ....171 E2
   WBAY NE26 ....41 E6
   WD/WHPE/BLK NE5 ....60 C3
Windsor Dr *CLDN/WHIT/ROK* SR6 ....107 D1
   HLH DH5 ....171 D4
   RDHAMSE DH6.........187 E4

STLY/ANP DH9	146	B3
SUNDSW SR3	160	C1
WLSD/HOW NE28	68	C3
Windsor Gdns *BDLGTN* NE22	7	E4
FELL NE10	100	B2
HAR/WTLS NE34	89	D1
NSHW NE29	54	C5
WBAY NE26	40	B3
Windsor Pk *WLSD/HOW* NE28	66	B3
Windsor Pl *JES* NE2	81	D1
RDHAMSE DH6	206	C1
SMOOR NE27	51	E3
Windsor Rd *CLS/BIR/GTL* DH3	118	A6
LWF/SPW/WRK NE9	119	D3
MONK NE25	40	A5
SEA/MUR SR7	175	E3
Windsor St *WLSD/HOW* NE28	67	D4
Windsor Ter *GOS/KPK* NE3	64	A2
JES NE2	80	C1
SEA/MUR SR7	188	C1
WBAY NE26	41	E6
Windsor Wy *GOS/KPK* NE3	45	E5
Windt St *DIN/WO* NE13	32	C5
Windy Nook Rd		
LWF/SPW/WRK NE9	100	A4
Windy Ridge Vls *FELL* NE10	100	B3
Wingate Cl *BW/LEM/TK/HW* NE15	77	D2
HLS DH4	170	C2
Wingate Gdns		
LWF/SPW/WRK NE9	100	C6
Wingrove Av *ROWG* NE39	110	C3
Wingrove Cl		
CLDN/WHIT/ROK SR6	109	D6
ELS/FEN NE4	79	E2
Wingrove Gdns *ELS/FEN* NE4	79	E2
Wingrove Rd *ELS/FEN* NE4	62	A5
Wingrove Rd North *ELS/FEN* NE4	54	A6
Winifred St *CLDN/WHIT/ROK* SR6	127	D1
Winifred Ter *SUND* SR1	5	E4
Winshields *CRAM* NE23	22	B4
Winship Cl *HAR/WTLS* NE34	88	B6
Winship St *BLYTH* NE24	16	B1
Winship Ter *BYK/HTN/WLK* * NE6	82	B2
Winskell Rd *HAR/WTLS* NE34	87	E4
Winslade Cl *SUNDSW* SR3	144	A6
Winslow Cl *BOLCOL* NE35	87	E6
BYK/HTN/WLK NE6	83	F2
SWCK/CAS SR5	100	D1
Winslow Gdns *SEA/MUR* SR7	175	E3
Winslow Gdns *LWF/SPW/WRK* NE9	99	D5
Winslow Pl *BYK/HTN/WLK* NE6	83	F2
Winsten *WASHS* NE38	137	F5
Winston Cl *CRAM* NE23	23	F6
Winston Grn *MLFD/PNYW* SR4	143	D2
Winton Cl *HLS* DH4	139	E6
Winton Cl *CRAM* NE23	22	B4
Winton Wy *GOS/KPK* NE3	62	D1
Wishaw Cl *CRAM* NE23	22	B4
Wishaw Ri *BW/LEM/TK/HW* NE15	77	D1
Witham Rd *HEBB* NE31	85	E5
Witherington Cl *LGB/HTN* NE7	66	A3
Withernsea Gv		
ASHBK/HED/RY SR2	161	F1
Witney Cl *SWCK/CAS* SR5	107	D6
Witney Wy *BOL* NE36	105	D3
Witton Av *BDN/LAN/SAC* DH7	178	B1
HAR/WTLS NE34	89	F2
Witton Ct *GOS/KPK* NE3	46	A6
SUNDSW SR3	144	A4
Witton Gdns *JRW* NE32	86	A5
Witton Garth *PLEE/EAS* SR8	208	B5
Witton Gv *DHAM* DH1	193	E2
HLS DH4	170	B3
Witton Rd *BDN/LAN/SAC* DH7	178	A2
HEBB NE31	68	B6
SMOOR NE27	52	B1
Witty Av *HEBB* NE31	85	E3
Woburn *WASHS* NE38	138	C2
Woburn Cl *CRAM* NE23	13	F5
WLSD/HOW NE28	66	B3
Woburn Dr *BDLGTN* NE22	8	B2
SUNDSW SR3	160	C2
Woburn Wy *WD/WHPE/BLK* NE5	60	C4
Wolmer Rd *BLYTH* NE24	17	E1
Wolseley Cl *GATE* NE8	98	B1
Wolseley Gdns *JES* NE2	64	C6
Wolseley Ter *MLFD/PNYW* SR4	143	F1
Wolsey Ct *HAR/WTLS* NE34	88	B2
Wolsey Rd *SEA/MUR* SR7	175	D4
Wolsingham Ct *CRAM* NE23	21	E1
Wolsingham Dr *DHAM* DH1	180	C6
Wolsingham Rd *GOS/KPK* NE3	63	D2
Wolsingham St *ELS/FEN* NE4	79	F5
Wolsingham Ter *STLY/ANP* * DH9	146	B4
Wolsley Rd *BLYTH* NE24	11	D4
Wolveleigh Ter *GOS/KPK* NE3	63	F1
Woodbine Av *PLEE/EAS* SR8	201	E6
WLSD/HOW NE28	67	D4
Woodbine Pl *GATE* NE8	99	D1
Woodbine Rd *DHAM* DH1	179	F5
GOS/KPK NE3	63	E2
Woodbine St *GATE* NE8	99	D1
SSH * NE33	71	F3
SUND	5	G3
Woodbine Ter *BLYTH* NE24	11	E6
FELL NE10	100	A2

MLFD/PNYW SR4	125	E4
Woodbine Vls *GATE* * NE8	99	D1
Woodbrook Av		
WD/WHPE/BLK NE5	60	C6
Woodburn *FELL* NE10	101	D5
STLY/ANP DH9	131	B6
Woodburn Av *ELS/FEN* NE4	62	A5
Woodburn Cl *BLAY* NE21	93	F2
Woodburn Dr *HLS* DH4	170	B1
WBAY NE26	40	A3
Woodburn Gdns *DUN/TMV* NE11	97	F4
Woodburn Sq *WBAY* NE26	39	F3
Woodburn St		
BW/LEM/TK/HW NE15	76	B2
Woodchurch Cl *LGB/KIL* NE12	65	F2
Woodcroft Cl *CRAM* NE23	34	C1
Woodend Wy *GOS/KPK* NE3	45	E4
Woodfield *PLEE/EAS* SR8	208	B2
Woodford *LWF/SPW/WRK* NE9	117	E3
Woodford Cl *SWCK/CAS* SR5	125	E1
Woodgate Gdns *FELL* NE10	102	A1
Woodgate La *FELL* NE10	84	A6
Wood Gn *FELL* NE10	102	A1
Wood Gv *BW/LEM/TK/HW* NE15	77	E1
Woodhall Spa *HLS* DH4	156	C4
Woodhead Rd *BYK/HTN/WLK* NE6	66	A6
Woodhill Rd *CRAM* NE23	22	B4
Woodhorn Gdns *DIN/WO* NE13	33	D4
Woodhouses La *WICK/BNPF* NE16	95	D4
Woodhurst Gv *MLFD/PNYW* SR4	141	F4
Woodland Crs		
BW/LEM/TK/HW NE15	78	A4
Woodland Dr *MLFD/PNYW* SR4	143	D2
Woodland Gra *HLS* DH4	169	E1
Woodland Ri *SUNDSW* SR3	160	A2
Woodlands *BW/LEM/TK/HW* NE15	57	E4
GOS/KPK NE3	63	E3
NSHW NE29	54	C4
WASHS NE38	137	D6
Woodlands Cl *MONK* NE25	38	C5
Woodlands Dr		
CLDN/WHIT/ROK SR6	107	F2
Woodlands Gra *LGB/KIL* NE12	50	A3
Woodlands Park Dr *BLAY* NE21	76	C6
Woodlands Rd		
BW/LEM/TK/HW NE15	76	C1
CLDN/WHIT/ROK SR6	107	E2
ROWG NE39	110	C2
Woodlands Ter *FELL* NE10	100	B2
SSH * NE33	71	F2
Woodlands Vw		
CLDN/WHIT/ROK SR6	107	F2
Wood La *BDLGTN* NE22	8	A3
Wood Lea *HLH* DH5	171	F3
Woodlea *LGB/KIL* NE12	49	F3
Woodlea Cl *HLH* DH5	171	F6
Woodlea Ct *NSHW* NE29	70	A3
Woodlea Crs *NSHW* NE29	70	A3
Woodlea Gdns *GOS/KPK* NE3	48	A5
Woodlea Sq *NSHW* NE29	70	A3
Woodleigh Rd *MONK* NE25	40	A4
Woodleigh Vw		
WD/WHPE/BLK NE5	62	A3
Woodman St *WLSD/HOW* NE28	69	D3
Woodmans Wy *WICK/BNPF* NE16	95	D6
Woodnansey Cl *PLEE/EAS* SR8	208	A1
Woodpack Av *WICK/BNPF* NE16	95	E4
Woodside *ASHBK/HED/RY* SR2	4	B3
BDLGTN NE22	8	B3
BLYTH NE24	11	E6
Woodside Av		
BW/LEM/TK/HW NE15	58	A4
MONK NE25	24	C6
Woodside Cl *RYTON* NE40	74	A3
Woodside Crs *LGB/KIL* NE12	50	A4
Woodside Gdns *DUN/TMV* NE11	97	F2
STLY/ANP DH9	149	D5
Woodside La *HLS* DH4	183	D3
RYTON NE40	74	A4
Woodside Rd *RYTON* NE40	74	A3
Woodside Ter *SUNDSW* SR3	159	E2
Woodside Vw		
BDN/LAN/SAC (off Daisy Hl) DH7	164	A4
Woodside Wk *ROWG* NE39	110	B3
Woodside Wy *RYTON* NE40	74	A3
SSH NE33	88	A1
Woods Ter *GATE* NE8	99	E1
SEA/MUR SR7	188	C1
Woodstock Rd		
BW/LEM/TK/HW NE15	77	F3
LWF/SPW/WRK NE9	117	F2
Wood St *CLSW/PEL* DH2	152	A1
DUN/TMV NE11	97	F2
MLFD/PNYW SR4	125	F5
WICK/BNPF NE16	111	F6
Wood Ter *FELL* NE10	84	A6
JRW NE32	85	F4
SSH NE33	71	F6
Woodthorne Rd *JES* NE2	64	A3
Woodvale Dr *HEBB* NE31	84	B4
Woodvale Gdns		
LWF/SPW/WRK NE9	100	B4
Woodvale Rd *BLAY* NE21	94	C1
LGB/KIL NE12	35	E6

Woodville Ct *MLFD/PNYW* SR4	143	D2
Woodville Crs *MLFD/PNYW* SR4	143	D2
Woodville Rd		
BW/LEM/TK/HW NE15	59	F6
Wooler Av *NSHW* NE29	68	B2
Wooler Crs *GATE* NE8	98	B2
Wooler Sq *ASHBK/HED/RY* SR2	145	D3
DIN/WO NE13	33	E3
Woolerton Dr		
BW/LEM/TK/HW NE15	77	D1
LWF/SPW/WRK NE9	100	A4
Wooler Wk *JRW* NE32	85	F4
Wooley Dr *BDN/LAN/SAC* DH7	192	B5
Wooley St *WLSD/HOW* NE28	67	D5
Woolmer Ct *LGB/HTN* NE7	66	A3
Woolsington Ct *MLFD/PNYW* SR4	125	E6
Woolsington Gdns *DIN/WO* NE13	44	B4
Woolsington Pk South		
DIN/WO NE13	44	B4
Woolsington Rd *NSHW* NE29	53	E5
Woolwich Cl *SWCK/CAS* SR5	107	E6
Woolwich Rd *SWCK/CAS* SR5	107	E6
Wooperton Gdns		
WD/WHPE/BLK NE5	78	B1
Worcester Cl *CLS/BIR/GTL* DH3	167	F3
Worcester Gn *GATE* * NE8	81	D6
Worcester Rd *DHAM* DH1	180	C5
Worcester St *ASHBK/HED/RY* SR2	4	B5
Worcester Ter *ASHBK/HED/RY* SR2	4	B5
Worcester Wy *DIN/WO* NE13	33	D5
Wordsworth Av *BLYTH* NE24	16	B1
CLSW/PEL DH2	152	A6
HEBB NE31	85	D2
HLH DH5	186	C4
SEA/MUR SR7	175	D3
WICK/BNPF NE16	96	A2
Wordsworth Crs		
LWF/SPW/WRK NE9	119	E3
Wordsworth St *GATE* NE8	99	F1
Worley Cl *ELS/FEN* NE4	79	E3
Worley St *ELS/FEN* NE4	80	A3
Worm Hill Ter *WASHS* NE38	139	D5
Worsdell St *BLYTH* NE24	11	D3
Worsley Cl *WLSD/HOW* NE28	66	B3
Worswick St *CNUT* NE1	3	E3
Worthing Cl *WLSD/HOW* NE28	66	B3
Worton Cl *RDHAMSE* DH6	206	B1
Wouldhave Ct *SSH* NE33	71	F3
Wraith Ter *ASHBK/HED/RY* SR2	162	A2
Wraysbury Ct *GOS/KPK* NE3	45	F5
Wreigh St *HEBB* NE31	84	C3
Wreken Gdns *FELL* NE10	102	B2
Wrekenton Rw		
LWF/SPW/WRK NE9	118	B2
Wren Cl *WASHS* NE38	137	F3
Wren Gv *SWCK/CAS* SR5	124	B3
Wretham Pl *JES* NE2	3	C1
Wright Dr *CRAM* NE23	34	C3
Wrightson St *CRAM* NE23	14	C3
Wright St *BLYTH* NE24	10	C4
Wright Ter *HLS* DH4	156	C4
Wroxham Ct *ASHBK/HED/RY* SR2	145	D4
WD/WHPE/BLK NE5	61	D2
Wroxton *WASHS* NE38	138	B3
Wuppertal Ct *JRW* NE32	86	A2
Wychcroft Wy		
WD/WHPE/BLK * NE5	61	E4
Wych Elm Crs *LGB/HTN* NE7	65	E3
Wycliffe Av *GOS/KPK* NE3	62	B3
Wycliffe Rd *MLFD/PNYW* SR4	143	E2
SEA/MUR SR7	175	D3
Wye Av *JRW* NE32	86	B5
Wye Rd *HEBB* NE31	85	D5
Wylam Av *MONK* NE25	25	E6
Wylam Cl *HAR/WTLS* NE34	89	D3
WASHN NE37	121	D3
Wylam Gdns *WLSD/HOW* NE28	68	B2
Wylam Gv *SUND* SR1	5	F4
Wylam Rd *NSHW* NE29	70	B3
STLY/ANP DH9	148	C1
Wylam St *JRW* NE32	86	A1
STLY/ANP DH9	149	E6
Wylam Ter *STLY/ANP* DH9	131	E6
Wylam Vw *BLAY* NE21	76	A6
Wynbury Rd *LWF/SPW/WRK* NE9	99	F5
Wyncote Ct *LGB/HTN* NE7	65	D4
The Wynde *HAR/WTLS* NE34	88	B3
Wyndfall Wy *GOS/KPK* NE3	62	C3
Wyndham Av *GOS/KPK* NE3	62	B3
Wyndham Wy *NSHW* NE29	53	D4
The Wynding *BDLGTN* NE22	7	D2
CRAM NE23	34	C1
Wyndley Cl *WICK/BNPF* NE16	95	E5
Wyndley Pl *GOS/KPK* NE3	62	B4
Wyndsail Pl *GOS/KPK* NE3	62	C3
The Wynd *BW/LEM/TK/HW* NE15	57	F5
CLSW/PEL DH2	152	A2
GOS/KPK NE3	62	A3
LGB/KIL NE12	50	A3
TYNE/NSHE NE30	54	C4
Wyndtop Pl *GOS/KPK* NE3	62	C3
Wyndways Dr *STLY/ANP* DH9	129	D5
Wynn Gdns *FELL* NE10	101	E1
Wynyard *CLSW/PEL* DH2	152	C5
Wynyard Dr *BDLGTN* NE22	8	B1

Wynyard Gdns
  LWF/SPW/WRK NE9 ....118 B2
Wynyard Gv *DHAM* DH1 ....195 E4
Wynyard Sq *ASHBK/HED/RY* SR2...145 D3
Wynyard St *DUN/TMV* NE11............97 E2
  HLS DH4 ....169 F2
  SEA/MUR SR7....................................176 C5
  SUNDSW SR3 ....160 C1
Wyvern Sq *ASHBK/HED/RY* SR2 ....145 D4

Y

Yardley Cl *SUNDSW* SR3 ....160 C3
Yardley Gv *CRAM* NE23 ....13 F6
Yarmouth Cl *SEA/MUR* SR7 ....175 F4
Yarmouth Dr *CRAM* NE23 ....13 F6
Yatesbury Av *WD/WHPE/BLK* NE5 ...61 D4
Yeadon Ct *GOS/KPK* NE3..................45 E5
Yelverton Ct *CRAM* NE23 ....13 F6
Yelverton Crs *BYK/HTN/WLK* NE6 ....83 E5
Yeoman St *NSHW* NE29 ....71 D2
Yeovil Cl *CRAM* NE23 ....13 F6
Yetholm Av *CLSW/PEL* DH2 ....153 D6
Yetholm Pl *WD/WHPE/BLK* NE5......60 C1
Yetholm Rd *GATE* NE8......................98 A1

Yetlington Dr *GOS/KPK* NE3 ....62 C2
Yewbank Av *DHAM* DH1 ....196 A3
Yewburn Wy *LGB/KIL* NE12 ....49 D6
Yewcroft Av
  BW/LEM/TK/HW NE15 ....77 E2
Yewdale Gdns *LWF/SPW/WRK* NE9...99 F6
Yewtree Av *SWCK/CAS* SR5.............125 E2
Yew Tree Dr *BDLGTN* NE22................7 E2
Yewtree Gdns *BYK/HTN/WLK* NE6....66 C5
Yewvale Rd *WD/WHPE/BLK* NE5 ......61 F5
Yoden Av *PLEE/EAS* SR8 ....201 E6
Yoden Crs *PLEE/EAS* SR8.................201 E6
Yoden Rd *PLEE/EAS* SR8 ....208 C1
Yoden Wy *PLEE/EAS* SR8 ....209 E2
York Av *JRW* NE32..............................86 A4
  PLEE/EAS SR8 ....209 E1
York Cl *CRAM* NE23 ....13 F6
York Ct
  BYK/HTN/WLK (off York Dr) NE6......66 C5
York Crs *DHAM* DH1 ....180 C4
  HLH DH5 ....171 E6
Yorkdale Pl *BYK/HTN/WLK* NE6 ......83 F2
York Dr *WLSD/HOW* NE28 ....66 C5
York Gv *BDLGTN* NE22........................6 C2
York Rd *CLS/BIR/GTL* DH3 ....136 B5
  PLEE/EAS SR8 ....200 B6
  WBAY NE26 ....41 D5

Yorkshire Dr *DHAM* DH1 ....196 C3
York St *ELS/FEN* NE4 ....80 A3
  FELL NE10...101 F1
  HLH DH5 ....185 D3
  JRW NE32..85 F2
  STLY/ANP DH9 ....146 B3
  SUND SR1 ....4 C2
York Ter *CLS/BIR/GTL* DH3 ....153 F6
  *FELL** NE10..100 C1
  NSHW NE29 ....70 B3
York Wy *HAR/WTLS* NE34 ....89 F2
Yorkwood *HEBB* NE31........................84 B3
Young Rd *LGB/KIL* NE12 ....50 B3
Young St *DHAM* DH1 ....195 E4

Z

Zetland Dr *MONK* NE25 ....54 B2
Zetland Sq *CLDN/WHIT/ROK* SR6 ....127 D3
Zetland St *CLDN/WHIT/ROK* SR6 ....127 D3
Zion St *SUND* SR1 ....5 F2
Zion Ter *SWCK/CAS* SR5 ....126 B1

Index - featured places

Abbey Road Industrial Estate
  DHAM DH1 .... 180 A4
Abbey Sports Centre
  DHAM DH1 .... 180 B4
Abbeywoods Business Park
  DHAM DH1 .... 180 A4
Acre Rigg Junior & Infant School
  PLEE/EAS SR8..................... 200 A6
Adamsez West Industrial Estate
  BLAY NE21 .... 77 E4
Addison Industrial Estate
  BLAY NE21 .... 75 E3
Airport Industrial Estate
  GOS/KPK NE3 .... 45 F6
Akhurst Preparatory School
  JES NE2................................ 64 B4
Albert Elliott County Junior Mixed
  School
  HAR/WTLS NE34 .... 88 B6
Albert Road Surgery
  JRW NE32............................ 86 A2
Alexandra Business Park
  MLFD/PNYW SR4................. 125 D4
Algernon Industrial Estate
  SMOOR NE27 .... 52 B3
All Saints Business Centre
  CNUT NE1 .... 3 E4
All Saints Junior Mixed School
  HAR/WTLS NE34 .... 88 A4
Amberley First School
  LGB/KIL NE12 .... 36 A6
AMF Bowling
  ELS/FEN NE4 .... 79 E3
AMF Bowling
  WASHS NE38........................ 138 B1
Amphitheatre
  SSH NE33 .... 72 A3
Annfield Plain County Junior
  Mixed School
  STLY/ANP DH9 .... 146 C5
Annfield Plain Cricket Club
  STLY/ANP DH9 .... 146 A5
Annfield Plain Infants School
  STLY/ANP DH9 .... 146 B5
Appletree Gardens First School
  MONK NE25 .... 40 A6
Arbeia Roman Fort & Museum
  SSH NE33 .... 71 E2
Archbishop Runcie C of E School
  GOS/KPK NE3 .... 47 F6
Archibald First School
  GOS/KPK NE3 .... 63 D1
Arcot Hall Golf Club
  CRAM NE23.......................... 20 C5
Argyle House School
  ASHBK/HED/RY SR2................ 4 A6
Armstrong Industrial Estate
  WASHN NE37 .... 119 F5
Armstrong Industrial Park
  ELS/FEN NE4 .... 79 F5
Arnison Centre
  DHAM DH1 .... 180 A4

The Art Gallery
  SUND SR1 .... 4 C3
Arthurs Hill Clinic
  ELS/FEN NE4 .... 80 A2
Ascham House School
  GOS/KPK NE3 .... 63 E2
Ashburne Medical Centre
  ASHBK/HED/RY SR2.............. 145 D2
Ashleigh School
  TYNE/NSHE NE30 .... 71 D1
Ashley Road County JMI School
  HAR/WTLS NE34 .... 88 B2
Assembly Rooms
  DHAM DH1 .... 194 B5
Astley Community High School
  MONK NE25 .... 24 B5
Atkinson House School
  CRAM NE23.......................... 23 E6
Atkinson Road Primary School
  BW/LEM/TK/HW NE15 .... 78 B4
The Avenues Medical Practice
  GOS/KPK NE3 .... 63 E3
Aykley Heads Business Centre
  DHAM DH1 .... 194 A2
Ayton Primary School
  WASHS NE38........................ 137 E3
Backworth Business Park
  SMOOR NE27 .... 37 E6
Backworth County First School
  SMOOR NE27 .... 37 D5
Backworth Golf Club
  SMOOR NE27 .... 37 E6
Bailey Green First School
  LGB/KIL NE12 .... 35 E6
Balliol Business Park
  LGB/KIL NE12 .... 48 C4
Balliol First School
  LGB/KIL NE12 .... 49 D6
Baltic Business Centre
  GATE NE8 .... 81 F5
Baltic Industrial Park
  NSHW NE29 .... 70 A3
Barbara Priestman School
  ASHBK/HED/RY SR2.............. 144 A2
Barley Mow Primary School
  CLS/BIR/GTL DH3 .... 136 C4
Barmston Medical Centre
  WASHS NE38........................ 139 E1
Barmston Village Primary School
  WASHS NE38........................ 139 E1
Barnes Junior School
  MLFD/PNYW SR4................. 143 E2
Barnwell Primary School
  HLS DH4 .... 140 A6
Barrington Industrial Estate
  BDLGTN NE22........................ 8 A1
Bassington Industrial Estate
  CRAM NE23.......................... 12 C6
Battle Hill First School
  WLSD/HOW NE28................. 67 F1
BBC North & Radio Newcastle
  ELS/FEN NE4 .... 79 F1
Beaconhill County First School
  CRAM NE23.......................... 21 D2

Beacon Shopping Centre
  NSHW NE29 .... 71 D1
Beamish County School
  STLY/ANP DH9 .... 149 F1
Beamish Park Golf Club
  STLY/ANP DH9 .... 132 B4
Beamish, The North of England
  Open Air Museum
  STLY/ANP DH9 .... 132 C5
Bebside County Middle School
  BLYTH NE24 .... 9 E4
Bede Infant School
  FELL NE10........................... 82 A6
Bede Trading Estate
  JRW NE32............................ 87 D2
Bedewell Industrial Park
  HEBB NE31.......................... 85 F2
Bedewell School
  HEBB NE31.......................... 85 D4
Bedlington Community
  High School
  BDLGTN NE22........................ 8 C2
Bedlingtonshire Golf Club
  BDLGTN NE22........................ 7 E5
Bedlington Station
  County First School
  BDLGTN NE22........................ 8 C1
Bedlington Stead
  County First School
  BDLGTN NE22........................ 8 B3
Belford House Sports Club
  ASHBK/HED/RY SR2.............. 144 C3
Bells Close Industrial Estate
  BW/LEM/TK/HW NE15 .... 77 D3
Bellway Industrial Estate
  LGB/KIL NE12 .... 50 B5
Belmont Business Park
  DHAM DH1 .... 196 A2
Belmont C of E (Controlled)
  Junior School
  DHAM DH1 .... 196 B3
Belmont Comprehensive School
  DHAM DH1 .... 196 B3
Belmont County Infant School
  DHAM DH1 .... 196 B3
Belmont Grange Clinic
  DHAM DH1 .... 196 B2
Belmont Industrial Estate
  DHAM DH1 .... 194 B4
Belmont Industrial Estate
  DHAM DH1 .... 196 A1
Belvedere Retail Park
  GOS/KPK NE3 .... 45 E6
Benedict Biscop C of E School
  SUNDSW SR3 .... 159 F3
Benfield Business Park
  BYK/HTN/WLK NE6 .... 84 A1
Benfield Comprehensive School
  BYK/HTN/WLK NE6 .... 66 A5
Bensham District Clinic
  GATE NE8 .... 98 C2
Bensham Synagogue
  GATE NE8 .... 98 C1

Bensham Trading Estate
GATE NE8 .... **98** C2
Bentall Business Park
WASHN NE37 .... **121** E5
Benton Park Primary School
LGB/HTN NE7 .... **65** D2
Benton Square Industrial Estate
LGB/KIL NE12 .... **51** D3
Benwell Hill Cricket Club
BW/LEM/TK/HW NE15 .... **78** A1
Bernard Gilpin Primary School
HLH DH5 .... **171** D2
Bessie Surtees House
CNUT NE1 .... **3** E5
Bewicke Health Centre
WLSD/HOW NE28 .... **68** C4
Bewicke Road Industrial Estate
WLSD/HOW NE28 .... **68** C4
Bewick Road Medical Centre
GATE NE8 .... **81** E6
Bexhill Primary School
SWCK/CAS SR5 .... **123** E1
Biddick Hall County Infant School
HAR/WTLS NE34 .... **87** F5
Biddick Hall County Junior School
HAR/WTLS NE34 .... **88** A4
Biddick School
WASHS NE38 .... **139** D3
Bill Quay Cricket Club
FELL NE10 .... **84** A6
Birtley East Primary School
CLS/BIR/GTL DH3 .... **118** B6
Birtley Golf Club
CLS/BIR/GTL DH3 .... **136** C3
Birtley Lane Surgery
CLS/BIR/GTL DH3 .... **136** B2
Birtley St Josephs RC School
CLS/BIR/GTL DH3 .... **136** B2
Birtley Sports Complex
CLS/BIR/GTL DH3 .... **136** B4
Birtley Swimming Pool
CLS/BIR/GTL DH3 .... **136** B3
Blackfell Primary School
WASHN NE37 .... **119** F6
Blackfriars Craft Centre
CNUT NE1 .... **2** B3
Black Gate
CNUT NE1 .... **2** D5
Bladen Street Industrial Estate
JRW NE32 .... **85** F1
Blakelaw Comprehensive
School & Leisure Centre
WD/WHPE/BLK NE5 .... **61** E4
Blakelaw Health Centre
WD/WHPE/BLK NE5 .... **61** E4
Blaydon Business Centre
BLAY NE21 .... **77** D5
Blaydon Business Park
BLAY NE21 .... **77** E4
Blaydon Cricket Club
BLAY NE21 .... **76** B6
Blaydon Haughs Industrial Estate
BLAY NE21 .... **77** D4
Blaydon Industrial Park
BLAY NE21 .... **76** C5
Blaydon Rugby Football Club
WICK/BNPF NE16 .... **95** E1
Blaydon Swimming Pool
BLAY NE21 .... **77** D6
Blaydon West Primary School
BLAY NE21 .... **76** B5
Blezard Business Park
DIN/WO NE13 .... **33** D1
Bloemfontein Co
Junior Mixed School
STLY/ANP DH9 .... **148** C5
Blyth Delaval County
Middle School
BLYTH NE24 .... **16** C1
Blyth Golf Club
BLYTH NE24 .... **16** A2
Blyth New Delaval County
First School
BLYTH NE24 .... **15** F2
Blyth Newsham County
First School
BLYTH NE24 .... **16** B1
Blyth Plessey Road County
First School
BLYTH NE24 .... **11** E5
Blyth Power Station
BLYTH NE24 .... **10** B1

Blyth Spartans A F C
BLYTH NE24 .... **11** D6
Blyth Sports Centre
BLYTH NE24 .... **10** C5
Blyth Tynedale County High School
BLYTH NE24 .... **9** F5
Blyth Tynedale County
Middle School
BLYTH NE24 .... **9** F5
Bobby Shafto Caravan Park
STLY/ANP DH9 .... **133** F5
Boker Lane Health Centre
BOLCOL NE35 .... **106** A2
Bolam Business Park
CRAM NE23 .... **12** C6
Boldon Business Park
BOLCOL NE35 .... **105** D2
Boldon Comprehensive School &
Leisure Centre
BOLCOL NE35 .... **105** F2
Boldon Golf Club
BOL NE36 .... **106** A4
Boldon Lane Health Centre
HAR/WTLS NE34 .... **88** B4
Bolingbroke Sports &
Recreation Hall
SSH NE33 .... **71** F4
Bow School
DHAM DH1 .... **205** E1
Bracken Hill Business Park
PLEE/EAS SR8 .... **207** E3
Brama Teams Industrial Park
GATE NE8 .... **98** A1
Brandling Primary School
FELL NE10 .... **100** C1
Brandon Cricket Club
BDN/LAN/SAC DH7 .... **203** F3
Brandon Modern School
BDN/LAN/SAC DH7 .... **203** D4
Brandon United Football Club
BDN/LAN/SAC DH7 .... **203** E3
The Bridges Shopping Centre
SUND SR1 .... **4** B3
Brighton Avenue Primary School
GATE NE8 .... **98** C1
Brinkburn School
HAR/WTLS NE34 .... **88** C3
Broadway East First School
GOS/KPK NE3 .... **47** F5
Broadway Junior School
MLFD/PNYW SR4 .... **142** C2
Broadwood Junior &
Infant School
BW/LEM/TK/HW NE15 .... **77** E1
Brockwell Clinic
CRAM NE23 .... **14** A6
Brockwell County Middle School
CRAM NE23 .... **14** A6
Browney County Primary School
BDN/LAN/SAC DH7 .... **203** F5
Browns Gallery
JES NE2 .... **64** A4
Brunswick Beech Special School
DIN/WO NE13 .... **32** C4
Brunswick Park Industrial Est
DIN/WO NE13 .... **32** B4
Buddle Industrial Estate
WLSD/HOW NE28 .... **67** D6
Bugatti Industrial Park
NSHW NE29 .... **69** E1
Builder's South Retail Park
BLYTH NE24 .... **10** C4
Bullion Lane Primary School
CLSW/PEL DH2 .... **153** D6
Burnmoor Cricket Club
HLS DH4 .... **156** A4
Burnopfield Primary School
WICK/BNPF NE16 .... **111** E6
Burnside County First School
CRAM NE23 .... **14** B5
Burnside High School
WLSD/HOW NE28 .... **67** F4
Burnside JMI School
STLY/ANP DH9 .... **149** D3
Burnside Primary School
HLS DH4 .... **170** C1
Burradon First School
CRAM NE23 .... **35** E5
Business and Innovation Centre
SWCK/CAS SR5 .... **125** E3
Business Enterprise Centre
SSH NE33 .... **71** D5
Byermoor Industrial Estate
WICK/BNPF NE16 .... **112** B5

Byermoor RC Aided Junior &
Infant School
WICK/BNPF NE16 .... **112** C5
Byker Business Development
Centre
BYK/HTN/WLK NE6 .... **82** A2
Byker Primary School
BYK/HTN/WLK NE6 .... **82** A3
Caedman Primary School
GATE NE8 .... **99** D1
Camden Square Secondary
School
SEA/MUR SR7 .... **176** B3
Camperdown Industrial Estate
LGB/KIL NE12 .... **35** D6
Carr Hill Infant & Junior School
LWF/SPW/WRK NE9 .... **100** A2
Cartmel Business Centre
FELL NE10 .... **101** F1
Carville First School
WLSD/HOW NE28 .... **67** D6
Castle Dene Special School
GOS/KPK NE3 .... **64** B2
Castle Keep
CNUT NE1 .... **3** E5
Castle Leazes Halls
JES NE2 .... **80** A1
Castle View School
SWCK/CAS SR5 .... **123** F3
Catchgate Primary School
STLY/ANP DH9 .... **146** A4
Cedars Special School
LWF/SPW/WRK NE9 .... **117** F1
Central First School
WLSD/HOW NE28 .... **67** F4
Central High School
GOS/KPK NE3 .... **63** E2
Central Newcastle High School
JES NE2 .... **64** A6
Central Surgery
SUND SR1 .... **4** D3
Cestria Health Centre
CLSW/PEL DH2 .... **152** B6
Cestria Primary School
CLS/BIR/GTL DH3 .... **153** F5
Chainbridge Road Industrial
Estate
BLAY NE21 .... **77** D4
Chapel House Middle School
WD/WHPE/BLK NE5 .... **59** D4
Chapel Park Shopping Centre
WD/WHPE/BLK NE5 .... **59** F2
Chase School
WICK/BNPF NE16 .... **96** A3
Cherry Knowle Hospital
ASHBK/HED/RY SR2 .... **162** A3
Chester-le-Street C of E
Junior School
CLSW/PEL DH2 .... **153** D4
Chester-le-Street Cricket Club
CLS/BIR/GTL DH3 .... **153** F6
Chester-le-Street Golf Club
CLS/BIR/GTL DH3 .... **154** B6
Chester-le-Street Health Centre
CLS/BIR/GTL DH3 .... **153** F4
Chester-le-Street Leisure Centre
CLS/BIR/GTL DH3 .... **153** F5
Chester Road Surgery
MLFD/PNYW SR4 .... **143** F1
Cheveley Park Medical Centre
DHAM DH1 .... **196** C3
Cheveley Park Primary School
DHAM DH1 .... **196** C2
Cheveley Park Shopping Centre
DHAM DH1 .... **196** C2
Cheviot County Junior
Mixed School
HAR/WTLS NE34 .... **72** C6
Cheviot First School
WD/WHPE/BLK NE5 .... **60** C2
Chevyside Middle School
WD/WHPE/BLK NE5 .... **60** C2
Childrens Hospital
SUNDSW SR3 .... **143** F2
Chillingham Industrial Estate
BYK/HTN/WLK NE6 .... **82** C1
Chillingham Road Primary School
BYK/HTN/WLK NE6 .... **65** E6
The Chorister School
DHAM DH1 .... **194** B6
Christ Church C of E
Primary School
JES NE2 .... **3** F2

Churchill Playing Fields Track
WBAY NE26.................................. **40** B5

Church of England Primary School
WLSD/HOW NE28......................... **68** A4

Church View Medical Centre
SUNDSW SR3................................ **160** C1

City of Newcastle Golf Club
GOS/KPK NE3............................... **47** C5

City of Sunderland College
ASHBK/HED/RY SR2...................... **145** D4

City of Sunderland College
HLS DH4....................................... **157** D3

City of Sunderland College
SUND SR1..................................... **4** C2

City of Sunderland College
SWCK/CAS SR5.............................. **124** C2

City of Sunderland College
SWCK/CAS SR5.............................. **126** B2

City Pool
CNUT NE1..................................... **2** D1

City Stadium
JES NE2.. **81** F2

Civil Service Sports Club
LGB/KIL NE12................................ **66** A1

Claremont Footcare Surgery
WBAY NE26................................... **40** A3

Clayton Street Indoor Mini Market
CNUT NE1..................................... **2** C4

**Cleadon Village C of E
Infant School**
CLDN/WHIT/ROK SR6.................... **108** A1

Cleadon Village County JM School
CLDN/WHIT/ROK SR6.................... **107** A1

Cold Hesledon Industrial Estate
SEA/MUR SR7................................ **189** E1

College of St Hild & St Bede
DHAM DH1.................................... **195** D4

Collierley County Primary School
STLY/ANP DH9............................... **128** B6

Collingwood Primary School
NSHW NE29................................... **69** F1

Concordia Leisure Centre
CRAM NE23................................... **21** E2

Condercum Industrial Estate
BW/LEM/TK/HW NE15.................... **78** C3

Coquet Park First School
WBAY NE26................................... **40** C4

Corpus Christi RC Primary School
GATE NE8..................................... **99** D2

Corrymella Scott Gallery
JES NE2.. **64** A5

County Durham Health Authority
PLEE/EAS SR8............................... **208** D2

County Hospital
DHAM DH1.................................... **194** A4

County Junior & Infant School
BDN/LAN/SAC DH7......................... **192** A3

**County Junior Middle &
Infant School**
STLY/ANP DH9............................... **150** B2

Cowgate Leisure Centre
WD/WHPE/BLK NE5........................ **61** F3

Cowgate Primary School
ELS/FEN NE4................................. **62** A5

Cowpen Crematorium
BLYTH NE24.................................. **10** B4

Cragside County First School
CRAM NE23................................... **22** A4

Cragside Primary School
LGB/HTN NE7................................ **64** C3

Craigievar School
CLDN/WHIT/ROK SR6.................... **127** D1

Cramlington Football Club
CRAM NE23................................... **22** C2

The Crematorium
WBAY NE26................................... **40** B1

Crofton Mill Industrial Estate
BLYTH NE24.................................. **11** E6

Crook Hall
DHAM DH1.................................... **194** B3

Crookhill Junior School
RYTON NE40.................................. **75** D3

Crowther Industrial Estate
WASHS NE38................................. **137** E2

**Crowtree Leisure Centre &
Ice Rink**
SUND SR1..................................... **4** B3

Cruddas Park Health Centre
ELS/FEN NE4................................. **79** F4

Cruddas Park Shopping Centre
ELS/FEN NE4................................. **79** F5

Cullercoats Primary School
TYNE/NSHE NE30........................... **55** E1

Dame Allans Boys School
ELS/FEN NE4................................. **79** D1

Dame Dorothy Street School
CLDN/WHIT/ROK SR6.................... **127** D4

Davenport School
HLH DH5....................................... **171** D4

Dawdon Industrial Estate
SEA/MUR SR7................................ **177** D6

Deerness Park Medical Centre
ASHBK/HED/RY SR2...................... **5** F1

Delaval Primary School
BW/LEM/TK/HW NE15.................... **78** A3

Delaval Trading Estate
MONK NE25................................... **24** B3

Denbigh Community First School
WLSD/HOW NE28........................... **68** C3

**Dene House County
Mixed Modern School**
PLEE/EAS SR8............................... **209** F2

Deneside Junior & Infant School
SEA/MUR SR7................................ **175** F4

Deneside Medical Centre
SEA/MUR SR7................................ **176** A3

Dental Hospital
JES NE2.. **80** B1

Denton Park Middle School
WD/WHPE/BLK NE5........................ **60** B4

Denton Park Pool
WD/WHPE/BLK NE5........................ **60** A4

Denton Road Primary School
BW/LEM/TK/HW NE15.................... **77** E3

Derwenthaugh Industrial Estate
BLAY NE21.................................... **77** E5

Derwent Infant School
GATE NE8..................................... **98** B1

**Diamond Hall Junior &
Infant School**
MLFD/PNYW SR4........................... **125** E5

Dinnington Village First School
DIN/WO NE13................................ **31** E3

Dipton Surgery
STLY/ANP DH9............................... **128** B6

Discovery Museum
CNUT NE1..................................... **2** A5

Donwell Primary School
WASHN NE37................................. **120** B3

Downhill Primary School
SWCK/CAS SR5.............................. **106** A6

Dragonville Industrial Estate
DHAM DH1.................................... **196** A4

Dragonville Industrial Park
DHAM DH1.................................... **196** A4

Dr Chandys Surgery
PLEE/EAS SR8............................... **209** F1

The Drive Primary School
FELL NE10.................................... **101** D2

Dr Krishnans Surgery
GATE NE8..................................... **98** C2

Dr Reg Carrs Surgery
BLYTH NE24.................................. **11** E5

Drum Industrial Estate
CLSW/PEL DH2.............................. **153** D1

Dryburn Hospital
DHAM DH1.................................... **193** F2

Dry Docks
WLSD/HOW NE28........................... **67** E6

**Dubmire County Junior &
Infant School**
HLS DH4....................................... **169** F2

Dubmire Industrial Estate
HLS DH4....................................... **170** C3

Dubmire Industrial Estate
HLS DH4....................................... **170** A1

Dudley Business Centre
CRAM NE23................................... **21** E6

Dudley Surgery
CRAM NE23................................... **35** D2

Dunholme School
DHAM DH1.................................... **194** A1

Dunston Activity Centre
DUN/TMV NE11............................. **97** F2

Dunston Federation Football Club
DUN/TMV NE11............................. **97** D1

Dunston Health Centre
DUN/TMV NE11............................. **97** D2

Dunston Hill Hospital
WICK/BNPF NE16.......................... **96** D1

Dunston Hill Junior & Infant School
DUN/TMV NE11............................. **97** D2

Dunston Industrial Estate
DUN/TMV NE11............................. **97** D1

Dunston Riverside Primary School
DUN/TMV NE11............................. **97** E1

Dunston Swimming Pool
DUN/TMV NE11............................. **97** D3

Durham Baths
DHAM DH1.................................... **194** C5

**Durham Blue Coat C of E (aided)
Junior School**
DHAM DH1.................................... **180** B6

Durham Business Centre
BDN/LAN/SAC DH7......................... **204** A3

Durham Castle
DHAM DH1.................................... **194** B5

Durham Cathedral
DHAM DH1.................................... **194** B5

**Durham CCC - County Ground,
Riverside**
CLS/BIR/GTL DH3.......................... **154** A6

**Durham City Amateur
Football Club**
DHAM DH1.................................... **196** A2

Durham City Cricket Club
DHAM DH1.................................... **195** D5

Durham City Golf Club
BDN/LAN/SAC DH7......................... **204** B5

Durham City Rugby Club
DHAM DH1.................................... **195** D5

Durham County N H S Trust
DHAM DH1.................................... **179** D5

Durham Crown Court
DHAM DH1.................................... **194** C5

**Durham Gilesgate
Comprehensive School**
DHAM DH1.................................... **195** F3

Durham High School
DHAM DH1.................................... **205** D3

**Durham Johnston
Comprehensive School**
DHAM DH1.................................... **193** F4

**Durham Johnston
Comprehensive School**
DHAM DH1.................................... **195** D6

**Durham Light Infantry
Museum & Durham Art**
DHAM DH1.................................... **194** B3

**Durham Newton Hall County
Infant School**
DHAM DH1.................................... **180** B6

Durham Road Trading Estate
CLS/BIR/GTL DH3.......................... **136** B6

**Durham St Hilds C of E (Aided)
School**
DHAM DH1.................................... **195** F4

Durham School
DHAM DH1.................................... **194** A6

Durham Sixth Form Centre
DHAM DH1.................................... **194** B4

Durken Business Park
CRAM NE23................................... **23** E6

Earls House Hospital
DHAM DH1.................................... **179** D6

Easington C of E School
PLEE/EAS SR8............................... **199** F3

Easington Comprehensive School
PLEE/EAS SR8............................... **199** F3

Easington District Leisure Centre
SEA/MUR SR7................................ **176** A3

Easington Lane Primary School
HLH DH5....................................... **186** C4

East Boldon Junior School
BOL NE36..................................... **106** B3

Eastcliffe Grammar School
GOS/KPK NE3............................... **63** F2

East Durham Community College
PLEE/EAS SR8............................... **208** C2

East End Pool & Library
BYK/HTN/WLK NE6........................ **82** B2

East Herrington Primary School
SUNDSW SR3................................ **159** E1

Eastlea First School
CRAM NE23................................... **14** B6

East Rainton JMI School
HLH DH5....................................... **170** B6

Eccles Industrial Estate
SMOOR NE27................................ **37** E6

Eden Hall Infant School
PLEE/EAS SR8............................... **209** D1

Edmondsley JMI School
BDN/LAN/SAC DH7......................... **164** A3

Eldon Gardens Shopping Centre
CNUT NE1..................................... **2** C2

Eldon Square Shopping Centre
CNUT NE1..................................... **2** C2

Elemore Golf Course
HLH DH5....................................... **185** F4

Elemore Leisure Centre
HLH DH5 .... **186** B3

Ellison C of E JMI School
JRW NE32 .... **86** A2

Elswick Park Leisure Centre & Pool
ELS/FEN NE4 .... **79** F4

Elswick Way Industrial Estate
BOL NE36 .... **106** C2

Elswick Way Industrial Estate
HAR/WTLS NE34 .... **87** F2

Emmanuel College
DUN/TMV NE11 .... **97** E5

Empire Theatre
SUND SR1 .... **4** A2

English Martyrs RC Primary School
SWCK/CAS SR5 .... **125** D2

Epinay Special School
JRW NE32 .... **86** B2

Eppleton Cricket Club
HLH DH5 .... **171** F4

The Evergreen Gallery
CNUT NE1 .... **2** C5

Ever Ready Industrial Estate
STLY/ANP DH9 .... **130** C4

Fairfield Industrial Estate
FELL NE10 .... **83** F6

Farne First School
WD/WHPE/BLK NE5 .... **60** C3

Farnham Medical Centre
HAR/WTLS NE34 .... **88** B2

Farringdon School and
Leisure Centre
SUNDSW SR3 .... **159** F1

Farrington Infant School
SUNDSW SR3 .... **142** C6

Farrington Junior School
SUNDSW SR3 .... **142** C6

Fatfield Junior & Infant School
WASHS NE38 .... **138** C4

Felldyke Primary & Infant School
LWF/SPW/WRK NE9 .... **118** C1

Fellgate JMI School
JRW NE32 .... **104** A1

Felling Business Centre
FELL NE10 .... **82** C6

Felling Pool
FELL NE10 .... **101** F4

Felling Shore Industrial Estate
FELL NE10 .... **82** C5

Fellside County Primary School
WICK/BNPF NE16 .... **95** F4

Fell Tower Medical Centre
LWF/SPW/WRK NE9 .... **99** E6

Felstead School
MLFD/PNYW SR4 .... **124** C6

Fenham Pool
ELS/FEN NE4 .... **61** F6

Finchale County Infant School
DHAM DH1 .... **181** D5

Finchale Priory
DHAM DH1 .... **182** A1

Fire Station
CNUT NE1 .... **3** E3

Fire Station
SUND SR1 .... **126** A5

Fisher Industrial Estate
BYK/HTN/WLK NE6 .... **84** A1

Flag Court Health Centre
SSH NE33 .... **71** F3

Fleming Business Centre
JES NE2 .... **63** F6

Fordley Clinic
CRAM NE23 .... **34** C2

Forest Road Industrial Estate
SSH NE33 .... **71** E4

Fox Cover Industrial Estate
SEA/MUR SR7 .... **176** C6

Framwellgate Moor
Comprehensive School
DHAM DH1 .... **180** A6

Framwellgate Moor
Junior & Infant School
DHAM DH1 .... **180** A6

Freeman Hospital
LGB/HTN NE7 .... **64** C2

Front Street Industrial Estate
RDHAMSE DH6 .... **187** E5

Front Street Industrial Estate
RDHAMSE DH6 .... **206** C1

Front Street Junior &
Infant School
WICK/BNPF NE16 .... **95** F3

Fulwell Grange Christian School
SWCK/CAS SR5 .... **126** B1

Fulwell Junior School
CLDN/WHIT/ROK SR6 .... **109** D6

Fulwell Medical Centre
CLDN/WHIT/ROK SR6 .... **108** C6

Fyndoune Community College
BDN/LAN/SAC DH7 .... **178** B2

The Gables Medical Group
BDLGTN NE22 .... **8** C2

Galactic Zoo
CNUT NE1 .... **2** B5

Galleries Retail Park
WASHS NE38 .... **120** B6

The Galleries Shopping Centre
WASHS NE38 .... **138** B1

The Gallery
CLSW/PEL DH2 .... **166** A3

The Gambling Man Gallery
TYNE/NSHE NE30 .... **71** D2

Garden Park Surgery
WLSD/HOW NE28 .... **68** C2

The Garrick Gallery
STLY/ANP DH9 .... **148** A2

Gateshead Area Health Authority
BLAY NE21 .... **77** D6

Gateshead Area Health Authority
DUN/TMV NE11 .... **97** F4

Gateshead Area Health Authority
GATE NE8 .... **98** B1

Gateshead Area Health Authority
GATE NE8 .... **99** D1

Gateshead Area Health Authority
LWF/SPW/WRK NE9 .... **100** B4

Gateshead Area Health Authority
WICK/BNPF NE16 .... **96** A3

Gateshead College
LWF/SPW/WRK NE9 .... **99** E3

Gateshead Fell Cricket Club
LWF/SPW/WRK NE9 .... **99** F4

Gateshead Health Care
FELL NE10 .... **102** A4

Gateshead Health NHS Trust
LWF/SPW/WRK NE9 .... **99** E3

Gateshead Hospitals NHS Trust
GATE NE8 .... **98** C3

Gateshead International Stadium
FELL NE10 .... **82** B5

Gateshead Leisure Centre
GATE NE8 .... **99** E2

Gateshead Little Theatre
LWF/SPW/WRK NE9 .... **99** E3

Gateshead Magistrates Court
GATE NE8 .... **81** E6

Gateshead & South Tyneside
Health Authority
SSH NE33 .... **71** F3

Gateshead Talmudical College
GATE NE8 .... **99** D1

George Stephenson High School
LGB/KIL NE12 .... **49** F2

George Washington Hotel Golf &
Country Club
WASHN NE37 .... **120** B1

Gibside School
WICK/BNPF NE16 .... **95** F5

Gilesgate County Infant School
DHAM DH1 .... **195** F3

Gilesgate County Junior School
DHAM DH1 .... **195** F3

Glebe School
WBAY NE26 .... **40** A2

Glebe Village Primary School
WASHS NE38 .... **138** C1

Glen Dene School
PLEE/EAS SR8 .... **199** F2

The Globe Gallery
TYNE/NSHE NE30 .... **71** D1

Glover Industrial Estate
WASHN NE37 .... **121** E5

Glynwood Primary School
LWF/SPW/WRK NE9 .... **99** F5

Goathland Primary School
LGB/KIL NE12 .... **49** E6

Gosforth Business Park
LGB/KIL NE12 .... **48** B5

Gosforth Central Middle School
GOS/KPK NE3 .... **47** E6

Gosforth Cricket Club
GOS/KPK NE3 .... **63** E2

Gosforth East Middle School
GOS/KPK NE3 .... **47** E6

Gosforth Golf Club
GOS/KPK NE3 .... **47** F5

Gosforth High School &
Leisure Centre
GOS/KPK NE3 .... **47** E6

Gosforth Industrial Estate
GOS/KPK NE3 .... **47** F6

Gosforth Memorial Health Centre
GOS/KPK NE3 .... **63** F1

Gosforth Pool
GOS/KPK NE3 .... **63** E1

Gosforth West Middle School
GOS/KPK NE3 .... **63** D1

Grainger Market
CNUT NE1 .... **2** C3

Grange First School
GOS/KPK NE3 .... **47** D6

Grange Park Primary School
SWCK/CAS SR5 .... **126** B2

Grangetown Family Dental
Health Centre
ASHBK/HED/RY SR2 .... **145** D4

Grangetown Junior &
Infant School
ASHBK/HED/RY SR2 .... **145** E3

Greencroft Comprehensive
Lower School
STLY/ANP DH9 .... **147** D4

Greencroft Comprehensive School
STLY/ANP DH9 .... **146** A4

Greencroft Industrial Estate
STLY/ANP DH9 .... **146** A6

Greenesfield Business Centre
GATE NE8 .... **81** D5

Greenfields Special School
HEBB NE31 .... **85** E1

Greenland County JMI School
STLY/ANP DH9 .... **147** F4

Green Lane Industrial Estate
FELL NE10 .... **101** F2

Grey College
DHAM DH1 .... **205** E1

Grindon Infants School
MLFD/PNYW SR4 .... **142** A3

Hadrian JMI School
SSH NE33 .... **71** E2

Hadrian Park First School
WLSD/HOW NE28 .... **52** A5

Hadrian Park Middle School
WLSD/HOW NE28 .... **52** A5

Hadrian School
BW/LEM/TK/HW NE15 .... **78** B2

Halls of Residence
MLFD/PNYW SR4 .... **126** A6

Hancock Museum
CNUT NE1 .... **80** C1

Hannington Works
WICK/BNPF NE16 .... **77** F6

Harelaw Industrial Estate
STLY/ANP DH9 .... **146** A1

Hare Law School
STLY/ANP DH9 .... **146** A2

Harlow Green Infant School
LWF/SPW/WRK NE9 .... **117** F2

Harraton Primary School
WASHS NE38 .... **138** A5

Hartlepool Community Care
NHS Trust
PLEE/EAS SR8 .... **208** C2

Harton School
HAR/WTLS NE34 .... **89** F2

Hatfield College
DHAM DH1 .... **194** B5

Havelock Primary School
MLFD/PNYW SR4 .... **124** C6

Hawick Crescent Industrial Estate
BYK/HTN/WLK NE6 .... **82** A4

Hawthorn House Medical Centre
BYK/HTN/WLK NE6 .... **82** B2

Hawthorn Primary School
ELS/FEN NE4 .... **79** F4

Hawthorns Hospital
PLEE/EAS SR8 .... **209** D3

Hazlewood Community
Primary School
DIN/WO NE13 .... **33** D5

Headway Theatre
BLYTH NE24 .... **11** E4

Heathfield Senior High
School & Leisure Centre
LWF/SPW/WRK NE9 .... **99** E4

Heaton Manor Lower School
LGB/HTN NE7 .... **64** C4

Heaton Manor Upper School
LGB/HTN NE7 .... **65** E2

Hebburn Baths
  HEBB NE31 .... **85** D3
Hebburn Community Centre
  HEBB NE31 .... **84** C2
Hebrew Synagogue
  WBAY NE26 .... **40** C5
Heddon-on-the-Wall
  C of E Controlled First School
  BW/LEM/TK/HW NE15 .... **56** A4
Hedworthfield Comprehensive
  School
  JRW NE32 .... **104** A1
Heritage Centre
  DHAM DH1 .... **194** C5
Herrington Medical Centre
  HLS DH4 .... **157** E3
Hertburn Industrial Estate
  WASHN NE37 .... **121** D5
Hetton Health Centre
  HLH DH5 .... **171** F6
Hetton Lyons Industrial Estate
  HLH DH5 .... **186** A1
Hetton Lyons School
  HLH DH5 .... **185** F2
Hetton Primary School
  HLH DH5 .... **185** E1
Hetton Secondary School
  HLH DH5 .... **185** E1
Hetton U D C Swimming Baths
  HLH DH5 .... **185** E1
Heworth Golf Club
  FELL NE10 .... **102** B4
Heworth Grange Comprehensive
  School & Leisure Centre
  FELL NE10 .... **101** E2
High Farm Middle School
  WLSD/HOW NE28 .... **67** D1
High Fell Special School
  LWF/SPW/WRK NE9 .... **99** F3
Highfield County Infant School
  HAR/WTLS NE34 .... **72** C5
Highfield Hospital
  CLS/BIR/GTL DH3 .... **153** E3
Highfield Junior & Infant School
  ROWG NE39 .... **110** A2
High Spen Industrial Estate
  ROWG NE39 .... **111** E1
Hillcrest Day Special School
  CRAM NE23 .... **22** A2
Hill Top School
  LWF/SPW/WRK NE9 .... **101** D6
Hillview Clinic
  ASHBK/HED/RY SR2 .... **144** C4
Hillview Infant School
  ASHBK/HED/RY SR2 .... **144** C4
Hill View Junior School
  ASHBK/HED/RY SR2 .... **144** C4
Hilton Primary School
  WD/WHPE/BLK NE5 .... **61** D4
Hindu Temple
  ELS/FEN NE4 .... **78** C2
HM Prison
  DHAM DH1 .... **194** C5
HMS Calliope Cadet
  Training Centre
  GATE NE8 .... **3** G5
The Hobart Gallery
  GOS/KPK NE3 .... **63** E2
Hobson Industrial Estate
  WICK/BNPF NE16 .... **129** F1
Hobson Municipal Golf Club
  WICK/BNPF NE16 .... **130** A1
Hollyhurst Medical Centre
  BLAY NE21 .... **93** F1
Holly Park Primary School
  WASHS NE38 .... **137** E3
Holmside & South Moor Hospital
  STLY/ANP DH9 .... **148** C4
Holy Cross RC Primary School
  WLSD/HOW NE28 .... **68** B2
Holystone First School
  SMOOR NE27 .... **51** E2
Holystone Trading Estate
  HEBB NE31 .... **84** C2
Holywell County First School
  MONK NE25 .... **25** E6
Hookergate Comprehensive
  School & Leisure Centre
  ROWG NE39 .... **110** A1
Horden & Easington RC
  Primary School
  PLEE/EAS SR8 .... **201** E5
Horton Grange First School
  BLYTH NE24 .... **9** E4

Hotspur Primary School
  BYK/HTN/WLK NE6 .... **81** F2
Houghton Colliery Welfare
  Cricket Club
  HLS DH4 .... **170** B1
Houghton Health Centre
  HLH DH5 .... **171** D2
Houghton Kepier School
  HLS DH4 .... **170** C2
Houghton-le-Spring Golf Club
  HLH DH5 .... **172** A2
Houghton Sports Centre
  HLS DH4 .... **170** C1
Howden Gas Works
  WLSD/HOW NE28 .... **68** C4
Howdon Works
  WLSD/HOW NE28 .... **69** D4
Howletch Lane Junior &
  Infant School
  PLEE/EAS SR8 .... **208** A2
Hudson Road Primary School
  SUND SR1 .... **5** E4
Hylton Castle
  SWCK/CAS SR5 .... **124** A2
Hylton Castle Health Centre
  SWCK/CAS SR5 .... **124** A2
Hylton Castle Junior School
  SWCK/CAS SR5 .... **123** E2
Hylton Retail Park
  SWCK/CAS SR5 .... **124** B3
Imex Business Centre
  CLS/BIR/GTL DH3 .... **136** A1
Indoor Market
  GATE NE8 .... **81** E5
Inland Revenue
  DHAM DH1 .... **195** D5
Ivy Road Primary School
  LGB/KIL NE12 .... **50** A4
Jesmond Pool
  JES NE2 .... **64** A4
Jewish High School
  GATE NE8 .... **99** D1
Jewish Infant School
  GATE NE8 .... **99** E1
John Spence Community
  High School
  TYNE/NSHE NE30 .... **54** C4
Joseph Swan School
  LWF/SPW/WRK NE9 .... **117** D1
Jubilee Industrial Estate
  BDLGTN NE22 .... **8** B2
Jubilee Infant School
  SEA/MUR SR7 .... **188** C1
Kenton Comprehensive School
  GOS/KPK NE3 .... **61** F2
Kenton Lodge Residential School
  ELS/FEN NE4 .... **63** D4
Kenton Park Shopping Centre
  GOS/KPK NE3 .... **62** C3
Kenton Park Sports Complex
  GOS/KPK NE3 .... **62** A1
Kepier Clinic
  DHAM DH1 .... **195** F3
Kibblesworth Primary School
  DUN/TMV NE11 .... **116** C6
Killingworth Middle School
  LGB/KIL NE12 .... **49** F2
Killingworth Sports Centre
  LGB/KIL NE12 .... **49** F1
King Edward Junior &
  Infant School
  TYNE/NSHE NE30 .... **55** D5
Kingfisher Industrial Estate
  SEA/MUR SR7 .... **175** F2
King George Comprehensive
  School
  HAR/WTLS NE34 .... **89** E5
Kingsmeadow Comprehensive
  School
  DUN/TMV NE11 .... **97** D2
Kings School
  TYNE/NSHE NE30 .... **55** F5
Kingston Park Primary School
  GOS/KPK NE3 .... **45** E6
Kingsway First School
  BLYTH NE24 .... **11** D6
Kitty Brewster Industrial Estate
  BLYTH NE24 .... **9** E3
Knoplaw First School
  WD/WHPE/BLK NE5 .... **59** E4
Laing Art Gallery
  CNUT NE1 .... **3** E2
Lancaster University
  CNUT NE1 .... **2** D5

Langley Moor Primary School
  BDN/LAN/SAC DH7 .... **204** A2
Larkspur Primary School
  LWF/SPW/WRK NE9 .... **100** B6
La Sagesse Convent High School
  JES NE2 .... **64** A3
Laurel Avenue County
  Junior & Infant School
  DHAM DH1 .... **195** E5
Laygate Lane County
  Infant School
  SSH NE33 .... **71** E5
Laygate School
  SSH NE33 .... **71** E5
Leafield House School
  CLS/BIR/GTL DH3 .... **136** C3
Leechmere Industrial Estate
  ASHBK/HED/RY SR2 .... **144** C5
Lemington Clinic
  BW/LEM/TK/HW NE15 .... **76** C2
Lemington First School
  BW/LEM/TK/HW NE15 .... **76** C2
Lemington Middle School
  BW/LEM/TK/HW NE15 .... **59** F6
Lightfoot Leisure Centre
  BYK/HTN/WLK NE6 .... **83** E4
Linden School
  LGB/KIL NE12 .... **49** F4
Lindisfarne County
  Primary School
  GATE NE8 .... **81** E6
Lingey House Primary School
  FELL NE10 .... **102** A3
Linhope First School
  WD/WHPE/BLK NE5 .... **60** B4
Littleburn Industrial Estate
  BDN/LAN/SAC DH7 .... **204** A3
Little Theatre
  CLDN/WHIT/ROK SR6 .... **107** F1
Live Theatre
  CNUT NE1 .... **3** F5
Lizard Lane Caravan &
  Camping Site
  CLDN/WHIT/ROK SR6 .... **91** D6
Lobley Hill Junior & Infant School
  DUN/TMV NE11 .... **97** F5
Longbenton Community College
  LGB/KIL NE12 .... **49** E5
Longrigg Medical Centre
  FELL NE10 .... **101** F3
Lord Chancellors Department
  CNUT NE1 .... **2** C5
Lord Lawson of Beamish
  School and Leisure Centre
  CLS/BIR/GTL DH3 .... **136** C3
Louisa Surgery
  STLY/ANP DH9 .... **148** A2
Low Fell Clinic
  LWF/SPW/WRK NE9 .... **99** F6
Low Fell Junior & Infant School
  LWF/SPW/WRK NE9 .... **99** E5
Lumley County Infant School
  CLS/BIR/GTL DH3 .... **167** F2
Lumley Junior Middle &
  Infant School
  CLS/BIR/GTL DH3 .... **168** A3
Lynnwood Business Centre
  ELS/FEN NE4 .... **79** E3
Malvins Close County First School
  BLYTH NE24 .... **10** B4
Manor Walks Shopping Centre
  CRAM NE23 .... **21** F2
Maplewood School
  SWCK/CAS SR5 .... **125** D1
Marden Bridge Middle School
  MONK NE25 .... **40** C6
Marden High School
  TYNE/NSHE NE30 .... **55** D3
Marine Avenue Medical Centre
  WBAY NE26 .... **40** B5
Marine Park Jmi School
  SSH NE33 .... **71** F3
Market Hall
  DHAM DH1 .... **194** B4
Market Place Industrial Estate
  HLH DH5 .... **171** E1
Marley Hill Primary School
  WICK/BNPF NE16 .... **113** F4
Mary Trevelyan Primary School
  ELS/FEN NE4 .... **79** F5
Maurice Road Industrial Estate
  WLSD/HOW NE28 .... **67** D6
Maxwell Street Industrial Estate
  SSH NE33 .... **71** E5

Mayfield Medical Centre
 JRW NE32 .... 85 F2
Meadowfield Clinic
 BDN/LAN/SAC DH7...................... 203 F4
Meadowfield Industrial Estate
 BDN/LAN/SAC DH7...................... 203 F5
Meadowfield Industrial Estate
 PONT/DH NE20 .... 28 A4
Meadowfield Sports Centre
 BDN/LAN/SAC DH7...................... 203 F4
Meadow Well Primary School
 NSHW NE29 .... 69 F2
Megabowl
 LGB/KIL NE12 .... 50 C5
Mercia Retail Park
 DHAM DH1 .... 180 B4
Metrocentre East Business Park
 DUN/TMV NE11 .... 78 C6
The Metro Centre
 WICK/BNPF NE16 .... 96 B1
Metro Retail Park
 WICK/BNPF NE16 .... 78 A6
Middlefields Industrial Estate
 HAR/WTLS NE34............................. 88 A2
Millbank Industrial Estate
 SSH NE33 .... 71 D4
Millburngate Shopping Precinct
 DHAM DH1 .... 194 B4
Mitre Industrial Estate
 SSH NE33 .... 88 A1
Modern Mixed School
 RDHAMSE DH6 .... 206 B1
Monkhouse Primary School
 TYNE/NSHE NE30............................. 55 D3
Monkseaton Clinic
 MONK NE25 .... 40 A6
Monkseaton High School
 MONK NE25 .... 54 A2
Monkseaton Medical Centre
 MONK NE25 .... 39 F6
Monkseaton Middle School
 MONK NE25 .... 40 A6
Monkton Business Park
 HEBB NE31 .... 85 D6
Monkton County Infant School
 HAR/WTLS NE34............................. 87 F4
**Monkton County Junior
 Mixed School**
 HAR/WTLS NE34............................. 87 E4
Monkton Hall Hospital
 HEBB NE31 .... 85 E4
Monkton Stadium
 JRW NE32 .... 85 F4
Monkwearmouth Health Centre
 SWCK/CAS SR5 .... 126 C4
Monkwearmouth Hospital
 SWCK/CAS SR5 .... 126 B2
**Monkwearmouth Railway Station
 Museum**
 SWCK/CAS SR5 .... 126 C4
Montagu Junior & Infant School
 WD/WHPE/BLK NE5 .... 62 A3
Monument Mall Shopping Centre
 CNUT NE1 .... 2 D2
Moor Edge First School
 LGB/KIL NE12 .... 49 D1
**Moorside Community
 Primary School**
 ELS/FEN NE4 .... 79 F2
Morgan Business Centre
 LGB/KIL NE12 .... 35 D5
Morrison Industrial Estate
 STLY/ANP DH9 .... 146 C6
Morrison Industrial Estate North
 STLY/ANP DH9 .... 146 C5
**Mortimer Comprehensiv
 School & Leisure Centre**
 HAR/WTLS NE34............................. 88 C1
Mountbatten Medical Centre
 HEBB NE31 .... 84 C3
Mountfield Primary School
 GOS/KPK NE3 .... 62 A1
**Mount Oswald Manor &
 Golf Course**
 DHAM DH1 .... 205 D2
Mulberry Trading Estate
 FELL NE10 .... 100 B1
Murton Primary School
 SEA/MUR SR7 .... 188 C1
Museum of Antiquities
 JES NE2 .... 80 C1
Music School
 DHAM DH1 .... 194 B5

The Natural Therapy Clinic
 TYNE/NSHE NE30............................. 54 C6
Nature Reserve
 LGB/KIL NE12 .... 51 E5
Nelson Health Centre
 NSHW NE29 .... 54 C6
Nelson Industrial Estate
 CRAM NE23....................................... 12 C5
Nettlesworth Primary School
 CLSW/PEL DH2 .... 165 E6
Nevilles Cross Primary School
 DHAM DH1 .... 193 E5
Newbottle Primary School
 HLS DH4 .... 157 E5
New Brancepeth Primary School
 BDN/LAN/SAC DH7...................... 202 B1
Newburn Hall Motor Museum
 BW/LEM/TK/HW NE15 .... 58 B6
Newburn Industrial Estate
 BW/LEM/TK/HW NE15 .... 75 F2
Newburn Leisure Centre
 BW/LEM/TK/HW NE15 .... 58 A6
Newburn Manor First School
 BW/LEM/TK/HW NE15 .... 58 B6
**Newcastle Antiques & Independent
 Museum**
 CNUT NE1 .... 2 C4
Newcastle Area Health Authority
 BW/LEM/TK/HW NE15 .... 78 A3
Newcastle Area Health Authority
 ELS/FEN NE4 .... 79 F4
Newcastle Arena
 ELS/FEN NE4 .... 80 B5
Newcastle Business Park
 ELS/FEN NE4 .... 79 D5
Newcastle Clinic
 JES NE2 .... 64 A3
Newcastle College
 ELS/FEN NE4 .... 80 A4
Newcastle College Concert Hall
 ELS/FEN NE4 .... 80 A4
**Newcastle Falcons RFC -
 Kingston Park**
 DIN/WO NE13 .... 45 D5
Newcastle Nuffield Hospital
 JES NE2 .... 64 A6
**Newcastle Playhouse &
 Gulbenkian Studio Theatre**
 CNUT NE1 .... 80 C1
Newcastle Preparatory School
 JES NE2 .... 64 A6
Newcastle Racecourse
 GOS/KPK NE3 .... 47 F1
Newcastle Reform Synagogue
 GOS/KPK NE3 .... 62 C2
Newcastle Road Baths
 SWCK/CAS SR5 .... 126 B2
Newcastle United FC (St James Park)
 CNUT NE1 .... 2 B2
Newcastle United Golf Club
 ELS/FEN NE4 .... 62 B5
The New City Medical Centre
 SUND SR1 .... 5 E3
New College Durham
 DHAM DH1 .... 193 F6
New College Durham
 DHAM DH1 .... 193 F1
Newgate Shopping Centre
 CNUT NE1 .... 2 C4
New Herrington Industrial Estate
 HLS DH4 .... 157 E2
Newker Junior & Infant School
 CLSW/PEL DH2 .... 153 D6
New Seaham Primary School
 SEA/MUR SR7 .... 175 E1
Newtown Industrial Estate
 CLS/BIR/GTL DH3 .... 136 B3
New York Industrial Park
 SMOOR NE27................................... 52 C4
Noble Street Industrial Estate
 ELS/FEN NE4 .... 79 E5
Norfolk Clinic
 SUND SR1 .... 4 D2
Norham Community High School
 NSHW NE29 .... 69 F1
**North Balkwell Farm
 Industrial Estate**
 NSHW NE29 .... 53 D5
North Biddick Club House
 WASHS NE38.................................. 138 C6
North Blunts Primary School
 PLEE/EAS SR8................................ 208 C2
Northburn County First School
 CRAM NE23....................................... 14 A5

North Durham Cricket & Rugby Club
 GATE NE8 .... 81 D6
North Durham NHS Trust
 CLS/BIR/GTL DH3 .... 153 E6
North East Aircraft Museum
 SWCK/CAS SR5 .... 122 C2
North East Industrial Estate
 PLEE/EAS SR8................................ 200 C5
Northern Land & Leisure Centre
 DHAM DH1 .... 194 A2
Northern Rugby Club
 GOS/KPK NE3 .... 47 E4
North Fawdon Primary School
 GOS/KPK NE3 .... 46 B5
North Heaton Sports Club
 BYK/HTN/WLK NE6 .... 65 E6
North Industrial Estate
 NSHW NE29 .... 53 D6
North Nelson Industrial Estate
 CRAM NE23....................................... 12 C4
North Sands Business Centre
 CLDN/WHIT/ROK SR6.................... 127 D4
North Shields Rugby Club
 NSHW NE29 .... 54 B4
North Tyne Industrial Estate
 LGB/KIL NE12 .... 50 C4
**North Tyneside Area
 Health Authority**
 LGB/KIL NE12 .... 49 F1
**North Tyneside Area
 Health Authority**
 NSHW NE29 .... 54 B6
**North Tyneside Area
 Health Authority**
 WLSD/HOW NE28............................ 52 A5
**North Tyneside Area
 Health Authority**
 WLSD/HOW NE28............................ 67 E3
North Tyneside College
 WLSD/HOW NE28............................ 68 A1
**Northumberland Area
 Health Authority**
 BLYTH NE24 .... 10 A5
**Northumberland County
 Cricket Club**
 JES NE2 .... 64 B6
Northumberland Golf Club
 GOS/KPK NE3 .... 47 E1
**Northumberland Mental Health
 NHS Trust**
 CRAM NE23....................................... 22 A1
Northumbria Sports Centre
 WASHN NE37.................................. 121 D1
North West Industrial Estate
 PLEE/EAS SR8................................ 199 E6
**Novacastrians Rugby
 Football Club**
 LGB/HTN NE7 .... 65 D2
Oakfield College
 ELS/FEN NE4 .... 78 C2
Oakfield Junior School
 LWF/SPW/WRK NE9 .... 117 E1
Oakleigh Gardens School
 CLDN/WHIT/ROK SR6...................... 90 A6
Old Lily Brickworks
 ROWG NE39.................................... 111 E1
Old Shire Hall
 DHAM DH1 .... 194 C5
Old Tyne Iron Works Cottage
 BW/LEM/TK/HW NE15 .... 76 C3
Onix Industrial Estate
 NSHW NE29 .... 53 E6
The Open University
 GOS/KPK NE3 .... 47 E6
Oriental Museum
 DHAM DH1 .... 205 D1
The Osborne Clinic
 JES NE2 .... 64 B5
Our Lady of Peace RC School
 HLS DH4 .... 156 C1
**Our Lady & St Annes
 Primary School**
 ELS/FEN NE4 .... 80 A3
Ouston County Infant School
 CLSW/PEL DH2 .... 135 E5
Ouston Junior School
 CLSW/PEL DH2 .... 135 D5
Oxclose Community School
 WASHS NE38.................................. 137 F2
Pallion Health Centre
 MLFD/PNYW SR4 .... 125 E6
Pallion Industrial Estate
 MLFD/PNYW SR4 .... 124 C5

Pallion Primary School
MLFD/PNYW SR4 .... 125 D4
Pallion Retail Park
MLFD/PNYW SR4 .... 125 D4
Pallion West Industrial Estate
MLFD/PNYW SR4 .... 124 C4
Palmer Community Hospital
JRW NE32 .... 86 A1
Parklands Golfing Complex
GOS/KPK NE3 .... 34 A6
Parkside Infant School
SEA/MUR SR7 .... 176 A5
Parkside Middle School
CRAM NE23 .... 22 A1
Parkside School
WLSD/HOW NE28 .... 66 C1
The Parks Sports Centre
NSHW NE29 .... 70 B2
Park View Community School
CLS/BIR/GTL DH3 .... 153 F5
Park View Comprehensive School
CLS/BIR/GTL DH3 .... 153 E1
Parkway Medical Centre
WD/WHPE/BLK NE5 .... 59 E4
Parkway School
WD/WHPE/BLK NE5 .... 59 F4
Parsons Industrial estate
WASHN NE37 .... 120 A4
Pattinson Industrial Estate
WASHS NE38 .... 122 A6
Pattinson Industrial Estate
WASHS NE38 .... 139 F3
Pelaw County Infant School
CLSW/PEL DH2 .... 153 D3
Pelaw Industrial Estate
FELL NE10 .... 101 F1
Pelton County Junior &
Infant School
CLSW/PEL DH2 .... 152 B1
Pelton Fell Surgery Building
CLSW/PEL DH2 .... 152 A4
Pelton Health Clinic
CLSW/PEL DH2 .... 152 B1
Pendower Clinic
BW/LEM/TK/HW NE15 .... 78 A3
Pennywell Business Centre
MLFD/PNYW SR4 .... 142 B1
Pennywell Comprehensive School
MLFD/PNYW SR4 .... 142 A1
Pennywell Industrial Estate
MLFD/PNYW SR4 .... 141 E3
Pennywell Shopping Centre
MLFD/PNYW SR4 .... 142 A2
Percy Main Cricket Club
NSHW NE29 .... 69 F3
Percy Main Primary School
NSHW NE29 .... 69 F4
Percy St Johns Primary School
NSHW NE29 .... 70 A3
Peterlee College
PLEE/EAS SR8 .... 208 B1
Peterlee Leisure Centre & Swimming
Pool
PLEE/EAS SR8 .... 208 C3
Philadelphia Cricket Club
HLS DH4 .... 157 E3
Phoenix Theatre
BLYTH NE24 .... 11 E5
Plawsworth Road County
Infant School
BDN/LAN/SAC DH7 .... 178 B1
Playhouse
WBAY NE26 .... 40 C4
Plessey Road County Junior School
BLYTH NE24 .... 11 E5
Point Pleasant Industrial Estate
WLSD/HOW NE28 .... 68 B5
Ponteland County First School
PONT/DH NE20 .... 28 B3
Ponteland County High School
PONT/DH NE20 .... 28 A5
Ponteland County Middle School
PONT/DH NE20 .... 28 B5
Ponteland Golf Club
PONT/DH NE20 .... 28 C4
Ponteland Health Centre
PONT/DH NE20 .... 28 A3
Ponteland Leisure Centre
PONT/DH NE20 .... 28 B4
Portberry Street Industrial Estate
SSH NE33 .... 70 C6
Portland School
SUNDSW SR3 .... 143 F4

Portobello County Junior Infant School
CLS/BIR/GTL DH3 .... 136 C4
Portobello Industrial Estate
CLS/BIR/GTL DH3 .... 137 D2
Post Office Sorting Office
CNUT NE1 .... 2 C6
Preston Grange County
Primary School
NSHW NE29 .... 54 A3
Prestwick Industrial Estate
PONT/DH NE20 .... 43 E1
Primrose Community Association
JRW NE32 .... 86 A4
Primrose Hill Hospital
JRW NE32 .... 86 B4
Prince Bishops Shopping Centre
DHAM DH1 .... 194 B4
Prince Consort Industrial Estate
BYK/HTN/WLK NE6 .... 84 B1
Princess Louise First School
BLYTH NE24 .... 10 C5
Princess Road Junior School
SEA/MUR SR7 .... 176 B3
Priory Primary School
TYNE/NSHE NE30 .... 55 F4
Priory Theatre
TYNE/NSHE NE30 .... 55 F4
Queen Elizabeth Hospital
LWF/SPW/WRK NE9 .... 100 B4
Raby Cross Medical Centre
BYK/HTN/WLK NE6 .... 82 A2
Raich Carter Sports Centre
ASHBK/HED/RY SR2 .... 145 E2
Rainton Bridge Industrial Estate
HLS DH4 .... 170 B3
Ramside Hall Golf Club
DHAM DH1 .... 197 D1
Ramside Hall (Hotel)
DHAM DH1 .... 183 D6
Ravenswood Infant &
Primary School
BYK/HTN/WLK NE6 .... 65 E5
Ravensworth Golf Club
LWF/SPW/WRK NE9 .... 118 A1
Ravensworth Surgery
SSH NE33 .... 72 A5
Ravensworth Terrace
Primary School
CLS/BIR/GTL DH3 .... 136 B2
RC JMI School
BDN/LAN/SAC DH7 .... 164 A6
Recreation Centre
CNUT NE1 .... 2 C3
Redesdale First School
WLSD/HOW NE28 .... 66 B2
Red House Junior Mixed School
SWCK/CAS SR5 .... 124 C2
Red Rose Primary School
CLS/BIR/GTL DH3 .... 166 C1
Regent Farm First School
GOS/KPK NE3 .... 46 C6
Regional National Blood
Transfusion Centre
JES NE2 .... 80 A1
Rehabilitation Centre
JES NE2 .... 62 C6
Rekendyke Industrial Estate
SSH NE33 .... 71 D6
Richard Avenue Primary School
MLFD/PNYW SR4 .... 144 A2
Richard Coates Church of England
Middle School
PONT/DH NE20 .... 28 A3
Richardson Dees First School
WLSD/HOW NE28 .... 67 F4
Rickleton Primary School
WASHS NE38 .... 137 E6
Riverside Business Park
WLSD/HOW NE28 .... 68 C5
Riverside Stadium
CLS/BIR/GTL DH3 .... 167 D1
Riverview House Business Centre
SUND SR1 .... 4 D1
Robins
DHAM DH1 .... 194 B5
Roman Road Primary School
FELL NE10 .... 101 F5
Ronald Moore Gallery
TYNE/NSHE NE30 .... 55 D5
Ropery Walk Primary School
SEA/MUR SR7 .... 177 D3
Ropery Works
CLDN/WHIT/ROK SR6 .... 126 C3

Roseberry Grange Golf Course
STLY/ANP DH9 .... 150 C3
Roseberry Primary School
CLSW/PEL DH2 .... 151 E3
Rowlands Gill Infant School
ROWG NE39 .... 111 E1
Rowlands Gill Junior School
ROWG NE39 .... 111 E1
Rowletch Burn Industrial Estate
CLS/BIR/GTL DH3 .... 136 A2
Royal College of Nursing
CNUT NE1 .... 2 D4
Royal Grammar School
JES NE2 .... 81 D1
Royal Industrial Estate
HEBB NE31 .... 68 B6
Royal Quays Outlet Shopping
NSHW NE29 .... 70 A4
Royalty Theatre
MLFD/PNYW SR4 .... 126 A6
Royal Victoria Infirmary
JES NE2 .... 80 B1
Rye Hill Sports Centre
ELS/FEN NE4 .... 80 A4
Ryhope General Hospital
ASHBK/HED/RY SR2 .... 162 B3
Ryhope Golf Course
ASHBK/HED/RY SR2 .... 162 A1
Ryhope Health Centre
ASHBK/HED/RY SR2 .... 162 A1
Ryhope Junior & Infant School
ASHBK/HED/RY SR2 .... 162 A1
Ryhope Village C of E
Primary School
ASHBK/HED/RY SR2 .... 162 B2
Ryton Industrial Estate
BLAY NE21 .... 75 F3
Sacred Heart Primary School
ELS/FEN NE4 .... 78 C1
Sacriston Cricket Club
BDN/LAN/SAC DH7 .... 178 A1
Sacriston Industrial Estate
BDN/LAN/SAC DH7 .... 178 B1
Sacriston Junior School
BDN/LAN/SAC DH7 .... 178 B2
Sacriston Swimming Baths
BDN/LAN/SAC DH7 .... 178 A1
St Aidans College
DHAM DH1 .... 205 D1
St Aidans RC
Comprehensive School
ASHBK/HED/RY SR2 .... 144 B2
St Albans Medical Group
FELL NE10 .... 100 C2
St Aloysius RC Infants School
HEBB NE31 .... 85 D1
St Aloysius RC Junior School
HEBB NE31 .... 85 D1
St Andrews RC Aided First School
BLYTH NE24 .... 10 B5
St Annes Mixed High School
SSH NE33 .... 72 A6
St Annes RC Primary School
MLFD/PNYW SR4 .... 142 A1
St Anthonys Health Centre
BYK/HTN/WLK NE6 .... 83 E1
St Anthonys RC School
ASHBK/HED/RY SR2 .... 4 A5
St Augustines RC Infant School
FELL NE10 .... 101 E4
St Bede Medical Centre
CLDN/WHIT/ROK SR6 .... 127 D4
St Bedes First School
BDLGTN NE22 .... 7 D3
St Bedes RC Comprehensive
School
PLEE/EAS SR8 .... 208 B2
St Bedes RC Infants School
JRW NE32 .... 86 B1
St Bedes RC JMI School
JRW NE32 .... 86 B1
St Bedes RC Primary School
BW/LEM/TK/HW NE15 .... 77 E1
St Bedes R C Primary School
SSH NE33 .... 71 E4
St Bedes RC Primary School
WASHN NE37 .... 120 C3
St Benet Biscops RC High School
BDLGTN NE22 .... 7 D4
St Benets Primary RC School
CLSW/PEL DH2 .... 135 E5
St Benets RC Primary School
CLDN/WHIT/ROK SR6 .... 126 C2

St Bernadettes RC First School
WLSD/HOW NE28.............................. 67 D1

St Catherines RC Primary School
JES NE2 .... 64 B6

St Chads College
DHAM DH1 .... 194 B5

St Charles RC Primary School
GOS/KPK NE3 .... 47 D6

St Columbas RC First School
WLSD/HOW NE28.............................. 66 C4

St Cuthberts C of E Junior School
GATE NE8 .... 98 B1

St Cuthberts High School
BW/LEM/TK/HW NE15 .... 78 A2

St Cuthberts RC Lower School
BW/LEM/TK/HW NE15 .... 78 A2

St Cuthberts RC Primary School
BW/LEM/TK/HW NE15 .... 58 B4

St Cuthberts RC Primary School
CLS/BIR/GTL DH3 .... 153 F6

St Cuthberts RC Primary School
GOS/KPK NE3 .... 61 F2

St Cuthberts RC Primary School
NSHW NE29 .... 70 C1

St Cuthberts RC School
SEA/MUR SR7 .... 175 D2

St Cuthberts Walk Shopping Centre
CLS/BIR/GTL DH3 .... 153 E5

St Edmunds RC
Comprehensive School
LWF/SPW/WRK NE9 .... 100 C6

St Georges RC Primary School
BW/LEM/TK/HW NE15 .... 76 C3

St Godrics RC Junior &
Infant School
DHAM DH1 .... 180 B6

St Hildas RC School
SWCK/CAS SR5 .... 125 F2

St John Bosco RC Primary School
SWCK/CAS SR5 .... 105 F6

St John Boste RC Primary School
WASHS NE38................................... 137 F1

St Johns College
DHAM DH1 .... 194 B6

St John Vianney School
WD/WHPE/BLK NE5 .... 59 F5

St Joseph RC Junior Primary School
BW/LEM/TK/HW NE15 .... 78 B4

St Joseph's Business and
Training Centre
LGB/KIL NE12 .... 49 F2

St Josephs Infant School
CLS/BIR/GTL DH3 .... 136 A1

St Josephs RC School
DHAM DH1 .... 195 F4

St Josephs RC School
MLFD/PNYW SR4 .... 125 E5

St Josephs RC School
SEA/MUR SR7 .... 188 B2

St Josephs School
NSHW NE29 .... 70 A2

St Josephs School
ROWG NE39 .... 110 A2

St Josephs School
WASHS NE38................................... 120 C6

St Lawrence RC Primary School
BYK/HTN/WLK NE6 .... 82 B2

St Leonards Junior &
Infants School
SUNDSW SR3 .... 144 A6

St Leonards RC
Comprehensive School
DHAM DH1 .... 194 A3

St Margarets C of E
Infants School
DHAM DH1 .... 193 F6

St Margarets C of E Primary School
DHAM DH1 .... 194 A6

St Marks RC Primary School
WD/WHPE/BLK NE5 .... 60 B2

St Marys College
ELS/FEN NE4 .... 78 C1

St Marys Junior & Infant School
STLY/ANP DH9 .... 148 B4

St Marys RC
Comprehensive School
LGB/HTN NE7 .... 64 C1

St Marys RC Primary School
ASHBK/HED/RY SR2....................... 144 A2

St Marys RC Primary School
JRW NE32 .... 86 C5

St Marys RC Primary School
TYNE/NSHE NE30............................. 54 C2

St Marys RC Primary School
WICK/BNPF NE16............................. 96 B3

St Mary's Roman
Catholic Cathedral
CNUT NE1 .... 2 B5

St Matthews School
JRW NE32 .... 86 A6

St Michaels Industrial Estate
BYK/HTN/WLK NE6 .... 82 A3

St Michaels RC Primary School
ELS/FEN NE4 .... 79 F5

St Nicholas Cathedral
CNUT NE1 .... 3 E5

St Oswalds C E Junior
Mixed & Infant School
HEBB NE31 .... 85 E1

St Oswalds Clinic
FELL NE10 .... 100 C2

St Oswalds C of E Infants School
DHAM DH1 .... 194 C6

St Oswalds RC Infant &
Junior School
LWF/SPW/WRK NE9 .... 118 B1

St Patricks RC School
ASHBK/HED/RY SR2....................... 162 B2

St Patricks RC School
BDN/LAN/SAC DH7......................... 204 A3

St Pauls RC First School
CRAM NE23 .... 22 A3

St Peter RC Junior & Infant School
LWF/SPW/WRK NE9 .... 99 F4

St Peters JMI School
JRW NE32 .... 69 E6

St Peters RC Middle School
CRAM NE23 .... 22 A4

St Robert of Newminster RC
Comprehensive School
WASHS NE38................................... 138 C4

St Stephens RC Primary School
LGB/KIL NE12 .... 49 D5

St Teresas RC Primary School
BYK/HTN/WLK NE6 .... 65 D6

St Thomas More RC (Aided)
Comprehensive School
BLAY NE21 .... 76 A5

St Thomas Mores RC School
DHAM DH1 .... 196 C3

St Thomas Street Business Centre
CNUT NE1 .... 2 C2

St Vincents RC Primary School
BYK/HTN/WLK NE6 .... 83 D4

St Wilfreds RC Junior &
Infant School
FELL NE10 .... 82 A6

St Wilfrids Middle School
BLYTH NE24 .... 10 C5

St Wilfrids RC Comprehensive School
HAR/WTLS NE34.............................. 88 C2

Sam Smiths Sports Ground
BYK/HTN/WLK NE6 .... 66 A5

Sanderson Hospital
GOS/KPK NE3 .... 63 D2

Sandhaven Caravan &
Camping Park
SSH NE33 .... 72 A3

Sands Industrial Estate
WICK/BNPF NE16............................. 95 F1

Saville Clinic
CNUT NE1 .... 2 D2

Scotswood Sports Centre
BW/LEM/TK/HW NE15 .... 77 E2

Seaburn Centre
CLDN/WHIT/ROK SR6...................... 109 E5

Seaburn Dene Primary School
CLDN/WHIT/ROK SR6...................... 108 C5

Seaham College
SEA/MUR SR7 .... 176 C3

Seaham Comprehensive School
SEA/MUR SR7 .... 175 E1

Seaham Grange Industrial Estate
SEA/MUR SR7 .... 162 A6

Seaton Delaval Whytrig County
Middle School
MONK NE25 .... 24 A4

Seaton Sluice Middle School
WBAY NE26.. 26 A1

Sea View Industrial Estate
PLEE/EAS SR8.................................. 201 E6

Sedgeletch Industrial Estate
HLS DH4 .... 156 C6

Segedunum Business Centre
WLSD/HOW NE28.............................. 67 E5

Segedunum Roman Fort, Baths &
Museum
WLSD/HOW NE28.............................. 67 E5

Seghill County First School
CRAM NE23....................................... 36 B1

Seghill Industrial Estate
CRAM NE23....................................... 36 B1

Shanklea First School
CRAM NE23....................................... 22 A1

Sherburn Hospital
DHAM DH1 .... 196 C6

Shieldfield Health Centre
JES NE2 .... 3 G1

Shield Row Junior & Infants School
STLY/ANP DH9 .... 131 F6

Shiney Row Primary School
HLS DH4 .... 157 D2

Shipley Art Gallery
GATE NE8 .... 99 E2

Shiremoor First School
SMOOR NE27 .... 52 A1

Shiremoor Middle School
SMOOR NE27 .... 38 B6

The Shopping Centre
STLY/ANP DH9 .... 148 B3

Shotton Colliery Industrial Estate
RDHAMSE DH6 .... 206 C1

Shotton Colliery Primary School
RDHAMSE DH6 .... 206 B1

Shotton Hall
Comprehensive School
PLEE/EAS SR8.................................. 208 A4

Shotton Hall Junior School
PLEE/EAS SR8.................................. 208 A4

Shotton RC JMI School
RDHAMSE DH6 .... 206 A1

The Side Gallery
CNUT NE1 .... 3 E5

Sidegate Gallery
WICK/BNPF NE16........................... 114 A1

Silksworth Health Centre
SUNDSW SR3 .... 160 C1

Silksworth Sports Complex Track
SUNDSW SR3 .... 143 E5

Silverbirch Industrial Estate
LGB/KIL NE12 .... 35 D6

Silverlink Business Park
WLSD/HOW NE28.............................. 52 C6

Simonside First School
WD/WHPE/BLK NE5 .... 60 B1

Simonside Industrial Estate
HAR/WTLS NE34.............................. 87 D3

Sir G B Hunter Memorial Hospital
WLSD/HOW NE28.............................. 67 E4

Sleekburn Business Centre
BLYTH NE24 .... 10 C1

Sloping Masonry Business Park
WLSD/HOW NE28.............................. 68 B5

Souter Lighthouse
CLDN/WHIT/ROK SR6....................... 91 E3

South Benwell Primary School
ELS/FEN NE4 .... 79 D4

South Cramlington
Industrial Estate
CRAM NE23....................................... 34 B1

Southdene Medical Centre
RDHAMSE DH6 .... 206 C1

South Gosforth First School
JES NE2 .... 64 A2

South Hetton Health Centre
RDHAMSE DH6 .... 187 E5

South Hetton Industrial Estate
RDHAMSE DH6 .... 187 E5

South Hetton Primary School
RDHAMSE DH6 .... 187 E5

South Hylton Primary School
MLFD/PNYW SR4 .... 123 F6

Southlands Middle School
CRAM NE23....................................... 22 A5

Southlands School &
Swimming Pool
TYNE/NSHE NE30............................. 54 C4

South Moor Golf Club
STLY/ANP DH9 .... 148 C5

Southmoor School
ASHBK/HED/RY SR2....................... 145 D3

South Nelson Industrial Estate
CRAM NE23....................................... 13 D6

Southridge First School
MONK NE25 .... 39 F4

South Shields FC
JRW NE32 .... 86 C2

South Shields Golf Club
HAR/WTLS NE34.............................. 90 A3

South Stanley
Comprehensive School
STLY/ANP DH9 .... 148 A3
South Stanley County Junior
Mixed School
STLY/ANP DH9 .... 148 A3
South Street County Primary School
GATE NE8 .... 99 E1
South Tyneside Area
Health Authority
HAR/WTLS NE34 .... 89 F1
South Tyneside College
HEBB NE31 .... 84 C6
South Tyneside College
SSH NE33 .... 72 A6
South Tyneside District Hospital
HAR/WTLS NE34 .... 88 C3
South Tyneside Health Care Trust
HEBB NE31 .... 85 D3
South Tyneside Magistrates Court
SSH NE33 .... 71 D4
South Wellfield First School
MONK NE25 .... 39 D4
South West Industrial Estate
PLEE/EAS SR8 .... 207 E2
Southwick Health Centre
SWCK/CAS SR5 .... 125 F3
Southwick Industrial Estate
SWCK/CAS SR5 .... 125 D2
Springfield Clinic
GATE NE8 .... 99 E2
Springfield Comprehensive
School & Leisure Centre
JRW NE32 .... 86 A3
Spring Terrace Health Centre
NSHW NE29 .... 54 C6
Springwell Health Centre
SUNDSW SR3 .... 143 D3
Springwell Village
Primary School
LWF/SPW/WRK NE9 .... 119 E3
Stadium Industrial Park
FELL NE10 .... 82 A5
Stadium Industrial Park
FELL NE10 .... 100 C1
Stanfield Business Centre
ASHBK/HED/RY SR2 .... 5 G5
Stanhope County Infants School
SSH NE33 .... 88 B1
Stanhope County Junior Mixed School
SSH NE33 .... 88 A2
Stanhope Parade Health Centre
SSH NE33 .... 71 E6
Stanley Health Centre
STLY/ANP DH9 .... 148 A2
Stanley RC Junior Mixed &
Infants School
STLY/ANP DH9 .... 148 B1
Stargate Industrial Estate
RYTON NE40 .... 75 D5
Stella Gill Industrial Estate
CLSW/PEL DH2 .... 152 A3
Stephenson Industrial Estate
LGB/KIL NE12 .... 49 E2
Stephenson Industrial Estate
WASHN NE37 .... 121 D2
Stephenson Railway Museum
SMOOR NE27 .... 52 C5
Stonelaw County Middle School
CRAM NE23 .... 21 E4
Studio Gallery
TYNE/NSHE NE30 .... 55 F5
Sulgrave Industrial Estate
WASHN NE37 .... 121 D3
Sunderland A F C Club Shop
SUND SR1 .... 4 C2
Sunderland Bowling Centre
SWCK/CAS SR5 .... 126 B3
Sunderland Counselling Services
MLFD/PNYW SR4 .... 142 B1
Sunderland County Court
SUND SR1 .... 4 D3
Sunderland Cricket &
Rugby Football Club
ASHBK/HED/RY SR2 .... 144 B2
Sunderland Eye Infirmary
ASHBK/HED/RY SR2 .... 144 C3
Sunderland FC Stadium of Light
SWCK/CAS SR5 .... 126 B4
Sunderland High School
ASHBK/HED/RY SR2 .... 4 D6
Sunderland Museum &
Winter Gardens
SUND SR1 .... 4 D3

Sunderland Retail Park
CLDN/WHIT/ROK SR6 .... 126 C3
Sunderland Royal Hospital
MLFD/PNYW SR4 .... 125 E6
Sunderland Talmudical College
GATE NE8 .... 99 E2
Sunderland University
SUND SR1 .... 4 D2
Swalwell Cricket Club
BLAY NE21 .... 95 E1
Swan Industrial Estate
WASHS NE38 .... 139 E2
Talbot House Special School
BW/LEM/TK/HW NE15 .... 58 A4
Tanfield Lea County Junior
Mixed & Infant School
STLY/ANP DH9 .... 130 C6
Tanfield Lea Industrial Estate
STLY/ANP DH9 .... 131 D5
Tanfield Lea
Industrial Estate North
STLY/ANP DH9 .... 130 B5
Tanfield Lea
Industrial Estate South
STLY/ANP DH9 .... 131 D6
Tanfield View Surgery
STLY/ANP DH9 .... 148 A2
Team Valley Business Centre
DUN/TMV NE11 .... 98 C4
Team Valley Trading Estate
DUN/TMV NE11 .... 98 B3
Team Valley Trading Estate
DUN/TMV NE11 .... 116 C1
Tedco Business Park
JRW NE32 .... 68 B6
Tedco Business Works
SSH NE33 .... 71 E4
Temple Park Centre
HAR/WTLS NE34 .... 89 D4
Theatre Royal
CNUT NE1 .... 2 D3
The Shopping Centre
STLY/ANP DH9 .... 148 B4
The Valley Shopping Village
DUN/TMV NE11 .... 98 C6
Thomas Bewick Special School
WD/WHPE/BLK NE5 .... 59 E4
Thomas Hepburn
Community School
FELL NE10 .... 101 D3
Thornhill Comprehensive School
ASHBK/HED/RY SR2 .... 144 A2
Thornley Station
Industrial Estate
RDHAMSE DH6 .... 206 C4
Thorpe Maternity Hospital
PLEE/EAS SR8 .... 200 A4
Throckley First School
BW/LEM/TK/HW NE15 .... 57 E4
Throckley Industrial Estate
BW/LEM/TK/HW NE15 .... 57 F3
Throckley Middle School
BW/LEM/TK/HW NE15 .... 57 E4
The Toco Gallery
JES NE2 .... 64 A4
Toner Avenue County
Infant School
HEBB NE31 .... 84 C5
Townend Primary School
SWCK/CAS SR5 .... 105 E6
Trevelyan College
DHAM DH1 .... 205 E1
Trinity Maritime Museum
CNUT NE1 .... 3 F4
Trinity Medical Centre
SSH NE33 .... 71 E5
Trinity School
BLAY NE21 .... 95 D1
Trouts Lane School
DHAM DH1 .... 179 D5
Tynemouth Business Centre
TYNE/NSHE NE30 .... 55 D6
Tynemouth College
NSHW NE29 .... 54 B6
Tynemouth Crematorium
NSHW NE29 .... 54 B5
Tynemouth Cricket Club
TYNE/NSHE NE30 .... 55 D4
Tynemouth Golf Club
TYNE/NSHE NE30 .... 55 D5
Tyne Point Industrial Estate
JRW NE32 .... 87 D2
Tyneside General Hospital
NSHW NE29 .... 54 A3

Tyneside Golf Club
RYTON NE40 .... 74 A2
Tyneside Retail Park
NSHW NE29 .... 53 D6
Tyneside Works
JRW NE32 .... 69 D6
Tyne Tees TV Studios
CNUT NE1 .... 3 H4
Tyne Theatre and Opera House
CNUT NE1 .... 2 A4
Tyne Tunnel (Tynemouth)
Trading Estate
NSHW NE29 .... 69 D1
Tyneview Primary School
BYK/HTN/WLK NE6 .... 83 F3
Tyne View Primary School
GATE NE8 .... 80 B6
Univeristy Halls of Residence
SUND SR1 .... 5 E1
University College
DHAM DH1 .... 194 B5
University for Industry
SUND SR1 .... 4 C2
University Library
DHAM DH1 .... 194 B5
University of Durham
DHAM DH1 .... 194 C5
University of Durham
DHAM DH1 .... 196 A1
University of Durham
DHAM DH1 .... 205 E2
University of Newcastle Upon Tyne
CNUT NE1 .... 2 B2
University of Newcastle Upon Tyne
JES NE2 .... 64 A6
University of Newcastle upon Tyne
LGB/HTN NE7 .... 65 E3
University of Northumbria
at Newcastle
CNUT NE1 .... 3 E1
University of Northumbria
at Newcastle
LGB/HTN NE7 .... 65 E2
University of Northumbria Officers
Training Corps
ELS/FEN NE4 .... 79 F1
University of Sunderland
ASHBK/HED/RY SR2 .... 4 C5
University of Sunderland
CLDN/WHIT/ROK SR6 .... 127 D4
University of Sunderland
MLFD/PNYW SR4 .... 125 D4
University of Sunderland
SUND SR1 .... 4 A3
University of Sunderland
SUND SR1 .... 126 A6
University of Sunderland
SWCK/CAS SR5 .... 124 A4
University of Sunderland
WASHN NE37 .... 119 F5
University of Sunderland (Library)
SUND SR1 .... 4 A4
University Technology Park
ASHBK/HED/RY SR2 .... 4 A4
Usworth Colliery Junior School
WASHN NE37 .... 121 D3
Usworth Grange Primary School
WASHN NE37 .... 121 E3
Usworth Secondary School and
Leisure Centre
WASHN NE37 .... 120 C2
Valley Road Infant School
ASHBK/HED/RY SR2 .... 145 E2
Valley Road Junior School
ASHBK/HED/RY SR2 .... 145 E2
Valley View County Infant School
JRW NE32 .... 86 A4
Vance Business Park
DUN/TMV NE11 .... 98 A2
Van Mildert College
DHAM DH1 .... 205 D2
Victoria Industrial Estate
FELL NE10 .... 84 B5
Victoria Medical Centre
HEBB NE31 .... 84 C2
Victoria Road Health Centre
WASHN NE37 .... 120 C4
Viking Gallery
JRW NE32 .... 86 A1
Viking Industrial Park
JRW NE32 .... 68 C6
Village Gallery
WICK/BNPF NE16 .... 96 A3

Wagonway Industrial Estate
HEBB NE31 .... **68** A6

**Walker Comprehensive School
and Leisure Centre**
BYK/HTN/WLK NE6 .... **83** E2

Walkerdene Special School
BYK/HTN/WLK NE6 .... **83** E2

Walker Gate Hospital
BYK/HTN/WLK NE6 .... **66** A6

Walkergate Infant School
BYK/HTN/WLK NE6 .... **66** A6

Walker Riverside Industrial Park
BYK/HTN/WLK NE6 .... **84** A5

Walker Riverside Industrial Park
BYK/HTN/WLK NE6 .... **84** A3

Wallaw Cinema
BLYTH NE24 .... **11** D5

Wallsend Business Centre
WLSD/HOW NE28 .... **67** E5

Wallsend Golf Club
WLSD/HOW NE28 .... **66** B4

Wallsend Sports Centre
WLSD/HOW NE28 .... **66** B4

Wardley Primary School
FELL NE10 .... **101** F2

War Memorial
SUND SR1 .... **4** D4

Warner Village
JES NE2 .... **3** F2

**Washington Albany
Infants School**
WASHN NE37 .... **120** A5

Washington Football Club
WASHN NE37 .... **120** C5

Washington Hospital
WASHN NE38 .... **137** D6

Washington Leisure Centre
WASHS NE38 .... **138** B2

Washington Old Hall
WASHS NE38 .... **121** D6

Washington Pit Museum
WASHN NE37 .... **120** B5

**Washington Secondary School &
Leisure Centre**
WASHN NE37 .... **120** C5

**Washington Village
Primary School**
WASHS NE38 .... **121** D6

Waterloo Medical Group
BLYTH NE24 .... **10** C4

Waterville Primary School
NSHW NE29 .... **70** B2

Waverley First School
BW/LEM/TK/HW NE15 .... **77** D2

Waygood Gallery & Studios
CNUT NE1 .... **2** D4

Wear Industrial Estate
WASHS NE38 .... **138** A4

Wearside College
SUNDSW SR3 .... **143** E3

Wearside Golf Club
MLFD/PNYW SR4 .... **140** C3

Weetslade Industrial Estate
CRAM NE23 .... **21** E6

Welbeck Primary School
BYK/HTN/WLK NE6 .... **82** C3

Wellbank Special School
WASHN NE37 .... **120** A3

West Boldon Junior Mixed School
BOL NE36 .... **105** F2

**West Chirton (Middle)
Industrial Estate**
NSHW NE29 .... **53** D5

**West Chirton (North)
Industrial Estate**
NSHW NE29 .... **52** C5

**West Chirton (South)
Industrial Estate**
NSHW NE29 .... **69** E1

West Chirton Trading Estate
NSHW NE29 .... **53** E6

West Denton First School
WD/WHPE/BLK NE5 .... **59** F5

**West Denton High School &
Leisure Centre**
WD/WHPE/BLK NE5 .... **60** A4

West Denton Retail Park
WD/WHPE/BLK NE5 .... **60** C4

Westerhope Clinic
WD/WHPE/BLK NE5 .... **60** B3

Westerhope First School
WD/WHPE/BLK NE5 .... **60** A3

Westerhope Golf Club
WD/WHPE/BLK NE5 .... **60** A2

Westerhope Small Business Park
WD/WHPE/BLK NE5 .... **60** A2

**Western Approach
Industrial Estate**
SSH NE33 .... **71** E4

Western First School
WLSD/HOW NE28 .... **66** C4

Western Infant School
NSHW NE29 .... **70** B2

Western Middle School
WLSD/HOW NE28 .... **66** C5

Westfield School
GOS/KPK NE3 .... **63** D3

West Gate Community College
ELS/FEN NE4 .... **78** C2

West Gate Community College
ELS/FEN NE4 .... **79** E2

Westgate Hill Primary School
ELS/FEN NE4 .... **79** F3

West Jesmond Junior School
JES NE2 .... **64** A5

West Lane Junior & Infant School
BLAY NE21 .... **93** F2

Westlea Junior School
SEA/MUR SR7 .... **175** D2

West Line Industrial Estate
CLSW/PEL DH2 .... **136** A4

West Moor First School
LGB/KIL NE12 .... **49** E3

Westmoor Middle School
LGB/KIL NE12 .... **49** D3

Westmorland Business Centre
ELS/FEN NE4 .... **2** A5

Westoe Gallery
SSH NE33 .... **71** F4

Westovian Theatre Society
SSH NE33 .... **72** A2

West Rainton Primary School
HLS DH4 .... **183** E2

West Walker School
BYK/HTN/WLK NE6 .... **83** F4

Westway Industrial Park
BW/LEM/TK/HW NE15 .... **57** F3

**Whickham Comprehensive
School & Leisure Centre**
WICK/BNPF NE16 .... **95** F4

Whickham Golf Club
WICK/BNPF NE16 .... **95** D6

Whickham Industrial Estate
WICK/BNPF NE16 .... **95** E1

**Whickham Parochial C of E
Junior & Infant School**
WICK/BNPF NE16 .... **95** E5

**Whickham Thorns Outdoor
Activity Centre**
DUN/TMV NE11 .... **97** D2

Whinfield Industrial Estate
ROWG NE39 .... **110** B3

**Whitburn Comprehensive
School & Leisure Centre**
CLDN/WHIT/ROK SR6 .... **109** F2

Whitburn Cricket Club
CLDN/WHIT/ROK SR6 .... **109** E2

Whitburn Golf Club
HAR/WTLS NE34 .... **91** D3

Whitburn Junior Mixed School
CLDN/WHIT/ROK SR6 .... **109** D2

Whitburn Surgery
CLDN/WHIT/ROK SR6 .... **109** D2

Whitehouse Business Park
RDHAMSE DH6 .... **207** E4

Whitehouse Industrial Estate
BW/LEM/TK/HW NE15 .... **78** B4

Whitehouse Primary School
NSHW NE29 .... **53** E5

Whitehouse Primary School
NSHW NE29 .... **54** A4

Whitley Bay Cricket Club
MONK NE25 .... **54** C1

Whitley Bay Football Club
MONK NE25 .... **54** C1

Whitley Bay Golf Club
WBAY NE26 .... **40** A2

Whitley Bay High School
MONK NE25 .... **40** A4

Whitley Bay Ice Rink
MONK NE25 .... **54** B1

Whitley Bay Rockcliff RFC
MONK NE25 .... **54** C1

Whitley Lodge First School
WBAY NE26 .... **40** A2

Whitley Memorial School
BDLGTN NE22 .... **7** F4

Willington High School
WLSD/HOW NE28 .... **68** B1

**Winchester House Community
Business Centre**
SWCK/CAS SR5 .... **105** E6

Windmill Industrial Estate
CRAM NE23 .... **12** B5

Windy Nook Primary School
FELL NE10 .... **100** C4

Wingrove Primary School
ELS/FEN NE4 .... **79** D2

Winlaton Park Junior School
BLAY NE21 .... **94** B2

Winlaton Vulcans Rugby Club
BLAY NE21 .... **94** B1

Witherwack Primary School
SWCK/CAS SR5 .... **107** E6

Woodlands Park Health Centre
DIN/WO NE13 .... **33** D5

Woodlea County Primary School
HLS DH4 .... **169** D1

Wrekenton Health Centre
LWF/SPW/WRK NE9 .... **118** C1

Yates Jewish School for Girls
GATE NE8 .... **99** D1

The Yemeni School
SSH NE33 .... **71** D5